Charles F. Marden

Rutgers, The State University

Gladys Meyer

Barnard College

MINORITIES
in American Society

Third Edition

Van Nostrand Reinhold Company

New York   Cincinnati   Toronto   London   Melbourne

VAN NOSTRAND REINHOLD COMPANY *Regional Offices:*
Cincinnati   New York   Chicago   Millbrae   Dallas

VAN NOSTRAND REINHOLD COMPANY *Foreign Offices:*
London   Toronto   Melbourne

Manufactured in the United States of America

Published by VAN NOSTRAND REINHOLD COMPANY
450 West 33rd Street, New York, N.Y. 10001

15 14 13 12 11 10 9 8 7 6 5

FOREWORD

This third edition of *Minorities in American Society* retains the central features of the earlier editions but introduces some major changes. The focus remains structural and interactional: it deals with stabilized and dynamic aspects of intergroup relations of a dominant-minority character. The plan of organization remains broadly the same. Chapters 1 through 5 introduce the subject in both descriptive and analytical ways. Chapters 6 through 18 consider each of the dominant-minority intergroup situations separately, beginning with the first contact and continuing to the present. The order of presentation moves from those with primarily cultural or religious distinctiveness toward those with increasing degrees of racial visibility. Chapters 19 and 20 consider this whole field in the light of sociological theory, interpret the phenomena, and discuss the current situation with regard to its problem aspects and social policy.

Turning to the changes, it will be seen that the various substantive chapters have been organized around a three-fold schema: the establishment of dominance, the maintenance of dominance, and the decline of dominance. Another difference, in degree of emphasis at least, over the previous editions is the elaboration of the pluralistic as distinct from the integrationist theory of assimilation in line with the course of events and in the corresponding sociological thought. The fact that religious identification has tended to supplant nationality identification as a basis of subcommunality has prompted the addition of an analytical chapter on religion. Finally, the dramatic course of Negro-white relations has called for a completely new chapter on the challenge to dominance as presented by the ongoing Negro Revolt.

The authors wish to express their appreciation to the following persons who have given, in various ways, generous assistance in the preparation of this new edition: Harry H. L. Kitano, of the Graduate School of Social Work, University of California at Los Angeles; Raymond E. Sakumoto, of the University of Hawaii; George K. Hesslink, of Rutgers, The State University; S. Frank Miyamoto, of the University of Washington; Edith Loewenstein, of the American Council for Nationalities Service; Joan Gordon, of New School for Social Research; Eleanor Russell Cate; Chia-Ling Kuo, of Rutgers, The State University; Madeline Engel, of Hunter College; and to our students whose questions and investigations always stimulate a new look at minority issues.

Dr. Marden wishes to acknowledge his appreciation for the extensive assistance given by his wife, Freda, for a wide range of contributions from typing and editing to critical comment on his part of this edition.

CONTENTS

3. *Race: Myth and Science*   *54*

4. *Religion and Minority Status*   *70*

The Significance
of Minorities in American Society

FIRST NEGRO APPOINTED TO SUPREME COURT   MER-
EDITH GRADUATES FROM "OLE MISS"   NORTHTOWN
BOARD OF EDUCATION APPOINTS FIRST NEGRO PRIN-
CIPAL   FIRST PUERTO RICAN SENATE PAGE BOY AP-
POINTED   INDIAN PROTEST INCREASING   NATION-
ALITY QUOTAS ABANDONED IN NEW IMMIGRATION
LAW   MEXICAN-AMERICANS TAKE   OVER   TEXAS
CITY GOVERNMENT   ECUMENICAL MOVEMENT AD-
VANCES   MORE NORTHERN SCHOOLS CHANGE DIS-
TRICTS TO CREATE BETTER RACIAL BALANCE
"QUOTAS" FOR JEWISH COLLEGE APPLICANTS VIR-
TUALLY ABOLISHED   BLACK POWER ADVOCATES
GAIN INFLUENCE   MEREDITH SHOT ON "VOTING
MARCH" THROUGH MISSISSIPPI   UNION DISCRIMINA-
TION AGAINST NEGROES FOUND PERSISTENT   PUER-
TO RICANS RIOT IN CHICAGO   REPORT SHOWS
INDIANS POOREST OF ALL MINORITIES   FOREIGN
PROFESSIONALS LOST TO UNITED STATES   POVERTY
AND PREJUDICE BLIGHT LIVES OF MEXICAN-AMERI-
CANS   STUDY SHOWS CHRISTIAN BELIEFS PERPETU-
ATING ANTI-SEMITISM   NEGRO COUPLE GIVE UP
LIVING IN WHITE NEIGHBORHOOD DUE TO WHITE
UNFRIENDLINESS VANDALS DESECRATE SYNAGOGUE

Headlines like the above illustrate recent events demonstrating crosscurrents in the situation of minorities in the United States.

In the first edition of this book (1952) we characterized the period following World War II as one in which emerging national self-consciousness concerning dominant-minority relations was the prevailing theme. During those years the recurrent concern with related subjects in all the mass media reflected an enormously accelerated public interest in the condition of minorities. At long last, discrimination was being recognized as a leading national problem. This new focus on "race relations" led to increased activity on the part of liberal elements aimed at reducing if not eliminating discrimination. Since up to 1954 the trend toward increasing acceptance of minorities was gradual and sporadic, the opposing elements were on the whole publicly dormant.

The 1954 Supreme Court decision, outlawing school segregation precipitated a "crisis" in race relations, so that our second edition (1962) gave special emphasis to conflict in Negro-white relations, especially in the South, while noting declining discrimination against other minorities. As we come to our third edition, the crisis in Negro-white relations continues at an accelerated pace and has become nationwide. Despite the optimism engendered by civil rights legislation, it is becoming clearer that a stabilized resolution of this conflict is far from reached, and it is not clear what form of stabilization will emerge. The dramatic character of this world-publicized conflict has tended to overshadow the situation of other minorities. However, focus of national attention on the "alienated poor" who do not share in the general national affluence has perforce generated increased awareness of other minorities, for example, Puerto Ricans, Mexican-Americans, and Indians.

Social science investigations have continued apace along three lines: (1) empirical research designed at understanding dominant-minority relations; [1] (2) research aimed at insight on how to effect peaceful change; and (3) increasing attention to the theory of intergroup relations. [2] Policy makers increasingly turn to the behavioral scientists for guidance. To quote from Chief Justice Warren on the Supreme Court decision reached in the school cases: "Whatever may have been the extent of psychological knowledge at the time of Plessy vs. Ferguson, this finding [that segregation in the public schools has a detrimental effect on colored children] is amply supported by modern authority." [3]

The purpose of this book is to present a comprehensive description of the most important minority situations in the United States; to analyze and inter-

[1] One of the most sophisticated and extensive of such researches is Robin Williams, *Strangers Next Door: Ethnic Relations in American Communities* (Englewood Cliffs, N.J.: Prentice Hall, 1964).

[2] See for example, Milton M. Gordon, *Assimilation in American Life* (New York: Oxford University Press, 1964), and Tamotsu Shibutani and Kian M. Kwan, *Ethnic Stratification: A Comparative Approach* (New York: The Macmillan Company, 1965).

[3] 347 U.S. 483. The citations given refer to various social science studies.

pret the relations of the dominant group to minority groups within a sociological framework; to state the general principles which emerge from such a study; and, finally, to indicate how our present knowledge may be brought to bear on social policy. The central focus of the book is the interaction which takes place between the dominant and minority, the discrimination imposed and maintained by the former, and the reaction of the latter.

In this opening chapter a preview of the range and scope of our inquiry will be indicated by (1) a preliminary summary of minority situations in United States history; (2) a preliminary statement of some of the principal ways these intergroup relations have affected our national life, and the nature of the problems they create; and (3) a brief historical summary of dominant-minority relations throughout the world in the modern era.

Minorities in the United States

Indians

From the earliest settlements in the colonial period until 1871, white people increasingly encroached on the land possessed by American Indians. Until 1871 Indian-white relations were considered formally, if somewhat fictionally, as contractual relations between sovereign political entities. Tribes were often called "nations." In 1871 Indians became official wards of the United States Government and thus formally, as well as actually, a minority. During the wardship period neither the welfare nor the status of the Indians improved much until 1934, when the broad policy established under the New Deal began helping the Indians improve their economic welfare with maximum possible retention of their tribal identities and cultures. Controversy now exists between those white Americans who retain this New Deal approach and those who want to see the tribes liquidated and Indians as individuals put on their own like other Americans. The policy of the federal government toward Indians continues to reflect these contrasting viewpoints.

Negroes

Importation of Negro slaves to the English colonies began in 1619. Thus the new nation, born in 1776, inherited a slave minority brutally forced into subservience. In spite of their long residence in this country and considerable improvement in their welfare, Negroes still occupy the lowest status of all American minorities. The nation as a whole is in the midst of a major crisis in Negro-white relations which will continue for some time ahead.

European Immigrants

Even before American Negroes moved from slavery to the status of a minority caste, there began an influx from Europe which was destined to change the character of the United States profoundly. First came the Irish, Scandinavians, and Germans, later the southern and eastern Europeans. The customs of these various peoples differed markedly from those of the "natives." The relation of these various peoples to the older residents followed a similar pattern, beginning with indifference, antagonism, and conflict and ending with acceptance as real Americans.

Once restriction of European immigration went into effect with the Immigration Act of 1924, an important era in United States history came to an end. While there remain some immigrants who will live out their days never fully assimilated into American life, their children and certainly their grandchildren have been, or are being assimilated. This era of our minority relations drew to a close as the result of indirect social forces rather than any direct and purposeful planning. Compared with the situation involving other minorities, it is no longer a problem. A study of America's immigration era, however, still has significance. First, from an analysis of it we learn much that may be applied to the analysis of other minority situations. Second, as a consequence of international developments following World War II, the problem of displaced persons continues to require a reconsideration of our immigration policy.

Oriental Immigrants

Overlapping chronologically with European immigration was that of the Chinese and the Japanese, who concentrated in West Coast communities. At first they were tolerated with condescension as exploitable labor. But as these people, particularly the Japanese, began to succeed in competition with native whites, further immigration was curtailed by the government. Those who remained here were fixed in a pattern of segregated minority status little altered until the drastic relocation of the Japanese during World War II. This latter unique epoch in the history of American minorities, from any long-range view an unfortunate episode, revealed a certain ineptitude and immaturity in the handling of minority group problems. Since the War the economic status of both the Chinese and the Japanese has improved, and discrimination against them has markedly declined.

While evacuation dispersed the Japanese somewhat, many of the evacuees returned to the West Coast. Of all non-European minorities, the native-born Japanese have achieved the highest welfare, and are widely accepted as good Americans although largely still identified also as Japanese. Substantial segments of the Chinese, partly by their own choice, are still considerably insulated in Chinatowns. Immigration of both Chinese and Japanese has greatly increased since the passage of the postwar immigration legislation.

Mexicans

Following the restriction of European immigration, a large influx of Mexicans into the Southwest began. The usual pattern of native-immigrant interaction occurred: welcome as menial laborers; discrimination otherwise; and acculturation, slow up to World War II, and accelerated since then. In the whole United States persons descended from former or current Mexican national lineage number now well over four million, thus being one of the larger minority groups. In the Southwest also there are descendants of the Spanish-speaking people who inhabited the region when the Anglos invaded and subsequently annexed the area. Known as "hispanos" they make up a substantial part of New Mexico's population. While they have never been formally discriminated against, hispanos still constitute a distinct ethnic component. Their economic and health conditions for years ranked among the lowest in the nation.

Filipinos, Hawaiians, Puerto Ricans

For still another phase of our minority group history, one must go back to the turn of the century, when the United States became a world power and added overseas territories to its domain. In the process of this expansion, the United States acquired new peoples: the Filipinos, the Puerto Ricans, and the peoples of Hawaii. The political and economic emissaries from the dominant homeland treated their new national compatriots as a minority group, although the upper classes were given special consideration. Filipinos migrating to the States, easily recognized as Orientals, encountered the same differential treatment accorded other Asians.

Hawaii presents a distinctive picture of ethnic relations. Though this small archipelago has an amazingly heterogeneous ethnic composition, the general impression prevails that it is a paradise of harmonious interracial relations. The impression needs some qualification in the light of the relation between Caucasian and non-Caucasian groups. But the admission of Hawaii to statehood in 1959 reflects the weakening influence of mainland racist ideology, a factor which had been previously an important obstacle to the territory's admission.

A more recent new minority situation arises out of the influx of a substantial number of Puerto Ricans to the mainland. At first largely localized in New York City, Puerto Ricans are now spreading across the nation. They have encountered the usual problems of an immigrant group adjusting to a strange cultural environment. As a people with linguistic and varying degrees of physical visibility, they have encountered discrimination and exploitation.

Religious Minorities: Catholics and Jews

Since the United States has been primarily a Protestant nation, residents with non-Protestant backgrounds have generally had some degree of minority status. Protestant discrimination against Roman Catholics and Jews has been a constant phenomenon, although its more overt manifestations have been intermittent. Antipathy toward the Irish, for example, has been directed as much toward them for being Catholic as for being Irish, partly because of the aggressive leadership of the Irish in American Catholicism. The later immigrant groups of predominantly Catholic background—Italians, Poles, Mexicans, and Puerto Ricans—were viewed more as "foreigners" than as Catholics.

The story of Americans of Jewish ancestry presents several unique and in some ways baffling facets for the student of intergroup relations. Broadly speaking, Jews accommodated to American life more quickly and successfully than other non-Protestant European immigrants. Gentile discrimination against them has been a constant phenomenon at least since the 1880's. The Jews are not a race, nor do they fit the common definition of a nationality. Their identification with a distinctive religion and related cultural elements and their long struggle in the Diaspora to maintain their distinctiveness has given them a persistent collective identity. The status of Jews in the United States today is a subject of much dispute among scholars. With certainty we can state that there is among Gentiles a substantial volume of prejudice against Jews and, perhaps small in total amount but often virulent, anti-Semitic activity; and among Jews there are clearly identifiable subcommunities heavily concentrated in metropolitan areas.

The Refugee Groups

While some minor portion of the earlier immigration from Europe was motivated by either political or religious persecution, a number of international political events since 1930 has prompted thousands of Europeans, and more recently Asians, to flee from their homelands. Chronologically, these have included "refugees" from the Nazis in the thirties; persons "displaced" in Europe as a result of Communist expansion during and since World War II; and more recently, "escapees" from Communist China and Cuba.[4]

The manner in which the United States has reacted to this situation reflects the crosscurrents of liberal internationalism and nativistic isolation. As the most affluent and not overpopulated democratic nation, the United States could hardly ignore responsibility for harboring some of these persons. A limited number were admitted under special legislation; however, the specific limitations of the Displaced Persons Act of 1948 were considered to reflect anti-Semitic and anti-Catholic attitudes. While in some localities where there was some conspicuous concentration of refugees a minor stir of local nativistic antagonism arose, on the whole they were quickly absorbed into the expanding economy. Their absorption into the society was facilitated by the presence here of groups of their own respective nationalities and a more positive government program to assist them in the initial stages of their adjustment.

---

[4] The Immigration and Naturalization Service Annual Report for 1965 states (1) "Since January 1, 1959, when Castro seized power, some 227,000 Cubans have been admitted in temporary status, and 56,526 have entered as immigrants. (2) A total of 13,619 Chinese persons had been paroled to the United States by the end of June 1965" (not as permanent lawful residents of the United States).

The Size of Minority Groups

Altogether the number of persons who have experienced minority status throughout American history has been substantial. Table 1–1 presents the best available current census counts or estimates of the size of most of these groups. The problems involved in estimating the size of each component are taken up in the separate ethnic chapters. At this point we merely call advance attention to crucial points. (1) Since whether Catholics per se are still a minority in status is debatable, we leave them out here. (2) Official reports of the number of Mexican Americans are estimates varying on whether language or nationality lineage is chosen for counting. (3) The 1960 census figures for the Asian peoples now include the Hawaiian components. (4) The numbers of all the groups where we have used the 1960 census figures are all larger now.

TABLE 1–1. *Estimated Numbers of Minorities in the United States*

Negroes	1966	21,598,000**
Jews	1963	5,600,000***
Mexican-Hispanos	1960	5,189,839****
American Indians	1960	546,225*
Japanese	1960	473,170*
Chinese	1960	236,084*
Filipinos	1960	181,614*
Puerto Rican (Mainland)	1960	855,704*

   * U.S. Census, 1960, Final Report P.C. (2) 1 c p. IX.
  ** U.S. Census Bureau Report released through Associated Press, Washington, D.C., June 2, 1967. Estimate of Negro population as of July 1, 1966.
 *** Population Estimate for 1963, American Jewish Year Book, 1964, p. 3.
**** A special census report, Persons of Spanish Surnames, Southwestern States, P.C. (2) —1 B, Table A, p. IX, indicates 3,466,999 in this region. The Bureau estimates the figure above for the U.S. as a whole.

Preliminary Consideration of the Social Problems Created by Dominant-Minority Relations

Sociologists have taken the position that whether certain social facts constitute a problem or not depends on the value system of the viewer of the facts. For example, to many Americans the segregation of Negroes is simply in the natural order of things, while to many others any group discrimination is a moral issue. Furthermore, the definition of the problem varies with personal value systems. To a traditional white Southerner the rising militancy of Negroes ignites the problem of "how to keep them in their place," while to the liberal the problem is "how best to cooperate with these minority efforts to advance toward complete equality." The value system we shall adopt in this text derives from two beliefs: (1) that democracy is the most desirable form of social organization; and (2) that the welfare of the society as a whole, either the nation or the community, properly takes precedence over the welfare of any special groups within this whole. This preliminary consideration focuses on the main ways in which discrimination against minorities creates problems defined according to these values. Relevant further discussion will be found in subsequent chapters.

Ineffective Use of Abilities

All minorities are discriminated against to some extent in the choice of their employment; some are discriminated against in training for specific occupations. Since there is a wide range of mental capacities in all minorities, occupational discrimination results in ineffective use of potential manpower. This waste was brought to public attention during World War II when, for example, the restriction against trained Negro nurses in white hospitals greatly aggravated severe personnel shortages.

Adverse Effect on National Income

It has been argued that minority discrimination retards the growth of national income. In regard to the traditional disparity in Negro income with that of whites, Broom and Glenn indicate that "the income gap closed appreciably during World War II but very slowly and erratically during the postwar period." [5] Still further rise in the relative purchasing power of minorities would stimulate the demand for consumer goods. Many factors conspire to make the Deep South the poorest economic region of the nation, but the poverty of their large Negro population is clearly one of the most important reasons. And discrimination is an important factor contributing to this poverty.

Deviant Behavior

The belief has been widely held by people with dominant status that minorities furnish more than their share of sociopathic behavior, such as juvenile delinquency, adult crime, mental disease, or other "pathologies." Research sometimes indicates that a particular minority does in fact show a disproportionate amount of some of these phenomena; sometimes the facts show the minority group to manifest less than their proportion. We shall examine the facts in more detail as we proceed in our study of particular minorities. Social science finds three broad factors provocative of disorganization: (1) the inevitable strain which a people of different culture faces in adjusting to a new situation; (2) the influence of the environmental conditions associated with the spatial and economic position of the minority, such as living in slum areas; and (3) frustrations and resentments growing out of discrimination itself. It is this last class of causes which is least generally recognized and which more directly

[5] Leonard Broom and Norval Glenn, *Transformation of the Negro American* (New York: Harper & Row, Publishers, 1965), pp. 115–116.

pertains to our analysis. A Negro boy may steal because he is poor, but he may also steal as a way of "getting even" with white people. In the latter instance, the direct influence of minority status as a causal factor in delinquency is evident. Whatever the incidence of disorganization among minorities, part of it may be properly attributed to the impact of minority status on personality.

Intergroup Tension and Violence

Dominant-minority group situations, especially in rapidly changing societies, inevitably create intergroup tensions which intermittently produce violent conflict with attendant bloodshed and economic waste. This was a permanent fact for a long time prior to the current "Negro Revolt." The North experienced many race riots before World War II. Lynching of Negroes was long a practice in the South. While in the decades before 1954 lynching had greatly declined, the present heightened conflict in Negro-white relations has increased violence and created new modes of its expression. In the North, for example, white violence toward Negroes has taken the form of damaging homes of Negro families moving into hitherto white areas. Among the developments in the South is violence directed against participants in "protest" activities, including white sympathizers as well as Negro people.

Inconsistency in Values

The status of minority groups in American society constitutes a basic ideological conflict, which is viewed by many people as a moral or ethical problem. Gunnar Myrdal, the Swedish social scientist, who made the most incisive interpretation of Negro-white relations in the United States up to 1940, considers the violation of the American Creed in our treatment of the Negroes a basic point:

> From the point of view of the American Creed the status accorded the Negro in America represents nothing more and nothing less than a century-long lag of public morals. In principle the Negro problem was settled long ago; in practice the solution is not effectuated. The Negro in America has not been given the elemental civil and political rights of formal democracy, including a fair opportunity to earn his living, upon which a general accord was already won when the American Creed was first taking form. And this anachronism constitutes the contemporary "problem" both to the Negroes and to whites.[6]

While several studies have raised considerable doubt as to how far American citizens concern themselves with this moral dilemma, viewed objectively it is a gross inconsistency in values.[7]

[6] Gunnar Myrdal, *An American Dilemma* (New York: Harper & Brothers, 1944), p. 24. By permission.
[7] See James W. Vander Zanden, *American Minority Relations*, 2nd ed. (New York: Ronald Press, 1966), pp. 158–165, for a summary critique of the Myrdal hypothesis.

Adverse Effect on America's Position in World Affairs

The moral dilemma which Myrdal highlighted has had an incalculably adverse effect on the image of the United States abroad. Of this, Arnold Rose writes:

> At least since 1940, instances of racial discrimination and violence in the United States have been important news items all over the world and have been reacted to very negatively. The implications of this situation are worth closer scrutiny.
>
> Let us start with some of the characteristic reactions of colored peoples, who constitute a majority of the world's population. They tend to identify with Negroes and imagine that if they were in the United States they would receive the same extreme treatment that is reported in the "scare" headlines of their newspapers. As A. M. Rosenthal says in a story in *The New York Times* of October 8, 1957, "The attitude of many an educated Indian toward the United States is conditioned by the fear that if he went there he might be mistaken for a Negro, treated badly and humiliated." In fact, in May, 1964, the head of India's Socialist Party was arrested in Jackson, Mississippi, because he went into a "white" restaurant and asked for service. We have troops stationed in Korea and Japan, and the friction, sometimes serious, which arises between our soldiers and their nationals is attributed to the racism in American culture. The shooting by an American military policeman of a Japanese woman who was salvaging shells near a military reservation is explained by informed Japanese in the same terms as they would use to interpret a case of violence in Mississippi. Perhaps they are partly right. People in other parts of the world are no longer just shocked by these stories of what is going on in the United States—they have come to regard such events as characteristic of American society. In Japan, for example, racism is spoken of as "America's incurable disease." [8]

Whatever the past costs in international relations of American discrimination, the present and future costs should be calculated in the light of the handicap that discrimination imposes on America's position in the United Nations and our efforts to contain the spread of Communism.

In December, 1948, after long deliberation, the United Nations accepted the Universal Declaration of Human Rights. Among the thirty articles of this document are these statements: "Everyone is entitled to all the rights and freedoms set forth in this Declaration, without distinction of any kind such as race, color, sex, language, religion, political or other opinion, national or social origin, property, birth, or other status." "All are equal before the law and are entitled without any discrimination to equal protection of the law." "Everyone, without any discrimination, has the right to equal pay for equal work."

The prominent role of the United States in the United Nations and the location of U.N. headquarters in New York City has placed the nation's treatment of its own minorities in a new perspective. The pattern of discrimination against nonwhite people in the United States causes numerous em-

---

[8] "American Race Relations and World Opinions" in Arnold M. and Caroline B. Rose, eds., *Minority Problems* (New York: Harper & Row, Publishers, 1965), pp. 9–10.

barrassing circumstances in relation to nonwhite representatives to the United Nations, such as refusals of service in public places outside New York and subtle rejections of housing accommodations even in the New York metropolitan area. Thus the task of implementing the Declaration our nation has subscribed to is a considerable one.

Dominant-Minority Relations Around the World

The phenomenon of dominance of some ethnic groups over others is not peculiar to the United States. It has a long history throughout the world. While what happened in the United States in intergroup relations is explainable in some measure by forces peculiar to its own history, dominance should be viewed in worldwide perspective.

In this brief overview, we shall examine four patterns of dominant-minority relations that have evolved in the past four hundred years and indicate post-World War II developments.

The Slavery Pattern

While slavery is an ancient institution, it was the enslavement by Europeans of African people and their forced immigration to the newly established colonies that was important for the modern era. The British ultimately restricted their slave trade to the Negro but pursued it with characteristic efficiency. The Latins made slaves of Indians and whites as well as Negroes, but they accorded slaves status as human beings, established rules to limit the rights of masters, set up procedures by which freedom might be obtained, and once the slaves were freed, accepted them as free men.[9]

Except for some still-remaining pockets in remote areas of the world, slavery was abolished by the twentieth century.

The Annexation Pattern

Through wars, European nations have annexed portions of their neighbors' lands and have imposed special discriminations on the newly acquired subjects designed to force the assimilation of the minorities into the dominant culture pattern. Alsace-Lorraine, alternately French and German; Poland, attempting to resist Russification under the Tsars; Magyar dominance over various Slavic folks in Hungary—all are illustrations in which minorities arise by means of political annexation.

Since World War II, the large Communist nations, Red China and the Soviet Union, are the only nations that have formally annexed previously independent nations. China annexed Tibet. The Soviet Union annexed Lithuania, Estonia, and Latvia, and has extended a sphere of de facto control over various nations of Eastern Europe. While the imposition of the communist way

[9] Frank Tannenbaum, *Slave and Citizen* (New York: Alfred A. Knopf, 1947).

of life upon these nations has inevitably brought about considerable erosion of the traditional cultures, it has not established formal patterns of dominant-minority relations. The establishment of the State of Israel in 1949 in the ancient homeland of the Jews with a large Arab population precipitated difficult interethnic relations, further complicated by the Israeli-Arab War of 1967.

The Colonial Pattern

The colonial pattern developed along several lines, all best illustrated by Great Britain. The development of a great trading economy, strengthened by the Industrial Revolution and rapid population growth, enabled the British to establish political control over various parts of the world and to dominate the economic life of these vast areas. Where these areas were densely populated by native peoples, control was maintained by placating the upper-class rulers, as in India, and applying military force when needed. According to Raymond Kennedy, the outstanding characteristics of this system have been the political and economic subordination of the native population; poor development of social services especially education, for natives; and the color line with its rigid social barriers between the white ruling class and the subject people. Of these, the most important feature for the study of minorities is the last—the color line. Concerning this, Kennedy writes: [10]

> The colonial code that dictates complete social segregation of the races is rationalized either by the commonplace assertion that natives are ignorant or unclean or uninteresting; or by the claim that they do not desire whites to become familiar with them; or by the argument that informality, camaraderie and, most of all, intermarriage would weaken the prestige of the ruling class in the estimation of their subjects. . . .
>
> The British colonial code draws the most rigid color line of all. Paradoxically, the greatest colonizers in the world are the most provincial in their attitudes towards strange groups and cultures. The British have been in contact for a longer time with more dark peoples than any other western nation, yet they hold aloof from their subjects to an unequalled degree. They refuse to associate freely or make friends with other races, and this exclusiveness had engendered a reciprocal feeling toward them on the part of their colonial peoples. The attitude of the latter varies from indifference to active dislike, but, except in isolated instances, it never approaches friendliness. Natives often express a grudging admiration for the moral rectitude, financial incorruptibility, and legalistic fairness of Britishers, especially government officials, in the colonies; but bonds of mutual friendship and affection are lacking. . . .

Where the areas of British expansion were thinly populated, the British themselves often settled, pushing back and partly annihilating the native pop-

[10] Raymond Kennedy, "The Colonial Crisis and the Future," *The Science of Man in the World Crisis,* ed. Ralph Linton (New York: Columbia University Press, 1945), pp. 318, 320. By permission of the publisher, Columbia University Press.

ulation to take over the area, as in North America, Australia, and New Zealand. The remaining remnants of these native peoples eventually became units of the British commonwealth.

The French, the Dutch, the Belgians, the Italians, and the Portuguese also engaged in colonialism that reinforced the development of deep-seated antagonisms toward the white man in Asia and Africa.

Colonization on the part of European nations in South America went through the same phases but much less successfully. Spain and Portugal early lost most of their colonial empires, though descendants of the European colonists came to occupy controlling upper-class status. In their relations with the native populations, the Mediterraneans have never drawn the color line very rigidly. They have exploited native populations, but in their personal relations they have never been strongly influenced by the idea of racial superiority. Intermarriage has been frequent. Latin America has had a more rigid class system than Anglo-Saxon America, but it has never been so preoccupied with race as a determiner of superiority or inferiority.

The dominant-minority pattern of South Africa represents a mixture of the two foregoing types of development. Here the British settled, defeated their Boer rivals, and then joined them to establish a nation based on a pattern of interracial segregation with 20 percent white dominant and 80 percent black subordinate, with Indians and mixed-bloods, called "coloured" to distinguish them from the natives, in between.

The pattern of European dominance and native subordination developed in South Africa has been made more explicit and more rigid by the policy of *Apartheid* pursued by the Nationalist governments continuously in power since 1948.[11] *Apartheid* has two main aspects: (1) the improvement of the economy and welfare of the natives in their own "reserves," presumably with eventual greater political autonomy in their own areas; and (2) the maximum possible segregation of natives and Europeans in areas of mixed residence, with complete domination, political and otherwise, by the Europeans. Since this approach to the race problem is directly opposite to the broad trend found elsewhere in the non-Communist world, it has evoked increasing resistance from the natives within the Republic and increasing criticism from abroad, frequently expressed through the United Nations.

Race relations in South Africa are now at a highly critical point. The Union withdrew from the British Commonwealth in March, 1961, because the other member nations insisted on a declaration disapproving its racial policy. Currently *Apartheid* is so strongly entrenched by repressive measures that change in South Africa is likely to be effected only by revolution, aided by the newly

---

[11] The Nationalist government is dominated by the Afrikaners (Dutch descended), found more in the rural areas, while the opposition, the United Party, is dominated by those of British descent, more concentrated in the urban areas, and slightly more moderate on the race issue.

developed Black African nations, or by strong pressures from the powerful nations of the West through the United Nations or otherwise.[12]

Rhodesia presents a broadly similar pattern in which a small component of dominant whites have resisted the insistent efforts of the British government that plans for the gradual civic integration of natives be formulated. Rhodesia reacted by declaring independence. British attempts to force Rhodesia back into the Commonwealth with an integrated policy have to date failed and the outcome is in doubt. The "rebel" government of Rhodesia does not appear as intransigent over total white dominance as does the nationalist government of South Africa.

The era of colonialism is virtually over.[13] Since World War II the former colonial nations have been surrendering their political control. Many former colonies, now independent nations, have chosen to retain nominal ties with their previous rulers—with the Commonwealth, for example, in the British case. Thus all influence of the former colonial powers has not been eliminated. It is still a fact of life that through investments the affluent nations exercise much influence on the economies and governments of these new nations. Before granting independence the British, French, and the Dutch had made some effort to train the natives in self-government and economic and technical competence. Much of the Congo crisis developing in the last decade relates to the failure of the Belgians to pursue a similar policy earlier.

Equally pertinent to our interest are the relations between the Euro-American residents and emissaries in these areas and the native peoples. For the most part, Euro-Americans residing in these former colonial areas—or anywhere in Asia and Africa for that matter—live and interact within a substantially separate and exclusive subcommunity of an obviously upper-status level. Although lacking the political power to be truly dominant, their conspicuous high-class status makes them in a sense a socially dominant, though foreign, component of many Asian and African states. While there is some "social" interaction with the upper class of the native population, the native population being non-Caucasian, the Euro-Americans tend to draw not only the class line but the "color" line as well. It is this sort of behavior which fosters the image of "the ugly American" among nonwhite people the world over, offset in part by the missionaries and more recently by the Peace Corps.

The Voluntary Immigrant Pattern

The fourth pattern of dominant-minority relations arose out of the voluntary immigration of peoples from nations other than those of the original colonists. The main destination of these peoples was the United States; Canada,

---

[12] See Pierre L. Van den Berghe, *South Africa: A Study in Conflict* (Middletown, Conn.: Wesleyan University Press, 1965), pp. 262–264.

[13] Even the Communist propaganda agencies now tend to use the rather illogical term "imperialist" in condemning what they call Western exploitation.

Australia, and New Zealand have restricted immigration largely to British peoples, thus preserving a large measure of cultural homogeneity at the expense of more rapid population growth and industrial expansion. Of these Commonwealth nations, Canada continues to have difficulties in the relation between its numerically dominant British-descended and its minority French-descended peoples.

Immigration to South America largely from Europe, occurred in the late nineteenth and early twentieth centuries, chiefly to Brazil and Argentina.[14] Of all South American countries, Argentina had the greatest amount of European immigration, mostly from Italy and Spain. This largely explains why Argentina is the "whitest" of the continent's nations. Not more than ten percent of its population is *mestizo,* and there are probably less than 60,000 full-blooded Indians and almost no Negro genetic element.[15] The Republic therefore has little group tension based on ethnic or racial lines.

Immigration to Brazil has not been so great as to Argentina. From 1874 to 1957, slightly under five million immigrants are reported as having entered the country.[16] The official 1950 census reported the following percentages of its population by color as White 61.7, Black 11.0, *Pardo* (mixed and Indian) 26.5.[17] Brazil has developed what amounts to a "veritable cult of racial equality." [18] Thus while widespread discontent is to be found among the masses, tension and conflict on the basis of racial or ethnic differentiation play no important role in it.[19]

Within the restrictive limits placed on immigration by the recipient nations there has been substantial voluntary immigration to various nations since World War II. Considerable numbers of Italians and Spanish migrated to Germany to meet the needs for filling the labor shortages at the menial levels of an expanding economy. More critical in regard to racial tension has been a moderate influx of Jamaican Negroes to Great Britain that has engendered problems somewhat similar to those of Northern communities in the United States in the early stages of Negro influx.[20] A recent officially sanctioned study of Britain's "colored" immigrants reports severe and extensive discrimination in such matters as housing, jobs, and the use of other facilities.[21] Finally the perennial problem of refugees from behind the Iron Curtain continues. Partly

[14] See Maurice R. Davie, *World Immigration* (New York: Macmillan Co., 1947), pp. 353–364, for a brief general account.
[15] *Encyclopaedia Britannica,* 1964, vol. 2, pp. 368–369.
[16] T. Lynn Smith, *Brazil: People and Institutions,* rev. ed. (Baton Rouge, La.: Louisiana State University Press, 1963), p. 121.
[17] *Ibid.,* p. 68.
[18] *Ibid.,* p. 151.
[19] *Ibid.*
[20] See Sheila Patterson, *Dark Strangers* (London: Tavistock Publications, 1963).
[21] The study was made by the Race Relations Board and the National Committee for Commonwealth Immigrants. See Anthony Lewis, "Severe Racial Bias Noted in Britain," in *The New York Times,* April 18, 1967, pp. 1, 7.

because the Communist countries strenuously ban it, thus keeping the numbers small, this kind of immigration has presented minimal problems to the receiving nations.[22]

Chinese in Southeast Asia

The emigration southward of substantial numbers of Chinese to other nations in southeast Asia—notably to Thailand, Malaya, Singapore, Indonesia, and the former Indochina area (now Vietnam, Cambodia, and Laos)—has been another main immigration trend. The Chinese in these areas have generally adjusted successfully. While they are not all middle class, enough of them are that they are identified as such by the native peasant class. Despite economic adjustment and considerable intermarriage, the Chinese remain a group apart. This failure to assimilate has been due in part to the political-legal discrimination imposed on them by the host countries or their colonial rulers, but it is due as much to their own retention of Chinese culture. Comparison with Western minority situations has often led Western writers to refer to the Chinese immigrants in Southeast Asia as "the Jews of the East." [23]

The current struggle for influence in Southeast Asia between the Communist—now more apparently Chinese than Russian—and the democratic nation may accentuate intergroup conflict in this area. Anxiety by the governments of these nations concerning the loyalty of their Chinese components, if China becomes more expansionist, is paralleled by anxiety on the part of the outgroup Chinese. Recent news reports, for example, indicate concern for their status among the Chinese in Indonesia since the 1966 coup which oriented the government away from Communist influence.

Soviet Russia and Minorities

In view of the struggle between the Communist and the non-Communist world, it seems pertinent to conclude our brief overall view of minority situations outside the United States with special attention to Soviet Russia. Within the Soviet Union itself, there have been three minority situations: (1) non-Slavic peoples with sufficient cultural distinction to have a special ethnic or religious identity—nearly 200 of such groups together comprised roughly a fifth of the Union's population at the outset of the Communist regime; (2) groups that were largely Mongoloid and non-Christian in religion; and (3) about three million Jews.[24]

[22] See for example Edmund Dahlstrom, "Estonian Refugees in a Swedish Community." Paper presented to the Second World Congress of the International Sociological Association, Liege, Belgium, 1963. Reprinted in Arnold M. and Caroline B. Rose, *Minority Problems,* pp. 98–107.
[23] Maurice Freedman, "The Chinese in Southeast Asia," in *Race Relations* in *World Perspective,* ed. Andrew Lind (Honolulu: University of Hawaii Press, 1955), Ch. 17.
[24] William H. Chamberlin, *Soviet Russia* (Boston: Little Brown & Co., 1930), p. 13.

In the formal organization of their society, the Soviets aimed to remove all manifestations of ethnic and racial discrimination. Ethnic equality was made explicit in the Soviet constitution in 1936 and its violation punishable by law. In their efforts to expand their influence among other peoples, the Soviets have made much of this in their propaganda. The actual practices reveal considerable divergence from this formal statement of policy.

In general the policy of the Soviets has been toward the standardization of culture within the Union among the lines serving the purpose of a monolitic regime—a modern-day Russification. Neither local culture nor nationality sentiment has been permitted to stand in the way of this process. During Stalin's time, the policy was drastic. "Three autonomous republics (Crimean Tartars, Kalmucks, and Chechens-Ingushi) were disbanded because of alleged disloyalty . . . in time of war. . . . The peoples concerned were just thrown into the vast Soviet Russian melting pot and disappeared. . . . No statistics or other official information can be obtained about them." [25]

World Jewry supported by many Gentile writers is strongly convinced that the Soviet government is intent on the destruction of Jewish culture and collective identity. Goldhagen has traced the fluctuations in the policy and practice of Russian communists throughout Marxian history. [26] Even the pre-Revolutionary European socialist movement itself in the early period tended to look upon the Jews "with unfriendly eyes, regarding them as the embodiment of these qualities which socialists denounced as evil. . . ." However, the succeeding generation of Russian revolutionaries changed this attitude, and those who dominated the revolutionary scene would not tolerate anti-Semitism in the movement.

Goldhagen describes four phases in the policy of the Soviet government. (1) "After the October Revolution the Bolsheviks adopted an uncompromising attitude against anti-Semitism." (2) In the 1930's under Stalin's nationalism a climate less congenial to Jews was created and discrimination against Jews in influential occupations became manifest. (3) This developing intolerance was, beginning with 1948, carried to outright repression of Jewish cultural institutions. "From then on until Stalin's death Soviet Jews lived under a reign of terror amid rumors of their imminent mass deportation." (4) Stalin's heirs aimed at relenting the terror and tolerated some revival of the separate nationality cultures but excluded the Jews specifically from this policy. "The terror relented. But the fundamentals of Stalin's policy toward the Jews were retained." Thus finally there continues to prevail what Goldhagen calls the policy of "assimilation through attrition."

This policy is more calculated on realpolitik than on emotional anti-

[25] Walter J. Kolarz, "Race Relations in the Soviet Union," in *Race Relations in World Perspective* (Conference on Race Relations in World Perspective, Honolulu: University of Hawaii Press, 1955), p. 192.

[26] Erich Goldhagen, "Communism and Anti-Semitism," *Problems of Communism,* vol. IX no. 3, 1960, pp. 35–43. The quotations used are also taken from this article.

Semitism of the traditional type. It is based on the inability of any totalitarian regime to tolerate any substantial "cultural pluralism" and a distrust of Jewish culture in particular as being "cosmopolitan," identified with world Jewry and with a foreign state, Israel.[27]

Whether or not Soviet citizens of Jewish lineage can avoid any discrimination if they give up their Jewish visibility is a debatable matter even among Jewish scholars.[28]

Topics for Projects and Discussion

1. Collect from any current newspapers or magazines items pertaining to minorities. Bring them to class prepared to relate them to this chapter.
2. In the family or neighborhood in which you were reared, what were the attitudes expressed toward peoples of different racial, religious, or nationality backgrounds?
3. If you have traveled abroad, cite any instances of the behavior of Americans in foreign lands indicative of their attitudes toward other peoples.
4. Prepare a 10-minute talk designed to convince a dominant-status audience that discrimination is costly to them.
5. Cite any current events concerned with minorities having implications that affect America's position in international affairs.
6. If you were an American representative in the United Nations, what would you say in reply to an attack by a Communist representative on the treatment of minorities in the United States?

Suggested Reading

Barron, Milton L., ed., *Minorities in a Changing World*. New York: Alfred A. Knopf, 1967.

> *Part II of this book of readings has several articles on minorities in various societies.*

Hunter, Guy. *South-East Asia: Race, Culture and Nation*. New York, London: Oxford University Press, 1966.

> *Chapter III, "The Immigrant Races," treats the Chinese and Indians as ethnic components of Southeast Asian nations.*

Paterson, Sheila. *Dark Strangers*. London: Tavistock Publications, 1963.

> *A comprehensive study of the nonwhite population of Great Britain and their interaction with the white British population.*

Rose, Arnold, and Caroline B. Rose. *Minority Problems: A Textbook of Readings in Intergroup Relations*. New York: Harper & Row, Publishers, 1965.

> *Part I, "The Nature of Minority Problems in the United States," and Part II, "Minority Problems in Other Parts of the World," are supplemental to this chapter.*

[27] See also Solomon M. Schwarz, *The Jews in the Soviet Union* (New York: The American Jewish Committee, 1951, published by the Syracuse University Press), for a broadly similar version of this topic.

[28] See Samuel Rozin, "I speak as a Soviet Jew," in *The Minority of One*, vol. 5, May, 1963, pp. 13–15, and Moshe Decter, "The Truth about Soviet Jewry," *The Minority of One*, vol. 5, July, 1963, pp. 15–17.

Shibutani, Tamotan, and Kian M. Kwan. *Ethnic Stratification: A Comparative Approach.* New York: The Macmillan Co., 1965.

> *An original approach to a theory of ethnic intergroup relations on a worldwide scale.*

Smith, Richard F. "The Refugees," *The Annals of the Academy of Political and Social Science,* Vol. 367 (September, 1966), pp. 43–52.

> *An account of the recent "refugee" immigration to the United States, including short discussion of Cuban immigration.*

Smith, T. Lynn. *Brazil: Its Peoples and Institutions,* rev. ed. Baton Rouge, La.: Louisiana State University Press, 1965.

> *Part Two: "The People," includes Chapter IV, "Racial Composition" and Chapter VIII, "Immigration."*

Van Den Berghe, Pierre. *South Africa: A Study in Conflict.* Middletown, Conn.: Wesleyan University Press, 1965.

> *An outstanding substantive and theoretical work on South African race relations.*

2

Introduction to the Sociology of Minorities

The situation of minorities is a special focus within the general problems of social analysis. This chapter will deal with some key *concepts* (the tools of sociology), and apply them to dominant-minority relations in general and to American society in particular.

Sustained relations between groups of people take place in two dimensions: within an established pattern of expected behavior (social structure) and, over time, in repeated contact that is affected by and in turn affects social structure (social process).

Some Basic Terms for Analysis of Social Structure

Values

Values are beliefs governing action. Shared values are the basis of voluntary group cohesion. Any existing society maintains its social order through the dominance of one configuration of values. These may not be consistent at all points, but even in their lack of consistency they show some central assumptions. For example, contemporary Western culture has been described as having the following ways of viewing the fundamental questions of the relation of man to his environment: that nature is to be *overcome* and controlled (the value basis for scientific and technological activity); that the *future* should have more emphasis than the past or present; that the normal mode of relations between men is individualistic and competetive. These orientations are the foundation of the derivitive expectations of behavior. The individual acquires values in hierarchical relationship to persons in authority: parents, teachers, employers and civic models. They are reinforced by myths and hero figures. They are acquired by indoctrination and emulation.

It is the nature of values that they seem to the group that holds them to be "the best," "the right." Values are acquired so early in the socialization process —in the family, in the school, in the community—that for most people they

20

are largely unconscious assumptions, governing action much more than it is governed by consciously professed creeds.

Variant values is a term for subcultural values. For example, among rural Spanish Americans of the southwestern United States, the individual is socialized and becomes integrated into a traditional culture different from the "Anglo" culture of the dominant group. His actions and expectations are therefore with reference to the subculture, and they may be inappropriate to the dominant culture.[1]

Both dominant and variant value systems are sets of *official values* designed to maintain cultural continuity and give a frame for expectations, and they are acquired hierarchically. *Unofficial values,*[2] on the other hand, are concerned with present interest and are acquired and supported by present experiences which lack hierarchical character. These are sometimes also called *deviant* values. Unofficial values may be of many kinds, but they contain some elements which are in conflict with official values, though there may be areas in which the two overlap. They may be values held by an artist group, a political protest group, a religious sect. In a period when official values are changing deviant values can be obsolete values clung to by groups whose interests are suffering through change. Members of minority groups are often attracted to groups that adhere to unofficial values because it may seem harmonious with their present interest to protest or deny official values, especially as these appear discriminatory, and, too, it may be a way of minimizing minority status by forming associations with a different group of people. Upholders of the official system in conflict with groups expressing unofficial values have sometimes linked unofficial values with "foreign" and used anti-minority sentiment against them.[3] Thus early miner's unions were described as "drunken, fighting Irish."

Norms

Norms are the implicit rules of behavior—that is, the group, *according to its values* defines what actions are approved, or "good," or "taken for granted" (normal). There are norms governing, for example, the conduct of family life, economic life, political behavior, religious participation, and education. When

---

[1] Florence Rockwood Kluckhohn, "Dominant and Variant Value Orientations," *Personality in Nature, Society and Culture,* rev. ed. Clyde Kluckhohn and Henry Murray with the collaboration of David M. Schneider (New York: Alfred A. Knopf, 1953), pp. 342ff.

[2] Milton L. Barron, *The Juvenile in Delinquent Society* (New York: Alfred A. Knopf, 1954), p. 203.

[3] A fair fist fight (between men of equal strength) and a drinking bout at the local tavern on Saturday night were legitimate outlets in Irish peasant culture. See Conrad M. Arensberg and Solon T. Kimball, *Family and Community in Ireland* (Cambridge, Mass.: Harvard University Press, 1940). These modes of behavior were "foreign" to Puritan America and later used to arouse sentiment against groups of Irish coal miners seeking to unionize. At this period unions represented unofficial values.

these norms have persisted across generations we speak of them as *institutionalized,* or a particular configuration establishing some segment of social behavior we call an *institution,* such as marriage as an institution of family life, a contract as an institution of economic life, the state as an institution of political life.

Within these institutionalized patterns individuals carry out their lives. The performance of their functions from day to day is a *role,* and there are expectations (norms) of how roles should be fulfilled: the "loving" mother, the "reliable" workman, the "efficient" secretary are rubrics expressing some aspect of role definition. The failure to carry out the institutional roles in the manner defined by the dominant culture is a major justification offered by dominants for devaluation of minorities: "They don't *do* right." The explicit or implicit definition of roles in the institutions of society ensure continuity and a reasonable degree of order. On the other hand, this very function of continuity often makes for lag in appropriate or useful adaptation to change.

Status

Status defines the relative position of a person or a group with regard to others persons or groups in the hierarchy of prestige. Honored positions in the society go to those who best fulfill significant dominant institutional roles. The overall problems of status are usually linked with the problem of social class (access to the opportunity structure), or caste (absolute barriers to selective types of social participation). We are interested primarily in the relationships between dominants and minorities with regard to their relative status. Though this is, as we shall see, intertwined with questions of social class, it can be considered a separate matter. While some actions unite dominants and minorities on the basis of class interests (as in some labor unions, political parties, etc.), more common in the past and to a considerable extent in the present is the alliance of dominants across class lines to keep minorities in subordinate status.

These key factors in social structure give us a background against which to define what is *dominant* and what is *minority.*

The Dominant Group: A Definition

The dominant group in a society is one whose appearance and ways of behaving are considered the "normal ones" of the society. Members of the dominant group share a common value system, a common language, and a common history. Dominant norms are historically derived, and their pre-eminence is established by custom and by law. The survival of the society is believed to depend on these norms to such an extent that subgroups which do not fully share them are restricted, formally or informally, to a greater or lesser degree, from full and equal participation in the life of the society.

Before the rise of national states, dominant-minority relations existed be-

tween kinship groups (tribes, clans, "peoples") or religious groups, where varying patterns of subordination or "tolerance" of outgroups were to be found. In
the modern world, the secular state has the military and legal prerogative to
determine the protection and participation of the people within its geographic
borders and, in many instances, within its extended political hegemony. The
state is distinguished from the other great institutions, such as the family and
the church, by its "exclusive investment with the final power of coercion." [4]
Therefore, the state is the territorial unit within which one must consider any
contemporary analysis of dominant-minority relations. We shall consider a
dominant group, then, *as one within a national state whose distinctive culture
and/or physiognomy is established as superior in the society and which treats
differentially and unequally other groups in the society with other cultures or
physiognomy.*

Minority: A Definition

The anthropologists Charles Wagley and Marvin Harris, in presenting case
studies in the Western Hemisphere from materials which, in part, were prepared for UNESCO by social scientists of five countries, have arrived at the
following definition of a minority, which we have adopted as the fullest and
most appropriate:

> (1) Minorities are subordinate segments of complex state societies; (2) minor-
> ities have special physical or cultural traits which are held in low esteem by the
> dominant segments of the society; (3) minorities are self-conscious units bound to-
> gether by the special traits which their members share and by the special dis-
> abilities which these bring; (4) membership in a minority is transmitted by a rule
> of descent which is capable of affiliating succeeding generations even in the absence
> of readily apparent physical or cultural traits; (5) minority peoples, by choice or
> necessity, tend to marry within the group.[5]

This statement gives us five criteria which can be applied to the designation
of a group as a minority in a contemporary society. First, to be a member of a
minority is not only to be part of a social group vis-à-vis another social group,
but to be so within a political unit. Thus the political power groups, as well as
the legal structure, will profoundly affect the situation of minorities. Second,
attitudes of dominant members toward minorities are bound up with a system
of values which devalues certain physical and cultural traits. Third, minorities
are conscious of themselves as groups. In some cases members of a minority
group deliberately adhere to values which vary from those of the dominant
group and which they wish to preserve; sometimes they share disabilities arising

[4] Robert M. MacIver and Charles H. Page, *Society* (New York: Rinehart & Company,
1937), p. 456.
[5] Charles Wagley and Marvin Harris, *Minorities in the New World: Six Case Studies*
(New York: Columbia University Press, 1958), p. 10.

from historical attitudes and discrimination. Fourth, one is a member of a minority without choice.

The chief limitation of the definition we have quoted is its failure to stress discrimination. Minority status is an *imposed* status except for sectarian separatist groups, and has validity only as dominants possess the power and opportunity to sustain it. Similarly we should prefer to state Wagley and Harris's fifth point the other way around. Minority peoples tend by *necessity* or choice to marry within their group. The minority's resistence to outmarriage may be due to regard for a particular cultural heritage, or to fear that outmarriages will result in unhappiness, or to a combination of these reasons.

Relations of the dominant group to any particular minority must always be understood in a *historical dimension*. Present attitudes derive from past patterns of interaction, even when there are now changed relations between the dominant group and the minority.

Ethnicity

Ethnic is an increasingly popular term in dealing with the subject of minorities. Often it is used adjectivally as an equivalent of the term *minority*. This is of course inaccurate. *Ethnic* is a term which emphasizes the cultural ethos (values, expectations, behavior) of a group and formerly, quite properly, was limited in reference to groups whose cultural characteristics are their prime distinguishing factor. *Dominants as well as minorities are members of an ethnic group*. An ethnic group, unlike a nationality group, is a population which has preserved visible elements of a tradition without primary reference to former loyalties to a nation-state. The French emigrés who came to New Orleans after the French revolution were a nationality group. The present French-Canadians are an ethnic group. Minority status may strengthen ethnicity, just as ethnicity may contribute to minority status.

Some Basic Terms for the Analysis of Social Process

All groups interacting over time go through phases of relationship. Sometimes these phases are sequential, and sometimes to an extent at least, they may be simultaneous. Some writers have claimed that initial contacts are dominated by curiosity, mutual assistance, and silent trade or barter, as for example the initial contacts of Europeans with American Indians.[6] But it is equally true of history that some initial contacts have been hostile on the part of both groups. One of the first sociologists to be concerned with contacts between races and cultures attempted to subsume these under three basic modes of interaction: *cooperation, competition,* and *conflict*. Sometimes these modes have been treated as a basic sequence which occurs in this order.[7]

[6] Franklin Frazier, *Race and Culture Contacts in the Modern World* (New York: Alfred A. Knopf, 1957).
[7] Robert E. Park, *Race and Culture* (Glencoe, Ill.: The Free Press, 1950).

Another way of viewing social processes is not in terms of patterns of inter-action, but as dynamic aspects of the social structure. These processes can then be *sustaining, differentiating, disjunctive,* or *integrative.* These, also, are some-times treated as sequential.[8] In the analysis in the following pages we shall employ both approaches. It is important to remember, however, that though one process may seem more predominant in one historical situation in one particular place, in any complex society such as the United States, all of these processes are *always* going on. One or another assumes pre-eminence in a given place or period depending on other factors creating increase or diminution of stress, such as heavy migration, depression, war.

We are now ready to turn to the framework of our discussion of dominant-minority relations as they take place within the social structure and social processes of American life.

The Establishment of Dominance

When peoples meet, the outcome might theoretically be a pattern of inter-group relations of a coordinate status character. Something of this sort appears to have happened between the peoples of German, French, and Italian descent in Switzerland. More generally, however, the outcome has assumed a super-ordinate-subordinate form.[9] Contributing to this are two conditions: a dif-ferentiation between the two peoples that makes each group identifiable to the other and an unequal power situation.

Since the establishment of dominance depends on each group recognizing the other as different we have called this factor *visibility*. The traits that are perceived as "different" may be physiognomic ("racial") or cultural, or both.

Biological Visibility

PHYSICAL TYPE   The traits that are highly valued in American culture are the Caucasoid features. Any variation from the ideal type is held in less esteem in the popular culture. Where differences from the Caucasoid type are per-ceived, as illustrated by those physical features of the Japanese or the Chinese which distinguish them from the white, we speak of biological visibility.

LINEAGE   Lineage is invisible visibility. We consider it an aspect of biological descent. In cases of severe devaluation of minorities, even a small proportion of minority ancestry is enough to designate membership in a minority. "Negroes" who are so completely Caucasoid in their physical features that they cannot be identified by sight are identifiable as Negroes by the general knowledge of their Negro lineage. In periods when dominant elements strongly desire to ex-

---

[8] For example see the organization of the discussion in Tamotan Shibutani and Kian M. Kwan, *Ethnic Stratification: A Comparative Approach* (New York: Macmillan, 1965).
[9] See Stanley Lieberson, "A Societal Theory of Race and Ethnic Relations," *American Sociological Review* (Vol. 26, No. 6, December 1961, pp. 902–910), for a discussion of types of initial contact and the conditions for superordination.

clude minorities from privileges and participation and when the latter's visibility is becoming too attenuated for the purpose, rules of descent have been made official, as in the case of the Jews in Nazi Germany.

Cultural Visibility

LANGUAGE AND NONVERBAL COMMUNICATION   The practice of speaking another language in the family or among close associates may serve as a mode of identification in both a derogatory sense for the dominant group, or in a sense of cultural pride for the minority. The language of gesture, facial expression, posture, emotional tone, all express cultural learning and vary from culture to culture. Different societies allow different ways of expressing emotional reactions to joy or pain or trouble, and these reactive patterns also are used to identify minorities in a derogatory way. For example, one study has shown that doctors and nurses with Anglo-Saxon norms of reserve in emotional expression often fail to understand and are impatient with the reactions to their illness of patients from non-Anglo-Saxon societies.[10]

DRESS   Although there are only a few highly coherent minorities that maintain traditional modes of dress—for instance the Amish, Hassidic Jews, and Navahoes (on the reservation)—dress has in the past been a major symbol of cultural identity. Nationality societies whose members have long since adopted the dominant modes of dress for everyday living, often still wear the traditional "costume" to celebrate patriotic or religious festivals. Modes of hair style and ornamentation may also indicate a particular cultural heritage. Sometimes an insecure group will adopt a mode of dress as part of a struggle for identification, as for example, the Zoot suits that were affected by young Mexican Americans in the early 1940's.

INSTITUTIONAL BEHAVIOR   Different ways of behaving in family, economic, political, and religious life often make members of minorities conspicuous. For example, filial obligations and parental authority may make a young person different in his group participation from his schoolfellows. A minority member with different religious practices in a highly coherent Protestant community may in this sense be visible to his neighbors.

ASSOCIATIONS   An aspect of visibility frequently ignored in the discussion of minorities is what we shall call *associational visibility*. An individual may have no visible traits that would designate him a member of a minority, but he identifies himself by the group with which he generally associates, particularly in his most intimate contacts. While as a means of identification associational visibility is derivative from other bases, it acquires significance through long practice.

OVERLAP OF TRAITS   A minority is sometimes identified only by physi-

---

[10] Mark Zborowski, "Cultural Components in Responses to Pain," *Social Perspectives on Behavior*, eds. Herman D. Stein and Richard A. Cloward (Glencoe, Ill.: The Free Press, 1958).

ognomic traits, but usually there is an overlap of physiognomic and cultural traits. Sometimes there are only cultural traits which may occur in any of several combinations. Perhaps only two minority groups can easily be fitted into a simple visibility scheme: the immigrants from the north of Europe who differ in ethnic culture without basic religious difference, and contemporary American Negroes, who are distinguished almost solely by their physiognomic features.

A useful clue to arranging minorities in a classification based on visibility may be found by considering the ways in which the dominant-status group has reacted to the visibilities involved. Proceeding in this manner, it can be observed that the dominant groups in the United States have conceived of minority groups in three ways: as "foreigners," as "colored," and as non-believers in the faith of the dominant group. While in most specific situations the dominants look on the minority in some combination of these three ways, in each case it seems possible to accord priority to one. For example, although the great majority of Italians are known to be Catholics, it is that entire configuration of cultural elements which compose the Italian "ethos" which identifies them most prominently. Again, while the Japanese are often thought of as foreigners, it is their physiognomic visibility which comes first to the mind of the person of dominant status when the word "Japanese" is mentioned. The leading element in the consciousness of the dominant in his conception of the Japanese is appearance. In spite of the fact that "color" is one of the less accurate traits to employ in "racial" classifications of mankind, it is consciousness of color which has loomed largest in the white man's concept of the other peoples of the earth. Wherever color difference is associated with other differences in the United States, it has always taken precedence over other factors in retarding assimilation.

Numbers and Concentration as Related to Visibility

A few dispersed individuals or families, whatever their physical or cultural traits, are less likely to be subject to all of the disabilities of minority position. They may be viewed with curiosity, tolerated, or ignored. When there are large numbers of a particular minority in a community, however, there is more likely to be a consensus of differential treatment. This is all the more so if they are forced to cluster in a given area of the community, or if they do so from choice. They are then not only visible as individuals, but visible as a segment of the community.

Differential Power

The establishment of dominance occurs, as we have pointed out, when one group, as contrasted with others, succeeds in superimposing its values and its institutions as normative, with the concomitant inferior valuation for those who adhere to different norms. Sometimes this is achieved by military conquest, sometimes through superior technology and/or organization, sometimes through superior numbers, or, in the case of voluntary migrants, when historically established norms confront them and they may find themselves culturally ill-equipped for immediate adjustment. This dominance nevertheless takes place through the *use of force* or through the *threat of force,* which covertly underlies other mechanisms of devaluation. Minorities respond by sporadic conflict, by negotiation, by separatism, and by accommodation.

CONFLICT   Since the interests of minorities and their share in the power, authority, and usually, therefore, the opportunities of the society, are disadvantaged, there is always potential conflict in dominant-minority relations. At times when force and the power of reprisal are overt, conflict will be sporadic, or it may be displaced against other powerless groups in the society.

NEGOTIATION   Negotiation can occur when it seems possible to establish regular channels for communication between disparate interests. Thus, though Indians were displaced from the Atlantic seaboard, and subsequently from most of the rest of the productive land of the United States, they were dealt with under treaty arrangement until the mid-nineteenth century. Throughout American history there have been negotiations for needed labor force, sometimes through agents directly with foreign workers, sometimes with foreign governments. Negotiation depends upon both parties accepting the terms (Indians accepting lands in the West, laborers accepting laborer's status). Negotiation can only occur when both parties have something to offer, and can be sustained only as long as both sides keep the agreement (explicit or implicit). Thus when white settlers sought to displace Indians in the West, conflict recurred, and when laborers wished to share in power and authority conflict emerged.

SEPARATISM   In the period of colonial expansion, from the seventeenth to the nineteenth centuries, there were many groups who sought to set up enclaves in the New World which were geographically separate and in which they could maintain their particular way of life. A number of such German-speaking groups came to the colonies in the eighteenth century, of which the Amish still persist. So too, those dissenting "minorities" from England who were discriminated against in the sphere of political power—Puritans, Quakers, Catholics—saw in the establishments of new settlements an opportunity not only to survive, but to control and develop their communities according to their own values. Thus William Penn wrote to his son in 1700:

> Remember these points, that it was the Government which engaged me and those that adventured with me.... The Government was our greatest inducement, and upon that public faith we have buried our blood and bones, as well as estates, to make it what it is: for being Dissenters, we therefore came that we might enjoy that so far of which would not be allowed us any share at home.[11]

[11] "Papers Relating to Provincial Affairs," in *Pennsylvania Archives of History and Biography,* Second Series, Vol. VII, p. 11.

Separatism represents the decision to eschew the structure of the dominant society in order to retain values which have led to discrimination in the society from which the group has separated. Throughout the nineteenth century there were separatist settlements in the United States with religious or nationality identities which they wished to preserve. With the closing of the frontier, separatism became a less common solution. Although it persists, occasionally even in the midst of an urban community, as with Hassidic Jews, it is no longer an easy solution.

ACCOMMODATION   If the individuals in a minority remain within the framework of the dominant society and are a powerless segment, they must of necessity accept conditions they cannot control; they must to a degree conform to subordinate positions and rules of behavior vis-à-vis the dominant group.

Conflict and negotiation are social *processes* that indicate that both *disjunctive* and *sustaining* forces are at work simultaneously in the establishment of dominance, with different foci toward different minorities. There was no negotiation with Negroes, although there are many instances of Negro rebellion. There was with Indians.

The positions assumed by the "different" peoples, therefore, were accommodative if they were not negotiable; or separatist, if they could claim by physical or moral force to be treated as equal partners to an agreement.

By far the most important factor in the establishment of American dominant-minority relations, other than the displacement of the Indians, is that English-speaking peoples arrived first in the largest numbers, became entrenched under the English government, with English values and institutions, and in time edged out the French, Dutch, or Spanish attempts to hold part of the terrain. The American experience has been in large part the attempt of the entrenched White Angle-Saxon Protestants (WASPS)[12] to maintain their privileges, their values, their institutions in the face of heavy in-migration of peoples whose values, language, customs, and often appearance have been different.

The Stabilization of Dominance

We have seen the conditions and processes of the establishment of dominance. How and why the stabilization of dominance is effected is our next consideration.

Law and Custom

Law and custom replace force to sustain over time the achieved dominance, and the initial definition of subordinate groups is augmented to apply to other visible groups that may be added to the population. Force, or the threat of

---

[12] The initials WASP have now become usage in some academic writing. The term, originally a "popular" contraction also initially carried an edge of derogation. We find it useful as a reminder that WASPS are also an ethnic group.

force, however, remains the ultimate sanction for maintaining dominance. It may be legitimately used (law enforcement) to ensure the preservation of established relationships, or, in periods of tension, it may be used in defiance of law.

In stable periods the law has pre-eminence, with *authority* to enforce. Thus political control of the state by adherents to dominant norms will ensure laws upholding these norms. In the creation of policy toward minorities, the state may, for example, grant or deny citizenship, as in America for a long time it excluded Orientals and defined limited citizenship for the conquered American Indians. Furthermore, the state plays its role in the subjugation of minorities not only through law and policy, but through its system of education. It presents historical models of esteemed behavior: the founding fathers and other "great men." Conversely, only too often, idealized subordinate roles are also presented in the official education: Pocahontas and Uncle Tom become the faithful protectors and upholders of Anglo-Saxon dominance. Public rituals and symbols constantly stimulate or reinvoke sentiments of loyalty, affection, and commitment to dominant values.

Custom governs the whole web of traditionally appropriate behavior. When dominance is maintained in a relatively unchanging society, custom ensures the continuance of previously defined appropriate ways of interacting. These may even be elaborated into a rigid etiquette which amplifies the fact of dominance in all spheres of life. Probably the extreme example of this is the pattern of relations between whites and Negroes in the more traditional sections of the South. The common understanding of what is expected and allowable between the two groups governs almost every phase of contact.

In the American legal system, resting as it does on English common law, there can never be too wide a gap between enforceable laws and accepted customs. The problem emerges most clearly in the tension between local or regional customs and the local and state laws which are coherent with them, and federal laws, which have responded to a broader legislative representation that includes many who do not share the regional or local patterns.

In order to maintain a stable pattern of dominance, specific patterns of action and attitude are incorporated into the social system and become self-understood or taken for granted on the part of dominants. These attitudes and actions are sustaining processes; they also ensure the restriction of people with other patterns of action or other attitudes from full participation in power and economic opportunity.

From time to time in American history there have been legal restrictions on the right of movement and of assembly. These have applied primarily to Negroes, slave and free before the Civil War, and to white indentured servants as long as the indenture system controlled the labor supply. American-born Japanese were confined in internment camps along with their Japanese-born parents in World War II.

Categorical Discrimination

Discrimination—differential and unequal treatment by the dominant of the minority—is an essential feature of the dominant-minority relationship. Discrimination is categorical when it is applied to all members of the minority. For example, Irish immigrants arriving in Boston in pre-Civil War days found signs at places of employment saying "No Irish need apply."

Discrimination may operate in hotels, jobs, social organizations, admissions to schools, colleges, and universities, and so forth, wherever there is categorical exclusion or categorical limitation of numbers. Discrimination may also operate to create unequal rewards for work that is done, in wage differentials, or in access to promotion. It may operate in the sphere of political rights, thus limiting access to the ultimate channel of power or redress. Provisions like the poll tax effectively deprive many people from their share in the political decision-making process.

POLITICAL DISCRIMINATION   American political institutions exhibit the many variations that occur through the different balances of statutory democracy and the right to private property. Because our Constitution guarantees civil equality to all regardless of race, creed, or national origin, political institutions have become the major focus for efforts to reduce discrimination. On the whole, great strides have been made, and political discrimination persists only in localities and regions where state and local laws obtain. The several problems of political discrimination that remain are generally subsumed under the term "civil rights." Segregation in public education, rights for Indians, access to tax-supported facilities, such as recreation areas, and so forth, are also within the sphere of political discrimination.

ECONOMIC DISCRIMINATION   The problem of economic discrimination is more complex, since attempts at regulation by law can in many instances be interpreted as unwarranted interference with the rights of private property. Types of economic discrimination include discrimination in employment, either by announced policy or by private agreement, and also the subtler problem of the promotions and privileges available in certain occupational channels. Another type of economic discrimination is residential discrimination, where informal agreements of property owners exclude some minorities from some residential sections.

The economic sphere has been increasingly invaded by state regulation in the twentieth century, and legislation has barred certain types of economic discrimination in some places. Economic pressure through threat of boycott or unfavorable publicity has lessened discrimination in those sectors of business most vulnerable to such mechanisms: transportation, hotels, and retail stores, for example. Discrimination in trade unions is another type of economic discrimination.

SOCIAL DISCRIMINATION   Discrimination in the private areas of life is not subject to control by law and will be the last to disappear. Most amenable to change, even in defiance of local sentiment on occasion, have been the religious institutions, though this is not occuring without struggle. Country clubs, fraternities, private schools, and other voluntary organizations may set their own rules and will maintain varying degrees of discrimination depending on how strong the in-group feeling of their membreship is. The final area through which discrimination can continue to operate longer is in the family and its attitudes, from social invitations through the spectrum of private life to intermarriage. All practices, formal and informal, which limit admission to groups, or situations that are primarily sociable or prestige-defining, are what we shall in conformity with common practice refer to as *social discrimination,* without particular reference to their institutional base.

Segregation

Segregation is an enforced pattern of settlement, or a pattern in the use of facilities which has the effect of categorically defining inferior status. Formal and informal restrictions may operate to exert these limitations. The dislike of many dominants of entering into close contact with various minorities leads to residential restrictions and/or to segregation in the use of public services. Local law and custom may require a member of a minority group to enter a public building by a separate entrance, to work in industry on a separate floor, to use separate waiting rooms and railroad cars, to attend separate schools. Segregation may be viewed as either ecological or institutional in character. It may be formally established, or formally demanded, but it is usually informally enforced.[13]

Segregated communities almost always represent a poorer average level of living with respect to quality of housing, public services, health, and education. Thus, in the long run, segregation is a cost to the total community. Where formal and informal residential restriction has kept in inferior conditions of life those people who wished to move out, the situation is analogous to the medieval ghetto and is indeed often referred to as such in sociological writing and popular discussion of minorities. The original use of the term "ghettoizing" in relation to the American subcommunity occurred in Louis Wirth's book, *The Ghetto.*[14] At the time Wirth wrote, the situations he described obtained for many nationality subcommunities in America's cities. Although these have declined in number and size, the problem of segregation is still very real for several of the minority groups.

Prejudice

Whereas segregation and discrimination are *actions,* prejudice is an *attitude* unfavorable to or disparaging of a whole group and all the individual members of it.

[13] Robin Williams, Jr., *Strangers Next Door* (Englewood Cliffs, N.J.: Prentice-Hall, 1964), pp. 28–77.
[14] Chicago: University of Chicago Press, 1928.

PREJUDICE AS FALSE PERCEPTION   Sometimes prejudice is the result of a false perception of a minority as learned from the various socializing agents to which children and youth are exposed. It is probable that most dominant-status persons who consciously or unconsciously take the advantage over minorities accruing from their dominant status do so simply as a result of behaving in a customary way, without any individual animus and often with limited experience of contact with the minority.

False perceptions are enhanced by *stereotypes*. A stereotype is an over-simplified generalization that emphasizes only selected traits of another group. It tends to evoke a generalized reaction to any member of that group. To some extent stereotypes arise out of the tendency to save time and effort. As one author points out, "It is much easier to have a definite opinion as to the type of creatures women are, and behave accordingly, than to analyze and study each woman anew." [15] What is significant in a stereotype of a minority group is that the selected traits tend to be those that emphasize difference from the dominant norm, and they tend to make up the whole image of an entire group, thus serving as an excuse for differential treatment. The assumption is that these traits are innate and hereditary and therefore that no change in the treatment of the stereotyped minority is warranted. Since newspapers and magazines and other forms of mass communication depend on popular approval for their sales, they often serve as reinforcing agents in the maintenance and continuance of such generalized popular stereotypes. They often help create a stereotype of the dominant groups as well. Minorities often have stereotypes regarding dominants, especially if they have a strong cultural tradition with different values from those of the dominants.[16]

PREJUDICE AS PERSONALITY STRUCTURE   Anthropology and psychiatry have called our attention to the fact that some personalities need to feel superior in order to have a secure self-image. In general, as far as we know from research, one can identify this need for dominance with an insecure person who has been brought up by very dominating adults. No community problems may occur if there are other outlets for his need to be superior—if, for example, the person may with cultural approval in turn dominate his children, or his servants, and if no major threat to his way of life occurs. When external circumstances challenge his way of functioning, his livelihood, his personal security, he may need to lay the blame for this at the door of members of the society whom he believes are of lesser worth—"aliens," "trouble-makers," "competitors." This is the person whose prejudices grow out of his *personality needs*. His prejudices develop with regard to any given important social stereotype that impinges on his environment. It may be a "native" in colonial Indonesia, an African in Afrikander South Africa, a Japanese on the West Coast, a Jew in Nazi Germany. Some societies seem to produce fewer of this type of personality, while

[15] Gerhart Saenger, *The Social Psychology of Prejudice* (New York: Harper & Brothers, 1953), p. 68.
[16] See Chapter 7 for a description of the Puerto Rican stereotype of the "Real American."

in other societies this type of personality seems to be more nearly the norm. No culture is composed *entirely* of one type of person or another.

It is these personalities that form the hard core of prejudiced citizens who resist change in the position of minorities and who refuse to surrender their stereotypes of minority groups. Persons who do not have such a personality structure may also have stereotypes which they acquired through learning in their environment, but they can relinquish them when given an opportunity for relearning. The personality type that needs prejudice to support its precarious self-esteem usually cannot modify through learning.

PREJUDICE AS PANIC REACTION   A third type of prejudice may be brought into play in situations of generalized anxiety where persons are played upon by propaganda or mob psychology to share attitudes against a minority which they would not have imagined for themselves in a time free of stress and of which they are often ashamed later. The existence of dominant-minority patterns provides an outlet for frustrations which can under some circumstances be mobilized into temporary aggression against a minority.

The "Vicious Circle"

Once established, the dynamics of dominant-minority relations set in motion a continuous series of reciprocal stimuli and responses which has been frequently called the "vicious circle." Discriminatory practices operate to keep a minority in disadvantaged circumstances which may lead to low standards of living, health, education, and morals. These poor conditions then give support to the dominant group's rationale for discrimination. The discrimination and the low standards mutually "cause" each other. Myrdal points out that,

> If things remain about as they are, or have been, this means that the two forces happen to balance each other.... If either of the factors changes, this will cause a change in the other factor, too, and start a process of interaction where the change in one factor will be continuously supported by the reaction of the other factor....
>
> If, for example, we assume that for some reason white prejudice could be decreased and discrimination mitigated, this is likely to cause a rise in Negro standards, which may decrease white prejudice still a little more, which would again allow Negro standards to rise, and so on through mutual interaction. If, instead, discrimination should become intensified, we should see the vicious circle spiraling downward.[17]

Minority Responses to Restrictive Processes of Dominance

When dominance has been established, dominants also define the appropriate responses of minorities to their subordinate position. If the differentiating traits are very marked, and the barriers to opportunity for the minority rigid, a

[17] Gunnar Myrdal, *An American Dilemma* (New York: Harper & Brothers, 1944), pp. 75–76.

pattern of stabilized accommodation will be characteristic, as the dominants expect it and the members of the minority have no choice.

Stabilized Accommodation

This mode of adaptation is one in which both superior and subordinate positions are taken for granted. Both dominant and minority members accept the same rationalizations for the existing pattern. Both may equally defend it. A high degree of *personal* sympathy and understanding may in some instances develop between dominant and minority individuals under these circumstances, as separateness is clearly understood and both are interdependent parts of an established social system.[18]

The psychological costs of this system are high. For the minority person it may affect his perception of reality. Indeed it was testimony to this effect by psychologists that was taken into consideration by the Supreme Court in the school desegregation issue. A stabilized subordinate position may create difficulty for a member of the subordinate group in handling repressed hostility and inevitable resentment. A variety of devices often develop to help him ease his psychic burden: clowning, intragroup aggression, fantasy, as well as psychological disorder of greater or lesser severity.[19] Even when occasional direct protest occurs it is doomed to failure, not only because of the power of reprisal, but because of the overwhelming difficulty of assessing the situation correctly for success. For the members of the dominant group too, there are greater costs than are often recognized. The need to maintain such a rigid system puts strains on the individual, especially in the period of childhood socialization, and often results in covert envy and sadistic exploitation of the subordinate group.

It is true, however, that some individuals may *choose* an accommodative adaptation even when the barriers against the whole group are not severe enough to maintain this pattern for all members. This will be a matter of temperament, skill, or previous social experience.

Acculturation

Acculturation is one of the sustaining processes whereby minorities are incorporated into the dominant culture. The term, when used to define a process, refers to the changes in individuals (and, if sharing the same experiences, groups of individuals) whose primary learning has been in one culture and who take over traits from another culture. Dominants expect minorities to acculturate, to a degree at least. Since dominants, like all ethnic groups, assume *their* values and social system to be the best, and since some degree of familiarity with the dominant language is assumed essential to reciprocal communication,

[18] E. Franklin Frazier, *Race and Culture Contacts in the Modern World* (New York: Alfred A. Knopf, 1957). Chapter 13 describes this in a discussion of the plantation as a social institution.
[19] Gunnar Myrdal, *An American Dilemma* (New York: Harper & Brothers, 1944), Chapter 44, pp. 956–994.

there is always some pressure for some acculturation even under severe restrictive patterns.

The process of acculturation takes place on two levels, often referred to as "external" and "internal." *External* acculturation is behavioral, in which material culture (refrigerators, cars, telephones, nylon stockings, etc.), everyday language, and secular (work, for example) roles are acquired. Key attitudes and behavior in the private spheres of life remain subcultural if acculturation is only external.

If the cultural element is paramount in differentiating the minority group the degree of discrimination will vary directly with the degree of external acculturation. This is, however, often perceived with different priorities by dominants and by members of minorities. For the dominants fluent, unaccented language and performance of institutional roles according to dominant norms are the most important. The minority member may on the other hand perceive the material aspect of acculturation as paramount: the labor-saving device or the big car. Even under the condition of extreme barriers to minority participation in the full range of opportunity in the society, more recognition and respect has usually gone to the more acculturated.

Occupational roles are key factors in the acculturation process. Improved occupational positions with the accompanying roles are much sought by minorities and are the point of interaction where much pressure and counterpressure is exerted. Conflict usually can be resolved only by minority members' learning new role behavior.

Although occupational roles are perhaps the most significant, other institutional roles are important also as focal points in dominant-minority relations. When the Irish entered politics the role of the political leader was defined by them in the light of their political heritage of protest and insurgence, the present necessity of vote-getting, and lack of access to the prerequisites of political leadership available to John Adams conservatives. The immigrant group created a new structure of urban politics and new roles, in the ward boss and the local party boss, which brought bitter but not always successful opposition.

Family roles as defined by one group may be alien to the other. For example, a Southern Negro mother, especially from a rural area, may take it for granted that she leaves her children for her mother to bring up. This is a carry-over from an antebellum pattern when older slaves took care of children and working-age women worked.[20] A social worker from the dominant culture may note this as "maternal rejection," which it may not be at all. A Puerto Rican mother may quit her job and apply for public assistance because her daughter has reached puberty and in the cultural framework it is now the mother's duty to stay home and chaperone her daughter. A father, in many European societies,

[20] E. Franklin Frazier, *The Negro Family in America* (New York: The Dryden Press, 1948).

who sees his paternal role as providing for a good marriage for his daughter may be bewildered when a college scholarship committee tells him she is not eligible for scholarship aid as long as her dowry is in the bank.

Internal acculturation occurs where the cultural *attitudes* of the dominant culture have been acquired. If there is close congruence between the dominant and minority cultural values, internal acculturation may precede external, as with the North Europeans and to some extent the Japanese. On the whole, however, as our non-northern-European populations have come largely from pretechnological tribal or feudal societies, the other sequence has been more common. Behavior changes first, then dominant norms are internalized and become the assumptions from which behavior emanates spontaneously.

The level of acculturation as a mode of adaptation in minority groups is typically generational—that is to say, the child of the immigrant becomes more acculturated than his immigrant parents and thus as a parent himself socializes his children to more of the dominant culture and less of the immigrant culture.

Minorities may, however, *choose stabilized acculturation and resist complete assimilation* as a mode of adaptation. This may be because they value a specific historic tradition of which they are part. Or they may feel that identity with a group that shares the same cultural tradition gives security. Or it may be their assessment that even with total acculturation all barriers to participation in the society will not be lifted for them.

The Class Structure as a Stabilizing Factor

The American colonies inherited the British class structure based on wealth and occupation, with the significant difference that at its apex there was no hereditary aristocracy. Until the first decade of the nineteenth century class position was demarcated by customary dress, and since, apart from Massachusetts, there was no free public education until the 1830's (and even later in new states) modes of speech also characterized class levels.

The urgent need of the new continent was for unskilled and semiskilled labor. Immigrants were recruited under the indenture system and subsequently under contract labor and finally as free labor to supply this need in the north, while imported slaves provided the agricultural and domestic labor force for the agrarian south. The vast majority of migrants (voluntary or forced) therefore started low on the class scale. On the other hand, individual improvement in economic circumstances and social status is a historic norm in the American tradition. Discrimination gave "native" Americans a competitive advantage in the upward climb. A Senator from Massachusetts in 1852 describes the mechanism clearly:

> That inefficiency of the pure Celtic race furnishes the answer to the question: How much use are the Irish to us in America: The Native American answer is, "none at all." And the Native American policy is to keep them away.

A profound mistake, I believe ... We are here, well organized and well trained, masters of the soil, the very race before which they have yielded everywhere besides. It must be, that when they come in among us, they come to lift us up. As sure as water and oil each finds its level they will find theirs. So far as they are mere hand-workers, they must sustain the head-workers, or those who have any element of intellectual ability. Their inferiority as a race compels them to go to the bottom; and the consequence is that we are, all of us, the higher lifted because they are here ...[21]

Increasingly as larger numbers of "different" peoples came, minorities were forced to seek improved positions within separate subcultural hierarchies. In the caste situation of the antebellum South parallel class structures occurred even more dramatically. Differences of prestige became established between house servants, skilled workmen, and field hands on the plantation, and between Negro craftsman and unskilled Negro workmen in the cities. Such a parallel hierarchy persisted in much of the South through custom and local ordinance even after the legal position of slaves and freedmen had changed.[22]

The overall class position of minorities, then, from the mid-nineteenth century until after World War II could be described by the following diagram.

Figure 2–1. *The Relation Between the Dominant-Minority Structure and the Class Structure*

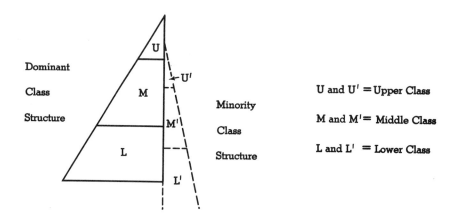

$$
\begin{array}{l}
\text{U and U}' = \text{Upper Class} \\[4pt]
\text{M and M}' = \text{Middle Class} \\[4pt]
\text{L and L}' = \text{Lower Class}
\end{array}
$$

[21] Edward Everett, "Letters on Irish Emigration," in *Historical Aspects of the Immigration Problem, Select Documents,* ed. Edith Abbott (Chicago, Ill.: The University of Chicago Press, 1926), pp. 462–463.
[22] See John Dollard and Allison Davis, *Children of Bondage* (Washington, D.C.: American Council on Education, 1940), for a description of Negro class structure in Natchez and New Orleans, and Gunnar Myrdal, *An American Dilemma,* Ch. 32.

A classic study of stratification in a New England small industrial city elaborates this.[23] Taking ethnic as distinct from "racial" minorities it was found that in 1933 in "Yankee City" they distributed over several segments of the six-fold class structure. For example, some Italians were found as high as the lower middle class. They were thought of, however, as Italians and reacted to accordingly. Within each class level to which they rose, the ethnics were thought of as somehow not quite the same as the native members of the same class— that is, until as individuals they became assimilated. If one examines the status of ethnic minorities in the United States, the conclusion seems inescapable that it represents a combination of the horizontal and vertical principles of social differentiation. The test of the existence of a minority is to verify dominant behavior toward it within the same class.

Assimilation

Throughout the period of the stabilization of dominance the expectation of the dominant culture is that "others" will either stay separate or subordinate or will be assimilable. Assimilation as viewed until nearly the close of the nineteenth century expected and allowed for *individuals* at all class levels to become part of the dominant society. At this time it meant that one must be "white," have acculturated externally and internally, speak English like a native (perhaps anglicize one's name), feel identity and loyalty as an American, and subscribe in behavior and feelings to the Protestant ethic. Indeed, in all but the very highest levels of society, the visible manifestation of Protestant affiliation was necessary. At the very top, men of wealth and talent might preserve a separate affiliation if their behavior and values were congruent with those of the dominants. This was more true of individual Jews than of Roman Catholics, except in local hierarchies (like Baltimore and New Orleans) where there had been old Catholic settlement.[24]

This was a possible adaptation for individuals, not for groups. As such it kept alive the expectation of mobility and success for the aspiring, and incorporated talents into the dominant structure. In this sense, *selective, individual assimilation* was a stabilizing factor in the society. The only *group* that was easily and almost totally assimilated in the nineteenth century was the British (not including the Irish).[25]

[23] See W. Lloyd Warner and Paul S. Lunt, *The Social Life of a Modern Community* (New Haven: Yale University Press, 1941), Ch. 5, "How the Several Classes Were Discovered," and p. 225, Table 7, "Class and Ethnic Groups." Although it is now recognized, as theory of stratification has developed, that the "Yankee City" studies are classifications of "status" (prestige) rather than "class" (access to economic positions), we have retained the original terminology.

[24] E. Digby Baltzell, *The Protestant Establishment: Aristocracy and Caste in America* (New York: Random House, 1964), p. 73.

[25] Rowland Tappan Berthoff, *British Immigrants in Industrial America, 1790–1950* (Cambridge, Mass.: Harvard University Press, 1953).

The attempts to assimilate sizable groups of "others" were first of all not possible in periods where sufficient continuing migration reinforced and kept alive old cultural attachments. In the second place it would have aroused, and eventually did (1880–1940), so much anxiety and apprehension on the part of segments of the dominant population that barriers which had not existed before were erected against the complete acceptance of "others." [26]

Nevertheless, although discrimination and prejudice increased for three quarters of a century, the dominant society succeeded in imposing *cultural,* if not always institutional, dominance, despite the incorporation of some external, peripheral culture traits from the migrating groups.

The operating concept of assimilation has now largely changed in the second half of the twentieth century, as we shall discuss below; but this could not occur until large, sufficiently acculturated groups had brought great pressure to bear on the dominant segment of the society.

The Decline of Dominance

The stabilization of dominance may become so embedded in the controls of beliefs, customs, and institutional roles that it can continue virtually unchanged for long periods of time, as with slavery in the South. When the whole society is adapting to general changes it may, for a time at least, undergo even more severe enforcement, as with South Africa today. The twentieth century in America, however, has witnessed the modification and gradual decline (not without struggle) of WASP dominance. This has been made possible through three broad processes: (1) general social changes which, in our national history, have led to (2) modification of the structure of dominance as new needs had to be met, and this in turn has (3) made possible and effective the direct challenge and protest of certain minorities themselves.

General Social Trends Affecting Minorities

INDUSTRIALIZATION   The transition from a predominantly agricultural and merchant to a predominantly industrial nation dominated the second half of the nineteenth and first quarter of the twentieth century in the United States. This affected the recruitment of the growing industrial labor force, the change in the status of workmen, and the attitudes toward immigrants.

As Warner and Low [27] point out with regard to "Yankee City," in the early days of industrialization industrial workers had the status which had obtained for free white wage earners under the handicraft system. There was an opportunity for able individuals to rise to supervisory or management positions or

---

[26] See Baltzell, *The Protestant Establishment,* Ch. V., and John Higham, *Strangers in the Land: Patterns of American Nativism 1860–1925* (New York: Atheneum, 1965).
[27] W. Lloyd Warner and J. O. Low, *The Social System of the Modern Factory* (New Haven: Yale University Press, 1941).

eventually to become entrepreneurs, much as the journeyman had once been able to become a master craftsman, setting the standards for his workmen, marketing his product, and being a small merchant capitalist. As industrialization grew and the factory system became the dominant pattern of production, the competition to cut labor costs brought a lower wage standard and a decline not only in the style of life of the industrial worker but in the prestige of his occupational group. Since immigrants contributed largely to this growing labor force, they shared and increased the lowered position of the American industrial workers. As more and more immigrants came, there was a tendency to identify all industrial labor as "foreign," all the more so when tensions grew up around the struggle to form labor unions. A study in the 1940's of a small industry in a midwest community showed that the industrial workers were referred to as "Poles," though in fact 50 percent of this group were of native American stock.[28]

In dominant-minority relations today, the most significant aspects of the industrialization process are the impact on the South of recent and increasing industrialization and whether or not companies will follow local or national standards of hiring and promotion of minorities; structural changes in the occupational field with advancing technology; the situation of the minority agricultural labor force (mostly Mexican American) in relation to the large corporation farms and vineyards of the Pacific Coast; and the progressive, but by no means universal elimination of discrimination in unions.

URBANIZATION   The growth of our urban, multi-group society has had a significant effect on minority participation. Folk cultures, with their kinship patterns, language, and folk beliefs, have been brought in contact with other cultures, and subjected to the secularizing influence of dominant economic, educational, and legal systems. The institutional balance of folk cultures, where family and religion take precedence, is borne upon by the multi-group urban community, where the dominant institutions are economic and political.

Another aspect of urbanization has been that the size, density, and heterogeneity of cities have made possible segmentation of roles, so that public and private roles need not necessarily overlap. This has aided the acculturation process.

It is significant that over half the population of the United States now lives in metropolitan areas—that is, in a big city or its suburbs. Although suburban patterns of dominant-minority relations vary from the patterns of the central city, the economic dependence of suburbs on the city, as well as other ideological influences emanating from the metropolitan core, has an impact which is being felt more and more.

THE WELFARE STATE   The problems of an industrial society, the urban balance in national politics, the experiences of the great depression of the 1930's and of world wars have led to an increasing centralization and extension

[28] August B. Hollingshead, *Elmtown's Youth* (New York: John Wiley & Sons, 1941).

of federal power. National responsibility has been accepted for at least a bare minimum guarantee of health and welfare, and America, like the industrial nations of Western Europe has become a welfare state. The change in national ideology from *laissez faire* to public regulation and responsibility has opened the door to a succession of legislation designed to ease the pressures on the least fortunate citizens. The Social Security Act, the Fair Labor Standards Act, the National Labor Relations Act, all passed in 1935, as well as the more recent Civil Rights legislation have done much to influence local practice and to extend guarantees to all Americans.

INTERNATIONAL PRESSURES   One large force which has affected dominant-minority relations in the United States is this country's new role in world affairs. With the rising strength of the Asian and African nations, the virtual end of colonialism, and the desire of America and Western Europe to uphold the prestige and influence of a social system of private enterprise and political democracy, it has been necessary for our nation to see to it that it is not vulnerable in its relations to those of its own population who are of other than Nordic origin.

Social Structural Changes Affecting Minorities

Overall adaptation to the needs of an urban industrial society have modified some structures and created new channels for members of minorities to improve their status.

THE LABOR MOVEMENT   The success of the trade union movement provided new channels for minority members to improve their position individually and to achieve leadership roles; it also improved the standard of living of American organized labor to the extent that many blue-collar workers have been able to see their children in middle-class positions.

In recent years the more open policy in employment, the membership policy of the AFL-CIO, both perhaps given impetus by the temporary wartime legislation against discrimination in employment, have opened jobs to Negroes from which they had previously been barred, and are paving the way for the same improvement which affected the older immigrant workers.

PUBLIC EMPLOYMENT   The civil services increased in scope with the growth of cities and the enactment of federal welfare provisions. Local civil service in the north and all federal civil service has been by law nondiscriminatory. Emergency programs such as those of the Depression or the present Anti-poverty efforts have given minorities opportunities for employment and/or skills in areas where these opportunities were not open to them. The requirement of nondiscriminatory hiring in industries receiving federal contracts has had some impact on local practice also.

THE GROWTH OF THE MILITARY   The extension of the armed forces since World War II has brought the young men of America into military training (dominants and minorities alike) and in Korea and Southeast Asia into common participation in military engagement. The desegregation of the army during the Korean war opened army career channels to some, and the studies of World War II have shown that the associations in the armed services were effective in many instances in changing the attitudes of both dominants and minorities in positive directions.

EDUCATION Historically the establishment of free compulsory education was probably the greatest single acculturative channel for minorities, however imperfectly it often fulfilled this function. At the present stage of dominant-minority relations the significant gains have been in the marked reduction of discrimination in higher education, and the concern with and beginning effectiveness of improved "integrated" public school education.

The Modification of Political Dominance

The possibility of modifying the political dominance of "the Protestant Establishment" has meant that the contenders must have sufficient acculturation to be able to use the political processes. It is not surprising that the Irish were the first to take advantage of political channels, for they were English-speaking and had the experience of having been a cultural minority within the United Kingdom. The urban political machine became an instrument for minorities to obtain local power. For several decades it operated, through its patronage system, as a welfare agent for minorities who supported it. Changes in the welfare structure of the nation have made this function (though not always this practice) obsolete. The machine also opened career channels in politics to minority members. It became an arena for intergroup integration between various national minorities, and subsequently during and after the Depression of the 1930's, a channel for the integration of dominants and minorities. The character of the machine has changed as its functions have changed and as urban politics has been more closely related to the national political structure.

As significant as the legislative structure has been the judicial structure, not only in the composition of the local magistrates' bench, but, particularly in the present, the Supreme Court. Although legal restrictions on minorities have received different adjudication in different periods, according to the composition of the bench and the spirit of the period, the Supreme Court has had the chief responsibility for the definition and interpretation of the rights of minorities, and the federal judiciary the responsibility for implementation of federal legislation on behalf of minorities.[29]

For half a century there have been members of religious or ethnic minorities appointed to the Supreme Court (and in 1967 the first Negro was appointed).

[29] See Jack Walter Peltason, *Fifty-Eight Lonely Men* (New York: Harcourt, Brace & World, 1961), for a discussion of the pressures on southern federal judges charged with the responsibility of implementing school integration.

Cases are argued before the highest court by lawyers who are members of minorities. The success of one minority in obtaining a favorable ruling emboldens others to use the same (though prolonged) process of redress. After the Supreme Court decision terminating the exclusion of Negroes from juries (a southern regional practice) Mexican Americans were able successfully to use the same channel. Even religious minorities such as the Amish or Jehovah's Witnesses whose beliefs and value system are opposed to participation in secular affairs of the state have modified sufficiently to employ counsel from outside their membership and seek recourse to the courts.[30]

The Challenge to Dominance

Although some challenge to dominance is continually going on, we have suggested that this is small and largely unsuccessful in a period when a nation is stabilizing its institutional patterns, or when, as in America, the expanding economy (and, historically, the expanding frontier) creates sufficient hope for individual improvement within the system that the pressure for modification is counteracted by the prospect of new rewards within the status quo. Thus the growing movement against slavery in the early decades of national independence was set back by the development of the "cotton culture" made possible by the cotton gin and the steamboat. For the minorities of European descent, in the period of national expansion the expectation persisted *both* on the part of dominants and of minorities that the immigrants would assimilate and share in the opportunities of the developing country. One must recognize, however, that increasing acculturation brings increasing restlessness with restraints of the dominant society. For many the process was too selective and too slow.

MARGINALITY   In the theory of minority adjustment which assumed that minority groups moved through a series of steps to ultimate assimilation, there were certain groups, as we shall see in subsequent chapters, that were at some time declared "unassimilable." Within this theoretical frame groups were sometimes defined as being in a marginal *stage*.[31] This referred to the fact that the direction of leadership and membership was toward the incorporation of dominant values and goals, emulating even if imperfectly dominant institutional roles, although "visible characteristics" of the minority and discrimination persisted. The group then took on a double identity illustrated by the self-designation of hyphenated status: "I am an Italian-American." [32]

Another way of discussing marginality is to see it as an *individual adaptation* to minority status. Robert K. Merton has defined the marginal person as one whose reference group (the group from which he takes his norms) is different from the group of which he is a member. That is to say, he emulates and

---

[30] See Chapter 4, "Religion and Minority Status."
[31] Robert E. Park, *Race and Culture* (Glencoe, Ill.: The Free Press, 1950).
[32] Baltzell refers to this (in *The Protestant Establishment*) as *marginal culture* **without any** implication of its being a stage in a sequence, pp. 62–70.

strives to be accepted by a group of which he is not yet, or is only peripherally, a member.[33] Viewing marginality this way, it can be said to occur whenever an individual is abandoning the mode of adaptation that has prevailed in the group of which he is a member. This usually makes him, to a greater or lesser degree, an "outsider" to both groups.

Internally the marginal person may suffer from conflict of values and conflict of loyalties. This may operate to make him anxious and to lower his efficiency in fulfilling the roles he is seeking to carry out. His anxiety may even keep him from perceiving the subtler aspects of role behavior in the group toward which he is striving. If he is able to rationalize his striving to the point where he suppresses or disciplines any conflicts in abandoning one group for the other, he risks being regarded as a renegade by the group he strives to leave and as an "operator" by the group he is moving toward.

His problem is often easier if he does not have to carry a double burden of class marginality along with race or culture marginality. Too often, however, there is this double burden as the minority member comes to accept the dominant American norm of class mobility. Since the institutional patterns of a culture are its guarantees of continuance, honored positions in the society go to those who best fulfill significant dominant institutional roles. People who have had prolonged subordination often have no opportunity to perceive or learn these roles, or feel they must reject them because they are impossible. Others cling to roles defined by variant value systems. Yet increasingly there is the rising aspiration for the benefits to be derived from improved positions, which leads to role relearning, role conflict, or role modification. This is where the real personal crises of dominant-minority relations occur.

For Baltzell, the marginal individual (as contrasted with the marginal culture) is the completely acculturated person who is still identified (sometimes by choice, though not necessarily) as a member by descent of a religious, ethnic, or "racial" minority.[34] According to Baltzell's analysis the top elite, nationally, can absorb a modest percentage of marginal men of high talent (bankers, federal judges, etc.) and does so, whereas the levels below, and to a large extent the *local* hierarchies of status, tend to persist in a parallel status structure.

COMPETITION   The marginal *individual* challenges dominance by the successful competition for honorific occupational positions. This is possible in a technological or developing society so long as particular skills and/or abilities clearly contribute to the needs of the society at the decision-making level.

Where individual competition shows some degree of success, there has been in the past, and may persist, a tightening of *social* barriers against successful persons of minority identification or descent (however tenuous the minority

[33] Robert K. Merton, *Social Theory and Social Structure* (Glencoe, Ill.: The Free Press), pp. 290–291. In Merton's definition marginality may apply equally to movement between any contiguous groups, as for example, upward or downward mobility between social classes.

[34] Baltzell, *The Protestant Establishment,* pp. 62–70.

tie). This may filter down from top levels and become not only social but more general discrimination for people lower on the status scale who fear that their opportunities for moving up are being jeopardized.

THE STRUGGLE FOR POWER Marginal *groups* who have taken on enough aspects of the dominant culture to share its goals and have some frame for perceiving what means will help them achieve as a group rather than as individuals, express their challenge to dominants in a struggle for legitimate or illigitimate power. This has been illustrated by the degree to which political organization depending on minority support and supporting minority interests in one period captured East Coast city politics and perhaps changed the character of large city politics throughout the nation. For a time city politics was linked with rackets and other nonlegitimate avenues to affluence, often attracting minority ability where legitimate channels were closed through discrimination.[35]

Nonviolent civil rights efforts represent an innovating attempt to achieve legitimate power, in the sense that they exert pressure for the state to modify patterns of discrimination, for channels of economic opportunity to be opened, and for civil participation within the legitimate structure.[36]

At another level people who have neither the confidence in nor knowledge of the legitimate channels will be vulnerable to spontaneous outbreaks of protest. If these become widespread (like riots spreading from city to city) it makes an impact on the Establishment. If this kind of protest is an isolated instance, it is usually ineffective. Sometimes it also retards the efforts of other modes of protest which seek more sophisticatedly to modify existing structures. As a phenomenon of protest it is most often the weapon of the most depressed of the minorities who are under the double pressure of severe discrimination and poverty, as with the Irish in the nineteenth century and the Negroes today.

NATIVISM Any organized protest effort of any sizable minority group has the effect of creating reactive movements designed to legitimately or illegitimately restrain minorities. Conflict increases polarization of interest and *nativistic* movements on the part of dominants who seek to, and sometimes for a time are able to, increase discrimination and stimulate latent prejudice. The largest number of followers of such movements may themselves be (in the general sense) marginal, economically, socially, or even sometimes ethnically. This situation is likely to emerge and become even stronger if the total society is undergoing confusing changes, such as rapid industrialization or urbanization.

Dominant nativistic movements seek to maintain a particular historical value system and status as expressed in an idealized historical image. Polariza-

[35] For a description of this interlocking and its meaning to one minority neighborhood in a large eastern city see William Foote Whyte, *Street Corner Society* (Chicago, Ill.: The University of Chicago Press, 1943).

[36] See Everett C. Hughes, "Social Change and Social Protest: An Essay on Marginal Man," *Phylon,* Vol. X, First Quarter, 1949, on the relation of marginality to protest.

tion also gives rise to minority nativistic movements which reach for an idealized past as a locus of identification. The marginal character of adherents to such movements is clear as the image of the idealized past which they project is expected to include the benefits of the contemporary society, thus indicating the duality of reference groups. No Zionist sought a biblical society in Israel. Black Muslims have taken a great ethical, progressive and "world" religion as the locus of their identity and combined it with a modern idea of power. The Garvey movement which advocated the return of Negroes to Africa did not envisage return to a tribal society.

The processes of conflict and protest are of course *disjunctive processes*: they disrupt the ongoing social pattern. For those people who have adapted and conformed to the system, disruption in itself is anxiety producing. *Yet no social change occurs without disruption for some* (like the displacement of some people who are used to a neighborhood in order to build better housing for more people). Disjunctive processes are part of the ongoing social experience, and although they are often focal at a particular time they do not preclude simultaneous sustaining processes, or integrative processes which grow out of the new demands on the society.

INTEGRATION   As we pointed out early in this chapter, when minorities have enough power (economic or political), cooperation has been through negotiation in the form of an implied contractual relationship between one group as a group and the other as a group. When individual cooperation between dominants and minorities *on the basis of equality* occurs we have the phenomenon of integration. Thus children within an integrated school may be friends and equals. Neighbors in an integrated neighborhood may cooperate as equal members of a taxpayers group or a community committee or as members of a neighborhod parish. Integration occurs in the equal association of individuals when the minority still identifies itself as a minority. In this way it differs from assimilation.

Protest movements, despite their disjunctive effect on the previously existing social equilibrium may be integrative factors in dominant-minority relations. This may be true *internally* through the opportunity they provide for committed members of both the dominant group and the minorities to come into frequent interaction as they work toward a common goal. They contribute *externally* to the degree they have a successful impact on the social situation. The *internal* integrative effect will be minimized if the majority of the membership of a given movement is either dominant (as with the antislavery movement) or minority (as with the National Congress of American Indians). The *external* effect will be minimized if the movement fails to change institutional patterns, not merely to achieve official abrogation of discrimination. Another limitation to the integrative impact of protest movements is their contemporaneous focus. If in addition to their immediate demands they become ongoing organizations they may lose flexibility in adapting to changing needs of a new generation of membership.

Assimilation in a Pluralistic Society

The history of America has been that of absorbing many peoples. As long as the migration was predominantly northern European it was assumed that all those of Caucasian stock would "disappear" as separate identities. For many this has been true. Coupled with this assumption was the designation of some peoples as "unassimilable." This was particularly a public argument regarding Asiatics on the West Coast, and was used as a platform for limitation of Asiatic migration. At one point, at the turn of the century, there was a variant of the older belief about assimilation: the *melting pot theory*, which claimed that from the merging of the many ethnic heritages a new type of person—the "American" —would evolve. At this time the public mind viewed people whose style of life was American and whose language was English as "assimilated," so long as there were no alien racial characteristics.

In contradistinction to the "melting pot" view was the concept of *cultural pluralism*. The heavy migration of the turn of the century with the resulting urban nationality subcommunities had an impact on political and social thinking within the urban milieu. Social workers, like those of Chicago's Hull House, were concerned with supporting the dignity of cultural heritage of immigrants confused by the impact of the new American environment. Politicians were recognizing subcultural identity in their bids for the "Italian vote" or the "Polish vote." Ethnic groups often controlled one type of operation, one floor in an industry, or one local of a labor union.

The dangers to the state of really diverse value systems within it is real, for to preserve justice and public order there must be a common understanding of norms, of what is a "fair" way of dealing with others. Furthermore, the latent effect of a really established cultural pluralism can lead to the mechanism "divide-and-rule." The maintenance of a total (or largely) separate cultural identity has often had the effect of increasing visibility and discrimination and deterring minorities from challenging their subordinate position. Effective challenge to dominance, as we have tried to show, can only come when at least some institutional acculturation has taken place.

What has happened in America has been that truly separatist communities, by choice, like the Amish, or by force, like the American Indians, have been small groups who kept their cultures intact by geographic and institutional separation. The rest of the groups, in interaction with others, acculturated to a greater or lesser degree as far as *secular* institutional participation was concerned (public schools, politics, jobs), and such pluralism as was retained was traditional religion, festival ritual, food, and other aspects of the personal rather than the public world. Cultural pluralism in the visionary sense of the early decades of the twentieth century proved incongruent to the effective needs both of minorities and of the total society, however humanistically appealing it was as a philosophy.

Stabilized Acculturation and Structural Pluralism

Association in work, in politics, and public life do much to break down "social distance" between disparate groups. The public recognition of the achievement of minority individuals has enhanced the "respectability" of minority descent. As large segments of the ethnic minorities have moved into middle-class occupations and become acculturated to middle-class norms, ethnicity, at least in the large urban multi-group communities, becomes more and more a private matter or a symbolic appeal in some public or political situations. Blue-collar workers, too, are more American than ethnic in their life styles.[37] To some extent this process may be observed also with regard to "racial" minorities if housing patterns permit interracial community contact.

"Respectability" means, then, that at least in the secular spheres of life, acculturation, at whatever class level, has taken place. It means, furthermore, that minority institutional patterns have modified and become more coherent with dominant norms.[38] Yet within this frame of acculturation there persists, it is argued, a preference for intimate associations with people whose cultural and/or religious and racial heritage is like one's own. We have called this mode of adaptation *stabilized acculturation*. More recently Milton M. Gordon has used the term *structural pluralism*.[39]

> We have chosen to focus on the nature of group life itself in the United States as constituting the social setting in which relationships among persons of differing race, religion, and national origin take place. For these 190 million Americans are not just individuals with psychological characteristics. They belong to groups: primary groups and secondary groups, family groups, social cliques, associations or formal organizations, networks of associations, racial, religious, and national origins groups. And the nature of these groups and their interrelationships has a profound impact upon the way in which people of different ethnic backgrounds regard and relate to one another.
>
> In particular, we have called attention to the nature of the ethnic group itself as a large subsociety, crisscrossed by social class, and continuing in its own primary groups of families, cliques and associations—its own network of organizations and institutions—in other words as a highly structured community within the boundaries of which an individual may, if he wishes, carry out most of his more mean-

---

[37] For a discussion of the persistence of token recognition to ethnicity and interethnic balance in the political situation of New York in 1960, see Nathan Glazer and Daniel Patrick Moynahan, *Beyond the Melting Pot* (Cambridge, Mass.: The M.I.T. and Harvard University Press, 1963).

[38] See Chapter 4, Religion and Minority Status.

[39] Milton M. Gordon, *Assimilation in American Life* (New York: Oxford University Press, 1964), pp. 235–236.

ingful life activities from the cradle to the grave. We have pointed to the considerable body of evidence which suggests that the ethnic varieties of Americans, excepting the intellectuals, tend to remain within their own ethnic group and social class for most of their intimate, primary group relationships, interacting with other ethnic and class varieties of Americans largely in impersonal secondary group relationships. The United States, we have argued, is a multiple melting pot in which acculturation for all groups beyond the first generation of immigrants, without eliminating all value conflict, has been massive and decisive, but in which structural separation on the basis of race and religion—structural pluralism, as we have called it—emerges as the dominant sociological condition.

This is to say that the majority of the members of minority groups in urban America at the present time, if the primary differentiating characteristics have been religious and cultural, and they are second or third generation, are assimilated at the appropriate class level in the spheres of work and political life and in their external life style. In the sphere of sentiment and intimate association, however, there are still strong religious and/or ethnic bonds. (This is equally true of WASPS as an ethnic group.) Gordon makes an exception for the intellectuals as a true interethnic stratum. We pointed out earlier in this chapter Baltzell's observation that at one time, and perhaps re-emerging today, the business and political elite associated as equals within the top echelons, despite differences of descent and affiliation. We might also add that protest movements in many instances create an interethnic associational base. Bohemias, the sections of metropolitan centers where the artists and their satellites congregate, have traditionally been exceptions to the pattern of structural pluralism.

The effect of the clustering of ethnic groups in the manner presented by Gordon has one dysfunction in that it may perpetuate some of the stereotypes of "others" among the different groups. Gans, in his study of an Italian working-class community, suggests that often this stereotyping of neighbors who are Irish, or bosses who are Jewish, is completely without malice.[40] Nevertheless there is always the risk, as Gordon points out,[41] that stereotyping has a direct relation to prejudice and, as we have indicated, in times of general social stress can be used to mobilize insecure people to action against the stereotyped group.

We shall discuss in the chapter on religion and minorities the idea that there is no absolute reason why this kind of pluralism cannot be viable. In a certain sense the image of such a stabilized pattern is Utopian, because it assumes that, as in an ideal marriage, private sentiments never interfere with the common good. Indeed, however, there has been recognition increasingly that "respectable" differences are allowable. Even with regard to the most visible differences (physiognomic) there is no longer, as there once was, public, national, and academic argument that certain peoples are unassimilable.

Structural pluralism is a solution for a minority group in adjusting to the

[40] Herbert J. Gans, *The Urban Villagers* (New York: The Free Press, 1962), p. 36.
[41] Gordon, p. 236.

dominant society which may be held as ideal (and this ideal may be shared by some dominants). For others it may be seen not as ideal but as a transitional reality to be followed by complete incorporation of the dominant values and affiliations including the private spheres of behavior and sentiment.

To see any direction of movement one must relate the mode of adaptation to *possibilities* as well as to goals. Louis Wirth has posited four possible goals for minority groups: secession, pluralism, assimilation, and achievement of dominance.[42] As Wagley and Harris point out, at the present time only two of these alternatives have any significant place in minority aspirations in the Western Hemisphere: pluralism and assimilation.[43]

Amalgamation

Amalgamation is the biological merging of previously distinct "racial" or "subracial" stocks. Amalgamation always takes place to some degree with or without formal approval when members of one group live in constant inter-action with members of another. With members of both groups having a similar degree of acculturation and a similar position in the overall status system, cross-marriages begin to take place even in the face of group disapproval. The character of the American family as a nuclear family and the geographic mobility of Americans have facilitated this process. Similarly, there have frequently been cross-marriages at upper-status levels where the frame of reference is international rather than national, as with some intellectual and social elites. And finally, when there is a pattern of severe exploitation and subjugation of the minority by the dominant group, sexual exploitation will be one facet of the configuration.

The Point of View of This Book

Recent approaches to the study of minorities have selected various emphases, and recent research has contributed to these selected foci. There are authors who have stressed culture: the richness and right to integrity of variant cultures within the national state. There are psychologically oriented authors who are primarily concerned with attitudinal and perceptive aspects of intergroup relations. Still another approach is comparative, to discover and delineate recurring and perhaps generic problems of dominant-minority relations in a number of national states.

Our concern is to write about the position of minorities within the social structure of the United States today. In a society as dynamic as that of America the situation of minorities is increasingly fluid. Therefore, when we can we will identify trends. Much conflict between dominants and minorities in the last

---

[42] Louis Wirth, "The Problem of Minority Groups," in *The Science of Man in the World Crisis*, ed. Ralph Linton (New York: The Columbia University Press, 1945), pp. 354–364.
[43] Wagley and Harris, *Minorities in the New World*, p. 286.

decade has been institutionally focussed. Minorities have increasingly pressed for political and economic incorporation with equality of chances and equality of sanctions. Great gains have been made in this area. But in the end the fundamental issues of dominant-minority relations will depend on how people in communities regard one another and how they associate with one another.

We have chosen *differential visibility* as the basis for the classification of minorities which governs our material. We have emphasized, though not exclusively, *discrimination* as the significant mechanism by which minorities are held in subordinate status. Our substantive material has been drawn, where possible, from *community studies,* as local and regional variations and variation in structure and type of community will affect both dominants and minorities. We have noted changes in public policy which affect communities, as community sentiments in turn affect policy. The process of interaction between dominants and minorities is a *reciprocal* one. Changes in either the behavior of dominants or of minorities will bring about reactive behavior, favorable or unfavorable, in the other group and thus affect the pattern of relationship.

Topics for Projects and Discussion

1. How do you perceive "dominant American values"? Have these to do with sentiments you cherish; with expected action; with material gains? Are the elements you have included consistent?
2. Can you describe the feelings of a minority member who cherishes some way of behaving, or some obligation that is not congruent with the expectations of the dominant group? Have you felt or observed such a situation in your community? Among your friends in college? How do you feel about their loyalties?
3. Does your state have laws against discrimination? How are they implemented?
4. With what stereotypes of "others" have you grown up? How do you think these stereotypes developed?
5. Are there people in your community who would never be invited to your home or your circle of friends? Are these "class" attitudes or dominant-minority attitudes?
6. How would you classify, in terms of visibility, the following people living in America who come from various backgrounds: Pakistani rice growers in California, an Eskimo white-collar worker in Seattle, an East Indian professor of Economics, a Turkish merchant, an Armenian priest?

Suggested Reading

Countryman, Vernon, ed. *Discrimination and the Law.* Chicago: University of Chicago Press, 1965.

> *Papers and discussion on legal aspects of discrimination in employment, education, public accommodations, housing.*

Frazier, E. Franklin. *Race and Culture Contacts in the Modern World.* New York: Alfred A. Knopf, Inc., 1957.

> *A discussion of patterns of contact, with illustrations from many countries.*

Gordon, Milton M. *Assimilation in American Life.* New York: Oxford University Press, 1964.

An analysis of choices and trends affecting urban minorities.

Wagley, Charles, and Harris, Marvin. *Minorities in the New World: Six Case Studies.* New York: Columbia University Press, 1950.

Presentations of selected minority situations in the Western Hemisphere, based on studies by five UNESCO social scientists.

Williams, Robin M., Jr. *Strangers Next Door: Ethnic Relations in American Communities.* Englewood Cliffs, N.J.: Prentice-Hall, Inc., 1964.

Prejudice, segregation, discrimination, and conflict affecting three minority groups in cities in four regions of the United States.

3

Race: Myth
and Science

In dominant-minority relations "race" is a basic category and provides the most obvious cue to visibility or identification. The term is placed here in quotation marks because its meaning and significance in the popular thinking and behavior of dominants are vastly at variance with current scientific thinking. One contemporary anthropologist has suggested that, in general usage at least, the term be discarded altogether.[1] That the beliefs about race which have become established in popular sentiment may well constitute, as Montagu's title suggests, "man's most dangerous myth" was anticipated in the 1880's by a French pro-Aryan writer, Vacher de Lapouge, when he wrote, "I am convinced that in the next century millions of men will cut each other's throats because of one or two degrees more or less of cephalic index." [2]

While the wars that have ensued since de Lapouge made this prophecy have not been based primarily on race antagonism, the idea of race was employed in the propaganda—for example, in the stereotype of "the Hun" in World War I, and in that of "the Jap" in World War II. Because these beliefs about race are so powerful a stimulus to social conflict, it is of the utmost importance that the student of social relations learn what race really is and how significant—or, actually, how insignificant—it really is. To the student of dominant-minority relations in particular, understanding the myth and the reality of race is indispensable. For over two centuries racialist thinking in international relations has fostered the dominance of white Europeans over colored peoples. As we shall see, the beliefs about race arose after the white subordination of colored peoples began. They gave to the dominants plausible intellectual and moral justification for a pattern of relations highly disadvantageous to the minorities.

Before the scientific developments of the present century, the term *race* was

---

[1] M. F. Ashley Montagu, *Man's Most Dangerous Myth: The Fallacy of Race,* 4th ed., rev. and enl. (Cleveland: The World Publishing Co., 1964).

[2] Vacher de Lapouge, cited by Ruth Benedict, in *Race: Science and Politics,* rev. ed. (New York: The Viking Press, Inc., 1945), p. 3.

often used to designate a nationality or a culture group, or some other broad class of human beings. Webster's definition illustrates how widely it has been used and how various are the nuances it may suggest:

> The descendants of a common ancestor; a family, tribe, people, or nation, believed or presumed to belong to the same stock; a lineage; a breed; also more broadly, a class or a kind of individuals with common characteristics, interests, appearance, habits, or the like, as if derived from a common ancestor; as the *race* of doctors, the *race* of birds. "The whole race of mankind"—Shakespeare. "When the long race of Alban fathers came."—Dryden.[3]

The research of the last fifty years, in physical anthropology primarily but also in related fields, has given an entirely new perspective on the physiological groupings of man. There is now consensus in anthropology, biology, psychology, and sociology as to what races are and are not. In 1950, UNESCO published a series of research monographs that represent international scientific agreement on what is known about races. The understanding of the physiological phenomena of "race" has depended on the development of the sciences. In populations without basic scientific orientation the term "race" is connotive of social attitudes derived from historical social experience, the universal ethnocentrism of isolated peoples, or folk superstition. It is therefore important to know clearly what is fact about race as a correction for traditional usages.

What "Race" Is

Origin of "Races"

To begin with, mankind apparently started out as one race. Since *Homo sapiens* evolved thousands of years before written history, it is not possible to know the racial features of prehistoric man with any exactitude. However, contemporary anthropology generally accepts on the basis of fossil evidence and the logic of evolutionary and genetic principles a monogenetic rather than a polygenetic theory of man's origin. Montagu has put it thus:

> Concerning the origin of the living varieties of man we can say little more than that there is every reason to believe that a single stock gave rise to all of them. All varieties of man belong to the same species and have the same remote ancestry. This is a conclusion to which all the relevant evidence of comparative anatomy, palaeontology, serology, and genetics points. On genetic grounds alone, it is virtually impossible to conceive of the varieties of man as having originated separately as distinct lines from different anthropoid ancestors.[4]

---

[3] Quoted in Harry L. Shapiro. *Race Mixture* (Paris: UNESCO, 1953), p. 8.
[4] Montagu, p. 83. By permission.

Differentiation of "Races"

Long before written history, the major differentiation of mankind into the main varieties occurred as a result of migration, and of natural selection as it affected the survival of certain variations in their environments. Ever since Linnaeus, the Swedish botanist, started the classification of plant and animal life in the eighteenth century, geneticists and physical anthropolcgists have been examining the differences in the physical characteristics of man. Linnaeus established four categories of man—*americanus, europaeus, asiaticus,* and *afer.* Since the eighteenth century these categories have been refined so that some discussions include seven major groups with many subgroups. The criteria for grouping depend on such factors as cephalic index, blood type, shape of facial features, degree of body hair, and so forth. Since no group is totally homogeneous in all of these indices, these older categories are now primarily of interest to researchers in the biological sciences and physical anthropology. What the groups of people represent in actuality are societies which through geographic isolation and barriers of social organization have intermarried for thousands of years, bringing into prominence selected dominant biological traits. These are sometimes referred to as "Mendelian populations," a term derived from the geneticist Mendel, who demonstrated the existence of dominant strains and recessive strains in inbreeding and crossbreeding. From this point of view the tall Watusi of Uganda, the pockets of blond Andalusians in Spain, and the Sherpas of Nepal are "Mendelian" populations.

> Such physical traits as the color of the eyes or hair and the pigmentation of the skin do pass through the genes from parents to children. The carriers have been identified and described. We know now that a group of individuals with common characteristics will procreate offspring with the same characteristics. Mankind is composed of a variety of populations which differ among themselves in the frequency of many genes. These Mendelian populations will reproduce themselves across time.[5]

Twentieth-century research has shown that physical type is not only the result of genetic transmission but is dependent on other factors as well. Selection affecting physical type can take place because of environment. Before the advent of modern medicine the physical type best suited to survival in geographic regions gradually emerged as dominant, and high infant mortality eliminated variations. Cultural factors such as language over time affect the mouth formation necessary to produce a selected sound. As a contemporary physical anthropologist writes, ". . . culture, which has affected other free-living animals too, has probably affected us more profoundly than it has any others because we created it, we cannot escape it, we have been constantly exposed

---

[5] Oscar Handlin, *Race and Nationality in American Life* (Garden City, N.Y.: Doubleday Anchor Books, Doubleday & Co., Inc., 1957), p. 151. (Reprinted by arrangement with Little, Brown & Co., Boston, Mass.)

to it as long as there have been men on earth, and we could not live without it." [6]

Since agreement on categories is basic to thinking and research, most scholars today work within the broad categories Caucasoid, Mongoloid and Negroid. These refer very generally to groups of people with visible physical traits. The designations, however, are matters more of convenience than of accuracy. As Ruth Benedict aptly writes:

> No one doubts that the groups called Caucasoid, Mongoloid, and Negroid each represent a long history of anatomical specialization in different areas of the world; but the greater numbers of individuals cannot be assigned to one or another of these races on the basis even of several ... [physical] criteria.... There are Whites who are darker than some Negroids; dark hair and eyes are common among all races; the same cephalic index is found in groups of the most diverse races; similar hair form is found among ethnic groups as distinct as native Australians and Western Europeans.[7]

Instability of Racial Type

Throughout history great migrations alternating with long periods of endogamous mating created and recreated visible subtypes. The American Indian illustrates the process of subtype development. The ancestors of the Indians came from Asia and possessed general Mongoloid feature. Natural selection and thousands of years of isolation, limiting the range or variability to that present in the original migrating groups, perfected a distinctive Indian type.

While throughout all history mixing has occurred across main divisions, in the past few centuries the wandering and mixing of peoples has created many new subtypes, involving combinations of traits from the main racial divisions. We may cite the Pitcairn Islanders, of *Mutiny on the Bounty* fame, and the American Negro. The present Hawaiian situation, where the various ethnic groups are intermarrying with increasing freedom, is a most interesting example of racial change going on today.

From the foregoing it can be seen that race is a highly unstable phenomenon. The racial variability of *Homo sapiens* has undergone more or less continuous modification. This changing nature of race makes the idea of a "pure" race meaningless. The greatest homogeneity in "racial" traits is found among small groups of people long isolated from the main currents of human travel and exchange.

All historical evidence makes us accept the inevitability of the crossing of strains wherever peoples come in contact with one another. But biological crossing is not the only modifying factor. In the early part of this century, Franz Boas, conducting an anthropological study of immigrants at the request of the United States Immigration Commission, was the first to show that a supposedly un-

---

[6] Carleton S. Coon, *The Living Races of Man* (New York: Alfred A. Knopf, 1965), p. 23.
[7] Ruth Benedict, *Race: Science and Politics,* rev. ed. (New York: The Viking Press, 1945), pp. 45ff.

changeable index of physical type was mutable. He found that the cephalic indices of immigrants from south and eastern Europe, as compared with their children, altered according to the length of time spent in the American environment. Furthermore, they all altered toward a uniform type more nearly in accord with the measurements of older American stock. Japanese who emigrated to the United States are physically different from their siblings who stayed in Japan. During the last two centuries, Americans of British descent have grown three and a half inches taller than their Revolutionary ancestors, and proportionately heavier. The cephalic index may drop dramatically in a single generation among people who have abandoned cradling.[8]

Race and Physiology

Comparative studies of the physiology of samples of racial groups have shown in some cases significant differences, in others mutability over time, and in others no differences at all. There is much current research on how and why people are different from one another physiologically, and at the present time one can relatively accurately delineate how, but only hypothetically why; although Coon suggests that the "why" answers to the relationship between physical environment and physiological phenomena may not be far away.[9]

In the cluster of traits which make up visible differences the most relevant one to the American popular mind is *skin color*. According to contemporary research skin color depends on the differences in melanin production in the body and on such secondary factors as disintegrated hemoglobin. That is, we know now the biological and physiological factors which make for darker or lighter skin. Coon thinks we are approaching the period where we will know why natural selection favors one or the other in different environments, for example, darker skins among people living in the wet tropics, or why the skin color of American Indians varies regionally. For Indians, skin color is darkest where radiation is at the peak, but in the tropical forests of South America (at high altitude) it is quite light, as is true of the inhabitants of rain forests in Borneo.

Another comparative dimension is immunity to disease. What seems to be apparent is that natural selection and adaptive mechanisms stabilize over time resistances to particular diseases in particular environments. Change in the environment may make people differentially susceptible to new diseases or may weaken resistance patterns to those endemic to their former environment. Coon suggests that malaria, so acutely debilitating to Europeans in Africa and Southeast Asia, and to which "native" populations have developed resistance may actually have preserved these people from the onslaughts of technically superior and better organized Caucasians and Mongolians. He further cites the suggestion that malaria may have increased in these areas in the shift from a

[8] Coon, Ch. 10.
[9] *Ibid.*, Chs. 8 and 9.

hunting-gathering economy to agriculture, which brought about cleared forests, pockets of still water in which mosquitos could breed, kept people anchored to specific places and allowed human and animal excreta to accumulate.[10]

As a final illustration we refer to "blood," about which so much superstition has developed. The four types of human blood, designated by the labels O, A, B, and AB, are inherited. But whites, Negroes, and Mongols have all these blood types. Blood plasma derived from various racial groups was utilized for the wounded in World War II irrespective of their race, with no effect on the personality or physiology of the recipients.

Race Crossing

Random observation of people in large metropolitan areas of the United States will readily reveal persons of hybrid characteristics of the main races of mankind whose external features are well proportioned and handsome. An occasional unpleasing-looking hybrid may be noted, but the same can be found among persons who are not hybrids. What science has to say about the effects of race crossing may be approached by first considering some conclusions drawn from specific studies of particular interracial crossings.[11]

POLYNESIAN-WHITE CROSSING The hybrid descendants of English mutineers and Tahitian women are taller than the average Englishman or Tahitian, and are more vigorous and healthy. They are perfectly alert. The physical type of the descendants is in every way harmonious, with white characteristics predominating.

AUSTRALIAN-WHITE CROSSING All unprejudiced observers agree that the offspring of aboriginal-white crossings in Australia are of an excellent physical type and that both the aborigines and the hybrids possess considerable mental ability.

IN HAWAII Here are hundreds of varieties of mixed types, involving native Hawaiians (Polynesians), Japanese, Filipinos, Koreans, Chinese, and whites of many nationalities. The descendents of mixed Hawaiian unions have a much higher fertility rate than other ethnic groups and in height, weight, and other physical characteristics tend to be intermediate between their Hawaiian and non-Hawaiian forebears.

INDIANS-WHITE MIXTURES Boas showed that the "half-blood" Indian was taller and more fertile than the parental Indian and white stock. Krogman concludes that Seminole Indians of Oklahoma, who are the descendants of a mixture of runaway Creek Indians, Negro slaves, and whites, are on the whole good physical types, and often beautiful. There is not the slightest evidence of degeneration or disharmony in development.

The verdict of biological and anthropological science is clear and unequivocal: race crossing per se has no deleterious biological consequences. On the

10 *Ibid.,* pp. 277–278.
11 The examples given are taken from Montagu, Chapter 8.

contrary, and most disconcerting to the exponents of racism, the preponderance of evidence points to at least an initial biological superiority of the progeny of the first hybrid generation over that of the respective racial parental generation. The phenomenon of "hybrid vigor" well known in plant and animal biology is indicated in many human interracial crossings. Of this the biologist Jennings writes:

> In view of the immense number of genes carried by individuals of each race, and their separate history up to the time of the cross, the relatively few defects that have arisen are almost certain to affect genes of different pairs in the two. Hence when the races cross, the individuals produced will receive a normal gene from one parent or the other in most of their gene pairs; and since the normal gene usually manifests its effect, the offspring of the cross will have fewer gene defects than either of the parents.[12]
>
> Thus the offspring of diverse races may be expected to be superior in vigor, and presumably in other characteristics. . . . Data on this point are not abundant, but it is possible that hybrid vigor is an important and advantageous feature of race crosses in man.[13]

The merits of race crossing may be argued at the social level, but those who argue against it will find no support from biological science.

What Race Is Not

Race and Culture

"Race" as it is used today only emerged as a concept in the sixteenth and seventeenth centuries. Until this time for Europeans the definition of "others" was Christian vs. non-Christian. As European expansion and imperialism began to develop peoples were encountered whose culture, values, and ways of life were different from the known and familiar. Since these people also looked different, there was the naïve assumption that their ways of behaving were related to the way they looked. Thus in the period of imperialist expansion for most people the concepts race and culture became inextricably intertwined. If one recognizes that culture is man's way of adapting to his environment, as we have indicated above, it is more likely that culture affected race than race, culture. The separation of physiognomic adaptations and cultural solutions did not become explicit until the development of the physical and social sciences. For almost three hundred years then, from the 17th to the 20th centuries, there was no factual basis for interpretation of differences, although always there were some sensitive individuals who appreciated other cultures without regard to visible physiognomic differences. As the fact or the spirit of imperialism grew,

[12] H. S. Jennings, *The Biological Basis of Human Nature* (New York: W. W. Norton & Company, 1930), p. 280. By permission.
[13] H. S. Jennings, "The Laws of Heredity and Our Present Knowledge of Human Genetics on the Material Side," in *Scientific Aspects of the Race Problem*, H. S. Jennings et al. (New York: Longmans, Green & Co., 1941), p. 71.

visible differences became the rationalization for what were really cultural conflicts. The technological superiority of the Europeans and European-descended peoples established dominance over less technologically developed societies and externally rationalized this on the basis of the confusion of race and culture. A European naïveté and ethnocentrism justified dominance in terms of "the white man's burden." As acculturation to the European dominance spread, the racial emphasis became more pronounced as the justification for subordination.

The institutionalization of dominant-subordinate relationships depends on the preservation of norms across generations. But norms are derived from values. Differences in the content and emphasis of values will give a different cast to patterns of subordination. For example again, in Brazil, Catholic Christianity was sufficiently in control of the value system in the early period of settlement that imported Negroes and indigenous Indians were accepted by Europeans and incorporated into the social system according to their education and ability if they were Catholic. It is true that as Brazil developed there was cruel exploitation of Indian labor, and Negro slaves coming in the later importations had less access to channels of opportunity. The result has been that lower classes tend to be darker. But in contrast to the North American traditional pattern, Negro or Indian descent has never been per se a barrier to entry into economic or social elites. In early Brazil intermarriage was frequent, manumission frequent, the family structure of slaves was protected, and tribal groups were often kept in tact. In contrast in North America, the indigenous social structures of African peoples were shattered, sexual exploitation rather than Catholic marriage was more typical, and manumission, although it occurred, was less frequent than in Brazil. One factor in the North American situation was a less unified superordinate religious value system.

When the institutionalized pattern is threatened with change additional supporting arguments are marshaled to uphold the existing structure. Thus the first arguments about the nature of "races" were based on Biblical Old Testament "authority," and later the beginning of the scientific study of man, which, like all *beginning* scientific endeavor must deal with categories of phenomena and with differences, laid a base for a belief in biological determinism—that is, that ability and behavior are determined by physical type. The racialist writers are one special group of biological determinists. In essence they hold that what determines differences in the cultures of ethnic groups is the distinctive genetic racial heredity of each. One such group of writers was the "Aryan" school. From philological research that revealed similarities in the languages of the Persians and Indians and those of the western Indo-Europeans, the Greeks, Romans, Teutons, Celts, and Slavs, they concluded that all languages derived from a common source, and they posited a primitive Aryan tribe from which all the later Aryans descended. Considering these languages superior and assuming without question that language and race are related, this school expounded the theory of the "superior Aryan race." It would take us too far afield to summarize the criticisms of the Aryan theories. In brief, the wide variation in both physical characteristics, as determined by anthropologists, and the cultures among the alleged Aryan peoples indicate that these theories have little scientific foundation.

Race and Nationality

The tendency to identify race and nation is perhaps the most widely held of all beliefs relating race to culture. It is in Europe, the very region where racialist theories were most earnesty expounded, that the lack of correlation between racial subgroups and national culture is most clearly illustrated. This is notably true of Germany, France, and England, where Nordic, Alpine, and Mediterranean traits have been shown to be harmoniously blended in the citizenry of each nation. Dominian wrote "Northern France is perhaps more Teutonic than southern Germany, while eastern Germany is, in many places, more Slavic than Russia.[14] Hankins points out that within Germany, "a relative purity of Germanic elements along the Baltic and North Seas (but mixed even there with Slavic Poles and Wends) gradually gives way to the southward to an increasing complexity in which Alpine and Mediterranean elements increase." [15]

Since the English were racially mongrelized within the broad Caucasian limits, it follows that the old American stock was correspondingly a mongrel mixture of European varieties. In a study of Americans descended from this English stock, Hrdlicka showed that they ranged widely in skin color, hair color, and eye color, with intermediates predominating over either the alleged Nordic type with fair skin, blue eyes, and blond hair, or the swarthy-complexioned, brunet, Mediterranean type. Altogether, the measurements indicate extensive hybridization in the old American stock.[16]

Beyond all this, the exhaustive study of the nature of culture and its processes which has gone on for the past few decades indicates that it is the common experience of living together that develops cultural similarities, irrespective of race. Thus American Negroes, whose lineal continuity with the American scene is almost as old as that of the English, were more Americanized in the cultural sense at the turn of the century than any of the recent white immigrant groups.

Social Race

From the foregoing discussion it is apparent that the term "race" as traditionally used has neither descriptive accuracy nor categorical validity. Nevertheless, this traditional concept persists in cultures as a mode, among others, of ranking people socially. This is what Wagley calls "social race."

[14] Leon Dominian, *Frontiers of Language and Nationality* (New York: Henry Holt & Co., 1917), pp. 3–4.
[15] F. H. Hankins, *The Racial Basis of Civilization* (New York: Alfred A. Knopf, 1926), p. 286.
[16] Alec Hrdlicka, *Old Americans* (Baltimore: The Williams & Wilkins Co., 1925), Chapter 3.

"Social race" (i.e., the way in which the members of society classify each other by physical characteristics) is one of a series of values which give individuals rank and determine their social relations.[17]

In analyzing populations in rural Brazil, Wagley found he had to resort to the term "race" for the concept of "social race" because this was the common term not only in the popular vocabulary but also in the collection of census statistics.

> Throughout this report, when the term "race" is used, the authors hold no brief for its validity as a physical or genetic classification. In one sense or another, the term is always used in this volume in a social and cultural sense. It is well known that colour or race data in population statistics reflect the social categories of the census takers, and it is interesting to reflect upon the variety of social definitions of "race" which would inevitably be involved in any census of Brazil.... Even our own observations as to the probable "racial" affiliation of an individual or group of people are by necessity "naked eye" judgements certainly coloured by our own social and cultural experiences. Throughout this report, then, we are interested in the social definitions of "race"... and in their effects upon the life of the people of the communities studied, while exact physical classification is of little interest for our purposes.[18]

In keeping with Wagley's position, we too shall have to discuss race with the understanding that we are referring only to popular social categories which affect the way in which groups behave toward one another.

Ethnic

In much contemporary writing on intergroup relations, the term "race" has been abandoned and the word "ethnic" substituted. In this book when the term "ethnic" is used in connection with groups which are distinguishable by physiognomic as well as cultural traits, we will be emphasizing the cultural ethos of the group. When the group is referred to as a "race" we will be emphasizing the barriers that are erected against them within the dominant pattern of race attitudes.

Equality and Inequality

Such myths as the belief that any races other than the European were less evolved species are now so long exploded that they do not need to be recapitulated and refuted. The growth of cultural anthropology has given a new perspective on cultures and their ability, whether simple or complex, to solve the problems of their natural environment, so that we are no longer prone to use the terms "savage" or "backward," which imply a set of criteria in which the highest

[17] Charles Wagley, ed. *Race and Class in Rural Brazil* (Paris: UNESCO, 1952), p. 14.
[18] *Ibid.,* p. 14. By permission.

development of Western European cultures is the standard of measurement. There is by no means the assurance of former times that the technologically developed world is morally superior to peoples whose modes of living still feature human labor and simple agricultural practices. With the widespread increase in education and communication, most of the literate world now knows that European civilization is not the only great civilization of history, that many technical processes were known on the continent of Africa while Europe was still tribal, and that the Oriental civilizations were in many respects far in advance of Western Europe in the Middle Ages and the beginnings of the modern period of our history.

The issues of equality of ability between the races fall again, as all the other previous arguments we have discussed, into the patterns of social relations between peoples. An issue which has been of major concern in dominant-minority relations in the United States has been the question of whether on the various mental tests the minority populations are as "bright" as native American groups.

> When the tests were first applied to representatives of different ethnic groups, it was usually in the belief that the method was capable of measuring native ability, and that the results could be so interpreted. . . . The history of the mental testing of ethnic or "racial" groups may almost be described as a progressive disillusionment with tests as a measure of native ability, and a gradually increasing realization of the many complex environmental factors which enter into the result.[19]

Many illustrations of the effect of environmental handicaps on performance in mental testing can be cited. Striking examples were the army tests in World War I, in which Negro recruits of Ohio, Illinois, and New York obtained higher scores than did whites of Mississippi, Kentucky, and Arkansas.[20] In most tests, American Indians generally obtain low test scores, but in a study of American Indian foster children living in white homes, Garth found an average I.Q. more than 20 points higher than the general Indian average.[21]

Klineberg refers to a statement by the southern sociologist Odum that among the "errors of sociology" is "the assumption that races are *inherently* different rather than group products of differentials due to the cumulative power of folk-regional and cultural environment." [22]

The Origins and Persistence of Racialism

Racialism a Corollary to European Expansion

As we have pointed out, the emphasis on race as a differentiating and determining factor in human behavior did not arise until about the eighteenth

[19] Otto Klineberg, *Social Psychology*, rev. ed. (New York: Henry Holt and Co., 1954), p. 305.
[20] *Ibid.*, p. 307.
[21] *Ibid.*, p. 310.
[22] *Ibid.*, p. 311.

century. It arose and became incorporated in the beliefs and practices of North Europeans in particular, and diffused among other peoples of North European descent.

> In the long history of the world men have given many reasons for killing each other in war: envy of another people's good bottom land or of their herds, ambition of chiefs and kings, different religious beliefs, high spirits, revenge. But in all these wars the skulls of the victims on both sides were generally too similar to be distinguished. Nor had the war leaders incited their followers by referring to the shapes of their heads. They might call them the heathen, the barbarians, the heretics, the slayers of women and children, but never our enemy Cephalic Index 82.
>
> It was left for high European civilization to advance such a reason for war and persecution and to invoke it in practice. In other words, racism [23] is a creation of our own time.[24]
>
> When we examine the scientific literature of the seventeenth century with a view to discovering what beliefs were held concerning the variety of man, we find that it was universally believed that mankind, was comprised of a single species and that it represented a unitary whole.... Physical differences were, of course, known to exist between groups of mankind, but what was unfamiliar was the notion that the differences exhibited by such peoples represented anything fundamental.[25]

In all modes of social conflict in the eighteenth and nineteenth centuries "racism" became involved. It was invoked by the nobles of France to justify their superiority to the bourgoisie, and later espoused by reactionary political theorists throughout nineteenth-century Europe.[26]

Racialism became the support of nationalist rivalries by adding to the cult of nationalism the idea that "our nation (or a dominant segment of it) is a superior race." But, most pertinent to our interest, racism became a strong support of slavery and imperialism. In the process of establishing their economic hegemony over most of the world and in developing less settled areas under this domination to their own greatest advantage, white Europeans, particularly the English—who passed on this tradition to the Americans—developed a caste-like relation to the "natives" of their colonies and, under an even more indisputably inferior status, to the forcefully imported slaves. In fact, it seems clear that in actual time sequence, the white men first exploited native labor and brought in slaves and then expounded a theory of the inferiority of the "colored" peoples to support their *de facto* status.[27] As Benedict points out,

[23] The use of the word "racism" in place of "racialism" is becoming increasingly common. It might serve a useful purpose to retain the more traditional term to refer to the literary apologia for the phenomena concerned and to use the newer term for the behavior manifesting this point of view. We shall, however, use the two terms synonymously. [Authors' note.]

[24] Benedict, pp. 3–4. By permission.

[25] Montagu, p. 16. By permission.

[26] See Jacques Barzun, *Race: A Study in Superstition,* rev. ed. (New York: Harper & Row, 1965), Chapter 2, "The Nordic Myth."

[27] See Chapter 10 for a discussion of the philosophical justification of slavery in the United States long after the first slaves were imported.

Racism did not get its currency in modern thought until it was applied to conflicts within Europe—first to class conflicts and then to national. But it is possible
to wonder whether the doctrine would have been proposed at all as explaining
these latter conflicts—where, as we have seen, the dogma is so inept—if the basis
for it had not been laid in the violent experience of racial prejudice on the
frontier.[28]

In summary, the doctrine of racism appears to have developed in relation
to the colored races as an ideological and moral justification for a system already
established and highly useful to white dominants. It has been continued for the
same reason. The fact that at the time of contact the native races were sufficiently colored to be identified and also were at a level of civilization actually
inferior (by the standards of white civilization) offered plausible demonstration
of the white man's allegation of their inferiority. Once systems of dominant-
minority relations became established, with the doctrine of white supremacy to
reinforce them, two vicious circles were set in motion: the perpetual conditioning of subsequent generations of white children to accept the racist doctrine,
and the impact of the system on the minority which served to keep them in large
measure inferior by impeding the development of their capacities.

Racialism: An Adjunct of Nationalistic Movements

The potential power of racism in stimulating group conflict can be further
illustrated by its application to two twentieth-century phenomena: the Japanese pan-Asiatic movement and the rise of the Hitler Reich. While it would be
oversimplification to explain the aggressive policy pursued by Japan in the
twentieth century wholly on the basis of their notion of race superiority, that
this notion was prevalent and served a useful purpose in developing morale for
aggressive political policies should not be overlooked. According to the Japanese
scholar Hirata, "from the fact of the divine descent of the Japanese people proceeds their unmeasurable superiority to the natives of other countries in courage
and intelligence." [29] While like all tribes and nations, the Japanese were always
ethnocentric, the development of distinct "racial pride" as part of the cultural
paraphernalia essential to whip up national enthusiasm for military, imperialistic
expansion was a part of the great borrowing of Western ideas and knowledge
which characterized modern Japan.

In the Nazi ideology, racialism was a dominant theme. It was not, however,
a new point of view, but rather the logical culmination of selected strains of
political argument throughout the nineteenth century. As Barzun states, "the
race-overtones are nothing new and the rearrangement of Tacitus's Nordic myth
was peculiar to France only in its details. Hitler showed how readily it applies

[28] Benedict, p. 111. By permission.
[29] Willard Price, "Japan's Divine Mission," *The New Republic*, Nov. 17, 1937.

to the Third Reich." [30] Whereas French writers were debating the superiority of Franks to Romanized Celts and the English were dreaming of Anglo-Saxon encirclement and hegemony of the world, the Nazi's applied the argument against the Jews, who in the century since the establishment of full civil rights for them in Germany had risen in status and made so many contributions to German enterprise and German thought. In the critical period of economic, political, and social reorganization after the defeat in World War I, the Nazi philosophers expounded the notion that the development of a pan-Nordic (German) state was the only bulwark against chaos, and that the German nation must be "purified" from the deteriorating "international" influence of the Jewish "race." In practice, the Nazis subjected Jews to persecution and extermination. Once the German Nordic "race" itself was thus purified, the rest of the "race" was to be incorporated into a pan-German state, and Germans in other parts of the world, notably the United States, were to be encouraged to retain their racial purity and to foster Nazi ideas.

Racialism in the United States

The doctrine of racialism is widely prevalent in the thinking of large segments of the population of the United States. How these racialist beliefs and attitudes serve to support dominant discrimination against minorities will be indicated repeatedly as we consider the stories of each minority group separately. At this point we shall limit our treatment of racialism in the United States to its literary expression. Writings of a racialist character directed specifically at showing the inferiority of the Negro and thus attempting to give moral justification to slavery appeared in the South in the decades before the Civil War. It was in the second and third decades of the twentieth century, however, that the racialist thesis found its greatest literary expression by the apostles of the Nordic movement, beginning with the publication by Madison Grant of *The Passing of the Great Race*.[31] Borrowing heavily from the European Nordic protagonists, Grant examined the United States. He considered the "melting pot" thesis anathema and warned the "native" Americans—that is, Nordics—to protect their heritage from being destroyed by new, non-Nordic elements. The same general thesis gained more academic respectability through the writings of Henry Fairfield Osborn, a professional paleontologist. Osborn belonged to the school of scientists who considered heredity far more determinative of human events than environment. He further believed that the Nordic racial group was superior to the Alpine and Mediterranean elements, and thus saw the gradual dying out of Nordic hereditary traits as the greatest single danger to the future of the country. Lothrop Stoddard, like Grant a lawyer, expanded the Nordic theme to encompass the doctrine of white supremacy over colored peoples. The

[30] Barzun, p. 23.
[31] Madison Grant, *The Passing of the Great Race* (New York: Charles Scribner's Sons, 1916).

title of one of his best known works, *The Rising Tide of Color Against White World Supremacy*, clearly indicates his basic theme.[32]

It is significant that this period in which the Nordic movement was receiving its greatest literary development coincides with the enactment of restrictive legislation against European immigration, beginning in 1921. While it is impossible to determine what effect these writings may have had on legislation, it is clear that the high quotas accorded the allegedly "Nordic" countries and the low quotas allotted the "non-Nordic" nations harmonized with the beliefs of these pro-Nordic writers.

The popularity of these pseudoscientific Nordic proponents stimulated vigorous research and writing which was ultimately to demolish, in intellectual circles, not only Nordic doctrine but all other expressions of racialism. From this exploration has emerged the scientific view of race presented earlier in the chapter. If the elimination of minority discrimination depended solely on "debunking" the racialist doctrine, such discrimination would disappear in a generation. But as the history of racialism suggests, belief in its doctrine does not rest solely on inadequate knowledge of its objective error but partly in the desire of the dominant to believe it.[33]

Race-thinking, to use Barzun's term,[34] is, as he points out, a superstition—literally, an idea that "stands over" facts. Philosophers of racism, (with the aid of other intellectual disciplines) have contributed in the past to "the astonishing enterprise of super-superstition." [35] It has been so pervasive a part of Western thought for some centuries that it has subtly infected us all so that surprising sentiments may be heard to emerge with regard to the French-Algerian conflict, the Arab-Israeli conflict, the inverted racism of "Negritude" in former French Africa, or "Black Power" among American Negroes. The urge to build theories about collectivities in order to mobilize collective hostility is still with us. Any hope for social peace lies in "turning group antagonisms into consciously economic or political struggles by removing their racist covering." [36] There are established channels for dealing with economic and political conflict. There are none for the undefined group aggressions of the confused, the frightened, the egocentric, the alienated, who subsume groups as identically capable or incapable, reliable or treacherous, lovable or hateful.

Topics for Projects and Discussion

1. Find out how many of your fellow students have heard of the UNESCO series of pamphlets entitled *The Race Question*. What kind of reactions do you get to

[32] See also L. L. Snyder, *Race: A History of Modern Ethnic Theories* (Chicago: Alliance Book Co., 1939), Chapter 14, "Racialism Invades the United States."
[33] See Gerhart Saenger "The Effectiveness of the UNESCO Pamphlet Series on Race," *International Social Science Bulletin*, Vol. VI, No. 3. Dr. Saenger found many resistances to using the UNESCO material in schools and colleges.
[34] Barzun, Preface to the second edition, p. x.
[35] *Ibid.*
[36] *Ibid.*, p. xix.

this inquiry that shows you something about attitudes toward other "races"? Toward UNESCO? Are these publications in your college library? In any library in your community?

2. Suggest as many reasons as you can why the comparative scores of two racial groups on mental tests may not reflect their relative mental abilities.

3. Read Hitler's *Mein Kampf,* Chapter 11, "Nation and Race," and write a critical review from the contemporary scientific view of race.

4. Find illustrations of the concept of "social race" in examples of differential treatment of several "racial" minorities. Explain the historical and other social factors that are relevant to these differences of acceptance.

5. The term "race" is frequently incorrectly used in written and oral speech. Collect as many such uses as possible. Classify your material and make an interpretative summary of your findings.

6. Discuss the inverse racialism of some militant Negro groups in the light of how they have historically perceived their group identity.

Suggested Reading

Barzun, Jacques. *Race: A Study in Superstition,* rev. ed. New York: Harper & Row, 1965. Also available in Harper Torchbook edition.
>   *European ideologies of race.*

Gossett, Thomas F. *Race: The History of an Idea in America.* Dallas: Southern Methodist Univ. Press, 1963.
>   *A recent book on racialism in the United States.*

Handlin, Oscar. *Race and Nationality in American Life.* Boston: Little, Brown & Co., 1950. Also reprinted 1957 by Doubleday Anchor Books.
>   *A discussion of American minorities today with special emphasis on the role of concepts of race.*

Klineberg, Otto. "Racial Psychology," in *The Science of Man in the World Crisis,* ed. Ralph Linton. New York: Columbia University Press, 1945, pp. 63–77.
>   *A critical examination of the belief that races have innate psychological differences.*

Montagu, M. F. Ashley. *Statement on Race.* New York: Henry Schuman, 1951.
>   *An expanded and annotated account of the statement on race issues by United Nations Educational, Scientific and Cultural Organization (UNESCO).*

Thompson, Edgar T., and Hughes, Everett C., eds. *Race: Individual and Collective Behavior.* Glencoe, Ill.: The Free Press, 1958.
>   *An extensive selection of readings ranging widely over the field of race relations.*

Wagley, Charles. *Race and Class in Rural Brazil.* UNESCO, 1952.
>   *A discussion of the social relations of persons of the three racial stocks and their mixtures which constitute the population of Brazil. An example of how ideology and the social system effect attitudes toward and opportunities for persons of different racial strains.*

4

Religion and
Minority Status

Race, religion and national origin are the differentiating concepts which separately or in combination have served to rationalize attitudes of prejudice and acts of discrimination at various times and in various places in the United States.[1] In this chapter we shall consider the problems of religious identification as they are associated with dominant or minority status; as they have been focal points in discrimination; as they have provided areas of conflict in the society, and what adjustments have taken place. We shall also consider briefly the role of religious conviction in challenging discrimination, not only for its own membership bodies, but also as leading to active participation in seeking to eliminate discrimination based on other factors than religion.

The problems of religious minorities differ from the problems of other minorities in the sense that religion *per se* is not as visible unless it is reinforced by cultural or racial factors. One may anticipate that in any modern society there is potential intergroup conflict among groups of people whose belief systems vary. This may often also lead to institutional conflict, a situation germane to all complex societies undergoing change where one institutional pattern is more coherent with the change than another. To the extent that these intergroup conflicts or institutional conflicts are the adjustments between equal segments of the community we can hardly describe it as a minority situation. Furthermore, ideally, members of a religious minority, if there is no other minority factor present in the situation, could move from minority religious status to dominant religious status without discrimination. For example, it is unlikely that a former Amishman would be discriminated against in the dominant society if he had left the Amish community.

Whereas such an ideal view of religious affiliation is hypothetically possible, and in individual instances has occurred, for most minority religions there is an identification with the group that is rooted in very early socialization and

[1] Note the title of Gordon's book quoted in Chapter 2: *Assimilation in American Life: The Role of Race, Religion, and National Origins* (New York: Oxford University Press, 1964).

deep emotional bonds. Individual "renegades" may assimilate but there are strong group pressures from the minority itself to retain its members. Religious minorities seek pluralistic equality for which they have some hope in the Constitutional provisions for freedom of religion. Their effort for equal coexistence has also strengthened the possibility of greater equality of all minorities within a pluralistic society.

Some Background

The history of religious minorities in the United States may suggest a variety of facets of dominant-minority relations. In the first place, it points out that dominant-minority relations are dependent not only on dominant attitudes but on loyalty to minority belief systems which in some circumstances and on some issues take priority over dominant beliefs. This loyalty is usually not only to the content of the beliefs themselves but to the members of the groups who hold the beliefs in common. Sometimes the sense of communality is so strong that it governs all the personal and social relationships of the members. In other situations, in line with the theory of structural pluralism discussed in Chapter 2, it is possible to have a variety of associations that are not limited to one's own community of belief, while at the same time maintaining in one's personal life a minority religious group participation.

The formal acknowledgement of religious equality or freedom before the law does not guarantee freedom from community conflict when contents of belief are divergent on matters of public policy. There are, for example, issues between Catholics and Protestants on appropriate legislation. Furthermore in the past there has been local conflict, discrimination and even persecution of religious groups whose beliefs seemed at crucial variance with the rest of the community. Anti-religious feeling is sometimes truly based on a difference of beliefs, but very often it is merely an overt focus for what is really "anti-foreign," or "lower-class," or otherwise alien in the view of the pillars of the dominant society. This may be especially true at a time when social change is threatening the position of leaders in the dominant group.

The Colonial Heritage of Religious Discrimination

The American colonies were settled in a period when Europe had not yet resolved the problem of separation of religious identity and national identity. The nations of Western Europe in consolidating the authority of the state against powerful feudal interests had leaned on the support of religion by designating an "established" church. Northern Europe and countries whose powerful elites were anti-Roman-Catholic developed national Protestant churches supported by state funds. Other European countries remained Catholic and gave important political roles to powerful members of the Church hierarchy. It was not until nearly the end of the eighteenth century that the long struggle for the centralized state as opposed to feudal and regional interests was sufficiently over for religious tolerance to develop and civil discrimination against those not members of the established religion to be abandoned.

The established churches acted as a conservative force, upholding the prerogatives of the joint political and religious power structure. They were effective in continuing traditional order. But with the growth of economic enterprise and the entry into economic power of groups not favored by the establishment, both religious and secular, there were further moves of disaffection. These were manifestly (that is, consciously expressed as) religious movements. People found new ways of expressing beliefs and then found themselves deprived of a voice in political affairs. The movements were, therefore, also latently political. These "dissenters" were eventually offered a solution in migration to the New World.

Though much of the labor force in colonial times as in later immigration crossed the Atlantic primarily for economic opportunity, powerful (in the new country) groups and individuals came so that they could have a society in which they could follow their beliefs without economic or political disadvantage. For some there was the Utopian hope of creating a homogeneous world, and when this hope was threatened they took reprisals against "aliens" or *their* dissenters. In the seventeenth century, New England Calvinist-puritans drove out "heretics" like Roger Williams, and persecuted Quakers. This pattern repeated itself as long as there was open land for new settlement. Religious groups formed new societies and if they could not achieve dominance, participation, or tolerance migrated elsewhere.

The American colonies were subject to the religio-legal restrictions of the mother country. Thus, even in Pennsylvania, which offered freedom of religion, Jews could not vote and an Alsatian gentleman was denied citizenship on the grounds that he was Roman Catholic.[2]

The Principle of Disestablishment

The Crown colonies tended to be chiefly Anglican (Church of England) in the enfranchised population, because of the position of the Governor and the military. Other colonies, however, were strongly "disestablishment": Pennsylvania under Quaker dominance, Maryland as a Catholic colony, Massachusetts still strongly Puritan, Connecticut as the refuge of Congregationalists. It was the "disestablishment colonies" who controlled much of the commerce, and who had been most restless with British rule. Thus in the formation of an independent nation the principle of disestablishment prevailed. This meant that there would be no *official* religion, and that no public funds would go for the support of any ecclesiastical body.[3]

The American Constitution in its First Amendment guaranteed that there

[2] Gladys Meyer, *Free Trade in Ideas* (New York: The King's Crown Press, 1941), p. 36.
[3] A special note should be made here of the distinctive position of the Religious Society of Friends (Quakers). This body was so prestigious at the time of the American Revolution that it retained certain concessions won in colonial times: exemption from legal oaths, exemption from "bearing arms." This was also true for Mennonites and their splinter group the Amish who had settled in colonial Pennsylvania.

was to be no state religion, implying thereby no religious requirement for citizenship, for franchise, or for office-holding; and there was to be no meddling by the State in private religious practice. The statements were brief and general and were from time to time subsequently abrogated by state laws. This separation of church and state, as the principle has come to be called, differentiates between the claims of two bodies of authority. It has been said that Jefferson was interested in the principle in order to protect the state from the church, and that Roger Williams was interested in it to protect the church from the state.[4]

The Nature of Religion

Before we analyze the multi-religious situation in America it is important to look briefly at the nature of religion, its place in the social structure and some of its particular American forms.

Religion as a Value System

Religion is an internalized commitment to a value system. It endows certain central values as *sacred*—that is, apart from the ordinary and not subject to utilitarian or empirical judgment. Durkheim describes the sacred as something experienced by and affecting human beings. It makes demands upon worshipers as well as being experienced by them with feelings of power and awe. In this sense it is a *relationship* with something ultimate. Freud sees it as man's confrontation with his powerlessness when he perceives himself in the hazardous crises of the human life cycle, or of nature's scarcity and the struggle for survival. William James points out that out of such experience theologies arise. They are inevitably influenced by the social experience of a particular milieu— a group, a terrain, a historical time.[5]

Religion and Culture

Religion in any organized form is a group experience and reflects the history and beliefs of the group. This experience is transmitted from generation to generation by means of symbols, myths, hero stories, festivals and rituals, and ethical obligations. Because religion is so linked to the life experiences of a group, there will be variations between groups even if the central beliefs are held in common. Thus Irish Catholicism and Italian Catholicism will differ to an extent from one another. Where a particular religion has dominated and pervaded a whole national group, ethnicity and religion seem inseparable. As one first-generation Polish worker said, "To be Polish *is to be Catholic*." This close interweaving of religion and culture, especially in traditional societies, has also made possible religious rationalizations for prejudice against "foreigners" when

[4] Earl Raab, *Religious Conflict in America* (Garden City, New York: Anchor Books, Doubleday and Company, 1964), p. 7.
[5] Thomas F. O'Dea, *The Sociology of Religion* (Englewood Cliffs, N.J.: Prentice-Hall, 1966), Ch. 2.

the real points of conflict were not so much religious as ethnic. Similarly, American experience has given rise to particular varieties of American sects with their belief in individualism and manifest destiny reflecting nineteenth-century American experience. So close are religion and culture that the destruction of religion may mean the demoralization of a people, as with the Sioux Indians when central religious ceremonies were prohibited. (See Chapter 16.)

Religious Organization

Religious organizations differ from one another not only in their deeper felt orientations that both affect society and are affected by it. They differ in their use of symbols, ritual, and liturgy. It is these extrinsic factors that often make them at first visible. They may further differ in the way they provide for leadership and authority within the organization.

In folk societies religion permeates all the life processes—is diffuse throughout the whole peoples. From time to time it is revitalized by outstanding leaders whose personal impact attracts followers. Their small personal followings are *cults*. Cults usually develop idiosyncratic behavior that sets them off from others. Often such cults are the beginnings of genuine religious movements that ultimately survive the demise of their leader. This may be the more true if they are shut out by the larger society, driven "underground" as were the early Christians, so that they strengthen their own solidarity. But to survive across generations they will have to establish norms of leadership, routinize their religious behavior so that it can be learned, in other words make the transition to some form of institutionalization.

An institutionalized church now has the problem of coming to terms with the secular society. It has the choice of becoming accommodated to the society and its other institutions—that is it may develop a spirit of compromise; or it has the choice of rejecting the society. The former pattern is usually defined as a *church* (ecclesia); the latter as a *sect*. The church attempts to be inclusive; membership is by birth and theology is explicit. The sect is based on voluntary joining, is exclusive of all who have not shared its experience of regeneration. As it does not, initially at least, seek compromise with the secular society, it is apt to be austere and ascetic. However, such austerity may also, under the conditions of the modern world, lead to prosperity and to a mitigation of the separatism from the secular world. In the historical pattern of America at such a point the sect becomes a denomination and a church. Some sects, however, like the Old Order Amish discussed below, remain "established sects," withdrawn from or critical of the secular world.

Religion and Class

Established religious bodies, whatever their theology, which have worked out acceptable (to them) compromises between the church and the world appeal to the classes that are also the most established in the world. In an open-class society like that of the United States this means that the older denominations are the most prestigious. (This hierarchy and prestigious religious affiliation could not apply to a situation where there was an identity of religion and culture, or where there was a closed class system, or an established national church.) In America, the denominations of the founding fathers (in the East) or of the pioneer evangelists (in the South and West) with their emphasis on either ritual or preaching have become the respectable or honored churches. On the other hand, the sects that have sought to relieve stress with the hope of a new messianic coming, or through a weekly experience of religious enthusiasm have provided expression to people whose position in the secular opportunity structure is by choice or necessity cut off from worldly success.[6]

Some Protestant churches, like Catholics, not only claim universality for all strata, but organizationally attempt to provide for this through a central administration and dioceses and parishes, or their equivalent. However this may often turn out to be, within Protestantism, the church and chapel pattern (a wealthy church supports a chapel in a poor section as part of its parish); or the "home missionary" effort of some other denominations.

Another aspect of the class differences in religious membership is related to the education of the clergy. Within Protestantism and Judaism the educated congregations prefer and insist on humanistically as well as theologically educated clergy. The working class and agrarian populations are more concerned with the "spirit" and traditional exposition of the scripture in their demands on clergy. In the expectations for clergy there are other issues which also in part reflect the differences between urbanism and rural or small community orientations. These are the felt conflicts between science and the authority of tradition; and also the difference between the church as (through its liturgy and sermons) primarily concerned with helping the congregation to be comfortable with the world or as primarily concerned with the compassionate mission of religion to help those in trouble.[7]

Religion and Status

In an open-class society where people are able to move from one position in the social hierarchy to another more prestigious one, religious affiliation often provides a visible anchor in the reference group one seeks to be part of. Thus Protestants may leave one denomination for a more prestigious one; Jews may shift from Orthodox to Reformed Judaism; Catholics may prefer a French to an Irish church. All of these are reflections of the larger national status picture in which roots in early settlement are part of the criteria for increasingly re-

[6] Werner Cohn, "Jehovah's Witnesses as a Proletarian Movement." (New York: The New School For Social Research, 1954), unpublished M.A. Thesis.
[7] For a discussion of some of these differences and conflicts see Gerhart Lenski, *The Religious Factor* (Garden City, New York: Doubleday and Co., rev. ed. for Anchor Books, 1963), Chs. 6 and 7.

spected status. As national values become more significant than local values there is a move toward the older established religious groups.

Religious Discrimination as Process

The Struggle for the Protestant Establishment

THE FIRST PHASE: 1789–1850   Until about 1850 Protestant dominance was sufficiently clear by virtue of numbers, early migration, and economic advantage that members of religious minorities could be incorporated in the secular life of the nation without having religion emerge as a categorical reason for discrimination.[8] This situation was able to persist till roughly the middle of the nineteenth century for several reasons. Conflicts of the period were regional, between the East Coast and the new Middle West. The major power struggles were those of the Eastern commercial classes against the workingmen of the East and the rural settlers of the Middle West. Both sides of the struggle were predominantly Protestant, but in religious terms they represented the established religious groups of the East: Episcopalians, Presbyterian, Congregational, versus the rising sectarian groups of the expanding nation: Methodists, Baptists, Disciples of Christ, etc., later to become the established denominations of the West. These popular evangelical, democratic, sectarian movements whose appeal was to farmers and workers contributed to the success of the Jacksonian revolution (eliminating, as it did, property qualifications for voting, imprisonment for debt, and advancing support of free public education). The period was one of lively theological controversy, not unmixed with belief in Divine intervention, Divine mission, a modicum of superstition, and an upstanding conviction of human worth as more significant than doctrinal designation.[9] Dissenters with significant numbers to be conspicuous in beliefs and practices different from the general community norms continued to find solutions in separatist colonies on the frontier. New forms of religion emerged out of the American experience developing from cult to sect to denomination over the century. Thus discrimination in this period was within the framework of class issues, with religious affiliation secondary. The "peculiar" people among native-born sectarians had the frontier to absorb them at a time when communication with the frontier was technologically limited.

A second factor of importance was that the largest body of non-Protestants did not migrate in great numbers until steamships were the common mode of trans-Atlantic travel. These were the Irish and the German Catholics. Although the Irish had come in a small steady stream since the mid-eighteenth century, the heavy Irish migration began in the eighteen-fifties, spurred by famine in Ire-

[8] Baltzell, E. Digby, *The Protestant Establishment: Aristocracy and Caste in America* (New York: Random House, 1964), p. 73.
[9] Thomas F. O'Dea, *The Mormons* (Chicago, Ill.: The University of Chicago Press, 1957). See Chapter I for a summary of the religious ferment of the period.

land, ship companies seeking fares, recruitment of unskilled labor for American industries, and a land tenure system which left large segments of the rural population landless. Irish labor crews built most of the railroads from the Alleghenies to the Rockies, and were miners in the Appalachian region. Many settled in Eastern cities and others in the newer communities of the Middle West and finally in the far West and California. Germans were much more widely distributed in the opening rural areas of the Middle West. Although many of them were Protestant, Chicago, St. Louis, St. Joseph, and various counties in Illinois, Missouri, Iowa, and Wisconsin had large contingents of German Catholics. Their arrival coincided with the opening of the railroad to Chicago and they dispersed to the West to follow their traditional occupations. The impact of these groups was certainly contributory to the rise of the first important nativistic movement, the Know-Nothing Movement (1850–1860), which was anti-immigration although the issues were defined ethnically rather than religiously. None the less the largely midwestern membership of the movement found Catholicism an "alien" religion. Among members of established Protestant denominations Freemasonry was strong throughout the nineteenth century (and later, also); this organized body was specifically anti-Catholic, inheriting its position from European anti-clerical struggles.[10]

The Jews of this period were present in sufficiently small numbers to be easily absorbed in the expanding opportunities of the developing country. They were merchants, professionals, or skilled workers and by the nature of their occupations largely urban. Some assimilated, joining one or another approved Protestant denomination. Some retained their Jewish religious affiliations and were respected according to their economic status, though often only marginally included in spheres of private social life. They neither sought nor had political influence. At the time of the Civil War they by and large supported the position of their regional location.

Non-European religions were ignored. The Chinese migrating to the West Coast and the Rocky Mountain area in the fifties were defined in terms of class and race (although many of the suspicions aroused against them were based on cultural differences.) American Indian religions were not given the dignity of recognition. There were efforts on the part of Catholics in Louisiana and California, as in the later annexed Southwestern territories, to Christianize them, and some Protestant groups sent missionaries among them. Sectarians (Quakers, Mennonites, Mormons) received them into membership; but little cognizance was taken of the integrity of their cultures, least of all their religious beliefs and practices.

THE SECOND PHASE: 1860–1924 The resurgence of religion as a rationalization for discrimination and the consolidation of WASP dominance is of course bound up with other struggles and social changes.

[10] See for example, Bernard Fay, *Revolution and Freemasonry, 1680–1800* (Boston, Mass.: Little, Brown & Co., 1935).

In the twenty years from 1860 to 1880 the dominant-minority issues were bound up first with the status of Negroes and subsequently with the Chinese. The only issue that had a religious dimension was the growth of anti-Irish feeling. Although for people in some places this was strongly linked to anti-Catholic feeling, the "Irish question" seems to have been based largely on involvement and subsequent leadership in early labor struggles. Mine workers and the Knights of Labor had strong articulate Irish membership. Part of the attempt to curb this insurgent class struggle was directed at the Irish as an ethnic group, not primarily as Catholics. The stereotype "Irish Catholic" came later. With the depression of the 1880's the Knights of Labor withered; this was the demise of the last widespread *political* labor movement. In subsequent decades the labor movement became a-political and "white"—anti-Oriental on the West Coast and anti-Negro in the East. This was probably inevitable as the nation was still expanding industrially and geographically and "white" labor had the real possibility of gains if it could eliminate the cheap labor of "alien" competitors.

The end of the nineteenth and the first decades of the twentieth century, however, saw the rise of real discrimination on religious grounds. On the part of the national elite it was first directed against the Jews. This temporarily successful effort to protect and consolidate WASP dominance was precipitated by several factors. The first, and not the least, of these was the displacement of the old commercial upper class by new wealth after the Civil War. First the transportation wealth and subsequently the industrial wealth pushed the old merchant families and their descendants into lesser positions of power. Some of the newly rich validated their social position by intermarriage with the old families. Some old families were clever enough to seize on the new developments. But for most, they were left without economic or political power and retreated into creating structures of social exclusion. One must see this movement against the backdrop of very rapid economic development. (The national income quadrupled between 1870 and 1900, and doubled again by 1914). The displaced patricians were supported in their attempt to create exclusive enclaves in "society" (resorts, elite boarding schools, metropolitan clubs and country clubs) by the new wealth which aped their parochialism in order to be "in." The result was "restriction" where this had never occurred formally before.[11]

The attitude leading to restriction filtered down. It was embraced by groups facing the heavy migration of Eastern European Jews whose folkways were conspicuously different and who were chiefly small merchants and industrial workers. It affected provincial cities undergoing the pangs of industrialization, affording them a scapegoat offered by the national models.

A phenomenon of this period was the rise of "old stock" associations with their emphasis on descent and date of migration as the criteria for social status.[12] As this movement spread it supported anti-Catholicism in New England and

[11] Baltzell, *The Protestant Establishment*, p. 110 and pp. 90ff.
[12] *Ibid.*, pp. 114ff.

the Middle West, anti-Orientalism among the "Native Sons of the Golden West" on the Pacific coast.

Another factor in the rise of religious discrimination was the religious literalism of many Protestant sectarians who saw industrial society encroaching on their agricultural way of life and were uneasy with intellectual trends in Protestant denominations. Perhaps even more they were resisting a permeating secularization in which they saw "success" emerging in place of "character" as the criterion for respect.

The rise of the urban political machine, in a number of cities largely in the hands of the Irish, with its patronage system of dispensing jobs or other aid and its frequent collusion with enterprises unacceptable to old Protestant mores, led to the anti-Irish-Catholic syndrome. This was the more true as Irish clergy dominated the American Catholic church at the time, and in some localities the church hierarchy had indirect controls on the local political machine. The response from many Protestants was the revival of the church-state issue.

Anti-Semitic and anti-Catholic feeling was at its height in the 1920's and even in the 1930's as World War I and the Depression made shockingly apparant the shift from a largely rural nation protected by two oceans to an industrial nation with international interdependence. The religious issue in dominant minority relations has never been so widespread since, although there have been sporadic resurgences. (See Chapter 18.)

Minority Adaptation to Protestant Dominance

The Sects—Protestant Revitalization Movements

America has historically been hospitable to migrating groups of sectarians from Western and Eastern Europe, and as we have indicated nineteenth-century America, and even twentieth-century America, has seen the emergence of a variety of indigenous religious sects. For many of these spatial separateness was once a viable solution. Now, however, in an era of increasing government demand on its citizens, sects have been caught in recurring conflict with the state; and mass communication influences attitudes toward these groups positively and negatively.

THE OLD ORDER AMISH An example of the dilemmas confronting a sect which has sought the historic pattern of ecological separatism is that of the Old Order Amish.

This group migrated to Pennsylvania in the eighteenth century. Although they are chiefly associated with Lancaster County, Pennsylvania, in the popular mind, they have settlements in Ohio, Indiana, Kansas, Illinois, Michigan, Iowa, North and South Dakota, Missouri, Nebraska, Oklahoma, and Oregon, as well. They number somewhat over 25,000. Religiously they are descended from the Mennonites and they in turn from the Anabaptists of sixteenth-century Bohemia. The Amish emphasize voluntary commitment represented by adult baptism, obedience to the literal teachings of the Bible, a return to the purity of the early

Christian (New Testament) communal congregational life. They renounce oaths, drinking, bearing of arms, and personal adornment. They are visible by their adherence to traditional dress and the fact that baptised males do not shave. These customs are symbols of their rejection of worldly values. The Amish are what one author has called a legalistic or objectivist sect—that is to say they are rule and symbol-oriented.[13]

They are patriarchal in family structure, with prestige and respect for the aged, and with clear separation of roles for men and women, women being subordinate. They are predominantly farmers, contact with the soil being a central value. They are opposed to modern technology, including electricity, automobiles, and farm machinery.

Amish religious services are carried on in homes rather than in church buildings, community services rotating from home to home. Church authority is vested in elders selected by the community. The sect is opposed to education beyond the eighth grade. An Amish proverb goes, "The more learned the more confused." Preference is for one-room schools with all age groups studying together, in the pattern of a large family. Amish religion is opposed to the teaching of evolution and science.

John A. Hostetler, a former Amishman, now sociologist, hypothesizes that both individual and social forces are creating restlessness and deviation among younger Amish.[14] This may be the result of ideological conflict with Amish doctrine, or personal frustration; or a result of division and instability in community leadership. Individual members have separated and reform groups have developed. The areas in which the Amish have had conflict with the state have been in their resistance to high-school attendance at consolidated schools where their children will associate with worldly companions and be exposed to technology and in their resistance to military service. Although they are exempted from bearing arms, they are subject to the draft and must do alternate service.

The Amish way of life, emphasizing soberness, righteousness, and hard work, has often won sympathy from other Americans. When a community in Pennsylvania lost a court case on the education issue the then governor of Iowa invited them to migrate to his state. However, non-Amish neighbors of these "queer" people are more often hostile, resorting to negative stereotyping in anti-Amish jokes, and even vandalism.

Although all Amish are American citizens, they have until recently rarely voted and have abjured public office. Now, however, many vote in local school board elections and some have held office on local school boards. Many showed great interest in the 1960 Presidential election, opposing John F. Kennedy.

The stresses and strains of change are being felt by Amish society. For some

[13] Elmer T. Clark, *The Small Sects in America,* rev. ed., (New York, Nashville: The Abingdon-Cokesbury Press, 1949), p. 147.
[14] John A. Hostetler, *Amish Society* (Baltimore: The Johns Hopkins Press, 1963), pp. 198–199.

communities this has led to modifications in the rules—a "controlled acculturation." In others it has meant a greater rigidity. Individual members, according
to Hostetler, are less likely to leave the more rigid communities in the absence
of acculturative agents to assist the out-movement. In the modified communities
there is more interaction with the salesman, the teacher, the neighboring
Mennonite who will drive the Amishman where he needs to go (since he may
not own or drive a car). In these contacts the way is opened to new associations
and new reference groups; the young Amish adolescent may move into another
sectarian group which gives him more emotional reward, allows him a more
liberal ideology and some benefits of the dominant society. The future of the
Amish probably lies less in the problem of conflict with the state than with the
potential decimation of the Old Order through reform splintering and individual defection.

THE MORMONS A contrasting solution to sectarian separateness may be
seen in the Church of Christ of the Latter Day Saints (the Mormons). With
two branches and four small splinter groups it has nearly two million members,
and has grown from a frontier revival sect to a world denomination. Founded in
Northern New York in 1830, the initial movement offered a combination of
Calvinism, evangelical Protestantism, the sense of present revelation, and the
authority of the prophetic mission. Unlike the Amish who took as their model
the early Christianity of the New Testament, the Mormons based their theology
on the Old Testament, with the concept of "peoplehood," destiny, and earthly
mission. They admitted the principle of continuing revelation which has made
them able to be flexible. They have stressed the intrinsic (belief) rather than the
extrinsic (behavior) dimensions of religion. They are highly centralized and
tightly bureaucratically controlled in church organization. Because they are
missionary in commitment they did not originally seek separatism, but after five
migrations in which their beliefs aroused hostility in each place of settlement,
the largest body finally migrated by wagon to Utah in 1847. Although many
Mormons have become assimilated into urban occupations throughout the
United States (and indeed abroad), the majority of Mormons still live West
of the Mississippi and many are rural or small-town inhabitants. The strange-
ness of their theology and their initial practice of polygamy set them apart
("their creed singular and their wives plural"). Polygamy as a social practice
was officially abolished by the church in 1896. It had already been declining
because of the nearly equal sex ratio of the Mormon population. The Re-
organized Church of the Latter Day Saints with headquarters in Independence,
Missouri, always claimed that polygamy was undoctrinal.

A recent study of a small Mormon community, closely related geographically
and economically to settlements of four other cultures, gives some sense of how
they relate to dominants and minorities.[15]

[15] Evon Z. Vogt and Ethel M. Albert, eds., *People of Rimrock* (Cambridge, Mass.: The
Harvard University Press, 1966), especially Chapters 2 and 7.

Rimrock is a Mormon unincorporated village in western New Mexico, 38 miles south of U.S. Highway 66. Mormons first came here as missionaries to the Indians in 1870. After an epidemic of smallpox wiped out all but one family, the central church body "called" families from nearby Arizona to renew the community. At present in the Rimrock region there are settlements of Anglo "Texans," Spanish Americans (New Mexico Hispanos), Zuni Indians, and Navaho Indians. In the present hierarchy of the five subgroups in the region, "Texans" and Mormons rank equally and highest. Below them are the Spanish Americans, with Zunis equal or a little higher and Navahos at the bottom of the scale. There has been some Mormon-"Texan" intermarriage. Rimrock Mormons will work for "Texans" and "Texans" for Mormons. Neither will work for Indians and only rarely for Spanish Americans.

Mormons view Indian religion as an apostate degeneration of Ancient Israelite roots, and allow Indian converts to retain some participation in Indian ceremonials. Nevertheless they have absorbed some of the dominant attitudes toward Indians as "lazy, dirty" people. They regard Zunis as "better" because they are settled and agricultural, whereas Navahos are nomad. Nevertheless, the Mormon economic system in Rimrock depends on Navahos for labor and more especially for suppliers and customers as the Mormons are the brokers who sell Indian products to the wider market and supply trading post consumer items to Navahos. Recently there has been a revival of missionary activity and there are now 112 Navaho Mormons in Rimrock, two of whom have attained higher positions in the Mormon priestly hierarchy. Many Navahos, however, view Mormon religious profession a "lip-service religion" and charge them with increasing encroachment on Navaho lands and exploitation of Navaho laborers and consumers. Zunis have no economic dependence on Mormons and have largely resisted missionary efforts.

The Mormons have largely succeeded in separating church and state. In local situations their sense of corporateness can enable them to undertake cooperative effort beyond their neighbors. Thus in Rimrock they could assess each citizen for the paving of roads, which was not possible in the "Texan" neighboring community. They have not in this century come into open institutional conflict with the state except for some rural Mormons who still practice polygamy to the embarrassment of the parent body. Some urban Mormons have achieved high positions in the economic and political spheres. Nevertheless, there is for Mormons as a minority, and for the dominant society, the continuing dilemma of which takes priority, the church or the world. As O'Dea points out, the Mormons have thus far showed great inventiveness and stamina in trying to resolve these pulls.[16]

One remaining issue for Mormons, more serious today than a scattered few of their rural "fundamentalist" polygamous adherents, is the fact that they

[16] Thomas F. O'Dea, *The Mormons*, Ch. 9 "The Sources of Strain and Conflict."

do not admit Negroes to the Mormon priesthood. They welcome Negroes as members but give them no opportunity to enter the church elite. Some Mormons are now attacking this position, which one may suppose is derivative from the fact that the founder of Mormonism probably at the time of his revelation had never seen a Negro and that the Mormons have largely lived in areas where there was almost no Negro population.[17]

We have discussed two sects which have attempted two solutions to the problems of sectarianism (the church and the world). One is of European origin, one a native American product, both long established and both with a history of persecution. Both were originally rural and are largely still so. Both are concerned with the sense of communality of membership. They both provide for members that accept their dogma, the sense of belongingness in an inner way. One has held to simple communality and teaches a doctrine of accepting present troubles as the price for "the truth" and eventual salvation. The other has chosen, or developed perhaps from the American experience of expansion, a sense of the truth always being revealed. One is "democratically" decentralized; the other is highly centralized. For both, the internalized values of religion take priority over the demands of the secular state. Both uphold the fundamental "Protestant ethic" and neither suffer categorical discrimination. Indeed both are now met with sympathy and appreciation by the dominant society, except for lesser incidents.

Let us now look at a more recent militant sect which has become increasingly urban. As we have said, sectarianism arises out of social and emotional needs that are not met by the establishment at any given time. Within urban society the dominant-minority issues are more apt to take the form of institutional conflict.

THE JEHOVAH'S WITNESSES The sect now known as the Jehovah's Witnesses was founded in 1870 in Allegheny, Pennsylvania, and until 1931 was known by various names. It began as a Bible class. Followers in the United States and abroad now number nearly a million. Charles Taze Russell, its founder, was a member of the Congregational Church and of the YMCA. He was "converted" to the Adventist doctrine, which was fundamentalist and held to the literal interpretation of the prophecies of the book of Revelation that Christ would return to earth and reign for a thousand years. The central task for living men and women, then, in the belief of the Witnesses, is to convince others of the truth they hold, namely, the imminent violent end of this evil world. In order to be among those saved in the millennial reign one must bear witness to Christ in every act—that is all conduct is governed solely by religion. Every Witness is an ordained minister with a duty to preach. All free time must be spent spreading the gospel. The mode of proselytizing is chiefly through published tracts and the magazine, *The Watch Tower*, which are distributed in house-to-

[17] *The New York Times,* May 19, 1967, pp. 1 and 23.

house canvassing or on street corners, and engaging the recipients in persuasive discussion. The sect has survived the difficult problems of succession of leadership and is now a tightly knit organization controlled by three corporations, similar to an ecclesiastical autocracy.[18]

A Witness must refuse to obey any law that is contrary to God's law, as derived from fundamentalist theology. On the other hand, Witnesses must obey any laws which do not conflict and must never present the truth through lawless means. Witnesses are expected to bear action against them stoically and not to retaliate. Indeed many rejoice in adversity, which they interpret as foreshadowing an imminent millennium. Witnesses are opposed to all organized religious bodies, as diverting people from the truth, and they are particularly anti-Catholic.

The Witnesses have experienced persecution and violence on the community level and have many conflicts with the law. The violence against them either in direct outbreak or in illegal arrests was at a peak in 1940, with 335 incidents of mob violence.[19] As they are opposed to military service 4,300 served prison sentences for violation of the draft laws in World War II.[20] It is estimated that about six to ten thousand Witnesses were sent to concentration camps in Nazi Germany, and other governments abroad have taken action against them.

The Flag Salute Controversy

The Jehavoh's Witnesses came into prominence over their long battle to be exempt from saluting the American flag as a public-school requirement. The first flag salute statute was passed in 1898 in New York State. Thirty states and various localities in the remaining states had enacted such statutes by 1938, when the American Civil Liberties Union undertook to survey the question.[21] The requirement of the salute was pushed by patriotic organizations and reactionary nationalist groups. Manwaring cites the Ku Klux Klan (in 1925), the D.A.R. (1923) and various fraternal groups.[22]

Before the issue became focused around the Jehovah's Witnesses there had already been incidents of religious objection to the ritual from Mennonites and other sectarians. On September 30, 1935, in a Lynn, Massachusetts, high school, Carleton Nicholls, a Witness, refused to salute the flag and was expelled from school. On October 6, Rutherford, the then President of the Witnesses, de-

---

[18] Herbert Hewitt Stroup, *The Jehovah's Witnesses* (New York: Columbia University Press, 1945), p. 21 for description of corporate organization.
[19] See David R. Manwaring, *Render Unto Caesar: The Flag Salute Controversy* (Chicago: The University of Chicago Press, 1962), pp. 169–171, for charts of incidence of violence 1940–1943; and Stroup, pp. 145–9.
[20] Manwaring, p. 30.
[21] *Ibid.*, pp. 4–5.
[22] *Ibid.*, pp. 7–8.

livered a radio address upholding young Nicholls' act. The Witnesses employed legal counsel and filed a petition with the State Supreme Court for Nicholls' reinstatement. The court upheld the school.

It was decided not to appeal at the time. Nevertheless, the ground had been broken for litigation. The Witnesses had no prohibition against using the courts; indeed, Rutherford had been a practicing attorney for twenty-seven years before he became president of his sect. Furthermore, as a small and unpopular body, the Witnesses could not resort to political pressure for a change in the statute. The issue became increasingly serious to them as they equated the salute with the Hitler salute at a time when their members were being persecuted in Germany. The first case to reach the Supreme Court on the flag salute issue was that of Minersville School District vs. Gobitis in 1940. The Witnesses were defeated, Justice Frankfurter writing the majority opinion and Justice Stone presenting a dissenting opinion. This was a blow to the Witnesses, especially as they had just before been upheld by the Court on an issue (Cantwell vs. Connecticut) involving distribution of literature and public proselytizing. The liberal press and the religious press (including two Catholic publications), much of the law press, as well as much of the general press was adverse in its criticism of the decision. The decision came just before the wave of violence against the Witnesses in the summer of 1940 and the widespread nature of the outbreaks was generally attributed to the Court decision.[23]

In 1943 the Supreme Court heard the last of the flag salute cases (West Virginia State Board of Education vs. Barnette.) The decision this time was favorable to the Witnesses. Justice Jackson wrote the majority opinion. His central point distinguished between state requirements of educational substance such as American history and requirements of *ritual*.

The Jehovah's Witnesses are well equipped in organization, legal talent, and funds to carry on a long, hard legal fight. Under present leadership, and since their success in the courts, some of the militancy has mitigated, though the dedicated spirit still dominates members. Jehovah's Witnesses have no racial bars, as they see themselves obligated to save, by incorporation if possible, every man on earth.

The illustrations that have been chosen certainly do not represent the full spectrum of sectarian religious difference. Dominants often do not perceive ethnically Nordic sectarians in a discriminating manner. This is in part because the present focus on minorities is more centered toward "racial" visibility, as was discussed in the last chapter. Nevertheless the sects have had to meet, through protest or adaptation or both, the problem of conflicting belief systems. At the present time, those we have chosen for illustration have held to

[23] For analysis of the Supreme Court opinions and the reaction to the decision, see Manwaring, Chapters 7 and 8.

certain values of the historical, Protestant, and now secular value system: the regard for property, sobriety, and hard work. They have furthermore tended to range themselves on the side of the conservative influences in American society.

Minority Established Religious Bodies

As we have indicated, established sects, as well as sects that have become churches, have had to solve problems of the conflict of demands between the religion and the state. They have met this challenge in different ways. Let us now consider the large established minority religious bodies which have played an important role in American life.[24]

THE JEWS We are here considering the Jews solely in terms of religious difference, which is the characteristic that has distinguished them since the days of the Roman Empire. In a later chapter we shall discuss the Jews in another light, as their history of being a minority has, in some places and at some times, taken priority over their religious claims, both for dominants and for Jews themselves. As was pointed out, initially in America they were viewed as a religious group, and today there has been a revival of religious emphasis in Jewish identity, just as there has been a growth in religious participation on the part of Protestants and Catholics as well.

The significant aspects of Jewish demography are these: (1) Jews in the United States comprise less than 5 percent of the total population; (2) present population trends indicate the Jewish population is growing less rapidly than the general national growth; (3) no radical change has occurred in the urban concentration of Jews within the country.

Jews are divided by their religious affiliation into three groups: Orthodox, Reform, and Conservative. Orthodox Jews keep as closely as possible to the Mosaic Law and its Talmudic elaboration. This means that they observe their Sabbath (Saturday) as a day of absolute abstention from the work of the other six days. For example, they refrain on the Sabbath from using transportation, from cooking, and from secular reading. Orthodox Jews keep the traditional dietary laws, which include prohibitions of particular kinds of foods and ritualistic regulations concerning the preparation of food. Within Orthodoxy there are some sects, the largest of which are the Hassidim, that are distinguished by their dress, hair style, and the character of worship. Orthodoxy is characteristic chiefly of the Spanish-Portuguese elite and the older generations of

---

[24] Claims by religious bodies as to membership may vary depending on whether or not they count, in Christian churches, all baptized infants, or only present church members in good standing. For non-Christian groups, also, there is the question of affiliation by descent or by present participation. The current estimates on the basis of present participation are about 36 percent for combined Protestant bodies including sectarians; about 25 percent for Roman Catholics; about 5 percent for Jews, about 2 percent for Eastern Orthodox, and .03 percent for Buddhists, and the remainder nonaffiliated. See the tables in Arnold Rose and Caroline Rose, *Minority Problems* (New York: Harper & Row, 1965), pp. 62–64.

the eastern European immigrants. In recent decades it has had a revival among Jewish intellectuals.

Reform Judaism is an outgrowth of the philosophy of Enlightenment as it affected Jews primarily in Germany. The Reform movement attempted to adapt Jewish religious life to the dominant Protestant model without losing the essential characteristics of Judaism. This means that it is altered legally and ritualistically, leaving theology unchanged. Some Reform Jews adapt to the dominant culture in observance of Sunday as the Sabbath, and have incorporated in their temple services such modifications as organ music, mixed choirs, and the unsegregated seating of women. The Reform movement in the United States has its main center in Cincinnati and has grown among the German Jewish population. Despite some inroads from Conservative Judaism, it is still the dominant pattern for Mid-western and Southern Jews.

Conservative Judaism represents a compromise and is in part a protest against the extreme modification initiated by the Reform Jewish movement. Less rigid than Orthodox Judaism, it has nevertheless retained much of the liturgical emphasis of Orthodoxy and some of the social practices that preserve the distinctiveness of the Jewish community. Conservative Judaism has often been the comfortable solution for the second and third generation descendants of Orthodox Jews in America.

As a scripture-based religion, Judaism has always emphasized literacy and learning as a permanent value. The Jewish religion does not emphasize individual salvation, but rather group salvation. It does not allow a personal image of God, but rather casts the ideals of religion as abstract principles, such as Justice, Mercy, Righteousness, which are the attributes of God. Such a religion, with its group emphasis, logically requires of the Jew that he be a contributor to the community, that within his power he aid its preservation and development, and that no individual Jew be left outside the shelter of community concern. The secularization of this ideal has also led to the contributions of Jewish leadership and wealth to the general secular intergroup community.

The organization of Jewish religious bodies is decentralized. Wherever there are twelve adult male Jews they may form a congregation. They may meet in a home or have a building for worship with appropriate symbols and liturgy.

While Jews in the United States have become politically integrated in their communities, they have usually tended to comprise a liberal bloc. Werner Cohn believes this to be an expression of the insecure place Jews feel in the Gentile world.[25] Jews have been very strong supporters of the principle of separation of church and state.

Discrimination against Jewish people, and outbreaks of violence and anti-Semitic propaganda have such complex roots and are based on many other social and psychological factors that they warrant discussion in a separate chap-

---

[25] Werner Cohn, "The Politics of American Jews," in *The Jew: Social Patterns of an American Group* (Glencoe, Ill.: The Free Press, 1958), pp. 619ff.

ter. (See pp. 404–427.) Jews in present-day America have rarely had areas of distinctly religious conflict except in the observance of Saturday as the Sabbath, or occasional problems of abstaining from work or study on religious holidays. These conflicts only become issues in places where laws (like Sunday Blue Laws) are in effect discriminatory to Jewish merchants, who, having closed on Saturday, are not permitted to do business on Sunday; and among very strictly observant Jews.

There have been some issues, especially in suburban areas with regard to Jewish objection to Christian teaching, or celebration of Christian holidays and use of Christian symbols in public schools. Leo Pfeffer, in analyzing the situation, sees this in the framework of tensions of suburban migration and points out that more and more Jewish opposition to religious teaching in public schools is in terms of freedom for the nonbeliever and the larger principle of separation of church and state.[26]

THE ROMAN CATHOLICS   About 25 percent of the American population is Roman Catholic.

The problems of Catholics as a minority are bound up with, first, the historic factor that America was settled by Protestant groups that had a heritage of protest against the Church of Rome. Their own group solidarity was maintained, in part, by teaching to successive generations the nature of this protest.

There were both doctrinal and organizational foci for their opposition. Doctrinally all Protestants opposed the primacy and ultimate authority of the Pope.[27] Other doctrinal points of conflict were confession, penance, absolution, and indulgence. For most Protestants at the period of the Reformation, the Bible became the authority rather than "the church." Initially, of course, for all and still for some "fundamentalist" groups this authority was accepted literally. Since the nineteenth-century development of documentary re-examination of the Bible and its sources, literalism has declined especially among the urban populations, but there is still the heritage of Biblical training (Protestant) versus Church Doctrinal training (Catholic), the latter often interpreted as the disallowance of free judgment. Some Protestant groups were also opposed to the centralized, bureaucratized structure of the Roman Catholic Church. Large denominations that elected their own leaders saw the hierarchical appointments of Rome as antidemocratic. For antiliturgical Protestants the Catholic forms of worship with their rituals, vestments, and symbolic participation, seemed instances of worldly pomp and splendor, or idolatry. To a young nation engaged in settlement, with early marriage patterns, the celibate clergy, and the monasteries of monks and nuns wearing strange traditional garments and living in enclosed communities were objects of suspicion and mistrust. Thus in the

[26] Leo Pfeffer, "Changing Relationships Among Religious Groups," *Journal of Intergroup Relations* (Spring, 1960), pp. 81–93.

[27] See the *New York Times,* April 29, 1967, p. 1, column 4, "Pontiff Concedes Papacy is Barrier to Christian Unity."

problems of interreligious relations there were both doctrinal (intrinsic) and customary (extrinsic) areas of devaluation.

The Catholic Church in the nineteenth century was ill equipped to interpret itself to non-Catholics. Many of the priests were foreign born and many foreign trained. They felt their primary obligation to minister to the migrating ethnic populations for whom they made a link with the Catholic heritage of the home country. The fact that the Irish were English-speaking gave them an advantage in achieving major influence in the Catholic Church in America, especially in the East. The close communal ties of the urban Irish migrants inevitably created a situation in which the Church could influence politics. This was usually bitterly resented by Protestants.

With the restriction of immigration there has been a decline in the ethnic church in America, Protestant as well as Catholic. The concept American Catholic has now replaced "Irish Catholic," "German Catholic," "Italian Catholic" for many third-generation Americans of Catholic faith, though not perhaps so widely in the image of Catholicism for non-Catholics. The new decision held by the Ecumenical Council to permit the Mass to be said in the language of the people have revived the ethnic language in some parishes, but without new influx of non-English speaking people the vernacular masses will inevitably become masses in English.

An interpretation of the trends in Catholic-Protestant relations since the restriction of immigration requires keeping in mind our preliminary distinction between intergroup tension which results from institutional conflict and discriminatory conduct based on a dominant-minority situation. On the one hand, it appears in general that, ignoring short-time fluctuations, discrimination simply because they are Catholics against Catholic persons who apply for jobs, houses, or admission to social clubs has markedly declined. Illustrative of this decline in discrimination against Catholics are the results, indicated in Table 4–1,

TABLE 4–1 *Restriction in Job Orders 1956–1957 and 1958–1959* [28]

	1956–1957	1958–1959
Total number of job orders	218	303
Total number of firms	202	258
Restrictions against Jews	142	83
Restrictions against Negroes	62	162
Restrictions against Orientals	43	47
Restrictions against Catholics	2	2
Restrictions against Mexican-Americans	18	44
Restrictions against minorities (use of code term "All American," meaning "white Gentile")	...	30

[28] *Rights,* Vol. 2, No. 6, April–May 1961, p. 52. A report published by the Anti-Defamation League.

of a survey in the fifties, of restrictions stipulated in job orders placed with a sample of employment agencies. It is seen that restrictions against Catholics are negligible. The survey noted the appearance in the 1957–1958 period of the stipulation that the applicant be "All American," which was a new code name for "white Gentile," and apparently did not connote rejection of Catholics.

A frequent source of conflict between Protestants and Catholics persists in the area of family relations—for example, divorce and dissemination of contraception or availability or abortion. Many Protestant urban groups have sought changes in laws governing these areas of life and there has been a strong conservative position on the part of the Catholic Church. The issue is really a church-state issue inasmuch as the conflict has centered on legal revision. Catholics have the dilemma of choosing between church doctrine on these issues or considering wider social problems and changes that may be expressed in movements for legal revision. Another issue has been the question of federal aid to schools. Catholics have argued that since they educate a considerable segment of American children they should have state aid, as any public school might have, since they save the public taxpayer monies in relieving the population pressure on public schools. The whole question of aid to religious schools (not only Catholic) is still very much alive.

In recent years there has been a considerable effort on the part of the Catholic Church to convert Negroes. Religious orders have accepted Negroes in their communal membership. The number of urban Negroes attending parochial schools has risen. In part this is related to the fact that Negro Protestants have easily accepted the leadership of authoritarian clergy, as we shall discuss. Other factors are also involved: the search for integrated participation, for status, for better education, and the effort on the part of segments of the Church to extend its mission.

THE NEGRO PROTESTANT CHURCH   In Colonial times some Negroes were admitted to white congregations and some free Negroes preached to white congregations. This practice could still be found in the early nineteenth century in the free states and in some situations in those parts of the South not dominated by the plantation system. Methodist and Baptist evangelists preached to Negroes and white alike; [29] as Negroes in the South joined these denominations in large numbers they were eventually provided with separate churches. For some of the national denominations this precipitated a schism between the northern and southern branches. Parallel to this was the move on the part of free Negroes in the North to establish specifically Negro churches. The oldest of these was the African Methodist Episcopal Church, established in 1816 in Philadelphia.

Frazier has called the Negro church "a nation within a nation." [30] He describes the functions of the Negro church as first, an agent of social control,

[29] E. Franklin Frazier, *The Negro Church in America* (Liverpool: The University of Liverpool, 1963. Schocken Paperback edition, 1966), p. 23.
[30] *Ibid.*, Ch. 3.

supporting monogamous, patriarchal, family life; second, as a vehicle for economic cooperation, both in the building and maintaining of churches and in the development of mutual aid and benefit organizations; third, as supporter of schools for Negroes; and finally as an arena for political life. Since Negroes were eliminated from the political life of the American community the church was the main area in which Negroes could aspire to become leaders of men.[31] In the locally autonomous denominations such as the Baptists, Negro preachers, elected by the congregations, could develop an autocratic rule.

The dilemma of the Negro church in the period following World War II has been that of competition with secular influences, and the gradual lessening of occupational discrimination which has made for more interracial contact. Frazier sees the older functions becoming obsolete. With the rise of a new urban Negro white-collar and professional class there has been a shift from the predominant Methodist and Baptist affiliation in the cities to the prestigious denominations: Presbyterian, Episcopalian, and Congregational. Frazier also sees the increasing number of Roman Catholic Negroes as a reflection of the changing status system. This new middle class is rejecting much of the Negro heritage, including religious heritage—its opposition to spirituals and the secular exploitation of gospel singers are examples cited by Frazier.[32] On the other hand, poor Negroes in city slums have turned more and more to cultist and sectarian movements, which provide hope and emotional dimensions to relieve the barrenness of their lives. Frazier has seen the Negro church which still clings to the earlier patterns of communality as a force for continuing segregation. However, it is not surprising, in view of the role of the Negro church as for so long the sole channel for popular leadership, that Negro clergy have been significant in the secular political arena and in the secular protest movements of the present.

The Decline of Protestant Dominance

As we have indicated, there have been changes in the relations between religious minorities and "the establishment." Popular attitudes have modified in many places. Within some minority religions changes have taken place that make them more compatible with the general value system. One of the unique aspects of the American society has been its attempt, not always successful, to absorb many people of many beliefs and traditions into a common body politic with respect for individual rights. More recently, with regard to religious minorities, the issue has been one of group rights. There is a limit beyond which any society can be stable with a multiplicity of critical or defecting groups. For many people, as far as religious groups are concerned, this dilemma has been resolved in the principle of separation of church and state. Whereas this is an important position, coherent with the idea presented in Chapter 2 of structural

[31] *Ibid.*, p. 43.
[32] *Ibid.*, Ch. 5.

pluralism, there are still the problems of community conflict, or of categorical discrimination in the structure of opportunity within the secular society. Since religion is important for at least two-thirds of the American people, the way religious bodies tackle the problems of the multi-group world have some significance.

Religious Reform and the Ecumenical Spirit

In the search to overcome devisiveness there have been a number of efforts, both intergroup and intragroup. One such organization, now half a century old, is the Conference of Christians and Jews. An urban organization with national leadership, this has provided opportunities for middle-class adults and youth to meet and discuss and know each other.

In the same spirit the outcome of the Ecumenical Council has made for greater dialogue between Catholic and non-Catholic religious leaders. Protestant and Jewish observers were invited to the Ecumenical Council. There has been modification of Catholic dogma regarding Jews. Protestant seminaries have invited Catholic theologians to teach, as some Catholic universities have invited Protestant and Jewish teachers.

The Jews in America made religious modifications long before other groups, with the exception of the orthodox congregations and the Jewish sectarians (Hassidim). Catholics are now struggling with problems of internal reform: the inclusion of laymen in decision-making roles from parish to seminary; protests within religious orders and permitted changes to allow members of orders wider secular roles; challenges about the celibacy of the clergy.

Protestant churches are seeking to overcome their own devisiveness of denominationalism; their differences having grown out of historical sectarianism. A number of Protestant mergers have taken place, including the reuniting of denominations split by the Civil War. For the established churches, then, we are probably really entering a period of structrual pluralism. This entire trend in its effectiveness in the United States, however, is an urban phenomenon and one which is essentially middle class.

The Churches and Social Protest

The religions of the West have, as part of their heritage, a hortatory injunction to promote social justice.[33] The dilemmas of religious participation in reform have not only been the established wordly position of conservative members; they have stemmed from the exclusiveness of sectarian heritages; the preoccupation with changing "the hearts of men" rather than the social institutions; the concentration on institutional religious matters. So great have been these factors in the twentieth century, many have felt the church had no positive

[33] "Let justice roll down like waters, and righteousness like an everflowing stream" (Amos 5:24).

role to play in creative social change. The so-called religious revival of the twentieth century has been, it is claimed, a search for respectability within an institutional structure.[34] Others have held that churches simply come along tardily after reform is well under way.[35]

Nevertheless, for reasons self-evident, Negro clergy were in the vanguard of the civil rights movement, and were in some instances supported by white clergy of various faiths and by theological students. In the spring of 1963 the Conference on Religion and Race was held in Chicago, which included all the major religious bodies in the United States. Resolutions were passed with regard to investment of funds in enterprises practicing discrimination, and resolutions regarding open occupancy housing. By 1964 nineteen cities were reported implementing the recommendations of the Conference.[36] The National Council of Churches, in the summer of 1963, formed a Commission on Religion and Race, which supported church leaders in demonstrations of solidarity with civil rights demonstrators, to encourage clergy to support civil rights even in the face of congregational opposition and to organize churchgoers to support civil rights legislation.

The Anti-Defamation League of B'nai Brith is an older organization which has broadened its concern from counteracting anti-Semitism to an organization concerned with all minority groups, and serves as a clearing house for much research on minority questions. The American Jewish Congress and the American Jewish Committee have been active on minority issues beyond those specifically related to the Jewish minority.

The concern of central religious bodies with reform on minority issues is not easily paralleled in the grass roots of community congregations. Gerhart Lenski, in his study of religious groups in Detroit, found a limited relationship between formal church membership and the degree to which members of the different religions were part of a socio-religious subcommunity. Where such subcommunities have developed he feels they *"foster and encourage a provincial and authoritarian view of the world."* (Italics are Lenski's.) [37] In a study of a midwestern rural area, "Corn County," the authors found that the majority of those interviewed had no knowledge of any social policies or pronouncements of the religious body of which they were members or which they preferred. Interreligious friendships existed when there were common bonds of ethnicity or status.[38] Clark found in his study of a small northern industrial city that clergy

---

[34] Will Herberg, *Protestant-Catholic-Jew* (Garden City, N.Y.: Doubleday and Co., 1955) p. 15; and (for a challenge to this viewpoint) J. M. Yinger, "Religion and Social Change: Problems of Integration and Pluralism Among the Privileged," *Review of Religious Research*, IV, 3 (Spring, 1963) pp. 129–148.

[35] Henry Clark, *The Churches and Residential Desegregation* (New Haven, Connecticut: College and University Press, 1965), p. 29.

[36] *Ibid.*, p. 239, n. 62 for list of cities.

[37] Lenski, *The Religious Factor*, p. 328.

[38] W. Widick Schroeder and Victor Oberhaus, *Religion in American Culture: Unity and Diversity in a Midwestern County* (New York: The Free Press of Glencoe, 1964), p. 182.

were anxious to "do good" on public issues, but were naïve about politics and power, and when defeated in a specific effort had no sense of alternative procedures and tended to retreat into their traditional roles of preacher of moral pronouncements or of personal counselors.[39]

The areas of tension between the "establishment" and religious minorities arise on three levels. One certainly is that of institutional conflict between church and state where in this century we have been as a nation both in the political electorate and in the Supreme Court defining the separate areas of jurisdiction and responsibility. The feeling about the separation of powers here is best expressed by a strong advocate of church-state separation:

> The state is to show no preference for any church or anti-church group; these groups have no authority in the state. . . . Similarly religious organizations have no claim . . . to a right to impose their standards of belief or behavior upon those who are not members of their organizations. The state has no right to interfere with their religious exercise, except in the interest of public safety or decency. . . . The individual conscience is in some respects superior to the state because the state is made by individuals. This claim cannot be denied by a constitutional state. Churches also claim superiority to the state, by virtue of divine authority. This claim a constitutional state cannot allow, because it is not the proper agency to decide among conflicting divine authorities claimed by conflicting creeds.[40]

A second level of relationships is that between religious bodies themselves. For middle-class "respectable" urban American Herberg's analysis of the religious situation in mid-century United States is pertinent.[41] (1) He finds that with increasing assimilation of the European immigrants except in religion, religious difference—Catholic, Protestant, Jewish—has replaced ethnic difference as a major differentiation of the American population. (2) In the process of adjustment to American society, both Catholicism and Judaism, originally foreign, became Americanized." "Foreign observers sometimes find the various American religions more like each other than they are like their religious counterparts." For example, "The Catholic church in America has tended to be activist in a way which borders on what Pope Pius XII in 1950 described as the 'heresy of action': the notion that the world can be saved by external activity." The extensive social welfare program of the American Catholic Church illustrates this more worldly focus. Herberg adduces support for the opinion that American Catholicism has accepted the basic principle of separation of church and state, contrary to the traditional position of the Church. (3) The secularization of all three religions has proceeded so far that the theological distinctions

---

[39] Clark, p. 203.
[40] Joseph L. Blau, ed., *Cornerstones of Religious Freedom in America: Selected Basic Documents, Court Decisions and Public Statements,* rev. and enlarged ed. (New York: Harper & Row, 1964), pp. 28–9.
[41] Will Herberg, *Protestant-Catholic-Jew,* p. 95.

which serve to distinguish them give way to a common belief which is essentially a belief in the American way of life. "Belief in God" and identification with a congregation of one of the established religions qualifies an American as religious and as a "good" American at the same time. Thus Herberg concludes that all three of the religions are now considered equally American and their adherents all equal Americans.

Assuming acceptance of Herberg's thesis of the equality of these three religions does not preclude competition and conflict between them. But this conflict appears more now as that of two forces with fairly evenly balanced power, and in its interpersonal aspects, between persons occupying equal social status (within class). Hence it is more similar to the political conflict between Republicans and Democrats, in which the opponents view each other as formidable adversaries, not as superior or inferior people.

On the community level Lenski's point that the degree of communality of the group—that is, to what degree church associations, delimit and incorporate friendships, leisure time activities, etc.—is primary in the life of individuals will affect the understanding and tolerance of other groups. Clark found that in some instances status identification in community was more important than religious communality, but even under these circumstances where interreligious friendships occur in closed status groups, there was little sense of the content of belief of other religions than one's own. We might anticipate that as urban modes affect not only cities but smaller communities there will be some greater differentiation developing between a person's secular roles and his religious roles that will undermine religious communality. Whereas this may aid the growth of religious tolerance, such separation of dimensions of activity is stressful to many, and cults and sects may attract those who find these stresses too great. Belongingness is a basic need for most people.

The Outlook

Most writers on the problems of present day religious pluralism seem to agree that there is always potential conflict between the church and the state and between religious groups. The degree of conflict may be associated with how vigorously one upholds the principle of separation of church and state, but this relationship is not easy. Shall church property be tax exempt? Shall the federal government aid all schools that are decently educating American children?

With the decline of occupational discrimination people in cities associate more and more with members of other religious bodies than those in which they hold membership. Is this intergroup association a factor for secularization, on the one hand, or merely the preservation of particular symbols on the other?

For the religious believer who seeks more than formal designation of his identity with a group, the conflicts of conscience may be severe and real. Is it possible, as one scholar suggests, that the solution rests on enlarging the population of truly religious people (intrinsic religion) and the gradual decline of extrinsic religions who draw their support from doctrines of revelation, election, and theocracy? [42]

Topics for Projects and Discussion

1. Have there been any interfaith efforts in your community? Who participated? For what age group were they significant?
2. Have any clergy whom you know been active in civil rights efforts? How are they regarded by other members of their faith in general, and specifically by any congregations to which they are attached?
3. Which churches or sects have categorically forbidden their members to bear arms? What should the government position be about this?
4. What were the church-state issues in the Kennedy campaign and how were they resolved. Which groups were on which side and what were their arguments?
5. Toward which religious groups have you heard negative sentiments expressed by your own membership group? What grounds were offered as a basis for these sentiments; were they social or doctrinal?

Suggested Reading

Baltzell, E. Digby. *The Protestant Establishment: Aristocracy and Caste in America.* New York: Random House, 1964.

> *An account of the consolidation and beginning decline of Protestant dominance.*

Blau, Joseph L., ed. *Cornerstones of Religious Freedom in America: Selected Basic Documents, Court Decisions and Public Statements.* New York: Harper & Row (Harper Torchbooks), 1964, revised and enlarged edition.

> *Historical and contemporary documentary statements on the separation of church and state.*

Lanternari, Victor. *The Religions of the Oppressed: A Study of Modern Messianic Cults,* translated from the Italian by Lisa Sergio. New York: Alfred A. Knopf, 1963; also available in Mentor Books edition, 1965.

> *A crosscultural study of the meaning and types of contemporary religious movements depending on prophecy and promising liberation.*

Raab, Earl, ed. *Religious Conflict in America: Studies in the Problems Beyond Bigotry.* Garden City, New York: Anchor Books, Doubleday and Co., 1964.

> *A symposium by leading sociologists and theologians on religious dilemmas in contemporary America.*

Stahmer, Harold, ed. *Religion and Contemporary Society.* New York: The Macmillan Company, 1963.

> *Contemporary statements of religious position of the major faiths in America.*

---

[42] Gordon W. Allport, "The Religious Context of Prejudice," *Journal for the Scientific Study of Religion* (Fall, 1966), pp. 447–457.

5

National Origins and Minority Status: The Impact of the European Migration

In the rationalization of discrimination the term "national origin" has been a category used to indicate differential esteem. It is a term prominent in the debates which led to the restriction of European immigration. As we have seen, it was often interchangeable with the nineteenth-century use of the term "race" (i.e. the Celtic "race" to describe the Irish). It was often a cover for religious discrimination. "National origin" refers less to any allegiance to former nations than to a cultural ethos in which behavior patterns, and often language, were alien. In this chapter we will examine the impact of immigration from Europe as it has effected dominant-minority relations in America.

Immigration, as the United States of America has known it, has been a peculiarly American institution. One British author has described it as "the greatest folk migration in human history," and "the most persistent and pervasive influence" on the development of the United States.[1] The Great Atlantic Migration opened a continent, built an industrial nation, and was a demonstration of political democracy's capacity to survive religious, national, and racial heterogeneity. The survival of the political institutions on which identification as an American is so strongly based today did not occur without pressures and counter pressures in meeting the challenge of unity born of heterogeneity.

The European migration has traditionally been broken into three periods before the restrictive legislation of 1924: the colonial, the "old," and the "new" immigration. Although this classification has had an effect on public opinion and on policy, there is no valid reason for it. The reasons for which immigrants came at all periods were similar; the skills they brought, and their ability to adapt to the American environment show great consistency, however much groups differed culturally. Some came earlier, some later. The *impact* of immigration, however, varied; and the attitudes toward immigrants varied at different periods of the nation's development.[2]

[1] Maldwyn Allen Jones, *American Immigration* (Chicago, Ill.: The University of Chicago Press, 1960), p. 1.
[2] *Ibid.*, pp. 4–5.

Except for slaves and transported convicts, migration involved in most instances a *decision* and a risk, which to an extent may have strengthened self-reliance, adaptability, and enterprise. Despite lingering loyalties to distant lands, the experience of migration inevitably worked against traditional values. The absence of a hereditary ruling class, the existence of representative government, and the separation of church and state which had been necessary for the coexistence of multiple sects, were significant factors in making possible national unity in the face of difference.

Immigration before 1820

Public issues related to immigration in the American colonies before the Revolution involved any immigrants lacking visible means of support, those convicted of crimes abroad, and Catholics. The criteria for acceptance had to do with economics, religion, and "moral standing"; there was no nationality criterion, though from time to time the Scotch-Irish, the French, and the Germans briefly encountered hostile attitudes. The attitude toward immigrants could be summed up as "welcome tinged with misgiving." [3]

The power struggle of the Revolutionary and post-Revolutionary period assured the pre-eminence of English political institutions and the English language. The success of the War of Independence united diverse elements behind a leadership stemming from the predominance of Englishmen in the first two generations of settlement. Although only New England and the Tidewater areas of other colonies had a predominance of population of English descent, these were the entrenched and the powerful.

The newcomers, of whatever origin, so far removed from Europe by the three-month voyage, were nevertheless sufficiently identified with the new world to be able to take individual positions—loyalist or revolutionary—without needing to form nationality blocs. [4]

The immediate post-Revolutionary period saw growing concern for the political influence of new migrants: political conservatives feared the growth-by-immigration of the anti-federalists; the popular democratic front was suspicious of the acceptance of emigrés from toppling European aristocracies. The Alien and Sedition Acts of 1798 had "anti-foreign" implications and were accompanied by "anti-foreign" outbreaks. Attempts were made to lengthen the period of residence before enfranchisement from two, to five, to fourteen years, but the longer periods, though enacted, were evaded by states. The tension of establishing a new nation made itself felt.

Throughout the late eighteenth and early nineteenth centuries there was lively public discussion of the pros and cons of migration in both the European and the American press. On the one hand, European governments felt the in-

[3] *Ibid.*, p. 40.
[4] *Ibid.*, pp. 53ff.

roads on their artisan classes; on the other, movements to limit the participation of the foreign-born in public affairs recurred in the United States. Both the American Revolution and the Civil War acted to improve the integration and the status of the immigrant groups. But the periods of tension preceding and during wars and accompanying economic depressions occasioned outbreaks against "foreigners."

During the period from 1790 to 1812, because of restrictions in Europe on emigration of artisans, regulation of the number of passengers a ship might carry, and the conditions of embargo and war, the volume of migration temporarily diminished. Those who came were assimilated rather rapidly. But the beginning of the revolution in technology, which was to change transportation and create the factory system, brought evasion and eventual abandonment of restrictions on both sides of the Atlantic for the next half century.

The Great Atlantic Migration

The young nation of the United States in 1820 had a substantially common culture woven around three main elements: political democracy, private economic enterprise, and Protestantism with a strong Puritan tinge. Scattered in its population were other North European people in insufficient numbers to disturb the general homogeneity. Perhaps only in Louisiana, where people of French descent were concentrated, did the culture have a distinctly variant ethnic flavor. This young America was made up largely of small towns and rural communities, in which the close solidarity of primary groups prevailed. Class distinctions were not pronounced except in the few large cities and in the South, where the plantation system was built on slave labor. A vast frontier of enormous resources lay open for exploitation and settlement. The one large group of extremely different people were the Negro slaves (and some free Negroes), who in 1820 constituted approximately 18 percent of the population. This was the social setting in which the great drama of immigration was to begin and continue for a hundred years, influencing in many ways the subsequent development of the new nation.

"America Fever"

Although an accurate census of immigration was not available till 1820, when shipmasters were first required to submit passenger lists to customs, it is a fact that the five million immigrants who came to the United States between 1820 and 1860 were a greater number than the entire estimated population in 1790. By the outbreak of World War I in 1917 immigration had reached 30 million; but the war interrupted the flow and after 1924 immigration was severely limited. Most of the attention to migration in both the domestic and the European press (pro and con) throughout the nineteenth century was due to its being recognized as unique. Contemporaries spoke of emigration as a "fever."

Many modes of communication stimulated immigration: books, pamphlets,

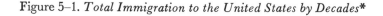

Figure 5–1. *Total Immigration to the United States by Decades**

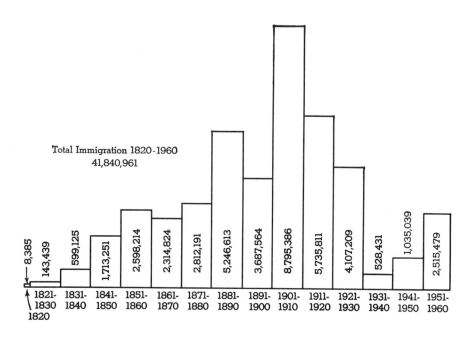

Total Immigration 1820-1960
41,840,961

* *Statistical Abstract of the United States,* United States Department of Commerce, Bureau of the Census, 1961, p. 92, Table 111.

letters from relatives, agents recruiting labor, transportation agents. The motives were mixed; economic improvement was paramount, but at no period was the economic motive exclusive. Jones believes that most of those who came for other than religious or political reasons or for adventure were not impoverished, but were in danger of loss of status as industrial and agricultural changes in Europe displaced old ways of life.[5]

Immigrants in the colonial period had been welcomed as buffers along the frontier. In the nineteenth century immigration only a small proportion became frontiersmen. Those who settled in agriculture followed and took over (and improved) land which had already been opened. Skilled workers (Welsh miners, Staffordshire potters, British and Scottish textile workers) tended to congregate in the American centers of their craft, creating ethnic enclaves. Climate, lack

[5] *Ibid.,* p. 107.

of artisan employment, and the presence of slave labor made for proportionately little immigration to the Southern states. Other regions took on distinctive ethnic flavors. At midcentury, two-thirds of the Irish were in the Northeast, one half the Germans in the upper Mississippi and Ohio valleys, and one half the Norwegians in Wisconsin.

Initial Reception of the Immigrants

The accumulation and assimilation of the nineteenth-century migrants depended on a number of factors. There was at the time a public policy against grants of land to ethnic groups, although several efforts were made to have such nationality enclaves established in the West. Dispersion greatly affected the rapidity of acculturation. Voluntary concentration on the part of the immigrants slowed their merging with the dominant Anglo-Saxon culture; but repeated nativistic movements also affected attitudes toward these new people. It is important here to distinguish between a passive dislike of foreigners based on ethnocentrism and the more violent mass zenophobia, marked by irrational hysteria, and often inspired by specific political interests.

Early nativism (pre-Civil War) had as its most prominent theme anti-"foreignism." Economic competition was not at this time a *manifest* issue. The Know-Nothing Party, which had its heydey in the two decades before the Civil War, revived the old Federalist efforts to limit office-holding to the native-born, to extend the period for naturalization, and to exclude criminals and paupers. Nativism re-emerged after the unifying interim of the Civil War, particularly on the West Coast. The restrictive acts of 1882–1885 were not an integrated attempt to deal with immigration, but rather a series of unconnected measures favoring special interests. The role of organized labor in "anti-foreign" efforts began to be felt, in California and in the Midwest, in mines, and in heavy industries, where new immigrants from Europe were used as strikebreakers or where other groups (such as Orientals) were willing to work for low wages. After the Haymarket bombing of 1886, the tendency to link the terms "foreign" and "radical" gained new impetus.

The nativistic movements of the nineteenth century reflected, in part, the struggles of the newly settled West to achieve a balance of national power; they reflected the unease of the agricultural sector, and of new industry with the efforts to create a strong labor movement; and they reflected the problems of growing cities. All these factors contributed to the attempt to consolidate the dominance of the Anglo-Saxon Protestant segment of the population. With the 1890 census the frontier was declared closed, and soon thereafter the myth of the frontier as the basic American experience began to take shape. Since most of the post-Civil War immigrants had little relation to the settling of the frontier, the myth helped to devalue latecomers.

But even more shaking change was ahead. In the last decades of the nineteenth and first two of the twentieth century the United States was to absorb a new labor force from East and South Europe, culturally more different than earlier migrants. America was to become an industrial nation of first rank. We were so involved in the First World War as to send our soldiers to European soil and our dollars to aid interests abroad. There was a crisis of feeling brought about by social changes too rapid for one generation to absorb.

The Consolidation of The Establishment:
The Restriction of Immigration

Immigration restriction is only one facet of the attempt, successful for a time, to ensure the dominance of one segment of the population, a population that bolstered its claim to legitimate privilege and leadership by descent, by language, and by having given, as it were, the *imprimatur* to "American" styles of thought and behavior. The heavy waves of immigration at the turn of the century were needed for growing industry. They were facilitated by better transport and encouraged by persecution or overpopulation in Europe. They precipitated a consolidation and articulation of the "Establishment" which manifested itself in social and political restrictive measures, despite the beginnings of reform movements and welfare efforts.

The problems were real, to an extent: between 1900 and 1920 approximately 3,400,000 Italians came to the United States (not all of them stayed; five-sixths were Southern Italians of peasant village origin); between 1880 and 1910 the Jewish population of New York City alone rose from 80,000 to 1,250,000, swelled by Eastern orthodox, Yiddish-speaking villagers fleeing from Russian Imperial repressive policies (See Chapter 18.); Baltic, Balkan, and other folk groups came in large numbers to Pittsburgh, Cleveland, Chicago, Youngstown, and the other rising centers of large industry. The situation was aggravated by the successful capture of local urban politics in many cities by the political machine largely, at this time, Irish. (See below, p. 112.) Furthermore, organized labor was in the unhappy dilemma of being viewed by the Establishment as the product of "foreign" insurgents, and itself having its gains threatened by the new labor force recruited often at Ellis Island as immigrants came off the boats.

THE DILLINGHAM COMMISSION   In 1907, when the nation was experiencing the greatest volume of immigration of all time, the Dillingham Commission was created to study the question of immigration and report to Congress. It was this Commission that coined the concept "old" and "new" immigration. The theme runs through the entire forty-one volumes of the report that the "old" immigration was of a different kind, had dispersed and entered all phases of American life, whereas the "new" immigration had congregated together in such a way that assimilation was impeded. The implication was that these late arrivals constituted pockets of people without American standards, values, or loyalties. In comparing "old" and "new," the Dillingham Commission's report took no account of the longer period of settlement of the "old" immigrant group. Furthermore, it lumped all old and all new into two simple categories without taking into account the vast differences in skill, motivation, and social organization within each category.

The Report came during a period of economic depression and gave support to a growing sentiment for immigration restriction. Indeed it provided the rationalizations on which the quota system subsequently was enacted. The anxieties of World War I, the increasing status of organized labor (won during the war), the fear of "radical" movements which appeared to be sweeping Europe at the close of the war, the psychological tests for the army which had showed low ratings for southern Europeans from peasant cultures, all increased the pressure for restriction.

The movement to restrict immigration gained backing from three public groups. The first, and prabably most influential, was organized labor.[6] Labor's position was based primarily on the practical consideration that immigrant labor accepted low wages and was generally more tractable, thus retarding union efforts to improve the workers' economic position. A second public favoring restriction was composed of those various individuals scattered throughout the country who attributed many of the nation's ills to the presence of "too many ignorant foreigners." These were the "racist"-minded people to whom the racialist writers mentioned in Chapter 3 appealed. In examining the newspapers and magazines from 1900 to 1930, Woofter found that from 1907 to 1914 there occurred a marked change in public sentiment toward immigration. "The undesirability of certain racial elements" was becoming more persuasive than economic argument against restriction.[7] Finally, there was a growing feeling among the more thoughtful and scientific circles that the nation could not go on indefinitely trying to assimilate such large masses of people of different cultures. This point of view is reflected in the report of the United States Immigration Commission in 1911, which recommended restriction on economic, moral, and social grounds. The first congressional act to give expression to these pressures was the measure to bar as immigrants any aliens who were illiterate (a measure passed in 1917 over President Wilson's veto).[8] This kind of test was aimed at curtailing southern and eastern European immigration. Actually, it failed to reduce materially the volume of immigration, and Congress turned to a system of numerical limitation.

The Quota System

Congress first passed the Immigration Act of 1921, the most important aspect of which was that it restricted immigration on a basis primarily numerical

[6] See Mary Beard, *A Short History of the American Labor Movement* (New York: The Macmillan Co., 1927), p. 72.

[7] T. J. Woofter, Jr., *Races and Ethnic Groups in American Life* (New York: McGraw-Hill Book Co., 1933), p. 31.

[8] Literacy test bills were passed by Congress in 1896 and again in 1909, but were vetoed by Presidents Cleveland and Taft.

—the first time this principle had been applied. The act provided that the number of aliens of any nationality admissible to the United States in any one year be limited to 3 percent of the number of foreign-born persons of such nationality who were residents of the United States in 1910. The Act did not apply to the Western Hemisphere or to countries otherwise regulated, such as China and Japan. The total yearly quota admissible under this Act was 357,803. The effect, although not the wording, of this law was discriminatory against southern and eastern European nationalities. The quotas set up permitted about 200,000 from the northern and western countries and 155,000 from the others. Since from 1910 to 1914 the average annual immigration from the northern European countries had been less than the quotas allowed, in practice the law did not greatly limit emigration from these areas. But it did greatly restrict southern and eastern European immigration, which had averaged 738,000 annually during the 1910–1914 period.

The Immigration Act of 1921 at its expiration was supplanted by the Immigration Act of 1924. Two different systems of quota apportionment were now set up, one temporary, in order to give the Immigration Commission time to work out proper quotas for the other, the permanent quota allotment. The temporary quota, which was to operate for three years, provided that "the annual quota of any nationality shall be 2 percent of the number of foreign-born individuals of such nationality resident in continental United States as determined by the United States Census of 1890, but the minimum quota of any nationality shall be 100." The effect of this Act was to reduce the number of yearly immigrants still further to 164,667 and to discriminate even more strongly against the "newer" immigrant countries. Northern and western Europe now was alotted 80 percent, whereas the southern and eastern nationalities had only 20 percent of the quota. The permanent provisions of the Act of 1924, which was to take effect in 1927, reduced the annual quota to 153,774.[9] The law called for the apportionment of the total quota among the countries to which the Act applied according to their relative contribution to the American population as enumerated in 1920. Correctly apportioning the quotas was a difficult task, which involved retracing the entire immigration figures almost since the beginning of the nation, for which many of the essential statistics were lacking. No records of immigration by nationality were kept before 1820, as we know; and the recording of the country of origin of persons born here of foreign-born parents was not started until 1890. The actual immigration at the time of the passing of the first restriction (1921) as compared with the quotas, for selected countries, will demonstrate the effect of the quota system. In 1921 there were 652,364 immigrants from Germany; the quota effective 1929 was 25,957. For Ireland there were 28,435 immigrants in 1921; the quota figure for 1929 was 17,853. For Italy there were 222,260 migrants in 1921; the 1929 quota was 5,802. Several

[9] The revised quota system under the Act of 1924 actually did not go into effect until July 1, 1929.

small modifications were made between 1929 and 1952 that represent the changed status of populations in the shifting of national borders or the creation of new nations.[10]

With the restriction of immigration the Great Atlantic Migration came to an end. The twentieth century was to be engaged in the problems of a fully industrialized nation, a world power, and the incorporation of the diverse peoples who had made this development possible.

Dominant Expectations of Immigrants

As we have stated in Chapter 2 the Anglo-Saxon English-speaking Protestants of America were an *ethnic group,* displaying the ethnocentricity characteristic of any group of people who share a common culture and a common historic tradition. In the eighteenth and nineteenth centuries the knowledge of and respect for other cultures was so limited that attitudes toward people who were "different" were inevitably devaluing. Immigrants were expected to "live right," were accorded a modest recognition if they worked hard, were thrifty, "sober" in manner, and learned to speak English. In a period absorbed in problems of settlement, development, and the maintenance of national unity, little thought was given until the close of the nineteenth century to adjustment problems of immigrants, although the newcomers were early made scapegoats for various ills and dysfunctions inherent in social change. It is not surprising that there was differential acceptance of immigrants.

The Northern Europeans

Although linguistically different, the Germans, Scandinavians, Swiss, and French Huguenots never suffered the categorical discriminations that most subsequent groups encountered. The more rapid acculturation and social acceptance of these northern Europeans was facilitated by many favorable circumstances. For one thing, they were less visibly different. Their cultures had more affinity to the dominant Anglo-Saxon culture. They were largely Protestant. They were more experienced in democratic political practices. And they possessed a heritage of independent agricultural occupation. The relatively small proportions that settled initially in cities were mainly skilled craftsmen or professionals. Most of the people settled beyond the heavily populated areas. While this semi-isolation enabled them to retain much of their Old World culture, it also provided opportunity for them to make their own adjustment to American life with a minimum of friction with the native population. That they were "looked down on" and "poked fun at" is illustrated by the following jingle quoted by Smith, directed at members of an immigrant group in Minnesota:

[10] Edmund Traverso, *Immigration: A Study in American Values* (Boston: D. C. Heath and Co., 1964), pp. 118–119.

Swedie, Swedie, stuck in the straw,
Can't say nuthin' but "Yaw, yaw, yaw."[11]

But with the acquisition of the English language, without an accent in their children's cases, most north Europeans became accepted Americans.

When north Europeans failed to join the mainstream of American life, one of the reasons was religious sectarianism. A number of Swiss and German separatist groups segregated themselves in distinctive colonies. Another type of sectarian adjustment was made by a group of Norwegians in "Jonesville," a community of about 10,000 in the North Prairie Region.[12] Here sectarian emphasis on the old rural Protestant ethic of work led this group to avoid the usual channels of mobility. Although some individuals have left the group and become easily absorbed in the overall social structure, the group has persisted for several generations content with low occupational status and strong ingroup values. This group, however, is not typical of the Norse-descended people of the surrounding region.

The heaviest period of northern European migration was in the four decades after 1850. Most of the immigrants came from agrarian backgrounds. Most were in part revolting against conservative consolidation in their home countries: required military service, the pressures of the state church against sectarian movements, the nepotism in the opportunity structure controlled by a stable class system. The largest area of settlement was the Middle West, reasonably accessible now that steamships plied the Atlantic and the railroad was open to Chicago and, after 1865, beyond. These people migrated intending to stay. They were chiefly initially rural, but by the second and third generation a large proportion of them became the merchant-entrepreneurial leaders of the developing cities of Wisconsin, Iowa, the Dakotas, and eventually of the Pacific Northwest. They intermarried (Germans and Scandinavians) in the second generation; in the third they outmarried and no longer spoke the language of their forefathers. They shared the Protestant ethic of hard work, improvement of self and land or enterprise, believed in education and founded colleges. In the private spheres of life there was still some intragroup life in which they shared a sense of common heritage and nuances of communication.[13] Like other American white Protestants of north European descent they maintained some sense of the country of their heritage, some interest in their traditional European roots, but the former "homeland" became, as one writer has called them "ghost nations," no longer experienced as real.[14]

[11] W. C. Smith, *Americans in the Making* (New York: Appleton-Century-Crofts, 1939), p. 149, n. 28.
[12] W. Lloyd Warner, *et al.*, *Democracy in Jonesville* (New York: Harper & Brothers, 1949), Chapter 11.
[13] Useem, John, and Ruth, "Minority Group Patterns in Prairie Society," *American Journal of Sociology*, March 1945.
[14] Nathan Glazer, "Ethnic Groups in America: From National Culture to Ideology," in *Freedom and Control in Modern Society*, eds. Morroe Berger, Theodore Abel and Charles H. Page (New York: D. Van Nostrand Company, 1954), p. 173.

Any such real sentiment for the "homeland" was put to the test for Germans in World War I and, for a later migration, Italians, in World War II. These two experiences show that there was no major loyalty or concern with nations at war with the U.S. by their American descendants except as the dominant society made them feel derogated. (There was a wave of hysterical anti-German feeling in America during World War I, related largely to the shock of sending American troops abroad; and in World War II some Italians as well as some Germans who, though American-born, had not enjoyed opportunities commensurate with their aspirations were attracted to neofascist groups or sentiments.)

Peasant Immigrants

THE IRISH The considerable number of Irish people who came to the colonies in the eighteenth century appear not to have been thought of as a people apart from the rest, except for a period when they arrived in large numbers. In the nineteenth century they were the first of the great ethnic migrations. They settled primarily in cities and stayed heavily concentrated in the North Atlantic states, except for those employed in mining and the construction of railways and canals. In the three decades before the Civil War they encountered much resistance and discrimination from the "native" population. For one thing, they were Catholic and anti-British. They were rural people who had settled largely in cities and towns. They entered the lower occupational ranks of unskilled work, thus starting with lower-class status at a time when class distinction was becoming more important.

This was America's first confrontation with a peasant culture.[15] The English, Scandinavians, or Germans who came to America in the nineteenth century came from towns or from freehold farming patterns. The Irish had been long exploited by the English landholding system. The unchallenged position of the Catholic church cemented bonds of identity. A history of famine, a family and inheritance system that led to late marriage and many unmarried men and women, the ambivalent situation of being English-speaking but not part of English-derived institutions, and migration in large numbers put the Irish in a peculiar relationship to dominants. Some welcomed them as a necessary working-class contingent; others engaged in flagrant discrimination. This discrimination is memorialized in an American folksong popular in the music halls of the 1860's.[16]

> I'm a decent boy just landed from the town of Ballyfad;
> I want a situation, and I want it very bad.

[15] For a description of Irish peasant social structure and factors leading to emigration, see Conrad M. Arensberg and Solon T. Kimball, *Family and Community in Ireland* (Cambridge, Mass.: Harvard University Press, 1940).
[16] Edith Fowke and Joe Glazer, *Songs of Work and Freedom* (Garden City, New York: Doubleday and Co., 1961), p. 154.

> I seen employment advertised, "It's just the thing," says I
> But the dirty spalpeen ended with "No Irish need apply."

Prior to the great migration resulting from the years 1846–1850, the Irish were distributed throughout the class structure. Glazer and Moynihan, writing on the Irish in New York today, find that this is once more true.[17] In the interim period they were far outstripped by some of the other groups migrating at the same time. Glazer and Moynihan attribute this in part to their Catholicism, which did not impart a strong ethic of individual success, to their immediate involvement and ultimate success in politics, which strengthened attitudes of discrimination against them, and to their high rate of alcoholism.[18]

The persistence of Irish identity these authors see as a reaction to discrimination and to their lively concern for Irish independence. Since the establishment of Eire this bond has been lost.

The Eastern and Southern Europeans

After 1880 until the restriction of immigration the largest migrations were from eastern and southern Europe. Almost all the migrants were of a different religious affiliation than either established or sectarian Protestants. Peasants came from Poland, Hungary, the Ukraine and other parts of modern Russia; Greeks from mountain and island villages; Italians, first from northern Italy and after 1900 in far greater number from southern Italy and Sicily; Jews from the little towns of Poland and Russia fleeing a policy of forced assimilation and sporadic concomitant persecution.

By the beginning of the twentieth century the absorbtion of older immigrants had considerably broadened what could now be called "native," but there is little evidence that this worked to lessen discriminatory attitudes toward the new groups; quite possibly the opposite was true. There was also in the North a new free Negro group whose opportunities for employment were curtailed by the great influx of immigrants. With regard to class, religion, and national culture the new groups were looked down on.

A picture of the layering of immigrant populations in a small New England industrial city can be seen in the classic study of "Yankee City." [19]

> The "natives" of "Yankee City" number 9,030, or 54 per cent of the population. They comprise mainly the descendants of colonial British stock. Included as natives, however, are a few descendants from French Huguenot stock and German

[17] Nathan Glazer and Daniel Patrick Moynihan, *Beyond the Melting Pot: The Negroes, Puerto Ricans, Jews, Italians, and Irish of New York City* (Cambridge, Mass.: The M.I.T. Press and Harvard University Press, 1963), p. 254.
[18] *Ibid.*, pp. 256–259.
[19] William Lloyd Warner and P. S. Lunt, *The Social Life of a Modern Community* (New Haven: Yale University Press, 1941). Condensed adaptation by Charles F. Marden of Warner and Lunt, pp. 213–217. By permission.

Jews who settled in the city early in its history. Also included are more recent immigrants from the British sources. "Predominant in number, this native group dominates the economic, political, and social structures of the community."

Of the remaining 7,646 individuals in "Yankee City" about half are Irish, the first large group of immigrants to enter, beginning around 1840. Though, like the Yankees, they spoke English, they differed in being Catholic and having a rural and agricultural background in a city whose economic life was geared to ship-building and maritime commerce.

The French-Canadians came next, around the 1880 period. They became more distinctive, a group apart, with high internal solidarity centering around their Catholicism, the French language, and a strong solidarity of family life. Next in order was the influx of Polish Jews beginning around 1903, which, added to a few German Jews who had come in earlier, formed a Jewish aggregate of 397 persons. The Jews differed from the rest in language, religion, and family and cultural tradition. Being, however, from urban occupational backgrounds, the Jews maintained their original occupational pattern, while the others did not. An Italian influx into "Yankee City" came about the same time as that of the Jews. Since their numbers were few—284 in 1933—they were not organized in separate parishes from the Irish. They were, however, split into antagonistic north and south Italian subgroups. The Armenian group at the time of the study was only slightly less than the Italian: 246. They had come into the city around 1900 and were more than other ethnic groups employed in one industry, shoe manufacture. This Armenian subcommunity lacked integration because it was split along religious lines between Congregational Protestants and eastern Orthodox communicants.

While the greatest movement of Greeks into "Yankee City" occurred in the 1920's, their number increased steadily, and in 1933 they were the fourth largest ethnic group, totaling 412. About two-thirds were employed in factory work; others were confectioners, restaurant owners, barbers. Their cultural accommodation centered around their separate Greek Orthodox Church and its parochial culture, their patriarchal type family, and their coffee houses. Still more recent arrivals were the Poles and Russians. The Poles had come to number 677, thus being the third largest ethnic group. First they worked in the textile factories, but following the decline of the textile industry found employment in other factories. Interestingly enough in view of the antagonism between Poles and Russians in Europe, the "Yankee City" researchers found "close and amicable relations existing between them in Yankee City." This arose from the knowledge of each other's language, from frequent and informal meetings in their local provision stores, and from the smallness of the Russian group.

Minority Adaptations to Dominance

A good deal of the classical description of the initial problems of immigrants stems from the tradition of the crusading journalists of the first decade of this century. At this period of heaviest immigration, particularly in the port city of New York, conditions were deplorable. We do not have data to estimate accurately the conditions that obtained for new migrants throughout the great century of migration from 1820 to 1920, but it is likely that they were similar. We know that it was a common pattern for immigrants to send for relatives and help establish them, as best they could, often house them, and induct them into some kind of community living. We know that until contract labor was made illegal in 1882 many came with committments to jobs, however low paid. Until the closing of immigration, agents of major industries waited at Ellis Island to meet the boats and to select skills or brawn as needed for America's industrial expansion. Skilled industrial workers were at a premium. There was also continually a small group of professionals or small businessmen with some capital who established themselves rather easily.

For most of the immigrants the voyage was hard, even with attempts to regulate the number of passengers and conditions of passage. Even when they were met by relatives, many experienced what is now termed "culture shock." Immigration officials were often harsh, and the Ellis Island interim with its great bare sheds, was a depressing end to an overcrowded voyage.[20]

In the later immigration many a self-respecting peasant felt a marked loss of status in a low-paid job (and in a home with no land). The added problem of imperfect communication for those who did not speak English compounded the distress of the newcomer. As we have said earlier, at various times, depending on many internal factors, the immigrant might be greeted with open hostility on the part of the natives. At other times he was largely ignored. Sometimes he was avidly seized upon: to serve in the Union Army; to be quickly naturalized in an election year; to become a strikebreaker for the Pinkerton agency.

The Ethnic Subcommunity

Wherever immigrants settled in considerable numbers they at first clustered with people from home. Sometimes they even had little sub-sub-communities, where they had discovered neighbors and friends not only from the home country but from the home district, and they brought their district or regional rivalries with them. Then, as now with the Puerto Ricans, they settled in the sections of the city which were least desirable residentially, since this was what was available to them. Then as now, landlords discovered that exorbitant rents could be extracted for little space and poor quality of housing. Families were forced to crowd into single rooms or "old law" tenements, some of whose rooms had no windows. In the evenings, the people spilled out on the street, weather permitting, and gossiped, quarreled, exchanged news from home, shopped from the pushcarts, and insofar as possible recreated the life of the home village. The Irish had their taverns, the Greeks a little restaurant that served as a

[20] Robert E. Park and Herbert A. Miller, *Old World Traits Transplanted* (New York: Harper & Brothers, 1921). Chapters 3 and 4 give documentary material on the demoralization of some immigrants in their early days in America.

coffee house for the men, the Germans their sport clubs. They read the foreign language press: *The Irish Echo,* the *Staatszeitung, Il Populo,* the *Jewish Daily Forward,* and so on. These subcommunities flourished through the first quarter of the century, renewed by a continued influx from the old country. They persisted in most of our large industrial cities until World War II, but now are gradually thinning out as a result of improved circumstances for the younger generation, efforts at urban renewal, and the dying out of the old generation.

This ecological separation of nationality groups let them build up an integrated subsociety which had little interaction with the dominant group except through economic, political, welfare, and occasionally religious contacts.

Acculturative Institutions

Initiated by Ethnics In the new environment, nationality groups developed formal associations for their own protection and improvement. Mutual benefit societies, limited to the members of a specific common nationality, replaced village informal patterns of mutual aid. Nationality societies—"Polish-American," "Hungarian-American"—preserved some of the old tradition, celebrated national holidays, but more importantly were a structure through which group interest could be expressed to the larger community in political and civic affairs. Participating in such formal organizations was in itself a training for established roles in American life, and thus contributed to the adjustment of the immigrant.

As we have seen, for almost every large immigrant group in America there arose newspapers printed in their own language, some with national and others with local circulation. Such papers printed news of activities in the old country and therefore have been considered as retarding assimilation. Yet, for those many immigrants who could not read English the newspapers brought a wider knowledge of American public affairs and the native cultural values.

Initiated by Native Americans The concern about immigrant welfare led to the development of organized efforts in their behalf on the part of various groups of native Americans. Most of these efforts were at first religiously motivated. The Methodists, for example, in the middle of the nineteenth century organized a German-speaking section of their denomination specifically to serve the German immigrants; later they extended their efforts to other immigrant nationalities and their publishing house for a time supported a religious press in several languages.

The initial motivation for the settlement movement was religious also; by now settlement houses have largely lost their religious orientation and have become secular. The settlement house was an institution developed at the end of the nineteenth century to aid the slum-dweller, which in the United States at that time meant the immigrant. Such centers as Hull House in Chicago and the Henry Street Settlement in New York became neighborhood centers providing educational, recreational, and cultural activities in immigrant communities. Though it cannot be claimed that the settlement movement reached the mass of immigrants, it did contribute significantly to all contemporary thinking about immigration and welfare. From the Henry Street Settlement the first visiting nurses went into homes to care for the ill, thereby creating the pattern of modern public health nursing. In New York and Chicago, settlement houses were active in promoting legislation concerning working conditions in factories, child labor, and housing and health. The first expressions of the value of cultural pluralism came from the settlements. As a direct service, settlement houses often tended to reach the more ambitious individuals anxious to move out of the immigrant world into the mainstream of American life. On the debit side, one study, made in Boston in 1940, has pointed out that settlement workers have often been unable to bridge the gap between their own middle-class American attitudes and the real needs and indigenous leadership of the immigrant group whose ways were alien.[21]

Interaction in the American Institutional Structure

The urban political party, the lower ranks of the civil service, and the trade union were each major modes of involving the immigrant in American life.

The involvement of the immigrant in politics is as old as the nation and the early struggles between the propertied and the popular parties. The immigrant vote was marshaled for every election, often with the individual voter understanding the issues only very vaguely at best. The heavy concentration of the Irish in the port cities of the East let them very early play an active role in organizing local politics. As urban centers grew throughout the nineteenth century, "machine" politics developed, seeking local control and party influence in the state and national elections. In the East, and to some extent in other industrial areas, the machine was Democratic and the leadership initially was Irish. The political machine operated on a basis of patronage and personal favors, which aroused the criticism of the "good government" organizations. However, the machine was able to make politics more personal for the immigrant, and therefore more meaningful, than could forces whose approach to civil life was impersonalized and abstract.[22]

Handlin describes machine politics as more characteristic of the second generation than of the immigrants themselves. Since the group that migrated

[21] William Foote Whyte, *Street Corner Society* (Chicago, Ill.: The University of Chicago Press, 1943).

[22] After the restriction of immigration, leadership passed from the Irish to other national groups, and by the 1948 national election the political pattern had changed so that the "ethnic vote" was no longer a meaningful category. Samuel Lubell, *The Future of American Politics,* 2nd ed., rev. (New York: Doubleday Anchor Books, 1956). See the index for analyses of nationality votes from 1929 to 1948.

often was too involved in other pressures, did not command the language, and had no history of political participation, it remained apathetic.[23]

During the nineteenth century, the lower civil service jobs in the cities became a channel for the establishment of immigrants and their children. The police force, the fire department, and the post office had their lower ranks filled from the new groups. The link between political patronage and the police allowed for a considerable amount of corruption, but it also kept the police of America free of the authoritarian and severe disciplinary attitude found in some of the immigrants' home countries.

The labor movement, too, involved the immigrant in an organizational structure which helped him adapt to the conditions of the new country. Throughout the nineteenth century, factories tended to deploy their labor force in a way that maintained ethnic solidarity, each department or shop having a particular ethnic character. Union locals therefore similarly were largely or exclusively composed of one ethnic group. But in the experience of a strike or in the conduct of union affairs above the shop level, native Americans, British, Irish, German, Welsh, Russian Jewish, Italian, and many others worked together. The major involvement of immigrant workers in unions came in the early twentieth century, but immigrants were prominent in the Workingmen's Party, a labor party, before the Civil War, in the Knights of Labor, and in the formation of the American Federation of Labor.

While the school was a more important factor in the assimilation of the native-born children of the immigrants, it deserves mention in relation to the immigrant generation as well. Many cities set up night-school programs for the instruction of adult immigrants, with the curricula stressing the English and civics necessary for naturalization. The main influence of the school on the adult immigrants, however, was largely indirectly mediated, through their children. For example, as Galitzi says of the Roumanians, "The children hearing the English language become the carriers of the new language and new ideas into the Roumanian home. They interpret to their parents the American standards of health, economic efficiency, civic duties, and fair play." [24]

But even with these bridges of contact with the dominant natives, the typical immigrant became only partially acculturated to American life. The pattern of subcommunal segregation described above retarded the process; yet, given the situation as it was, such a response was logical and necessary. Mass immigration was encouraged and tolerated because the rapidly growing industrial society greatly needed cheap labor. Yet, for the most part, the immigrant was not desired as a neighbor, a friend, or a competitor by the dominant natives. Segregation suited perfectly the natives' attitudes and arose in part in response

---

[23] Oscar Handlin, *The Uprooted* (Boston: Little, Brown & Co., 1952), Chapter 8.

[24] Christine A. Galitzi, *A Study of Assimilation Among the Roumanians in the United States* (New York: Columbia University Press, 1929), p. 228.

to them. And temporarily it met a need of the immigrant for a sense of self-respect, for expressing his accustomed mode of life, and for social security—the sense of belonging.

Generational Conflict and Marginality

The concentration of immigrants in subcommunities intensified the problems of the second generation. What gave security to their elders created conflict for the children of the immigrant growing up in America. Like all other parents, immigrant parents conditioned their children to their accustomed social heritage. The children, as a result of their school experience and the other outside stimuli their growing knowledge of the English language opened to them, wanted to become Americanized. The children began to perceive that the culture of their parents was not American as defined by the outside dominant native world. Furthermore, the immigrant children learned that the ways of their parents were defined as inferior and that they, too, were socially rejected because of their background. Handlin discusses the fact that a great deal of the generational problem was compounded by the insecurity of the immigrant parents in their own roles. In the new environment a confusion came as to the old established rights and duties between husband and wife and parents and children. Without the protective cover of well-defined roles, father, mother, son, and daughter faced each other as individuals under the most trying conditions.[25]

While in the long run it was to be free education that assimilated the descendants of immigrants, in the short run too often the school fell far short of solving the emotional problems of these culturally marginal young people. Smith's appraisal of the school's impact epitomizes the dominant attitude toward the immigrant minorities:

> On the basis of the available data, we are forced to the conclusion that the American school, although well intentioned, has not dealt wisely with the children of immigrants. Unknowingly it has been actually ruthless in ignoring and belittling the cultural heritages of the diverse elements in our population while glorifying the dominant civilization, thereby bringing about permanent and often tragic estrangements. The school should have paid some attention to counteracting the various influences in the community which tend to produce conflicts between the two generations.[26]

The school not only tended to depreciate or ignore the cultural heritage of the children of immigrants, but the very models they presented of Americans and American life were alien to these children and contributed to their feeling of inferiority. Handlin points out that the elementary-school textbooks offered to immigrant children were based on the vocabulary and images of rural

[25] Handlin, *The Uprooted*, p. 239.
[26] W. C. Smith, *Americans in the Making*, p. 303. By permission.

America, which were unreal and meaningless to the children of urban slums. "Falsity runs through all the books, which were written to be used by other pupils in other schools; even the arithmetic sets its problems in terms of the rural countryside . . ." [27]

In the face of these two worlds of home and school, the children as they grew older developed perforce a life of their own, an intermediary world, whose locale was the street. Here they formed their own social groups and established their own code of behavior. Sometimes these groups were hostile and destructive. Sometimes they were merely friendship groups. Whyte has described one such group in detail in his study *Street Corner Society*. "Doc" and his gang, the "Corner Boys," rejected the dominant values as represented by school and settlement house, since they had been rejected by teachers and social workers. Theirs was a friendship group that "hung around together." Their chief norm was loyalty to and sharing with one another. Some of the difficulties for these Italian American boys are summed up by Whyte.

> Some ask, "Why can't those people stop being Italians and become Americans like the rest of us?" The answer is that they are blocked in two ways: by their own organized society and by the outside world. Cornerville people want to be good American citizens. I have never heard such moving expressions of love for this country as I have heard in Cornerville. Nevertheless, an organized way of life cannot be changed overnight. As the study of the corner gang shows, people become dependent upon certain routines of action. If they broke away abruptly from these routines, they would feel themselves disloyal and would be left helpless, without support. And, if a man wants to forget that he is an Italian, the society around him does not let him forget it. He is marked as an inferior person— like all other Italians. To bolster his own self-respect he must tell himself and tell others that the Italians are a great people, that their culture is second to none, and that their great men are unsurpassed.[28]

Some of the second generation did become Americans in their incorporation of the American goal of achievement and success. The traditionally sanctioned means to business success was frequently closed to them, however, because of ethnic discrimination and low socioeconomic status. For many, achievement or monetary success could be found in politics or the rackets and, as Daniel Bell has pointed out, both politics and crime in the large urban areas have experienced successive invasions by ethnic groups.[29]

For those individuals who did correctly perceive the expectations and values of the dominant society, the situation in which they found themselves was often marginal. Taking the dominant group as their reference group and incorporating dominant norms and goals, they found themselves at a competitive dis-

[27] Handlin, *The Uprooted*, p. 246.
[28] Whyte, *Street Corner Society*, p. 274. By permission.
[29] Daniel Bell, "Crime as an American Way of Life," *Antioch Review*, Summer, 1953. Also in Bell, *The End of Ideology* (Glencoe, Ill.: The Free Press, 1960).

advantage, and were often made to feel inferior. Such a person, Chick Morelli, is described by Whyte. He identified with the schools, his teachers, the settlement workers, saved his money, got an education, tried to organize an "improvement" program in his community of "Cornerville," but came to see politics as the only career open to him despite his associations with people outside his subcommunity. He even came to believe that Italians themselves were to blame for the discrimination they received, yet he did not successfully establish himself in "native" middle-class society.[30]

To have been successful, that is to assimilate, he would have had to abandon his heritage more drastically, as is illustrated by a Polish young man in Yankee City. The first thing he did was anglicize his name: Paul Stanley

> Through the aid of his athletic prowess he had graduated from college and gone to law school while supporting himself working in the law office of a local lawyer of upper middle-class (native) status.
>
> Paul's father and mother had come from Poland when they were children. They had both worked in the shoe factory and had gone to an "Americanization school" to improve their English. They were proud of their home, which they owned outright, kept well painted, and landscaped with cast-off tires, a border of half-buried beer cans, and well-tended garden and lawn. They looked down on their less ambitious neighbors and also the Riverbrookers (lower-lower class people) with "native" status.
>
> Mr. Stanley was very fond and proud of his son, for whom education had opened the door to greater social heights. Their first serious rift came when Paul became interested in Annie Taylor, a Riverbrooker girl; Paul wanted to marry her and eventually did, much to the disappointment of his parents. Annie's family were a typical ne'er-do-well low-class family known to the truant officer. Annie herself was the most ambitious and respectable of the lot and had in school managed to be accepted in "better-class" cliques of girls. Because of all the in-law complications, Annie and Paul ran away to get married, causing a split in Annie's family, who said she had married a "damn foreigner" and a Catholic fellow. Following their marriage, the new Stanleys drew away from both sets of parents, who were not after all the kinds of parents they wanted their new friends to meet. Their new home was in a nonethnic neighborhood.
>
> After graduating from law school Paul had been invited to join the Caribous, made up mostly of Yankees, with only a few Poles. Within a year after his marriage, Paul became a member of the Antlers (higher social rating than the Caribous) and played bridge there several nights a week. He began to neglect his Caribou contacts. The Stanleys were now in a social clique made up of Yankee lower-middle class folks but were not, of course, ever invited to dinner at the home of the still higher-class Antlers whom Paul knew at the club, or ever called on by the nice ladies of Hill Street—upper class. "And anyway," they said, "we're going to see to it that our children have every advantage." [31]

[30] Whyte, *Street Corner Society*, pp. 52–56.
[31] Warner and Lunt, *The Social Life of a Modern Community*, adapted by Charles F. Marden, pp. 188–193. By permission.

The Peer Group Society

Although the second generation produced some marginal individuals and others who moved out and up, there was always a contingent—smaller or larger —which remained as part of an ethnic subsociety. The nationality neighborhoods of the first generation became interethnic as vacancies occurred and low-rent housing was in demand. Herbert J. Gans has studied one such urban neighborhood.[32] The largest ethnic group was Italian, although the neighborhood included Poles, Albanians, Ukrainians, Greeks, and a residue each of elderly Irish and elderly Jews. There was also a scattering of middle-class professionals and students attached to the nearby teaching hospital, artists, Gypsies, and groups of single men as well as some of the very poor, with the pattern of broken families and the mild pathologies of the psychologically disabled. Only seven percent of the population was "American" in background.

Gans gives a picture of the second-generation Italians of today as a "peer group society" in which sociability centers around a gathering of family and friends, occurring several times a week. "One could almost say that the meetings of the group are at the vital center of . . . life, that they are the end for which other everyday activities are a means." [33] The activities of such a group center largely around the exchange of news and gossip. This serves as a mechanism of social control, supplies information and advice, provides entertainment and drama about one's own group that are provided for others through the mass media.[34] This translated "village" social behavior reinforces group identity and interprets selectively the "outside" world. It protects the group from disorganizing influences, and substitutes for formal organizations.

Gans sees this tightly woven ethnic society threatened by larger social changes. In the specific instance, the neighborhood he studied had been designated for urban renewal, which would inevitably lead to the ecological dispersion of many of the families. The fact that the younger generation will stay in school longer will lead many of them out of the blue-collar occupational world of their parents. The discontinuance of arranged marriages will, despite the strong family controls, lead to increasing interethnic marriage.

The Challenge to Dominance

The European migration was disparate enough in cultural roots, and extended over a sufficiently long period of time, for the American economy to absorb at some level most of the migrants, so that "national" or "cultural" groups were not to any significant extent involved in protest for themselves as. groups demanding recognition and identity. On the whole they joined with others in the political and economic protests relevant to the problems of an

[32] Herbert J. Gans, *The Urban Villagers: Group and Class in the Life of Italian-Americans* (New York: The Free Press, 1962).
[33] *Ibid.,* p. 74.
[34] *Ibid.,* pp. 78–79.

industrially developed America. Immigrants, and even more their children, were involved in support of the North in the Civil War, the rising movements for organized labor, urban politics out of which grew a new look at public responsibility for social welfare, and moderate to extreme radical movements. All these were interethnic challenges, WASPS included. The northern Europeans of the 1850's, who mostly settled in the northern Middle West but also in northern cities, vigorously supported the antislavery position. The Irish, the British skilled workers of the 1870's and 1880's, the Italians, the Poles, the Lithuanians and other Eastern European groups, as well as WASP Western miners, all played a role in the American Labor Movement. The radical movements of the last quarter of the nineteenth and the first half of the twentieth century included immigrants, the children of immigrants, and WASPS seeking solutions to the upheaval of social change. This is in contrast to the protests of today, which ask respect for one's heritage and identity, first and foremost, as a prerequisite to all other goals. Possibly it was this experience of uniting in formal organizations for specific public goals that has accelerated the separation of public and private spheres of life in American society. Certainly the members of these participating groups, except perhaps for a leadership elite, lived much of their daily lives in the life style and associations of their own ethnic subgroups.

The Effect of the European Migration

Considering the long time span and the varieties of people who migrated to America it would be impossible to adequately discuss the contributions made to American life by each ethnic group.[35] Contributions were not always recognized; liabilities were often argued. Surveying the vast literature on immigration we would summarize the effects of European immigration as follows:

1. It accelerated the population growth of the United States during the period in which it took place and thus further advanced the position of the United States among world powers.

2. It expedited industrial expansion and urbanization.

3. It temporarily retarded the growth of unionism.

4. It facilitated the perpetuation of the "Tammany Hall" type of urban politics until such time as increasing assimilation of the native-born descendents and their class differentiation broke up any marked tendency toward ethnic political blocks.

5. In its total impact, it increased for a time the volume of personal maladjustment with particular reference to ethnic persons in marginal status positions.

[35] See Francis J. Brown and Joseph S. Roucek, *One America* (New York: Prentice-Hall, 1949), Part II, for the most exhaustive listing in one volume of the significant contributions of each of the 39 ethnic groupings described.

6. It elaborated the artistic and esthetic elements of the general culture, and facilitated the trend away from the Puritan outlook on pleasure and personal morality.

7. It retarded the trend from a supernaturalistic toward a secular approach to problems of human welfare, particularly, the application of newer social science approaches in human relations.

8. While innumerable specific items in the various ethnic cultures became incorporated into the general national or regional cultures, the minority status of ethnics limited the extent of this influence.

Immigration Since the Establishment of Restriction

Although there have been amendments, and two special acts affecting immigration outside the quota system, there has been no fundamental change in the policy of restriction. A review of the immigration situation until the first major amendment in 1952 shows the following.

IMMIGRATION ADJUSTS TO THE QUOTA LIMITS: 1925–1930 During this period practically all European nations utilized their quotas to the full. The fact that the total immigration exceeded the quotas is accounted for by the admission of nonquota immigrants as permitted by the Act of 1924, the largest group of which were the wives, husbands, or minor children of resident immigrants.

IMMIGRATION FAR BELOW THE PERMISSIBLE LIMITS: 1931–1935 The drastic decline in European immigration beginning with 1930 clearly reflects the economic depression of these years, which made coming to America less attractive to Europeans. In addition, the federal government instructed its consulates abroad to apply rigidly the clauses in the immigration legislation denying entry to persons likely to become public charges.

REFUGEES INCREASE THE TOTALS: 1936–1940 While the rise in European immigration beginning in 1936 may have reflected in part the improved economic conditions in the United States, it was substantially advanced by the arrival of thousands of Europeans who sought asylum from persecution in the expanding Nazi Reich.

WORLD WAR II VIRTUALLY CUTS OFF ALL IMMIGRATION: 1941–1946 Interestingly enough, because of the manpower shortage during the war, the United States imported on temporary visas from Mexico, Canada, and the West Indies some 350,000 laborers.

DISPLACED PERSONS INCREASE IMMIGRATION AFTER 1946.

The Refugees

Throughout our entire history American society has been added to periodically by immigrants who left their native lands primarily to escape persecution for political or religious opinions. The term "refugees" was applied to individuals who fled from the Nazi persecution beginning in Germany in 1933 and carried on further in the Nazi-occupied areas after 1938. To quote Davie and Koenig,

> The recent refugee movement has also been marked by (1) the extremely cruel treatment of the victims of political, religious, and "racial" persecutions; (2) by the difficulty which these victims encountered in escaping and in finding a secure refuge as Naziism spread to ever larger areas; (3) by the reluctance of the countries not immediately affected to admit them because of the deep economic depression then existing; and (4) by the breaking up of families on a scale previously unknown. Such has been the refugee movement which began with the rise of Hitler to power in 1933.[36]

Davie and Koenig estimate the total number of immigrants in the United States who can be called "refugees" at 243,862. The period from 1938 to 1941 marked the peak of this particular immigrant movement. America was not, as many natives put it, "swamped" with refugees, since the total amount of all immigration to our shores from Europe from 1933 to 1944 totaled only 365,955, only 16.8 percent of the total permissible from Europe under the quota laws. Over half the people came from Germany or Austria, with Poles, Czechoslovakians, Russians, French, Italians, and Hungarians following in this order. Of the entire group about two-thirds were Jewish, a fact explained by the Nazi persecution of Jews, which was most systematic and categorical. These refugees eventually distributed themselves throughout the country, although they settled largely in cities.

This particular group differed from the earlier mass immigration in having a far larger proportion of highly educated, professionally trained, and commercially experienced persons. For example, 5,000 were physicians; 25,000 merchants; 1,800 manufacturers; and 3,500 college and school teachers. The proportion of skilled and unskilled laborers was far below that of the earlier immigration. This unusual distribution of occupational backgrounds is explained by the difficulties of escaping and the need of some wealth to get away. Relatively more of the refugees were wealthy, although many of the well-to-do who did not come early were unable to bring their wealth with them.

Davie and Koenig sum up their answer to the question "What do Americans think of the refugees?" as follows:

> The general reaction of Americans toward the refugees may be summed up as one of compassion for the victims of persecution seeking a haven here. The refugees report that, on the whole, Americans have shown an attitude of friendliness and helpfulness. As the number of refugees increased, however, a certain amount of antagonism developed. Refugees began to be looked upon as serious

[36] Maurice R. Davie and Samuel Koenig, *The Refugees Are Now Americans,* Public Affairs Pamphlet, No. 111, 1945, p. 4. By permission.

competitors, especially by certain professional and wage-earning groups and in certain communities. These fears were allayed with the increased demand for labor brought about by the war.

Nevertheless, a certain degree of resentment has persisted in certain quarters and against certain groups of refugees.[37]

Within a short time these refugees became well adapted, if not assimilated, to American life. On the one hand, their relatively few numbers offered little serious competition to Americans except in an occasional locality; on the other hand, they had a beneficial influence out of proportion to their numbers. Some started new business enterprises and introduced new manufacturing processes; others were highly skilled workers in trades where a dearth of native trained workers existed. If in any sense the presence of the refugees constituted a "problem," it has long since ceased to be one.

Displaced Persons

In the years since World War II the United States has been receiving a new category of immigrants who have become technically designated "displaced persons." These people are Europeans who were rendered homeless through the destruction of the last war or who for various reasons could not with safety resume residence in their prewar community. By the end of 1950 the heart-rending task of resettling these people had been substantially accomplished. It would therefore perhaps be adequate for us to confine our discussion of the topic to indicating how many came to this country, who they were, and how they fared among us. But the role which the United States played in this co-operative world problem is a good barometer for evaluating the present climate of American sentiment toward certain minorities, and a good test of the attitude of the American people toward international cooperation. We shall therefore treat the topic of the displaced persons in detail.

The Circumstances Creating Displacement

During the period of the German conquest up to 1943, millions of persons were evacuated by the German army or fled before it. At the same time prisoners of war and slave labor from non-German nationals were taken to Germany. More than two million Poles, French-speaking Alsace-Lorrainers, and Slovenes were expelled from border areas incorporated into the Reich in order to make room for foreign nationals of German stock who were thus repatriated nearer the homeland. As the tide of the war reversed, a series of other population movements took place. Inhabitants of German cities, perhaps as many as six million, were evacuated to other places within the Reich. As Russian victories occurred, Reich Germans from eastern and southeastern

[37] *Ibid.,* p. 28. By permission.

Europe, together with some non-Germans who feared the Communists, fled back to the fatherland. At the conclusion of the war, the Allied armies liberated from the notorious Nazi concentration camps the surviving Jews and non-Jewish political opponents of the Nazi regime. And later on, as the Iron Curtain began to surround their countries, thousands fled from their homes to seek asylum in lands controlled by the Allied governments.

Characteristics of the Displaced Persons

Surveys made in Europe of the displaced persons indicated a fairly even sex distribution, a heavy concentration in the age groups 18 through 44, and a high birth rate in the camps of 35.5 per thousand.[38] One survey estimated 70 percent Roman Catholics and 20 percent Jewish.[39] The percentage of skilled laborers was high. Most of the displaced persons were Poles, Ukranians, Yugoslavs, and Balts.

The Role of the United States

The response of the United States to this problem was slow and cautious. During the early period, when the emphasis was on repatriation, the United States admitted 20,000 displaced persons, each of which was required to have a sponsor in this country who would guarantee that he would not become a public charge. The United Nations organized the International Refugee Organization in 1947, and in the first year about 200,000 displaced persons were resettled, of whom the United States admitted 16,836, a rather small number. One reason for this was that most of the displaced persons were ineligible for admission under our quota system. The Administration urged Congress immediately upon IRO's call to pass special legislation making it possible for a substantial number of displaced persons to be admitted on a nonquota basis. Congress did not act until the closing hours of its 1948 session, on June 2. The bill then passed had the following main provisions.

1. Permitted the admission of 205,000 displaced persons over a two-year period.
2. Charged the displaced persons entering up to 50 percent against future annual quotas of the countries of birth.
3. Restricted eligibility to those entering Germany, Austria, and Italy before December 22, 1945.
4. Required that at least 40 percent of the total admitted must be persons coming from areas annexed by foreign powers.

While the number allowed under this act was more commensurate with the size and position of the United States, the specifications made it difficult

[38] E. D. Kulischer, "Displaced Persons in the Modern World," *The Annals of The American Academy of Political and Social Science*, March, 1949, 262: 172–173.
[39] William S. Bernard, "Homeless, Tempest Tossed," *Survey Graphic*, April, 1948, 37: 189.

to find 205,000 displaced persons who could qualify. The cutoff date excluded the large number of Jews who fled from eastern Europe after December, 1945. The areas which had been annexed by foreign powers, from which 40 percent must be drawn, included the Baltic States, whose population contained substantial numbers of Protestants. Since, as indicated above, 90 percent of the displaced persons were either Roman Catholic or Jewish, it is not surprising that the bill was considered by many as highly discriminatory against peoples of non-Protestant faith. Sharing this sentiment, President Truman, in a statement released when he signed the bill, put it in these words: "In its present form, the bill is flagrantly discriminatory.... It is a close question whether this bill is better than no bill at all.... [It] discriminates in callous fashion against displaced persons of the Jewish faith.... [It] also excludes many persons of the Catholic faith who deserve admission." [40]

As admissions began to lag, the Administration pressed for revision of the 1948 Act, and on June 16, 1950, a new bill was signed by the President. This revised act permitted the entry of 228,514 displaced persons in addition to the 172,239 admissions already granted. It removed the qualifications as to occupation and nationality in the previous bill and the prior "cutoff date" for time of displacement, thus making eligible Poles, Roumanians, and Catholics in general who had fled in 1946 and 1947 from Communist-controlled countries. By the end of 1952, when the displaced persons legislation ended, the United States had admitted about 400,000.

The response of the American government and public to the various refugee problems reflects the ambivalence characteristic of its response to earlier immigration, but with certain changes. Opposed to acceptance of these refugees have been the various nativist publics, to whom "foreigners" are *ipso facto* undesirable, and the anti-Semitic public. As before, liberal elements have favored a generous policy in accordance with democratic principles. Unlike the early period, there has been a shift in the position of organized labor, which at least officially supported the admission of displaced persons. The growing recognition of the international responsibility of the United States and the "cold war" implications of the refugee problems made acceptance of a substantial share of these people imperative.

The admittance to the United States of these various refugee groups created no serious problems at all. They were dispersed widely enough that there was no marked visibility or noticeable economic competition with natives. The ethnic backgrounds were all from nationalities which already had furnished assimilated elements in the American population.

An outstanding new feature of refugee immigration has been the addition of new procedures. The screening of applicants and their preparatory orientation abroad, the preplanning of first home and job in this country before arrival, and the cooperative assistance of voluntary agencies with governmental officials

[40] See *The New York Times,* June 26, 1948, p. 7.

in facilitating the adjustment of the new arrivals marks a new approach to the handling of immigration. This new approach was utilized in connection with the admittance of some 25,000 Hungarian refugees from political persecution following the abortive Hungarian revolution of 1956, again by special legislation outside the quota system.

Changes in the Immigration Law

The McCarran-Walter Act, 1952

The McCarran-Walter Act did not change the policy of the quota system but involved setting up preferences within the same system. Immigration officials were ordered to give first preferences to persons with skills currently in short supply, and second preference to relatives of persons already in this country. Other provisions of the Act included codifying the entire series of immigration bills and allotting quotas for the first time to Asiastic nations, in most instances 100 per annum (185 for Japan). Immigration had been debated bitterly for the previous five years. The Act was passed over President Truman's veto and reflects the continuance of "nativist" preferences and a fear of possible "subversive" infiltration. The failure to liberalize the approach to immigration on the one hand and the tiny concession to naturalization of Asiatics on the other represents the fundamental unease and inevitable compromises in democratic political action, with a changing world and America's new role within these changes.

The 1952 Act made no real attack on the "national origins" bias of the quota system. It simplified the national origins formula of the 1924 Act by basing the annual quota on a flat one-sixth of one percent of the population of that origin in the 1920 Census. The total quota was 154,657.

President Truman's veto message [41] sharply criticized the quota system as defined in the Act, describing it as a "discriminatory policy." He cited the quota from Poland, for example, 6,500 as against 138,000 exiled Poles seeking to come here.

The Act of 1965

Sentiment against nationality quotas had been building up, and in the 1960 Presidential campaign both Republicans and Democrats included some statement in their platforms urging modification.[42] On October 3, 1965, further amendments to the immigration law were enacted which, beginning December 1, 1965, were to eliminate over a five-year period of transition "national origins" as a basis for selective entry into the United States. Although only 10 percent of the total quota may be admitted from any one country in a

[41] "House Document No. 520," *Congressional Record* (Washington, D.C.: Government Printing Office, 1952), 8225–28.
[42] Traverso, *Immigration: A Study in American Values,* pp. 143ff.

single year, the principle of preferential nationality has been supplanted by one more equitable.

In the amended law the preference system of granting visas is retained from the 1952 revision with only minor modification to admit more professionals and to allow some adjustments in health requirements. The law defines three classes of immigrants: those eligible for preference visas (relatives, professionals, skilled or unskilled labor in short supply, refugees) who come within the total quota. There are additional places for nonpreference immigrants. These, like skilled and unskilled workers (category six) must have certification from the United States Department of Labor. Western hemisphere immigrants enter freely, not as part of the quota, but also must have Labor Department certification. The 1965 amendment, in harmony with its relaxation of discrimination, adds free migration to Western Hemisphere colonials (largely Caribbean) on the same basis rather than as part of the applications of their mother country. The law still retains from the McCarran-Walter Act exclusion of members of "totalitarian" or "communist" political parties, a requirement often difficult to interpret justly.

The amendments since 1952 have made for greater justice and greater consistency in our immigration policy. They seem to indicate in the preference quotas recognition of the hardship of separated families and the easier adjustment of newcomers if they have family here. Preferential acceptance of scientists and artists certainly enriches America, although this may contribute to the "brain drain" abroad. That the new law has hardly solved all the problems it was intended to is indicated in the recent introduction of a bill to admit 100,000 Italians who are brothers and sisters of American citizens and their spouses (fifth preference) where, because of the limitation of 10 percent a year for any one nationality, the backlog of approved visas is such that an Italian in this category must have filed application by March 1, 1955, to be considered.[43]

Future Immigration Policy

It is obvious that all modern countries will make some effort to numerically limit influxes of population. A country such as the United States with a fully developed industrial economy and the technological threat of increasing automation can absorb only some of the people who seek a more congenial place to live and work. On the other hand, it is probable that our economy could absorb more than the present limitation.

Flexibility in the number admitted in any one year, for which there is precedent in our emergency acts of the forties and fifties, might be increased to correspond with business fluctuations and the varying need to provide refuge for groups in distress.

Whereas some limitations for each nation are necessary to give opportunity to all foreigners to compete for admission, American quotas still do not represent

[43] *The New York Times,* Aug. 11, 1967.

an equable distribution. It might be possible to anticipate that the unused quotas of nations might be pooled for the use of other nations.

Finally, the question of political affiliation must be considered. When a nation is engaged in a struggle against another nation, it is inevitable that it will want to bar as immigrants people whose loyalty is on the other side, as is the case with many European Communists today. A real danger to democracy in the application of political tests for admission to the United States is the danger of confusing beliefs—as, for example, Communism—with mere belief in social change.

Assimilation or Pluralism

The degree to which assimilation will take place depends on a number of variables. These may be grouped as (1) variables in dominant acceptance of persons of particular ethnic origin; (2) variables affecting the degree of cultural cohesion of ethnic groups; (3) variables in the social structure that accelerate or retard or limit interethnic association; (4) personality variables affecting individual choice.

The reception of persons of different ethnic background by dominants will vary with the climate of opinion in the community, and with the educational level of the dominant opinion leaders. The climate of opinion will incorporate some historical attitudes, it may be affected by the recency of the migration of an ethnic population; it may be related to the size and cohesion of the ethnic group; and it may be affected by the degree of difference between dominant and ethnic norms. Some attitudes will be related to the socioeconomic position of the ethnic group.

The degree of cultural cohesion of the ethnic minority will vary with degree of ecological separation and the degree of family control. Social structure barriers, especially in the opportunity structure—in type and quality of education available and in access to occupations and to formal associations—affect the degree and desirability of abandonment of the subculture. Finally, individual temperaments may rebel against membership in the subcommunity, or may find shelter in retaining it as the focus of their identity.

Today, then, we must say that the older assumption that all European immigrants would assimilate, in the nineteenth-century sense of submerging into the dominant culture, no longer fits. What seems to be happening is an interplay between a changing dominant society and dynamic subcultures. These subcultures bear increasingly less relation to the folkways of the countries from which they were derived, but their members participate with varying selectivity in a life flavored with meaningful elements that are not WASP.

European Migrants and Other American Minorities

There has always been some attitude of status superiority among those migrants who came before other migrants. Thus Irish looked down on Italians and both looked down on the Spanish.[44] There is also some rivalry, for example, between groups as discussed by Mario Puzo in his account of the American Italian Anti-Defamation League and the Anti-Defamation League of B'nai Brith, a rivalry he describes as that of brothers where one has been more successful than the other.[45]

The more important problem now, however, facing our pluralistic or totally assimilated European migrants is their relation to the non-European minorities in America. In the nineteenth century, the Irish were active in the West Coast movements against the Chinese. Many of the stable nationality settlements in cities, suburbs, or in small communities today find Indians, Mexicans, and especially Negroes too "different" to be acceptable neighbors, union members, or schoolmates. The crisis in American race relations is exacerbated by the communal bonds of many of the descendents of the European migration, "new" as well as "old."

The creation of a stable and dynamic society that is either ethnically pluralistic or religiously pluralistic depends on real respect for differences and equal access to the opportunities the society offers. Americans easily respond to pleas of injustice, but many Americans are provincial in their unease with *differences*. The future of America lies no longer in the hands of WASPS, but in those of all Americans who must transcend their communalities: people of different descent, different date of migration, different religion as neighbors, co-workers, and public authorities.

Topics for Projects and Discussion

1. How would you account for the fact that there has been little immigration to the United States from South America?
2. Recalling your high-school education, what did you learn about the cultural heritages of the immigrant groups to be found in the American population?
3. Ask a number of people who migrated to the United States from continental Europe to talk about their first year or two in this country. Try to direct the conversations to the difficulties they experienced, particularly how they got along with the natives. Write an account of these conversations.
4. Make a chart of your own family history since migration to this country. Show the ethnic identity, occupation, and place of residence of each generation. Summarize what this shows you about migration to and opportunity in the United States.
5. If you have had experience with a family which has foreign-born parents and American-born children, try to discover the chief areas of dispute between parents and children. To what extent are these similar or different in content and emphasis from the usual disagreements between American parents and children as discussed in popular magazines?
6. Select one group from the European migration and see what you can discover that their culture had contributed to American life: to language, (words, expressions),

44 Caroline F. Ware, *Greenwich Village* (Boston: Houghton-Mifflin Co., 1935), p. 141.
45 Mario Puzo, "The Italians, American Style," *The New York Times Magazine,* Aug. 6, 1967, p. 14.

foods, customs, enterprises, public service, scientific or artistic achievement, and so on.

7. Outline the major changes in the American population and in patterns of American life that account for the election of a third-generation Irish Catholic as President of the United States.

8. Discuss ways in which our present immigration law might be modified to make it fairer and more beneficial to the United States.

Suggested Reading

Bowers, David, ed. *Foreign Influences in American Life.* Princeton: Princeton University Press, 1944.

> *Essays on the influence of European immigrants on the politics, economic ideas, and cultural life of the United States.*

Davie, Maurice R. *Refugees in America.* New York: Harper & Brothers, 1947.

> *The most comprehensive account of the pre-World War II refugee immigration.*

Gans, Herbert J. *The Urban Villagers: Group and Class in the Life of Italian-Americans.* New York: The Free Press, 1962.

> *A provocative analysis of the subculture of blue-collar Italian Americans.*

Handlin, Oscar. *The Uprooted.* Boston: Little, Brown & Co., 1951.

> *A lively account of the voyage and settlement of American immigrants.*

Jones, Maldwyn Allen. *American Immigration.* Chicago, Ill.: University of Chicago Press, 1960.

> *A brilliant reappraisal by an Englishman of the great migrations to America.*

Park, Robert E. and Miller, H. A. *Old World Traits Transplanted.* New York: Harper & Brothers, 1921.

> *One of the earliest sociological studies of the process of immigrant adjustment with much interesting case material.*

Warner, W. Lloyd, and Srole, Leo. *The Social Systems of American Ethnic Groups.* New Haven: Yale University Press, 1945.

> *A classic study of the ethnic patterns in a small New England manufacturing city.*

6

The Mexican Americans

The Spanish-speaking people of the Southwest of the United States have designated themselves variously as "Latin Americans," "Spanish-speaking Americans," "Mexican Americans," "mexicanos," and "hispanos." [1] Each of these terms carries a nuance of identity related to status, degree of acculturation, and time of settlement. We have chosen the usage preferred today by those leaders concerned with the improvement of the status of their group: "Mexican American." For the dominant group we have used the term "Anglo American," or sometimes the common designation in the Southwest, "Anglo." [2]

The distinguishing feature of relations between dominants and Mexican Americans is the fact that long before the period of large-scale immigration from Mexico, the Southwest bore a cultural imprint of Spanish-Mexican origin as symbolized by the many "Los" and "Santa" community names in the region. In the area were many hispanos, especially in New Mexico, whose families held land grants from long before any Anglo Americans penetrated the area. Thus the migrating Mexicans, who began coming in large numbers about 1910, came to a part of the United States which was for them, in a sense, less alien than that into which the European immigrants came. By this time, however, Anglo American dominance had clearly been established and any incorporation of hispanic culture was largely superficial.

Size and Distribution of the Mexican American Population

The Mexican Americans make up the third largest minority in the United States. According to 1960 census figures the estimate was 5,189,837—2.89 percent of the population of the United States. Furthermore it is a young and

---

[1] The term "hispano," although often used by Spanish-speaking peoples interchangeably with other terms, has in the literature about this minority a particular designation. It refers to those Spanish-speaking settlers who were in the territory annexed by the United States before English-speaking people arrived.

[2] Celia S. Heller, *Mexican American Youth: Forgotten Youth at the Crossroads* (New York: Random House, 1966), pp. 6–7.

fast-growing population. The median age in 1960 was 20, as contrasted with 30 for "white" Americans as a whole. Figures for family size in five southwestern states in 1960 show double the percentage of families with more than four children for Mexican Americans than for Anglo Americans.[3]

Most of the Mexican American population is concentrated in five states of the Southwest: Arizona, California, Colorado, New Mexico, and Texas. Two-thirds live in California and Texas. About 80 percent are now found in urban areas, similar to the proportion for Anglo Americans. Mexican American communities are also found in a number of northern cities: Chicago, Detroit, Gary, Kansas City. There seems evidence that the migration to northern industrial centers is continuing and spreading out.[4]

Patterns of Migration

The greatest proportion of Mexican Americans have migrated since the annexation of the territories of the Southwest. Trends in immigration have largely been affected by the "pull" of employment opportunities, and the "push" of adverse economic or political conditions in Mexico. As with other groups, immigration declined sharply during the Depression. Then the great demands for manpower during World War II precipitated a rise which reached a peak about 1953. Until the enforcement of immigration restriction after 1929, Mexicans crossed the border freely. The majority came from the rural folk culture of Mexico, to some extent deviants from a feudal social system which viewed economic advancement of the individual as unworthy.[5] A minority came from more sophisticated strata in the hope of improving their financial position. Still others came as refugees from the political upheavals of Mexico.

Wetbacks

The enforcement of immigration restrictions led to the growth of illegal migration, with people popularly designated as "wetbacks." These people

[3] 15.5 for Anglos, 32.9 for Mexican Americans. *Ibid.* p. 33. The precise figures for this rapidly growing population are difficult to arrive at. The 1930 Census attempted to enumerate the Spanish-speaking people of the Southwest under the heading "Mexican," defining this group as people born in Mexico or children of people born in Mexico. This eliminated the older hispano population of the Southwest. In 1940 the census dropped this category, but attempted to determine the size of the Spanish-speaking and other foreign language groups by a five percent sample of "what language other than English was spoken in your home." This sample was relatively accurate for large cities, but not for small cities and rural areas. In 1960 a sample was taken in five states of people with Spanish surname, but this of course failed to include those who had anglicized their names or women who had intermarried. The chief source of figures for Puerto Ricans, the second largest Latin American minority is the Office of the Commonwealth of Puerto Rico in New York.

[4] See for example a study of in-migration in Racine, Wisconsin: Lyle W. Shannon and Elaine M. Krass, *The Economic Absorption and Cultural Integration of Immigrant Mexican-American and Negro Workers* (Iowa City: State University of Iowa, Department of Sociology and Anthropology, 1964).

[5] William Madsen, *The Mexican-Americans of South Texas* (New York: Holt, Rinehart and Winston, 1964), p. 24.

crossed the Rio Grande in large numbers. Illegal ferry services were maintained at designated points along the river. The crossing was made at night on flat-boats or rafts. Single men often swam the river pushing a log, holding their clothing above water. This type of illegal entry was hazardous and often un-successful. The border patrol returned thousands, but though most of the wet-backs came with the intention of working only for the crop picking season, some stayed on once they were here.

> Alfredo is a tall, handsome man in his fifties who proudly calls himself a Texan. He freely admits to his friends that he entered the United States as a wetback. "My determination to stay was great," he said, "fourteen times they caught me and threw me out but here I am." [6]

Braceros

Braceros came legally to the United States as agricultural labor under con-tract with the Mexican government. Many of them liked the United States and decided to stay. The statute admitting this type of seasonal labor was allowed to expire at the end of 1964 and braceros are no longer admitted to the country.[7]

Immigration restriction has affected the Mexican American as it has other migrants. Today 85 percent of Mexican Americans are native born and 50 percent are third generation.[8]

The Establishment of Dominance

Spanish-speaking people have been in the Southwest for over 350 years. Some of the villages north of Santa Fe, New Mexico, were founded in 1598. A century later Spanish settlements were made in Texas, and almost two centuries later, in California. In each of these three areas, distinctive Spanish cultures developed. Another influence was the relation of the Spanish to the many different Indian groups with which they came in contact. "Until about the middle of the nineteenth century, the *californios,* the *nuevo mexicanos,* and the *texanos* went their separate cultural ways, held together only slightly by, at first, the slender ties of Spain, and later, briefly, by the uncertain and flimsy bonds of independent Mexico." [9]

From the turn of the eighteenth century to the Mexican-American war, intergroup relations ranged from individual friendships to competition, an-tagonism, and, in many instances, violent conflict rising out of ethnic and racial distinctions. The Mexican society was sharply divided between upper-class

---

[6] *Ibid.,* p. 25.

[7] See Heller, *Mexican American Youth,* p. 11, for analysis of this statute, public law 78, and its termination.

[8] *Ibid.,* p. 12.

[9] We are indebted to Prof. George I. Sanchez, of the University of Texas, for supplying "Spanish-speaking People in the Southwest—A Brief Historical Review" (mimeographed), which has been drawn upon in this section.

property owners and peons. The invader-immigrant Anglos as individuals often competed and sometimes came in conflict with the upper-class Mexicans for economic gain; however, there were many who cooperated with the ruling Mexican elements and through intermarriage became part of Mexican society. Both upper-class Mexicans and Americans considered the peons an inferior, servile class. With the increasing infiltration of Americans, however, relations between Mexican and American became more antagonistic. In Texas, where by 1836 Americans far outnumbered Mexicans, this antagonism expressed itself in a successful revolution resulting in the formation of the Republic of Texas.

By the treaty of Guadalupe-Hidalgo, terminating the Mexican-American War, all the Mexican territory north of the Rio Grande became part of the United States. From this point on, American influence became dominant over Spanish-Mexican; some upper-class Mexicans attempted to join American society; the poorer and illiterate Mexicans became a distinct ethnic minority, notwithstanding the fact that they were now citizens of the United States. The antagonistic character of Anglo-Mexican relations is reflected in the terms "gringo" and "greaser," which each group came to apply to the members of the other, with contemptuous implication. In popular usage before the conquest, "gringo" referred to any foreigner who spoke Spanish with an accent. The term "greaser" referred to a native Mexican or a native Spanish-American, and was originally applied disdainfully by the Americans of the Southwestern United States to Mexicans.

Given this situation against the setting of the "trigger-fingered" frontier, it was not surprising that violence should frequently arise. Paul S. Taylor in his study of a border community testified to many instances of violence from both groups. He cites the comment of a local official: "Undoubtedly robberies and murders by Mexicans have continually been perpetrated in Texas, but in retaliation Americans have committed terrible outrages upon citizens of Mexican origin." [10] McWilliams notes that "the first person to be lynched in California was a Mexican," and Leonardo Cordoba, Clement Lopez, and Jesus Saguaripa were lynched in Tucson . . . (1873), with a coroner's jury defending the lynching.[11]

In 1914 when diplomatic relations between Mexico and the United States were temporarily severed the Mexican Americans of South Texas were frequently identified with "the enemy." As Madsen reports

> A wall of fear grew between Anglo and Latin communities. Recalling this period, a Mexican-American said, "All our people were afraid. And here we were in our own country but the Anglos thought we were not from here." [12]

[10] Paul S. Taylor, *An American-Mexican Frontier* (Chapel Hill: University of North Carolina Press, 1934), p. 65.
[11] Carey McWilliams, *North From Mexico* (Philadelphia: J. B. Lippincott Co., 1949), pp. 127–128.
[12] Madsen, *The Mexican-Americans of South Texas*, p. 9.

Dominance was achieved by military aggression and by Anglo-American astuteness in seizing economic advantage. After the annexation of Texas land speculators were able to buy up land confiscated for unpaid taxes. In 1877, a 3,027-acre original Mexican land grant whose Mexican American owner was in tax arrears was sold by the sheriff to an Anglo for fifteen dollars. The boom in land speculation continued until 1930.[13]

Differentiation

PHYSICAL DIFFERENCES The "racial" composition of the population of Mexico has been in this century approximately 10 percent white, 60 percent mestizo (mixed Indian and white) and 30 percent Indian.[14] Since the immigrants to the United States have been more numerous from the latter two population elements, especially the mestizo, it is not surprising that the results of the United States Census of 1930, enumerating the Mexican stock by racial designation as "white" and "colored" for the first and only time, showed less than 5 percent as "white," 65,968 out of 1,422,533 total Mexican stock listed.[15] This considerable admixture of Indian traits does not have any significance in relation to behavior capacities or traits, since there is no evidence that Indians are inferior in innate capacity. The mestizo cultures are more Latin-American than Indian. The Indian strain does, however, give the Mexican-American group a darker appearance. In the earlier days, this color visibility affected Anglo attitudes toward Mexicans. Writing about race consciousness in 1930, Gamio stated,

> The darkest-skinned Mexican experiences almost the same restrictions as the Negro, while a person of medium-dark skin can enter a second-class lunchroom frequented also by Americans of the poorer class, but will not be admitted to a high-class restaurant. A Mexican of light-brown skin as a rule will not be admitted to a high-class hotel, while a white cultured Mexican will be freely admitted to the same hotel, especially if he speaks English fluently.[16]

Thus Mexican Americans are not a homogeneous group in appearance, but are often identifiable. To the extent that they are predominantly now American born, they are also showing some physical changes, as have the children of other immigrants to the United States: increase in stature, hand length, and nasal index.[17]

[13] Ibid., pp. 5–6.
[14] Maurice R. Davie, World Immigration (New York: The Macmillan Co., 1936), p. 215. Also Encyclopedia Americana, 1960, p. 472.
[15] United States Census, 1930, Population, Vol. 2, pp. 27, 34.
[16] Manuel Gamio, Mexican Immigration to the United States (Chicago: University of Chicago Press, 1930), p. 53. By permission.
[17] Heller, Mexican American Youth, p. 29; and Marcus S. Goldstein, Demographic and Bodily Changes in Descendants of Mexican Immigrants (Austin: University of Texas, Institute of Latin American Studies, 1943).

Madsen quotes an uneducated Anglo (about 1960) as saying: "The Meskin's not a white man, but he's a hell of a lot whiter than a nigger."[18] A study of a California city of about the same date finds similar comparative attitudes on the part of dominants toward Mexican Americans and Negroes.[19] Madsen also points out that the South Texans whom he studied will only let the term "white" be used for an Anglo. He quotes one anglicized Mexican American as follows:

> I think like an Anglo and I act like an Anglo but I'll never look like an Anglo. Just looking at me, no one could tell if I am an American or one of those blasted Mexicans from across the river. It's hell to look like a foreigner in your own country.[20]

CULTURAL DIFFERENCES The value system of the Mexican Americans has been traditionally associated with the concept of *La Raza* (the race). In the sense this term is used it is nineteenth-century and has no relation to the racialism of North Europeans and American WASPS. Just as the French speak of themselves as a race, so *La Raza* is a cultural concept. It applies to all Latin-Americans who are united by cultural and spiritual bonds.[21] It implies that God has planned a great destiny for this people, though it never may be attained because of the individual sins of its members. In other words it is a concept of peoplehood and of destiny, creating deep psychic bonds. One can see the same phenomenon among Jews and, in the early periods of American history, nordic Americans. The central character of the value system of *La Raza,* however, reflects in the Mexican Americans the long history of feudalism from Spain, oppression in Mexico, and discrimination in the United States. For most of the older generation it is a Catholicized fatalism.

Heller, in her study of the metropolitan second- and third-generation Mexican American youth, suggests that the sense of *La Raza* is no longer very significant, although her data show many of the behavioral values associated with this cultural ideal. Madsen in his study of the Mexican Americans in southern Texas still finds it significant.

Acceptance and appreciation of things as they are, says Madsen, constitute the primary values of *La Raza*. He quotes as an expression of the world view of the Mexican American:

> We are not very important in the universe. We are here because God sent us and we must leave when God calls us. God has given us a good way to live and we should try to see the beauty of His commands. We often fail for many are weak but we should try. There is much suffering but we should accept it for it comes from God. Life is sad but beautiful.[22]

[18] Madsen, *The Mexican-Americans of South Texas,* p. 11.
[19] Alphonso Pinkney, "Prejudice Toward Mexican and Negro Americans: A Comparison," *Phylon* (First Quarter, 1963), pp. 355 ff.
[20] Madsen, *The Mexican Americans of South Texas,* p. 8.
[21] *Ibid.,* p. 15.
[22] *Ibid.,* p. 17.

Because God controls events the Anglo orientation to and planning for the future is alien to the true member of *La Raza*. For him, honor, to behave like "a whole man," to maintain dignity and courtesy, to show respect and to fulfill his obligations to the family of his birth as to the one he founds, these are the core values.

RELIGION   Religion and culture are closely intertwined in the average Mexican American household. The presence of a family altar in the house symbolizes the family-centeredness of the culture as much as it does the religious faith.[23] However, as Ruth Tuck points out, Mexican American Catholicism is not church-centered and she found in *Descanso* that men rarely went to church.[24] Conservative Mexican Americans may still name their sons Jesus, which seems peculiar and even sacriligious to Anglo Protestants. "We live with God while the Anglos lock Him in to Heaven." [25]

LANGUAGE   The principal language for Mexican Americans, whether first, second, or third generation, is some variant of Spanish. This is often a local dialect intermixed with hispanized English words, and there is considerable variation: from "Tex-Mex" to the Spanish spoken by the hispanos of New Mexico to that of the largely generational dialect, *Pachuco,* spoken by Mexican American urban youth.[26]

The greatest deficiency in the English of Mexican Americans is in informal English. Often they hesitate to speak English at all if they do not know it well as to do so might be discourteous. They do not encourage Anglos to speak Spanish to them. Heller suggests that they may perceive the imperfect Spanish of an Anglo as "talking down" to them. Also, they seem to be embarrassed for the Anglo for his poor Spanish.[27]

Spanish is spoken in the home as long as one identifies with the Mexican American community. Some parents speak some English to their children "so that it won't be so hard for them in school," and upper-class Mexican Americans pride themselves on perfect Spanish and English.

INSTITUTIONAL ROLES   Next to family roles, "manliness," (*machismo*) is the most important community ideal. To be a "whole man" involves a high degree of individuality, yet this is within the family framework as every Mexican American male is expected to represent his family with honor at all times. The manly role makes him sensitive to any authority or competition which would darken his public image with threat of devaluation or failure. According to Madsen, "ideally the Latin male acknowledges only the authority of his father and God. In case of conflict between these two sources of authority he should

---

[23] Madsen seems to indicate that the family altar is less conspicuous as one goes up the status scale of Mexican American society. It ceases to be in the living room and may rather be in the mother's bedroom. *Ibid.,* pp. 35–41.

[24] Ruth D. Tuck, *Not With the Fist* (New York: Harcourt, Brace and Co., 1946), p. 153. See also Heller, *Mexican American Youth,* pp. 17–19.

[25] Madsen, *Mexican-Americans of South Texas,* p. 7.

[26] Heller, *Mexican American Youth,* pp. 29–30, 59–62.

[27] *Ibid.,* p. 30.

side with his father. No proper father, however, would act counter to God's will for such behavior would make him less of a man." [28]

This sensitive pride leads the Mexican American to avoid associations that threaten him; to be punctilious about indebtedness, to avoid accepting charity, to occasionally seek personal revenge, to feel that the obligations of affiliation with formal organizations weakens his independence.[29]

Great value is put on male sexual virility with the resulting double standard of sexual morality. Girls are carefully guarded by their mothers and brothers, and wives by their husbands. The approved roles for women are within the household and the family. The Mexican American wife is expected to show her husband absolute respect. Her fulfilment is in helping her husband achieve his goals as he sees fit.

Father and mother alike share the task of teaching children how to conduct themselves. Proper relations to others in Mexican American society involve patterns of respect and formal courtesy. An "educated" person is one who has been well trained as a social being.

> As long as a Latin conforms to the rules of proper conduct, he is entitled to his own beliefs. One may resent another's actions but not another's opinions or interpretations. The view is expressed in the Mexican American saying, *Cada abeza es un mundo* (Each head is a world unto itself). A person may think as he pleases but he should not try to impose his ideas on anybody else. These concepts of propriety are a major factor in the hostility felt toward missionaries and public health workers who are trying to change Mexican American beliefs. A distinguished Latin citizen voiced his opinion on what he called "brain washing," "Americans have abandoned geographic imperialism, but to them mental imperialism is a wide open field." [30]

The Stabilization of Dominance

In broad outline, the process of adjustment of the Mexican immigrant group follows the pattern delineated for European immigrant groups. For the initial period, the studies of Paul Taylor in four different areas of the Southwest are the most extensive.[31]

Mexican immigrants in the Southwest found employment in unskilled occupations, chiefly as agricultural laborers. Their wages, in common with agricultural labor generally, were low—usually lower than that paid any Anglos

---

[28] Madsen, *Mexican-Americans of South Texas*, p. 18.
[29] *Ibid.*
[30] *Ibid.,* p. 21.
[31] Paul S. Taylor, *Mexican Labor in the United States* (Berkeley: University of California Press, Publication in Economics, Vol. 6, 1928). In this volume are included three monographs: No. 1 on Imperial Valley, California; No. 2 on the Valley of South Platte, Colorado; and No. 5 on Dimmit County, South Texas. Taylor also wrote *An American-Mexican Frontier* (Chapel Hill: University of North Carolina Press, 1934). While Taylor, an economist, was primarily interested in the labor situations of the Mexicans, his field of inquiry embraced the general pattern of social relations between the Anglos and Mexicans.

employed in the same kind of work. Employers often maintained that this differential was justified because Anglo laborers were more productive than Mexicans. These Mexican laborers were slow to become unionized. Earlier efforts at organization, opposed strongly by the agricultural employers, were generally unsuccessful. While by the late 20's an increasing number of the Mexicans were buying or building homes of their own, they did not buy farm land for themselves, and they showed little interest in sharecropping. Few opportunities existed for Mexicans in higher-ranking occupations, both because they were not equipped to fill them and because of the discrimination against their employment in occupations involving Anglo fellow workers or serving Anglo trade. Some Mexican clerks were employed in low-priced stores for the purpose of encouraging Mexican trade.

The housing of the more settled Mexicans was of the lowest standard; and that of Mexicans employed in agriculture of a nondescript variety, sometimes haymows or improvised shelters in the woods. In spite of these poor economic conditions, Mexicans were not often on relief rolls, partly because of their tradition of mutual aid. Nor did Taylor find their criminal arrests more than proportionate.[32]

Until World War II the usual devices were employed to keep Mexican Americans in subordinate status.

Spatial Segregation

In towns and cities with any sizable Mexican American population there are still today the residential enclaves where the majority of this ethnic group are concentrated. Mexican Americans refer to them as "colonia" and dominants as "Mextown" or "little Mexico." In 1954 John H. Burma estimated that about three-fourths of all the Mexican Americans in the United States lived in *colonia*.[33]

Discrimination

Whereas there were few legal restrictions against Mexican Americans except in some counties, in subtle ways they were "kept in their place." The pattern of discrimination was summed up in an extensive study of Texas communities conducted during the war years.

Economic Discrimination. (1) Unfair employment practices forcing low economic status upon the majority of Latin Americans. (2) Discrimination exercised by both management and Labor unions in the admission and upgrading of Latin Americans. (3) Exploitation in agriculture. (4) Demand of growers for cheap labor carried to the extreme of favoring illegal seasonal influx workers, thereby denying employment opportunities to resident workers.

[32] Taylor, *An American-Mexican Frontier*, p. 250.
[33] John H. Burma, *Spanish-Speaking Groups in the United States* (Durham: The Duke University Press, 1954), p. 88.

Inequitable Educational Opportunities. (1) Arbitrary segregation in public schools. (2) Inability of working children to attend schools. (3) Lack of interest of school administrators in enrolling Latin American children and encouraging attendance. (4) Improperly trained teachers and inferior buildings and equipment.

Social and Civic Inequalities. (1) Refusal of service in some public places of business and amusement. (2) Denial of the right to vote in some counties. (3) Denial of the right to rent or own real estate in many cities. (4) Denial of the right to serve on juries in some counties. (5) Terrorism on the part of law-enforcement officers and others.[34]

Minority Adaptations to Dominance

The Subcommunity

Ae we have pointed out the *colonia* is the center of life for a majority of Mexican Americans. A classic study of one such community is Tuck's account of "Descanso" in the early 40's.[35]

Descanso is a small Southwestern city set in a fertile valley, half cupped by mountains. It is a railroad junction, surrounded by large-scale farm operations. "Railroads and ranching...set the tempo" of its economy. While it lacks the clear-cut ecological pattern of Eastern cities, the tendency is for the east and north sections toward the mountains to be the preferred native residential section. The south section is the dilapidated area of shacks and cheap bungalows now inhabited about equally by Mexican-Americans, poor native Americans, and Negroes. It is in the western section, the Monticello district, that the Mexican colony lives. To quote Dr. Tuck:

> On both sides of Monticello Avenue, a small Mexican business district has grown up—cafés, grocery stores, *cantinas,* a barber shop, a bakery, a drugstore, and a couple of *tortillerias.* The hiring and provisioning agency for the Santa Fe is also here. Much of the life of the Mexican-American colony centers on this street, and the colony itself is larger, more homogeneous, and more progressive than the smaller group in Spring Valley. The district has one or two Italian families, a few Filipinos, and recently the area has experienced a considerable invasion of Negro families from its east end, close to the railroad tracks. Practically no Anglo-Americans live in the heart of the district, although, toward the north, Mexican-Americans of higher economic status are beginning to occupy houses on streets with Anglo-Americans.[36]

The social life of the *colonia* is rooted primarily in the family system, secondarily in the church. The family system follows the usual Latin patriarchal form: subordination of women, although much reverence for mothers; subordi-

[34] Pauline R. Kibbe, *Latin-Americans in Texas* (Albuquerque: University of New Mexico Press, 1946), pp. 271–272.
[35] Tuck, *Not With the Fist.*
[36] *Ibid.,* p. 5. By permission of the publisher.

nation of children, with differential training of the sexes in line with patriarchal ideals; permanency in family relations; strict parental protection for girls, together with a double standard of sex morality. "Most of the social life of the *colonia* is essentially informal in nature." [37] The *colonia* reinforces the pride in the subculture.

This self-respecting pride in one's background and origins strikes a rather new note in American immigrant histories. The man who changed his name, denied his background, and was ashamed of the old folks with the accented English and foreign ways is a commonplace type among other immigrant groups. He is a distinct rarity among Mexican-Americans, except for some badly confused adolescents; and his actions, rather than being admired as a hallmark of success are described as "his misfortune," as though he had a strange affliction. "Assimilation! I am tired of that word," said one of the *colonia's* leaders. "Fusion is what we want—the best of both ways." A young American of Mexican descent, speaking at a club luncheon, was told by a gentleman of Swedish ancestry: "We Scandinavians get ahead because we dropped our old-country ways." "Perhaps that was your misfortune," was the reply.[38]

While there are Mexican Americans who can honestly say they have never encountered any of the cruder forms of discrimination and others who experience them only infrequently, still "it is safe to say that the entire population . . . is aware of barriers against it." [39]

A young college graduate said—"Discrimination? Of course, all of my life, since I was a little boy. I make my way, I enjoy myself, I have good Anglo-American friends, in spite of it, but I never forget."

An extremely successful man [Mexican] by colony standards, said: "I don't know why it is, but I've had to fight ever since I first crossed the threshold of a public school. Even now, I seldom sit down in a restaurant without expecting the waiter to come up and say, 'Sorry, we can't serve you.' I'm careful to go where I know such things won't happen, but I still half expect them." [40]

The Parallel Status System

Descanso's *colonia* falls into a two-class division: the "big people" and their satellites; and the commoner folk. "The top group contains some persons whose origins in Mexico were 'folk,' many quasi immigrants whose parents had such origins, and an increasing number of second-generation persons who have risen within the structure of the *colonia*." [41] The criteria of class mobility are much

---

[37] *Ibid.,* p. 157.
[38] *Ibid.,* p. 134. By permission of the publishers.
[39] *Ibid.,* p. 52.
[40] *Ibid.,* pp. 52–53. By permission of the publishers.
[41] *Ibid.,* p. 133.

the same as with other people, with one exception. Higher education, higher status occupations, money, and service to the group raise one's status. The exception seems to be pride in being a Mexican.

Madsen gives a picture of a more differentiated status system in the Rio Grande community he studied.[42] At the top of the status structure is an old hispano elite, descendents of Spanish land grant families. A man's influence and prestige, irrespective of money, rests on his family and his ability to live up to the role he inherited. As one middle-class Mexican American is quoted as saying, "They are the real Texans and they are gentlemen." [43] They are devout Catholics and educate their children in parochial schools, private colleges, and sometimes universities abroad. The elite think of social stratification on the basis of caste rather than class. Other classes of Mexican Americans are viewed as peasants, tradesmen, or upstarts. Madsen finds in the community of "Magic Valley," five of the six status levels that Warner and his associates found in "Yankee City." There is no lower upper class, as the Mexicans who have risen since migration in this community have only attained upper middle class status.

Marginal Men

Madsen finds self-made Mexican Americans who have made it to the upper strata of Anglo American society in South Texas. They are owners of large business establishments, important ranchers, lawyers, and doctors. They are frequently ashamed of the poverty and superstitions of Mexican Americans. They seek residence in Anglo districts if they live in towns, and membership in recognized clubs. But according to Madsen, they are still sensitive and afraid to relax their defenses.[44]

Organizational Patterns

Before World War II Mexican Americans were weak in organizational structure. Tuck describes the situation in Descanso.

> The proliferation of societies, clubs, and associations which distinguishes American life has not yet intruded on the *colonia*. The number of kin of each family is extensive enough to provide a wide circle of friends. There is one large men's organization, the Confederation of Mexican Societies, a council of four mutual insurance groups, whose chief activity is to celebrate two Mexican national holidays. It rather vaguely acts for the "economic, moral, and cultural improvement of the Mexican people." Its constitution specifically restricts any civic activity which is political in nature. From time to time, other organizations had arisen which were more definitely political; however, "most of them have had brief, fitful lives." [45]

[42] Madsen, *The Mexican-Americans of South Texas*, Chs. 4 and 5.
[43] *Ibid.*, p. 42.
[44] *Ibid.*, p. 43.
[45] Tuck, *Not With the Fist*, p. 160.

Many Mexican Americans were discouraged from contemplating political action because of discrimination in various places through the poll tax and the disqualification of Mexican Americans for voting in Democratic primaries.[46] In the 1940's Ernesto Galarza complained that

> Mexicans are a political non-entity in the U.S. . . . They keep clear of political obligations and therefore do not take advantage of political opportunities. . . . Therefore all pleas to the state governor, the President of the United States, the legislature or Congress must be based on considerations of high human sentiment. In the American political system, however, such sentiments have always been found to fare much better when supported by precinct organization and votes in the ballot box.[47]

Dominant Attitudes Toward Mexican Americans

As is characteristic of dominant groups, southwestern Anglos tended to play down the extent of their discrimination and to rationalize what could not be denied by invoking an unfavorable stereotype of the Mexican American. Tuck put it thus:

> There is nothing Descanso will deny more stoutly than any intention of keeping its Mexican-Americans disadvantaged in order to derive an economic gain from their position. That is why it resents the words caste or semicaste being applied to its practices. Descanso argues, rather, that the bulk of its Mexican-Americans are so low in type that they could not profit by advantage. It seems rather odd to prove this point by making sure that they have continued inferior advantage, but Descanso sees no hint of a vicious circle in this procedure. The "low type" of Mexican, says Descanso, is getting about what he deserves. If he encounters segregated schooling, segregation in use of public facilities, unequal employment opportunities, unequal pay for equal work, or prejudiced law enforcement and justice—what of it? Descanso does not see that, in making these and a thousand other decisions, it is casting a vote that amends, not only the rights and liberties of a certain group, but the very nature of its democratic procedure. Descanso would not think of revising a certain historic document so that it guaranteed life, liberty, and the pursuit of happiness somewhat more to "high types" than to "low types." No, says Descanso, we are just making a few social distinctions, several million of which cannot possibly affect a democracy. You have to recognize, argues Descanso, that some people are just born inferior, generation after generation. As the leader of a church study group put it, "there are always hewers of wood and drawers of water." [48]

In a study of a south Texas community, Simmons found that the Anglo stereotype of the "mexicano" emphasized his inferiority, which seemed to the

[46] Kibbe, *Latin-Americans in Texas,* p. 227.
[47] Ernesto Galarza, "The Mexican American: A National Concern," *Common Ground,* 9 (Summer 1949), pp. 27–38.
[48] Tuck, *Not With the Fist,* pp. 53–54. By permission of the publishers.

Anglos self-evident.[49] He is identified with menial labor, but as a worker is considered improvident, undependable, childlike and indolent. Other features of the stereotype are uncleanliness, drunkenness, criminality, and spitefulness toward Anglos. Viewing the Mexican American in this unfavorable light, Anglos feel justified in their practices of exclusion. Even the favorable features of the stereotype reinforce the Anglo notion that "mexicanos" belong in subordinate status.

> Among those [traits] usually meant to be complimentary are the beliefs that all Mexicans are musical and always ready for a fiesta, that they are very "romantic" rather than "realistic" (which may have unfavorable overtones as well), and that they love flowers and plants and can grow them under the most adverse conditions. Although each of these beliefs may have a modicum of truth, it may be noted that they can reinforce Anglo-American images of Mexicans as childlike and irresponsible since they support the notion that Mexicans are capable only of subordinate status.[50]

In a study made in the 1950's which compares prejudice in Eastern, Midwestern, Southern, and California communities, Robin Williams, Jr., found that in the California community, where Mexicans do live, only 37 percent of the informants held a low and derogating stereotype of Mexican Americans, whereas in the Southern city studied where most respondents could not have had any contact with this minority the stereotype was endorsed by 79 percent of the informants. Furthermore, in the Southern city no differentiation was made between Mexicans and Mexican Americans.[51]

Williams describes stereotypes as "petrified expectations that are relatively unyielding to social change." [52] They increase the vulnerability of minorities and they also increase the anxieties of dominants as numbers of the minority increase, or become more visible; and the identity crises of minority members in the face of stereotypes, especially for youth, are particularly stressful.

The "Zoot Suit" Riot of 1943

One of the severest outbreaks against Mexican Americans occurred during the Second World War at a time when Mexico was our ally. It was the first of a series of riots that summer which in part reflected the tension of a country at war.

> The anti-Mexican riots in Los Angeles ranged from June 3, 1943, until June 9. This was wartime; a nearby naval base made Los Angeles the mecca for sailors'

[49] Ossie G. Simmons, "The Mutual Images and Expectations of Anglo-Americans and Mexican-Americans," *Daedulus: Journal of American Academy of Arts and Sciences,* Spring, 1961, 90: 286–299.
[50] *Ibid.,* p. 292. Reprinted by permission of the Editors of *Daedalus.*
[51] Robin Williams, Jr., *Strangers Next Door: Ethnic Relations in American Communities* (Englewood Cliffs, N.J.: Prentice-Hall, 1964), p. 75.
[52] *Ibid.,* p. 39.

leaves. The riots were touched off on June 3 by two incidents. Some servicemen walking through a deteriorated street in a Mexican section of the city were beaten up by a gang of Mexican boys. In a nearby precinct on the same evening some Mexican boys returning from a "club" conference at the police station on how to avoid gang strife were beaten up by a gang of non-Mexican boys. It does not seem as if the two incidents were connected. The police took no immediate action, but then after their regular duty was over, a so-called "vengeance squad" set out to clean up the gang that had attacked the sailors. They found no one to arrest, but great newspaper publicity was given to the incidents and to the policemen who had made the fruitless raid.

The following night about 200 sailors hired a fleet of 20 taxicabs and cruised the Mexican quarter. The Mexican adolescent boys had a fad of wearing long, draped jackets (zoot suits). Four times the taxicab brigade stopped when it sighted a Mexican boy in a zoot suit and beat up the boys, leaving them lying on the pavement. There was no mobilization of police. One police car did intercept the caravan, and nine sailors were taken into custody, but no charges were preferred against them. In the morning papers the war news was pushed off the front page with stories of the night before on a triumphal note of the sailor's move to clean up "zoot-suited roughnecks." The third night, June 5, scores of sailors, soldiers, and marines marched through the Mexican quarter, four abreast, stopping and threatening anyone wearing zoot suits. No sailors were arrested, either by the police, the shore patrol, or the Military Police, although twenty-seven Mexican boys were arrested. In various bars Mexicans were beaten up or their jackets torn off and ripped up. The police announced that any Mexicans involved in rioting would be arrested.

On the night of June 6 six carloads of sailors cruised through the area, beating up teenage Mexicans and wrecking establishments. The police came after them in mopping-up operations and arrested the boys who had been beaten up. In the morning forty-four severely beaten Mexican boys were under arrest.

Whipped up by the press, which warned that the Mexicans were about to riot with broken bottles as weapons and would beat sailors' brains out with hammers, the excitement erupted and two days of really serious rioting occurred, involving soldiers, sailors, and civilians, who invaded motion picture houses, stopped trolley cars, and beat up the Mexicans they found, as well as a few Filipinos and Negroes. At midnight on June 7 the military authorities declared Los Angeles out of bounds for military personnel. The order immediately slowed down the riot. On June 8 the mayor stated that "sooner or later it will blow over," and the chief of police announced the situation "cleared up." However, rioting went on for two more days. Editorials and statements to the press lamented the fact that the servicemen were called off before they were able to complete the job. The district attorney of an outlying county stated that "zoot suits are an open indication of subversive character." And the Los Angeles City Council adopted a resolution making the wearing of zoot suits a misdemeanor.[53]

The role of the police is to be understood only if one presumes that their refraining from interference was deliberate and related to an entirely different

[53] McWilliams, *North From Mexico,* pp. 244–253. Adapted by the authors.

matter. At the time of the riots a police officer was on trial in the courts for charges of brutality. Shortly after the riots, according to Carey McWilliams, a Hollywood police captain told a motion picture director that the police had touched off the riots to give a break to their colleague in demonstrating the necessity for harsh police methods. As a matter of fact, the charges against the officer were dismissed a month later.

The use of the stereotyped image of the zoot suit appeared in all the publicity and what was simply an adolescent fad was linked in the minds of the readers with the characterizations "gang," "roughneck," "subversive," and so forth. The press and the radio leaped on the bandwagon and were largely responsible in their unanimity for enflaming the population.

The tone of the press clearly reflects the war psychology and the support of servicemen. The servicemen themselves were young men away from home, uprooted from the normal community controls in the anonymous and sex-segregated climate of military life. Many of them engaged in actions that would have been unthinkable in their home environment.

The effect of World War II was not, however, only negative to Mexican Americans. The agencies of the federal government brought pressures to bear on employment and on local areas during the war to improve the positions of minorities. The Fair Employment Practices Commission did make for less discrimination in jobs for the duration of the war. Through the Office of the Coordinator of Inter-American Affairs committees were formed to improve relations between Anglos and Mexican Americans. Even more important, this office set up local community service clubs to "stimulate grass roots democracy." Many communities succeeded in special local programs for better recreational facilities, return of dropouts to school, health surveys, and other local issues. Such ameliorative measures certainly stimulated many individuals and communities so that there was some net gain. But at best this was only a potential underpinning for more lively participation and real voice for the future.[54]

Post World War II and the Challenge to Dominance

Mexican Americans were in the armed services in World War II and later in Korea. Immediately following the world war many veterans began to take active roles in community leadership. Tuck cites one such person:

> A discharged private in the infantry said: "I'm glad I'm going to have one of those little buttons to wear in my coat. And a flock of foliage to put on my uniform for Armistice Day parades. I'm going into politics. There's seven or eight of us, all from Southern California, who've talked it over. Things are going to happen in these colonies, and we're going to see that they do." [55]

[54] *Ibid.,* p. 279.
[55] Tuck, *Not With The Fist,* p. 221. Reproduced by permission of the publishers.

Many veterans were able to buy better homes, continue their education under the G.I. Bill, and were often able to obtain better employment. "Some even managed to get chosen, appointed or elected to public office." [56] In Los Angeles, four years after the zoot suit riots the first American of Mexican ancestry since 1881 was elected to a municipal office.[57]

Growth in Organizations

One of the most well known Mexican American organizations today is LULAC, the League of United Latin-American citizens. Although founded in 1929, it was more in the nature of a confederation of local social and civic clubs. The effectiveness as well as specific goals varied from one locality to another. It tended until recently to welfare and "betterment" type programs: encouraging youth to finish high school, "citizenship" education, etc. The organization has been ambivalently evaluated. Kibbe felt it was a strong organization contributing to improvement for Mexican Americans in Texas.[58] Heller feels that its scope is limited.[59] In a study of El Paso it is described as being the major vehicle for promoting Mexican American interests in the 1950's, but the author of this study, too, finds its scope limited.[60] The criticisms imply too little concern with political action, which is an understandable aspect of a long-established organization whose leadership is the older and more established segment of the Mexican American community. A 1967 article in *The Reporter* states, however, that LULAC now vies with other more specifically politically oriented organizations in bombarding state and federal officials with grievances.[61]

Political Participation

One of the outstanding developments of the past ten years has been the growth in political participation of Mexican Americans. The two main organizations, the Mexican American Political Association (MAPA) and the Political Association of Spanish-speaking Organizations (PASO) are more militant than LULAC and more directly involved in politics. Working together these organizations have achieved significant gains and their potential is even greater. They have been concerned with equal employment opportunities, with

[56] Raul Morin, *Among the Valiant: Mexican Americans in World War II and Korea* (Los Angeles: 1963), p. 278.
[57] See Beatice W. Griffith, "Viva Roybal—Viva America," *Common Ground*, 10 (Autumn 1949), pp. 61–70, for a description of the candidate and the mobilization of the Mexican American community for the election in which 15,000 new voters were registered.
[58] Kibbe, *Latin-Americans in Texas*, p. 264.
[59] Heller, *Mexican American Youth*, p. 100.
[60] William V. D'Antonio and William H. Form, *Influentials in Two Border Cities—A Study in Community Decision Making* (South Bend, Indiana: The University of Notre Dame Press, 1965), p. 245.
[61] Marvin Alisky, "Mexican-Americans Make Themselves Heard," *The Reporter* (February 9, 1967), pp. 45–48.

voter registration, and election of Mexican Americans to office. By 1951 there
were four councilmen of Mexican descent in Los Angeles. Mayors have been
elected in El Paso (1957) and in Crystal City, Tex., (1963). In El Paso the
election of a Mexican American did not alienate the business community, but
in Crystal City there was a split between Anglo economic power and Mexican
American political power. Economic reprisals were taken against some Mexican
American members of the City Council.[62]

A record number of Mexican Americans voted in the 1966 elections. Alisky
states, "many believe that the 1966 voting was a direct way of fighting the indifference of some conservative Democrats," and he forecasts that "as the
Mexican Americans become more politically articulate, the size of their voting
age population continues to rise. By 1975 there will be almost 20 million Latin
American U.S. citizens. In 1972 and even in the 1968 presidential elections the
Latins intend to get out the vote." [63]

Union Organization

In the 1940's and '50's there were sporadic attempts to organize by Mexican
Americans. In 1944 the CIO International Union of Mine, Mill and Smelter
Workers succeeded before the War Labor Board in eliminating discriminatory
wage rates. The San Antonio teamsters union aided in the Crystal City election.
But the critical problem for many Mexican Americans is that of low wages for
agricultural labor. Although there had been an attempt to organize grape pickers
in California in the 1930's these efforts were defeated. In 1966, however, a
successful strike was organized and carried out in the California vineyards of
Shenley industries.[64] Efforts to organize 1,500 farm workers, seeking a $1.25
minimum wage, in the lower Rio Grande Valley has received national attention
and created conflict with the Roman Catholic Bishop of Texas who disciplined
a priest active in organization efforts.

Mexican Americans Go to Court

Of what is probably the greatest significance, overt segregation of Mexican
children in the public schools has been eliminated to all intents and purposes. The
federal court cases in California, Arizona, and Texas—both those that came to trial
and those which did not—have made it abundantly clear that American children of
Mexican descent cannot be segregated in the public schools. Even where school
authorities have sought to use pseudo-pedagogical reasons for separating "Anglos"
from "Latins" the courts have either condemned the practices or have made it
patent that the proof of the pudding would be in the eating, thus discouraging the
use of subterfuges to cover up "racial" segregation. This break-through in school

[62] "Revolt of the Mexicans," *Time* (April 12, 1963), p. 25.
[63] Alisky, *Mexican-Americans Make Themselves Heard*, p. 48.
[64] "Another Civil Rights Headache—Plight of Mexican-Americans," *U.S. News and World Report* (June 6, 1966), p. 46.

cases has served as precedent for the attack on segregation in other public services, with wide-spread success. In all areas there still remain many fronts on which the civil liberties battle will have to be fought. Recalcitrant communities (rather, recalcitrant governing boards) will seek "legal" ways to perpetuate segregation—in education the devices will include "neighborhood schools," "free choice" in the selection of a school, "ability grouping," "special" provision for migrant children, and the like. Most of these subterfuges will be the subject not of court action but of political action, as has been demonstrated already in a number of communities.

In the area of civil liberties, the *Pete Hernández Case* (Supreme Court of the United States, No. 406, October Term, 1953) has not drawn the attention it deserves, for it is significant not only for Spanish-Mexicans in the United States but for all groups that are treated as a class apart. This case, about a "Mexican" who was tried and sentenced by a jury in a county where "Mexicans" had never served on juries, was carried on up to the Supreme Court of the United States by lawyers of Mexican descent who were financed entirely by funds raised by people of Mexican descent. The unanimous judgment of the Court, written by the Chief Justice, finding for the plaintiff, included the following:

> Throughout our history differences in race and color have defined easily identifiable groups which have at times required the aid of the courts in securing equal treatment under the laws. But community prejudices are not static, and from time to time other differences from the community norm may define other groups which need the same protection. Whether such a group exists within a community is a question of fact. When the existence of a distinct class is demonstrated, and it is further shown that the laws, as written or as applied, single out that class for different treatment not based on some reasonable classification, the guarantees of the Constitution have been violated. The Fourteenth Amendment is not directed solely against discrimination due to a "two-class theory"—that is, based upon differences between "white" and Negro.

This far-reaching decision, handed down two weeks before the *Brown v. Board of Education* (segregation of Negroes) case, laid down a principle on which the Americans of Mexican descent (as well as others) can rely for protection against discrimination and the mistreatment of their class in every area of official public endeavor. The Hernandez case served another cause of equal importance: it gave heart to the "Mexican" leadership, a leadership whose sights had been raised with their victory in the previous Mendez and Delgado (school segregation) cases.[65]

The Outlook

That Mexican Americans are making themselves felt is signified by the Presidential establishment, in 1967, of a federal office for Mexican American Affairs. This will increase the lines of communication to the national government, and, combined with the increasing political activity of Mexican Americans, should have some broad effect on improving the position of this group in the national image and in the access to opportunity. We may anticipate that

[65] From an unpublished summary of recent trends prepared for the authors by George I. Sanchez, University of Texas.

for a time this will increase conflict, as the economic position of the majority of Mexican Americans is still very low. The Office of Economic Opportunity has encouraged self-help programs and pressure channels have been made visible to many of the Spanish-speaking poor. As two recent researchers in the ongoing University of California study of Mexican Americans point out,

> Local poverty programs are giving Mexicans a high degree of self-consciousness. And the immediate result of nearly every poverty program in nearly every community is social conflict. Sometimes the Anglo power structure must be fought in order to get assistance, as is happening in South Texas. Sometimes the spoils must be divided with other minorities.[66]

Some of the problems that face the Mexican American group in addition to wishing a proportionate share in the benefits of the national society cannot be resolved merely by obtaining a political voice. Probably the most important of these may be their relation to the Negro population of the United States. In all status studies that have included both groups, the Mexican Americans rank next to the bottom, with Negroes at the bottom. Nevertheless, Negro protest has been a model for many Mexican American younger leaders. Traditionally Latins have had a very tolerant attitude toward "race" differences. Yet in the competition for improved place economically and statuswise they are thrown in conflict with Negro Americans. The Negro Americans have the advantage of being a larger and better organized minority. They do not have the pulls of a hereditary culture and language. In metropolitan centers like Los Angeles and New York the educational level of Negroes is higher than that of Spanish-speaking Americans, and Negroes are more willing to compete with dominants for jobs.[67] Many Mexican Americans have eschewed the militancy of the Negro protest model. Heller found that the Los Angeles youth whom she studied had no sense that Mexican Americans had in fact benefited from the Negro effort.[68]

For the present it would appear that subcultural pulls and competition in the larger society will hold most Mexican Americans to a pluralistic definition of their relation to the larger society of the United States. Because of their large numbers and potential political strength they may influence the total society toward a greater acceptance of ethnic pluralism.

Hispanos: A Variant

As we have noted, included in the population of the Southwest are those Spanish-speaking people who are descended from Spanish-Mexican lineage indigenous to the area at the time of the annexation, some of whose ancestry goes

---

[66] Joan W. Moore and Ralph Guzman, "The Mexican-Americans: New Wind from the Southwest," *The Nation* (May 30, 1966), p. 648.
[67] Pinkney, "Prejudice Toward Mexican and Negro Americans," p. 138.
[68] Heller, p. 101.

back to the sixteenth century. In view of the general statistical confusion concerning Americans of Latin ancestry, their numbers and proportion are difficult to establish. It is clear, however, that in New Mexico and southern Colorado a large proportion of the Spanish-speaking people derive from this hispano lineage as distinct from migrant Mexican lineage; in Texas and Southern California the situation is roughly reversed.

Hispanos in New Mexico

Hispanos comprise about half the population of the state. There are several counties where they number more than 80 percent of the population. Both Spanish and English are official languages in the state. Compared with the obvious minority status of immigrant Mexicans in other southwestern states, hispanos do not appear at first to be a minority at all. They are all citizens, and no efforts are made by Anglos to deny them civic privileges. All over New Mexico there are hispanos who participate actively in politics, and in counties where they predominate heavily they frequently run the government. Free and equal access to all public places is accorded all ethnic and racial elements—the Indians and the relatively few immigrant Mexicans, as well as the hispanos. In the entire Southwest region, New Mexico exhibits the least "racial" intolerance. The reason for New Mexico's distinctiveness in this connection appears to lie in the fact that through a long part of the state's history as United States territory, Anglos were a distinct numerical minority, and that, therefore, a pattern of racial tolerance was developed at the outset of Anglo-Hispano contact which has been strengthened by tradition. But beneath the surface of this substantial intergroup harmony lie subtle discriminations against the Spanish-speaking people of middle-class status and until recently the pitifully low welfare status of the lower-class hispanos.

The Hispanos of Rimrock [69]

Spanish *conquistadores* and other travelers, officials, and priests passed through this area from 1540 to the annexation. The present hispano settlement, however, descends from migrants from eastern New Mexico who settled in the region in the 1860's. They were scattered and relatively prosperous ranchers. Their largest village, Atrisco was founded in 1882. Since the 1920's Atrisco's population has declined so that in 1950 it had only 89 residents. The other cultural groups in Rimrock are Indians (Zuni and Navajo), Mormons who came in the 1870's, and Texans who came in three small waves beginning at the turn of the century and ending in the 30's.

Anglo-hispano relations in Rimrock have been characterized by the ac-

---

[69] Evan Z. Vogt and Ethel M. Albert, *People of Rimrock: A Study of Values in Five Cultures* (Cambridge, Mass.: Harvard University Press, 1966). The Mormons of Rimrock are discussed in Chapter 4.

quisition of dominance by the Texans, not without conflict and abrasion of feeling at various times. Before migration the Texans had known Spanish-Americans only in the depressed position of field labor. Mexicans were considered as Negroes. The migrants were distressed to discover that their children would have to attend school in a hispano village, and that many county officials were "Mex." On the other hand, the hispanos were initially tolerant of the newcomers, many of whom they pitied because they were so poor.[70]

Friction began when Texans began to fence land and acquire title to acreage that had been traditionally open range. The first outbreak of hostility occurred in 1934 when a Spanish-American teacher, the son of one of the most respected families in Atrisco, was assigned to the newly constructed Homestead school in the Texan village. In the first weeks of school the windows were broken at night and signs appeared: "We Don't Want Any Chile Pickers for Teachers." Finally the schoolhouse was burned down. It is now the consensus of both groups that the fire was started by a Texan extremist.

By 1938 the high school was shifted from Atrisco to Homestead and a few years later the grade school in Atrisco was closed so that hispano children must now go to school in Homestead.

Another serious conflict occurred in 1947. It started with a fight between a Texan and a hispano at a dance; the fighting spread and continued for several days. This outbreak (nicknamed "the Spanish American war") has not been forgotten by either group. The antagonism between the groups remains, and such relations as there are between them are sustained by the pattern of employee-employer relations (hispanos always employed by Texans, never the reverse), pupil-teacher, storekeeper, and the tenuous associations at public dance places. Three couples in the Rimrock area represent Anglo-hispano intermarriage. One couple moved away. Both groups talk a great deal about the other two couples (two daughters of the former *patrón* of Atrisco each married a Texan). Texans tend to call the children half-breeds; hispanos refer to them as coyotes, meaning unpredictable—that is impossible to say how they will turn out. The children are being raised as Catholics and one Texan husband has converted to Catholicism.

Rural Hispanos: "Forgotten People"

In Northern New Mexico live a hispano folk who Sanchez calls "forgotten people." [71] Relatively isolated for generations, these rural hispanos developed a "folk" community life based on a subsistence, noncommercial agricultural economy organized along semicommunal lines. Over the years since annexation, the encroachment of Anglo "big business' agriculture whittled down their domain, so that their economic resources, coupled with their outmoded tech-

[70] *Ibid.*, p. 59.
[71] George I. Sanchez, *Forgotten People* (Albuquerque: University of New Mexico Press, 1940).

niques, brought them to a pitifully low economic level. Their culture did not so much change in its traditional character; rather it deteriorated as a result of their unequal struggle to survive in a modern civilization. Their low welfare status was reflected in New Mexico's statistics on health and literacy. In 1930 the state had a death rate of 13.8, almost 3 more deaths per 1,000 population than the nation at large. Its percentage of illiteracy in 1930 was 13.3, placing it third from the lowest among the states.[72]

These isolated rural hispano New Mexicans were not so much discriminated against, in the usual dominant-minority sense, as neglected. They were exploited in the impersonal ways characteristic of the free enterprise system where groups are unequally able to compete.

Tijerina's Republic of San Joaquin del Rio de Chama

A symptom of the circumstances of these northern depressed, rural hispanos is the revitalization or nativist movement of the Federal Alliance of Land Grants, which claims millions of acres to which titles are held from original Mexican land grants valid before annexation. This group, led by Reies Tijerina ("king tiger") wishes to establish a separate hispano state. To dramatize their cause members of this group marched to Santa Fe in the summer of 1966. In October they held a great rally in the National Forest in the foothills of the Rockies. The membership is estimated to be about 20,000.[73]

The governor of New Mexico met with leaders of the movement and felt there was little threat to stability and order from the group. The Santa Fe District Attorney, however, (who has a Spanish surname, but it is not clear whether he is hispano or Mexican American) is an active member of the American Legion and saw the movement as "communist," "subversive," and believed it had a great cache in the mountains of rifles and machine guns. Therefore in 1967 when an annual meeting of the Alliance was scheduled, again in the northern picnic preserves of the National Forest, he arrested several of the leaders and confiscated the membership lists. In retaliation fifteen Alliance members swept down on the hamlet of Tierra Amarilla and attempted to present a warrant for a citizen's arrest of the District Attorney. A fight ensued in which two policemen were wounded and a reporter taken as hostage by the Alliance members. The governor, who was out of state and may have been misinformed, panicked and called the National Guard. Two tanks were sent up into the hills, and after a five-day search in which fifty people, including women and children, were held for two days without food, water, or sanitary facilities, Tijerina was arrested. The charge is kidnaping, which in New Mexico is a capital offense.

[72] *Ibid.*, pp. 29–33. Sanchez cites 1930 figures but there is little evidence of much improvement of the isolated rural hispano.
[73] George W. Grayson, "Tijerina's Republic of San Joaquin del Rio de Chama," *The New Republic* (July 1, 1967), pp. 10–11.

The *average* annual income in these depressed northern counties is $1,100. This, of course, means that there are many with much lower income. In this mood of desperation Tijerina's movement has been attractive. It promises a "return" to justice, faith, salvation as expressed in the traditional feudal and pastoral life of the past. The Alliance is truly separatist. It has never sought the support of liberal Anglo-Americans. It is avowedly nonviolent (although the court house incident led to provocation of violence by one or both parties). Its members view Spanish Americans in office as "Tio Tomas's" (Uncle Tom's). Their disdain for things Anglo American is epitomized in their hatred of lawyers (who have defrauded them) and powdered milk. "Every time Spanish Americans begin acting up, they offer them powdered milk and eggs," says Tijerina.[74] He expresses a phrase of Professor Sanchez, undoubtedly a Spanish saying: "No queremos que nos den atole con el dedo": "we don't want to be fed mush with a finger." [75]

In Summary

Although many hispanos from the rural areas are migrating to the cities, they tend to be the newcomers who replace the upwardly mobile in the *colonia*. In the areas they leave there is an increasing population of older and very young people, with the consequent need for institutionalized Anglo-type services (welfare and health).[76]

At the present it seems that the cultural vitality of Spanish-speaking Americans is still very strong.[77] As long as spacial and social structural separation persist the attitudes of the old Spanish-Mexican elite will govern these old settled groups. An illustration is presented by Madsen.[78]

During a conversation with a wealthy Anglo, a Latin aristocrat made a subtle jest using the symbolism of Cervantes. When the Anglo looked confused rather than amused, the Latin said, "Of course, you have read Don Quixote," The Anglo brightened and replied, "No, but I saw the movie." The Latin later shrugged and commented to a friend, "What can you talk about to such people outside of cotton and the comics."

In summing up the situation of the Spanish-speaking Americans of the Southwest, we can at best quote Simmons: [79]

> This peculiar status of these Spanish-speaking peoples has made them unusually resistant to the superficial features of Americanization. Under no compulsion to repudiate the "old country" and to become 150 per cent American, they have clung

---

[74] *Ibid.*, p. 11.
[75] Moore and Guzman, "The Mexican-Americans: New Wind from the Southwest," p. 648.
[76] Lyle Saunders at the University of Denver made these observations for the authors.
[77] *Ibid.*
[78] Madsen, *The Mexican-Americans of South Texas,* p. 42.
[79] Simmons, "The Mutual Images and Expectations of Anglo-Americans and Mexican-Americans," p. 298.

tenaciously to their language and to other manifestations of their sense of identity. This in spite of widespread blind, misguided pressures by schools, employers, news media, and the like. In some public schools, children are still punished if they speak Spanish on the school grounds; and it is the exception, rather than the rule that by all reason should prevail, when a school system seeks to capitalize on the Spanish vernacular of its children. The pressures have been so great that, on occasion, a Spanish-Mexican leader has sought to champion the obliteration of this basic cultural heritage of his people. Fortunately, these instances have been rare and, in most cases, the proponent has recanted. One of the most encouraging of recent developments has been a conscious and vocal resistance to these pressures. This is in part the result of the action of the leaders, of whom there are many more with good education; in part this results from the increased maturity and sophistication of the entire society, which daily appreciates more the value of foreign languages; and in part the slowly spreading realization among educators that, instead of being a disastrous handicap, the Spanish mother-tongue of these Americans of Mexican descent can be transformed into a decided asset.

Topics for Projects and Discussion

1. Take the *Reader's Guide to Periodical Literature* for 1966 and 1967 and see how many articles are listed that deal with Mexican Americans, or Spanish Americans. Read a selection of these and assess the issues presented.
2. If there are Spanish-speaking Americans in your community make a survey among your friends and their parents of how they view this group. If you are of Spanish descent try to find out what your acquaintances and those of your parents' generation feel about Anglos.
3. If there are Spanish-speaking people in your area get your county figures on health and welfare for this group as compared with some other group for which they have figures. What does this tell you?
4. Do you know anything about Spanish culture as it is relevant to Spanish-speaking Americans? How would you find out?
5. What organizations (other than those mentioned in the text) or programs (local, state, federal) are dealing with the Spanish-speaking population? What are they doing?
6. How do you, your parents, your friends, and their friends feel about having neighbors of Mexican American descent? Is class more or less important than ethnicity?

Suggested Reading

Gamio, Manuel. *The Mexican Immigrant: His Life Story: A Community Study.* Berkeley and Los Angeles: The University of California Press, 1959.
>   *A classic study of Mexican immigrants, 1920–30, with personal life histories.*

Heller, Celia S. *Mexican American Youth: Forgotten Youth at the Crossroads.* New York: Random House, 1966.
>   *The conflicts and opportunity expectations of Mexican American Youth in Los Angeles.*

Madsen, William. *The Mexican-Americans of South Texas.* New York: Holt, Rinehart and Winston, 1964.

> *An anthropologist's examination of culture and mental health in the lower Rio Grande Valley.*

McWilliams, Carey. *North From Mexico.* Philadelphia: J. B. Lippincott, 1949.

> *An intelligent review by a writer of the relations between Anglo Americans and Americans of Mexican descent until the late 40's.*

Saunders, Lyle. *Cultural Differences and Medical Care: The Case of the Spanish-Speaking People of the Southwest.* New York: The Russell Sage Foundation, 1954.

> *A comprehensive analysis of the culture, social organization, and welfare of the Southwest's hispano population. Contains also a useful appendix on the demographic characteristics of this population.*

7

The Puerto Ricans
on the Mainland

At the close of the Spanish-American War Puerto Rico became a United States dependency, and Puerto Ricans became citizens of the United States. A modest migration began to New York City, which was the continental port for most ship passage from the island. In 1910 there were 500 people of Puerto Rican birth in New York.[1] By 1930 the number had risen to 45,000, by 1940 to 70,000. The group included some professional people and small business men, but the overwhelming majority were unskilled workers. A few settled in Brooklyn, but most settled in the East Harlem section of Manhattan, forming a sub-community, bordered on the north by Negro Harlem, and on the East by an Italian settlement and a declining population of Jews. This section of the city is called *El Barrio* by the Puerto Ricans and Spanish Harlem by the rest of New Yorkers.

Puerto Ricans have free migration as citizens; the initial upswing in migration was undoubtedly precipitated by the restriction on European immigration and propelled by the miserable conditions on the island from which they came.

Puerto Rico and the United States

Before 1932 the federal government assumed a laissez-faire attitude toward the island's economy, with the result that American investment in the development of Puerto Rico came from mainland private capital. The extent of absentee interest in the Puerto Rican economy was summarized in 1930 as follows:

> ... Sugar is 60 per cent absentee-controlled; fruit is 31 per cent, or more; tobacco is 85·per cent; banks are 60 per cent; railroads 60 per cent, or more; public utilities, 50 per cent; and steamship lines, approximately 100 per cent. There is no important

[1] Nathan Glazer and Daniel Patrick Moynihan, *Beyond the Melting Pot: The Negroes, Puerto Ricans, Jews, Italians, and Irish of New York City* (Cambridge, Mass.: The Harvard and M.I.T. Press, 1963), pp. 91–93.

source of wealth that is not partially in the hands of outsiders, and in some instances, such as steamships, outsiders control the entire business. Any estimate of Porto Rico dependence on absentees which places the total at less than 60 per cent of the island's wealth is certainly too low. Not all of the industries belong to absentees, but those which do not are so indebted to continental banks as to be virtually in their possession. Not all of the good land is in the hands of outsiders, but a large portion of it is, and much of the remainder is heavily mortgaged. And finally, there is that type of dependence on absentees which Porto Rico suffers, because of her long dependence on a monopolizing mother country, the necessity of importing vast quantities of food, clothing, machinery, chemicals and drugs. The control of the absentee is all but complete and with the aid of the Coastwise Shipping Act and the American Tariff bids fair to absorb all of the profitable enterprise.[2]

Under Franklin D. Roosevelt's early administrations, governmental effort at reorienting the Puerto Rican economy with more regard for the welfare of the islanders themselves was undertaken. The Puerto Rico Relief Administration was succeeded by the Puerto Rico Reconstruction Administration, which undertook irrigation projects, new highways, new schools, new houses and other development efforts. In 1942 Pattee said "There is little doubt that the present administration . . . postpones, at least, a collapse in Puerto Rican economy." [3]

"The Puerto Rico Reconstruction Administration . . . made definite progress but did not achieve that complete reform that was so desperately needed." [4] An indigenous reform program developed from the emergence of a new political party on the island, the Partido Popular Democrato. By somewhat faltering steps, democratic political institutions have been established, with increasing degrees of self-government permitted. On November 2, 1948, Puerto Rico elected its own governor for the first time. Except for the Presidential appointment of the auditor and supreme court justices, and for the power of the United States Congress to annul any law passed by the Insular Legislature (something which has not yet been done), Puerto Rico has attained complete self-government.

Early Conditions

Despite aid from the federal government conditions had not markedly improved. Although the death rate dropped, the birth rate remained one of the highest in the world. In 1898 83 percent of the population was illiterate. By 1940 it was only 31 percent, but policies had shifted back and forth as to which language, English or Spanish, was to be taught at what levels. This wavering led to a reduced effectiveness of education. Neither English nor the Spanish

---

[2] W. Bailey Diffie and Justine Whitfield Diffie, *Porto Rico: A Broken Pledge* (New York: The Vanguard Press, 1931), pp. 135–136. By permission.
[3] Richard Pattee, "The Puerto Ricans," *Annals of the American Academy of Political and Social Sciences,* Sept. 1942, 223: 52.
[4] *Ibid.,* p. 52.

cultural heritage were adequately transmitted. The island suffered heavily during the Depression because of the major dependence on the cash crop of sugar.[5]

Operation Bootstrap

Under self-government Puerto Rico launched "Operation Bootstrap," a development program to raise the levels of living on the island. In twenty years these efforts of the Puerto Rican government raised the per capita income on the island 307 percent. The program concentrated on two areas of economic improvement. The first was diversification of agriculture. Many of the large sugar areas have been made available for smaller landowners under the "500 acre law," which had been on the books since 1900 but was not enforced. Many new crops were introduced. The second effort was to encourage industry. By February, 1960, some 600 new factories had been established, creating jobs for 45,000 people. The government aided in the training of personnel by building factories for rent at reasonable rates, and by other measures. In 1956 the income from manufacturing surpassed the income from agriculture for the first time. Puerto Rico has surpassed every Latin-American country in increase in per capita income. The social aspects of Operation Bootstrap have included a major public health effort and marked achievements in education. Although Spanish is the primary language, English is a required subject from the first grade on. Now almost the only illiterates are older people. The number of school rooms, teachers, and pupils has more than doubled; higher education has tripled; extension services in education have been developed; and the Division of Community Education has become a focus of interest and training for workers from many countries engaged in development programs.

Despite these advances, in 1958–59 unemployment on the island averaged 90,000: 14 percent of the labor force. A large proportion of this has been and is being drained off into the labor market of the continental United States.[6]

The complex population problem has been met by Puerto Rico's government through free birth control clinics; the operation for the sterilization of women was made cheap and easy. This policy was bitterly opposed by the Roman Catholic hierarchy, but the opposition had the effect of publicizing the program. By 1950 the birth rate had begun to decline.[7]

Nevertheless, industrialization eliminated jobs as well as creating them. Perhaps even more the experience of Puerto Rican G.I.'s (65,000 in World War II and 43,000 in the Korean War) aroused aspiration for a new standard of material comfort.[8]

[5] Glazer and Moynihan, *Beyond the Melting Pot,* pp. 87–88.
[6] Clarence Senior, *Strangers—Then Neighbors: From Pilgrims to Puerto Ricans* (New York: Freedom Books, 1961), pp. 55–59.
[7] Glazer and Moynihan, *Beyond the Melting Pot,* p. 98.
[8] *Ibid.,* p. 96.

The Post-World War II Migration

During the war migration declined to a small trickle, but it picked up after the war, the peak year being 1953, when 58,000 Puerto Ricans migrated to the mainland.[9] Puerto Ricans, largely concentrated in New York City before the war, have now spread out to Chicago, Pittsburgh, the New England industrial centers (Bridgeport, Connecticut's population is 10 percent Puerto Rican),[10] to Ohio, Michigan, New Jersey and Wisconsin.[11] It is estimated that there are now 1.6 million.

The Puerto Rican migration has been the heaviest foreign language migration to the Atlantic states since before World War I. Up to 1947 and 1948, a large proportion of the Puerto Ricans who came to the continent were contracted for agricultural and domestic labor. There was much unethical traffic in human beings until the island legislature enacted legislation to control and correct the situation. Offices of the Commonwealth of Puerto Rico, set up to assist migrants, were established in New York and Chicago. At present the Migration Division of the Department of Labor of the Commonwealth of Puerto Rico maintains offices in San Juan and in twelve mainland cities. The division's personnel work in approximately one hundred mainland towns and cities each year. Cooperation has also been established between the Puerto Rico Employment Service and the United States Employment Service. Since Puerto Ricans are citizens, job orders from American industry pass through the United States Employment Service to the Puerto Rico Employment Service when qualified local workers are not available. Employers may recruit labor in Puerto Rico directly only with the approval of the Puerto Rican government, and only when a legitimate order is cleared through regular United States Employment Service channels.

In 1948 the Columbia University study [12] of Puerto Ricans in New York City found that 85 percent of the immigrants had quit jobs in Puerto Rico to come to the United States. What they sought was not so much any job but a *better* job. The data on age of immigrants also suggest that the principal motive for migration has been economic.

Other benefits, too, are sought. Education is thought by many to be better on the mainland, and the ultimate opportunity for improved status is encouraging. There are some for whom life in the home village has become unsatisfactory because of social situations. On the mainland, health and security benefits are easily available. Then there is the glamor of New York. And there are kinship ties to those who have already migrated.

One aspect of the Puerto Rican migration is the ease and frequency with

[9] *Ibid.*, p. 93.

[10] *The New York Times*, August 25, 1967, p. 37.

[11] Senior, *Strangers—Then Neighbors*, p. 22.

[12] C. Wright Mills, Clarence Senior, and Rose Kohn Goldsen, *The Puerto Rican Journey* (New York: Harper & Brothers, 1950).

which the migrants may return to Puerto Rico. Although it was also a feature of some of the older migrations to have a proportion of migrants who viewed their sojourn in the United States as a way to improve their economic circumstances, after which they would return home, for Puerto Ricans, because of the nearness to the island and their citizenship status, there is more turnover in population. There is also a considerable amount of seasonal labor, principally for agricultural work. Those who do establish permanent residence and intend to become part of mainland life still keep ties in the island and take frequent vacations "at home" when they can afford it.

Of the current migration, Senior reports that 40 to 45 percent of the new arrivals speak English, but many are timid about speaking it with strangers. In 1957, a survey found that 63 percent of the Puerto Rican families living in New York City speak English at home. Those who come from rural areas experience more difficulty in the cities than those who have had urban experience. Those who come from mountainous areas tend to be individualistic, while those from cane plantations are more accustomed to cooperative group actions.[13]

Puerto Rican labor is vital to the economic future of some American industries. The Harvard University study of the New York metropolitan region points out:

> The rate of Puerto Rican migration to New York is one of the factors that determine how long and how successfully the New York metropolitan region will retain industries which are under competitive pressure from other areas.
>
> To the extent that some of these industries have hung on in the area they have depended upon recently arrived Puerto Rican workers, who have entered the job market of the New York area at the rate of about 13,000 each year. But the New York area is beginning to lose its unique position. . . . [T]his stream of migration is now spreading to other mainland areas as well, and the spread promises to accelerate.[14]

Visibility

"Racial" Visibility

The Puerto Ricans at the time of annexation by the United States, had adopted and adapted Spanish institutions and Spanish culture to form their own variant of Latin-American civilization. Into the composition of the population had gone white, Negro, and Indian strains. The social structure was that of a plantation economy in which a small upper class, chiefly of landed proprietors, was distinguished from a peasantry, some of it on plantations, some in mountain villages.

Since the abolition of slavery in the island there has been no civic and public

[13] Senior, *Strangers—Then Neighbors*, pp. 63–64.
[14] Cited by Senior. *Ibid.*, p. 65. Recently it has been queried whether or not Negroes at least in the past decade could have supplied this labor.

discrimination in Puerto Rico because of race. None of the forms of inter-racial conflict or violence which have been found on the mainland has oc-curred. This formal absence of discrimination is similar to other patterns in Latin cultures in the Western hemisphere. Furthermore, the population of Puerto Rico presents so wide a range of combinations of physiognomic features that a pattern of dominant-minority relations based on "race" would be dif-ficult to maintain.

Although Puerto Rico is often cited for its absence of prejudice based on "color" visibility, and intermarriage between people of different racial heritages has long been recognized, there is some consciousness of differences. Taken to-gether with the factors of wealth and education color may affect status. "Whites" —very light-skinned people—are at the top if they also have wealth and educa-tion. Very dark-skinned people are at the bottom unless they have wealth and education. They are then sometimes designated as "trigueño" (brunet) as a circumvention for the term "Negro," or they borrow the French usage, "a man of color." "Indios" are an intermediary group; "grifo" designates the light-skinned, kinky-haired individual.

Padilla has made a chart which shows the differences in the way in which biological visibility is perceived by mainlanders, by other Puerto Ricans, and by individuals with regard to themselves.[15]

REFERENCES (MAINLANDERS)	REFERENCES OF INGROUP (HISPANOS)	REFERENCES OF INDIVIDUALS DESCRIBING SELF
White	White	White
	Trigueno Hispano	Hispano
	Grifo	Trigueno
	INTERMEDIATES*	
Puerto Rican	Negro	De Color (of color)
or	Trigueno	Trigueno
Mixed	Indio	Hispano
	Grifo	Indio
	Hispano	
Negro	Negro	De Color
	Trigueno	Trigueno
	Indio	Hispano
	Grifo	Indio
	Hispano	

* A category to include the numerous racial terms used by Puerto Ricans, used by C. Wright Mills, Clarence Senior, and Rose Kohn Goldsen, in *The Puerto Rican Journey*.

[15] Elena Padilla, *Up From Puerto Rico* (New York: Columbia University Press, 1958), pp. 47–48.

This table shows us that no individual in the group of migrants studied designates himself a Negro. Neither will he call himself Grifo. The Hispano group, however, may call him either of these, with implied derogation. When appearance is predominantly "white," the outgroup, mainlanders, may accept the individual as white where both Hispano individuals and the Hispano group will make some differentiation.

Color is clearly a problem for mainland Puerto Ricans. Mainland attitudes have produced ambivalent attitudes. On the island the greater differential was class rather than color. Furthermore when the earlier migration of Puerto Ricans came there were better relations with the Negroes than with the Italians who were contiguous to *El Barrio*. Italian youth were hostile to Puerto Rican youth and Negro youth more accepting.[16] Yet there is the memory of the fact that during World War II, army camps on the island segregated Puerto Rican troops, and the Navy would not take Puerto Ricans.[17] Puerto Ricans, unless very dark and with Negroid features are listed as white in New York City. The proportion of "colored" in the Puerto Rican population drops from census to census (4 percent in 1960).[18] Father Fitzpatrick, Professor of Sociology at Fordham University, made a study of Puerto Rican marriages in six Catholic parishes. He found, in the late 1950's, that 25 percent of the marriages of Puerto Ricans in these widely varying parishes involved people of different color.[19]

Cultural Visibility

Cultural visibility is especially marked among new migrants. Even without hearing the rapid Spanish chatter which goes on in the streets of New York, lower-class Puerto Ricans can usually be identified by their dress, especially the women. Styles favor bright colors. Movement is free, swinging, and graceful. In old-fashioned Puerto Rican families little girls' ears are pierced in babyhood and toddlers will wear earrings. Young men often affect bright jackets and shirts.

The value system of Puerto Ricans shares much with other Spanish cultures. The importance of *dignitad* (self-possession, pride) is paramount in the conception of the ideal person. The culture and social system are male dominated, with strong emphasis on proving masculinity. A man must be, ideally, stable and strong, sexually virile, honest and reliable in work, aggressive in combat, and sensitive to honor. He is logical and can reason. Women, on the other hand, are frail, illogical, and easily deluded. Therefore women must be guarded and accompanied by the responsible males of the family.

The human condition is such, in the value scheme, that man is buffeted by

[16] Glazer and Moynihan, *Beyond the Melting Pot,* p. 93.
[17] Maxine W. Gordon, "Cultural Aspects of Puerto Rico's Race Problem," *American Sociological Review,* June, 1950, p. 382.
[18] Glazer and Moynihan, *Beyond the Melting Pot,* p. 91 and 134.
[19] Joseph P. Fitzpatrick, "The Adjustment of Puerto Ricans to New York City," *Journal of Intergroup Relations* (Winter, 1959–60), pp. 43–52.

many forces. Fatalism underlies much of the thinking, operating sometimes to lower individual aspirations, or quite usually to explain failure and disappointment. Time is infinite. Hurry robs one of dignity; thus commitments within time have wide latitude. Gaiety is valued, singing and dancing enjoyed by all. Emotional expressiveness in word and gesture are the norm. Puerto Ricans sometimes refer to dominants on the mainland as "the cold people."

These values are carried out in the institutional patterns. Within the island social structure the family and the extended kinship form the dominant institutional configuration. Obligations of kinship are strong, as are those of village ties, which for rural families have been the *locus* of the extended family. Male virility is honored by the evidence of many children. Girls are watched over by their mothers before marriage and women by their husbands and mothers-in-law after marriage. The marriage age is early in rural Puerto Rico, often soon after the onset of puberty. "Consensual marriage," like the common-law marriage of the mainland's rural colonial heritage, is acceptable whether or not it is ever formally sanctioned by church or state.

Most Puerto Ricans are Roman Catholic. For many this is a nominal identification with only a tenuous discipline exercised by the affiliation. In New York City, a minority of Puerto Ricans, perhaps 20 percent, have been attracted to Protestant Evangelical groups. Store-front churches have sprung up, and the Pentecostal Holiness sect and Jehovah's Witnesses have been successful proselytizers. Some of the poorest stratum have embraced various Asiatic and Caribbean cults.[20]

Puerto Ricans come from a society which until recently had very marked stratification, with little chance for mobility. In migration the old criteria of status are weakened, though not destroyed. However, a new precedence is given to the united, stable family ("familia undia"). A family of this sort usually consists of several biologically related nuclear families which recognize mutual obligations toward each other. In the new environment it is the symbol of stability and respectability.[21] Income, occupation, and level of education affect a person's status, as do occupational position and familial connections in Puerto Rico before migration.[22] A small percentage of Puerto Ricans have established themselves as members of middle-class dominant society, or as members of the world of celebrities in the arts and sports.[23]

Status in the Spanish-speaking group in New York is otherwise largely related to "old residents," the "born and/or brought up in New York," and "new migrants." Old residents, unless they are middle-class and educated, may not speak much English, having considered themselves too old to learn—"that's for

---

[20] Glazer and Moynihan, *Beyond the Melting Pot,* pp. 105–106.
[21] Padilla, *Up From Puerto Rico,* p. 115.
[22] *Ibid.,* Ch. 2.
[23] Senior, *Strangers—Then Neighbors,* p. 59.

the children"—but they have adapted in other ways, survived, acquired know-how, offered advice and help to those who came later. They consider new migrants "very old-fashioned people," since the newcomers are often closer to the older folk beliefs and cultural ways of the island. Many old migrants are members of a united family, whereas newcomers may be single men, nuclear families, unmarried young women ("daughters of family"—that is, virgins) "women" (mujeres)—single women about whom there has been some scandal in the village and who it is hoped can start over again in the new environment, or disorganized persons.[24]

Patterns of Dominance

Spatial Distribution

In New York City, where more than half of the Puerto Ricans on the mainland live, the old subcommunity, *El Barrio,* south and East of Harlem has overflowed to many other parts of the city. There are concentrations of Puerto Ricans in Brooklyn and the South Bronx, but they still make up about a third of the population of Manhattan, creating different patterns of neighborhood relationships in different situations. Thus on Manhattan's West Side the avenues have large middle-class and upper middle-class apartment houses occupied by "continental whites," while the side streets are filled with Puerto Rican families crowded into converted former private residences that have been abandoned as single-family dwellings in the changing pattern of city and suburban living. Here social class as well as cultural barriers create social distance, and often tension, between mainlanders and migrants.

In New York's Lower East Side, housing conditions are often not as bad for the migrants because of extensive urban renewal in this district. Furthermore because of its historic role as an immigrant neighborhood, the Lower East Side is one of the best serviced and most intercultural subcommunities in New York City.

Many of the longer established Puerto Rican families are, like other New Yorkers, going to the suburbs, and to the less crowded boroughs of the city. In the deteriorating sections of the city the newcomers have found places in the slums with other slum dwellers.[25]

New York State and New York City both have fair housing laws, but since Puerto Rican median family income is the lowest of any group in the city ($3,811 in 1960), and families are large, most Puerto Ricans are automatically limited to poor and crowded housing. Many are benefiting from low-income

24 Padilla, *Up From Puerto Rico,* p. 58.
25 For a vivid description of the ecological distribution of Puerto Ricans in New York City, see Christopher Rand, *The Puerto Ricans* (New York: Oxford University Press, 1958), Ch. 1.

subsidized public housing, but there is not nearly enough of this to meet the need.

Discrimination

No other place in the United States, probably, gives as much lip service to the ideal of nondiscrimination against religious, ethnic, or racial minorities as does New York. Nevertheless, there is much discrimination through evasion of laws and in the areas of daily living not covered by special codes against it.

Since Puerto Ricans form such a large part of New York's unskilled labor force, they have found employment readily in the lowest paying jobs. Discrimination at the lower levels of the occupational structure seems to be linked with the factors of the language handicap, union policies, and traditional "corners" on certain types of employment that have been held by some other ethnic group. The old-line unions in the building trades and on the waterfront have succeeded fairly well in keeping out Puerto Ricans. However, other unions—in the garment trade, the hotel workers and the retail and department store union—have had antidiscrimination policies. Union control of a shop's choice of workers through hiring halls has sometimes been used to break the hold of a particular ethnic group on a shop by forcing mixed crews on the employers.[26] In the white-collar field, public employment is, for Puerto Ricans as for earlier immigrant groups, the chief channel of access.

One important issue is that of whether or not to license professionals trained in Puerto Rico. The Board of Education will take graduates of the University of Puerto Rico as Substitute Auxiliary teachers, a nonclassroom position designed especially to aid Spanish-speaking parents and children. The Department of Welfare has followed this precedent for special personnel. The acceptance of nurses whose examinations were not taken in English has been resisted, despite the urgent need for Spanish-speaking nurses for ward and clinic service in hospitals throughout the city.

Discrimination in good housing continues in many parts of the city. The housing law is new, and the enforcement agency is part of a larger section of city government with many other responsibilities. It is too soon to evaluate the adequacy of the law and the feasibility of enforcement. Eagle, in a study of the housing of Puerto Ricans in New York City, was surprised to find so few Puerto Ricans feeling themselves discriminated against. To the question, "Do you think you can live anywhere in the city if you have the money to pay the rent, 87 percent answered "Yes," and only 5 percent stated that they felt they had actually experienced discrimination in seeking housing. A partial clue to this apparent unawareness of discrimination lies in the fact that the great majority of Puerto Ricans can afford to seek housing only in the less desirable dwellings. The same study found that while only 3 percent of those who had lived in the

[26] *Ibid.*, pp. 143–144.

city three years or less complained of discrimination, 10 percent of those who had lived in New York longer voiced such a complaint.[27]

Political discrimination is primarily linked with the question of English language literacy. Some Puerto Ricans feel there is discrimination in the courts, since the procedure of American courts deprives them of a chance to plead their cause with emotion, gesture, and Latin eloquence.

Minority Adaptations to Dominance

The Hispanic Community

Some writers have argued that because of the neglect by Spain, the extreme poverty of most islanders until well into the twentieth century, and the intermixture of other Caribbean influences, Puerto Rican folk culture is both less rich than other peasant cultures and less Spanish than that of other Latin Americans.[28]

Puerto Ricans have not benefited as the Mexican Americans have from having an older Spanish-speaking tradition to build on in America, or an elite to perpetuate the idea of *La Raza*. Nevertheless, they are pridefully conscious of their Spanish heritage. They usually refer to themselves (if they are the migrating generation) as hispanos or latinos, linking themselves with other Western Hemisphere Spanish cultural groups.

> The Hispano group includes Puerto Ricans, their descendants who may or may not be Spanish-speaking individuals, and also Spanish-speaking persons from Latin America and Spain.... Sources of solidarity and bonds of understandings among Hispanos are partly derived from the historic common general cultural traditions of the peoples who are considered Hispanos. But, partly, too, they are a reaction to the position of the group as a minority in New York: [29]

Puerto Ricans gain on several counts from this sense of identity. It clearly differentiates them from American Negroes and is seen as protection from the threat of the racial attitudes of mainlanders. Among other Spanish-speaking people, Puerto Ricans gain status by being American citizens. According to Padilla, members of other groups of Spanish cultural origin often claim to be Puerto Rican when they are not.[30] Identity born of language and culture is consciously reinforced by symbolic and ceremonial efforts. Rand describes a Columbus Day celebration in which wreaths were laid at the statue of "the Spanish Columbus" in Central Park (as distinguished from the other statue of the presumably Italian Columbus in Columbus Circle). One placard at this demonstration read

[27] Morris Eagle, "The Puerto Ricans in New York City," in Studies in Housing and Minority Groups, eds. Nathan Glazer and Davis McEntire (Berkeley and Los Angeles: The University of California Press, 1959), pp. 166–167.
[28] Glazer and Moynihan, *Beyond the Melting Pot*, p. **88**.
[29] Padilla, *Up From Puerto Rico*, pp. 47–48.
[30] *Ibid.*, p. 11.

WE DO NOT KNOW WHERE

HE WAS BORN BUT WE DO KNOW

HIM AS A CITIZEN OF SPAIN

AND AS THE ADMIRAL

OF THE SPANISH EXPEDITION

IN WHICH THE NEW WORLD

WAS FOUNDED [31]

There are losses also from this sense of identity, for it is not strong enough to solve all the problems confronting Puerto Ricans in New York. The young person of Puerto Rican descent is subjected not only to conflicts of values and behavior patterns that persist in modified and transformed modes between hispano and mainland culture, but he must seek status and approval both within and outside the hispano group. Furthermore, the dominant culture presents no uniform set of standards in the variety of status and ethnic traditions in metropolitan New York.[32]

Obstacles to Acculturation

There are a number of areas that become focal points of attention in adjustments between traditional acceptable ways of the island and the dominant norms of the mainland. Adjustment has been eased to some extent by the fact that the people of the older urban migration were familiar with public education, wage systems, large hospitals, mass communication, and the electoral process. New migrants have increasingly had experience with these forms as a result of the development of the island. Rand mentions an informant in Chicago who felt that the Puerto Ricans had an advantage over the Mexicans in that city because of the longer exposure, in the island, to certain key structures of mainland society, as well as to entrepreneurial values.[33]

The most obvious problem of acculturation is language. Employers complain of a labor force with which they can communicate only through one or two bilingual members, and they are not sure whether or not directions are being communicated accurately. The Employment Service finds trouble placing workers with little English.[34] The problem for the schools is acute, since hundreds of children enter the public school system with little or no English. The language problem cannot be divorced, however, from the central cultural value of *dignitad*. Many Puerto Ricans understand more English than mainlanders realize, but their pride prevents them from speaking English if they do not speak it well.

The problem of punctuality is acute for the migrants from rural background,

---

[31] Rand, *The Puerto Ricans*, p. 158.
[32] Padilla, *Up From Puerto Rico*, pp. 88 ff.
[33] Rand, *The Puerto Ricans*, p. 144.
[34] *Ibid.*, pp. 142 ff.

who have not had the experience of industrial society, and for women who have been confined to a limited sphere of activity.

Since the family is the dominant institution in the island culture, it is in family patterns and roles that many adjustments are required. Consensual marriage is not recognized in New York State, which outlawed, by statute, common-law marriage nearly half a century ago. Thus the mother of children born in a consensual marriage is ineligible for welfare benefits which might accrue to her on the disability, death, or desertion of a husband in a registered marriage. The custom of early marriage comes in conflict with the New York State age of consent, which is sixteen with parents' permission and eighteen without. The role of women in traditional hispano culture is often at variance with the expectations for women in institutional structures. Independent participation in church and school activities may be denied a Puerto Rican woman by a conservative husband or by the extended kinship group. One finds the phenomenon of a husband having to take a leave of absence from his work to take his wife and children to the clinic, "since she could not go alone." Yet, because New York City is the center for the needle trades, and needlework has been a traditional skill among the women, many Puerto Ricans have found employment in the factories of the garment district and in the sewing rooms of custom dress shops. Often a woman in the garment industry can earn more money than the men of her family, a fact which creates conflict of roles within the family.

The American ideal of the nuclear family, if adhered to, often can neither provide security nor assure authority. Roles of parents and children become confused without the support of kinship and hispano community approval. Nevertheless, Puerto Ricans are criticized by mainlanders for kinship obligations that take precedence over work or school commitments.

Economically, Puerto Rican acculturation is retarded by the low skill level characteristic of many migrants. According to Rand, there has been some evidence that some Puerto Ricans have not accepted the possibility of moving on to more highly skilled jobs, and are content to remain at the level they have learned.[35]

In politics Puerto Ricans have been handicapped by the requirement for voters to pass literacy tests in English. Since most Puerto Ricans in New York read the Spanish daily papers, many people feel that literacy tests should be given in Spanish if, as it is claimed, the issue is literacy and not literacy-in-English. The participation of Puerto Ricans in city politics has been relatively slight, although it has increased in the last decade. Since the political machine has not the coherent power it had in the beginning of the century when the immigrant vote was wooed, there have only been sporadic efforts to reach the Puerto Ricans, and this usually by a factional group of one or another political party. On the whole, Puerto Ricans have not benefited in New York politics.

The role of the church, functioning primarily as it does in the sphere of

[35] *Ibid.,* p. 145.

personal belief and loyalty, and in welfare, is a point of conflict for the migrant in two areas. In education, parochial schools in New York City have not had the space or staff to accept the non-English-speaking child. Many middle-class Puerto Ricans, or those who are conservative, prefer parochial education, especially for the upper grades. They feel that discipline is better, that respect for the teacher is maintained, and they approve of the segregation of the sexes. It is the feeling of organizations concerned with public education in New York that Puerto Rican children with language or disciplinary problems are "dumped" on the public schools, that the best group is syphoned off to the parochial schools, thereby helping to maintain a derogatory image of Puerto Ricans and driving more middle-class families among the mainlanders to use private schools or to move to the suburbs. The second area of conflict within the institutional pattern of religion is that of family planning. Because the marriage age is low and because there are cultural values related to fertility, many young families find themselves with numerous children before they are thirty. We have noted that the government of Puerto Rico has had a public policy of fostering family limitation, but this is contrary to the established doctrine of the Roman Catholic Church. On the mainland, health and welfare agencies, reform groups, and often the hispano mothers themselves are interested in smaller-sized families, especially in the situations of low income and poor housing.[36]

"Eastville"

"Eastville" makes an interesting comparison with Tuck's study of the Mexican community, "Descanso," which we presented in Chapter 6. "Eastville" is not "El Barrio Latino." It is an interethnic slum, not a homogeneous nationality subcommunity.

> Regardless of how long they have been melting in the pot, the people of Eastville are seldom identified as just plain Americans. They are designated "Hungarians," "Puerto Ricans," "American Negroes," "American Indians," "East Indians," "Russians," "Italians," "Chinese"—and all of these group labels are conceived as indicating something about the personal, social and biological traits of various group members. It makes little difference in this categorizing whether the individuals were born or have lived all their lives in this country if they still possess characteristics —real or assumed—in physical appearance, in styles of wearing apparel, in knowledge of another language than English, and in their names, that allow them to be distinguished from "real Americans." The term "American" is used, as a rule, with reference to outsiders who do not live in the neighborhood and who, although they may themselves be members of ethnic groups, do not meet the criteria that suggest to Eastvillers membership in any particular group with which they are familiar.[37]

In "Eastville" there are ties of neighborhood that cut across ethnic lines and other identifications that are ethnic.

[36] *Ibid.*, p. 83.
[37] Padilla, *Up From Puerto Rico*, pp. 1–2. By permission.

Among Eastvillers there are levels on which feelings of neighborhood solidarity bind members of all ethnic groups together. By the process of discrimination and dislike people get involved in relationships of conflict, and by common understandings and participation in common activities sentiments of solidarity develop. Both the positive feelings and the negative ones work together to shape the social body that is the neighborhood. The idea that the neighborhood is a bad place in which to live is a shared one among Eastvillers. So, too, is their attitude toward discrimination by outsiders against them. . . .

On the other hand, it is difficult to organize programs of social action in Eastville when ethnic group barriers are ignored or when the sources of loyalty within an ethnic group are not recognized. Beneath the intergroup tensions and conflicts among ethnic groups are working interpersonal relationships among individuals, which override ethnic affiliation.[38]

Although there is neighborliness and often mutual helpfulness, the urban slum neighborhood lacks the homogeneity and long residence of the village.

First and last names are seldom known or recognized in Eastville. People are identified according to whatever characteristic they are best known by in the neighborhood—the man from Italy, the lady who owns the candy store, the woman from Ponce . . .[39]

Housing is a problem in "Eastville," although the overcrowding is not comparable to that in some districts where there are whole families in one room. The 1950 census reported an average of three persons per room for "Eastville." Apartments are self-contained units which include a bathroom (sometimes with the tub in the kitchen). Some are "old law" (pre-1911) tenements with windows only in the front and back rooms and airshafts for the intervening rooms. Rents in the middle 1950's, at the time of Padilla's study, ranged from $14 to $80 a month, with "under the table" fees from $800 to $1,500 "for the key." Utilities are extra. The entire area is rat-infested; repairs in electric installations, plumbing, and plaster must usually be undertaken by tenants themselves, as complaints are consistently ignored by the absentee landlords. When weather permits, much of the life of the neighborhood goes on on the street.

Strewn with garbage though they are, the streets and alleys are notable for the number of people of every conceivable ethnic group who spend a considerable part of their time there to get away from their apartments. Day and night the juke boxes in the candy stores deluge the streets with the tunes of the latest records of the season, and it is not strange to see youngsters or young adults dancing by themselves inside the stores or on the sidewalks to rock 'n' roll rhythms by the Velvets or to Xavier Cugat's mambos and meringues. Others watch and then try the ones they like under the tutelage of those who know the steps and proper motions for the dances. Noise of music and of words in Yiddish, Spanish, Italian and English, barking dogs, movement of people, cars' horns, are interwoven in a polyphonic soundtrack which records the pace of the neighborhood. Only very cold weather or news echoed through the grapevine that gang fights are scheduled, keep people off the streets. Otherwise

---

[38] *Ibid.,* pp. 11–12. By permission.
[39] *Ibid.,* p. 12.

the streets, the sidewalks, the stores, and the bars are filled with people meeting, chatting, and relaxing.[40]

Living in the midst of people who have conscious ties to ethnic groups, hispanos have continued the pattern of vesting individuals with ethnic identity. The principal ethnic groups recognized by hispanos in "Eastville" are Cubans, Americans, American Negroes, Italians, and Jews. Of these, Americans and Italians are the most highly rated. Jews, Cubans, and American Negroes are, as a rule, less favored, especially the two latter groups.[41]

> An undisputed American, or someone who is American and nothing else, is conceived as having a name that cannot be identified with or traced to a foreign origin; as being reddish and white in complexion, tall, blond and blue eyed; as doing professional work; and as not knowing Spanish or having an accent when speaking it. He does not understand the Hispano people. Americans are nice, honest, beautiful and funny. Should one or more of these traits be missing, the individual is suspected of not being a "real American," but something else instead.[42]

Adaptive Institutions

Formerly there were three Spanish language newspapers in New York City, one of which was a New York edition of a San Juan paper. Today a merger has taken place between the other two: a conservative daily that had addressed itself to the middle-class Spanish-speaking population with a great deal of news of Spain and South America, and the popular tabloid which most Puerto Ricans read. In addition to carrying the usual type of copy it offers itself now as the informant about night classes, the P.T.A., presents itself as the champion of the Spanish-speaking population against the police and other agents of authority who "do not understand the Spanish people." Neither of the merged papers was founded by Puerto Ricans,[43] but certainly the present journal acts as a force to unify the sense of identity of all the Latin-American community.

Labor unions, some with locals almost 100 percent Puerto Rican serve also as adaptive institutions. A 1959 survey found that 63 percent of the New York Spanish-speaking households surveyed had one or more union members.[44] These may not have been all Puerto Rican households, as Glazer and Moynihan point out that Mexicans and Cubans appear on the executive board of a major union, along with two Puerto Ricans, though the majority of the labor force in this local was Puerto Rican. The authors imply that Puerto Ricans have not yet achieved competitive leadership positions in proportion to their numbers.[45]

In Manhattan there has been an ongoing struggle for political leadership

---

[40] *Ibid.,* p. 9. By permission.
[41] *Ibid.,* p. 89.
[42] *Ibid.,* p. 90. By permission.
[43] Glazer and Moynihan, *Beyond the Melting Pot,* p. 103.
[44] Senior, *Strangers—Then Neighbors,* p. 68.
[45] Glazer and Moynihan, *Beyond the Melting Pot,* p. 102.

among the Puerto Ricans. In the Bronx a borough leader has clearly emerged. The Puerto Rican vote has risen to nearly a quarter of a million registered voters in New York City.

A number of indigenous organizations have developed. The Spanish Merchants Association has 200 Puerto Rican members. The Puerto Rican Civil Service Employees Association is thirty-five years old, owns its own building, and has established a successful credit union. The Spanish Club of the New York City Police Department has 250 members, mostly Puerto Rican. The Association of Puerto Rican Social Workers has more than 1,000 members. There are organizations of lawyers, ministers, teachers, nurses, electricians, barbers, bar owners, taxi owners and drivers, and baseball umpires. The Council of Puerto Rican and Spanish-American Organizations of Greater New York now includes fifty-four civic, social, cultural, religious and fraternal organizations. The Federation of Puerto Rican Organizations of New Jersey has thirty member groups.

The Decline of Dominance?

There was a period in which many social scientists felt that the Puerto Rican population would be split between the "lighter" and darker Puerto Ricans, with the latter sharing whatever possibilities were in store for American Negroes. This kind of split has not occurred. What has happened instead seems to be a division within the Puerto Rican community between the mobile and the very poor.

The mobile choose as their models the earlier immigration and expect that they, too, by the third generation will be absorbed into the mainstream of American life. Such a point of view is expressed in the organization *Aspira*, devoted to working with students and parents to understand and take advantage of educational and vocational opportunities.[46]

There is some justification for this hope. Both the 1950 and 1960 censuses have shown an increasing shift upward in the occupations of second-generation Puerto Ricans.[47]

In 1960 there were 4,000 independent small businesses owned by Puerto Ricans in New York City.[48] This is a large figure and attests to the entrepreneurial skill of a segment of the Puerto Rican population. On the other hand, considering the trends of the American economy, the future of small business is precarious.

One could probably assume that the expectation of the mobile group to blend into American society would be fulfilled with diminishing prejudice and discrimination were it not for the large number of poor Puerto Ricans. Their visibility and their share in the desperate problems of urban blight might possibly precipitate more discriminatory behavior toward all Puerto Ricans.

[46] *Ibid.,* p. 128 ; see also *The New York Times,* May 26, 1967, p. 49.
[47] *Ibid.,* pp. 115–116.
[48] *Ibid.,* p. 112.

As we have already indicated, the poor segment of the Puerto Ricans is large and at the bottom of the heap in the urban centers where Puerto Ricans are concentrated in large numbers. They migrated into an America that was a welfare state. They have large families. They have the usual disabilities of the poor. They create many problems for the educational system, the health departments, the welfare departments. They are a headache to city governments and an embarrassment to middle-class America. Nor do they have the claim to the American conscience that has been sometimes an effective weapon of the Negro.

Puerto Rican Welfare

More intelligent effort has been made to meet the problems of the Puerto Rican migration than was possible with the older European migrations. The structures of labor and welfare in the United States have changed. The development of the social sciences has made more knowledge available to influence planning. The position of Puerto Rico as a United States dependency facilitates coordination between the island and the mainland.

The Migration Division of the Office of the Commonwealth of Puerto Rico works both on the island and in its offices in the United States to aid the adjustment process. Each week twenty-nine radio stations throughout the island carry a program, "Guide to the Traveler," based on the experience of previous migrants. In 1960 there were thirty-five committees on migrant orientation in cities and towns in Puerto Rico. Television, radio, newspapers and printed leaflets are urging knowledge of English, giving information about climate and clothing, the documents needed for schools, the need for driver's licenses, and warning about installment buying and many other topics.

In New York the Migration Division has organized a campaign to urge the newcomer to go to night school. The Spanish-language press and Spanish-language radio carry these appeals, and there are thousands of leaflets distributed by clergy, social workers, health stations, settlements, and banks.[49]

Some progress is being made on the housing problem through efforts at urban renewal. New York City has a program of low-cost, subsidized housing in areas where there have been particularly bad slum dwellings. Renewal of the side streets between middle-class housing is beginning, and clergy, social agencies, and political clubs have aided in bringing negligent landlords to court.

The school system, where it is practicable, has attempted to draw zone lines so that the ethnic balance of a school's population will not exceed one-third Puerto Rican. The problem is aggravated, however, by the principle of homogeneous grouping, which syphons off the better students into separate classes. Since the number of Puerto Ricans who have qualified for these classes is still not large, the other classes have disproportionately more Puerto Ricans. The

[49] Senior, *Strangers—Then Neighbors,* p. 62.

Board Education has been experimenting with "culture-free" intelligence tests and with special programs for the gifted of less privileged background. There are about a hundred Spanish-speaking Substitute Auxiliary teachers assigned to schools in the city. The efforts of Negro parents and Negro organizations for improved schools and for revised testing have benefited Puerto Ricans also.

The public welfare agencies, the private nonsectarian welfare agencies, various Protestant denominations, and Catholic parishes and religious orders have given thought and effort to meeting the needs of the new migrant group.

Padilla gives an account of one "welfare" family in "Eastville":

> Mr. Rios was injured in an industrial accident in 1953. This later involved ortho-pedic surgery. Workmen's Compensation was paid for a short period and for the subsequent surgery, but after the discontinuance Mr. Rios continued to suffer pain, and with his injured arm could not find a job. A visiting nurse suggested the family should seek help from the Department of Public Welfare—"go on welfare," and she herself made the contact for the family. The case with the Compensation Board was reopened and Mr. Rios now receives $18 a week from this agency. Mrs. Rios and the three children have supplemental aid from the Department of Welfare. Mr. Rios has been attending night school, has finished grammar school and is now in junior high school. He still has pain and receives treatment from both public and private clinics. He still consults lawyers in the hope of getting indemnification for his injury. In the last seven years the rent has been doubled.
>
> The Rios family have been in New York for twenty years. They belong to a store front church, and the children have been to the church camp summers, although when the daughter reached puberty, her parents no longer allowed her to go to camp. The children are not allowed to play on the streets, though the boys are often "given permission" to go to the park. The children are doing well in school. Mrs. Rios earns a little money by caring for the children of working mothers in her home. Mr. Rios hopes when he "has completed his education" to be able to get a job so they can get off welfare. He is 45 years old.[50]

Mr. Rios represents the kind of need for which the welfare system was de-vised: the possibility of maintaining the thin line between despair and self-re-spect. On the other hand, the welfare system, being nationwide and bureaucratic cannot change flexibly, and it is significant that the landlord can raise the rent without the delays and counterpressure of a city administration or Congress. Furthermore, Mr. Rios lives in "Eastville," which is not as isolated or neglected as *El Barrio*.

The Puerto Rican Underclass

"Underclass" is a term now common for the very poor in cities. For the Puerto Ricans of New York, these are mostly found in the tenements of East Harlem. As the mobile move out, the poorest newcomers come in. Much of the housing is still "old law" (pre-1911): half a floor of an old private residence or

[50] Padilla, *Up From Puerto Rico,* pp. 134–141, adapted by the authors.

one initially built four- or five-story tenement, with the toilet in the outside hall for the use of the whole floor, a tub in the kitchen, two of the rooms with air shafts instead of windows, and rats. Garbage collections in these poor districts of New York is twice a week, whereas in middle-class residential sections it is every day.[51]

The anthropologist Oscar Lewis has given us a vivid portrait of a migrant to *El Barrio*.[52] Soledad, whose mother migrated to San Juan from rural poverty in Puerto Rico, brought her children up in a San Juan slum. Soledad came to the continental United States because one of her brothers had come. She came with her children and worked briefly as an agricultural laborer in New Jersey. She then wound up in *El Barrio* where she knew some people from San Juan. A woman not without strength and primitive intelligence, Soledad is a true product of "the culture of poverty."[53] She is confused, full of antagonism when confronted with the bureaucracy of the welfare department, the health clinic, the school system. Her colorful argot, her unstable relations to men, her overprotective yet harsh dealings with her children, her general personal disorganization (by any middle-class standard) still show a woman struggling against odds: some private clinging to bastardized religious beliefs; some great strength in enduring and fighting.

Lewis's *La Vida* has offended many Puerto Ricans, as they fear it will contribute to a derogatory stereotype of them as a group. But Soledad (the name means solitude—"alienation") is not of a hereditary national culture. She is of the culture of the most depressed of the urban poor. Without understanding Soledad one cannot understand why the only riot in New York City in 1967—that summer of desperate riots across the country—was in *El Barrio*. As one writer expressed it, "Some of the nation's most intensive community project work had been insufficient to counter the feeling of separation and rejection which had so long afflicted the Spanish-speaking ghetto."[54] To New York it was startling to have Spanish-Americans riot. Furthermore the riot, compared with others of the summer (Detroit, Newark, Cincinnati, New Haven) was not as destructive or as prolonged.

On the second day of the riot one of the local Roman Catholic parishes inaugurated a parade which continued for three days. It was led by some small, brave boys, followed by the priest and nuns and parishioners carrying votive candles and placards calling for peace in *El Barrio*. It passed under the elevated railroad tracks which take commuters to the suburbs. As the trains went by no one looked up from his newspaper to be concerned with "down below."[55] As

[51] Prof. Meyer found this to be true when working as a field supervisor for a study for the U.S. Dept. of Health, Education, and Welfare in 1965.
[52] Oscar Lewis, *La Vida: A Puerto Rican Family in the Culture of Poverty—San Juan and New York* (New York: Random House, 1965), pp. 127–245.
[53] For a discussion of the concept "the culture of poverty" see *Ibid.*, pp. xlv–lii.
[54] *The New Yorker*, August 5, 1967, pp. 19–23.
[55] *Ibid.*, p. 22.

the riot simmered down the Mayor and two prominent Puerto Ricans (one a sports figure and one a political leader of another borough of New York) toured the area, asked to meet with neighborhood representatives. The spokesmen of the neighborhood mostly resented the calling of the police Tactical Control Force. On the second day of the riot youths, still sullen and heckling, handed out handbills that called for more sanitation pick ups and for lower grocery prices.[56]

The Impact of Puerto Ricans on New York City

The most frequently cited contribution of the Puerto Ricans is economic. Without this labor force many industries would undoubtedly have left New York. It is possible, as Glazer and Moynihan point out, that southern Negro migrants would have filled the gap.[57] There is some conflict of interest between the two groups in the pressing needs of both for housing, for jobs, for advancement.

The cultural contribution of Puerto Ricans is less of high culture than of language. Today in New York almost all public notices are in English and in Spanish. An increasing number of New York City police are Spanish speaking. The banks, in their branches throughout the city have leaflets in Spanish explaining their services. Neighborhood organizations are incorporating Puerto Ricans and continental whites, and middle-class established people are learning Spanish to be able to work with their neighbors on common problems besetting their city. In addition to language, the Puerto Ricans have brought color and gaiety in to the city of the "cold" people.

Possibly their greatest potential contribution may come in the diffusion of their attitudes toward color. Whereas for purposes of public policy and pressure Negroes may polarize their position vis-à-vis whites, as neighbors the Puerto Ricans act as a leaven. (They never refer to Negroes as "you people.")

> They carry a new attitude toward color—an attitude that may be corrupted by continental color prejudice but it is more likely, since this is in harmony with the trends that are making all nations part of a single world community, that the Puerto Rican attitude to color, or something like it, will become the New York attitude.[58]

Trends and Prospects

The future of the Puerto Rican minority is bound up with many factors: · the development of the island, the dispersion of Puerto Ricans on the main-

---

[56] It is reported that in some poverty areas, local merchants raise grocery prices on the days the welfare checks come. On the other hand, the index on food prices for the nation has been steadily rising.

[57] Glazer and Moynihan, *Beyond the Melting Pot,* p. 131.

[58] *Ibid.,* p. 132.

land, the opportunity for advancement, the consciousness of themselves as a cultural minority, and the future position of racially visible people in the continental United States.

The amazing development of the island economy, if it continues at the present rapid rate, may change the pattern of migration. We have already noted a shift from the urban to the rural migrant. The development of the island may reduce the available cheap labor force by a considerable amount, especially if the Puerto Rican efforts toward population control begin to show effects. The preparation of migrants can be expected to improve also. Nevertheless, for some time to come, opportunities in the continental United States will outstrip those in Puerto Rico, and the remoter rural areas may still be a source of supply for the mainland labor force, and these rural people are the ones who will have the severest problems of adaptation to mainland urban life.

The future of the island politically is also a factor influencing both the increase or decrease in migration, as well as the feelings within the Puerto Rican group already settled in the United States. Various groups on the island have at one time or another favored either independence or statehood. Independence would at the very least create new problems, and perhaps new emphases, in the development of the island. Statehood would also slow development efforts, since Puerto Rico would then be subject to federal taxation, from which it is now exempt. The former Governor, Muñoz Marin, sees great cultural as well as economic benefits in the present relationship, which allows self-government within "a commonwealth of the American political system." He foresees a future in which Puerto Rico will carry its share of the federal financial burden, and he poses the question of whether eventually a new relationship may not be defined which is neither statehood nor independence. The political future of Puerto Rico, however, is also bound up with other developments in Latin America and the Caribbean, as well as with American policy.

Opportunity for advancement seems to be promising for Puerto Ricans as compared with most early twentieth-century immigrant groups. According to David W. Barry, Executive Secretary of the New York City Mission Society,

> No previous immigrant group so quickly numbered among its members so many policemen, welfare workers, teachers and social workers, office workers and independent business men, and even doctors and lawyers—after barely a dozen years in New York. And the signs of the future are in the substantial enrollment of young Puerto Ricans in the city's colleges and universities.[59]

Puerto Ricans are beginning to move into home-owning areas in the suburbs. One Cleveland, Ohio, realtor is quoted as saying, "they are becoming a credit to the community, although many old timers protested when they moved in." [60]

This rapidity of movement of some, however, does not offset the large con-

[59] Quoted in Senior, *Strangers—Then Neighbors*, p. 67.
[60] *Ibid.*, p. 70.

centration of urban poor, whose future depends on what solutions American society can find to the larger problem of suburban flight and deteriorating core cities.

Whether the Puerto Ricans will assimilate or whether their identity as a cultural minority will be strengthened will be influenced by larger trends in America, and in United States–Latin American relations. Even the efforts to achieve nondiscriminatory legislation in a city like New York heightens the awareness of descent as a criterion of identification. In the face of this there is an inevitable strengthening of cultural bonds, which may be reinforced if there is unabating migration.

For the dark-complexioned Puerto Ricans the future is bound up with the future of race attitudes. Many continue to segregate themselves from American Negroes and are a powerful factor in maintaining the Spanish cultural subgroup. But in the end their opportunity is associated with the ultimate opportunity of other dark-skinned Americans.

Topics for Projects and Discussion

1. Compare the Puerto Rican and the Italian migrations to the United States. How are they alike and how do they differ?
2. What are the gains and losses to an immigrant in a geographic nationality sub-community as compared with a mixed neighborhood?
3. Why are Negroes and Puerto Ricans sometimes treated as if they were a single "problem" group? Is this justified or not? Explain.
4. How do you account for the lack of organized crime among adult Puerto Ricans? How do you explain, then, the high rate of juvenile delinquency?
5. One of America's leading musicians, Leonard Bernstein, has made young Puerto Ricans in New York the central figures in *West Side Story.* Listen to the songs from this musical. Compare it with Padilla's account of "Eastville." Do they agree or disagree in their presentation of young people in a city slum?
6. What arguments would you advance for and against the Puerto Ricans joining with Mexican Americans to form a political bloc of Spanish-speaking citizens?

Suggested Reading

Eagle, Morris. "The Puerto Ricans in New York City," in *Studies in Housing and Minority Groups,* eds. Nathan Glazer and Davis McEntire. Berkeley and Los Angeles: University of California Press, 1959.

> *Studies the housing of New York's Puerto Ricans and how they themselves view the situation.*

Handlin, Oscar. *The Newcomers: Negroes and Puerto Ricans in a Changing Metropolis.* Cambridge, Mass.: Harvard University Press, 1959.

> *A part of the New York Metropolitan Region Study. The new migrants' problems appraised in the light of the history of the New York City labor force.*

Lewis, Oscar. *La Vida: A Puerto Rican Family in the Culture of Poverty—San Juan and New York.* New York: Random House, 1965.

  Part II, "Soledad," describes a day with the poorest stratum of Spanish Harlem.

Padilla, Elena. *Up From Puerto Rico.* New York: Columbia University Press, 1958.
  A social anthropologist describes and analyzes the daily living of Puerto Ricans in one New York neighborhood.

Senior, Clarence. *Strangers—Then Neighbors: From Pilgrims to Puerto Ricans.* New York: Freedom Books, 1961.
  An up-to-date summary of facts about Puerto Ricans on the mainland, with an excellent bibliography.

Stycos, J. Mayone. *Family and Fertility in Puerto Rico.* New York: Columbia University Press, 1955.
  An analysis of the values governing family life among working-class Puerto Ricans in Puerto Rico.

Wakefield, Dan. *Island in the City: The World of Spanish Harlem.* Boston: Houghton Mifflin Co., 1959.
  A vivid description of life in "El Barrio Latino," the Spanish subcommunity of New York.

8

The Chinese
in the United States

In the mainland population of the United States there were in 1960 some 600,000 people of Asian lineage. There were 206,877 Japanese, 199,095 Chinese, and 107,240 Filipinos.[1] While altogether these people make up only a small percentage of the total mainland population, their relations with the dominant population have been significant, for their treatment by white Americans has had serious repercussions in the relations between the United States and Asian governments.

In broad outline, the interaction of these Oriental immigrants parallels that of all native-immigrant interaction. The discrimination displayed against them was, however, on the whole, much stronger. While, as we have seen, most of the subsequent generations of European lineage became assimilated, the Asian immigrants, up to World War II at least, remained only partially acculturated to American society. In part, of course, this may be explained by the fact that their cultures were in some aspects more alien to the United States than that of the European immigrants. The ranking of Asian immigrant groups below that of European immigrant groups on social distance scales indicates that they have seemed more different. Yet today, even on the West Coast which has had the most anti-Oriental sentiment in the past, they rate above Mexican Americans.[2]

The picture in the mind of the average American of the Chinese in this country is probably more compounded of myth and legend than is true of any other minority. The word "Chinatown" is associated with things exotic, mysterious, curious, and alien to American life. The population stereotype is derived

[1] The Asian population of Hawaii is given in Chapter 17. These figures were obtained by subtracting the data for Hawaii from the United States total as given in the Advance Reports of the 1960 Census. Data for Asian Indians, Koreans, and Polynesians are not given, but all other Asians living in mainland United States are few in number.
[2] Robin Williams, Jr., *Strangers Next Door: Ethnic Relations in American Communities* (Englewood Cliffs, N.J.: Prentice-Hall, 1964), p. 72. In "Valley City" in California this study found the rank order of minorities from the most acceptable to the least acceptable as follows: Jews, Indians, Chinese, Japanese, Mexican, Negro.

more from the movies and mystery novels than from actual contact with the Chinese themselves. The lack of real knowledge of the Chinese is explained by their small numbers and their concentration in a few large cities. But it also arises from the fact that even in the communities where they do live, the Chinese have been until rcently the most socially isolated of all minorities, a point which takes on added significance when we remember that the Chinese immigration antedated the period of later European immigration.

The Chinese Population in the United States

Chinese immigration to the United States, as Table 8–1 shows, beginning in large numbers in the 1850's rose to a peak in the decade of the 1870's and declined sharply after the First Exclusion Act (1882). Beginning with the depression through World War II, there was little immigration at all. Since the war,

Table 8–1. *Chinese Immigration to the United States and Population of Chinese Ancestry as Recorded by Census*

Year	Total Admitted*	Total Recorded**	Per Cent Increase or Decrease
1820 to 1830	3	————	———
1831 to 1840	8	————	———
1841 to 1850	35	758	———
1851 to 1860	41,397	34,933	———
1861 to 1870	64,301	63,199	80.9
1871 to 1880	123,201	105,465	66.9
1881 to 1890	61,711	107,488	1.9
1891 to 1900	14,799	88,869	−16.4
1901 to 1910	20,605	71,531	−20.4
1911 to 1920	21,278	61,639	−13.8
1921 to 1930	29,907	74,594	21.6
1931 to 1940	4,928	77,504	3.4
1941 to 1950	16,709	117,140† (150,005††)	51.8
1951 to 1960	9,657	190,095† (237,292††)	62.3 (58.2††)
Total	408,539		

* *Annual Report of Immigration and Naturalization Service,* Washington, 1960, Table 13, p. 41.
** *United States Census* for each decade.
† Includes mainland United States without Hawaii.
†† Includes Hawaii.

immigration has increased sharply again. How are we to account for the fact that, while during 140 years more than 400,000 Chinese have migrated to the mainland of this country, there are apparently not half that number living in the country in the 1960's?

Chinese Immigration to the United States

First, the Chinese Exclusion Act drastically curtailed, though it did not completely eliminate, further immigration after 1882. Second, during several decades the number of Chinese returning to China exceeded the number of arrivals. "From 1908, when records of departures began, to 1930, while 48,482 Chinese immigrant aliens were admitted, 72,796 departed, thus showing a net loss." [3] Third, normal natural increase was prevented by the disproportion of the sexes. In 1910 there were 1,430.1 males to every 100 Chinese females; in 1920, 695.5; and in 1940, 258.3. Finally, because of exclusion there had been an undue proportion of elderly Chinese in the population which accounted for a relatively high death rate for the group. Thus the Chinese population declined from a peak of 107,488 in 1890 to a low of 61,639 in 1920. From 1921 to 1940 the Chinese in America increased but slightly, to a 77,504 total in 1940.

The 1940–1950 decade showed an increase of 51.8 percent in the Chinese population. Part of this may reflect a more accurate census count gained through the use of Chinese recorders for the first time. But it is a question if even this measure succeeded in getting all the resident aliens counted, since many avoid official contacts because of illegalities in their status—fraudulent claims to derivative citizenship, "jumping ship" by seamen, crossing borders without detection, and "smuggling." Much of the increase actually occurred in the postwar years, when an unprecedented number of female immigrants admitted under the War Brides Act helped bring the sex ratio of this population to 1.89. (In 1890 there had been 27 Chinese males to every 1 Chinese female.)

Most of the Chinese who came in the nineteenth century were poor villagers. Within the pattern of the Chinese family system the men came, leaving their wives and children, if they had them, within the shelter of the kinship circle in China. Many of them came as contract laborers, especially for railroad construction. They made no particular effort to settle in agriculture, perhaps because American agriculture was alien to their patterns of cultivation at home. Some returned to China for a time, or several times, to invest their earnings in a strip of land in the home village, to pay the bride price for a wife, or to contribute to the joint family purse. Others saw as their goal small entrepreneurial enterprises in America, where they were free from the "squeeze" of officialdom or the limitations of the class system. Whereas they shared the social structural ways of behaving characteristic of China, they shared little of the great Chinese culture of the Confucian literati. Obviously as the Chinese population increased, merchants came also to the principal centers to maintain the supply of familiar

[3] Maurice R. Davie, *World Immigration* (New York: The Macmillan Co., 1936), pp. 315–316. By permission.

Chinese goods. Many of these merchant families were related through organizations of merchants or through family ties to others in other cities of America. They became the power structure of the Chinese subcommunities of the large cities. In smaller centers in the West there was more opportunity for migrating laborers to rise to the position of small merchants.

Sojourners

This term applies to the Chinese who have lived in this country with the idea of making enough money to return to the homeland to live at a higher-status level. Siu describes this category thus: [4] "The Chinese sojourners maintain a psychological and social separateness from the larger society and insulate themselves against the full impact of the dominant societies' values, norms, attitudes, and behavior patterns." With this attitude, the sojourner lives a dual existence "which contributes to his sense of non-belongingness in both societies, a fact that is seldom admitted by the sojourner." It is this psychological orientation which marks a Chinese as a sojourner whether foreign or native-born, irrespective of his class position, or whether the time ever comes that he feels affluent enough to return to his homeland.

Students and Intellectuals

From 1847, when an American missionary brought three Chinese boys to study at an American academy, to 1954, some 18,000 Chinese nationals have studied in the United States. Most American institutions of higher learning have trained some Chinese nationals. The peak of Chinese student enrollment came in 1949, at 3,916. Since most of this student group have come from the upper strata of Chinese society, their relations with dominant people have been different from those of other Chinese.

The "Slot Racket"

Unique to the Chinese in the United States has been the so-called slot racket. A section of the 1870 citizenship law passed by Congress recognized the right to confer citizenship on Americans born abroad. Chinese residents in this country have made much use of this law to secure entry of others, especially relations with the same surnames. As we have seen, many male Chinese immigrants returned to China from time to time for protracted visits to their families abroad and conceived children there. In countless instances, "sons never born" were reported, thus creating a "slot" on the family tree. Those "slots" enabled people to claim derivative citizenship and enter the United States. Persons claiming derivative citizenship, if born before 1934, were eligible for admission to this country if they could prove that their fathers or grandfathers resided in the United States at one time. The "racket" aspect has been

---

[4] Paul C. Siu, "The Sojourner," *American Journal of Sociology,* July, 1952, pp. 34–44.

in the selling of these "slots" by legitimate claimants. Arrangements are made to sell the "slots" through Hong Kong brokers for prices ranging from $2,500 to $6,000.[5]

The above considerations explain why there was such a high percentage increase in the census figures for the Chinese population on the American mainland from 1950 to 1960 (62.3 percent). In addition to more accurate counting, some Chinese students stranded in the country by the Chinese revolution who were given permanent entry, the large number of relatives of Chinese American nationals, and refugees from the mainland of China—mostly merchants and scholars—all swelled the total. For example, of the 5,722 immigrant aliens from China admitted for the 1959 period, 1,348 were wives of American citizens.[6]

The new immigration law has benefited the Chinese under the preferences for skills, relatives, and refugees. Many of the Chinese becoming citizens under these provisions already had been granted permanent residence in the United States.

The American Chinese population is highly urbanized. By 1950, as many as 94 percent were officially counted in cities of various sizes, and according to Lee only 1 percent could be said to have really rural residence.[7] The trend has been toward concentration in a few large cities. In addition to San Francisco, with the largest Chinatown in the nation, enough Chinese to form a local "colony" are found in Chicago, Detroit, Los Angeles, Brooklyn, New York, and Philadelphia. The most interesting recent change in the geographical distribution of the American Chinese population has been the southward movement. In 1950 there were 10,432 in the South. While this was still a small percentage of the then 117,629 national total, it represented an increase over 1940 of 112.5 percent. Of this Lee writes:

> The southern movement gathered momentum during the depression, when the South surpassed all other regions in attracting families who owned and operated general merchandise, food, and service establishments. The Chinese function as middlemen in a multi-racial society where the social relations between the whites and Negroes are strained and hostile. They also play this role in the Southwest, where Mexicans and American Indians are numerous and the Chinese cater to all groups. This is similar to the position the Chinese occupy in South-East Asia, the Caribbean, and elsewhere.[8]

It is of interest to find that in 1940, a hundred years after the Chinese immigration started, for the first time the American-born Chinese exceeded the foreign born Chinese population. The exceptional tendency for Chinese immi-

---

[5] *Time,* January 20, 1958, p. 17.

[6] *Annual Report of the Immigration and Naturalization Service,* Washington, D.C., 1959, p. 17, Table 6.

[7] Rose Hum Lee, *The Chinese in the United States* (Hong Kong: Hong Kong University Press, 1960), p. 38. Distributed in the United States by the Oxford University Press.

[8] *Ibid.,* p. 39.

grants to return to their homeland and the long period in which the group had had an excessively high male preponderance account for the delay.

The Establishment of Dominance

Visibility

To the Westerners settling the Pacific Coast and the Rocky Mountain area, the Chinese appeared particularly alien. Although the China trade had been active for some decades, few of these "pioneers" had ever seen an Asiatic. They were immediately subject to derogating attitudes as a "race."

Actually, however, what struck Anglo-Americans, were cultural characteristics, more than racial. The peculiarities of the Chinese language, with its high sing-song intonation and its ideographic writing, bore no relation to any spoken or written language they had known. The men, who were in preponderance and hence most visible, still dressed according to the old-style Chinese custom: long queues, felt slippers, cotton blouses, and little round hats. They were also ridiculed because they accepted domestic work at a time when there were few women available to do it. This did not fit American ideas of a masculine role.

Religiously, none of the nineteenth-century migrants were Christian, although soon the Protestants and subsequently in the twentieth century, the Catholics, began to proselytize among the new migrants.

Discrimination

The discovery of gold in California was a magnet for the first Chinese as it was for many Americans. The Chinese have developed mining all over Southeast Asia, and the pattern for overseas enterprise for the son of a joint family is centuries old. Perhaps much of the peculiarly violent and rough treatment accorded these first Chinese immigrants can be understood when it is remembered that Chinese-native-white interaction first took place in the especially lawless setting of the frontier. Opposition arose to the Chinese as gold miners because they were industrious and persevering, often taking on mining locations that whites considered worthless and making them pay. Thus began the cry that the Chinese depressed the wages and the living standard of the whites, an allegation that was to dog the Chinese as they subsequently became laborers in all the menial occupations available—in railroad construction, on the farms, and in domestic service. Antagonism toward the Chinese expressed itself in lawless violence, in discriminatory city ordinances and state legislation, and finally in successful persuasion of the federal government to exclude further Chinese immigrants.

Acts discriminating against the Chinese, imposing special taxes on them and prohibiting them from entering the state, were passed by the California legislature in the 1850's and 1880's. Opposition to the Chinese was manifested also in city ordinances that attempted to reach the Chinese indirectly. For example, "San Francisco had a laundry ordinance imposing a license fee as follows: on laundries using a one-horse vehicle, $2 per quarter; two horses, $4 per quarter; no vehicle, $15 per quarter. The Chinese laundries commonly used no vehicle. It was made a misdemeanor for any person on the sidewalks to carry baskets suspended on a pole across the shoulders—a typical Chinese practice." [9]

Frequently the Chinese were exposed to violence, especially in periods of hard times. As a result of the panic of 1873, riots occurred during which the Chinese were robbed, beaten, and murdered by hoodlums who made the Chinese the scapegoats for the ills of the times. Eye-witness accounts report that "it was a common sight in San Francisco and other cities to see the Chinese pelted with stones or mud, beaten or kicked, having vegetables or laundry stolen from their baskets, and even having the queues cut." It was also reported that their wash-houses were set afire, and when they tried to escape from burning houses they were beaten and sometimes compelled to die in the flames. The police afforded little protection against these outrageous attacks and the victims did not retaliate. The Chinese government, however, demanded an indemnity, which was paid by the United States government.

Agitation for the exclusion of the Chinese rose throughout the 1870's. At first, there was little support in Congress as most people east of the Rockies had not encountered many Chinese, if any, and the Southern states were watching to see whether, after Emancipation, they might not need to replace Negro labor with Chinese. With the collapse of Reconstruction, the Southerners in Congress supported the Californians, and the Chinese Exclusion Act was passed in 1882, suspending all Chinese immigration for ten years. This was repeated for another ten years in 1892; and in 1902 suspension of Chinese immigration was extended indefinitely. This remained the status of Chinese until 1943, when, under the pressure of the war situation, China was added to the quota immigrant nations and allotted 105 annual entries.

The exclusion of the Chinese by federal legislation is a clear illustration of Congress yielding to the specific will of one of its individual states in the absence of any general national demand. McWilliams has noted the following factors in the situation which help explain it: (1) All but one of some eight anti-Chinese measures passed by Congress were passed on the eve of national elections and for avowed political purposes; (2) the interrelationship of the Southern attitude toward the Negro and the California attitude toward the Oriental prompted Southern representatives to side with California on a *quid pro quo* basis; (3) there was no real knowledge of the Chinese on the part of white Americans throughout the nation, and they failed to recognize the issue as related to national interest.[10]

[9] Davie, *World Immigration,* pp. 311–312.
[10] See Carey McWilliams, *Brothers Under the Skin* (Boston: Little, Brown & Co., 1943), pp. 87–96, for an extensive account and interpretation of the legislation against the Chinese.

Minority Adaptations to Dominance

The Chinese reaction to conflict with dominants was one of passivity and withdrawal. They sought niches in which they would be inconspicuously tolerated.

Occupations

The Chinese moved primarily out of rural areas, and developed occupations that either served their own group (such as restaurants, bakeries, small businesses), or served the outside the community in positions where there was a labor shortage (such as in laundries, domestic service, etc.)

Residence

Like other minorities, the Chinese clustered in special sections. This was, in part, natural and voluntary, because of their cultural ties, but it was maintained as a result of discrimination because other housing was not open to them. Chinatowns have spread to all the major cities in the United States where there is any sizable population.[11]

These Chinatowns became worlds of their own, with their own system of organization. In the end, they did harm to the public image of the Chinese, as they seemed to be alien and mysterious places. They were, indeed, in former times, not only residential subcommunities, but centers of illegal activities.

Old San Francisco Chinatown: The Anti-Chinese Stereotype

The largest Chinatown in the United States has always been in San Francisco, for many years the most powerful in the network of associational relationships for Chinese in America. Many activities, illegal in America, merely reproduced acceptable behavior in old China. For example, opium has always been smoked in China since the British introduced it in the nineteenth century. It is not surprising, therefore, that a great deal of the narcotics smuggling of former times was located in Chinatown and fortunes were made from the drug traffic. Opium smuggling and opium consumption was at its height in the 1880's, and has gradually declined since then.[12] Then, too, there was active prostitution, since apart from the well-to-do merchants, very few Chinese brought wives, and the predominant immigrant population was male. The Chinese were great gamblers, and gambling houses were part of the Chinese picture. The existence of these illegal activities helped create a stereotyped image of the Chinese, which probably reached its height in the fictitious character of the nefarious Dr. Fu Manchu.

[11] There are no Chinatowns to be found in cities under 50,000 population and no Chinatowns in states having fewer than 250 Chinese. D. Y. Yuan, "Voluntary Segregation: A Study of New York Chinatown," *Phylon* 3rd quarter, Autumn, 1963, pp. 255–265.
[12] Leong Gor Yun, *Chinatown Inside Out* (New York: Barrows Mussey Inc., 1936), p. 216.

San Francisco was also headquarters for some of the major "tongs." These are merchant associations and in former times there were often violent outbreaks as they attempted to control a particular street or territory. The national press often played up these "tong wars."

The slot racket had seriously disorganizing consequences in the American Chinese community: (1) It added an illegal activity. In addition to "paper" families, many Chinese men had wives in China whom they could not or would not bring to this country. In time these men remarried here, thus victimizing native-born girls and their offspring. (2) It increased the tendency for the Chinese to fail to cooperate with American authorities. Even innocent resident Chinese who might have wanted to expose the perpetrators were likely to fear to do so. (3) The "slotted" residents led a dual life, fearful of exposure which might lead to deportation. (4) It helped perpetuate the tongs, because many slotted individuals relied on them to protect their false status or that of their "illegal" families in the United States. The attention given to these factors by the police and the press obscured the fact that thousands of Chinese lived out their lives in Chinatown in an orderly and structured fashion.

The Social Structure of the Subcommunity: New York Chinatown [13]

New York City has the second largest Chinatown in the United States. An examination of it will delineate the social structure of the immigrant Chinese community as it has been preserved in Chinatowns throughout the nation. New York can also illustrate the changes and the problems that confront members of this subcommunity. New York City Chinatown is the nodal center for an estimated 60,000 Chinese in the Metropolitan area. (The Chinese population is believed to be much larger than the census figures.) The sex ratio in 1950 was 4:1 male-female; the age distribution, predominantly middle-aged. The major economic strength of the district was restaurants and laundries.

Chinatown serves social, economic, cultural, and political functions. Socially, Chinatown is indispensable for Chinese, as such a high proportion have no nuclear family life. (There are many single males, living alone, scattered through the Metropolitan area and having no social contact with their local neighborhoods.) Economically, Chinatown is an entrepôt for the redistribution of Chinese goods, especially foods for the great Chinese restaurant industry. Culturally, it supports five Chinese newspapers, three Chinese schools, book stores, printing houses, and Chinese movie theaters. Politically, it houses the headquarters of all political and social organizations. Today Chinatown has about 160 voluntary organizations. These make up the network of the power structure of Chinatown at whose apex is the Chinese Consolidated Benevolent Society.

[13] The authors are indebted to Miss Pauline Fung for her analysis of the social structure of New York Chinatown in 1966 in a senior paper for Barnard College Sociology Department.

The stated purpose of the Chinese Consolidated Benevolent Society is to maintain a Chinese school, to keep peace and order, to do charitable work, and to supervise immigration and other activities of Chinese residents. It was registered in 1911 with the Peking Imperial Court as the supervisory organization for overseas Chinese. It was responsible not to the government of China, but to the great families of China for their overseas kin. In the 1920's it was registered in New York State as a charity organization. It has been, in the past and for the older generation, the "supreme" organization. Its present situation is that of authority for the older generation. This means, however, there is still considerable authority because of the Chinese age-grading system. However, it is being challenged by the younger Chinese who have formed such organizations as The Chinese Democratic Club and the Chinese Junior Chamber of Commerce.

Family Associations

The simplest form of organization in Chinatown is the family association. These are societies of people bearing the same surname. They do not need to be blood relations. Generally, there will be one family association in each Chinatown that is the most powerful. Not all family names have enough people to support an organization, in which case a few of the weaker families will make a combined group. However, these combinations are not at random. They find some justification for association in Chinese history or literature. The family association is subdivided into a smaller group called a *fong* which is organized according to the village from which the immigrants came. The family associations have social and economic functions. They find jobs, provide capital, finance education, adjudicate disputes among members, provide housing, contacts, and so on. The social functions (mostly held on Sundays) are also important for the dispersed, isolated members of the family group.

Territorial Associations

Most of the Chinese in New York Chinatown are from Kuangtung Province (the Province of Canton). Within this territory there are associations of people from four counties who speak variants of the same Cantonese dialect. Then there are the Haka-speaking people who have an association, and there are several smaller groups from Eastern provinces and one for the Northern Mandarin-speaking Chinese. The territorial associations form the intermediate power structure. The most powerful of them alternate in providing the President of the Chinese Consolidated Benevolent Society (usually for a two-year term). They have social functions, especially for the older people, but they do not have jurisdiction in disputes. This is the prerogative of the family associations.

The Tongs

These, as we have said, are merchant associations. In New York the two major Tongs control each of the two major business streets, Mott Street and

Pell Street. They also control dispersed businesses outside of Chinatown. Their major purpose is to limit competition and assure thereby a reasonable livelihood for each of their merchants. Their control outside of Chinatown is declining.

Changing Chinatown

The structure of Chinatown was first challenged a generation ago with the organization of the Laundry Alliance in 1933. Until this time the Chinatown power structure controlled the lives of the little people with the pattern of gentlemanly "face" and power structure "favor" and a considerable amount of official "squeeze" in the best style of Chinese officialdom. It is probable that the laundrymen would never have had the boldness to organize—so humble was their position in the hierarchy—had not outside circumstances threatened their very existence. The large American laundries instituted a systematic campaign against the Chinese laundries, displaying placards showing Chinese laundrymen spitting on white shirts. The Chinese Consul-General protested and with the aid of the city police succeeded in having most of the placards removed. The Chinese Consolidated Benevolent Society assessed each laundryman a dollar as an "anti-placard" fee. In March of 1933 there was a proposed city ordinance to license public laundries with a $25 fee and a $1,000 security bond required. The liberal *Chinese Journal* took up the cause of the laundrymen. The CCB, through the editor's prodding, had to take some action, but it was concerned to keep control. However, an able leader, Louis Wing, emerged from among the laundrymen, and with the help of the editor of the *Chinese Journal* in space rented from the Roman Catholic Church on Mott Street, an organization was formed that became an independent, self-determining body. There were many struggles to bypass the Chinatown power structure, and at one point the *Chinese Journal* was boycotted, but both the Alliance and the *Journal* survived. The organization grew, it cooperated with the efforts for improved conditions of other organizations of service trades and by 1935 moved its headquarters outside Chinatown.[14] Its trucks may be seen all over New York today.

During the 1930's and 1940's there was a considerable exodus from Chinatown. The younger, the better educated, in the better occupational positions tended to go to newer sections of metropolitan New York.[15] Chinatown in the early 1950's was left with an older, poorer, less well-educated general population, which for the oldest generation contained a sharp cleavage between the power elite and stranded sojourners.[16] Many of the American-born second generation are more conservative than the newest immigrants, as Chinatown has managed

[14] Leong, *Chinatown Inside Out,* Ch. 5, pp. 85–106.

[15] D. Y. Yuan, "Chinatown and Beyond: The Chinese Population in Metropolitan New York," *Phylon,* Fourth Quarter, Winter, 1966, pp. 321–322.

[16] Stuart H. Cattell, *Health, Welfare and Social Organization in Chinatown, New York City.* A Report Prepared for the Chinatown Public Health Nursing Demonstration of the Department of Public Affairs, Community Service Society of New York, August 1962, p. 52. (Mimeographed.)

to preserve a form of Chinese culture that disappeared in China decades ago.[17] The teenagers of the third generation are often in open conflict as they seek to emulate American behavior patterns.

Cattell describes many barriers that aggravate the situation of many Chinatown families. There is unfamiliarity with and cultural resistance to using the health and welfare services available. Yet there is a high incidence of illness and of mental illness. In a sample study of 105 cases (1958–60) the highest percentages were infective diseases and nutritional diseases.[18] These reflect some of the principal problems of Chinatown: low income and bad housing.

Of the 2,323 Chinese families living in Chinatown in 1950, 37 percent had incomes of less than $3,000, and 55 percent had less than $4,000. The New York State Housing Survey of 1950 reported that more than 30 percent of the dwelling units did not contain flush toilets; 48 percent had no bathtub or shower; 40 percent lacked hot water; 71 percent did not have central heating.[19]

The New Migration to Chinatown

In the 1930's New York's Chinatown was threatened by an invasion of Italians from the north. Leong felt, in 1936, that it might be swallowed up.[20] Quite the opposite has happened. Chinese have driven the Italians out of Mulberry Street to the north. This is largely due to the influx of immigrants, many from Hong Kong, Taiwan, and Singapore, which began with the 1965 revision of the immigration law. This has changed the balance of population as well as increased the numbers. The older social structure is not equipped to handle this influx; where formerly the population was predominantly male, today there are many women and children. Delinquent gangs have emerged for the first time; the surrounding public schools have had the proportion of Chinese pupils rise markedly. Chinatown has set up a garment industry within its borders, now organized into Local 23 of the International Ladies Garment Workers Union. With all this ferment, some Chinese Americans are moving back to Chinatown from outlying small communities.[21] Some new housing has been built adjacent to Chinatown.

The Decline of Dominance

World War II opened many occupational opportunities to the American Chinese, especially in white-collar and technical-professional positions. A large and increasing proportion of this minority are more American than Chinese. Some of them now occupy top-ranking teaching, executive, managerial, and

[17] Ibid., p. 48.
[18] Ibid., p. 58 and Table following.
[19] Yuan, "Chinatown and Beyond," pp. 324–325.
[20] Leong, Chinatown Inside Out, p. 238.
[21] Paul Hoffmann, "New Wave of Immigrants Floods Chinatown, Bringing Challenge and Change," New York Times, June 28, 1967, pp. 47, and 91.

research positions in American corporations, banks, and universities. They participate in formal organizations of the larger society in their communities, including some country clubs. They have in some instances married Anglo Americans. They do not experience major value conflicts. They feel that they have not experienced discrimination. They include the dispersed suburban Chinese and some of the modern leaders in the urban Chinese subcommunities. To what extent then may we consider them assimilated?

A contemporary study of two Chinese American clubs in suburbia shows us something of the pattern of friendship, community participation, and sense of identity of Chinese Americans.

The Chinese of Long Island [22]

Miss Kuo studied two social clubs: *The Circle* and *The Center on Long Island*. These serve a dispersed membership in various suburbs within commuting distance of New York City. The families live in Anglo neighborhoods and represent the same socioeconomic status as their neighbors. The informants report no incidents of hostility. Miss Kuo attributes this in part to the fact that they are dispersed rather than heavily concentrated. Furthermore she emphasizes three other factors that gain them acceptance: they maintain an appropriate style of life consistent with their neighbors; their children are well behaved and often achieve high academic status in school; they are courteous in their attitudes and behavior toward their neighbors.

The Circle is a women's club of about 70 members. It is composed of a young group (average age 30) of American-born Chinese who are teachers, social workers, and white-collar workers. Their husbands have occupations that are skilled, professional, or business. Miss Kuo estimates their average annual income for the family as about $10,000. Some of these women are college educated. This club has a typical American cast. It provides social events for adults, teenagers, and children; it raises scholarship funds for able young Chinese Americans.

Most of the members of *The Circle* did not grow up in Chinatown. English is the first language for them, though many can speak Chinese to elders or relatives in Chinatown. Most of their parents were skilled workers. In their homes, only English is spoken. They share the American dream of mobility, have aspirations for their children, and have frequent contacts and some friendships with other Americans.

We see this group of American Chinese, then, to be like any other mobile descendents of immigrants in their values and their behavior. Their need to form a "circle," however, suggests that on the one hand they are aware of themselves as a distinct minority and find pleasure and security in associations with people of their own ethnic background and similar socioeconomic level.

The Center has about a hundred members, men and their wives of a more

[22] The authors are indebted to Miss Chia Ling Kuo, Instructor in Anthropology, Rutgers, The State University of New Jersey, for the use of material from her unpublished study.

successful stratum. They are a more recent migration, persons who came from China to the United States for advanced training and could not return after the fall of the Nationalist government. They are of upper middle class and upper class origin in China and have maintained or improved their status in America. (This organization does not include the most elite of the New York Chinese such as Professor Wu, the Nobel prize winning physicist, or Pei, the architect, or Tsai, the eminent member of the New York Stock Exchange.) Nevertheless they are engineers, professors, managers and owners of small factories, consultants and accountants.

The Center consciously works to further Chinese-American cultural relations. The programs are designed on the one hand to widen the membership's knowledge and appreciation of American culture, and on the other hand, to acquaint the American-born children and the non-Chinese community with Chinese art, philosophy, drama, and the classical Chinese language.

According to Miss Kuo this group is unevenly acculturated. Those who were upper class in origin, or who were raised in the large coastal cities of China, or who were raised in Christian high schools and universities are the most acculturated because of early and constant exposure to Western culture in China. Those who belong to only one or none of these categories are still in the process of acculturation. Most of the men associate with non-Chinese at work. They are active in local civic organizations. Eighty percent of the women are active in church groups. In their daily life they live like other Americans of similar economic status. Since they are a more highly trained group than the young members of *The Circle* they are in a higher income bracket, have larger and better furnished homes, celebrate American New Year with open house for their neighbors, take up tennis, swimming, dancing. They feel they have not encountered prejudice, but they are more ethnocentric in their attempts to preserve for their children and communicate to the non-Chinese community their regard for scholastic achievement, filial piety, harmony, and compromise in human relations as presented in Confucian ethics. Although these families speak English at home, and their children, who go to private schools and Ivy League colleges do not speak Chinese, their children are more familiar with Chinese history and culture than the children of the American-born group studied.

Miss Kuo concludes that the Chinese on Long Island are partially integrated into American life through formal group participation; that those with high technical skills are structurally assimilated regardless of degree of acculturation; and the Chinese desire for complete assimilation is real despite the fact that at present they still seek primary-group contacts among themselves.

New Wind in Chinatown

In 1966 the first Chinese American in New York, Edward Hong, an Illinois-trained lawyer, ran for Congress for the district that includes Chinatown. He was defeated, but his candidacy foreshadows the imminent participation of Chinese in American politics. The Chinatown Chamber of Commerce met in June, 1967, to plan development projects for their subcommunity. Federal funds have been secured through the Chinatown Planning Council, which is establishing preschool, tutoring, and youth programs. More and more people are using the services of public and private health and welfare agencies as the ineffectiveness of the old Chinatown organizational structure to meet contemporary problems becomes apparent. Mr. Hong feels it is time for the 90,000 Chinese in the New York metropolitan area who have never had a judge or a deputy commissioner to have a political voice.[23]

Changing Dominant Attitudes to the Chinese in America

The last two decades have seen a marked change in the opening of the American opportunity structure to Chinese. The days when a Chinese graduate of an American university didn't have a chance of getting work other than as a waiter or in a laundry have passed. There is a general recognition that the traditional Chinese values of hard work, ambition, respect for education, mesh very well with the American values. The public image of the Chinese, in most instances based largely on mass communication has been aided by the stratum of successful men who were stranded here by the change of government in China.

Chinatowns, not only in New York, but equally in San Francisco, Chicago, Los Angeles, and Boston have passed through the phases of being centers of illegal activities, segregated subcommunities or tourist traps, and are dispersing their populations, as well as receiving a new and more modern influx; and they are forcing, albeit modestly, recognition for their members in the larger society. In some places, and perhaps more frequently on the West Coast, where there is a long tradition of anti-Oriental sentiment, Chinese still find some discrimination in housing.

THE SOUTHWOOD CASE   A China-born student who served in the Chinese army, advancing to the rank of captain in World War II, came to this country in 1943 and graduated from an American College intending to go in the consular service of his country. Following the Communist revolution, he decided to remain in this country, having in the meantime married an American-born Chinese girl. They settled in an apartment in a South San Francisco suburb and the husband worked as an airplane mechanic. This couple answered an "ad" of a house for sale, bought it successfully, and were preparing to move in when the "news" of their coming leaked out and spread through the neighborhood. Late that afternoon, a neighbor paraded up and down in front of the house, shouting with raised fist, "The Chinese are coming." The white sellers received irate letters and were later threatened with economic reprisals. The Chinese couple received threatening phone calls and letters. Not easily dissuaded, the young couple called for a public meeting in the area to discuss the situation. This was followed by informal voting on the matter. The tally

[23] Paul Hoffman in *The New York Times,* June 28, 1967, p. 91.

was 174 I object; 28 no objection; and 14 no opinion. The couple gave up the house.[24]

The above case is not cited to suggest that the entrance of a Chinese family to all Caucasian neighborhoods is always opposed in this fashion. Lee indicates that many Chinese families have settled in the suburban neighborhoods of San Mateo and Burlingame. And even in Southwood this couple had some white supporters and received many expressions of regret from various dominant status people.

Although still not a large number, there has been some intermarriage in the upper-status groups between dominants and Chinese. (Because of the predominance of males in the older migration there has always been some intermarriage with other minorities in the lower socioeconomic groups, largely Chinese men to Mexican, Puerto Rican, and Negro women.)

As the dispersion and integration of the Chinese progresses they have often been local community leaders in "race relations," serving as buffers between dominants and more depressed minorities.

The Outlook

Many factors are operating to forecast complete assimilation of the Chinese in America. They are not a large minority. Many of the traditional values (as contrasted with social organization) are coherent with American values. They have made real contributions to the intellectual, professional, and business life of America. They are urban and suburban with behavioral and social structural patterns that are now the dominant ones in America. Because of the history of the older migration they have some contribution to make to the total problems of an interethnic society. They are becoming more vigorous in their participation in American institutions other than the economic. Most middle-class Chinese in America are Christian and active members of churches.

Their vulnerability is not, however, eliminated. Whether there will be a revival of anti-Chinese sentiment will depend on the international situation. If the present Chinese government in China becomes a major target for finding a devil, there may be repercussions on American Chinese as scapegoats. For example, in the Korean war:

> In Woodland, California, a family lost their son recently in the battlefield in Korea. When the Defense Department notified them, parents, wife and brother were deeply grieved. Filled with a desire for revenge, they gathered their friends and relatives and headed toward a Chinese restaurant in that town. They broke into the establishment and destroyed everything within. Dishes, glasses, furniture, etc. were all ruined. The damages were estimated to be very great.[25]

[24] Adapted from Lee, *The Chinese in the United States*, pp. 315–319. By permission.
[25] The excerpt is from an editorial in the *Chinese Journal*, New York, December 1, 1950. The editorial warned the Chinese in America that they face close scrutiny from the F.B.I. under the present circumstances, particularly those who would be classified as enemy aliens in the case of formal declaration of war.

That some of the Chinese are aware of this threat is indicated in the full page advertisement in *The New York Times,* November 5, 1965.[26] It spoke for 16 million overseas Chinese against the present government of China. The countries represented in the advertisement were Australia, Austria, Belgium, Brazil, Canada, Chile, Colombia, Costa Rica, Curaçao, the Dominican Republic, Ecuador, Fiji, France, the German Federal Republic, Guatemala, Honduras, Hong Kong, India, Italy, Jamaica, Japan, Korea, Laos, Macao, Mexico, Mozambique, New Zealand, Nicaragua, Panama, Peru, the Philippines, Portugal, the Ryukyus, El Salvador, South Africa, Spain, Surinam, Tahiti, Thailand, Timor, the United Kingdom, the United States, Uruguay, Venezuela, and Vietnam. In the United States fourteen Chinese organizations were signers of the advertisement in ten cities. They ranged in type from Chinese Consolidated Benevolent Societies, to Anti-Communist Leagues, to the Chinese American Alliance of Houston, Texas, to the On Leong Chinese Merchant Association.

Indications thus far are that the Chinese in America will be a conservative political force with regard to values, a private-enterprise economic system, and a technological society. On the other hand, they are a leaven in the difficult problems of an ethnically and racially multigroup society.

Topics for Projects and Discussion

1. Are there any Chinese in your community? How many? What type of organizations have they? How are they viewed in the public schools?
2. Using the back files of *Time* find out what you can about distinguished Chinese who have made major creative contributions to American society.
3. Make a little study among your friends and your parents' friends as to how they would describe the Chinese; would they welcome, object, be indifferent to Chinese neighbors?
4. Find out what you can about Confucian values and compare them with your understanding of American values.
5. Discuss the implications of the changed international situation for Chinese in the United States. Can you find anything that gives you a sense of what the Chinese communist government has done for villages and poor people?

Suggested Reading

Barth, Gunther. *Bitter Strength: A History of the Chinese in the United States, 1850–1870.* Cambridge, Mass.: Harvard University Press, 1964.
> *A vivid account of the life conditions and work conditions of Chinese in the U.S. in the period of heaviest nineteenth-century migration, with excellent source materials.*

Lee, Rose Hum. *The Chinese in the United States of America.* Hong Kong: Hong Kong University Press, 1960. Distributed in the United States by Oxford University Press, New York.
> *The most comprehensive and informative single volume on the Chinese in the United States*

[26] *The New York Times,* Nov. 5, 1965, p. 38.

Leong, Gor Yun. *Chinatown Inside Out*. New York: Barrows Mussey, 1936.

> *A picture of the old Chinatowns with excellent prints and photographs, by a journalistic author who sees the potentials of change. (The author, by name, is clearly related to one of the great merchant associations operative in many cities of the United States.)*

McWilliams, Carey. *Brothers Under the Skin*. Boston: Little, Brown and Co., 1943.

> *A summary of dominant actions against Chinese, especially on the West coast.*

Waln, Nora. *The House of Exile*. Boston: Little, Brown and Co., 1933.

> *A beautiful account of life in an upper-class Chinese family by an American Quaker, which gives a vivid sense of ideal Chinese values and social structure.*

9

The Japanese in the United States
Mainland

Like the Chinese, the Japanese settled on the West Coast, but in a more stable period in that region's history. While eventually they may have incurred more antagonism from the natives than the Chinese did, they were spared the physical violence suffered by the Chinese in the lawless frontier days. Japanese culture was Asiatic, like that of the Chinese, but Japan had already entered a period of technological development so that their literacy was greater and their skills better suited to rapid economic adjustment. It is perhaps because of this superiority from the standpoint of making a living that their subsequent relations with the natives followed a different course than those of the Chinese.

Although most of the Chinese remained on the West Coast, a considerable number scattered in cities throughout the northern part of the country. But up to the time of their relocation the Japanese remained highly concentrated in the Pacific coast states. While the Chinese reacted to native opposition with extreme passivity, as has been shown, the Japanese were less tractable. They held their ground, refusing to disperse like the Chinese, and made ingenious adaptations to the various economic discriminations inflicted on them, such as devising a plan whereby an alien father bought land in the name of his native-born son. Consequently, while the native population came to think of the Chinese in stereotype A—the inferior, humble, and ignorant, who could be condescendingly tolerated—the Japanese came to be treated according to stereotype B—the aggressive, cunning, and conspiratorial, requiring more active and outright dominance to keep them "in their place."

Like the Chinese, the Japanese retained a greater interest in their homeland than the European immigrants, as manifested in the large number constantly returning to Japan. Yet the Japanese population in the United States shows an almost steady rise, while up to 1930, as we have seen, that of the Chinese showed some years of decline. Finally, both groups suffered from the humiliation of severe legislative discrimination, culminating in drastic federal laws. The manner, however, of handling the federal restriction of immigration was noticeably more diplomatic in the case of the Japanese, a contrast attributable to the greater power of the Japanese government, a government able to protest more effectively against the discriminatory treatment of their nationals in this country.

Japanese Population Trends

For over 200 years, from 1638 to 1868, Japanese citizens were forbidden to go abroad, and foreigners, with few exceptions, were forbidden to enter Japan. The first to go out from the Land of the Rising Sun were students sent to gain knowledge from the rest of the world. Soon after, a limited number of laborers were permitted to leave. But it was the agreement signed by the Japanese government and certain Hawaiian sugar plantation owners in 1885 by which Japanese contract laborers were permitted to go to Hawaii that set emigration into momentum. From then until 1924 there was considerable Japanese migration to Asiatic Russia (302,946), to Hawaii (238,758), to the United States (196,543), and to China (105,258); and, in more limited numbers, to Canada, Brazil, the Philippines, Peru, Korea, and Australia. Considering the enormous rate of population growth in Japan during these decades and the consequent population pressure, the relatively modest amount of emigration is surprising. The failure to emigrate in larger numbers to the areas of the world settled by Europeans was due in part to the unfriendly manner with which the Japanese were received and to the legal restrictions imposed. The special circumstances leading to substantial Japanese immigration to Hawaii are discussed in Chapter 17.

With overlapping in the 1881–1890 decade, Japanese immigration to the continental United States takes on where Chinese immigration falls off. Tables 9–1 and 9–2, respectively, show the number of Japanese immigrants admitted from 1861–1965 and the total Japanese population, which of course includes the native-born, at the decennial years with 1961–65 included.

The increase in the Japanese population from 1880 to 1910 was due largely

TABLE 9–1. *Japanese Immigration to the United States* [1]

1861–70	186
1871–80	149
1881–90	2,270
1891–00	25,942
1901–10	129,797
1911–20	83,837
1921–30	33,462
1931–40	1,948
1941–50	1,555
1951–60	46,250
1961–65	19,126

[1] *Annual Reports of the Immigration and Naturalization Service.*

TABLE 9–2. *Japanese Population in Mainland United States* [2]

Census Year	Number	Decade	Percentage Rate of Increase
1860	0		
1870	55		
1880	148	1870–80	169.1
1890	2,039	1880–90	1,277.7
1900	24,326	1890–00	1,093.0
1910	72,157	1900–10	196.6
1920	111,010	1910–20	53.8
1930	138,834	1920–30	25.1
1940	126,947	1930–40	− 13.1
1950	141,768	1940–50	11.6
1960	260,887*	1950–60	83.3**

* The 1960 Census includes Hawaii, giving a total Japanese population of 464,332.
** Based on mainland figures without Hawaii. The percentage increase of the Japanese population for the United States including Hawaii for the 1950–1960 decade was 42.3.

to immigration itself, since the great preponderance of the newcomers were male. After the agitation on the West Coast for restricting Japanese immigration, President Theodore Roosevelt negotiated directly with the Japanese government, and the so-called Gentleman's Agreement was made in 1907. It provided that Japan would not issue passports for the continental United States to laborers unless they were coming to resume a formerly acquired domicile, to join a parent, husband, or child, or to resume control of a farming enterprise which they had left. This agreement did not completely close the door to Japanese immigration, and the growth of the population was due partly to that continued, though greatly diminished, immigration. More significant, however, is the fact that many of the immigrants after 1907 were women, frequently "picture brides." By 1930 the sex ratio among the Japanese in this country had declined to 143.3 males for every 100 females—much more normal than that of either the Chinese or the Filipinos living here. The only decennial decline in Japanese population occurred in the 1930–1940 decade, during which the number of returning homeland emigrants exceeded 8,000, while slightly fewer than 2,000 new immigrants came in. This trend apparently continued up to the time of Pearl Harbor, since the estimated population in 1942 was only 122,000.

As Table 9–2 shows, the population of Americans of Japanese descent on the mainland has continued to increase, reaching 260,887 in 1960.[3] The surprising increase in the 1950–1960 decade cannot be accounted for by births or by the allocation to Japan of an annual quota of 185 for the first time under the

[2] *Advanced Reports,* United States Census, 1940, Vol. II, Table 4, p. 19; also *Advanced Reports,* 1960, Annual Population Characteristics, P. C. (A2)–1, Table 1, p. 4.
[3] Figure obtained by subtracting the Japanese in Hawaii in 1960 (203,445) from the total Japanese population of the United States (464,332). See note in Table 9–2.

McCarran-Walter Immigration Act in 1952. It is largely due to the admission of wives of male American citizens, Oriental or Caucasian. From 1961 to 1965, of the 19,126 Japanese immigrants admitted to the country, 13,601, or 68 percent, were wives of American citizens.[4]

As we have noted, the Japanese population, unlike the Chinese, remained heavily concentrated on the West Coast, particularly in California, up to the time of the attack on Pearl Harbor. In 1940, of the 127,000 Japanese, both foreign-born and native-born citizens, 111,000, or about 88 percent, resided on the West Coast. California alone had 83 percent, and most of these were in Los Angeles County. Outside of the West, the only two cities having enough Japanese to form a distinctive colony were Chicago and New York. Chicago had a larger Japanese population than any other city except Los Angeles, estimated at 15,000 to 20,000.[5] In New York a Japanese colony has existed since the late nineteenth century, reaching at one point nearly 5,000, but at the outbreak of the war numbering about 2,000.[6] The relocation of the Japanese resulting from their evacuation from the West Coast and their resettlement has considerably changed the pattern of distribution as will be discussed below.

The Establishment of Dominance

The Characteristics of the Japanese

The Japanese immigrants were Mongoloid in "racial type" and therefore easily identifiable as different by white Americans, even though not always distinguishable physiognomically from the other Asians.

The culture in which the Japanese immigrants had been reared differed more markedly from that of America than the culture of the European immigrants; yet in some aspects it prepared the Japanese for more successful adjustment to life in this country. Before the period of Japanese immigration, Japan had begun transforming itself from a semifeudal into a modern industrial nation. Thus its culture was a mixture of the traditional and the new. Basic in its traditional culture was the intricate set of mores which defined the strong obligation of the individual to the group, to the family, to those of superior class, and to the state. The authoritarian character of Japanese social organization produced markedly obedient and self-effacing personality traits in the Japanese people. The strong sense of subordination of the individual to the welfare of the group was reflected in the solidarity of Japanese groups in this country. Deriving also from long tradition was the intricate pattern of etiquette

[4] Annual Reports of the Immigration and Naturalization Service. For each annual report during these five years, see Table 9–1.

[5] *People in Motion: The Postwar Adjustment of the Evacuated Japanese,* United States Department of Interior Publication (Washington, D.C.: Government Printing Office, n.d.), p. 168.

[6] Bradford Smith, *Americans from Japan* (Philadelphia: J. B. Lippincott Co., 1948), p. 336.

and ritual which prescribed the proper way of behaving in every situation. To conform punctiliously to these elaborate social rituals was a major drive in the Japanese personality, accounting for the reputation for courtesy and good manners which the nineteenth-century Japanese acquired.

The ferment of rapid change had begun in earnest at the beginning of the Meiji Era (1868–1912). The conscious policy of the ruling elite was to transform Japan into an industrial nation with Western technological methods under a centralized government. To the already great skill in farming, necessitated by population pressure and little tillable acreage, new scientific agricultural methods were added. Public education was developed to a high level. The development of scientific medicine and programs of public health were encouraged. While it is difficult to know how much all these new influences affected the mass of the Japanese people, nevertheless, in the willingness to learn and to experiment in matters technological and economic, the Japanese did surpass not only all other Asians but many European immigrant groups.

Native Reaction to the Japanese

The West Coast region to which the Japanese first came was greatly undersettled and provided economic opportunity for population growth and economic development with many menial jobs to be filled. The Japanese were therefore welcomed by the natives in the capacity of laborers. The first Japanese in the United States were employed in domestic service. As their numbers increased, some became engaged in a wide variety of menial jobs and others began to operate small shops. Because at first their numbers were small and the jobs they took did not affect the employment opportunities of white American workers, little opposition was felt. Beginning about 1890, however, antagonism began to be displayed by members of labor unions. In that year Japanese cobblers were attacked by members of the shoemakers' union. In 1892, a Japanese restaurant in San Francisco was attacked by members of the local cooks' and waiters' union.[7] From then on, anti-Japanese activity grew steadily in California, rising to a climax in the famous School Board Affair in 1906, when the San Francisco Board of Education passed a resolution requiring the segregation of all Oriental children in one school. At the time there were ninety-three Japanese attending twenty-three different public schools of San Francisco. The resolution brought protest from the Japanese government and precipitated a crisis between the Imperial Government and that of the United States, which led to the signing of the Gentlemen's Agreement in 1907.

The rising antagonism toward the Japanese in the cities led them to turn to agriculture.[8] They started out as farm laborers and by the late 1890's out-

[7] Yamato Ichihashi, *Japanese in the United States* (Stanford: Stanford University Press, 1932), pp. 229–230.

[8] *Ibid.,* see Chs. 11, 12, 13, for an account of the progress of the Japanese in American agriculture.

numbered the Chinese laborers. By 1909 they constituted a large part of the
farm labor force in the western states. It was natural for the Japanese to turn
to agriculture. They brought with them knowledge of intensive cultivation of
the soil superior to that of many American native farmers. It was likewise
natural that more and more of them should aspire to operate farms themselves.
By 1909 there were 6,000 Japanese operating farms, the greater number by far
as tenants.[9] They experimented with small-scale farming, finally concentrating
on fruits and vegetables. They were adaptable, thrifty and industrious, and the
number of Japanese-operated farms increased until 1920.[10]

The success of the Japanese in moving from laborer to entrepreneur, even
though on a small scale and usually involving the payment of rent to white
owners, led to opposition from white farmers, culminating in the passage in
California of the first alien land holding act in 1913. Under this legislation,
aliens ineligible for citizenship could lease agricultural land for periods not
to exceed three years but could not own it. When it was discovered that the
Japanese were buying stock in land-owning corporations and acquiring land
in the name of their native-born children, further pressure resulted in a new
act, which in substance prohibited the leasing of land by any method by
Japanese foreign-born. Similar laws were passed by other Western states, and
their constitutionality was upheld by the United States Supreme Court in a
test case in 1923. From then on the role of the Japanese in agriculture declined,
and return to the cities increased. Nevertheless, at the time of Pearl Harbor
they controlled large segments of California's berry and vegetable crops.

The Stabilization of Dominance

Adjustment of the Japanese as a Minority

As with all immigrant groups, the Japanese reacted to minority status by
forming separate subcommunities, which were a mixture of Old World traits
and accommodative institutions. On the West Coast the main little Tokyo's were
in San Francisco, Los Angeles, and Seattle. For the latter, Miyamoto made an
extensive study at the end of the 1930's from which we draw.[11]

> The traditional heritage was most clearly seen in the continuance of the patri-
> archal Japanese family, with its extreme emphasis on male authority and filial
> obligations. In recreation likewise, their play life tended "to revolve about activities
> that are essentially Japanese in character." The two Japanese daily newspapers in
> Seattle in 1935 were heavily devoted to activities of the homeland, and few of the
> foreign-born Japanese read American papers.
>
> Among the accommodative institutions were the economic "pools," the *tanamo-*

[9] *Ibid.,* p. 178.
[10] *Ibid.,* p. 193.
[11] Shataro Frank Miyamoto, *Social Solidarity among the Japanese in Seattle,* University of
Washington Publications in the Social Sciences, Vol. 11, No. 2 (Dec. 1939), pp. 57–130.

shi. While 31 percent of the Japanese were in domestic service and 45 percent in the trades, there were a substantial number operating small mercantile establishments of their own. But few could accumulate enough capital for these ventures; it required the help of friends and relatives for the start. Often kinfolk formed pools from which various members could draw in initiating new enterprises. Seattle's Japanese had a local branch of the Japanese Chamber of Commerce (*Ken-Jin*) which served social and charitable functions, as well as acting as an agency of social control throughout the Japanese community and representing it in its relations to the larger community.

The high value which Japanese placed on education served to accelerate acculteration. While most of the immigrants themselves lacked higher education, they encouraged their children not only to continue school but also to excel in their studies. The strong discipline of the Japanese parents over their children was employed to reinforce the authority of the school. Between 1930 and 1937 in the nine Seattle high schools fifteen Japanese students were either valedictorians or salutatorians of their classes.

In religion, it is somewhat striking to note that 1,200 Seattle Japanese belonged to Christian churches in 1936, more than belonged to all the Japanese religious groups combined. Miyamoto suggests that the many practical services rendered by the mission churches encouraged Japanese membership.

The American-Born Japanese

The increasing acculturation of the Nisei [12] developed cleavages in the closely integrated and self-sufficient Japanese community life. Cultural conflict similar to that noted in the European groups produced similar strains in family life. The younger Japanese considered their parents "too Japanesy" and began to defy their attempts to discipline them according to the traditional family pattern. The children became interested in American sports, desired freedom in their out-of-school life, and wanted to dress in the fashion of their white schoolmates. For the parents this Americanization brought much sorrow. They could not understand that this desire on the part of their children to act like Americans was dictated by the wish to be accepted as Americans.

The typical conflict between generations among immigrant groups was made more intense for the Japanese by the unusual age distribution of their population. The great disparity in the sex ratio of the earlier immigrant group resulted in a great preponderance of males in the older generation. The middle-age generation was proportionately small, and not until the third generation were large numbers of both sexes present. "As late as 1940, only 27,000 of the 80,000 Nisei were over twenty-one.[13] Many Japanese parents sent their children to Japan to be educated. In 1942 it was estimated that at least 25,000 United

[12] For convenience we use the Japanese designation Issei for the foreign born; Nisei, for the first American born; and Sansei for the second and later generations of native born. In addition, the term Kibei is used for those American-born Japanese who were sent back to Japan for their more advanced education.
[13] Bradford Smith, *Americans from Japan,* p. 245.

States citizens of Japanese ancestry had been educated in schools in Japan. Among these kibei, as they were designated, were the Japanese considered most probably disloyal in sentiment at the time of Pearl Harbor.

As with the Chinese, the conflict of the generations, typical in immigrant patterns, had a different sequel from that of the European nationalities. Anxious as the Nisei were to become Americans and forget Japan, they found that, despite their acculturation, the native community looked upon them as "Japs" because of their "racial" visibility. They continued to be discriminated against in three areas—employment, public places, and social contacts.

In employment the educated Nisei had three choices. He could accept prejudice for what it was, and assume the inferior tasks of houseboy, dishwasher, migratory laborer, cannery hand—just what the dominant group expected of him as an inferior. He could go to Japan and forsake America. Or, if he tried, he could get a job at a higher level, though far below his actual qualifications.

Many barbershops, restaurants, and hotels refused service to Orientals. Several large coastal cities had restrictive covenants which kept the Japanese out of any of the attractive neighborhoods. And there were other aspects of discrimination in the social sphere.

> The fear of rebuffs, the constant horror of being humiliated in public, made the Nisei draw together in a tight circle, even at college. . . . [Such] organizations only perpetuated their difficulties. They formed noticeable groups on campus. "There's a barrier between Nisei and the other students," said one. "You can feel it. They never feel easy with each other."
>
> Hostility in the social sphere did not as a rule become noticeable until adolescence. The fear of "miscegenation," the old superstitions about racial "hybrids," the fear that friendship might be construed as having a sexual intent introduced at the courting age, a stiffening of attitudes, yet the Nisei were quite as set against intermarriage as the Caucasians, their own fears and superstitions as deeply rooted.[14]

Evacuation and Relocation: A Case History in White American Dominant Behavior

The stabilized accommodation of the Issei-Nisei generations was rudely shattered by Pearl Harbor. On February 19, 1942, the Army was given authority to establish military zones from which any persons, citizens or alien, might be evacuated and excluded. All Japanese people were ordered to leave the West Coast. This action was the most unprecedented single national action against a large group of people in modern times. Analysis of its causes provides insight into the dynamics of dominant-minority relations in the United States. (We shall return to this after carrying forward an account of what happened to the Japanese after February 19.)

[14] *Ibid.,* p. 250. By permission.

At first the Japanese were given time to remove themselves. A few did leave, but it was soon discovered that they were not wanted elsewhere. A report from the *Los Angeles Times,* March 24, 1942, reads, "Japanese evacuees moving inland from California in a great mass migration will be put in concentration camps if they enter Nevada, Governor E. P. Carville warned tonight." [15] Therefore, on March 27, the Japanese were ordered to stay where they were pending their mass evacuation under military supervision. A new federal agency, The War Relocation Authority, was established to plan for the supervision of the Japanese under detention. Between then and August 8, all West Coast Japanese (over 110,000) were transferred to ten hastily built centers in the Rocky Mountain states and in Arkansas.

In addition to the shocklike psychological effect and the bitterness which evacuation engendered, the Japanese faced enormous economic losses. While the government took steps to protect the material property owned by the Japanese, the guarantees appeared so uncertain that many sold their effects— under the circumstances, of course, at a loss. A business enterprise and a crop in the field could not be "frozen." They had to be disposed of for whatever they would bring at hurried sale or lease, or be abandoned.

Life in the Settlement Centers

The War Relocation Authority faced a unique problem in American history. How the personnel met these problems and how life in the centers affected the Japanese have been extensively studied by highly qualified social scientists.[16] The policy of the WRA was to organize the community life with maximum self-control by the Japanese. All the evidence indicates that the personnel were highly sympathetic to the Japanese, an attitude criticized by the same elements of the white population that had clamored for evacuation. As was almost inevitable under such circumstances, a number of rebellious activities followed. Of these the most serious was a strike by some evacuees at Poston Center, Arizona, arising out of a feeling that two alleged attackers of a white official had been unfairly punished. In consequence of incidents of this nature, Tule Lake Center, California, became a segregation camp where active malcontents from all other centers were placed and controlled under strict discipline.

Resettlement

The other branch of the WRA's operation was engaged through regional offices throughout the nation in trying to find employment for the Nisei outside the center. The WRA also assumed responsibility for helping the resettler adjust to his new community, as well as to his job. One of its hardest

[15] Alexander H. Leighton, *The Governing of Men* (Princeton: Princeton University Press, 1945), p. 36.
[16] *Ibid.* See also Dorothy Swaine Thomas and Richard S. Nishimoto, *The Spoilage* (Berkeley: University of California Press, 1946).

tasks in this connection was to find a place for him to live. This phase of operations has not been given the systematic study which it deserves as a reflection of dominant attitudes. Its activities beginning in the spring of 1943 included the resettlement of the Japanese particularly in the Midwest and the Mountain States. Lack of extensive resettlement in the East was due to Army opposition. Most of those leaving the camps were young adult Nisei who, when they became successfully resettled, often sent for relatives to join them. In the large metropolitan centers it was fairly easy to place Japanese in a wide range of menial and semitechnical jobs. It was difficult to place them in industries with war contracts or in positions calling for contact with the public. Frequent opposition from unions arose. Among the reasons often given for not hiring the Japanese were distrust of their loyalty, the fact that other employers would resent it, that customers would resent it, and that "my son is in the Pacific." While many of the resettlers left their jobs for the same reasons one might under normal circumstances, they also left because of their interest in finding work where they could acquire new skills and get ahead.[17]

Up to January 1, 1945, the date after which evacuees were permitted to return to the West Coast, the WRA had resettled 31,625 Japanese in other parts of the country. Interestingly enough, when the opportunity came, the vast majority of the evacuees returned to their former communities. Since the date for terminating the WRA had been set, their choice had to be quick and the WRA was no longer able to give them individual assistance. It is probable also that many of the Japanese who had been resettled in other areas subsequently returned to the West Coast.

Analysis

As we have noted, the evacuation of all persons of Japanese ancestry from the West Coast and their subsequent internment was a government action without precedent in American history, involving constitutional issues of grave significance. The Supreme Court of the United States upheld the constitutionality of evacuation in wartime,[18] although strong dissents were written by a minority of the justices. However, in retrospect, the whole incident appears to have been a serious error in judgment. For this reason some analysis of the circumstances which led to the steps taken is highly pertinent to the study of dominant-minority relations. The central question engaging our attention is this: To what extent was the decision for evacuation and internment of the Japanese arrived at as a logical necessity for national security, or to what extent was the decision made in response to regional pressures unrelated to security?

THE MILITARY'S JUDGMENT   Since the Western Defense Command of the United States Army was responsible for the decision, it is appropriate to con-

[17] The authors are indebted to Gordon Berryman, a former employee of the WRA, for sharing these insights into the resettlement process.
[18] Koramatsu v. United States, 323, U.S. 214.

sider first the case which it presented in justification of its role in evacuation as presented in its final report.[19] This document referred to as fact some illegal signaling from shore to sea on the West Coast, although it presented no specific proof that Japanese were involved. It cited the result of one spot raid made by the Federal Bureau of Investigation on Japanese homes in which "more than 60,000 rounds of ammunition, and many rifles, shotguns, and maps of all kinds" were found. Such articles, as well as some others, had been declared contraband for enemy aliens. To what extent they were possessed by enemy aliens or by American citizens of Japanese ancestry and to what extent the articles found were evidence of conspiracy is not stated. The report indicated that in three instances in which Japanese submarines shelled West Coast areas, the particular spots chosen were the very ones most out of range of American coastal batteries at the time. It assumed that the Japanese Navy must have had "inside" information, although no evidence was presented to connect West Coast Japanese with this knowledge. The above is in substance the entire case made regarding acts of sabotage or espionage.

Much more of the case presented by the Western Defense Command concerning the security menace of the Japanese was based on the fact that the Japanese were in a position to do much damage and on the assumption that many of them would take such opportunities. The military authorities were much impressed by the residence distribution of the Japanese, which seemed too singularly adjacent to strategic points to be fully coincidental. Surprisingly enough for a military document, the report rested much ot its case on sociological phenomena. Reference was made to "ties of race" as well as strong bonds of common traditional culture that make the Japanese a tightly-knit group. Major emphasis was placed on the considerable number of Japanese associations on the West Coast whose purposes and activities reflected great interest in the ancestral homeland and in some instances involved contributions in behalf of Japan's war with China. Finally, the report stressed and statistically verified the fact that a considerable number of the American-born Japanese had been educated in Japan and subsequently returned to live in the States. The military authorities conceded that many Japanese living in the country were loyal but felt that the task of screening the loyal from the disloyal presented too great a problem and that therefore the only safe course was to evacuate everybody of Japanese ancestry.

The sociological observations just noted comprised facts about the Japanese in the United States well known to many people on the West Coast. In fact, the Japanese had been the subject of much detailed study by Pacific Coast social scientists long before Pearl Harbor. These students could have greatly assisted the military in making valid interpretations of Japanese society on the West Coast. In this connection Grodzins writes, "as later research has shown

[19] "Need for Military Control and for Evacuation," *Final Report, Japanese Evacuation from the West Coast* (Washington, D.C.: Government Printing Office, 1943), pp. 7–19.

military officers did not in a single instance rely on the large mass of scientific materials that had been gathered about American Japanese by such men as Steiner, Park, Strong, Bogardus, and Bailey." [20]

Espionage and sabotage are inevitable concomitants of war. It is reasonable to suppose that some of the enemy aliens would be engaged in the task, though it is also logical to suppose that among the enemy agents would be some who were not Japanese at all. Even in the absence of much specific proof of disloyal behavior on the part of Japanese Americans, the general logic of the situation clearly called for special vigilance over this group by the agents of the Justice Department and prompt action against any particular individuals, even perhaps on reasonable suspicion. With such a policy, actually already in practice before evacuation orders, few Americans, and perhaps even few Americans of Japanese ancestry, would have quarreled. This was, indeed, the policy advocated by the Justice Department. As late as January 12, 1942, Attorney General Biddle said, "Wholesale internment, without hearing and irrespective of the merits of individual cases, is the long and costly way around, as the British discovered by painful experience; for by that method not only are guiltless aliens themselves demoralized, but the nation is deprived of a valuable source of labor supply at a time when every available man must be at work." [21]

The case submitted was highly unimpressive as a justification for such drastic action as mass evacuation. How then is the evacuation to be explained? Two possible answers appear. One is that General De Witt, Commanding General of the West Coast Area, believed it necessary on the basis of his no doubt sincere, but sociologically inaccurate, judgment of the Japanese, and his judgment was accepted by various higher officials, including President Franklin D. Roosevelt, who finally issued the order. A second possible explanation is that De Witt was influenced by the pressure of people on the West Coast who were either fearful of or imbued with strong antagonism toward the Japanese.

PRESSURE GROUPS   Grodzins stresses the influence of pressure groups: "The most active proponents of mass evacuation were certain agricultural and business groups, chambers of commerce, the American Legion, the California Joint Immigration Committee, and the Native Sons and Daughters of the Golden West." [22] The list of pressure groups can be divided into those with economic motivation for getting rid of the Japanese and those with a nativist, anti-foreign orientation. The following excerpt from a resolution adopted by an Oregon American Legion Post illustrates the sort of pressure that was exerted:

> [that] this is no time for namby-pamby pussyfooting. . . . that it is not the time for consideration of minute constitutional rights of those enemies but that it is time for vigorous, whole-hearted, and concerted action . . . toward the removal of all enemy

[20] Morton Grodzins, *Americans Betrayed: Politics and the Japanese Evacuation* (Chicago: University of Chicago Press, 1949), p. 305.
[21] Leighton, *Governing of Men*, p. 17. By permission.
[22] Grodzins, *Americans Betrayed*, p. 17.

aliens and citizens of enemy alien extraction from all areas along the coast and that only those be permitted to return that are able to secure special permit for that purpose ...[23]

Ten Broeck and his associates [24] place greater responsibility on the commanding officer and his superiors, and on the people of the West Coast generally, among whom there was widespread fear and frustration engendered by the war and Japan's early military successes.

In summary, we suggest that the evacuation resulted from the interaction of a series of factors: (1) the well-established pattern of dominant-minority relations, long nurtured throughout the history of the relations between native Americans and the Japanese on the West Coast; (2) the crisis of war, engendering fear of those racially identified with an enemy nation; (3) a situation ripe for special groups antagonistic to the Japanese to exploit; (4) the failure of liberal West Coast native Americans to bring sufficient counterpressure; (5) the position of authority of a commanding officer with particularly unsophisticated sociological judgment; and (6) the fact that higher federal officials had to make a decision while beset with the enormous burdens of conducting a war.

THE HAWAIIAN CONTRAST   It is instructive to conclude the discussion of the evacuation episode with a brief account of a contrasting situation in Hawaii.

At the outbreak of war with Japan, persons of Japanese ancestry comprised about a third of Hawaii's population. Following Pearl Harbor, rumors arose of espionage activities on the part of some island Japanese. Both the military and the insular authorities, failing to find specific evidence, placed their official weight on the side of allaying the rumors and indicating their confidence in the loyalty of the Hawaiian Japanese as a group. Limited restrictions were imposed on the alien Japanese similar to those imposed on the West Coast, and a few Japanese whose records before the war rendered them suspicious were interned. But there were elements of the general insular population who, fearful of the possible dangers from the Japanese and other groups, called for firmer action. As Lind indicates, there was an increase in public demonstrations against Japanese persons, apparently more from the Filipinos in Hawaii than from the white or other ethnic elements.[25] Nevertheless, the authorities held firm to their policy of active vigilance over the Japanese and arrest of only those who acted in a suspicious manner. General suspicion and fear of the Japanese as a group subsided, and the relations of the Japanese to the rest of the archipelago's population resumed, in the main, their prewar character. The

---

[23] *Ibid.*, p. 42. By permission.
[24] Jacobus Ten Broeck, Edward N. Barnhart, and Floyd W. Matson, *Prejudice, War, and the Constitution* (Berkeley and Los Angeles: University of California Press, 1954).
[25] Andrew Lind, *Hawaii's Japanese* (Princeton: Princeton University Press, 1948), pp. 56–61.

correctness of the official judgment that the Japanese in general constituted no serious security threat to Hawaii was borne out by future events. Subsequent hearings on the charges of subversive activity by local Japanese brought forth emphatic denials from the War Department, the Federal Bureau of Investigation, and from various insular authorities.[26] On the whole, it can be said that the Japanese were cooperative in accepting the mild restrictions, continued their economic role in Hawaiian production, and ultimately made contributions to the armed services. Lind states that "The final count of Hawaiian war casualties revealed that 80 percent of those killed and 88 percent of those wounded throughout the war were of Japanese ancestry." [27]

How can we account for the strikingly different policies adopted in Hawaii and on the West Coast? Contrary to what one might at first think, the much greater proportion of Japanese in the islands operated against a policy of internment. To have tried to police one-third of the population would have been a costly process. More important, however, the removal of the Japanese from the general labor force would have drastically reduced the productive capacity of Hawaii just when a maximum increase in production was essential to the war effort.

Underlying the more favorable treatment of the Japanese were certain facets of the general pattern of intergroup relations in Hawaii, which are discussed in more detail in Chapter 17. At this point we shall briefly call attention to two factors which stand in sharp contrast to the West Coast situation. First, a more friendly and less discriminatory pattern of intergroup relations prevailed in Hawaii. Tradition frowned on any public or explicit color discrimination. Second, the economic position of the Japanese in Hawaii had developed few antagonisms based on competition. While by 1940 the Japanese as a group had moved far from their earlier role as plantation workers toward various city occupations, this transition had not yet brought them into much direct competition for jobs with the socially dominant white population.

The Effects of Evacuation

The short-range effects of the evacuation and temporary resettlement on the national welfare were costly indeed. Particular segments of the West Coast population, as we have seen, made substantial gains out of removal of the Japanese from competition. For these gains, the nation paid a heavy price. The removal of the Japanese retarded the war effort. While eventually many Japanese did find useful work during the war, they would have contributed more if they had remained where they were. In fact, there were so many high-paying opportunities in California created by the manpower shortage that many Mexicans and Negroes migrated there. The whole process of evacuation, the operation of the centers, and the effort of the WRA to relocate the evacuees

[26] *Ibid.,* pp. 38–47.
[27] *Ibid.,* p. 126.

cost time, money, and energy which could have been used to more constructive purpose.

The effect of the evacuation on the prestige of the United States in world opinion is difficult to appraise. Because of their imperialist activities in Asia, the Japanese abroad were thoroughly hated by many other Asiatic peoples. Nevertheless, the way in which the Japanese in this country were dealt with in contrast to the treatment of Germans and Italians reflected our color bias, and cannot have raised our moral stock with nonwhite people in general.

The Decline of Dominance

Following the end of the evacuation order on January 1, 1945, the Japanese were free to go where they wanted. As we have seen, many returned to the West Coast. In 1960, the number of Japanese in the states of California (157,317), Washington (16,652), and Oregon (5,016) was 178,985, accounting for 69 percent of the mainland Japanese population. Since in 1940 as many as 88 percent were concentrated on the West Coast, the difference reflects the dispersive effect of evacuation. The largest number located in any one community not on the West Coast was in Chicago. The Los Angeles–Long Beach area, with 81,204 in 1960, occupied first place ahead of Chicago, having about one-third of all the Japanese on the mainland.

Economic Readjustment

Bloom and Riemer have estimated that the evacuated Japanese sustained an economic loss of $367,500,000, if income losses were added to all other losses incurred from forced sale of their assets, loss of business goodwill, and other losses attendant on their rapid removal.[28] A sample survey of 206 Japanese American families found the median loss per family to be $9,870 at the 1941 value of the dollar.[29]

Some small part of this loss was compensated under an Act of Congress in July, 1948 (Public Law, 886, H. R. 2999), which empowered the Attorney General to reimburse any person not to exceed $2,500 for "damage to or loss of real or personal property. . . . that is a reasonable and natural consequence of the evacuation." Claims had to be filed within eighteen months, and any claims for loss of anticipated profits or earnings were excluded. Evacuees filed 24,064 claims. By March 1, 1956, all but 1,936 had been adjusted and paid. The delayed settlements involved claims in excess of the original $2,500 limit. In 1956, Congress amended the act to permit settlement up to $100,000. The problem in settling these claims involved the difficulty of proving the losses and the fact that few Japanese had obtained documentary proof of sale in anticipa-

[28] Leonard Bloom and Ruth Riemer, *Removal and Return* (Berkeley: University of California Press, 1949), pp. 202–204.
[29] *Ibid.*, p. 144.

tion of such indemnity. The last claim was settled in November, 1965; two of the original plantiffs had died.[30]

The evacuation undermined the occupational position of the Japanese and forced readjustment upon return at lower socioeconomic levels. Few farmers could re-establish themselves, and produce dealers were far fewer than before the war. Many went into contract gardening, which provided a measure of the independence they formerly enjoyed. The great shortage of housing available for the Japanese increased the number of boarding and rooming houses where the Japanese who did have homes added to their income by charging high prices of fellow Japanese. The housing shortage also increased the number of returnees who went into domestic service, which often provided housing. In general, the pattern of employment for the returnees involved a shift from being either independently employed or working for other Japanese to working for non-Japanese employers.

Reaction of Dominant Americans

On the West Coast, knowledge that the Japanese were coming back evoked reaction from racist-minded groups that had been instrumental in causing their evacuation. The American Legion, Veterans of the Foreign Wars, Native Sons of the Golden West, the California Farm Bureau all protested. New "Ban the Jap" committees sprang up. A number of newspapers ran scare headlines which made many Californians uneasy. "Hood River had jumped the gun by erasing the names of its sixteen Nisei soldiers from the honor roll" [subsequently restored].[31] In the first half of 1945 more than thirty serious incidents occurred throughout California.

This time, however, there was a second set of reactions, which had been missing before. Many individuals and groups demanded that the Japanese be given fair play and became active in insisting that they get it. The Fresno Fair Play Committee organized to file eviction suits in behalf of those Japanese unable to move back into their former homes. In Hood River a Christian pastor organized the League for Liberty and Justice, which "made a frontal attack on the shameful practice of refusing to sell groceries and other necessities to Nisei."[32] When machinists of the San Francisco Municipal Railway threatened to strike in protest against the employment of a Nisei, Mayor Roger Lapham averted the strike by going to the shop in person and explaining to the men why the Nisei was entitled to the job. Churches up and down the Coast were focal points of support for the Nisei. This second reaction finally won out.

The pressure of public opinion all over the country put California on the defensive. It came to a point where the civic pride of the several communities was chal-

---

[30] William Petersen, "Success Story: Japanese-American Style," *New York Times Magazine,* Jan. 9, 1966, p. 33.
[31] Bradford Smith, *Americans from Japan,* p. 346.
[32] *Ibid.,* p. 348.

lenged and race baiting lost favor. At the beginning of 1945 the West Coast papers had been four to one against the Japanese. A year later they were four to one in favor of fair and equal treatment.[33]

In the state of Washington, Schmid notes "Following World War II a revival of anti-Japanese prejudice which had its origin in the White River and Puyallup River valleys, spread to Seattle in the form of propaganda and a few public meetings. However, the reaction was short lived and, generally, since 1945 the economic, social, educational and political status of the Japanese has shown unprecedented improvement." [34]

Nisei Acculturation

Under more favorable circumstances the Japanese made rapid acculturative strides. By breaking up the continuity of the group life, the evacuation had weakened group solidarity. Leadership was gradually transferred to the Nisei. The experience in relocation gave the Nisei more independence, since they often earned more money by working in the vicinity of the camps than their parents. Many Nisei relocated in Eastern cities; and many chose their own mates. A government survey reported, "The institution of arranged marriages is very nearly out of the picture as far as Nisei are concerned." [35] Community-managed Japanese schools were not reopened. The number of Japanese language newspapers was fewer than before the war, and those published had smaller circulations.[36]

Chicago's Japanese Americans

An extensive study of the rapid acculturation of the nisei in particular is reported by Caudhill and Devos for Chicago in the 1947–1950 period.[37] Their main findings concern the marked acculturation of Chicago's Nisei to American middle-class norms. Objective measures of this phenomenon are seen in an educational level which exceeded that of the general American average, and in the occupational distribution. The authors found that, as early as 1947, of their sample, 35 percent were in white-collar employment, 6 percent owned small businesses, and 9 percent were professionals. Employed Nisei women were largely in white-collar occupations. As young adults, the Nisei were still moving up the occupational scale.

Since various studies had indicated that the range of mental ability of Japanese Americans conformed to the general population range, Caudhill and

---

[33] *Ibid.*, p. 349. By permission.
[34] Calvin Schmid and Wayne W. McVey, Jr., *Growth and Distribution of Minority Races in Seattle, Washington,* Published by the Seattle Public Schools, 1964, p. IV.
[35] *People in Motion,* p. 201
[36] *Ibid.*, p. 203.
[37] William Caudhill and George Devos, "Achievement, Culture and Personality: The Case of Japanese Americans," *American Anthropologist,* 1956, 58: 1102–1126.

Devos sought the explanation of such unusual occupational success in Japanese culture. The chief hypothesis emerging was that "There seems to be a significant compatibility (but by no means identity) between the value systems found in the culture of Japan and the value systems found in American middle class culture." [38] Thematic apperception tests indicated scores in positive achievement responses more comparable to those of the researchers' middle-class white sample (in fact higher) than their sample of white lower classes. The cultural influence, as mediated through the parents, was further confirmed in the still higher positive achievement responses of the Issei (who were themselves less successful) than those of the Nisei. The study further reports highly favorable opinions of the Japanese by employers, who attributed many middle-class virtues to the Japanese workers: efficiency, honesty, punctuality, neatness, good moral character. Significantly, the occasional negative evaluation took the form of criticizing the Nisei for being too ambitious, for wanting to move on to a better job too quickly. Thus in a new setting where no community pattern of hostility is traditional, the Japanese have created a highly favorable image of themselves as a group.

The Challenge to Dominance

The American Japanese have as a group made little formal challenge to the minority status accorded them. As we have seen, as individuals the majority have been diligent and alert to take the opportunities not denied them to improve their welfare and to rise in class status. The Issei when denied land ownership placed title in the names of their native-born children, for example. While evacuation came as a shock, as a whole, they put up with it with unusual grace.[39] We have already stressed their tendency to take full advantage of educational opportunities. Mainland Japanese Americans have not been as active in politics as some other minorities and thus have not made maximum use of political pressure to improve their status, although a few Japanese have been elected to state offices in California from areas of heavy ethnic concentration.[40] An occasional Japanese has challenged discrimination through the courts with considerable success, as the following indicates.

COURT DECISIONS   A number of court decisions invalidating laws and practices that discriminated against both the Japanese and the Chinese were handed down between 1948 and 1950. In June, 1948, the United States Supreme Court (*Takahashi* vs. *Game Commission of California*) declared unconstitutional a California law prohibiting the issuance of fishing licenses to persons ineligible for

[38] *Ibid.*, p. 1107.
[39] See Dorothy S. Thomas and Richard S. Nishimoto, *The Spoilage,* for an intensive study of those Japanese who became bitter enough to renounce their citizenship.
[40] Harry H. L. Kitano, *The Japanese Americans*, Prentice-Hall, Inc., Englewood Cliffs, New Jersey, forthcoming publication © 1968. Reprinted by permission.

citizenship. In October, 1948, the Supreme Court of California ruled that this state's law barring interracial marriages was unconstitutional.

Three significant court decisions bearing on West Coast laws prohibiting Oriental aliens from owning agricultural land were handed down in the same period. The United States Supreme Court in January, 1948, ruled in the case of *Oyama* vs. *California* that that section of the California alien land law raising presumption of fraudulent ownership and occupation of agricultural land by persons ineligible for citizenship was unconstitutional. In March, 1949, the Oregon Supreme Court held unconstitutional the state's 1923 Alien Land Law, which prohibited renting and leasing land to Japanese aliens. The District Court of Appeals, sitting at Los Angeles in April, 1950, held that California's law barring aliens ineligible for citizenship from owning land was contrary to the Constitution of the United States. In this case the Court made a further point of great significance when it stated that the law involved was contrary to the Charter of the United Nations.

WELFARE   Clearly the situation of Japanese Americans is the most favorable of all the non-European ethnic components in the United States. As to their welfare, the following data are impressive.

> As of 1960, the median years of schooling completed by the Japanese were 12.2 as compared with 11.1 by whites and 8.6 by Negroes. Japanese males had a much higher occupational level than whites—56 percent in white-collar jobs against 42.1 percent for whites. "According to California life tables for 1959–1961, Japanese Americans in the state had a life expectation of 74.5 years (males) and 81.2 years (females) ... six or seven years longer than that of California whites." [41]

DISCRIMINATION   White American prejudice and discrimination have obviously declined. Even by 1956 Gladwyn Hill reported from the West Coast, "The stereotype of the shadowy minority group with sinister alien ties has gone." [42] Bogardus found as early as 1946 that on his social distance scores the Nisei were being distinguished from the foreign-born Japanese and being given more favorable scores; and that "By 1956, the Americans of Japanese parentage had been accorded a still better rank order and a lesser distance score." [43]

More specifically, with reference to occupational discrimination Gladwyn Hill reported in 1956, "Instead of encountering prejudice when they apply for jobs, Japanese Americans are in special demand because of their reputation for keenness and intelligence." [44] By 1966, Kitano considers occupational assimilation substantially accomplished. But he makes some qualifications.

[41] William Petersen, "Success Story: Japanese American Style," *The New York Times Magazine,* Jan. 9, 1966, pp. 36, 38, 40.
[42] Gladwyn Hill, "The Japanese in United States Gaining Equality," *New York Times,* August 12, 1956, p. 38.
[43] Emory Bogardus, "Racial Distance Changes in the United States During the Past Thirty Years," *Sociology and Social Research,* Nov.–Dec., 1958, pp. 127–135.
[44] Hill, "The Japanese in United States Gaining Equality," p. 38.

[T]he opportunities to find positions commensurate with their training and experience appear to be better away from California. Once again, numbers play an important role, and it is probable that even in the East, there is upward mobility for only a small, select group of Japanese. There appears to be an unofficial quota system in operation; it would be unusual to see more than one person of Japanese ancestry in an executive position in the same American business, even on the East Coast.[45]

Decline in discrimination against Japanese is reflected by the sensitive index of housing opportunities. In the San Francisco Bay area in 1956, Kitano showed the Japanese more dispersed than before evacuation. Of a sample of Japanese, 39 percent indicated that they had been discriminated against in seeking better homes and 56 percent said they had not. Of this latter group Kitano wrote "probably many had 'played it safe' by finding houses through friends or Japanese real estate agents." [46] The same author ten years later feels able to state that "Housing is not a major problem for the Japanese. There are still areas which practice covert discrimination, but, in general, the nisei and the sansei can buy homes in 'desirable' neighborhoods, depending on their income and occupation." [47] So little is the current discrimination perceived by the Japanese that some supported the opposition to the 1964 ballot proposition calling for non-discriminatory housing.[48]

The small amount of Japanese outmarriage with Caucasians is not an adequate measure of current white attitudes concerning intermarriage because of the strong pressure to marry within the racial group. Of the various subgroups within the Japanese population, the only category which is maritally assimilated is that of the "war brides." Kitano however cites the following: "As an American airlines pilot once remarked to us, speaking of his Japanese bride, 'No one pays any attention to us since there was that movie (Sayonara) with Marlon Brando.' " [49] It may well be the Japanese (and to some extent the Chinese Americans) who are finally breaking down the long-nourished American white insistence on "color" visibility as a categorical barrier to assimilation. This would indeed be a significant turning point in the development of intergroup relations in the United States.

Thus the marked acculturation coupled with the marked decline in WASP discrimination suggests considerable probability that the future of the Japanese

[45] Kitano, *The Japanese Americans*. See footnote 40.
[46] Harry H. L. Kitano, "Housing of the Japanese-Americans in the San Francisco Bay Area," in Nathan Glazer and Davis McEntire, *Studies in Housing and Minority Groups* (Berkeley and Los Angeles: University of California Press, 1960), p. 183.
[47] Kitano, *The Japanese Americans*.
[48] *Ibid*.
[49] *Ibid*.

descended population is a matter of their own choice. Do they or will they come to wish to become totally assimilated into the general population, or do they and will they continue to want to retain a collective identity?

Pluralism versus Assimilation

It is clear that at present most American citizens of Japanese descent still remain identifiable as a distinct ethnic group both by themselves and other Americans. They form a separate community in places where their number warrants it. And even when they move into the suburbs they tend to form contiguous groups. "Few [nisei] are to be found randomly scattered in other neighborhoods." [50]

The maintenance of a separate social structure is reinforced by the high degree of intergroup marriage. Kitano found 97 percent of a sample of nisei parents preferring that their children marry other Japanese; however "a high proportion conceded that the idea of marriage to a Caucasian was not as disturbing as it once seemed." [51] The same author finds the norm of ingroup marriage weakened by "built-in structural factors which will literally force a change," and develops the point thus:

> The increased differentiation and stratification within the relatively small number of Japanese will inevitably lead to increased interaction with non-Japanese groups at all levels. For example, . . . the third generation Japanese Ph.D. social scientist will probably find few sansei females with comparable background, interests, and values. The old model "Just so long as she [or he] is Japanese" will no longer be satisfactory . . . And the same story will be repeated on all levels of the Japanese social structure. The social expectations of group members will not be fully satisfied within the ethnic community.[52]

A current assessment by Kitano of the degree of assimilation as measured by various indices and of the regional variations involved are seen in Table 9–3. Disregarding Hawaii which we treat separately in Chapter 17, assimilation lags most on the West Coast and increases progressively moving to the Midwest and to the East Coast. As would be expected, except for war brides married to non-Japanese, the sansei are the most assimilated of the various Japanese subgroups.[53] Their acculturation is now nearly complete. English is the predominant language even in private, and more pertinently their interests and values are substantially identical with the Caucasian group. "They are members of Little Leagues, fraternities . . . and other organizations designed upon American mod-

[50] *Ibid.*, op. cit.
[51] *Ibid.*, op. cit.
[52] *Ibid.*
[53] See Kitano, "Paradigm of Assimilation Applied to Selected Japanese Groups in the United States."

TABLE 9–3. *Area of Residence and Assimilation in Terms of Cultural, Social-Marital Occupational, Housing and Political Variables* [54]

	Cultural	Social-Marital	Occupational	Housing	Political
California (West Coast)	Yes	No	Partially	Partially	Beginning
Midwest (primarily Chicago)	Yes	Beginning	Yes*	Yes*	No
New York— New England	Yes	Partially	Yes*	Yes*	No
Hawaii	Yes	Partially	Yes*	Yes*	Yes

* Substantially Yes.

els within the ethnic sub-community." [55] In a special study Kitano found a shift in the achievement patterns of Japanese high school students between 1940–1960: from a decreasing participation in academic and honor groups toward an increasing participation in multi-club activities. The trend is toward an all-round personality with the scholarly role no longer desirable.[56] Further indices of the "Americanization" of the Japanese are found in increasing crime and delinquency rates,[57] and some evidence of increasing divorce.

It is increasingly evident that the sansei are American Japanese and not "Japanese" Japanese. Peterson put it as follows concerning sansei students:

> On a campus where to be a bohemian slob is a mark of distinction, they wash them-selves and dress with unostentatious neatness. They are mostly good students, no longer concentrated in the ultilitarian subjects of their fathers but often majoring in liberal arts. Most can speak a little Japanese, but few can read more than a few words. Some are opposed to intermarriage, some not; but all accept the American principle that it is love between the partners that makes for a good family. Con-scious of their minority status, they are seeking a means both of preserving ele-ments of the Japanese culture and reconciling it fully with the American one; but their effort lacks the poignant tragedy of the earlier counterpart.[58]

In concluding the theme of pluralism vs. assimilation, it is instructive to com-pare the Japanese with the Jewish minority. Much similarity can be seen. (1) The stereotypes held by the dominants of both Jews and Japanese bear consid-erable similarity. (2) Both groups have internalized strongly the basic American middle-class value system and (3) have succeeded in achieving this status. (4)

---

[54] *Ibid.*
[55] *Ibid.*
[56] Harry H. L. Kitano, "Changing Achievement Patterns of the Japanese in the United States," *The Journal of Social Psychology*, 1962, vol. 58, pp. 257–264.
[57] *Ibid.*
[58] William Petersen, "Success Story: Japanese-American Style," p. 40. By permission.

In regard to 2 and 3, they both had original cultures more in tune with middle-class norms. (5) Both have low rates of deviant behavior in general. (6) In both groups, it is interesting to note a revival in the third generation of interest in their ancestral heritage as against some repudiation of this as characteristic of the second generation, although evidence is less marked with the Japanese than with American Jews.

There are several differences. (1) Perhaps foremost is the racial visibility of the Japanese, although many Gentile Americans think of Jews as a "social race." But we have already noted marked decline in the "white" negative reactions to the color "yellow." (2) While both groups possess power vulnerability, this is more marked with the mainland Japanese. However, so far as localized dominant attitudes are concerned, the high degree of concentration of both groups within limited areas partly offsets the fact that nationally they represent a small percentage of the population. (3) While there are historic regional (West Coast) prejudices against the Japanese in the United States, Jews have been a perennial minority throughout centuries in the Euro-American world.[59]

There is some basis for hypothesizing that in the future the Japanese could become totally assimilated if that should be what future generations of Sansei want. That by choosing to maintain a distinctive identity in a "pluralistic" America they might more enrich the national life is of course a value judgment shared by many non-Japanese Americans.

Topics for Discussion and Projects

1. How do you account for the currently more assimilated situation of the Japanese than that of the Chinese in the United States?
2. Collect pictures of various Oriental people including Japanese, Chinese, and Filipinos. Arrange them without designation of their national identity. Show them to a sample of your fellow students and ask them to identify their nationality. Report your results.
3. Observe the reactions of white passersby to seeing mixed pairs of white and Japanese, or other Oriental people who may be married or simply dating. Report your observations.
4. In view of the greater antagonism toward Orientals on the West Coast, how do you account for the fact that the great majority of the evacuated Japanese returned to this region after release from internment?
5. Discuss the significance of white-Oriental relations in the United States in connection with the present international situation.

Suggested Reading

Benedict, Ruth. *The Chrysanthemum and the Sword.* Boston, Mass.: Houghton Mifflin, 1946.
   An interpretation of the patterns of culture of twentieth-century Japan.

[59] See below, Chapter 18, especially pp. 404–427.

Caudhill, William, and De Vos, George. "Achievement, Culture, and Personality: The Case of Japanese Americans," *American Anthropologist*, 1956, 58:1102–1126.

    An outstanding study of the Chicago Japanese in the 1950's.

Kitano, Harry H. L. "Japanese-American Crime and Delinquency," *The Journal of Psychology*, 1967, 66:253–263.

    An up-to-date study of deviant behavior among Japanese-Americans.

Miyamoto, Shotaro Frank. "Social Solidarity among the Japanese." University of Washington publication in *Social Science*, Vol. 11, No. 2, Dec. 1939, pp. 57–130.

    One of the most complete community studies of the Japanese Americans as of the 1930's.

Petersen, William. "Success Story: Japanese American Style," *New York Times Magazine*, Jan. 9, 1966, pp. 4, 5, 33, 36, 38, 40, 41, 43.

    The story of the Japanese Americans from evacuation to the later 1960's is widely covered by a professional sociologist.

Ten Broeck, Jacobus, Barnhart, Edward N., and Matson, Floyd W. *Prejudice, War and the Constitution.* Berkeley and Los Angeles: University of California Press, 1954.

    A scholarly account of the Japanese evacuation during World War II with special emphasis on the legal aspects.

Thomas, Dorothy S., and Nishimoto, Richard S. *The Spoilage, Japanese-American Evacuation and Resettlement.* Berkeley and Los Angeles: University of California Press, 1946.

    An intensive study of those Japanese who became bitter enough about evacuation to renounce their citizenship.

10

Negro-White Relations: Biology and Background

Among the various dominant-minority situations in the United States Negro-white relations obviously occupy first place as a social problem and currently a social problem of the utmost gravity. We therefore devote more attention to this intergroup situation than to the others.

The Negro minority constitutes a little over a tenth of the nation's population. It is the oldest minority, the first Negro slaves having been bought in Jamestown in 1619.[1] This minority has the lowest status rank of all ethnic and racial groups. A large portion of the Negro population has a very low standard of living, even though with the emergence of a class structure within the population, the welfare within the group as a whole is at present highly variable. Differing from the other minorities, the continuity between its original African cultural heritage has virtually disappeared through the long years of servitude and caste conditions so that such distinctiveness as Negroes may have is largely derived from the experience of slavery and discrimination.

The two most important factors which explain why Negroes have so long remained a minority are that they are Negroid in their physiognomic characteristics or in their known lineage; and (2) that their ancestors were in the vast majority of cases slaves. In the first of these chapters devoted to Negro-white relations we shall deal briefly with the period of slavery and its aftermath.

The Growth and Distribution of the Negro Population

Growth

Table 10–1 shows that the number of Negroes in the United States has increased each decade since 1790. It also shows that with temporary decennial rises the proportion of Negroes to the total population declined until 1930. This proportional decline is due primarily to the great increase in the white population by immigration from Europe.

[1] Indian-white relations did not become dominant-minority relations in the true sense until the Indians became wards in 1871.

221

TABLE 10–1. *Growth of the Negro Population Since 1790* *

Census Year	Number of Negroes	Percentage of Total Population	Percentage Increase of Negroes During Decade	Percentage Increase of Whites During Decade
1960	18,871,831	10.5	25.4	17.5
1950	15,044,937	9.9	17.0	14.4
1940	12,865,518	9.8	8.2	7.2
1930	11,891,143	9.7	13.6	15.7
1920	10,463,131	9.9	6.5	15.7
1910	9,827,763	10.7	11.2	21.8
1900	8,333,940	11.6	18.0	21.2
1890	7,488,676	11.9	13.8	27.0
1880	6,580,793	13.1	34.9	29.2
1870	4,880,009	12.7	9.9	24.8
1860	4,441,830	14.1	22.1	37.7
1850	3,638,808	15.7	26.6	37.7
1840	2,873,648	16.8	23.4	34.7
1830	2,328,642	18.1	31.4	33.9
1820	1,771,656	18.4	28.6	34.2
1810	1,377,808	19.0	37.5	36.1
1800	1,002,037	18.9	32.3	35.8
1790	757,208	19.3		

* United States Bureau of Census, *Negroes in the United States, 1920–1932*, pp. 1–2 ; *Sixteenth Census of United States, Population*, Vol. II, p. 19. 1960 Census, P. C. (A2)–1, p. 4.

From 1930 on the percentage of the total national population counted as Negro began to increase slightly from 9.8 in 1940 to 10.5 in 1960. It will also be noted that it was in the 1951–1960 decade that a considerably greater proportional increase in the Negro as against the white population occurred—25.4 for the former as against 17.5 for the latter. The relatively greater proportional increase of the Negro over the white population has continued through the 1960's. The Census Bureau estimated that as of July 1, 1966, Negroes comprised 11 percent of the national population as compared with 10.5 percent in 1960. The birth rates of both the white and Negro population declined during this period: white live births per 1,000 women decreasing from 22.7 in 1960 to 17.5 in 1966; live births per 1,000 Negro women declined from 32.9 in 1960 to 26.5 in 1966.[2]

Regional Distribution

Through the entire national period up to 1910 the Negro population was highly concentrated in the South—over 90 percent. Within the region under

[2] U.S. Census Bureau Report released through the Associated Press on June 2, 1967.

slavery, Negro migration was of course governed by the owners and traders of slaves. The southern and southwestern expansion of the plantation economy from the upper South was paralleled by a corresponding expansion of the Negro population in these areas. In spite of the technical freedom for Negroes to move where they desired after the Civil War, very few migrated to the North, and almost none to the West. There was considerable shifting about in the South itself, the net result of which was to increase the proportion of Negroes living in southern cities. From 1910 on there has been a marked migration out of the region (slowed down somewhat by the depression decade), so that by 1960 the proportion of the total Negro population in the South had dropped to 60 percent. Until 1940 this exodus from the South was to the North East and the North Central regions. A small but hitherto unprecedented trend toward the West began in consequence of the labor demands in that region created by World War II. Most of this migration was to California, which led all the other states in the percentage rise in Negro population during the 1951–1960 decade—90 percent, giving the state a Negro population of 883,861 in 1960. A prime factor accounting for this trend out of the South has been the increasing job opportunities outside the region. In their studies Karl and Alma Tauber did not find any clear support for the thesis that among the "push" factors was the desire to escape the southern discriminatory pattern of race relations.[3] However, many autobiographies of Negroes do show that the desire to escape from the southern system was a compelling motive in some instances.[4]

Urban Trend

The second outstanding shift in the Negro population over more or less the same period of time has been migration from rural to urban areas. This trend has been characteristic of the national population as a whole. In the South both racial groups moved cityward in about equal proportions. In 1960 58 percent of the southern Negro population lived in cities against 59 percent of the southern whites. In the North and West Negroes are more highly urbanized than whites. In 1960 the percentages of each racial population living in cities were, in the North, 96 percent for Negroes and 73 percent for whites, and in the West, 93 percent for Negroes and 78 percent for whites. The most crucial aspect of the Negro migration has been to bring about heavy concentrations of Negro populations in the leading urban areas. While this has been characteristic of the South for fifty or more years, since World War II it is in the North and West that this has been most marked. The Taubers' adaptation of the U.S. Census data of 1960 indicates that the five cities with the greatest number of

[3] Karl E. and Alma F. Tauber, "The Negro Population in the United States," Chapter 2 of John F. Davis, ed., *The Negro Reference Book* (Englewood Cliffs, N.J.: Prentice-Hall, 1966), p. 111.
[4] See for example Richard Wright, *Native Son* (New York: Harper & Brothers), 1940; and Horace Cayton, *Long Lonely Road* (New York: The Trident Press, 1965).

Negroes were New York, 1,088,000; Chicago, 813,000; Philadelphia, 529,000; Detroit, 482,000; and Washington, D.C., 464,112. The five non-southern cities with the highest percentages of their population being Negro were Washington, 53.9; Newark, New Jersey, 34.1; Detroit, 28.9; Philadelphia, 26.4; and Chicago, 22.9. That the same phenomenon now is being repeated in the West is attested by the fact that Oakland and Los Angeles, California, which do not appear in the 1910 list of 25 cities with the largest percentages of Negro population, in 1960 showed marked increases. Oakland had a 22 percent Negro population (84,000 in number), and Los Angeles 13.5 percent (335,000 in number).[5]

The movement of Negroes out of the South and the westward trend has continued since 1960. Federal government studies show that in the years from 1960 to 1965 more than two million Negroes migrated from the South.[6] The proportion of the Negro population living outside the South may now exceed the proportion within it. These studies estimated that in 1965 53.6 percent of the nation's 20,940,000 Negroes lived in the South, a decline from the 60 percent of the 18,850,000 Negroes living in the region in 1960. The continuing westward trend is attested by the estimated 8.2 percent of the national Negro population residing in the West in 1965 as compared with 5.7 percent in 1960.

The implications of these striking changes in the distribution of the Negro population will be discussed in later chapters. In conclusion here we point out that the national Negro population is expected to increase a little more proportionally than the white population but to remain a definite numerical minority, one important factor in power vulnerability. On the other hand, the uneven concentration already has had two effects: (1) providing in some local areas such a substantial number as to give it potential political power[7]; and (2) markedly accentuating interracial tension in such areas.

Characteristics of the Negro Population

The minority status of Negroes in the United States has rested in large measure on the beliefs developed and sustained in the minds of the white population that being Negroid in racial ancestry means that Negroes are innately inferior in many ways. In our Chapter 4 on race, it was seen that contemporary social science seriously challenges this belief. In the first place, how actually Negroid is the population counted as such in the United States?

Ancestry of the American Negro Population

The "visibility" of the Negro population is accounted for by the fact that all the members have some genetic lineage from Negro ancestry. In the United

---

[5] Karl and Alma F. Tauber, in Davis, p. 119.

[6] Studies made by the U.S. Census Bureau and the U.S. Department of Labor as reported in *The New York Times,* Dec. 1, 1966, p. 14.

[7] Actually, since at least 1960, Negroes have been a numerical majority of the population of Washington, D.C. It appears probable that among the considerations which have up to now led Congress to refuse voting privileges to the residents of this capitol city is that Negroes could become the predominant political influence.

States a person is considered a Negro if he has any known Negro lineage, whether he can be identified by his appearance or not. There is no precise data indicating what distribution of the basic Negroid traits are now present in the population known as Negro. The United States Census count in 1920—the last year a distinction between mulatto and black was made—gave the figure of 15.9 percent for mulattoes, which all students of the question consider a gross undercount. Obviously, census takers are not physical anthropologists. When a study was made by Herskovits combining genealogical and anthropometric methods, a high correspondence between the measurements and the genealogical data was found.[8] Only 22 percent of his sample of 1,551 Negroes were pure bred Negro, the rest showing varying degrees of Caucasian and American-Indian admixture. Although Herskovits' sample contained a disproportionate number of more educated Negroes, having a greater percentage of white ancestry, the probability that many Negroes in his sample did not know of white ancestry from several generations back may have served to counterbalance the selective bias. Pettigrew estimates that one-fourth of the Negro gene pool consists of genes of Caucasian origin.[9]

Most Negroes in the United States show one or more of the basic Negroid traits: dark skin, thick lips, "wooly" hair, and prognathism; in a minor proportion, the evidence of these traits are so faint that one cannot be sure of identifying them; and in a relatively small percentage there is absolutely no somatic evidence of Negro lineage, but either the individuals themselves, or others who know them vouch for some Negro ancestry. The American Negro population of today is, biologically speaking, quite different from that of colonial days. The processes by which this change has come about will now be described.

Selective Mating Processes

INTERTRIBAL MATING   While knowledge of the ancestry of American Negroes is not too precise, it is considered that most of the present Negro population traces the Negro part of its ancestry back to slaves who originally came from the West Coast of Africa. Since under slavery their mating was not tribally endogamous, the first process was the intermixing of these original tribal variations. This would have produced a new, but African, Negro type if it had not been for the crossing of slaves very early with both Indians and white people.

NEGRO-INDIAN CROSSING   In the United States before the nineteenth century there was extensive intermingling between Indians and Negroes, with the result that some of the admixtures disappeared into the Indian population. Herskovits found 27 percent of his Negro sample to have some Indian lineage.[10]

[8] Melville Herskovits, *The American Negro: A Study in Racial Crossing* (New York: Alfred A. Knopf, 1930).

[9] Thomas Pettigrew, *A Profile of the Negro American* (Copyright 1964, D. Van Nostrand Company, Inc., Princeton, New Jersey), p. 71.

[10] Herskovits, *The American Negro*, p. 9.

Additional Indian genetic strains resulted from the increasing importation, in the later periods, of slaves from the West Indies, where "crossing" with Indians had occurred. However, later studies suggest that the amount of Indian admixture in the Negro population is not so high as in Herskovits' sample, but genetic data on Indians have been based on those groups less likely to come in contact with Negroes, not from Indian Southerners.[11]

NEGRO-WHITE CROSSING The population from which the African slaves were recruited already had some admixture of Caucasian genes, as a result of miscegenation with the Portuguese who settled on the Guinea Coast for slave trading purposes and through contact in Europe, whence some slaves were brought to the West Indies.

In the colonies themselves, indications are that the first extensive Negro-white crossing took place between indentured white servants and Negro slaves. As the indentured servant disappeared and the Negro slave system developed, mating between white and colored people continued through the access to Negro slave women which the system gave the white male owners and white men in general. Mulatto women were most frequently chosen.

The next stage came with the Civil War and its aftermath. "The Northern army left an unknown amount of Yankee genes in the Southern Negro people.[12] Under the caste system which supplanted slavery, interracial crossing resumed more or less in the same pattern of white male exploitation of Negro women, although the women had somewhat more freedom than under slavery. While evidence is scarce, most writers agree that the amount of miscegenation has declined in the twentieth century. Among the factors frequently cited to account for this tentative conclusion are, on the part of the white people, a decline in sexual congress with Negro women because of an increasing casualness in white female sexual behavior and, on the part of the Negroes, the increasing number who have adopted white middle-class attitudes toward sexual conventionality and have developed a maturing sense of racial pride.

"LIGHT" SELECTION IN THE NEGRO POPULATION It is generally acknowledged even by Negro students of race relations that mate selection within the Negro population itself has been in favor of those Negroes who possessed the greater visible indices of Caucasian traits. The higher status of mulattoes has been due not only to their "lightness" but also to the fact that the dominant white population has been somewhat more favorably inclined to them. Thus in general mulattoes have had more economic and educational opportunity. This selective mating bias among Negroes has had the effect of increasing the distribution of white genetic factors in the Negro population.[13] The effect may

---

[11] Pettigrew, *A Profile of the American Negro,* p. 68.
[12] Gunnar Myrdal, *An American Dilemma* (New York: Harper & Brothers, 1944), p. 127.
[13] For further discussion of this subject, see Otto Klineberg, ed., *Characteristics of the American Negro* (New York: Harper & Brothers, 1944), Pt. V, Ch. 9, "The Future of the Hybrid," by Louis Wirth and Herbert Goldhammer.

be partially offset, however, by the tendency of "lighter" Negro couples to imitate the white middle-class standard of having smaller families. On the other hand the development of Negro race pride, stimulated by certain elements of Negro leadership, may well reverse the effect of the process here being considered. To the extent that a trend toward the devaluation of lightness increases, the Negro population will veer toward a mulatto norm and toward greater homogeneity about that norm.

PASSING   By "passing" is meant the successful and permanent assumption of "white" status by a person who knows he has Negro ancestry. In studying the African ancestry of the white population in the United States, Stuckert, using the method of genetic probability tables, estimated that during the years 1941–1950 an average annual mean of 15,500 Negroes passed. There was an annual rate of 1.21 per 1,000 Negro population, and the rate was found to be increasing.[14] The effect of passing is the removal from the Negro population of strains which would increase the Caucasian admixture in the Negro population. The process adds some Negroid admixture to the white population, but very little, since the Negroes who pass have very few Negroid genes to add. The Negroid influence is further diluted by the tendency of "passers," when they marry, to select either white mates or equally white Negro mixtures. In this connection, it is pertinent to call attention to the fear which many white people and many "passable" Negroes have concerning the possible Negroid characteristics of children resulting from marriages of two white-appearing Negroes or of one of them to a white person. The genetic probabilities from such unions are known. Representative of the accepted view are these summary statements by Julian Lewis, a biologist:

> Two very fair-complexioned Negroes will produce children 18 percent of whom are pure white, 65 per cent the same color as the parents, and 17 per cent a shade darker than both parents.
>
> When a white person mates with a very fair Negro who is sometimes able to pass for white but not of the "pure white" type, 40 percent of the resulting children are of the same color as the white parent, less than 60 percent are the color of the Negro parent, and less than 1 per cent is darker than the Negro parent. The possibility of this one exception frequently causes untold worry and concern in such unions.
>
> Some of the children of matings involving fair Negroes are pure white according to accepted standards of whiteness. Such types are known to geneticists as "extracted whites." When an extracted white mates with a full white or another extracted white, none of the children will ever be darker than the parents.[15]

[14] Robert P. Stuckert, "African Ancestry of the White American Population," *The Ohio Journal of Science*, May, 1958, 58:155–160. The main finding of this study was that 28 million "white" persons have some African ancestry.

[15] Julian Lewis, "What Color Will Your Baby Be?" *Negro Digest*, Nov., 1945, 5: 6–7. By permission. For fuller treatment see Julian Lewis, *The Biology of the Negro* (Chicago: University of Chicago Press, 1942).

Trends in Racial Characteristics

The wide range of the degree of Negroid characteristics within the Negro population is clear, but the frequencies at various intervals of the range are not at all well known. Future trends in the biological composition of the Negro population depend on social and cultural factors. In general, there appear two alternative possibilities. First, the Negro population may tend toward a more homogeneous type, which may be indicated by the term "brown Americans." This development would be favored by the continued decline in miscegenation, by passing, and by the continued increase in the development of the Negro race consciousness and pride. The second possibility is the gradual disappearance of the Negro population through absorption in the white population. Even a marked increase in Negro-white intermarriage, certainly not now taking place, would fail to bring about amalgamation for many generations. Therefore, as a possible "solution" of America's twentieth-century Negro problem it may be for all practical purposes dismissed.

Personality Characteristics of the Negro People

In discussing other minorities it has been noted that certain personality and behavioral traits tend to characterize each group. What, if any, such traits characterize American Negroes in general which differentiate them from whites? [16]

If one seeks the answer from the stereotypes of Negroes held generally by most twentieth-century white Americans, it runs about as follows: The Negro is lazy, won't work unless he has to, and doesn't know what to do with money when he gets it. He is dirty, smelly, careless in appearance, yet given to flashy dressing. He is much more "sexy" than the white man, and exercises little restraint in sexual expression. He has low mental ability incapable of anything but menial labor. He is naturally religious, but his religion is mostly emotion and superstition. On the other hand, in his simple way, the Negro is a likeable fellow, clever in a childlike way, and has natural abilities as a singer, dancer, and actor which surpass those of most white folks. Obviously, by this time an increasing number of white Americans no longer hold this image of the Negro, and even those who hold it in diluted form are at least rationally forced to exclude the rising number of educated and middle-class Negroes.

Students of sociology are aware of the long controversy existing in the behavioral sciences in attempting to discover the part played by genetics and by

[16] In view of the heterogeneous ethnic composition of the population of the United States we shall for operational purposes consider the white, north European lineage, Protestant portion of the population as the prototype of the "white" population and shall mean in Negro-white comparisons (except where official government figures are used) that this is the white group together with those other European-descended and Catholic people who are for most purposes considered normative Americans. For short, as we have done elsewhere, we shall sometimes call them WASPS.

environmental influence in determining group characteristics as well as individual differences within groups. We noted in Chapter 3 on Race a marked tendency to emphasize the latter as accounting for significant differences found between large groups. Before turning to more detailed discussion, let us consider part of the findings of one of the more recent reviews of research on Negro-white differences:

> In psychophysical and psychomotor functions, differences appear between whites and Negroes which may not be accounted for by differential environment conditions. However, a tendency is prevalent in the literature to indicate that most differences of this nature may be leveled off when social and economic variables are controlled.... In temperament ("personality") studies, Rorschach, T.A.T., PAT., and P-F Studies, differences are found, but again there is insufficient evidence to determine the relative contributions of genetic constitution and experiences. At least in those reactions which indicate responses to a dominant group culture, experience seems to be the major, if not sole determinant. Overall likeness in psychodynamics appears more extensive than differences.[17]

Since intelligence is the single most important personality trait affecting achieved status, it deserves special mention. The results of most studies show the following: (1) On comparative mental testing, Negroes generally have lower average scores than whites. (2) Extensive overlapping exists in the distribution of the scores with a substantial number of Negroes scoring above the white median. (3) Improvement occurs in the scores of Negro children when exposed over time to a more favorable environment. Neither Dreger and Miller's review or an even more recent (1964) review by Klineberg[18] suggests that there has been any basic change in the scientific view of this matter since 1944 when Myrdal summed up as follows:

> The large amount of overlapping brought out the fact that both Negroes and whites belonged to the same human species and had more similarities than differences. The averages themselves tended to come nearer each other when the measurements were refined to exclude more and more the influence of differences in environment, such as education, cultural background and experience, socioeconomic class; and the social factors in the test situation itself, such as motivation and rapport with the tester.
>
> The intensive studies of these last influences proved, in addition, that no psychological tests yet invented come even close to measuring innate psychic traits, absolutely undistorted by these influences. *They rather rendered it probable that average differences would practically disappear if all environmental factors could be controlled.*[19]

[17] Ralph M. Dreger and Kent S. Miller, "Comparative Psychological Studies of Negroes and Whites in the United States," *Psychological Bulletin,* Sept., 1960, pp. 393–394. By permission.

[18] Otto Klineberg, "Negro-White Differences in Intelligence Test Performance: A New Look at an Old Problem," *American Psychologist,* Vol. 18, 1963, pp. 198–203.

[19] Gunnar Myrdal, *An American Dilemma,* p. 147. Italics ours. By permission of the publishers, Harper & Brothers.

Social science has further contributed to an understanding of group differences where minorities are involved through more sophisticated analysis such as that provided by Elkins in his study of slavery.[20] There emerged under slavery a stereotype of "Sambo" which Elkins described thus:

> Sambo . . . was docile but irresponsible, loyal, but lazy, humble but chronically given to lying and stealing; his behavior was full of infantile silliness. . . . His relationship with his master was one of utter dependence and childlike attachment; it was indeed this childlike quality that was the very key to his being. Although the merest hint of Sambo's manhood might fill the Southern breast with scorn, the child "in his place" could be both exasperating and lovable.[21]

Was this white man's stereotype of Sambo a myth or a reality? It was, of course, a necessity for the white Southerner to believe it in order to rationalize the institution of slavery. But to fully understand its element of reality it is necessary for analytical purposes to distinguish two types of what appears outwardly to be the same behavior: (1) that of the slave growing up under slavery who really internalized the self-image of himself as called for in the stereotype, and (2) that of the type of slave who behaved according to the stereotype in order to get along better with white people but whose self-image did not fit the stereotype at all. There is no possible data to determine the frequencies of these two types of self-images among the slaves.[22] We have drawn this distinction for its value in understanding Negro behavior under the later caste system and under the still prevailing minority situation of Negroes throughout America today. Behavior which social science has call *role playing* and that involving internalized self-derogatory conceptions may go together but quite often do not. In essence our point is that much of the behavior which in fact does fit the stereotype is role playing.

Cultural Characteristics of Negroes

All the minorities previously treated started out in this country with distinctive ethnic cultural differences which have been passed on to native-born generations in increasingly diluted form. The situation of Negroes in this respect is considerably different. The sharp impact of slavery went far to destroy the many tribal cultures which the Negroes brought with them. Scholarly controversy prevails among the students of the history of the Negro in the New World concerning the extent to which African culture traits have survived, or to what extent Negro cultural adaptations in the New World were influenced

[20] Stanley M. Elkins, *Slavery: A Problem in American Institutional and Intellectual Life* (Chicago: The University of Chicago Press, 1959).
[21] *Ibid.*, p. 82.
[22] Elkins further develops his thesis by describing what happened to adults in the Nazi concentration camps under Hitler. See especially pp. 104–105 of *Slavery*.

by their aboriginal culture.[23] A considerable number of scattered, specific cultural traits have been found in specific Negro groups which can be directly traced to African origin. It is significant, however, that more of these have been found among Negro groups in the West Indies, and that among those found in the United States the groups involved were especially isolated. For other, more prevalent aspects of American Negro culture and behavior which present a vague, general similarity to African cultural forms, the continuity of African heritage is highly debatable. For example, is the frequency of common-law marriage in Negro rural life derivative from African customs, or can it be explained by the highly destructive impact of slavery on the stability of Negro family life? Is the predilection of American Negroes for the Baptist denomination, which features total immersion, due to the surviving influence of West African "river cults," as Herskovits speculates, or is it more simply attributable, as Frazier suggests, to the vigorous proselytizing activities of the Baptist denomination.[24]

So far as African heritage is concerned Elkins writes: "No true picture... of African culture seems to throw any light at all on origins of what would emerge in African plantation society as the stereotype 'Sambo personality.' " He further concludes that the cultural level and the social organization of the various African societies from which the slaves were obtained "entitles one to argue that they must have had an institutional life at least as sophisticated as Anglo-Saxon England." [25] Thus if Elkins' conclusion is accepted it follows that most of any cultural distinctiveness of the Negro minority in America has developed out of their experience in the United States. Any aggregate of people who are collectively isolated from the mainstream of the broader society in which they reside develop some cultural distinctiveness. Despite the plethora of books recently written on America's race problem, Broom and Glenn write "the present state of knowledge does not permit an accurate estimate of the extent to which there is a distinctive Negro American way of life different in kind from that of the surrounding whites." [26] We will return to this topic again in Chapter 15 in connection with the goals of the Negro Revolt. Here we note that in regard to significant aspects of culture, American Negroes are Christians, heavily Protestant, speak English, and that their subcommunity social structure parallels that of the white community.[27] Thus of all American minorities the Negro minority most resembles the WASP prototype.

---

[23] A brief introduction to this historical problem is found in Frazier, *The Negro in the United States,* (New York: The Macmillan Co., 1949), Ch. I, "Significance of the African Background." For fuller discussion of the topic, see Melville J. Herskovits, *The Myth of the Negro Past* (New York: Harper & Brothers, 1942).

[24] Frazier, pp. 10–18.

[25] Elkins, *Slavery,* p. 97.

[26] Leonard Broom and Norvall Glenn, *The Transformation of the American Negro* (New York: Harper & Row, Publishers, 1965), p. 22.

[27] With the possible exception of the family and sex-role differences generally.

The white American stereotype of Negro personality, behavior, and culture has been largely unfavorable. Much of the comparative figures show a larger percentage of "sociopathic" behavior (as viewed by whites) by Negroes than for whites. Negroes are disproportionately found on police records and in penal institutions and have higher rates of recorded illegitimacy, ingroup violence, homicide, gambling, drug addiction, and drunkenness. While written as a recapitulation of data on Negro-American crime, the following puts well an interpretation of the so-called Negro "pathology" in general.

> White supremacists are quick to interpret these data as further evidence for their theories of the genetic inferiority of Negroes as a "race." There is, however, no scientific evidence to support such claims. But there are considerable data which indicate that a multiplicity of social factors produce these criminal patterns among Negroes.
>
> One broad set of factors is socio-economic in character. When compared with white Americans, Negroes are concentrated in those social sectors which exhibit high crime rates regardless of race. Thus, Negroes are more often lower class and poor, slum residents of the nation's largest metropolitan areas, victims of severe family disorganization, Southern in origin, young, and unemployed. Note that each of these characteristics is an important social correlate of crime apart from race—and especially for those violations with the highest Negro rates.
>
> The other, closely related set of factors involves the special type of discrimination inflicted upon Negroes. As with other minority groups who find discriminatory barriers blocking their path toward the mainstream of success-oriented America, many Negroes turn to crime. Crime may thus be utilized as a means of escape, ego-enhancement, expression of aggression, or upward mobility. The salient feature of Negro Americans is that they have accepted and internalized American culture, but are generally denied the chief rewards and privileges of that culture. High crime rates are but one consequence of this situation.[28]

Background: Phases of Negro-White Relations

The centuries-old interaction between Negroes and whites in the United States has followed a more complicated course than that of other minority situations, which requires some adaptation of our general three-phase schema. Again we repeat that in all points in this interaction some opposition by Negroes to dominance has occurred and much resistance by whites to any attempts to change the status quo has always taken place. For this reason, the dates used to mark off each phase are somewhat arbitrarily chosen. With these considerations in mind, let us examine the phases of Negro-white relations, using the following outline: (1) Slavery: white dominance over Negroes as slaves 1619–1863; (2) Early reconstruction: decline in white dominance 1866–1875; (3) Later reconstruction: the re-establishment of white dominance 1875 to circa 1900; (4) The maintenance of the dominant white Southern bi-

[28] Pettigrew, *A Profile of the Negro American,* pp. 155–156.

racial system, circa 1900–1954; (5) The establishment and maintenance of white dominance in the North, from World War I to World War II; and (6) The decline in white dominance in the North from World War II and in the South from May, 1954, and still in process.

The System of Slavery: The Colonial Period

Dominance of white Americans over Negroes was established at the outset from the time the first twenty slaves were bought by Virginia settlers in 1619. However, since there was no precedent in English law at this time, it seems to have been assumed that the status of slaves was similar to that of white indentured servants, with stipulated ways of being manumitted. But early in colonial history, differential treatment of Negroes began. For example, when three bound servants, two white and one Negro, had been brought back to Virginia from Maryland after attempting escape from servitude, the court, having ordered thirty lashes for all three, further ordered that the white servants should serve three years in bondage, but that the Negro should serve his master for the rest of his life.[29] By court actions such as these, the differential status of Negroes evolved into a clear pattern of slavery, which eventually became established by more explicit law. In Virginia the slave status was fixed by a law making all non-Christians who came into the colony as servants from across the seas slaves for the rest of their lives. In 1682 this law was repealed and in its place another substituted "making slaves of all persons of non-Christian nationalities thereafter coming into the colony, whether they came by sea or land and whether or not they had been converted to Christianity after capture."[30]

Although early developing into a fixed institution, Negro slavery grew indispensable only as the plantation system of agriculture became important and more widespread. This system involved the large-scale production of a staple crop for commercial exchange and required cheap labor. At a time when land was either free or cheap, white men wanted to work as independent farmers, not as wage earners. Thus Negro slaves filled the increasing manpower demand. The colony of Georgia, founded in 1735, first prohibited the importation of Negro slaves, but by 1750, as the plantation system began to spread into the new colony, the act was repealed. The number of Negroes in Georgia increased from a reported 349 in 1750 to 15,000 by 1773.[31] The nexus between the plantation economy and slavery is further illustrated by the difference between the two Carolinas. In North Carolina the plantation economy failed to develop on a large scale and so did slavery; in South Carolina, where the plantation system developed on a large scale, "the number of Negroes had become so numerous that it was felt necessary to encourage the importation of white serv-

[29] Frazier, *The Negro in the United States*, p. 24.
[30] *Ibid.*, p. 26.
[31] *Ibid.*, pp. 32–33.

ants to secure the safety of the colony." [32] Finally, in the North, where there was no plantation economy, no large-scale slavery developed. By 1790, when the first federal census was taken, the proportion of free Negroes to those in slavery ranged from the all-free Negro population (5,462) in Massachusetts to other states where from a third to a half of the resident Negroes were still slaves.[33]

The introduction of slavery into the colonies came as an extension of the institution already established in the West Indies. The slave trade was carried on largely by the British, although subsequently colonists themselves took a hand in it, especially New England port merchants.[34] This trade was a highly hazardous and adventuresome occupation. It was not easy to get the slaves or to deliver them since, aside from the problem of holding them by force, great mortality occurred from the usually overcrowded conditions in the "Middle Passage" journeys. However, when things went well, as they obviously often did, the profits were high. Franklin writes, "It was not unusual for a ship carrying 250 slaves to net as much as £7,000 on one voyage. Profits of 100 percent were not uncommon for Liverpool merchants." [35] The exact number of slaves imported to the colonies, and later to the states, is not known, but estimates range from 500,000 to 700,000. And, in spite of the fact that the importation of slaves was officially prohibited after 1808, the evidence is incontrovertible that a substantial contraband trade continued after that date. Collins estimates that about 270,000 slaves were imported into the United States between 1808 and 1860.[36]

From all accounts the total number of slaves imported from Africa to all the New World from the fifteenth to the nineteenth century must be reckoned in the millions. Williams writes, "The importation into Jamaica from 1700 to 1786 was 610,000, and it has been estimated that the total import of slaves into all the British colonies between 1680 and 1786 was over two million.[37] Bearing in mind the number who died resisting capture and the heavy mortality on shipboard, it can be seen that the slave trade constituted a great drain on the manhood of Africa, particularly in the West Coast area, and especially since the traders tried to take the youngest and healthiest men.

From the Revolutionary War to the War Between the States

In spite of the fixed position of slavery in the colonial economy during and for a short period following the Revolutionary War, there were signs that the

[32] *Ibid.*, p. 32.
[33] *Ibid.*, p. 34.
[34] Maurice R. Davie, *Negroes in American Society* (New York: McGraw-Hill Book Co., 1949), p. 18.
[35] John Hope Franklin, *From Slavery to Freedom* (New York: Alfred A. Knopf, 1947), p. 57.
[36] Winfield H. Collins, *The Domestic Slave Trade of the Southern States* (New York: Broadway Publishing Company, 1904), p. 20.
[37] Eric Williams, *Capitalism & Slavery* (Chapel Hill: University of North Carolina Press, 1944), p. 33.

slavery system might be abolished. Slavery was coming under increasing attack from a moral viewpoint, not only from Northerners but from enlightened slaveholders such as Washington and Jefferson. The first President desired "to see a plan adopted for the abolition of it [slavery]"; [38] and Jefferson wrote in his autobiography, "Nothing is more certainly written in the book of fate than that these people are to be free." [39] The attitude of the public was affected by economic interests as well as moral idealism. Frazier indicates that opposition to slavery was expressed in Delaware, Maryland, and Virginia, where a diversified agriculture was supplanting the production of tobacco, whereas in the lower South, where the production of tobacco, rice, and indigo was still important, there was strong opposition either to suspending the slave trade or to the emancipation of the Negro.[40] In the midst of these conflicting attitudes toward slavery, the Constitution of the new republic compromised on the issue by setting 1808 as the date after which the importation of slaves was to be abolished. The abolition of slavery in many state constitutions in the North and its declining economic significance led many people to share with Jefferson the belief that slavery was on its way out.

But the hopes of those opposed to slavery were destined to be dashed by the invention of the cotton gin. With this invention Southern cotton planters were able to meet the rapidly growing demand of the English market. The expansion of cotton economy increased by leaps and bounds, especially from 1815 on. This development was accompanied by the growth of the slave system and the slave population. (See Table 10–2.)

TABLE 10–2. *Growth of the Slave Population in the United States, 1790–1860* [41]

Census Year	Slave Population	Percent of Decennial Increase
1790	697,624	
1800	893,602	28.1
1810	1,191,362	33.3
1820	1,538,022	29.1
1830	2,009,043	30.6
1840	2,487,355	18.8
1850	3,204,313	28.8
1860	3,953,760	23.4

From 1790 to 1803 the natural increase of the slave population was supplemented by foreign importation of over 100,000 slaves. Although, as Table 10–2

[38] Myrdal, *An American Dilemma*, p. 85.
[39] *Ibid.*
[40] Frazier, *The Negro in the United States*, p. 35.
[41] United States Bureau of the Census, *A Century of Population Growth*, p. 132.

shows, the percentage of increase after 1810 declined, a substantial number of slaves was smuggled in to augment the natural increase. And since there was an increasing demand for slaves because of the prohibition, a domestic slave trade developed. As the plantation system spread south and west away from Maryland, Virginia, and Kentucky, many slaves were bred for sale by their first owners to work in the new areas.[42]

Having built not only its economy but a total society on the foundation of slavery, the South needed rationalizations which would justify it. Thus there began to emerge in the pre-Civil War period learned treatises solemnly concluding that "the Negro" was naturally meant to be a slave and that he was obviously inferior to the white. Many of these treatises invoked Biblical sanction and two of the most scholarly were written by Presbyterian ministers.[43] The growing intellectual support for the established system reached its climax in the words of Chief Justice Taney, who in his famous decision in the Dred Scott case declared, "A Negro has no rights which a white man need respect." [44]

Thus it appeared clear that, far from declining, the slave system during the early nineteenth century in the South grew constantly stronger. This is important to keep in mind as we turn to the reconstruction days. It does much to explain why the Emancipation Proclamation, which freed slaves in the legal sense, did not protect them from the caste barriers that were erected to supplant those of slavery.

The American Slave System: Comparison with Latin America

Among the many instances of slave systems, there is considerable variation. The degree of authority accorded to the master is affected by many factors, of which the economic role of the slaves and the character of the other institutions in the society are important. The actual exercise of the permitted authority is always influenced by the human qualities of affection, on the one hand, and of aggressiveness and cupidity on the other, qualities which are in part structured by the general culture but which always vary to some extent with individual personalities. Too, the responses of slaves to their condition vary with their cultural level and their personality variables.

In Latin America, where a slave system flourished for many years, law, re-

[42] Frazier, *The Negro in the United States*, p. 42.
[43] *Ibid.*, pp. 46–47.
[44] Part of the decision rendered in the Dred Scott Case (Mar. 6, 1857) as quoted in *The Columbia Encyclopedia* (New York: Columbia University Press, 1940), p. 1728. Dred Scott, a Negro slave, was taken by his master from the slave state of Missouri into free territory. Upon return, Scott sued for his freedom on the ground that residence in Illinois, a free state, and in Minnesota, a free territory, made him a free citizen. The case came up in the Missouri courts, but after Scott was purchased by a citizen of New York, suit was filed in the federal courts. Financed by Abolitionists, the case reached the Supreme Court, where Chief Justice Roger B. Taney rendered the opinion taken as that of the majority. (1) It upheld the Missouri courts in declaring that Scott, still a slave, was not a citizen. (2) It declared the Missouri Compromise unconstitutional. The Negro was branded inferior, "altogether unfit to associate with the white race."

ligion, and the mores of the society made the status of slaves vastly different from, and on the whole superior to, that of slaves in the British-settled area of South America and in southern United States. First, in Latin America, slaves had rights protecting them against many specific abuses from their masters. The power to inflict certain physical punishments upon slaves was limited by law, and slaves could obtain legal redress if the master overstepped these bounds. Married slaves could not be separated from each other against their will. "The children followed the status of their mother, and the child of a free mother remained free even if she later became a slave." [45] By contrast, in the American system, the slave had practically no protection by law from the arbitrary exercise of authority by the master.[46] He had no property rights. Married partners could be separated from each other, and children from their parents. That they were is attested in a number of advertisements, of which the following is typical.

> NEGROES FOR SALE. A negro woman, 24 years of age, and her two children, one eight and the other three years old. Said negroes will be sold SEPARATELY, or together, *as desired*. The woman is a good seamstress. She will be sold low for cash, or EXCHANGED FOR GROCERIES. For terms, apply to Matthew Bliss and Co., 1 Front Levee.[47]

Second, the Latin system favored manumission, and a more-or-less steady change from slavery to freedom was going on all the time. "A hundred social devices . . . encouraged the master to release his slave, and the bondsman to achieve freedom on his own account." For example, in Cuba "a slave worth six hundred dollars could buy himself out in twenty-four installments of twenty-five dollars each, and with each payment he acquired one twenty-fourth of his own freedom." [48] The American system operated to prevent manumission. While some slaves were freed, as the system grew in strength during the early nineteenth century the pressures against freeing slaves became greater.

A third contrast is seen in the difference in the status of former slaves once they became free. In Latin America the freed person, whatever his racial lineage, assumed a place equal to that of all others in the civic community. Authorities differ as to whether or not Negro ancestry might have been a handicap in the class status system of Latin America, but there seems little doubt that many Negroes came to occupy high public position and that white-colored intermarriage was never looked upon with the abhorrence that it is looked upon in the United States. Although the position of the Negro freed before general abolition was in some respects higher than that of those still enslaved, the fact that he was still a Negro meant that he was considered an inferior person.

Among the various social forces which Tannenbaum offers in explanation

[45] Frank Tannenbaum, *Slave and Citizen* (New York: Alfred A. Knopf, 1947), p. 49. Most of the material for this comparison is derived from Tannenbaum.
[46] Myrdal, *An American Dilemma*, pp. 530–531.
[47] *New Orleans Bee*, quoted in Tannenbaum, p. 77. By permission of the publishers, Alfred A. Knopf.
[48] *Ibid.*, pp. 53–54.

of the contrasts in these two slave systems was the presence in the Latin-American legal system of Spanish law, with its established precedents of specific definition of slave status, and the absence of any corresponding precedents in British law. He further notes the influence of Catholic doctrine in contrast to the position of Protestantism. Although the Church did not interfere with the institution when the domestic law accepted it, it had early condemned the slave trade and officially prohibited Catholics from participating in it, even though not altogether successfully. Still further, the Church considered that slave and master were equal in the sight of God, gave slaves the right to baptism, and insisted that masters bring their slaves to church. This stands in sharp contrast to the total neglect of Negroes by the Episcopal Church in the British West Indies, and to the position of the Protestant denominations in the South of the United States. After 1700 there was no systematic opposition to teaching the Christian doctrine to the Negro slave, but the churches in the South generally made no attack on the institution of slavery itself.

Slavery as a Social System

Slavery as a system of human relations cannot be maintained without the use of force. While most slaves states passed statutes designed to protect the slave from unnecessary sufferings, Myrdal writes, "In general, the Negro slave had no 'rights' which his owner was bound to respect." [49] Thus the disciplining of Negroes was left largely to the master or his white overseer, who in exercise of this function was restrained only by his own conscience and such group pressure as the white mores of the community brought to bear. When it was felt to be necessary, the masters did inflict corporal punishment and even death on the slaves.

Nevertheless, the relations between the two racial groups came to be ordered by a system of etiquette and ritual which more or less explicitly defined the proper reciprocal behavior whenever members of the two races were together. The actual relations between groups never perfectly coincide with the formal status. White-Negro relations under slavery were often overlaid with a sense of mutual responsibility and reciprocal affections. This was particularly true with house servants who identified themselves with the family, and who were often biologically related to it.

Aptheker has called attention to the fact that there were some rebellious reactions. He has noted about 250 slave insurrections and rebellions involving ten or more people.[50] Better known is the fact that many slaves attempted to flee to free territory, some successfully. The odds, however, against either rebellion or escape were so overwhelming that some form of accommodation to the

[49] Myrdal, *An American Dilemma*, p. 530.
[50] Herbert Aptheker, *American Slave Revolts* (New York: Columbia University Press, 1943), p. 162.

inevitable was the price of survival. Accommodation to slavery required taking on—at least as role playing—all the traits of servility and dependence.

Reconstruction

BRIEF CHALLENGE TO WHITE DOMINANCE The emancipation of slaves and the end of the Civil War were followed by a brief challenge to white dominance. But emancipation was forced upon the South against its will, of course, and the implication of freedom could be carried through only by a costly, large-scale federal program and the application of considerable pressures upon the South. The problem was twofold: how to implement and guarantee the new political status of Negroes as free men; and how to reconstruct the economy of the South in such a manner that Negroes would have a secure economic position.

The war had wrought enormous material property losses on Southern whites, as well as taking away their slaves. Many of the freed slaves who, both during the war and immediately after it, had flocked to the cities or to the vicinity of Northern army camps found no means of livelihood. In 1865 the Bureau of Refugees, Freedmen, and Abandoned Lands was established to aid in, among other things, the economic rehabilitation of the freedmen, as well as the property-less whites, and to promote an educational program for the Negroes. The general plan was to furnish land and tools with which the freedmen and landless whites might become self-sustaining farmers.

However, during the seven years of its existence (1865–1872), the Bureau was unable to accomplish its economic objectives. It had woefully inadequate funds for the size of the job. The amnesty granted former Confederates restored to them the land which had already been leased to Negroes, who consequently became landless again. When efforts were made to resettle both white and Negro tenants on public lands in the Gulf areas, inability to raise enough capital and general discouragement with the whole program spelled failure. The desire of the more influential portion of the white South to retain the traditional system of agricultural production and to keep the Negro in his servile place did nothing to help. And the half-hearted support of Northerners contributed to the failure of the government to carry through the program. The lukewarm support was due in part to the usual reluctance to appropriate the rather large funds needed for the task. Northerners, although believing in theoretical freedom for Negroes, were far from advocating that they be accorded full, equal status. The combination of proprietary interest in the South and the traditional white attitudes toward the proper status of Negroes, shared by many Northerners as well as nearly all the white South, conspired to defeat what appears in retrospect to have been a validly conceived plan for the economic rehabilitation of the South.

The same combination of interests and attitudes appeared in opposition to the fulfillment of the other objective in the Northern plan for reconstruction of the South: the civic and social integration of Negroes and the rehabilitation of Negroes as first-class citizens. Soon after the close of the war, eight Southern states instituted the so-called Black Codes. By various statutes affecting apprenticeship, labor contracts, debts, and vagrancy, these codes went far to reestablish the servile position of Negroes. Of the examples of these codes which Frazier cites, the following is significantly illustrative.

> The Florida code states that if any person of color failed to fulfill the stipulations of a contract into which he entered with a plantation owner or was impudent to the owner, he should be declared a vagrant and be subject to punishment for vagrancy.[51]

When the Republican government of the North realized that the South was in fact nullifying the Emancipation Proclamation, it set about to exert pressure to force acceptance. Through the Fourteenth Amendment to the Constitution, declared effective in 1866, abridgement of the full civic equality of all citizens was declared unlawful, and the supplementary Fifteenth Amendment, effective in 1870, specifically denied the right to abridgement of the voting privilege "on account of race, color, or previous condition of servitude." Still further, Congress passed in 1867 a series of reconstruction acts which called for the temporary governing of the South by military rule until such time as genuinely democratic elections could be held and governments so elected should get under way. In the governments which followed, many Negroes were elected to state assemblies, and twenty were sent to Congress. Some of these Negro officials demonstrated unusual ability.

In these turbulent years the majority of Southerners naturally resented the attempt of the "carpetbaggers" to reconstruct their society, aided by their own "scalawags," as the Southerners who co-operated with the Yankee officials were called. They made much of the point that complete civic equality for Negroes would give the colored population control over the South. Actually, in no state were Negroes ever the dominating factor in the government, though in several states they constituted about half the population. The Southern attitude toward the Negro was not reconstructed, as the testimony of Carl Schurz indicates:

> Wherever I go . . . I hear the people talk in such a way as to indicate that they are yet unable to conceive of the Negro as possessing any rights at all. . . . The people boast that when they get freedmen's affairs in their own hands . . . "the niggers will catch hell."
>
> The reason of all this is simple and manifest. The whites esteem the blacks their property by natural right, and however much they admit that the individual relations of masters and slaves have been destroyed by the war and by the President's emancipation proclamation, they still have an ingrained feeling that the blacks at large belong to the whites at large.[52]

[51] Frazier, *The Negro in the United States*, p. 127.
[52] Report of Carl Schurz, Senate Executive Document, No. 2, 39th Congress, 1st Session, cited by W. E. B. DuBois, *Black Reconstruction in America* (New York: Harcourt, Brace & Co., 1936).

The next phase of the reconstruction drama opened as the Republican Congress began to weaken. In 1872, the disabilities imposed on the former Confederate leaders, which prevented their participation in political affairs, were removed. The Freedmen's Bureau was abolished, depriving many Negro laborers and tenants of much-needed economic support and moral aid. The climax came when the Civil Rights bill of 1875 was declared unconstitutional. This bill, as Myrdal puts it, "represented the culmination of the Federal reconstruction legislation, was explicit in declaring that all persons . . . should be entitled to the full and equal enjoyment of the accommodations, advantages, facilities, and privileges of inns, public conveyances on land and water, theaters, and other places of public amusement . . . applicable alike to citizens of every race and color, regardless of previous condition of servitude." [53] When the bill was declared unconstitutional, at least as far as the "social" equality phases were concerned, the North seems to have given up.

From 1875 on, the door was open for the unreconstructed white Southerners to carry out their own program of reconstruction. The result was the biracial pattern of race relations in which the dominance of white over colored was assured. This social system has remained broadly intact down to the present and will be the subject of detailed examination in the next chapter. Reconstruction on this biracial basis involved the use of both legal and illegal procedures. Since in the white Southern view Negroes had already advanced too far, it was first necessary to apply illegal force and terror to compel a return to their original status. This phase of the reconstruction was spearheaded by a number of secret societies, of which the Ku Klux Klan is the most widely known. Extralegal activities were supplemented by further Black Code legislation, which segregated Negroes and otherwise accorded them unequal privileges. While it took some years to accomplish the task, the white South succeeded in establishing a color-caste system.

Reconstruction: An Object Lesson

What happened in the reconstruction period is an excellent object lesson in social science. It illustrates the consequences of attempting swift and radical social change without adequate social planning. In hindsight, it is clear that the federal government attempted to accomplish too sweeping objectives in too short a time against too strong a set of opposing forces and with too little public support from the North itself. For example, how could it have been expected that white Southerners, long steeped in the tradition of slavery, could change their complex attitudes and habits concerning Negroes overnight? Again, how could it have been expected that slaves, held to such a low level of literacy and moulded into a servile, dependent, personality pattern, could immediately become self-reliant and civically active? Furthermore, how could it have been

[53] Myrdal, *An American Dilemma*, p. 579. By permission.

expected that such a program could be carried on without a greater consensus of Northern opinion to support it? To raise such questions in hindsight and to leave the matter there is obviously unfair to the many intelligent and socially conscious white people, both North and South who set the objectives and tried to carry them out. Neither the theoretical knowledge of human nature and social processes nor the accumulated practice of social engineering had advanced to a point in 1865 to have made success possible. We cite the lesson for its value at the present time.

The United States is now in an extraordinary period of disequilibrium in white-Negro relations, precipitated by the Supreme Court's school desegregation decision. We face this period with a considerably greater body of social theory, techniques, and practices in intergroup relations. In areas of the nation where the attitudes of the dominant group are not too intransigent, some of this knowledge has been usefully applied. As we have before commented, social knowledge affected the decision of the Court itself. The nature and scope of this accumulated knowledge will be discussed in Chapter 19.

Topics for Projects and Discussion

1. Discuss the relative importance of (a) sociological factors and (b) biological factors in determining whether an American is or is not a Negro.
2. The "Negro" population of the United States could decline even with higher birth rates and lower death rates among people of Negro ancestry. Explain how this could happen.
3. Discuss the various effects on Negro-white relations which you would see following from the increasing development of race pride among American Negroes.
4. Trace carefully the role which economic and technological factors played in the development of the slavery system in the South.
5. Consult appropriate historical sources to determine the extent to which Negroes in the South following the War between the States were or were not prepared for citizenship.

Suggested Reading

Aptheker, Herbert. *American Negro Slave Revolts.* New York: Columbia University Press, 1943.
    The most complete history of the subject.
Berry, Brewton. *Almost White.* New York: Macmillan Co., 1963.
    A study of pockets of people with mixtures of Indian, white, and Negro lineage found in over 200 communities in the Eastern United States occupying anomalous status position.
Elkins, Stanley M. *Slavery: A Problem in American Institutional and Intellectual Life.* Chicago: The University of Chicago Press, 1959.
    An institutional approach to the subject.
Franklin, John Hope, "Brief History of the Negro in the United States," Chapter 1 of the

American Negro Reference Book. Englewood Cliffs, N.J.: Prentice-Hall, 1966, edited by John P. Davis.

> *An outstanding historian of the American Negro summarizes the subject in seventy-five pages.*

Frazier, E. Franklin. *The Negro in the United States,* rev. ed. New York: The Macmillan Co., 1957.

> *Part I, "The Negro under the Slave Regime," and Part II, " Racial Conflict and New Forms of Accommodations," are pertinent to this chapter.*

Lewis, Julian H. *The Biology of the Negro.* Chicago: University of Chicago Press, 1942.

> *Most complete summary and analysis of the subject.*

Myrdal, Gunnar, *et al.* An American Dilemma: *The Negro Problem and Modern Democracy.* New York: Harper & Brothers, 1944.

> *The most comprehensive assemblage of facts about Negroes in relation to whites in American society. The Swedish writer has presented his own interpretation of the data and researches provided by scores of American scholars. Chapter 7, "Population"; Chapter 8, "Migration"; and Chapter 10, "The Tradition of Slavery," bear on this chapter.*

Styron, William. *The Confessions of Nat Turner.* New York: Random House, 1967.

> *In this literary tour de force, the novelist provides a fascinating biography of the leader of an abortive slave revolt of 1831.*

11

Negro-White Relations: The Traditional Southern Pattern

The previous chapter delineates briefly the process by which the white South re-established dominance in a new pattern of race relations after the abortive attempt to develop an integrated pattern following emancipation and the Civil War. This chapter will describe this system and consider its implications for the South and the nation. By 1910 it had been crystallized and remained essentially intact to World War II. In view of the postwar changes, we employ the past tense generally but it should be understood that much of this pattern still prevails especially in the Deep South. The still strong resistance to change in the South is better understood by keeping in mind that today's adult white Southerners have been conditioned since birth to the biracial system here described.

The South includes seventeen states and the District of Columbia. The following states are considered border states: Delaware, Kentucky, Maryland, Missouri, Tennessee, Oklahoma, and West Virginia. The term "Deep South" is not so definite geographically. It certainly includes Alabama, Georgia, Louisiana, Mississippi, and South Carolina. Arkansas, Florida, North Carolina, Texas, Virginia, and the District of Columbia account for the rest of the South.[1]

Caste System

In common with many other, although not all, students of minorities, we shall designate this Southern interracial pattern as a caste system. In its ideology and in the institutions which governed race relations, the categorical segregation of the two races in a large number of social relations was clear. Intermarriage was flatly prohibited. While specific identification with a particular occupation, as was characteristic of the traditional Hindu caste system, was not so marked, nevertheless the Southern pattern did not generally permit the performance together of the same tasks by members of the two races. Furthermore, the rising

[1] To Southerners "Deep South" meant the areas where the plantation economy earlier was extensive and vigorous.

244

middle class of Negroes in the South was in the main segregated from the white middle class. It was the absence of explicit religious sanctions in support of its biracial system which mainly distinguished the Southern pattern from other caste systems.

The Southern caste system had two main features—segregation and the so-called caste etiquette. The former involved the physical separation of Negroes from whites; the latter included the rules to be followed when interaction must unavoidably take place between one or more members of each race. Both the patterns of segregation and the caste etiquette always symbolized the superordination of the white people and the subordination of the Negroes.

Housing Segregation [2]

Residentially, in rural areas, Negroes were scattered but did not live close to whites except on plantations, where the mansion was separated conspicuously, though often not far, from the Negroes' shacks. In small towns there was a clustering of Negro homes on edges of the community. In Southern cities there were varieties of Negro residential patterns: the back-alley residence plan, as seen in Charleston; the isolated community, as in Tulsa; the one large Negro area with smaller scattered clusters found in many cities. Interestingly enough, Southern whites did not appear to object to having Negro families live near them, as Northern whites did. However, in the South when homes of Negro families were spatially proximate to those of white families, there was usually some outward manifestation of the superior-inferior status—for example, whites facing the streets and Negroes the alley, or the comparatively more run-down appearance of the Negro homes. Neighborliness prevailed, but always in conformance to the etiquette of race relations.

Education

Seventeen states had entirely separate school systems. No contact at all took place between the teachers or pupils of the two systems except the unavoidable contact of the superintendent, who was white. This separation in schooling during the early years went far to root firmly in the attitudes and habits of children of both races the practice of race segregation. Negroes were not admitted generally into public libraries in the South, and a Negro had no access to library facilities unless he could get a white friend to take out a book for him. In a few large cities Negro branch libraries were established.

Social Discrimination

Public recreational facilities were generally scarce in the South outside the large cities, and whites in the nonurban areas did not share those that existed

[2] See Charles S. Johnson, *Patterns of Negro Segregation* (New York: Harper & Brothers, 1943), for the fullest single-volume discussion of segregation at the height of the development of the system.

with the Negroes. In Southern cities, Negroes were generally excluded from public parks, and only a few cities had parks for Negroes. Except in a few instances where a special section of a public playground was set aside for them, the colored people were not permitted to use public playgrounds. At one time, a fairly common sign in Southern parks was "Negroes, Soldiers, and Dogs Keep Out."

In hotels and restaurants the segregation was absolute and complete. Outside the larger cities, where some Negro hotels and restaurants existed, it was impossible for Negroes who were traveling to get a meal or lodging unless some Negro family gave them hospitality. In public buildings, such as post offices, tax offices, an so on, Negroes usually waited in line until every white person appearing had been served. Separate toilets for each race was the general rule in public places where both races were admitted. The best-known device of the segregation system was "Jim Crow" transportation. In local transportation, where the vehicles were often not physically partitioned, Negroes had to go to the rear and whites to the front, the dividing line being set on each trip by the proportion of each race aboard. Of this Johnson wrote: "The operator is empowered to regulate the space occupied by each race in accordance with the respective number of passengers. This system is subject to abuse since it permits the attitude of the operator to become a factor in segregation." [3]

A striking example of segregation was in hospitalization. In some places there were isolated wards for Negroes. But more often the hospitals would not admit Negroes, and there were few Negro hospitals. Instances occurred of Negroes in need of emergency operations dying because the nearest hospitals would not admit them.

Economic Discrimination

Segregation in economic life had two main aspects: in employment and in the role of the Negro as a customer. In regard to employment, the basic principle was that Negroes must not work alongside whites on equal functional terms. For instance, one restaurant might have all Negro waitresses and another across the street all white waitresses, but no restaurant would mix the two. The first would probably have a white cashier; the second would probably have Negro dishwashers; but here the functional differentiation was clear. This principle operated to limit Negro employment to those occupations which whites did not care to enter. (The one important exception was tenant farming, in which both races engaged but in which they did not work together.) As a result, occupations which were the most menial and the poorest paid were left for the Negroes. When technological improvements came along to make any particular occupation more rewarding, the whites tried to keep the Negroes

[3] *Ibid.,* p. 49.

out, as they did following the introduction of farm tractors and the mechanical cotton picker.

Until 1935 labor unions in the South excluded Negroes from membership, or at most permitted them to organize in separate auxiliary locals. Since the earlier days of the caste period, Negroes had become a majority in certain semiskilled or skilled trades; the development of unions had the effect of driving them from these occupations. The elimination of Negroes as engineers on railroad locomotives and the gradual decline in the number of Negro firemen and brakemen correlated with the rise of the railway workers' unions.

The color line was less rigidly drawn against the Negro as a customer in commercial establishments. Two generalizations held largely true. The cheaper the price level of the goods to be sold, the more welcome was the Negro trade. Thus the five-and-ten-cent stores and the chain food stores generally welcomed Negro trade and provided reasonably courteous service, while the more exclusive stores either refused or discouraged Negro patronage through discourtesy. The other general rule was that the more intimate the personal relationship involved in a commercial transaction, the more likely the Negro was to be excluded. In beauty parlor and mortuary services the races were strictly separated. But when the services rendered, though involving considerable interpersonal relationships, were such that the position of the vendor was clearly superior to that of the buyer, as in the case of medical or legal counsel, white professional people often would take Negro clients.

The Code of Race Etiquette

Since Negroes were an important part of the economic life of the South, they could not be totally segregated. To allow for some interpersonal relations there developed an elaborate pattern of racial etiquette,[4] the function of which was to make clear the superordinate and subordinate caste positions. For example, a white man did not shake hands with a Negro when introduced to him. An exception would be when a white man visited a Negro college or, sometimes, a Negro home. The white person did not address the Negro person as "Mr." or "Mrs.," but rather by his first name or by his last without the courtesy title; the Negro always addressed the white person as "Mister," "Marse," or "Misses," or better still by some such title as "Colonel," which often the white man did not actually possess. Interestingly enough, professionally trained Negroes could be addressed as "Professor," "Doctor," or "Reverend." Thus most Negro male school or college teachers were "Professors," however limited their education may have been. Negro women were never referred to as "ladies," but either just "women," or, irrespective of age, as "girls." Negro men were expected to doff

[4] See Bertram W. Doyle, *The Etiquette of Race Relations in the South* (Chicago: University of Chicago Press, 1937), for a fuller description of the subject.

their hats when they spoke to white men, but the latter were not expected to reciprocate. Whenever Negroes had occasion to call at or enter white men's homes, they did so at the rear door; the white man, of course, always appeared at the front door. Whenever circumstances brought Negroes and white people together at mealtime or on recreational occasions, the races were not expected to sit together at the same table or play together. Thus when a white person visited a colored home, if the Negro hostess wished to provide food for her guest, etiquette prescribed that they not eat together. With the exception of quite young children, Negroes and white did not ordinarily play together. A significant exception was where there was opportunity for the Negro to serve his white companion in a servile role, as in hunting or fishing.

Endogamy is the primary principle of caste. Marriage across caste lines was not recognized and was forbidden by law in Southern states. Most adamant of all the taboos was the one against any sort of casual interpersonal relations between a white woman and a Negro man. No one thing was more dangerous to a Negro male than to be in a situation that could be even remotely construed as indicating personal interest in a white female. That Negro men understood this and acted accordingly can be seen in the following instance. A white woman, the wife of a white man in charge of a migrant labor camp for Southern Negroes in the North, attempted to engage Negro men in the camp in friendly conversation and was nonplussed at their attempts to avoid the situation. Brought up to know that the rope or faggot awaits the Negro accused—falsely or otherwise—of "sexual" interest in a white woman, Negro men in the South, as a general rule, avoided white women.

The Interrelation of Class and Caste

In the South the class system was linked with the caste system in significant ways. In most Southern communities, particularly in cities, class differentiation had developed within the Negro caste as well as in the white caste. Negroes performing higher-ranking functions—for example, ministers, teachers, doctors, farm agents—had achieved a higher-class status within their racial group. The class position of such Negroes was generally recognized by the white people, and the Negroes so recognized were accorded differential treatment from that accorded the lower-class Negroes. Frequently upper-class whites came to the defense of upper-class Negroes who got into trouble with lower-class whites. Warner and Davis cite the case of a colored professional man who accidentally ran down and killed with his car a drunken lower-class white man. Local bankers offered money for the Negro's defense, and upper-class white women called at his place of business to indicate that they supported him in his difficulty.[5] This class bond which cut across caste lines prompted upper-class whites on occasion

[5] W. Lloyd Warner and Allison Davis, "A Comparative Study of American Caste," in *Race Relations and the Race Problem,* ed. Edgar T. Thompson (Durham: Duke University Press, 1939), p. 243.

to attend special functions conducted by upper-class Negroes, and at such occasions special courtesies not generally accorded Negroes by caste etiquette might be extended by the whites, such as addressing the Negro women as "Mrs."

This class-differentiated aspect of the caste system operated more to strengthen caste, however, than to undermine it. While it accorded upperclass Negroes some differential privileges, these were limited and always fell clearly short of equality. And to receive these class privileges upper-class Negroes had to accept caste, at least outwardly. This special relation also served practical purposes in the maintenance of the biracial system. While caste relations are fundamentally antagonistic, they cannot exist without some degree of cooperation. In spite of the vastly superior power position of the whites, an orderly community under caste required cooperation from the Negro group. In their function as leaders, the middle- and upper-class Negroes were expected to exert their influence to control the Negro masses in the interest of preserving order.[6]

Methods of Enforcing Caste

The methods employed for sustaining this caste pattern of race relations in the South may be conveniently treated under the headings of legal methods, illegal force and intimidation, and custom. Bearing in mind that at many points these three methods of social control reinforce each other, we shall discuss each separately.

Legal Methods

Specific local and state laws required segregation of the two races in many of the categories of interaction noted above. Southern state supreme courts upheld these laws, and for a long time the Supreme Court of the United States upheld Southern segregation laws in the cases reaching it. One important exception concerns housing segregation by state or municipal law. In 1915, a Louisville, Kentucky, city ordinance forbidding Negroes to reside in certain areas was declared unconstitutional by the United States Supreme Court.[7] It further ruled that the segregated public facilities and services provided Negroes should be equal to those provided for whites. As we shall presently indicate, every description of the facilities for Negroes in the South documented the fact that Negroes did not have equal public facilities, in spite of this interpretation of the Constitution. Segregation continued to be upheld by local law.

---

[6] These class-linked relations should not be confused with the intergroup relations which are in substance nonconformity to caste. There have been, of course, throughout the whole period considered, a few white people here and there, more particularly in cities, who did not believe in caste and who, with due deference to the personal costs of nonconformity, have participated in informal mixed gatherings on a plane of social equality.

[7] See Johnson, *Patterns of Negro Segregation*, p. 175.

Illegal Violence and Intimidation

Not all segregation and race etiquette, however, was upheld by law. The part of it not so covered was reinforced by intimidation and extralegal violence. The Negro who violated the customary etiquette found himself brought to order by whites by abusive language and warnings. If he persisted in violation or if the breach was considered particularly heinous from the dominant caste's viewpoint, he might be physically maltreated or even lynched. If the violations appeared to be in any sense en masse, a whole Negro street or area might be destroyed by white groups as a way of "teaching the nigger to keep his place." The authors of the book *Deep South* write:

> In fact, it is considered entirely correct for the white person to resort directly to physical attack upon the Negro. Thus, if a Negro curses a white, the white may knock the Negro down; and the failure to do so may even be considered as a failure in duty as a white....
>
> It is a common belief of many whites that Negroes will respond only to violent methods. In accordance with the theory of the "animal-like" nature of the Negro, they believe that the formal punishments of fines and imprisonments fail to act as deterrents to crime.[8]

A planter puts the traditional Southern white viewpoint thus:

> The best thing is not to take these young bucks into the court house for some small crime but to give them a paddling. That does them more good than a jail sentence. If I catch a Negro stealing a hog or some chickens, what is the use of taking him into court? He would get a fine or a jail sentence and unless I pay him out he will lie up in jail, and when he gets out he will keep on stealing.[9]

As a result of this traditional support of intimidation and violence, law itself was caste-patterned, applying very unequally to the two races. When any altercation occurred involving a white and a Negro, the Negro was usually presumed to be wrong. The word of a white person was ordinarily taken against that of a Negro, even when many whites knew that the white person was lying. Furthermore, the law failed to protect the Negro against extralegal violence on the part of whites. It was generally impossible to get anybody to testify that he had any knowledge about illegal acts of violence perpetrated against Negroes. As a result, lynching after lynching occurred in the South. Even those reported in the national press, where the fact of lynching was incontrovertible, seldom resulted in indictments and trials. Negroes were carefully kept off juries in the South. However, Federal Supreme Court reversals of Negro convictions where the defense argued successfully that Negroes in the communities involved were pur-

[8] Allison Davis, Burleigh Gardner, and Mary R. Gardner, *Deep South* (Chicago: University of Chicago Press, 1941), pp. 45–46. By permission.
[9] *Ibid.*, p. 46.

posely not called to jury duty began to break this caste practice to a degree.[10] For a long time the only chance for some measure of justice for the Negroes was if they had a white protector who would intercede for them. Frequently an employer would say a good word for his Negro employee and get the case dismissed or the sentence lightened.

Custom

The casual traveler in the South would not have noticed the intimidation we have mentioned. He saw for the most part an orderly pattern of segregation and race etiquette. On the surface he saw no resentment. But, although indications of intimidation were not present each day, no Negro brought up in the South was unaware of the threat of violence. Negro children were taught by their earliest experience with white people to conform to the established pattern. Negro parents had to punish the rebellious inclinations of their children who naïvely approached white persons as equal human beings.[11] And the white children in the South were, of course, conditioned to assume all the appropriate attitudes and behavior patterns of the dominant caste. Any tendency to really like Negro children had to be sternly disciplined to make sure that they were not treated as equals. Thus the Southern caste pattern was supported by the conditioning and custom of the Southerners of both races to assume the reciprocal social roles required to keep it intact—the white to be arrogant, exploitative, superior; the Negro to be submissive, exploited, and inferior. Most of the time this combination of implicit intimidation and habituation worked quite successfully. The Negro who occasionally threw caution to the wind and rebelled against the pattern was dealt with summarily. The white person whose conscience occasionally pricked him submerged his inclination under the pressure of public sentiment.

Caste Control Illustrated: Keeping Negroes from Voting

The mixture of law, intimidation, and custom in sustaining caste is well illustrated in the devices by which Negroes in the South were prevented from exercising the ballot. Between 1890 and 1910, eleven Southern states adopted special requirements for voting designed to deny Negroes the franchise. One was the poll tax, requiring the citizen to pay a special tax of a dollar or two for the privilege of voting. While not a large sum, by various other devices it was made to serve its purpose. Sometimes the tax was retroactive—that is to say, in order to vote in any one year, poll tax receipts for a number of years had to be shown if asked for by the election official. An arrearage of, say, $10 was effective in keeping a Negro from voting.

[10] Myrdal, *An American Dilemma* (New York: Harper & Brothers, 1944), p. 549.
[11] See Calvin C. Hernton, *Sex and Racism in America* (Garden City, New York: Doubleday and Company, 1965), pp. 53–58, for personal testimony.

Negroes were barred from voting in the Democratic primary with the excuse that any political party may restrict its membership. Before 1941 the United States Supreme Court in decisions concerning these white primary regulations failed to overrule the specific laws in this connection. Other qualifications for voting left opportunity for discrimination through their administration. For example, educational tests were sometimes stipulated. By asking Negro applicants for registration questions concerning government which they could not possibly answer, officials could keep them off the list. Or such devices as giving the Negroes only a day for registration when the white officials were not available were further employed.

In addition to these state statutes of questionable constitutionality, and to administrative discrimination, white Southerners at times resorted to intimidation and violence for the purpose of preventing Negroes from voting. Davie furnishes the following example: "There are numerous instances of Negroes who attempted to register or vote being driven away, beaten up, or killed. More generally the opposition took the form of intimidation. For example, a Negro went to the registration booth in his county and asked if he could register. The white official replied: 'Oh, yes, you can register, but I want to tell you something. Some God-damn niggers are going to get killed about this voting business yet.' " Intended to terrorize Negro citizens who might seek to vote in the primaries in Dennison, Texas, in the fall of 1932, handbills were scattered throughout the town reading as follows:

NIGGER!

The white people do not want you to vote Saturday.

Do not make the Ku Klux Klan take a hand.

Do you remember what happened two years ago, May 9?

George Hughes was burned to death, the county courthouse destroyed.... For good reason.

Riots on election day in which both whites and Negroes were killed occurred in various sections of the South.[12]

Effects of the Caste System

In discussing the effects of the race caste system as it operated in the South we will consider its effect on personality and behavior, on the welfare of the Negro, on social organization in Southern communities, and on the political and economic development of the region.

Effect of the Southern Racial System on White Personality

The value of treating the social structure as an independent variable and the normative behavior of the people reared in it as the dependent variable is

[12] By permission from *Negroes in American Society*, by M. R. Davie. Copyright 1949. McGraw-Hill Book Co., p. 266.

well illustrated by considering how being reared in the Southern biracial system affected the personality of the white Southerner. One of the earliest and best-known field studies of the Southern racial system was that of John Dollard of a cotton community.[13] Dollard analyzed the gains accruing to white people under the caste system which were in turn "losses" to the Negroes. First was the economic gain, enabling white people to exploit Negroes as workers and consumers. A typical year for the Negro tenant farmer ran as follows: After the cotton had been sold and the Negro had paid his debts, he was broke. The land-lord advanced him "furnish" to carry him through the next harvest. The charges for this "furnish" were not regulated and, since the Negro lacked education, the accounting was typically in the landlord's hands. Dollard does not main-tain that this exploitative advantage was always completely utilized, but it was difficult for the Negro to get justice if his accounting differed from that of the landlord.

Second, Dollard mentions the "sexual gain." The system operated to give white men exploitative sexual opportunity with Negro women, which we have already noted, while any sexual advances of Negro men toward white women were absolutely tabooed and infractions often punished by death. The caste system did not require Negro women to accept the sexual overtures of white men, but the economic and social advantages to Negro women often made ac-ceptance of these advances attractive. While not all white men took advantage of this opportunity, the white caste ideology considered Negro women sexually promiscuous and therefore relations with them were hardly to be taken seriously in an ethical sense.

The third gain Dollard saw accruing to the white caste was "ego" gratifica-tion. The daily expressions of superiority toward all Negroes which the whites could indulge and the responses of submissiveness by the Negroes bolstered the self-esteem of the whites, especially those among the less privileged ranks.

The normative white Southerner was (still is) a person who assumed the superordinate role toward Negroes which involved considerable ambivalence. The role called for "bullying" and exploiting Negroes, and for treating with kindness and friendliness those Negroes with whom whites interacted so long as the Negroes involved acted in the appropriate subordinate role. It also called for unwavering defense of the system—ideological and behavioral. There were two types of deviant white Southerners: those who carried the superordinate role too far, who were over bullish and exploitative, lost repute but not status and were not otherwise punished for such behavior, even though it was often illegal. The other deviant type of white Southerner was rare, one who openly called for and occasionally participated in some organized attempt leading to challenge of the established system.

Departing from our time sequence, we call attention to some studies made

[13] John Dollard, *Caste and Class in a Southern Town* (New Haven: Yale University Press, 1937).

more recently on the feelings of white Southerners about their racial system. Campbell found little evidence of guilt about segregation among 112 in a sample of 279 white students but much moral defense of the traditional system.[14] Campbell and Pettigrew in a study of ministers in Little Rock, following that city's school desegregation crisis, found little guilt among sectarian leaders of the clergy of the established churches.[15]

Among the white professional literary writers and novelists dealing with the Southern scene was Lillian Smith, who depicts the effect of the system on white Southerners. In *Killers of the Dream* she describes her own childhood experience when her parents had taken into their family an apparently white child living with a Negro family only to return the child again to its adopted parents when it was discovered that in fact the child had Negro lineage. Miss Smith wrote as follows:

> Something was wrong with a world that tells you love is good and people are important and then forces you to deny love and to humiliate people. I knew, though I would not for years confess it aloud, that in trying to shut the Negro race away from us, we have shut ourselves away from so many good, creative, honest, deeply human things in life. I began to understand slowly at first but more clearly as the years passed, that the *warped, distorted frame we have put around every Negro child from birth is around every white child also.* Each is on a different side of the frame but each is pinioned there. And I knew that what cruelly shapes and cripples the personality of one is as cruelly shaping and crippling the personality of the other. I began to see that though we may, as we acquire new knowledge, live through new experiences, examine old memories, gain the strength to tear the frame from us, yet we are stunted and warped and *in our lifetime cannot grow straight again* any more than can a tree, put in a steel-like twisting frame when young, grow tall and straight when the frame is torn away at maturity.[16]

Effects of Caste upon Negro Behavior and Personality

Dollard's study essentially covers the range of possible personality and behavioral adjustments of Negroes to the inevitable frustrations of being brought up in such a system.[17] However, in line with more recent theoretical analysis we distinguish between the normative type of adjustment and the more deviant adjustments. The normative adjustment was to accept the role assigned to a Negro under the system—to be docile, servile, and to adhere to the rules of etiquette and segregation. This type of behavior was sometimes accompanied by an internalization of the white stereotype of the Negro; and in other instances

---

[14] Ernest Campbell, "Moral Discomfort and Racial Segregation—An Examination of the Racial Hypothesis," *Social Forces,* March, 1961, pp. 228–234.

[15] Ernest Campbell and Thomas Pettigrew, *Christianity in Racial Crisis: A Study of Little Rock's Ministry* (Washington, D.C.: Public Affairs Press, 1959).

[16] Reprinted from *Killers of the Dream* by Lillian Smith. By permission of W. W. Norton & Co., Inc. Copyright © 1949, 1961 by Lillian Smith.

[17] See Dollard, Ch. 12.

was merely *role playing* of necessity in order to get along better under the system. This tendency of most Southern Negroes most of the time to act normatively under the system furnished the basis for one of the major elements in the race ideology of the white Southerner, namely that on the whole "their" Negroes were content with the system. The fact that Negroes seldom openly manifested hatred for white people should not be interpreted to indicate that they do not cherish such a feeling inwardly. Warner and Davis wrote that "Anyone who believes that the hostile statements uttered by Southern whites toward Negroes are extreme should be allowed to hear those uttered by Negroes, even Negro children and adolescents toward whites." [18]

Deviant responses as adjustments to the frustrations of caste status were numerous.[19] (1) *Ritualistic*. Certain Negroes whose circumstances and/or ability permitted strove to achieve higher status within the Negro community, for example as professionals, civil servants, through pursuing the goals of the white value system. Ironically, the very existence of the segregation system afforded this opportunity and this higher status of such Negroes was recognized by whites, as well as by Negroes, as long as they did not challenge the system. (2) *Retreatist*. Escape from the frustrations of caste by retreating from the tension took several forms. (a) *Hedonism*. Enjoying as fully as possible those pleasures not denied by caste. Here one may distinguish those activities closer to the normal responses of all mankind such as taking an unexcused day off from work to go fishing and losing a day's exploitative pay, or casual sexual activity; and those responses more personally disorganizing such as drinking, drugs, and the other so-called vices.[20] (b) *Intragroup aggression*. Another way of coping with frustration is to fight other Negroes. There is much data on homicide among Negroes.[21] (3) *Rebellion*. Some (but, under the caste system, few) Negroes responded to systematic discrimination by attacking either white persons or the system. The first were almost always impulsive acts since all Southern bred Negroes knew it would lead to violent reprisal. The second was deliberate, for example, participation in some planned activity usually by a group asking for some improvement in welfare. Sometimes if carried on with due deference such a response met with success.

While the life of Southern American Negroes under these established patterns of dominance was not a total vale of tears, there is ample empirical material to show that coping with the frustrations of caste left deep psychic scars.

[18] Lloyd Warner and Allison Davis, "A Comparative Study of American Caste," in Edgar T. Thompson, ed., *Race Relations and the Race Problem*, p. 237.

[19] The terms used in our schema here are closely related to the meaning given them in Robert Merton's classic exposition in "Social Structure and Anomie," in *Social Theory and Social Structure* (Glencoe, Ill.: The Free Press, 1957), pp. 130–160.

[20] See Harry Bredemeier and Jackson Toby, *Social Problems In America: Costs and Casualties in an Acquisitive Society* (New York and London: John Wiley & Sons, 1960), Chapters 7 and 8.

[21] While homicide is, of course, active in a sense, we place this under retreatism because it is taking out one's aggression on the wrong category of persons.

Mark of Oppression

Many years ago Herbert A. Miller referred to the high prevalence among minorities of the attitudes of fear, hatred, resentment, jealousy, suspicion, and revenge—which he labeled the "oppression psychosis." The essential point made by Miller has been substantiated by research, even though the term "psychosis" may be applicable only to those more intensely affected by discrimination. Kardiner and Ovesey, after studying twenty-five Negro males by personality tests and psychoanalytic techniques, concluded as follows:

> On the whole we must be satisfied that the conclusions derived from the three different experimental approaches—the psychodynamic analysis, the Rorschach test, and the T.A.T.—are essentially the same. The major features of the Negro personality emerge from each with remarkable consistency. These include the fear of relatedness, suspicion, mistrust, the enormous problem of the control of aggression, the denial mechanism, the tendency to dissipate the tension of a provocative situation by reducing it to something simpler, or to something entirely different. All these maneuvers are in the interest of not meeting reality head on.... The defects in adaptation are not of mysterious or racial origin but owe their existence entirely to the arduous emotional conditions under which the Negro in America is obliged to live.[22]

Karon studied a small but rigorously selected sample of Northern and Southern Negroes and Northern whites, employing the Tompkins-Horn Picture Arrangement Test. His findings were that caste sanctions have an effect on the personality structure of Negroes born and reared in the South in eleven characteristics, six of which are related to the problem of handling aggression. This research rejects the formerly oft-stated hypothesis that the Southern Negro, because he lives in a consistent interracial system, is not disturbed by caste sanctions, in contrast to the Northern Negro, who lives in a more ambiguous racial situation. Karon's findings show a consistent relationship between the severity of the caste sanctions and the appearance of these disturbed traits. Rural Southern Negroes are "worse off" than the urban Southern Negroes; Northern Negroes born in the South are worse off than those born in the North. In fact, the latter quite closely resemble the white Northern sample, which the author attributes possibly to the inadequacy of the tests to determine small discriminants.[23]

Dreger and Miller in their review of studies up to 1960 conclude that "On the basis of the evidence available it does appear that Negroes more frequently (than whites) experience psychiatric difficulties, particularly of a severe nature."[24]

---

[22] Abram Kardiner and Lionel Ovesey, *The Mark of Oppression* (New York: W. W. Norton & Company, 1951), pp. 337–338. By permission.

[23] Bertram A. Karon, *The Negro Personality* (New York: Springer Publishing Company, 1958), pp. 169–175.

[24] Dreger and Miller, p. 392. See Horace R. Cayton, *The Long Lonely Road* (New York: The Trident Press, 1963) for a dramatic personal illustration.

The Welfare of the Negroes in the South

In practically all indices of welfare, the Negro population continued through the first half of the twentieth century to rank well below that of the white population. Since this has been so amply demonstrated we will simply summarize the main points.[25]

Negroes were highly concentrated in the lowest occupational levels with a small percentage scattered in middle levels. Average family incomes were about one-third that of white families. Negroes were paid less for the same type of work at all levels. Negro housing was of poorer quality than that of whites. Comparative studies show markedly disparate health for Negroes and higher death rates. Associated with this was the lack of medical services, particularly hospitalization directly due to segregation.

Comparing the educational level of the Negro population in the South in 1930 with its level at the time of emancipation indicates tremendous strides. In 1870, 81.4 percent of Negroes were illiterate; in 1930, this figure had been reduced to 16.3 percent.[26] Comparing the educational facilities for Negroes with those of white persons in the South at any given time, however, reveals gross disparities. During the year 1939–1940, the Southern states spent $55.69 per white child in average daily attendance in schools as against only $18.82 for each Negro child.[27] At the higher educational levels the differential opportunity of Negroes was even more striking. In 1933–1934 only 19 percent of the Negro children of high-school age were in high schools, as compared with 55 percent of the white children of the same age.[28] Education of Negroes at the college level in the South before 1890 was exceptionally limited, and the schools available were supported largely by private contributions, chiefly from Northern religious denominational sources. In 1890 an amendment to the original Morrill Act adopted in 1862 required that federal funds be divided fairly between the white and the Negro institutions in states having the dual system. Subsequently, seventeen land-grant agricultural and mechanical colleges for Negroes were established, receiving some of their support from federal funds under this Act. But wide disparities continued to exist in both the quantity and the quality of Negro higher educational institutions in the South.

The Impact of the Caste System on the South

Tension and Violence

Despite the facade of a smoothly operating biracial system, racial tension was constantly present in the region in those local communities with sizable Ne-

[25] See Gunnar Myrdal, *An American Dilemma*, Ch. 16 ; Maurice Davie, *Negroes in American Society* (New York: McGraw-Hill Co., 1949), Chs. 5, 6, 10, 11, and 12 ; and E. Franklin Frazier, *The Negro in the United States*, rev. ed. (New York: The Macmillan Company, 1957), Part 5.
[26] Davie, *Negroes in American Society*, p. 139.
[27] See Frazier, *The Negro in the United States*, p. 437.
[28] *Ibid.*, **p.** 436.

gro populations. It is inevitable that where constant tension exists, violence will sporadically occur. Making some allowance for the tendency of novelists to dramatize, the writings of Southern novelists, as Erskine Caldwell, for example, suggest that interpersonal violence in which individual white Southerners maltreated individual Negro people was more or less an everyday occurrence. On a larger scale and more sporadically, the two characteristic modes of expression of this violence have been lynchings and riots. In American history lynching of native-status and of minority persons other than Negroes has taken place. Statistics of lynchings were provided by Tuskegee Institute for the years since 1882. (See Table 11–1.) In 1884, lynchings of white people still exceeded the lynching of Negroes by a substantial margin—whites, 160, Negroes, 51. The peak year of Negro lynching was 1892, and for each year from 1891 through 1901 the number was over a hundred. From 1892 on, Negro lynchings greatly exceeded white lynchings. With minor fluctuations, the trend was sharply downward.[29]

TABLE 11–1. *Lynchings, Whites and Negroes, 1882–1959 by Decades* [30]

PERIOD	WHITE	NEGRO
1882–1891	751	732
1892–1901	381	1124
1902–1911	76	707
1912–1921	50	553
1922–1931	23	201
1932–1941	10	95
1942–1951	2	25
1952–1959 (8 years)	1	4

With the closing of the frontier, lynching became primarily a Southern phenomenon (see Table 11–2). As with other characteristics of the caste system, in total number of lynchings the Deep South exceeds the border states. It is also of interest to note that the four non-Southern states listed are adjacent to the Southern region: Illinois, Kansas, Ohio, and Indiana.

Concerning lynching the Myrdal study found:

Lynching is a rural and small town custom and occurs most commonly in poor districts. There are some indications that lynchings go in waves and tend to recur in the same districts. The accusations against persons lynched during the period for which there are records were: in 38 per cent of the cases for homicide, 6 per cent for felonious assault, 16 per cent for rape, 7 per cent for attempted rape,

[29] After 1936 the recorded number was under ten annually. In 1952, for the first time, no lynching was reported. From 1952 through 1959 this record was broken by three lynchings in 1955 and one in 1959.

[30] Tuskegee Institute, Department of Research and Records.

TABLE 11–2. *States in Which Highest Number of Negro Lynchings Occurred, 1882–1959, by Rank Order* [31]

MISSISSIPPI	538	NORTH CAROLINA	84
GEORGIA	491	VIRGINIA	83
TEXAS	352	OKLAHOMA	40
LOUISIANA	335	WEST VIRGINIA	28
ALABAMA	299	MARYLAND	27
FLORIDA	257	ILLINOIS	19
ARKANSAS	226	KANSAS	19
TENNESSEE	204	OHIO	16
SOUTH CAROLINA	156	INDIANA	14
KENTUCKY	142		

7 per cent for theft, 2 per cent for insult to white persons, and 24 per cent for miscellaneous offenses or no offense at all. In the last category are all sorts of irritations: testifying at court against a white man or bringing suit against him, refusal to pay a note, seeking employment out of place, offensive language or boastful remarks. Regarding the accusations for crime, Raper testifies: "Case studies of nearly one hundred lynchings since 1929 convince the writer that around a third of the victims were falsely accused." The meaning of these facts is that, in principle, a lynching is not merely a punishment against an individual but a disciplinary device against the Negro group. . . .

The actual participants in the lynching mobs usually belong to the frustrated lower strata of Southern whites. Occasionally, however, the people of the middle and upper class take part, and generally they condone the deed, and nearly always they find it advisable to let the incident pass without assisting in bringing the guilty before the court. Women and children are not absent from lynching mobs; indeed, women sometimes incite the mobs into action.[32]

Conditions suggested as related to lynching were poverty and economic fear, social fear that the Negro was "getting out of place," the dullness and general boredom of everyday life in the rural areas and small towns of the South.

Lynching had a "psychological importance out of all proportion to its small frequency." [33] Analyzing its effects, the Myrdal study has this to say:

The effects of lynchings are far reaching. In the locality where it has happened and in a wide region surrounding it, the relations between the two groups deteriorate. The Negroes are terror stricken and sullen. The whites are anxious and are likely to show the assertiveness and suspicion of persons with bad, but hardened, consciences. Some whites are afraid of Negro retaliation or emigration. Every

[31] Tuskegee Institute, Department of Research and Records.
[32] Myrdal, *An American Dilemma,* by permission of the publishers, Harper & Brothers, pp. 560–562. See Arthur Raper, *The Tragedy of Lynching* (Chapel Hill: University of North Carolina Press, 1933), for an extensive analysis of the lynching problem.
[33] *Ibid.,* p. 564.

visitor to such a communty must notice the antagonism and mutual lack of confidence between the two groups.[34]

Lynchings in the United States unfailingly received wide publicity abroad with adverse consequences to the nation's prestige.

It should be mentioned that, however committed they were to segregation as a basic policy for the South, many white Southerners deplored lynching. Influential in this connection was the organization in 1930 in Atlanta of the Association of Southern Women for the Prevention of Lynching. This association succeeded in securing the signatures of 50,000 white women of the South to its pledge, which read in part, "We solemnly pledge ourselves to create a new public opinion in the South which will not condone for any reason whatever acts of mobs or lynchers." [35]

Race riots have been more characteristic of the Northern scene and will be discussed in that connection. In the South, they tended more to be mob action by whites directed at defenseless Negro areas.[36]

Political Effects

The South as a region has had a political development which differs from that in the rest of the country. (1) The proportion of people who participate in politics has been markedly smaller than in the rest of the nation. We have already referred to the virtual disfranchisement of Negroes. Bunche estimated that in eight Southern states, the so-called Deep South, never more than 80,000 to 90,000 Negro votes had been cast in general elections up to 1940, and only a handful in the primaries, the elections that really count.[37] The proportion of the white electorate which participated in politics was also decidedly less than in the rest of the nation. In 1940 only 28 percent of the adult population of twelve Southern states went to the polls, in contrast with 53 percent for the rest of the country. (2) The South for all practical purposes has had a one-party system, the Democratic party. The primary contests in this party constituted in essence the final decision. (3) From this it followed that political opposition was more confined than elsewhere to rivalries between factions and personalities in which the basic issues contested in the nation as a whole were not debated. Since the Democratic party in the South represented traditional and conservative influence in the national Congress, the same kind of liberal political pressures which had arisen elsewhere in the nation, representing broadly liberal and human welfare interests as opposed to conservative and propertied interests, had not manifested themselves in any marked degree in the South. Since wide

[34] *Ibid.*, p. 564, by permission of the publishers, Harper & Brothers.
[35] Davie, *Negroes in American Society*, p. 355.
[36] For dramatic accounts of violence in the Southern scene, see Walter White, *A Man Called White* (New York: The Viking Press, 1948).
[37] Ralph J. Bunche, "The Negro in the Political Life in the United States," *Journal of Negro Education*, July, 1941, 10: 567–584.

exercise of the franchise, a two (or more) party system, and the vigorous debate of new ways to further the democratic ideal are signs of a healthy democracy, the democratic political process in the South may properly be regarded as having been retarded.

To what extent are these distinctive developments in Southern politics attributable to the effect of its system of race relations? Since we adhere to the general principle that the causal factors in such complex social phenomena are always multiple and interact with one another, we shall not suggest that the system of race relations is all-determinative. Nevertheless, the interrelationship between the phenomena of race relations and these political developments is highly impressive. The elaborate devices to limit the electorate arose primarily as a way of preventing Negroes from exercising active citizenship. The one-party system, with its "white" primary, developed for the same reason. Once established, these political phenomena furthered the politicoeconomic interests of the middle and upper classes of the white South in opposition to those of the lower-class whites. The failure of the latter group to generate more effective political expression of its interests is in considerable measure related to its preoccupation with "keeping the Negro in his place." [38]

Effect on the Economy of the South

Rupert Vance, an outstanding student of the Southern region, described the South's position (1930) in the national economy in these terms: "The statistical indices of wealth, education, cultural achievement, health, law and order reduced to a per capita basis combine in every instance to give the Southern states the lowest rankings in the Union." [39] After a careful appraisal of the natural resources of the region, Vance concluded that it was not lack of adequate natural resources which accounted for the South's relative poverty. He found the chief explanation in the manner in which the Southern economy had been organized.

After the Civil War, Southern economic reconstruction called for carrying on the plantation agricultural economy, with chief emphasis on cotton production and such modifications as the emancipation of the slaves required. Since this economy required cheap labor, the caste system developed in part as a means of guaranteeing the continued employment of Negroes in their accustomed role at subsistence wages. Furthermore, in order to hold its place competitively in a national economy generally more efficient than its own, the South was forced to exploit the soil to the point of diminishing returns. In this way, a cycle of reciprocal forces was established which operated to retard the economic development of the region. The relatively inefficient economy could provide only subsistence wages for the laborers involved. Their marginal in-

[38] See Lillian Smith, pp. 154–168.
[39] Rupert B. Vance, *Human Geography of the South* (Chapel Hill: University of North Carolina Press, 1932), p. 442. By permission.

come in turn retarded the regional demand for goods which would have favored the development of industrial enterprise. Furthermore, the marginal economy was unable to produce enough to furnish the capital needed for industrial development. This capital had to be furnished, therefore, from outside the region, which meant that part of the gains were drained from the region itself. In order to get this capital, the South offered the inducement primarily of cheap labor costs, which still further aggravated the low standard of living, extending it to a wider segment of its white population. While the expanding industrial economy offered some opportunity to transfer Negroes from farm work to city work, the caste system prevented their employment in other than the lowest-paying capacities.

Clearly, many factors are involved in interpreting the cycle just described. Nevertheless, the influence of the caste system is apparent at every turn. As Vance has written: "The South holds the Negro back; the Negro holds the South back; and both point in recrimination." [40]

Variation in the Southern Pattern

The foregoing description has disregarded variations in order to indicate the general Southern pattern. Some significant rural-urban contrasts, however, should be noted. The city environment permitted some relief to Negroes from the omnipresent impact of caste through the opportunity it afforded to build a separate community structure. At least within this area, Negroes could live their own lives.[41] Compared with the smaller places, there was less actual personal interaction between the members of the two races in the city. Since traditionally the caste system carried with it much direct personal dependence of individual Negroes on particular white people, through which conformity to the mandates of caste could be closely scrutinized, the greater drawing apart of the two races in the Southern cities placed the control of caste on a more impersonal basis.

The Border States

The major variation in the Southern pattern of race relations is seen by considering certain border states, including Oklahoma, Kentucky, West Virginia, Missouri, Maryland, and Delaware, and The District of Columbia. In none of these was the "white primary" to be found; among them, only Oklahoma had "Jim Crow" streetcars. In these states the code of etiquette was frequently less explicit and less binding. However, in all of them intermarriage

[40] *Ibid.,* p. 43.
[41] One of the authors was told by a Negro physician in a Louisiana city that the members of his family went "down town" as seldom as possible because they so profoundly disliked the caste requirements.

between Negroes and whites was prohibited by law, and the segregation of Negroes in schools remained up to 1954.[42]

The pattern of race relations in Washington, D.C., is naturally of particular significance, not only because it is the capital but because it is visited by foreign officials of all other nations. On the one hand, Washington, as part of the Southern area, reflected in many ways the Southern attitude and behavior in Negro-white relations. On the other hand, the influence of the federal government imposed certain exceptions to the traditional Southern pattern. Thus Negroes were not "Jim Crowed" in District transportation; they had equal access to all institutions and services directly operated as federal government property. Before World War II, the national government employed a limited number of Negroes in higher-ranking occupations, qualified by the tendency to place them in special assignments dealing with Negro problems. But generally, Washington in the period before World War II presented substantially the same picture as other border cities. School segregation, for example, prevailed, and Negroes were denied the use of general restaurant and amusement facilities in the city.

Changes in the Southern Pattern

Between 1880 and World War II race relations in the South revealed changes that went rather rapidly in one direction and rather slowly in another. As we have seen, most of the gains made by Negroes following Emancipation were lost by the establishment of the caste system. On the other hand, the welfare of Negroes improved somewhat along with the general national trend, even though at all times with wide discrepancies with the welfare of the whites. Circumstances operating to improve Negro welfare were the opportunity presented by World War I for Negroes to find employment in the North, the tendency of the federal government to require more equitable use of federal funds for Negroes, especially during the depression years of the 1930's, and the beginnings of some breakdown of segregation in labor unions in the mid-1930's.

The earnest efforts of a small group of Southern white liberals in behalf of Negroes deserve recognition as an influence in keeping the Southern pattern somewhat unfrozen. The group comprised a few writers, journalists, educators, and some club women, whom Myrdal has described as "mostly a fraternity of individuals with independent minds, usually living in, and adjusting to, an uncongenial social surrounding." [43] Because for the most part they possessed high social prestige either through their lineage from Southern aristocracy or through the national pre-eminence they had acquired in professional fields, their espousal of the Negro's cause was tolerated. Their first efforts were directed

---

[42] See Myrdal, p. 1072, Table 1, for a checklist of the various features of the caste system for each Southern state.
[43] *Ibid.*, p. 467.

at striving for equal justice, particularly against lynching, and gaining for the Negro a fairer share of public monies spent for education, health, and other aspects of welfare. They were unable to challenge the system of segregation itself. The Southern liberals were not able to influence political life to any marked extent, and their influence was largely confined to the higher social and educational levels of Southern society. The main organization through which Southern liberalism found expression was the Commission on Interracial Cooperation, founded in 1919. In Myrdal's judgment its most far-reaching effect is *"to have rendered interracial work socially respectable in the conservative South."* [44]

Finally, we consider the effect of Negro leadership and organization on the course of Southern race relations during the caste period. Under slavery the organized activities of Negroes in their own behalf consisted, as we have seen, largely of abortive slave revolts. The outstanding leader among Negroes in the nineteenth century was Frederick Douglass. Following emancipation, which he had urged upon Lincoln, he worked to secure full equality for the Negroes, but saw the fight lost during the Southern reconstruction. Organized movements among Negroes subsequently divided into "protest" or "accommodative" patterns. The former, which Douglass espoused, aimed to secure full equality for Negroes; the latter aimed to secure the betterment of conditions without challenging the institution of caste itself. During the early twentieth century the protest type of activity was almost exclusively confined to Negroes in the North, which we shall consider in Chapter 12. In the South the unquestioned spokesman for the Negroes was Booker T. Washington, who is generally considered a leader of the accommodative type, though some of his biographers think the extent of his compromising has been overstressed, particularly in view of the circumstances which he faced. Rose summarizes the role which Washington played and the philosophy behind it:

> It is wrong to characterize Washington as an all-out accommodating leader. He never relinquished the right to full equality in all respects as the ultimate goal. But for the time being he was prepared to give up social and political equality, even to soft-pedal and protest against inequalities in justice. He was also willing to flatter the Southern whites and be harsh toward the Negroes—if the Negroes were allowed to work undisturbed with their white friends for education and business. But neither in education nor in business did he assault inequalities. In both fields he accepted the white doctrine of the Negroes "place." In education he pleaded mainly for vocational training. Through thrift, skill, and industry the Negroes were gradually to improve so much that later the discussion could again be taken up concerning their rights. This was Washington's philosophy. [45]

[44] *Ibid.,* p. 847. Italics in original.
[45] Arnold Rose, *The Negro in America* (New York: Harper & Brothers, 1948), p. 240. By permission.

However one views the relative merits of the protest as against the accommodative program of action, beyond question Washington had the greatest influence of any single Negro on the development of Negro welfare during his time. His influence was most concretely evidenced in the development of Tuskegee Institute, over which he presided for many years.

Topics for Projects and Discussion

1. Interview some mature Northern white adults who had traveled in the South before World War II and some Southern-bred whites who had traveled in the North at this earlier time. Ask each to talk about his reactions to his first experience with the different pattern of race relations he encountered outside his region. Report.
2. Debate the topic—Biracial segregation in principle is consistent with equality of opportunity for both groups.
3. How would you account for the fact that some Negro women in the South accede voluntarily to the sexual overtures of some white men?
4. Discuss the topic—The effects of the Southern caste system on the personalities of Southern white people.
5. How do you account for the apparently greater overt antagonism manifested by lower-class Southern whites as compared with that shown by middle- and upper-class whites?

Suggested Reading

Chalmers, David M. *Hooded Americanism: The First Century of the Ku Klux Klan.* New York: Doubleday & Co., 1965.
> *A full-length and scholarly history of this well-known "nativistic" organization.*

Lewinson, Paul. *Race, Class and Party: A History of Negro Suffrage and White Politics.* New York: Grosset and Dunlap, Universal Library Edition, 1965.
> *A pioneer historical study of the interrelation of race and class in Southern political life from slave days to 1930.*

Davis, Allison, and Dollard, John. *Children of Bondage.* Washington, D.C.: American Council on Education, 1940.
> *An intensive study of eight Negro adolescents in the Deep South indicating the effects of the Southern pattern on the Negro personality.*

Lewis, Hylan. *Blackways of Kent.* Chapel Hill: University of North Carolina Press, 1955.
> *A comprehensive and intimate account of the life of Negroes in a typical biracial community of the Piedmont area.*

Meier, August. *Negro Thought in America 1880–1915.* Ann Arbor, Michigan: The University of Michigan Press, 1966.
> *Analyzes the racial ideologies of Negro leaders in the age of Booker T. Washington.*

Pettigrew, Thomas P. *A Profile of the Negro American.* Princeton, N.J.: Van Nostrand Co., 1964.

Chapter 1, "The Role and Its Burdens," and Chapter 2, "Reactions to Oppression," examine the impact of white domination on the Negro personality.

Rohrer, John H., and Edmonson, Munro S. *The Eighth Generation: Cultures and Personalities of New Orleans Negroes.* New York: Harper & Brothers, 1960.

An intensive follow-up study of the subjects of Davis and Dollard's study of the children of bondage who as adults comprise the eighth generation of New Orleans Negroes.

12

The Pattern
of Northern Dominance

Since the number of Negroes living outside the South was so few before World War I, this chapter will center on the pattern of Negro-white relations which developed in the North during the period between the two world wars.

In the North, Negroes were discriminated against substantially everywhere, but not in as many aspects of life nor so intensely as in the South. The welfare of the Negro in the North was the lowest of all large minorities, but the relatively higher general standard of living in the North was reflected in the higher standards of Northern Negroes as compared with those of Southern Negroes.

A basic difference between the Northern and Southern situation has been the absence in the North of any such precise institutionalization of the minority position of Negroes as the Southern caste pattern involved. In the South, caste relations were well defined in law and in the regional mores; and control mechanisms for maintaining the system had become standardized through years of practice. In the North the discrimination and segregation which did exist lacked such explicit sanction in the mores; and there were also lacking such established control devices for holding the Negro in minority status. For Southern white people in general the attitudes and values of the caste system were an integral part of their personalities; and for Southern Negroes brought up under this system the reciprocal attitudes and behavior patterns were deeply structured in their personalities. Caste was an intrinsic part of the Southern social structure and daily touched the lives of the people of both races. In the North the segregated position of Negroes was only a fragmentary aspect of Northern community life, and many white people, even in communities with sizable Negro populations, were scarcely aware of its presence.

The many contrasting circumstances in the two regional situations accounting for this basic difference can be stated only briefly in this overview. The North did not have the tradition of slavery, having abolished slavery decades before Emancipation. And in no Northern community did the number of Negroes approach a majority. Thus, while Negroes were highly useful to the economy of the North, their labor was never considered essential to Northern economic life, especially as long as European immigration furnished cheap labor. The concentration of Negroes in the larger cities of the North, where their residential segregation resembled that of other ethnic and racial minorities, made their position appear less sharply in contrast to the dominant white community than in the South, where Negroes were the only considerable minority.

The Establishment and Maintenance of Dominance

The Pattern of Discrimination

A close-up view of the general pattern of Negro-white relations in the North may be obtained from the comprehensive study of Chicago made by Drake and Cayton. In essence their book, *Black Metropolis,* typifies the Northern situation. Much of the material was gathered for this volume in the 1930's, though some of it refers to the impact of World War II.[1] Since 1940 there have been enough changes in the situation in Chicago, as well as elsewhere in the North, to prompt the use of the past tense in this chapter. Much of the description which follows, however, is still applicable in this day.

RESIDENTIAL SEGREGATION   Negroes in Chicago were highly concentrated in residence; 337,000—90 percent of all—lived in the Black Belt.[2] The difference between this and other ethnic colonies found in cities was that while the others tended to break up in time, the Negro area became increasingly concentrated. The particular area was on the lower South Side, long considered by Chicago planning boards a "blighted area." The extent of congestion is indicated by the fact that Negroes were living 90,000 to the square mile, as compared with 20,000 in neighboring white apartment house areas.[3] This high degree of spatial segregation "is primarily the result of white people's attitudes toward having Negroes as neighbors. Because some white Chicagoans do not wish colored neighbors, formal and informal controls are used to isolate the latter within congested all-Negro neighborhoods."[4]

The real force of the measures to contain the Negro area began when the mass migration took place. "It was only after 1915, when 65,000 migrants came into the city within five years, that resistance became organized."[5] Property-owners associations began to take active steps to forestall sale and rent of property to Negroes outside the Black Belt. "A wave of violence flared up, and between July 1917 and March 1921 fifty-eight homes were bombed.... The victims of the bombings were Negro families that had moved into white neighborhoods, as well as Negro and white real-estate men who sold or rented

---

[1] St. Clair Drake and Horace R. Cayton, *Black Metropolis* (New York: Harcourt, Brace & Co., 1945).

[2] *Ibid.,* p. 174.

[3] *Ibid.,* p. 204.

[4] *Ibid.,* p. 174.

[5] *Ibid.,* p. 177.

property to them." [6] The major device for controlling the Negro community was the restrictive covenant—an agreement between property owners within a certain district not to rent or sell to Negroes.

Since the consequences of housing discrimination remain the key to analysis of the Northern interracial situation, we reserve fuller discussion for Chapter 14. It is pertinent here, however, to point out that attempts to upset restrictive covenants legally were for a long time unsuccessful.[7] In 1917 the Supreme Court (245 U.S. 60) ruled that a municipal zoning ordinance which segregated Negroes and whites was unconstitutional, but it was not until 1948 that the highest tribunal declared that restrictive covenants in private housing transactions could not be upheld by law (334 U.S. 1–1948).

OCCUPATIONAL DISCRIMINATION   Discrimination in jobs can be seen in the tendency to deny Negroes jobs when white people were out of work. Drake and Cayton state that in 1940, *"while Negroes made up only 8 percent of the available workers, they constituted 22 percent of the unemployed.... Almost half of the Negro domestic servants, a third of the semiskilled workers, and a fourth of the unskilled were unemployed in 1935."* [8] Negroes were substantially barred from numerous pursuits. "The job ceiling for Negroes ... [tended] to be drawn just above the level of semiskilled jobs, with the skilled, clerical, managerial, and supervisory positions reserved for white workers." [9] Again Negroes had not consistently held their competitive position in certain occupational fields. For example, during the depression Negroes lost out to whites in restaurants and hotel jobs. In the occupational areas where Negroes and whites competed for jobs, it should be remembered that before World War II, whites in general were able to refuse to work with Negroes in the same level job. Thus if a restaurant wanted to employ white waitresses, there could not be any Negroes in a similar capacity.

As small compensation for these inequities, Negroes had a substantial monopoly in the two occupations of Pullman porter and redcap, where "the earnings and the prospects of advancement are dependent upon cheerful and, if necessary, ingratiating service.... Even very well-educated Negroes did not scorn such jobs." [10]

The low economic position of Negroes was in part explainable by their relative lack of skills and training for the higher ranking jobs, and by the tendency of Southern Negroes to flock to the North in numbers in excess of the job opportunities available to them. But in considerable measure it was due to racial discrimination: to the tendency of white workers to refuse to work alongside Negroes and of employers to assume that this was always so; to the

[6] *Ibid.,* p. 178.
[7] See Robert C. Weaver, *The Negro Ghetto* (New York: Harcourt, Brace & Co., 1948), Chapter 13, "The Villain-Racial Covenants."
[8] *Ibid.,* p. 217. By permission. Italics in original.
[9] *Ibid.,* p. 262.
[10] *Ibid.,* p. 237.

tendency of white customers to resent being waited on by Negroes, except in the most servile services, and of employers to assume the universality of this reaction by white clients; and to the tendency to consider the Negro as somehow different, "not quite one of us," and therefore inferior.

SOCIAL DISCRIMINATION   In contrast to the South, Negroes in Chicago were not segregated in their utilization of many public facilities. Public parks, public transportation facilities, stores, and public toilets were open to them. However, the more intimate the situation, the more doubtful the acceptance of Negroes on equal terms. In theaters, restaurants, and particularly swimming places, Negroes were discouraged by every possible means from associating with whites. In the Midwest metropolis, bathing beaches and swimming pools were among the primary tension points. The Negro press reported:

POLICE OBJECT TO MIXING OF RACES ON BEACH; ARREST 18. SAY THEY ARE TRYING TO PREVENT RACE RIOT.[11]

While the color line was seldom drawn in theaters or at large public gatherings, in recreation situations that emphasized active participation as distinct from merely looking on, Negroes were barred; and in all situations where men and women participated together, there was a rigid line. Whatever may have been their ultimate hope, Negroes themselves put less stress on the desirability of achieving equality in this more intimate sphere than in others. This difference in the relative importance attached to social equality by the two races was favorable to facilitating adjustment in Negro-white relations in the North. In such borderline situations as "social affairs" held by civic or occupational clubs with biracial membership, Negro members present resented either being ignored or being dealt with as "a special problem." [12]

CIVIC "EQUALITY"   In marked contrast to the South was the civic "equality" accorded Northern Negroes. However, the term "equality" is here placed in quotes because what Negroes had in Chicago and elsewhere in the North was limited by the framework of dominant-group attitudes toward minority groups. It is hard to prove that a teacher "looks down" on Negroes, or that a juror will not believe Negro testimony when it contradicts that of a white person. But one cannot study the events without being convinced that equality was qualified by prejudice.

Drake and Cayton wrote that "To Negro migrants, fresh from the South, Midwest Metropolis presents a novel experience—a substantial measure of equality before the law. Here, they can expect a reasonably fair trial in the courts, with a choice of colored or white counsel. There are no lynchings." [13] Negroes had full political rights. Even though they were thought of as a mi-

11 *Ibid.*, p. 105.
12 *Ibid.*, p. 123.
13 *Ibid.*, pp. 108–109.

nority group, their right to vote and participate in political organization was not denied. What this opportunity to be a citizen meant to Negroes is described as follows:

> Politics became an important, perhaps the most important, method by which the Negro sought to change his status. It was often the only avenue open for struggle against caste tendencies. This struggle invested his political behavior, even when corrupt, with an importance and a dignity that similar behavior could not command in any other portion of the population.[14]

As a result of their political activities, Negroes made substantial gains in Chicago.

> Within a decade after the Great Migration, Black Metropolis had elected two Negro aldermen, one State Senator, four State Representatives, a city judge, and a Congressman.... Wielding such political power, Negro politicians have been in a position to demand appointive positions for a few hundred individuals and equitable treatment in the courts for the masses (as well as dubious "benefits" from the great Chicago enterprise of "fixing" and "rigging" everything from traffic tickets to gambling dens). They have also been able to expose and check discrimination in the administration of the civil service laws and in the enforcement of the Civil Rights Law. They have created, among influential white politicians of all parties, an awareness of the Negro's desire for equal opportunity.[15]

The minority status of Negroes was reflected, however, in politics as in all other phases of their lives. Of this Drake and Cayton write:

> The color line in politics is also reflected in the types of political plums that go to Negro politicians and their henchmen. The big contracts and the heavy graft are reserved for whites. Negroes get the petty "cuts" from gambling and vice protection. In fact, a tradition has developed that Negroes will not demand big political rewards.... Political leaders in Midwest Metropolis, balancing the pressures of ethnic, economic, and religious blocs, are forced to grant some of the demands of Negroes, and Negro politicians shrewdly demand all that they think the traffic will bear.[16]

EDUCATION Curiously, in view of their exhaustive coverage of Negro life in Chicago, Drake and Cayton wrote very little about education. For the North in general during this period, Myrdal, however, noted the following:

> There is little school segregation required by law in the Northern and Western states: Arizona requires it in elementary schools and makes it permissive in secondary schools; Kansas, Wyoming, Indiana, and New Mexico make school

[14] *Ibid.,* p. 343. By permission.
[15] *Ibid.,* pp. 109–110. By permission.
[16] *Ibid.,* p. 111. By permission.

segregation permissive in the elementary grades and sometimes also in the secondary grades. Some communities in the southern parts of New Jersey, Indiana, Pennsylvania, Ohio and Illinois use organized pressure contrary to law to segregate Negroes in at least the elementary grades. In practically all other areas of the North there is partial segregation on a voluntary basis, caused by residential segregation aided by the gerrymandering of school districts and the system of "permits." This segregation is fairly complete for elementary schools, except where Negroes form only a small proportion of the population, but there is much less segregation in secondary schools. In few cases—if any—is this segregation accompanied by discrimination, however, except that form of discrimination which inevitably arises out of isolation. In fact there is probably more discrimination in the mixed schools than in the segregated ones in the North; frequently Negroes in mixed schools are kept out of swimming, dancing, and other athletics, and out of social clubs. There are, however, some Negro teachers in mixed schools in many Northern cities, and Negroes sit on the boards of education in a few big Northern cities.[17]

The opportunity for Negroes to acquire higher education in the North was less than for secondary schools. Northern state universities did not prohibit Negro enrollments, but the vast majority of the private institutions either categorically did not accept Negroes or accepted only a "token" Negro or two. Myrdal concludes that there was no serious restriction on higher education of Negroes in the North, supporting his view by pointing out that only four Negro colleges, all of these established before the Civil War, were located in the North. However, it is pertinent to note that before 1940 a large number of Northern Negroes had gone South to attend Negro colleges—3,000, for example, in 1938–1939.[18] They may have done this because these colleges were less expensive or because they received scholarships. However, it is also possible that they had the feeling that they would face a number of unpleasant discriminations in Northern colleges. Caliver writes that Negro students "seldom lived on campus and in general, they seemed not to belong in the same way that white students felt themselves a part of the university." [19] Discrimination in higher education was likewise seen in the fact that before World War II not more than five white colleges had a Negro on their faculties.

Methods of Maintaining Dominance

Generally speaking, segregation outside the South was not supported by law. A few non-Southern states banned intermarriage; and certain local communities officially segregated Negroes in schools, but such laws were usually overridden by court decisions. In some communities the police attempted to keep Negroes out of certain public areas, such as beaches, but these actions

---

[17] Myrdal, *An American Dilemma* (New York: Harper & Brothers, 1944), p. 633. By permission of the publishers.
[18] Ambrose Caliver, *United States Office of Education, National Survey of Higher Education of Negroes,* Vol. IV (Washington, D.C.: Government Printing Office, 1942–43), p. 13.
[19] *Ibid.*

were nowhere legally supported. Subterfuges, like making the commercial recreational place a "club," were sometimes successful. In a left-handed way law-enforcing agencies frequently supported segregation by refusing to arrest whites who molested Negroes.

Segregation was upheld by common practice—practices by whites to keep Negroes within the bounds of minority status and the reciprocal practices of Negroes to accept this status. While Negroes bitterly resented this, to have some peace of mind, they put up with discrimination most of the time. The fact, however, that these practices were of doubtful legality meant that Negroes could challenge civic discrimination on occasion, and by this means kept the pattern of relationships unfrozen. Sporadic gains here and there were made. Generally, when Negroes pressed cases of discrimination involving civil rights they won them. But, of course, since legal vindication is a costly process, such cases were not numerous.

As in the South, the Northern pattern was supported by the prevalence of the "racial ideology" which looks upon Negroes in the mass as inferior. There was, however, a wider variation in racial attitudes and beliefs in the North. What in comparison appears clearest is that Northern attitudes were not crystallized into any uniform public opinion. As Drake and Cayton wrote: "In the South, every white man feels impelled to protect every white family, clique, and church from 'Negro contamination.' In Midwest **Metropolis**, each person is concerned only with his own." [20]

Variations in the Northern Pattern

In minor aspects the picture of Chicago's Negro community and its relation to the larger community is affected by its particular locale; but less extensive studies of other large cities indicate that *Black Metropolis* was a typical picture of Negro-white relations in the metropolitan areas of the North, where the far larger proportion of the Northern Negro population lived.[21] Variations in the Northern pattern were in the main related to three situational factors: (1) the recency of the migration of substantial numbers of Negroes into any particular community; (2) the smaller-city situation as against the large-city situation; and (3) the relative exposure of the community to Southern influence.

RECENCY OF MIGRATION   The status of Negroes in Northern cities varied with the extent to which a given city shared in the Great Migration. Generally the status of Negroes in the North as a whole declined in the years attending this migration. Furthermore, the occurrence of the depression of the 1930's, during which so large a proportion of Negroes were on relief, retarded improvement in welfare. Even in New England, which did not greatly share in the Great Migration, the traditional tolerance toward Negroes declined. Frazier

[20] *Black Metropolis,* p. 119.
[21] See for example, Robert A. Warner, *New Haven Negroes* (New Haven: Yale University Press, 1940).

writes, "The increase in the Negro population [of Boston] during and following World War I accentuated race consciousness among Negroes as well as whites." [22] He cites a study of a similar situation in Milton, Pennsylvania.

Confirmation of the principle that animosity to a minority rises with the sudden influx of a new group into a particular area comes from a study of the situation in the Northwestern communities to which Negroes migrated during World War II.[23] Before 1940, Negroes comprised less than 0.5 percent of the population covered in this study; by 1945 the Negro population had increased 300 percent. The very small and inconspicuous group of Negroes living in the area before this recent migration "had learned gradually to adjust themselves to white patterns, and whites had in turn more or less come to accept this small Negro minority as a natural part of the population." However, "with the appearance of new faces, unfamiliar with the community's mores, tensions began to be apparent." [24] Contributing to the tension was the fact that the white "newcomers" to these localities came from areas with more discriminatory patterns, and they translated their usual attitudes into behavior in the new situation. Furthermore, the change in white attitudes was resented by the old-time Negro families, whose status deteriorated in the face of the general rise of antagonism toward Negroes, producing friction within the local Negro group. Insofar as social policy can be brought to bear on future adjustment of Negro-white relations, these Northern and Western experiences point toward discouraging a large influx of Negroes over a short period of time into any one community.

THE SMALLER CITY VERSUS THE METROPOLIS   Since the major portion of the Northern migration went to the large cities, little attention had been given to Negroes in the smaller cities. In Muncie, Indiana, the Lynds found in 1929 that "the sense of racial separateness appears in widely diverse groups." Negroes were not permitted in the Y.M.C.A., for example. "News of the Negroes is given separately in the papers under the title 'In Colored Circles.' " [25] In 1935, in their post-depression study of the same city, the authors found Negroes had better leadership and organization but that they "occupy a more exposed position . . . than before the depression." [26] Rudwick states of East St. Louis, Illinois, that before World War I, "Negroes were expected to conform to a rigorous system of racial segregation." [27] In smaller communities, Negroes were further

[22] E. Franklin Frazier, *The Negro in the United States* (New York: The Macmillan Co., 1949), p. 254.

[23] T. H. Kennedy, "Racial Tensions Among Negroes in the Intermountain Northwest," *Phylon*, 1946, 7: 358–364.

[24] *Ibid.*, p. 360.

[25] Robert S. and Helen M. Lynd, *Middletown* (New York: Harcourt, Brace & Co., 1929), p. 479, footnote 1.

[26] Robert S. and Helen M. Lynd, *Middletown in Transition* (New York: Harcourt, Brace & Co., 1937), p. 465.

[27] Elliot M. Rudwick, *Race Riot at East St. Louis, July 2, 1917* (Cleveland and New York: The World Publishing Co.), 1966, p. 6.

handicapped because their numbers were inadequate to furnish for themselves a complete, separate community life.

INFLUENCE OF THE SOUTHERN PATTERN ON THE NORTH   In concluding the discussion of variables in the Northern scene, it is pertinent to note two influences of the Southern pattern on the North and West. First, the migration of white Southern workers to the North which, when recent and in substantial numbers, tended to disturb the pattern of toleration of Negroes in many Northern communities. This was notable as a factor in the tense Detroit situation of World War II. Second, in those Northern states bordering on a state with a Southern pattern, variation in race relations from south to north was noticeable. In New Jersey, for instance, before state government policies inaugurated in the 1940's, school segregation was more pronounced in the southern than in the northern portion of the state. The part of Illinois which dips down into the South still showed strong Southern caste influence.

All these variations make it clear that throughout the North white Americans normatively were unwilling to accord Negroes real equality.[28]

Impact of the Northern Pattern on Northern Communities

The kind of pattern of Negro-white relations which we have described in this chapter affected the life of those Northern communities with any substantial Negro population in many ways. We shall consider the following effects: (1) Negro minority status created and more or less perpetuated a "black ghetto," which as a physically deteriorated area yielded the high rates of crime, delinquency, ill health, and other social pathologies characteristic of slums everywhere. (2) The discrimination imposed on Negroes directly engendered frustrations in their personality sturcture, further provoking antisocial behavior. (3) The dominant-minority character of race relations created a continuous intergroup tension in community life which sporadically broke out into violent intergroup conflict. (4) The less rigid character of race relations in the North, on the one hand, led to confusion, handicapping adjustment, but on the other hand afforded greater opportunity than in the South for Negroes themselves to advance their race.

The Negro Ghetto: a Blighted Area

The assignment of Negroes to minority status in Northern cities resulted in separate subcommunal structures within the larger communities. While in many

[28] A notable exception to the rigid line of discrimination in the North has recently appeared from a field study by George K. Hesslink, published as *Black Gentry: Negroes in a Northern Rural Community* (Indianapolis: Bobbs-Merrill, 1967). Hesslink uncovered a Michigan village in which Negro descendants of pre-Civil War fugitive slaves interacted with whites on a mutually equitable basis from the early years. To the degree that tensions are generated in this community they tend to occur between the established white families. The study is significant because it underscores the different pattern of interracial relations in a smaller community not steeped in traditions of interracial hostility but whch is now faced with the potentially disruptive effects of migration and social change.

cities there were a few scattered Negroes living among whites, most Northern Negroes lived together either in one large area or in several scattered but compact Negro areas. And, though the area was small, there was a distinctive community composed of separate churches, clubs, recreational organizations, and civic groups. Off the job, Negroes associated almost exclusively with one another. The development of separate Negro communities fitted easily into the ecological pattern of Northern city life, where various ethnic colonies were no new phenomenon. But as time went on, while the ethnic colonies tended to disappear through assimilation of subsequent generations, the Negro separate colony, as we have noted, persisted and grew, posing a problem of serious dimensions. Resistance to admitting Negroes into new areas resulted in fantastic overcrowding. Weaver writes that in 1939 in Detroit rates for overcrowding were twice as high as for the white population.[29] When finally the walls of the black ghetto burst, infiltration of Negroes into other dilapidated areas began. However, when some Negroes did get a foothold, whites began to move out and more Negroes moved in, until the new block, or section, came to be generally Negro. This process was attended by considerable animosity between both racial groups, sometimes climaxed by race rioting. Through it all Negroes had substandard housing, for which they paid abnormally high rents.

It has been demonstrated that all slum areas, regardless of who lives in them, although highly profitable to particular special interests, are an economic drain on the community at large, and unvaryingly yield a disproportionate share of the social pathologies—delinquency, crime, high disease rates. That the presence of a Negro ghetto in a Northern community is no exception has been amply demonstrated by many studies of such areas.[30]

Northern Discrimination and Negro Personality

In Chapter 11 we discussed the effects of the Southern interracial pattern on Negro personality. It is here recalled that Karon found the same effects on Northern Negroes reared in the South, though in lesser degree. Illustrations of these effects are seen in the following cases.

> A young Negress in one of the Northern industrial centers who is engaged in housework is encouraged by her white teacher to take the civil service examination. She passes at the top of the list and is assigned to a public swimming pool. Negro patronage of this swimming pool has been prohibited; nor does the director wish to employ Negroes. His objections are overruled by the civil service authorities. He employs the Negro girl in a lower capacity than she merits—in cleaning work. The girl works without complaint. After a few weeks she thinks of swimming in the pool herself. Immediately a group of white boys approach her, treat

[29] Weaver, *The Negro Ghetto,* p. 115.
[30] See Robert Weaver, *The Negro Ghetto;* E. Franklin Frazier, *The Negro in the United States,* Part IV; and Gunnar Myrdal, *The American Dilemma,* Ch. 14.

her none too gently, make her stop swimming. The shock is so great that she not only quits her job but refuses to try for any other job to which she is eligible in the civil service. The white teacher from whom I got these facts told me that she came upon the Negress some time later as an elevator girl in a department store. The teacher tried to encourage her to apply once more for a civil service position, but the girl seemed to have lost all faith and all interest in anything better than a subservient place.

Such a degree of breakdown made me suspect that as a child this Negress had had particularly friendly relations with white children on an equal footing. An inquiry showed that she had indeed grown up in a group of children without discrimination between whites and Negroes.[31]

While in the above case discrimination led to withdrawal and passive reaction, in the following case of Arthur Brown, the ultimate result was aggression.

"Hey, you lazy 4-F," growled the cop, "why don't you get yourself a job and stop hanging out on street corners?" His nightstick swung menacingly.

Arthur Brown choked back the anger and resentment that rose in his throat. His fist itched to take the measure of that cop, but he knew too well that in Harlem that just didn't go. Hit a cop and the whole force gangs up on you.

"Mind your business," he said sharply. "I can take care of myself."

Actually Arthur had tried during the day to get employment as an International Business Machines operator or supervisor, work for which he was well qualified. While there were such positions open in the community at the time, Arthur was turned down for reasons indicated. In his first personal interview, he faced a woman employment officer in a Business Survey Systems Office. In turning down Arthur for the job, the white woman said:

"But you realize we've never had a colored supervisor. Now so far as I'm concerned, personally, I'd take you on in a minute. I haven't any prejudice at all. I have a great many Negro friends. But these girls we have here—they're young, impressionable—and some of them are very prejudiced. I just couldn't put you over any of them. They'd walk out on me—right smack out of the place."

Arthur tried his second reference, this time in the office of a shipyard building naval vessels. His conversation with the assistant general manager ran as follows:

"So they sent you down to get that I.B.M. job, huh?" he asked. "Well, son, I can't give you that."

"Nope. But I'm afraid you wouldn't fit into our office. We have five men on those machines. As it happens, they're all white."

"I'll get along with them."

[31] Kurt Lewin, *Resolving Social Conflicts* (New York: Harper & Brothers, 1948), pp. 172–173. By permission.

"Well—" The general manager chewed speculatively on a big cigar. "Maybe you would and maybe you wouldn't. My experience says you wouldn't."

"How about letting me try?"

"Nope, couldn't do it. And I'll tell you why. About five or six years ago I took a colored fellow outa' the yard and put him on an office machine. He was no good—just couldn't do the work. The other fellers said he balled up the whole department, and I had to take him out. I learned a lesson from that—colored boys are all right for the heavy yard jobs, but they don't work out in an office."

"But he wasn't competent," Arthur Brown argued. "I've had experience. Besides, you can't judge a whole race just by one guy—"

"Son—" The general manager's tone was patronizing. "When you've been in business as long as I have you learn what works and what don't work. We're too busy now with war orders to try out experiments. I'll give you a job, this minute, as a shipfitter's helper. It's a good trade for you to learn. But I'm not going to buck human nature and put you on an office job, and that's that."

Later the same evening, while walking up Lenox Avenue, Arthur spied a couple approaching in his direction.

Suddenly he ducked into the sheltering darkness of an unlighted storefront. A tall, good-looking brownskin girl brushed by without a second look at him. A merchant seaman held her arm, and they laughed together as at some great joke. Lucy!

Lucy was Arthur Brown's girl—or was she, any more? Since he'd lost his last job, since he'd no longer been able to take her out, buy her drinks, show her a good time—

Lucy was a fine girl. But after all, what more could he expect?

Arthur Brown walked along the avenue, shoulders hunched against the gathering twlight chill.

He paused before a theater, fingering the fifteen cents remaining in his pocket. He'd need the fifteen cents for breakfast in the morning.

He reached an intersection and stood there on the corner, watching traffic. He didn't see the cop until he tapped him on the shoulder.

"Hey," growled the cop, "didn't I tell you to stop hanging out around here? Why don't you get yourself a job—do some work to help the war effort?"

It was then he hit the cop. Why he did it he could never quite explain. He knew in Harlem that just didn't go. But somehow he didn't care.[32]

Such cases suggest that minority status imposed on Northern Negroes had effects on the personality structure and behavior similar to those of the caste system in the South. The passive reaction of the young woman in Lewin's case, in contrast to the aggressive reaction of Arthur Brown, may reflect the variables in the psychological constitution of the two as individuals; but the intensity of the reactions noted can be considered as arising from discrimination.

[32] Edward H. Lawson, "Arthur Brown Applies for a Job," *The Journal of Social Issues,* February, 1945, 1: 11–14. By permission.

Sporadic Violence

The presence of Negroes in minority status was a constant source of tension and a sporadic source of race rioting in Northern communities. While there had been race riots in the North before the Great Migration, such as one in Springfield, Illinois, in 1908, most of the serious riots occurred during and following the two great wars of this century. During World War I, aside from a notorious riot in Houston, Texas, involving servicemen of both races, the most important riot occurred in East St. Louis, Illinois, during which at least 39 Negroes and 9 whites were killed.[33] In 1919, riots occurred in at least 26 American cities. After this flurry of disturbances, race riots were relatively few until the beginning of World War II.

In Detroit in 1942 one of the worst race riots occurred. Myrdal writes of it:

> ... [I]n trying to move into a government defense housing project built for them in Detroit, Negroes were set upon by white civilians and police. The project was built at the border between Negro and white neighborhoods but had been planned for Negroes. Encouraged by the vacillation of the federal government and the friendliness of the Detroit police (many of whom are Southern born) and stimulated by the backing of a United States congressman and such organizations as the Ku Klux Klan, white residents of the neighborhood and other parts of the city staged protest demonstrations against the Negro housing project, which led to the riot.[34]

It will be noted that the outbreaks just mentioned occurred under conditions of stress or crisis in the larger society. This suggests the value of special analysis of the responses of dominant and minority people under such stressful conditions.

A somewhat different pattern of race riot was illustrated by the Harlem Riot of 1935. This was an outbreak of sporadic violence in the Negro area itself, an outgrowth of the inevitable high degree of social disorganization to be found in physically blighted, "burstingly" overcrowded, and socially depressed areas such as the black ghettos of the North. Ottley describes this riot in these words:

> The morning of March 20, 1935, the nation awoke to learn to its dismay that the home of happy feet, Harlem, had exploded into violence. Whipped to a frenzy by radical street speakers, upwards of ten thousand had tumbled from taverns and tenements, barber shops and basement dives, and surged through the streets grappling in hand-to-hand struggles with the police. They smashed store windows, hurled bricks and assaulted white merchants. Bands plundered and looted stores with amazing discrimination—choosing only those owned by whites. When the police finally restored order in the early morning, three Negroes had been killed,

[33] Elliot M. Rudwick, *Race Riot at East St. Louis, July, 2, 1917.*
[34] Myrdal, *An American Dilemma,* p. 568. By permission of the publishers, Harper & Brothers.

thirty-odd hospitalized for bullet wounds, and two hundred white and Negro persons treated for injuries. Two hundred shops were smashed and gutted, and two million dollars in property was destroyed. One hundred Negroes were in the lockup for inciting to violence, unlawful assembly, and looting.

The police hunted the answer in poolrooms, basements, and gambling joints, places where the criminal elements gathered. But actually the outburst was a manifestation of deep social unrest and unhappiness.[35]

Ambiguity of the Northern Pattern

Adjustment of adult migrants to a new social environment is usually characterized by a certain amount of disorganization. A large proportion of the Negroes living in the North, certainly before 1940, had been brought up in the South; and of the rest many were children born in the North to Southern-bred parents. Negro migration often involved movement from a rural or small-town Southern setting to a Northern, urban milieu. This alone would account for some of the problems arising from adjustment to Northern life. Adjustment was further complicated, however, by the fact that this migration likewise involved a shift from a clearly defined and firmly established pattern of caste relations to a less rigid and more ambiguous dominant-minority pattern.

The particular kind of conditioning which Negroes had had made the Northern scene peculiarly upsetting. The Southern Negro generally had adjusted himself, with whatever inner psychic costs, to a lifetime of minority status. In the North this pattern of adjustment was considerably upset. The Negro was in many ways freer to do things he could not do in the South, but was frequently at a loss to know just how much freer. He could go to this restaurant, but that one refused him service. He could play on the school team, but he could not go to the dances. And, while treating him like a minority person, the Northern practice at the same time held the Negro more accountable to behave according to the general norms of the community. Petty thievery was almost expected of the Negro by the white Southerner, and was dealt with as one ordinarily deals with it in the case of children. But the Northerners put him in jail for it. "Illegitimacy" in the South (often occurring within stable monogamic unions) was laughed off by Southern whites as "natural for darkies," but in the North it frequently brought investigation by a white welfare worker.

Finally, while the South held out no prospect to the Negro of ever rising above the confines of caste (allowing only for some upward class mobility within caste), the Northern situation, ill defined and perplexing as it was, was sufficiently fluid to encourage Negro aspirations. But since Northern white attitudes were by no means ready for the full step, Negroes' hopes were frequently raised too high, only to be dashed. The relatively better education offered the Negro in the North encouraged him to prepare himself for occupations em-

[35] Roi Ottley, *Black Odyssey* (New York: Charles Scribner's Sons, 1948), p. 258. By permission.

ployment in which he would subsequently be denied. His desire for better housing, and often the means to pay for it, was raised only to be frustrated by restrictive covenants. He was at the same time encouraged to develop higher cultural interests and refused a seat in a theater. Thus the lack of clear definitions of expected Negro behavior and the uncertainties and fluidity characterizing their relations with whites placed considerable strain on Negro personality.

Opportunity to Challenge Dominance

In spite of the disorganizing effect of the none-too-well defined situation of the Negro and of the very considerable discrimination against him, compared with the South, the North afforded two advantages: the opportunity for individual Negroes to reach higher levels of success and the greater opportunity to work effectively to advance the race.

Rise of Individual Negroes

Although Negro society in the South had some class differentiation, in the North the class structure was more elaborated, reaching, as with the white class structure, its greatest complexity in the metropolis. The social class structure of "Black Metropolis" is described as follows:

> The process of differentiation among Negroes in Bronzeville has given rise to a loose system of social classes which allows for mobility upward and downward. This class structure operates as a system of social controls by which the higher-status groups "protect" their way of life, but admit "strainers" and "strivers" who can make the grade. Individuals and organizations on the higher-status levels become models for imitation and also serve as an incentive toward social mobility. ... At the top are uppers, oriented predominantly around "Society" and Race Leadership, and with a small group of Gentlemen Racketeers who have gained some status as Race Leaders but who are not accepted socially. Below them is the middle class with four "centers of orientation"—church, social club, "racial advancement" (including *individual* advancement), and "policy." At the bottom is the lower class with a large "disorganized segment," but also with a "church-centered" group and a small group of "secular respectables" interested in "getting ahead." Underlying the whole structure is the "underworld" of the Black Ghetto.[36]

A few individual Negroes in the North had gained fame and fortune in areas competitive with white people: Joe Louis and, even earlier, Jack Johnson in prizefighting; Roland Hayes and Paul Robeson in concert singing; Paul Lawrence Dunbar, Countee Cullen, James Weldon Johnson in literature. The theme which the artists emphasized was often related to Negro life and problems.

For most of the Negroes who achieved higher social and economic status,

[36] Drake and Cayton, *Black Metropolis,* pp. 710–712. By permission.

it was the very separation of the Negro community from the rest that provided much of their opportunity.[37] Negroes had been conspicuously underrepresented in business, even compared with some other racial minorities, such as the Chinese and Japanese. Rose writes, "In 1939, there were not quite 30,000 Negro retail stores, giving employment to a total of 43,000 persons. The total sales in 1939 were less than 2/10 of 1 percent of the national total." [38] Nevertheless, the pattern of segregation itself created a monopoly for Negroes in certain kinds of business—those involving intimate contact with the person of the Negro, such as hairdressers, restaurant and hotel service, and undertaking.

In professional service, however, where the relationship to the client is less personal, aspiring Negroes, when they managed to hurdle the difficulty of acquiring professional training, were in competition with white professionals for the trade of the Negro population while being generally barred from competition for the white trade. In 1940 there were about 3,500 Negro physicians in the whole country, which means about forty-five times as many white doctors as Negro. Negro physicians were handicapped by the lack of hospitals for their patients, and frequently were not permitted to treat their patients in mixed hospitals. In 1940 there were 1,063 Negro lawyers in the United States. Although this was less than 1 percent of all lawyers in the country, the North provided an opportunity here which was substantially closed in the South. Thus two-thirds of this small number of Negro lawyers were to be found outside the South, where less than one-fourth of the Negro population lived.

The ministry in Negro churches was, of course, an exclusively Negro occupation. Clergymen were the second largest group among Negro professionals. Teaching exceeded the ministry, largely because in the South only Negro teachers were allowed to teach Negro children. While the influence of ministers as leaders of the church-going Negro people was strong, in the North their leadership was shared and sometimes overshadowed by other educated Negroes.

Interestingly enough, one of the largest of all Negro businesses was insurance. Frazier writes, "For the year 1945, the 44 member companies of the National Negro Insurance Association reported nearly 4,000,000 policies in force, of which 3,860,890 were health and accident and nearly 80,000 unspecified." [39] The opportunity here arose from the reluctance of general insurance companies to underwrite Negro policies on the same actuarial basis employed for whites because of the known wide differentials in risks in health and mortality between the two races. That the reluctance to underwrite Negroes was by no means absolute, however, is indicated by Frazier's statement that "one large white insurance company has insurance in force on Negro lives amounting to

---

[37] This is not to imply that many of these same people would not have achieved comparable status in competition with whites in a social structure in which racial distinctions did not prevail.
[38] Arnold Rose, *The Negro in America* (New York: Harper & Brothers, 1948), p. 108.
[39] Frazier, *The Negro in the United States,* p. 401.

more than twice the insurance in force in all the Negro insurance companies." [40]

Another occupation arose from semisegregation of Negroes in the North and the necessity of integrating them somehow into the civic life of the community, which provided an opportunity for some Negroes to become the liaison agents, or specialists, representing Negroes in community-wide civic activity. Much more in the North than in the South, although the tendency was increasing there, such liaison activity was assigned to Negroes. The very real participation of Negroes in Northern politics, as described previously for Chicago, afforded opportunity for leadership in party politics, with occasional appointment to public positions either as reward or through civil service.

Finally, it is inevitable that among a people so situated there should arise an "underworld," often abetted and patronized by whites, and affording opportunity for some Negroes to achieve financial, if not status, reward.

Thus the Northern scene afforded Negroes qualified opportunity for getting ahead and accounted for the growing upper and middle class in the Northern Negro communities. The values and modes of life among the middle-class Negroes were similar to those in the white middle class. Drake and Cayton put it thus:

> The whole atmosphere of middle-class life is one of tension, particularly at upper-middle-class level, or among people on the way up, but not yet secure in their position. The drive to get ahead, to "lay a little something by," to prepare for the education of children, and at the same time keep up "front" by wearing the right kind of clothes, having a "nice home," and belonging to the proper organizations—the pursuit of these goals brings into being definite social types which Bronzeville calls "strivers," and "strainers." With limited incomes, the problem of striking a balance between the conspicuous consumption necessary to maintain status, and long-range goals like buying property and educating children, becomes a difficult one. During the depression years particularly, Bronzeville's middle-class families faced a continuous crisis.[41]

This opportunity for the more educated and ambitious Negroes in the North to rise to higher status presented something of a dilemma regarding their attitudes toward advancing the race. Frazier pointed out that segregation protects certain Negro professionals to some extent from competition with whites in corresponding occupations—a competition which was keener and which he felt many of the Negro professionals could not meet successfully.[42] It is clear that a rapid breakdown of the segregated pattern would create much insecurity for the Negro middle class, and it is reasonable to hypothesize that, unconsciously at least, this would temper the vigor of the participation of its mem-

[40] *Ibid.*
[41] Drake and Cayton, *Black Metropolis,* pp. 667–668. By permission.
[42] See E. Franklin Frazier, *The Black Bourgeoisie* (Glencoe, Ill.: The Free Press, 1957), for fuller treatment of the rise of the Negro middle class.

bers in desegregation movements.[43] On the other hand, esteem among Negroes, as well as other minorities, was to be bestowed on those who championed the advancement of the race.

Organization of the Negro Challenge

We have seen that throughout the long history of the Negroes in the New World there have always been some members of the group who have actively protested against their minority status. Under slavery, Negroes organized rebellions; under Southern caste, Negro leadership took the accommodative road of trying to improve the welfare of the group without challenging the basic system of segregation. In the North in the early twentieth century, Negro leadership and organization to advance the race embraced a wider range of activities and programs.

ESCAPIST MOVEMENTS   Brief attention may be pertinently directed to those movements with an escapist character directed by charismatic leadership. Of these, the "Back to Africa" movement led by Marcus Garvey comes first.[44] Garvey, a West Indian full-blooded Negro, rejected the idea that Negroes in the United States could ever become fully assimilated into the general white society. He organized The Universal Negro Improvement Association, whose broad aim was the establishment of an African republic to be led by Negroes. Garvey was imprisoned in 1925 on the charge of using the mails to defraud in connection with his financial manipulations, and the movement collapsed. During the brief period of its existence, the Garvey movement elicited considerable response from the Negro people. Myrdal called it the first organized Negro activity of the protest variety which really gripped the imagination and enthusiasm of the Negro masses in this country.[45]

Likewise of an escapist variety, though in many other ways completely opposite to Garvey's movement, was the much-publicized movement by George Baker, generally known as Father Divine. Preaching a doctrine of love among all peoples, Father Divine established a cult in which those who joined one of his "heavens" turned over their possessions and lived under his protection and security. This remarkable leader was shrewd in managing the affairs of the movement and, on the whole, took care of the followers who placed their trust in him. While most of his followers were Negroes, some white people entered his "heaven."

"Glamour" personalities—Duke Ellington, Paul Robeson, Marian Anderson —often functioned as Negro leaders, not so much because of their actual civil

---

[43] This point is illustrated in the later school desegregation crisis. Many Negro teachers in the South viewed with anxiety the possible loss of jobs or demotion in administrative rank as a consequence of school integration.

[44] See Ira DeA. Reid, "Negro Movements and Messiahs," *Phylon*, 1949, 10: 362–368, for a brief treatment of the leading Negro movements of this century.

[45] *An American Dilemma*, pp. 746–749.

rights activities but because of the fame and fortune they achieved in the white man's world. Comparatively "glamorous" white people do not necessarily play a leadership role in community affairs. In the case of Negroes, however, a sort of "race" leadership is thrust upon them by the very novelty of their success whether or not they have the capacity or inclination to assume the role.

THE NEGRO INTELLIGENTSIA   The 1920's saw the emergence of a group of Negro intellectuals whose purpose was to enhance the self-respect of Negroes by glorifying the great accomplishments of Negroes past and present. Prominent among the leaders of this movement were W. E. B. DuBois, editor of *The Crisis;* Charles S. Johnson, editor of *Opportunity;* Alain Locke, editor of the volume *The New Negro;* and Carter G. Woodson, who had organized The Association for the Study of Negro Life and History in 1915 and begun the publication of *The Journal of Negro History.* This movement had much moral support and financial aid from liberal-minded white people.

The high position occupied by Negro college and university professors in the leadership of American Negroes during this period is worthy of note. To take the field of sociology alone, one may cite Dr. Charles S. Johnson, president of Fisk University; Dr. E. Franklin Frazier, professor of sociology at Howard University and subsequently president of the American Sociological Society; and Dr. Ira DeA. Reid, chairman of the sociology department of Haverford College.

ACTIVIST ORGANIZATIONS   The first effort to organize a movement among Negroes in protest against their minority status was launched in 1905, when twenty-nine Negro intellectuals met at Niagara Falls and planned the formation of a national organization to challenge all forms of segregation and discrimination. Such a bold program was opposed by Booker T. Washington and thus in a way challenged his accommodative leadership. Although the organization itself ceased to be effective after 1915, it prepared the way for the formation of the National Association for the Advancement of Colored People (N.A.A.C.P.), presently to be considered, through which in part the spirit of the Niagara movement lived on.

Following the Great Migration and World War I, some younger Negro leaders in the 1920's, of whom A. Philip Randolph, president of the Brotherhood of Sleeping Car Porters, was to become the most influential, saw the Negro's greatest hope in alignment with the postwar Socialist movements. It is clear, however, from the relative failure of urban radical movements as far as election results were concerned that the majority of Negroes aligned themselves politically with the major parties. Generally it appears that this element merged with the New Deal element of the Democratic Party except for an occasional convert to Communism.[46] As we shall see in our account of the trends since 1940,

---

[46] See Wilson Record, *The Negro and the Communist Party* (Durham, North Carolina: University of North Carolina Press, 1951), for a full treatment of the topic. The author finds membership of American Negroes in the Communist Party to have been inconsequential and doubts that up to 1950 it ever exceeded 8,000.

the protest line of activity continued to gain ascendancy over the accommodative approach.

The first two organizations that have continued to be the most influential in working for the improvement of Negro welfare and status are the National Association for the Advancement of Colored People and the Urban League. These two organizations are not exclusively Negro but interracial, with substantial white membership. While they operate in the South, their origin in the North and their greater support in this region make it appropriate to discuss them in this chapter.

The N.A.A.C.P. was formed in 1909 following a severe race riot in Springfield, Illinois, the previous year. It was started on white people's initiative, but its active workers have usually been Negroes. The long-run objective of the Association has always been to win full equality for the Negro as an American citizen. Its specific activities have been in the field of civil liberties, constantly fighting legal cases of discrimination, such as anti-lynching legislation, the abolition of poll taxes, and so on. The strategy of its approach has been practical and opportunistic. The Association did not conduct an omnibus legal campaign against the Southern caste pattern but selected strategically important cases in specific fields of discrimination. It saved many Negroes from unequal court treatment; prevented the extradition of Negroes from North to South for trial; and helped establish the precedents by which the exclusion of Negroes from jury service constitutes a denial of equal protection of laws as guaranteed by the Fourteenth Amendment—to select only a few of its many legal successes.

The Urban League was founded in 1910, also as an interracial movement on white initiative. It arose primarily to help the recent Negro migrants adjust to Northern city life. It became a general social welfare agency performing various welfare services: health work, recreational work, delinquency prevention, and acting as an informal employment agency for Negroes. In the postwar period, the Urban League has concerned itself more with advancing desegregation but, in contrast to the N.A.A.C.P., has used informal and educational methods in pursuing this goal rather than a legal approach.

In 1944 Myrdal wrote that one great weakness of both these organizations was their lack of support from the Negro masses.[47] This was due in part to the generally low educational and economic status of the Negro masses and the widespread prevalence among Negroes of a resigned and hopeless attitude as far as cracking the color line was concerned. The lack of mass support was also due to the fact that, as in all class structures, the interests of the Negro middle class and the Negro lower class were not identical in all respects.

Race Relations: A Regional Issue

Before turning to consider the trend since World War II, during which great changes in Negro-white relations have occurred, it is pertinent to em-

[47] *An American Dilemma*, pp. 835–836.

phasize that the very existence of regional attitudes and practices as disparate as those portrayed in the past two chapters had been a perennial source of regional conflict affecting in many ways the political and civic unity of the nation. The slavery issue threatened national unity until the close of the Civil War. From 1880 to World War I, the North in general tended to leave the Negro problem, as far as it was thought of as such, to the South. The Great Migration to the North brought the problem home. The discriminatory pattern that developed appeared at first to suggest a moving of the region closer to the view of the South. However, throughout the entire period a segment of Northern opinion continued to propagandize against discrimination toward Negroes. Finally there began to emerge a new definition of the problem as one of national significance. More Northern people began to believe that the prevailing patterns of dominant-minority relations between the two races could not permanently endure in a political democracy. This emerging new definition of the race problem received considerable impetus from the New Deal. In the operation of large-scale relief and in other government-planned projects, the tendency was toward providing Negroes a fairer share. Here and there Negroes were placed in new situations alongside whites. The number of Northern organized groups, especially religious groups, that became interested in democratizing race relations grew. Among the minorities themselves, a trend arose toward cooperation in protest activities in behalf of all, in which Jewish associations took a prominent lead.

While these new trends were developing in the North, there was no perceptible indication of the South's readiness to accept this redefinition of the race problem or to basically alter its traditional biracial system. Thus the approach of World War II found a long-standing regional issue assuming new dimensions, more sharply focused by the greater influence of the North—as the predominant center of national opinion-making—in the formation of national policy.

Topics for Projects and Discussion

1. Interview several white, and, if possible, Negro, people who grew to maturity before 1940 in Northern communities with a noticeable Negro population. Design a short questionnaire to use for your interview based on Drake and Cayton's *Black Metropolis* for the purpose of comparing their answers with the findings in the Chicago study.
2. It is frequently said that Negroes prefer to associate with their own kind. Do you think this is true?
3. Since the indications are that Negroes did have a considerably larger measure of opportunity in the North, how do you account for the fact that far more did not leave the South earlier?
4. Consider carefully all the reasons that occur to you to explain why it is that Negro youth, although accorded equal right in the North to complete their high-school education, do in fact drop out of school in larger proportions than white children.

5. Find out from the best available sources whether or not the delinquency rate is higher for Negroes than it is for non-Negroes in some delimited local area. Having established the comparative rates, study the situation and account for them.

Suggested Reading

Cantril, Hadley. *Psychology of Social Movements*. New York: John Wiley & Sons, 1941.
> *Chapter 5, "The Kingdom of Father Divine," interprets this movement as a search for satisfaction which the "real" society denies.*

Drake, St. Clair, and Cayton, Horace R. *Black Metropolis*. New York: Harcourt, Brace and Co., 1945.
> *The most comprehensive study of any urban Negro community in the North in the twentieth century. The picture drawn is of the late 1930's and early 1940's.*

Lee, Frank F. *Negro and White in Connecticut Town*. New York: Bookman Associates, 1961.
> *A study of race relations in a small town emphasizing the techniques of social control.*

Locke, Alain. *The New Negro*. New York: Albert and Charles Boni, 1925.
> *One of the first books surveying the literary and artistic contributions of the Negroes to American culture.*

Reid, Ira DeA. *The Negro Immigrant*. New York: Columbia University Press, 1939.
> *Most definitive account of the subject, treating especially the West Indian migrant.*

Spear, Allan H. *Black Chicago*. Chicago: The University of Chicago Press, 1967.
> *A historical study of the making of a ghetto in Chicago from 1890 to 1920.*

Waskow, Arthur I. *From Race Riot to Sit-In: 1919 and the 1960*. Garden City, New York: Doubleday Company, Anchor Books, 1966.
> *The first half of this volume describes and analyzes the major race riots of 1919 in the light of their origins, the riot process, and how they were dealt with.*

13

The Decline in Dominance:
The Southern Scene

The previous two chapters have dealt with the establishment and maintenance of white dominance over Negroes both North and South. The traditional
patterns indicated remained substantially crystallized to World War II. Because
since then change has predominated over stability, the focus of this and the
following two chapters become developmental. The net effect of change has
been a substantial decline in white dominance throughout the nation. The
movement of Negroes toward greater equality has been brought about by the
operation of broad general forces in the society at large and by direct action.
At all points resistance toward the predominating trend has been manifested
both from social forces and from white resistance to direct action. In this chapter
we shall first discuss the social forces and follow with the crisis of direct action as
it developed in the South. The next chapter will consider the changing North.
Early in the 1960's it became obvious that a massive challenge by Negroes, and
white sympathizers, was underway, and that a racial conflict of unprecedented
magnitude faced the nation. The fact that this still continues prompts the title
of Chapter 15, "The Negro Revolt."

Indirect Effect of Social Forces

The first social force indirectly affecting Negro-white relations was a temporary one, namely World War II.

The Impact of World War II

Crises characteristically make for some change, if only temporarily, in
established social structures. World War II had this effect on Negro-white relations. The main effect grew out of the labor shortages in the working force,
affording Negro men and women new opportunities for employment, more
steadily, and at higher wages with the consequent rise in the standard of living.[1]

[1] See Robert C. Weaver, *Negro Labor a National Problem* (New York: Harcourt, Brace
and Co., 1946).

Some change in status occurred in the employment area. In many war jobs Negroes worked alongside whites on equal terms, and were increasingly accepted into labor unions, to a limited extent even in the South, on an integrated basis.[2]

However, even under the urgency of war, acceptance of Negroes was not easy. Employers were reluctant to hire Negroes and white workers showed resistance to accepting them as co-workers.[3] In order to overcome as much as possible of this resistance President Roosevelt issued an executive order in 1941 establishing the Fair Employment Practices Commission, which aimed to require all government agencies and all private firms with government contracts not to discriminate on the basis of race or national origin. While this Commission had neither legislative sanction nor much real power of enforcement, substantial gains in the number of Negroes employed followed its establishment.[4]

Aside from these economic gains, the line of segregation held substantially the same. Even the National Capitol Housing Authority bowed to the prevailing housing pattern in building low-rent housing units.[5] In other more intimate areas of social relations, substantially no change took place.

THE ARMED SERVICES   The armed services practiced a policy of segregation. In the Army, Negroes were assigned to colored units, most of which were in supply services where the tasks were largely menial labor. A few thousand Negro officers were trained and placed over Negro troops, frequently under the command of a white captain. In army posts, separate recreational rooms were maintained, and nearly all communities which any considerable number of soldiers frequented—North as well as South—restricted colored troops to the Negro areas and set up separate USO's. For the most part, Negro units were kept out of combat. According to Rose, "In Europe there were some efforts made to keep Negroes from fraternizing with the civilian population, when no such bar was set up against the white troops." [6]

The policy of segregating Negro troops reflected the wishes of the white troops. A survey of the attitudes of servicemen made in March, 1943, revealed that about 80 percent of the white troops preferred to have the two groups separated in PX's, service clubs, and military units.[7] While over 90 percent of the Southern white respondents on each of the three counts listed above approved segregation, it is significant that over 70 percent of the Northern white

[2] See Drake and Cayton, *Black Metropolis,* pp. 309–310, for the Chicago picture during World War II.

[3] See Herbert R. Northrup, *Organized Labor and the Negro* (New York: Harper & Brothers, 1944), for an account of this subject.

[4] See *Fair Employment Practices Commission, Final Report, June 28, 1946* (Washington, D.C., 1947).

[5] See *Segregation in Washington, A Report of the National Committee on Segregation in Washington* (Chicago, 1948).

[6] Arnold Rose, *The Negro in America* (New York: Harper & Brothers, 1948), p. 138.

[7] Samuel A. Stouffer, et al., *The American Soldier,* vol. 1 (Princeton: Princeton University Press, 1949), pp. 566–570. Chapter 10 of this volume contains definitive research material gathered on how young adult males of both races looked at one another and felt about the race problem during the 1940's.

troops likewise indicated approval.[8] The Negro respondents showed far more opposition to being segregated, as would also be expected, but the detailed findings provide significant indication of how Negroes viewed their situation generally. Of the Negro sample, 37 percent disapproved separation in military units; 36 percent approved; 17 percent thought it made no difference; and 10 percent were undecided.[9] Comments by some of the antisegregation Negro soldiers emphasized primarily the democratic principle involved, for example: "Separate outfits shows that the Army continues segregation and discrimination. Is this the Democracy we are told we are fighting for?" [10] The 36 percent of Negro soldiers who approved of segregation did so on the basis of expediency, on a realistic appraisal of white prejudice. Among the reasons given by Negroes for taking the pro-segregation viewpoint were a fear of interracial friction— "A white soldier would call a colored soldier 'nigger' and it would be a fight"; a desire to withdraw from the situation of not being wanted—"so long as there are so many prejudiced white people, it would be too unpleasant"; a desire to prove that Negro groups can match the achievements of white groups; and finally, a desire to associate with those who understand one another—"I had rather be with my own color. Then I know where I stand." [11]

Some experiments in desegregated units were conducted toward the war's end without any important difficulties—paving the way for the postwar integrated policy which was to come.[12]

In spite of segregation policy and practice, the total impact of experiences in the armed services had effects disturbing to the traditional pattern of caste relations. More objectively measurable was the introduction of colored servicemen to new standards of welfare—in diet, health, and sanitation; and the increased training in many new skills, some of which could be useful in peacetime. A measure of the Negro soldiers' feelings about the value of their army training is seen in their answers to the direct question on this where 61 percent replied it would help them, compared with 39 percent who so replied among the whites.[13]

Less tangible but perhaps in the long run more significant was the impact of service experience on the attitudes of GI's of both races. Northern-born Negro servicemen trained in the South came face to face with the stricter Southern caste system. Southern Negro GI's stationed in the North experienced some measure of unaccustomed freedom. In Europe many Negro GI's found white people wishing to accept them like any other American soldier. Equally disturbing to traditional attitudes and habits was the impact of war service on

[8] *Ibid.,* pp. 568–570.
[9] *Ibid.,* p. 568.
[10] *Ibid.,* p. 575.
[11] *Ibid.,* p. 574.
[12] See Charles Dollard and Donald Young, "In the Armed Forces," *Survey Graphic,* Jan. 1947, p. 68.
[13] Stouffer, *The American Soldier,* p. 537.

many white Southerners. This is most dramatically illustrated in Margaret Halsey's account of her experiences operating a servicemen's center in a large Northern city.[14]

Economic, Technological, and Ecological Trends

The expanding economy offered some new jobs for Negroes and some at higher levels for qualified Negroes. This was in part offset by a decrease in demand for unskilled workers brought about by technological changes leading to large-scale unemployment. The nation in general became increasingly more affluent. In this Negroes shared but disproportionally to whites. Negroes also shared in the general urban migration. Their concentration in larger centers gave them increased localized political power, but aggravated slum conditions, and increased racial tension. Finally "rationalization" of the economic system favored job placement on the basis of achieved qualifications rather than ascribed status; and the keener competition for profit turned attention to the rising purchasing power of the Negro population.

Political and Governmental Trends

As we have already emphasized, the traditional basis of democratic governmental institutions pressed for more equality for Negroes as reflected in court decisions, civil rights legislation, and governmental administration particularly at the federal level and, outside the South, at some state and local levels. The growing Negro vote forced office-seekers to promise improvements and office-holders to act to give Negroes more rights—the rationale of the democratic political process. The general trend toward the "welfare state" sustained if not improved the welfare of Negroes, probably disproportionately since a larger percentage of Negroes than whites needed the aid. Provision of this aid, however, reinforced a traditional concept among whites that Negroes won't work and are glad to live on relief. Finally increasing sensitivity to adverse world opinion of the United States' racial system favored both official and voluntary action to offer more equality.

Cultural Trends

The general increase in educational facilities was shared by Negroes if unevenly and spottily, aside from the whole matter of desegregation, and had some effect on debunking the myth of innate Negro inferiority. The increasing dissemination of social science findings was creating a younger generation of white adults who at the intellectual level were more aware of the errors of the doctrine of racism and more conscious of the damaging consequences to American society of the persistence of the traditional intergroup pattern. Prodded by

[14] Margaret Halsey, *Color Blind* (New York: Simon and Schuster, 1946).

all these influences favoring the decline in discrimination, the leading organized religions were prompted to reassess the implication of their practices in regard to the race question.

The Elaboration of Mass Media

Finally we call attention to the elaboration of the mass media. Of all the social forces mentioned, there appears little research material to assess its bearing on changing race relations. The American press and magazines have in general given wide coverage to the events and have been objective in recording them. They have tended to editorialize in favor of the American Creed which should have had considerable influence on white thinking. Television, however, may be the medium that has the most powerful influence on both the dominant and the minority. Witnessing the jeering faces of white mothers as little Negro girls entered hitherto white schools might have been a powerful stimulus for the cause of racial justice. Likewise the televising of civil rights activities may arouse in other Negroes the desire to participate in the movement themselves. Finally, an important field for scientific investigation would be to determine the effect of television in the spreading of rioting from city to city particularly in 1967.

Since the net effect of the operation of these social forces was to improve the welfare and status of Negroes, it tended to raise the aspirations of Negroes still further and to spur more concerted direct action by Negroes and those whites committed to the Negro cause.

The Changing South

Before 1954

While the above-mentioned social trends were prompting a decline in discrimination nationwide, the pace in the South was quite slow and certainly held out no promise of equality for living Negroes. This is strikingly true if one focuses attention on certain significant developments in the Southern scene before 1954.

In the area of civil rights, the following developments may be noted: an increase in Negro voting—595,000 Negroes were on the voting rolls in 1947 and 1,008,614 in 1953;[15] some increase in Negro jury service prompted by a growing disposition of the federal courts to overturn convictions where the failure to call Negroes into service was attested; some beginnings of arresting and trying white people for crimes of violence against Negroes; the appointment of some Negro police officers to cover Negro areas. The Civil Rights pro-

[15] Margaret Price, *The Negro and the Ballot* (Atlanta: The Southern Regional Council, 1959), p. 9.

gram of the Truman Administration led to the formation of the States Rights party in the 1948 Presidential election, carrying the electoral vote of four Southern States. No precipitate rise in violence toward Negroes was apparent, although the virtual disappearance of lynching was somewhat offset by a rise in the bombing of Negro homes—more than forty being reported for a year and a half period during 1951 to 1952.[16] While there was some reactivation of racist organizations, such as the Ku Klux Klan, white public opinion against such extremists was evidenced by the outlawing of masked gatherings in some Southern cities.

In education, two significant developments in the postwar years were (1) a partial breach in the pattern of segregation in higher education at the graduate level. Estimates indicate more than 200 Negroes enrolled in hitherto exclusively white graduate schools in 1951. (2) A trend toward greater equalization of the segregated Negro school system as compared to the white system. A comprehensive study of public-school education in the South in 1952 found the two systems most nearly equal in regard to teacher salaries, levels of teacher preparation, and the number of days in the school year. Although some lessening of the disparity between the two systems since 1940 was found in the provision of better school plants, the number of and amounts spent for library books, and in various vocational offerings, the study concludes that "in spite of the rapid improvement of Negro schools . . . substantial further progress is needed before equalization can be achieved." [17]

Thus on the surface while some improvement in Negro welfare and status was occurring, in the main the Southern biracial system remained intact and race relations did not appear unduly critical. Then came the Supreme Court decision outlawing school segregation.

The Supreme Court School Desegregation Decision: May 17, 1954

This decision concerned five separate cases, which the court consolidated since the same legal question was involved in each of them. In each case Negro children through their legal representatives had sought admission to white public schools, had been denied this right by local courts, and eventually had appealed the unfavorable decisions to the Supreme Court of the United States. The core of the decision is found in the following excerpts:

> We conclude that in the field of public education the doctrine of "separate but equal" has no place. Separate educational facilities are inherently unequal. Therefore, we hold that the plaintiffs and others similarly situated for whom the actions have been brought are, by reason of the segregation complained of, deprived of the equal protection of the laws guaranteed by the Fourteenth Amendment. . . .

[16] "Blight, Bigotry, and Bombs," *The New South* (Atlanta, Ga.: Southern Regional Council, July, 1952).
[17] Truman M. Pierce, and others, *White and Negro Schools in the South* (Englewood Cliffs, N.J.: Prentice-Hall, 1955), p. 292. See pp. 291–292 for summary.

Segregation of white and colored children in public schools has a detrimental effect upon the colored children. The impact is greater when it has the sanction of law; for the policy of separating the races is usually interpreted as denoting the inferiority of the Negro group. A sense of inferiority affects the motivation of the child to learn. Segregation, with the sanction of the law, therefore has a tendency to retard the educational and mental development of Negro children and to deprive them of some of the benefits they would receive in a racially integrated school system. . . .

Whatever may have been the extent of psychological knowledge at the time of Plessy vs. Ferguson, this finding is amply supported by modern authority. Any language in Plessy vs. Ferguson contrary to this finding is rejected.[18]

The way the Court handled these cases indicated awareness of strong negative reactions and that enforcement would be beset with special difficulties. The decision was unanimous and read by Chief Justice Earl Warren giving it a sense of finality. The Court postponed its implementing order until May 31, 1955, when it ordered compliance "with all deliberate speed." This phraseology indicated that the Supreme Court did not expect affected states to integrate all schools at once, but that some reasonable plan for eventual complete integration should be made and a beginning announced. It was left to district federal courts to decide whether a particular plan presented in its area was designed to accomplish really complete integration in a reasonable time.

It is essential to emphasize that the implications of the school decision went far beyond the matter of schools alone. It appeared that the reasoning presented in supporting the decision had general application—in effect the court was saying that all state-imposed racial segregation was unconstitutional. By stating that it was reversing Plessy vs. Ferguson (1896), which held that segregation in public transportation was legal provided the facilities were equal, the Court seemed to imply this general application. Subsequent decisions by various courts

[18] 347 U.S. 483. The number 1 case was Brown, et al. v. Board of Education of Topeka, Kansas. Three other cases were linked together with Brown, et al.: Briggs v. Elliott (South Carolina) ; Davis v. County School Board of Prince Edward County, Virginia ; Gebhart v. Belton (Delaware). A separate decision in Bolling v. Sharpe, 347, U.S. 497, to the same effect was read following Brown, et al. This case concerned segregation of public schools in the District of Columbia and therefore involved the federal government directly.

Footnote 11 in the text of the decision lists the following writings: K. B. Clark, *Effect of Prejudice and Discrimination on Personality Development* (Midcentury White House Conference on Children and Youth, 1950) ; Witmer and Kotinsky, *Personality in the Making* (1952), c. VI ; Deutscher and Chein, "The Psychological Effects of Enforced Segregation: A Survey of Social Science Opinion," 26 *J. Psychol.* 259 (1948) ; Chein, "What are the Psychological Effects of Segregation Under Conditions of Equal Facilities?" 3 *Int. J. Opinion and Attitude Res.* 229 (1949) ; Brameld, *Educational Costs in Discrimination and National Welfare* (MacIver, ed., 1949), 44–48 ; Frazier, *The Negro in the United States* (1949), 674–681. And see generally Myrdal, *An American Dilemma* (1944).

See Albert P. Blaustein and Clarence C. Ferguson, Jr., *Desegregation and the Law: The Meaning and Effect of the School Desegregation Cases* (New Brunswick, N.J.: Rutgers University Press, 1957), for an extensive account of the legal proceedings and the text of significant cases related to the desegregation decision.

within the federal system in widely divergent fields further supported this interpretation. In short, the school desegregation decision appeared to undermine the entire legal, or *de jure,* basis of public racial discrimination throughout the United States. Obviously, for the South this legal situation was bound to create a crisis of a profoundly critical nature. Since we wish to discuss the Southern crisis in these broader terms, we will at this point summarize the main facts concerning school desegregation and later discuss the crisis period in broader terms.

School Desegregation in the Southern Region

Table 13–1 provides data on the extent of school desegregation state by state in the Southern region in 1966–67, twelve years after the Supreme Court's decision.[19] Focusing attention on the last column, one notes the wide variation in the percentage of Negroes in school with whites in the eleven states of the South and the Border States—15.9 for the former as against 75.7 percent for the latter. The other most striking variation is the Deep South as contrasted with the rest of the South; the former ranging from 2.5 percent in Mississippi to 8.8 in Georgia; the latter starting with 15.1 for Florida to 44.9 for Texas. Relatively speaking these variations have prevailed in general throughout the school desegregation process, as will be seen as we summarize the process from the beginning.

The most striking fact is the slow pace of desegregation. (1) The District of Columbia was the only area to desegregate all its schools immediately following the decision. (2) Substantial integration in the Border States occurred in the first few years so that by the school year 1960–1961 almost half (49 percent) of Negro pupils in those states combined were in school with whites and by now desegregation is substantially complete. (3) In the following seven of the eleven Southern States, a very few school districts desegregated before 1960 and even up to 1965 with one exception (Texas) the percentage of Negro pupils in school with whites was five percent or below. These seven states are listed in the order of the first school year in which any one school district officially desegregated: Texas, Arkansas, Tennessee, North Carolina, Florida, South Carolina, and Virginia. Most of this desegregation up to 1964 took the "token" form —that is to admit only a few Negroes into a white school and call it "desegre-

[19] Source of the table is *Statistical Summary of School Segregation-Desegregation in the Southern and Border States, 1966–1967,* p. 2, published by Southern Education Reporting Service, Nashville, Tennessee. In this summary, SERS provides similar data for preceding years. Except where otherwise specified, all the data we present are taken from this source. The U.S. Office of Education made a separate survey for 1965–66 and the Southern Regional Council has also published data. While the detailed figures of these other sources differ from those of SERS, the broad essential picture as to school desegregation is not altered from that of SERS.

The extensive coverage of the school desegregation process by SERS, in detailed accounts published in periodic issues of *Southern School News* (now changed to *Southern Education Report*) beginning in 1957 makes this subject probably the most thoroughly documented phenomenon in American history.

TABLE 13-1. *School Segregation-Desegregation in the Southern and Border States, 1966–1967 (Public Elementary and High Schools)*

NOTE: The table below summarizes the SERS statistics on school desegregation for 1966–67. It shows for Arkansas, as an example, that the state had 406 school districts, including 222 with whites and Negroes, and that 391 of the 406 are in federal compliance and 12 are not. (The USOE total of districts differs from the Arkansas official figure.) The state has 337,920 whites and 119,817 Negroes in public elementary and high schools this school year, with the USOE estimating that 18,100 Negroes, or 15.1 percent of the state's Negro enrollment, actually attend schools with whites.

	School Districts With Negroes		In HEW Compliance		Enrollment		Negroes In Schools With Whites	
	Total & Whites		Yes	No	White	Negro	No.	%
Alabama	118	118	66	52	571,200	273,800	12,000b	4.4
Arkansas	406a	222	391	12	337,920d	119,817d	18,100b	15.1
Florida	67	67	65	2	967,721	289,871	64,574	22.3
Georgia	195a	189	151	45	776,281b	388,140b	34,300b	8.8
Louisiana	67	67	46	21	502,870	317,785	10,697	3.4
Mississippi	148a	148	94	55	309,413d	295,831d	7,258	2.5
North Carolina	169	169	156	13	828,583c	355,107c	54,600b	15.4
South Carolina	107	107	89	18	377,077	265,400	14,853	5.6
Tennessee	151a	133	148	4	693,143	184,511	52,691	28.6
Texas	1,314a	862	1,306	6	2,185,000c	355,000c	159,400b	44.9
Virginia	135	127	127	8	760,758c	243,553c	61,500b	25.3
SOUTH	2,877	2,209	2,639	236	8,309,966	3,088,815	489,973	15.9
Delaware	49a	44	50	0	89,438	21,333	21,333	100.0
District of Columbia	1	1	1	0	13,369	133,275	114,976	86.3
Kentucky	200	167	200	0	613,919	60,540	54,571	90.1
Maryland	24	23	24	0	605,043	185,884	121,359	65.3
Missouri	878a	212	689	0	852,770c	130,000b	101,100	77.7
Oklahoma	988a	310	995	0	536,800b	61,600b	31,300b	50.8
West Virginia	55	44	55	0	403,246c	22,800c	21,300b	93.4
BORDER	2,195	801	2,014	0	3,114,585	615,432	465,939	75.7
REGION	5,072	3,010	4,653	236	1,424,551	3,704,247	955,912	**25.8**

a The sum of districts in and not in HEW compliance does not equal the state total because the Office of Education reports a different number of districts from that given by the State Department of Education. b USOE estimate c Unofficial estimate. d 1965–66.

Source: *Statistical Summary of School Segregation-Desegregation in the Southern and Border States, 1966–1967*, p. 2, published by Southern Education Reporting Service, Nashville, Tennessee.

gated." (4) Up to 1960 no public school desegregation at all had taken place in Louisiana, Georgia, Alabama, and Mississippi. Since all of the ingenious attempts by the white South to evade school desegregation have been overruled by federal courts and have been given much publicity, we pass over them here.

The first break in the Deep South come in New Orleans, where in November, 1960, under court order the Orleans Parish School Board admitted three Negro pupils to an elementary school and one to another school. (5) The year 1965–1966 marks the first sharp increase in desegregation in the South. Whereas the percentage of Negro pupils in school with whites had reached only 2.25 percent up to 1965, the following school year showed a rise to 6.1. This is accounted for by an order issued by the U.S. Department of Health, Education, and Welfare (permissible under Title VI of the Civil Rights Act of 1964) requiring all school districts to submit "affidavits of compliance" to the Court desegregation order as a requirement for securing any federal funds. By November, 1966, 97 percent of the school districts of the entire South had had such affidavits accepted by HEW. It is important to note that these pledges of compliance did not call for specific plans or time to implement them. In October 1966, federal action to disqualify 65 Southern school districts for federal aid was started. However, "Most of them appear indifferent to this threat and several had arranged to replace the money from local sources." [20] This new policy did result in another large rise in school desegregation in 1966–1967, but as Table 13–1 shows, the 15.9 percent of all Negro pupils in school with whites cannot be considered large-scale integration. And strong opposition to the Office of Education "guide lines" arose in the House of Representatives in 1967.[21]

School desegregation in the South has other difficulties. "Tokenism" slows up integration since the few Negro students, if not openly abused—as some of the first to enter were—are not socially accepted and therefore often Negro students selected have hesitated to enter; those who did enter sometimes withdrew. Moreover, where desegregation takes place with considerable Negro enrollment, resegregation, or decided imbalance, occurs through the withdrawal of white students.[22] Finally, there is the matter of *de jure* vs. *de facto* desegregation. The school board of a particular district may officially desegregate but in some areas within the district there may be no Negroes or no whites, so that while the district is counted as a desegregated district, the proportion of Negro students in school with whites may or may not be high. For example, the District of Columbia is a single school district (desegregated), but in 1966–67 the percentage of Negroes in school with whites was 86.3, whereas in Delaware of the state's 49 school districts five have no Negro students, but 100 percent of the Negroes are listed as going to school with whites. The housing segregation of

[20] *Southern Education Report,* Nov.–Dec. 1965, pp. 30–31.
[21] See "New Battles for Guide Lines," *New York Times,* June 11, 1967, 3 E.
[22] In 1960 in Orchard Villa School, Dade County, Florida, the admission of even a few Negro students brought white student withdrawals. At the end of the school year the school was all Negro.

Negroes plus the "flight to the suburbs" of whites (similar to the Northern situation) make this distinction between *de jure* and *de facto* significant.

The potentially adverse consequences of school desegregation for Negro teachers was recognized from the very start of the process but detailed data on the number of Negro teachers on desegregated faculties have only recently been available. In 1966–67, at least 41,403 Negro teachers in the South were reported to be serving on desegregated faculties, out of a total of its 113,557.[23]

Various analyses of the uneven progress of school desegregation broadly agree that the following factors favor desegration: (1) a smaller proportion of Negroes in the total population; (2) urban as distinct from rural areas; (3) higher educational level of the white person. In detail, however, fortuitous circumstances make the relationship between various social factors and the timing of desegregation difficult to predict. For example, the personal decision of influential politicians on whether to take an adamantly opposed or a moderate position on the desegregation issue can delay or expedite the process in their particular localities.[24]

The Southern Crisis

The school case decision of 1954 precipitated a crisis for the South, especially the Deep South. Since the implications of the decision were, from the Southern point of view, revolutionary, it is not surprising that what followed has been a bitter, continuous struggle between those committed to traditional continuity and those intent on basic change in the Southern interracial system. The active agents on the side of change in this struggle were national Negro leaders, supported by a growing body of the Negro population; the federal court system; and an influential and articulate body of Northern public opinion, expressed in mass media. In sequence the roles played by these agents follow the order as just presented. Courts act when cases are brought before them. It was therefore the deliberate decision of the National Association for the Advancement of Colored People to test the constitutionality of school segregation that brought on the crisis at this particular time. On the side of traditional continuity were the institutions of race discrimination and the corresponding attitudes which found a substantial majority of Southern white people psychologically unprepared and unwilling to accept the drastic changes implied by the various court decisions against segregation. Some open support was received from racist-minded Americans outside the South—who were not, however, persons of much influence.

[23] "Statistical Summary of School Segregation-Desegregation in Southern and Border States, 1966–67," *Southern Education Reporting Service,* April, 1967, p. 2.
[24] The need for federal intervention with the first token integration in Little Rock, Arkansas, in 1957 was related to the particular position taken by local authority in contrast with Atlanta, where local authority supported by the white establishment decided to comply. See Claude Sitton, *New York Times Magazine,* May 6, 1962, pp. 22, 123, 128, for a report on the Atlanta situation.

Following the school desegregation decision, tension and conflict between the races rose sharply. Biracial relations in most communities were polarized between active Negro groups and reactionary white groups, pitted against each other on the desegregation issue. Moderate white leadership was unable to exert influence; liberals faced extraordinary reprisals.[25] Effective communication between the white and Negro communities broke down. The situation was no longer one where white groups could debate among themselves, consult with accommodative Negro leaders over improving Negro welfare, or criticize particular whites who had abused the privileges of the system by maltreating a Negro. The issue had become the abolition or survival of the segregation system itself, a system for so long an integral part of the Southern way of life that the conflict between the races was raised to the level of a crisis.

The interracial struggle has followed a course which we will describe in the following phases: (1) Southern whites viewed the situation as a crisis and the prevailing segment reacted accordingly with strong resistance. (2) Negroes challenged further areas of segregation with considerable success. (3) Further extra-regional pressures were brought upon the South with reference to other forms of segregation: from Congress in the form of Civil Rights legislation which led to increasing intervention by the federal government, and from voluntary groups, such as the "Freedom Riders." (4) Under the impact of all these pressures, the resistance movement began to weaken and reluctant compliance with desegregation orders increased. (5) Finally, current trends and prospects are considered.

White Resistance

That the white South would react with strong resistance to the school decision, and to any other areas of desegregation, would be expected from an understanding of the Southern interracial system as described in Chapter 11. Further measure of the unreadiness of the white South to accept desegregation can be gained from public opinion polls. On the school issue itself, the extent of Southern white disapproval is indicated by a Gallup Poll in 1954 which found 71 percent of its Southern white sample disapproving the school decision, as compared with 30 percent outside the South and 46 percent for the nation as a whole.[26] The strength of Southern white support for the traditional system is further attested in another poll, where the respondents were requested to choose between "keeping the races apart," and "bringing them together" as the best solution to the Negro-white problem. Nearly three-fourths of the Southern white

[25] We define a segregationist as one who believes that retention of the biracial system is the most important thing to the South ; a moderate as one who believes in segregation but gives many other things priority to this issue and who is therefore willing to compromise on the race issue ; a liberal is the white Southerner who believes that desegregation in varying degrees of rapidity is desirable.

[26] Data furnished by American Institute of Public Opinion, Princeton, New Jersey, which has conducted polls on the question of desegregation since 1954.

respondents chose the former answer, as against about one-sixth who chose the latter.[27]

Given this attitudinal climate, it is not surprising that white Southern resistance to desegregation was intensified by so sweeping a challenge as the school decision. A report of increased tension in the area from 1955 to 1958 found 530 cases of violence, reprisal, and intimidation as an aftermath of the various court decisions.[28]

White Citizens Councils

Of the various movements arising to oppose school desegregation, the most prominent was the White Citizens' Council movement.[29] This organization originated in Mississippi shortly after the school decision and continued to be strongest in that state. Similar councils arose in other states, and some liaison between the various councils in the South developed. Members were recruited from people of considerable status and power, which may explain the fact that, in general, control was exercised to keep its activities nonviolent. In addition to influencing state legislation, the Councils' chief method was at first to apply economic pressure against both Negroes and whites who participated openly in desegregation. As criticism of the use of economic sanction arose, the movement abandoned it officially, though it may have continued to practice it covertly. At least temporarily, the use of economic pressures was quite effective in discouraging the desegregation efforts of Negroes and sympathetic whites.

The resistance methods had mainly a delaying effect, since federal courts tend to overrule municipal ordinances or state laws causing segregation directly or indirectly. Illustrating the effectiveness of economic reprisal was the widely publicized eviction by white landlords of Negro tenants from their rented farms in Fayette and Haywood counties, Tennessee (1960). The reason given for this action was that because of mechanical improvements the Negroes were no longer needed. The evicted tenants included Negroes who had been active in attempting to register to vote. A case carried to a federal district court on this matter resulted in an order to stop these evictions.

SUCCESS OF WHITE RESISTANCE   The white resistance movement met with considerable success. We have already noted the lack of speed in integration into the public schools. Further indications of effective resistance can be seen in the slowing down of the pre-1954 trend toward integration of Negroes in colleges

[27] Poll conducted by the Ben Gaffin Associates, research agency for *The Catholic Digest* in 1956. See Melvin M. Tumin, *Segregation and Desegregation* (New York: Anti-Defamation League of B'nai B'rith, 1957), p. 98.

[28] "Intimidations, Reprisal, and Violence in the South's Racial Crisis," published by the Southeastern Office, American Friends Service Committee, Department of Racial and Cultural Relations, National Council of Churches of Christ in the United States of America; and the Southern Regional Council, 1959.

[29] See Hodding Carter III, *The South Strikes Back* (Garden City, N.Y.: Doubleday & Co., 1959), for an extensive treatment of White Citizens' Councils.

and universities, and similarly, of the trend toward increased Negro voting.

The slowing down of integration of Negroes in Southern colleges and universities was documented in the 1961 report of the United States Commission on Civil Rights, which found six states still effectively resisting integration at this level. Excerpts from the report follow:

> Compliance in some degree with the requirements of the equal-protection clause in 55.9 per cent of the formerly segregated public white colleges and universities of the South is progress indeed, but unfortunately, in many of these institutions compliance is not complete. In some, Negroes are admitted only to the graduate division; in others, they are admitted to the undergraduate division, but only if they wish to enroll in a course of study not offered in the college for Negroes maintained by the state. Such limitations are clearly in violation of the Fourteenth Amendment.
>
> The most serious equal-protection problem in public higher education, however, does not arise from the occasional instances of discrimination that occur, but from overt official resistance to any desegregation at all.[30]

Efforts to limit the further extension of the franchise to Negroes in the South were effective. In some Louisiana parishes a movement to purge Negroes from the registration rolls gained much headway.[31] A Florida study shows that while the Negro major party registration increased from 5.5 percent of the adult Negro population to 37.5 from 1944 to 1956, the largest increases took place between 1944 and 1950.[32] The author comments: "Increasing tension over the segregation issue is making it more difficult for officials and candidates in the South to maintain a moderate position on this [the voting] issue, or to seek Negro support on other issues.[33]

The predominance of the resistance elements of the white South over moderates seems clear at least to 1960. The unseating of a moderate white southern Congressman, Brook Hayes, of Little Rock, Arkansas, in 1958 by a write-in vote sponsored by segregationists illustrates why other Southern politicians who may privately hold moderate views have not outwardly opposed the resistance movement. Further indication of the dominance and effectiveness of the segregationists influence comes from a study of the reaction of Little Rock's clergy to the school desegregation crisis in that city in 1957.[34] The main thesis of this study runs as follows:

> Those ministers who were openly or privately integrationist did not receive from any source, sufficient support to make their position viable. They were opposed

[30] United States Commission on Civil Rights, *Report on Racial Discrimination in Higher Education, 1961*, as reported in *The New York Times*, January 16, 1961.
[31] Margaret Price, *The Negro and the Ballot*, pp. 15–17.
[32] H. D. Price, *The Negro and Southern Politics: A Chapter of Florida History* (New York: New York University Press, 1957), p. 33.
[33] *Ibid.*, p. 106.
[34] Ernest Q. Campbell and Thomas F. Pettigrew, *Christians in Racial Crisis: A Study of Little Rock's Ministry* (Washington, D.C.: Public Affairs Press, 1959).

not only by the community-at-large but by their own congregations, and by the ministers of the sect churches as well. Denominational executives, while often integrationists in their attitudes, were inclined to give greater or at least equal weight to what amounted to a contradictory value, namely, the maintenance of congregational harmony. The desire to keep the congregational peace also moved the ministers themselves, inducing some to keep silent, others eventually to give up the hope of being able to fight their cause through. Despite the difficulties, a small handful of ministers continued to make their views manifest out of personal conviction, only to be confronted with economic pressures, or in some cases with transfer to parishes outside the South.[35]

Negro Reaction to the Crisis

To many white Americans the most surprising consequence of the new situation has been the reaction of the Negroes. Their surprise arises from long-held illusions concerning the real feelings and attitudes of Negroes in regard to discrimination and segregation. While there was an awareness that educated Negroes were discontented with their status,[36] it appeared to many white people that the Negro masses had resigned themselves to minority status and had worked out a reasonably contented way of life on this basis. Thus, while it would be expected that the school case decision would greatly encourage Negroes, whites were unprepared for the great outpouring of concerted action in their own behalf which Negroes North and South have manifested.

That the real feelings of Negroes in the United States were quite different than the whites thought had been well documented in a survey conducted among soldiers in 1943. A representative sample of all Army troops was asked the question, "If you could talk to the President of the United States, what are the three most important questions you would ask him about the war and your part in it?" After analyzing the replies of the Negro troops in this study, Stouffer and his associates had this to say:

> Four out of five Negroes came forward with at least one question, the same proportion as in a cross section of white soldiers queried at the same time...[H]alf of the Negroes who responded with questions to the President wrote explicit questions or protests about racial discrimination. Of the remaining comments, an unknown proportion were stated in terms which at least implied a racial emphasis but could not clearly be placed in this category on the basis of explicit statement. For this reason, the proportion of men reported as making racial comments is a minimum estimate of the racial response to the question. It will be noted that the question was so worded as to encourage focusing attention on the war and contained no manifest reference to race. While the results must be interpreted in the light of evidence...that the better educated and more critical were more likely to offer free answers, the fact that four-fifths of the Negroes volunteered at least

[35] Quoted from Paul Y. Glock, who reviews Campbell and Pettigrew, *Christians in Racial Crisis* in *Public Opinion Quarterly*, 1960, 24:378. By permission of the Editors.
[36] See Rayford W. Logan, ed. *What the Negro Wants* (Chapel Hill: University of North Carolina Press, 1944).

one response means that a correction for nonrespondents would not alter the picture much. The high incidence of "racial" comments, therefore, is evidence of the Negro soldiers' concern with racial questions.[37]

The wide discrepancy between the way the white people thought the Negro viewed the situation and the way the Negro actually viewed it arose in part from the social distance between the two groups. Whites seldom learned much of the Negroes' feelings. This was further aggravated by the tendency of Negroes when in conversation with white people to conceal their real feelings. Finally, the misinterpretation on the part of white people was in considerable measure a matter of wishful thinking. Many believed what they wanted to believe, which helped to justify the situation.

With the description of the Southern pattern delineated in Chapter 11 in mind, it is easily understandable that induration to minority status prevents many Negroes from active participation in the desegregation movement. Custom, with its associated habits and the experience of intimidation, are still deeply rooted in the personalities of Southern-born Negroes, particularly the older generation. Fighting for their rights is fraught with danger and is otherwise unpleasant. The experience of integration itself is often uncomfortable, which explains why many Negroes fail to exercise new rights even after they have been won. But this was not the prevailing mood in Negro response.

The Supreme Court's decision in the school cases raised the level of aspiration of American Negroes to new heights. For the first time since the Southern Reconstruction, younger Negroes began to feel that first-class citizenship was a possibility within their own lifetime. This is the key to understanding what has seemed to many Americans the most "unexpected consequence" deriving from a single event—the school decision—the previously unparalleled amount of united action among American Negroes themselves to press the advantage which the more favorable social climate presented. For an increasing number of American Negroes, "Uncle Tom" was now dead.[38] This prevailing mood has been demonstrated in various protest movements to which we now turn.

THE MONTGOMERY BUS PROTEST   "Jim Crow" laws as applied to public transportation have always been a major source of irritation to the colored minority. Aside from the principle involved, they have been a practical inconvenience, heightened by the fact that Negroes use public transportation more than whites. The practice promotes inefficiency and is costly. It is therefore not surprising that a Negro challenge on this point should be one of the next steps.

As is often the case in such a situation, the precise time and the particular

---

[37] Stouffer, *et al.*, *The American Soldier*, pp. 503–504. By permission of publishers, Princeton University Press. Among the white troops asked the same question, there were no questions listed pertaining to racial discrimination.
[38] The name "Uncle Tom" has long been used among Negroes to designate those Negro leaders who have placated whites by not challenging the segregation system and thus strengthen the accommodative relationship while hindering attempts at social change.

place resulted from a fortuitous incident, in this instance in Montgomery, Alabama, in 1955. Montgomery's "Jim Crow" regulations were more than ordinarily cumbersome. Negroes were required to enter the front door of the bus, pay their fare, then disembark and go to the rear door to re-enter, and sit in a rear section.[39]

On December 1, 1955, a Negro woman refused to "move back" on a crowded bus so that a white woman could have her seat. For this the bus driver had her arrested. The Negro community of Montgomery reacted by organizing a boycott of the buses. The Negroes walked or arranged car pools. The movement was led by the Montgomery Improvement Association, formed for the purpose. The leader of the organization was the hitherto unknown Reverend Martin Luther King, Jr., who, as a result of his role in the protest movement, emerged as a nationally recognized Negro leader. A remarkable development in this affair was the practically unanimous and well-disciplined cooperation of the Negroes of the city. At the outset, the M.I.A. made the modest demand for a "first come, first served" procedure in bus seating, the Negroes to start from the rear, the whites from the front. Since this did not challenge the Jim Crow principle directly, the National Association for the Advancement of Colored People would not lend its assistance. However, when this modest demand was rejected, the M.I.A. adopted the N.A.A.C.P. viewpoint, calling for complete integration, and received the national organization's support.

The bus boycott continued for many months at great loss to the local bus companies, while a legal case was carried finally to the United States Supreme Court. On November 14, 1956, this Court upheld a previous district court decision declaring the transportation segregation laws of the State of Alabama unconstitutional. On December 21, 1956, integrated buses rolled down the streets of Montgomery for the first time, with Dr. King and other M.I.A. leaders sitting up front.

THE "SIT-INS" A new challenge to the caste system arose in 1960 in the form of "Sit-Ins." We have noted that the etiquette of the caste system prohibited whites and Negroes from eating together seated at the same table. Increasingly, large merchandizing establishments, especially of the chain store variety, have installed lunch counters as part of their business. No objections were forthcoming to Negroes shopping in such places; on the contrary, their patronage was welcomed. In deference to local custom, however, these stores adhered to the practice of not serving Negroes at their lunch counters. Early in 1960, Negro students in Rock Hill, South Carolina, sat down at a local store lunch counter and requested service, which was refused. This began the "sit-in" movement, which spread to other Southern cities. The management of the stores reacted at first by refusing service to Negroes and sometimes closed their counter

[39] See L. D. Reddick, *Crusader Without Violence: A Biography of Martin Luther King, Jr.* (New York: Harper & Brothers, 1959) Chs. 8, 9, and 10, for an account of the Montgomery bus protest movement.

service at the appearance of a Negro. Here and there "sit-inners" were arrested, and often high bails were set. Groups of white youths frequently gathered to jeer at the "sit-inners" and occasional physical abuse was used against them. On the other hand, some white Southern students joined in the sit-ins.

The movement caught the imagination of Northern college students, both white and Negro, who indicated their support by picketing the Northern branch stores of the national chains involved. These pressures and the Negro students' persistence led to a sweeping victory. Within a year, most of the Southern branch stores were ordered by their top management to serve Negro customers on the same basis as whites. Following the first such changeover, later ones tended to be put into effect without public announcement in order to avoid undue publicity or incidents.

Negro activity in the struggle for desegregation was marked by spontaneity, discipline, and, until recently, nonviolent techniques. While the Negro movements described above were aided by organizations once they were started, the origin of these and similar movements has often been in spontaneous acts by single individuals. Perhaps the most striking characteristic has been the orderliness maintained by Negroes in their various protest movements. News and television pictures of incidents arising in these protests usually show the whites in a most unfavorable light by comparison with the Negroes. The aid and training given the student "sit-inners" by organizations such as the Congress of Racial Equality (CORE) helped account for the discipline maintained. The widespread adoption of the techniques of passive resistance has been influenced by the leadership given by clergymen such as Dr. King, and laity motivated by Christian pacifism.[40]

These activities also reflect the increasing impatience of younger and more educated Negroes with the slowness of the integration process, and with what they feel is the too-conservative leadership of the National Association for the Advancement of Colored People. This is well illustrated in the Freedom Rider Movement.

THE FREEDOM RIDERS   In May, 1961, a group of Northerners of both races decided to test the extent to which certain Southern cities had complied or would comply with court rulings that segregation in the public facilities provided for passengers in interstate commerce was illegal. As the riders proceeded farther south they met with increasing resistance. Violence broke out in Alabama cities, culminating in a race riot in Montgomery. Finding evidence that the Montgomery officials had not attempted to protect the riders from white violence, Attorney General Robert F. Kennedy ordered federal marshals into the city, to remain until the immediate tension was abated. The freedom riders proceeded on to Mississippi, stopping in Jackson, where they were promptly arrested when they ignored police orders to leave a white waiting room. Despite the request by federal authorities to let matters "cool off," other, similar rides

[40] Reddick, *Crusader Without Violence*, pp. 133–135.

took place through various areas of the South, meeting with varying degrees of interference.[41]

Further Extraregional Pressures: Civil Rights Legislation

The next important development in the Southern conflict came from outside the region—from Congress and the Attorney General's office.

FEDERAL ACTION ON VOTING While the federal courts were continuing to issue orders of desegregation, the Congress of the United States made no supplementary moves to further the desegregation process until 1957, when the first Civil Rights Act for many years was passed.[42] Its main provisions were (1) to authorize the establishment of a Commission of Civil Rights, whose duties were: to study the entire problem, including specifically denials of the right to vote; to collect information concerning legal developments denying equal protection of the laws; and to appraise the laws and policies of the federal government with respect to equal protection, (2) to empower the Attorney General to seek court injunctions against interference with the voting rights of any individual, and (3) to establish a Civil Rights Division in the Department of Justice.

The Commission found that in 1956 only about 25 percent of the nearly five million Negroes of voting age as of the 1950 Census were registered, in contrast to 60 percent of voting-age whites. Further analysis showed relatively greater Negro registration in the large Southern cities such as Atlanta, Miami, and New Orleans, and from 5 percent to none at all in rural counties, where Negroes constitute a large proportion of the population.

The fact that the Commission waited five months before a single complaint was forwarded to it is strong testimony to the influence of the intimidation implicit in the Southern segregation system. Complaints finally came, first from Alabama and Louisiana. In the hearings held in these states, local authorities tried to resist the purpose of the Commission by refusing to testify on the basis of state law, and adopted other obstructive procedures.[43] The hearings amply documented registration discrimination against Negroes. But the Commission found that the federal government faced difficulties in prosecuting violations.

> The history of voting in the United States shows, and the experience of this commission has confirmed, that where there is a will and opportunity to discriminate against certain potential voters, ways to discriminate will be found. The burden of litigation involved in acting against each new evasion.... county by county, and registrar by registrar, would be immense. Nor is there any presently available effective remedy for a situation where the registrars simply resign.

[41] See *Report on Freedom Riders* (Atlanta, Ga.: Southern Regional Council, 1961).
[42] Students of the realities of politics and government in the United States will know how the Southern Congressional representation has special means at its command to block any legislation dealing with racial discrimination, for example, chairmanships of key congressional committees acquired through seniority.
[43] "With Liberty and Justice for All," an abridgement of the *Report of the United States Civil Rights Commission*, 1959, Chs. 4–5.

If any state were to pass forthrightly a law declaring colored citizens ineligible to vote, the Supreme Court would strike it down forthwith as in flagrant violation of the Fifteenth Amendment. The trouble, however, comes not from the discriminatory laws, but from the discriminatory application and administration of apparently nondiscriminatory laws.[44]

Reluctant Compliance

From roughly 1960 on Southern white reaction has taken the form of reluctant minimum compliance to federal law and attempting various forms of delay to put off desegregation as long as possible. Aside from the more publicized events numerous instances of desegregation take place without publicity as the following illustrates.

> Greenville, South Carolina, had separate branch library buildings for whites and Negroes. In the spring of 1960, some local Negro ministers and Negro high school students entered the white branch for service and were arrested. When the case was appealed, the library trustees and the city council closed the library. Subsequent decision by a federal court made it clear that the library must be operated on a nonsegregated basis. Two weeks later the trustees decided to open on an integrated basis but with the reading tables to be segregated by sex. While Negroes continue to use the Negro branch, a moderate number of them now make use of the former white branch because of its superior holdings. The sex segregation of tables is no longer maintained.[45]

Desegregation has generally occurred in "piecemeal" fashion—that is, by a particular desegregation in a particular locality. It is significant that there have been few instances in the Deep South where the appropriate white authorities initiated a specific desegregation. Change in the pattern in race relations has occurred typically in this manner: (1) Negroes have challenged a specific form of desegregation either by requesting that it be abolished or by deliberately violating a local law for the purpose of testing its legality. (2) White authorities then have denied the requests or arrested and found the Negroes guilty. (3) The Negroes, often with the aid of interested organizations, have carried cases to court, preferably and eventually to a federal district court. (4) When faced with a court order to desegregate, white authority has either closed the public facility or reluctantly complied. The pace of desegregation has been slowed by the failure of white authority to take the initiative in instituting voluntary desegregation. More recently white initiative has been spurred by the threat by a Negro or other organization to take a case to court, or the threat of federal intervention.

Strengthening the trend toward compliance are certain consequences of the increased tension and conflict which affect the region adversely: [46] (1) Un-

---

[44] *Ibid.*, p. 88.

[45] We are indebted to Mr. Charles Busha, a library intern in Greenville at the time of the incident, for this account.

[46] See *The Price We Pay*, prepared by Barbara Patterson and other staff members of the Southern Regional Council and the Anti-Defamation League, for extensive examples of the various costs of discrimination, particularly to the South.

favorable economic effects have been felt. The South loses national conventions because the cities are unable to guarantee nondiscriminatory treatment of Negro members. Certain businesses otherwise disposed to locate in the South are waiting until the racial atmosphere is clearer. (2) The education of whites as well as Negroes has been seriously disturbed. Southern universities have lost many faculty members and find difficulties recruiting new ones. (3) Southern politicians with aspirations for public office have found that the segregationist label, necessary for election in the South, is often a disqualifying mark outside the region.

Current Trends and Prospects

By "current" is meant the 1960 decade to date. Since, as seen in Chapter 15 the crisis in race relations is now clearly national rather than regional, some observations pertinent to the South are dealt with further in that connection. Here we shall deal with the following six main trends. (1) Negro welfare has continued to improve. (2) Substantial decline in segregation in the *public* sectors of community life continues. (3) Racial tension and violence have increased. (4) Southern white dominance remains essentially intact. (5) The Negro challenge has been slowed down. (6) The prospect for some years ahead is continuous overt racial conflict.

Negro Welfare

Along with the nation as a whole and American Negroes generally, the welfare of Negroes in the South has improved. On some indicants of welfare Negroes seem to be closing the disadvantageous gap between them and the white population; on others their relative gain is in doubt; but on all main indicants the gap remains wide. As to their economic situation here are some examples: "Poverty among Negroes in the South is about three times more prevalent than in the rest of the country." [47] A special study of the life time earnings of factory workers showed the comparative regional ratio for Negroes versus whites to be the lowest in the South. [48]

As to occupational distribution, the only outstanding difference in the South in 1960 was the lesser employment of Negro males in the clerical field. [49] Since then according to Elaine Burgess occupational advances by Negroes in the South have been slowing down. She writes, "the majority of Negroes remain at the lower levels of the occupational ladder, making them particularly susceptible to unemployment and other problems created by automation and technology." [50] Hill likewise finds that despite the South's great industrial development "a most disturbing aspect of the rapid growth of manufacturing facilities has been the

[47] Andrew F. Brimmer, "The Negro in the National Economy," Ch. 5 in Davis, p. 263.
[48] *Ibid.*, p. 261.
[49] Eli Ginsberg and Dale Hiestand, *The American Negro Reference Book*, p. 214.
[50] Elaine Burgess, in John C. McKinney and Edgar T. Thompson, *The South in Continuity and Change* (Durham, N.C.: Duke University Press, 1965), p. 350.

serious inability of the Negro worker to register significant gains in the new Southern industrial economy." [51]

Both the education and health of Southern Negroes has improved since 1940, but the wide disadvantageous gap compared with whites has not been closed. In some rural areas, Negro health and welfare has deteriorated.[52] A team of physicians made a special investigation of a sample of school children in the Delta area of Mississippi in May, 1967, and reported much hunger and disease among them.[53] Many were not receiving any government aid partly because Mississippi failed to take advantage of all possible federal funds.[54]

Decline in Discrimination and Segregation

Desegregation in the public sectors of Southern community life continues at an uneven pace from locality to locality.[55]

EMPLOYMENT   The erratic pattern of desegregation is seen in the South from Atlanta, where some movement of Negroes into minor "white collar" positions has begun, to Winterville, North Carolina, where of the high-school graduates in 1966, none found work in North Carolina itself above the menial level.[56] While the Civil Rights Act of 1964 prohibits discrimination by unions and bars segregated locals, Hill marshalls much documentary evidence that employment discrimination on the part of employers, unions, state government, and even the federal government still existed in the mid-sixties in the South.[57]

VOTING   Registration of and voting by Negroes has continued to increase, with local white resistance taking the forms of legal subterfuge, economic reprisal, and intimidation, more particularly outside the large cities of the region. The Civil Rights Bills of 1960, 1964, and 1965 added further provisions to overcome the legal subterfuges.[58] An important feature was to give the federal

[51] Herbert Hill, "Racial Inequality in Employment: Patterns of Discrimination," *The Annals of the American Academy of Political and Social Science,* Vol. 357, Jan. 1965, p. 39. Article reprinted in Barron, *Minorities in a Changing World,* pp. 223–248.

[52] See Rashi Fein, "An Economic and Social Profile of the Negro American," in *The Negro American* (Boston: Houghton Mifflin, 1966), p. 9. Most of the articles in this volume which we cite extensively were originally published by *Daedalus,* Fall 1965, Winter 1966. With some additions and some alteration, Houghton Mifflin Co., jointly with *Daedalus,* published these articles in book form under the editorship of Talcott Parsons and Kenneth B. Clark, with a foreword by Lyndon B. Johnson in 1966. We gratefully acknowledge the permission to quote from this volume by the editors of *Daedalus.* References hereafter will be to *The Negro American.*

[53] See Walter Rugaber, "The Delta: Poverty Is a Way of Life," reported in *The New York Times,* July 27, 1967, pp. 1, 16.

[54] Writing in the *New York Times,* Aug. 6, 1967, p. 60, Joseph Loftus reports that 21 states forfeited 1.8 million dollars a year in federal aid to families with children. Of these forfeiting states, all but eight are Southern.

[55] See Gene Roberts, "Integration in the South: Erratic Pattern," *The New York Times,* May 29, 1967, pp. 1 and 14 for a comprehensive review.

[56] *Ibid.*

[57] Herbert Hill, in Barron, pp. 221–248.

[58] See Caroline B. Rose, "Negro Representation and Voting in the South," in Rose and Rose, *Minority Problems* (New York: Harper & Row, 1965), pp. 205–209.

government authority to send special examiners to take over registration of Negroes in certain areas if necessary. However, hesitancy on the part of the federal government to exercise this new right and hesitancy on the part of Negroes to exercise it have limited the rise in both registration and actual voting. Between 1960 and 1966 the percentage of eligible Southern Negroes registered rose from 28 to 52.8.[59]

This increasing participation of Southern Negroes has already produced results. White politicians have begun to woo the Negro vote and in local areas where Negroes outnumber whites, an occasional Negro candidate wins office. In 1965, Macon County, Alabama, elected the first Negro sheriff. Governor Lester Maddox of Georgia, who formerly closed his restaurant rather than obey court orders to integrate, deals with a legislature with several Negro representatives. Even in Mississippi about 65 Negro candidates were campaigning in local primaries in the summer of 1967; and though the seven white candidates for gubernatorial nomination were avowed segregationists, only one of them made white supremacy a major issue.[60]

PUBLIC FACILITIES   The Civil Rights Act of 1964 made racial discrimination in places of public accommodation operated as a business illegal and its constitutionality was upheld by the Supreme Court (December 1964, 379 U.S. 241). The Act also barred further prosecution in the case of those arrested previously in activity aimed at securing these rights. In 1955 the Interstate Commerce Commission had ordered an end to passenger segregation on eleven Southern interstate railroads, but it took tests by civil rights groups to actually get discrimination eliminated in this field.

PROTECTION AGAINST VIOLENCE AND UNFAIR CRIMINAL PRACTICES   Laws protecting all persons living in the United States against such treatment have long been on the statute books. The difficulty in the nation, and in the South, in particular, has been the failure of local officials to enforce them and of Negroes to be fearful of suing against illegality in law enforcement. This subject is so interwoven with violence that we will discuss it further under the next heading.

Increased Tension and Violence

It is inevitable that in a period of heightened interracial conflict tension and violence should reach high levels. Abusive conduct of individual or small groups of white Southerners toward individual Negroes or their neighborhoods has been a commonplace feature of Southern life. Whether this sort of abusive behavior has increased or decreased is hard to measure. One index of the current increase of violence is that from 1955 through June, 1966, 108 persons are known to have been killed in race-related incidents.[61] An important difference

[59] "Voting in the South," *Southern Regional Council Report,* 1967.
[60] See Walter Rugaber in *The New York Times,* Aug. 9, 1967, p. 23.
[61] "Violence," *New South,* November, 1965, and a 1966 supplement, Southern Regional Council, Atlanta, Georgia.

developing in the current crisis has been the direction of violence against whites who participate in civil rights activity, several of whom are included in the killings noted above.[62] Also different in the current situation has been changes in the modes of violence. The earlier lynching has been repaced by shooting and rock-throwing and bombing of Negro homes.

The Southern Regional Council's reports also indicate that the number of convictions against whites for this illegal conduct has remained low. Indictments are rare; and convictions are few. However, the trend is changing. The white man pleading guilty to the shooting of James Meredith in June, 1966, was sentenced to three to five years in prison, which was the highest sentence yet given a white assailant in racially connected murders or attempted murders in ten years. There is also a tendency in serious cases of violence against Negroes to indict and try the white assailant on a lesser charge. "One of the white boys who killed the Negro boy on a bicycle has been convicted by an all-white jury of second degree manslaughter and sentenced to prison for seven months." [63] Negroes have been able sometimes to get convictions reversed on the grounds that members of their race have been until recently systematically barred from jury duty.

A landmark in the history of Mississippi justice occurred in October 1967, when an all-white Neshoba County jury presided over by a Mississippi-born Federal judge, found seven out of fifteen white Mississippians guilty of participating in a plot which had resulted in the death of three civil rights workers in 1964. One of the convicted defendants was the chief deputy sheriff of the county. At first the jury reported itself deadlocked but were "persuaded" by the judge to try again to reach a verdict.

Pace of Civil Rights Activity

In the early 1960's, hundreds of civil rights workers—white and Negro—coming mostly from outside the region, and including representatives of organizations and volunteers, engaged in a wide assortment of activities of a protest nature. In mid-decade this extensive activity greatly decreased so that the pace of extraregional pressure against the South markedly declined. This does not mean that further challenge to dominance and increasing desegregation has been ceasing. The momentum of the earlier thrust carries over; the pressure from federal courts and the federal government agencies continues, if somewhat muted; civil rights organizations still push for more equality; Southern Negroes, often college youth, still engage in demonstrations; and unorganized racial disorderly melees occur from time to time. Reference to Table 15–1 shows that

[62] See Jack Mendelson, *The Martyrs* (New York: Harper & Row, 1966) for an account of sixteen who were killed in the Southern interracial conflict, including several white persons.
[63] Constance B. Motley, *The American Negro Reference Book,* p. 516.

six of the thirty-one riots reported up to mid August for the year 1967 were in Southern cities.

Southern White Dominance Intact

Despite the foregoing account of Negro gains, the biracial—white dominant and Negro subordinate—character of social organization and life in the South still remains essentially intact. As Blumer has put it, the inner core of the color line persists.

> It is a serious mistake, however, to regard the achievement by Negroes of civil rights, as presently defined, as equivalent to removing the color line.... The contested area of civil rights is, as previously stated, but the outer band of the color line. Inside of it lies the crucial area of economic subordination and opportunity restriction—an area of debarment of Negroes which is exceedingly tough because it is highly complicated by private and quasi-private property rights, managerial rights, and organizational rights. Still further inside of the color line are the varied circles of private association from which the Negro is grossly excluded. Thus, the successful achievement of civil rights merely peels off, so to speak, the outer layer of the color line. By itself, it does not alter significantly the social positions of the two racial groups. It raises somewhat the position of the Negro on the dominance-subordination axis but leaves this axis of relationship essentially intact.[64]

Support for Blumer's assessment comes from the *Newsweek* polls of 1963 and 1966 which show little change in the attitudes of white Southerners during this interval. In 1966, nearly half of the Southern white sample still objected to even public integration in having Negroes sit beside them in a restaurant, a movie, or on a bus. In closer contact 69 percent claimed unwillingness to have a Negro family move into their neighborhood, and over 90 percent would object if a teenage white child dated a Negro, or if a close friend or relative married a Negro.[65]

The Prospect: Continuous Overt Racial Conflict

Previous discussion has indicated that Negroes in the South are already more integrated in fact than white Southerners want them to be. How do Negroes feel about their increasing, if limited, gains? Of this Blumer writes:

> That the satisfaction of demands for civil rights will neither dissolve the color line nor lessen the struggle waged against it can be appreciated further by recognizing how the struggle for civil rights has intensified racial consciousness. Such

[64] Herbert Blumer, *The South in Continuity and Change,* pp. 329–330.
[65] "Crisis of Color '66," *Newsweek,* Aug. 22, 1966, p .28. We wish the *Newsweek* pollsters had included a question to indicate white attitudes toward working alongside Negroes at the same kind of job and at equal pay.

intensification of racial consciousness has been particularly pronounced in the case of the Negro. The struggle has released, aroused, and mobilized the feelings of bitterness and resentment which Negroes experience as a result of their objectionable social position. Their attitudes, even though largely concealed, have hardened against the whites as a group—against "the Man." Evidence of this may be seen in their increased militancy, in their disparagement of "Uncle Tom" types in their own ranks, in the pressure on their leaders to take a more decisive and militant posture, and in an increasing suspicion of whites extending even to liberal sympathizers. The struggle for civil rights is leading Negroes to a renewed assessment of their disadvantaged social status, bringing into sharper focus the illegality and injustice of their social position, making them chafe under the seeming insensitivity of whites to their plight, and with their increased sense of common identity making them writhe with bitterness over publicized instances of wanton indignity and cruelty occurring in the resistance of whites. They have become increasingly sensitive and touchy with regard to the intentions of whites. To sum up, we are presented with the seemingly anomalous situation in which the struggle for civil rights, even as it moves toward achievement, intensifies the Negroes' sense of his disadvantaged position and reinforces his feelings that white society is lined up against him." [66]

Given the reciprocal white and Negro positions just presented, it is inevitable that interracial conflict with seriously disturbing consequences faces the South and the nation for some years ahead. Writing more particularly, but not exclusively, of the South, Killian and Gregg conclude: "There is no easy way out. The battle has been joined. The question is whether the conflict will rend the nation irreparably or draw its racially separated parts together in some yet unforeseeable future." [67]

Topics for Projects and Discussion

1. Why is it that in time of war the situation of minorities (other than those of enemy origin) tends to improve?
2. Assuming it practically unfeasible and attitudinally difficult for a Southern community which has not yet really desegregated its school system, what step-by-step plan aimed at full integration would you suggest? Why?
3. Expand the discussion of the effects of the general social forces on Negro-white relations beyond the brief points made in the chapter. What other social forces might have been added?
4. If you are a Northerner who has traveled in the South, cite any impression you derived about the Southern racial system. If you are a Southerner who has traveled outside the region cite any reactions you had of Negro-white relations in the areas visited.
5. Do you think many Americans view the racial situation as having such serious possibilities as that stated by Killian and Gregg in the last sentence of the chapter?

[66] Herbert Blumer, *The South in Continuity and Change,* pp. 330–331.
[67] Lewis Killian and Charles Gregg, *Racial Crisis in America* (Englewood Cliffs, N.J.: Prentice-Hall, 1964), p. 144.

Suggested Reading

Blumer, Herbert. "The Future of the Color Line," Ch. 15, in John C. McKinney and Edgar T. Thompson, eds., *The South in Continuity and Change.* Durham, North Carolina: Duke University Press.

A penetrating and hard-hitting analysis of the Southern racial scene.

Fishman, Jacob R., and Solomon, Frederic. "Youth and Social Action: Perspectives on the Student Sit-In Movement," *American Journal of Orthopsychiatry,* 33, 1963, pp. 872–882.

Analyzes the reasons why Negro young people participate in nonviolent demonstrations.

Griffin, John Howard. *Black Like Me.* New York: Signet Books, The New American Library, 1960.

The story of the experiences and feelings of a white man in the Deep South who altered his physical appearance to "pass" as a Negro.

Patrick, Rembert W. "The Deep South, Past and Present," in Robert Highshaw, ed., *The Deep South in Transformation.* University, Alabama: University of Alabama Press, 1964, pp. 111–134.

A Southern historian deals with the myths and realities of Southern history in relation to race relations.

Sarratt, Reed. *The Ordeal of Desegregation: The First Decade.* New York: Harper & Row, 1966.

Traces the various public reactions to the Southern school desegregation process and the causes of slow progress; projects the probable future in this movement.

Thompson, Daniel C. *Negro Leadership Class.* Englewood Cliffs, New Jersey: Prentice-Hall, 1963.

A discerning analysis of the means by which various types of Negro leaders operate under the Southern biracial system as studied in New Orleans.

14

The Decline of Dominance:
In the North

Following World War II, the pattern of Negro-white relations in the North resumed much of its prewar character; but the trend toward increasing acceptance of Negroes in the public sectors was slightly accelerated up to the widespread Negro revolt in the 1960's. The crisis precipitated in the South by the school decision did not immediately present any special challenge to the rest of the nation. Polls showed that Northerners approved of the decision and many Northerners were critical of the Southern resistance to the various desegregation court rulings. But it should not be overlooked that what the South was being ordered to do was accord Negroes the civil rights which for the most part the white North generally agreed in principle were due the Negroes despite extensive failure to put principle into practice. *Official* segregation in schools, and discrimination in voting and office-holding had long ceased. Some unofficial discrimination still existed in school assignments, more extensively in occupations and public accommodations, and very strongly in housing. The trend toward a decline in dominance was supported by the net effect of the social forces previously outlined. It was occasionally further supported by state and local antidiscrimination laws with special enforcement agencies. Discrimination was here and there challenged by individual Negroes or local groups ofttimes successfully and ofttimes not. This sort of piecemeal process was whittling away at discrimination in public and civic life in the absence of much direct action. But the rising aspirations of the Negro population precipitated more direct challenge in the form of both organized and unorganized revolt. For this the North was clearly not prepared.

In describing and analyzing this changing situation in the North we shall organize our discussion around four main phases: (1) The continued existence of the Negro subcommunity and the continued discriminatory status bestowed on its members; (2) the "Negro Revolt"; (3) the reaction of the white North to the Negro revolt; and (4) the current trends and prospects. This chapter will deal with the first phase, and the following chapter with the remaining phases.

Segregation and the Negro Community

That the social structure of the Negro community in the North had not fundamentally changed from that depicted by Drake and Cayton for Chicago in the 1940's (see Chapter 12) is attested by Grodzins' study of Pittsburgh in the 1950's. The mass media portrayals of the situation in the 1960's show little fundamental change in the structure of the Negro subcommunity from that summed up by Grodzins thus: "The picture for the future is clear enough: Large non-white concentrations (in a few cases numerical majorities) in the principal cities; large white majorities, with scattered Negro enclaves in their suburbs." [1]

Among the economic consequences of this phenomenon, Grodzins notes the decline of parts of the central city's business activity and associated values. The replacement of higher quality stores and amusement places with all-night jewelry auctions and hamburger stands is characteristic notably of sections of Chicago, Boston, and Los Angeles. While other factors contribute to this trend, minority concentrations certainly reinforce it.

Grodzins found these social consequences following from metropolitan segregation: (1) The spreading of the slums. Given limited space for a growing population, relatively low incomes, and disproportionally higher rents for substandard dwellings, overcrowding continued to be inevitable. Slum areas tend to be augmented by newcomers adjusting to a new environment. Thus the high rates of social pathologies characteristically associated with the above conditions may be expected to continue or increase. (2) Interracial conflict. It has been generally found that interracial conflict of the more explosive sort tends to occur along the boundary areas where the dominant race residents are trying to stem minority invasion. (3) Increased social isolation of Negroes from whites. Within the black belt, "hundreds of thousands of Negroes live, eat, shop, work, play and die in a completely Negro world with little or no contact with other people." [2] This statement appears to us to be too sharply drawn, particularly by including work with other phases of isolation. In fact, Grodzins refers to some participation of Negroes in mixed labor unions, some mixed blocks where friendly interracial neighborliness prevails, and a few newly formed interracial church congregations. Nevertheless, "the larger evidence is not that of integration nor intracommunity social gains. Rather it is in the direction of more uncompromising segregation and larger Negro slums." [3] Finally, these large Negro concentrations have political consequences. Negroes are in a position to use their increasing political power to gain advantages for their group, as witness the increasing number of Negro officeholders. There is always the disturbing possibility of sharpened political conflict along race lines in the city proper as the nonwhites

[1] Morton Grodzins, *The Metropolitan Area as a Racial Problem* (Pittsburgh: University of Pittsburgh Press, 1958).
[2] *Ibid.*, p. 11.
[3] *Ibid.*, p. 12.

threaten to become a majority. Similarly, there is potential political conflict between the Negro-dominated city proper and the white-dominated suburbs, an old type of political conflict in the United States, acerbated by the consciousness of racial difference.

Discrimination in Housing

Since it appears that discrimination in housing constitutes the key factor in blocking integration let us deal with it in more detail. In large cities with substantial Negro populations, the residential distribution of Negro people tends to follow this pattern: (1) There is a main Negro area—Harlem, for example— not far from the central business district, where a large part of the population dwells and major businesses and recreational enterprises catering to Negroes are located. (2) There are other smaller pockets of almost exclusive Negro residents, typically sections becoming less desirable for residence. (3) There are some mixed white-Negro areas in the inner core of the metropolitan area where the white people are of lower economic level. (4) Where Negroes have moved to the suburbs, the areas involved tend to become all Negro.

The process by which Negro residential segregation comes about is roughly as follows. Start with a sizable compact Negro area with population growing by births and even more by migration from the South. White resistance makes any movement directly outward or jumping to other low-rent areas difficult. However, some vacancies do occur in these other areas as upwardly-mobile non-Negro families move out. One or two Negro families thus manage to get into a new block or section. Whites, having tried first to prevent this "invasion" and failed, now react in panic and begin to move out rapidly. More Negroes move in, and the section becomes all Negro.[4]

White Reaction to Negroes as Neighbors

Aside from other factors, a substantial amount of concentration of Negroes in the less desirable housing areas would occur because of low income and because few white people seek such low-rent areas. However, there is a growing number of Negro families who could afford better housing but cannot get it.

The *Newsweek* poll of 1966 shows that 46 percent of all whites in their national sample replied that they would object to Negroes as neighbors.[5] Since more Southerners (69 percent) gave this objection, the figure for whites outside the region is considerably less. It is, however, essential to point out that verbal replies to this, in many instances hypothetical, situation are not an adequate measure of how such respondents would behave in an actual situation. Furthermore, such data are obviously no measure of the extent to which whites would or have actually encouraged Negro movement into their area.

[4] See "Where Shall We Live? *Report of the Commission on Race and Housing* (Berkeley and Los Angeles: University of California Press, 1958), Ch. 2.
[5] "Crises of Color, '66," *Newsweek,* Aug. 22, 1966, p. 28.

News accounts are frequent of adverse reactions by white families at the prospect of any Negro family becoming a neighbor. There are cases in which a Negro family after enduring for awhile the unfriendliness of their white neighbors have moved back to a Negro area.

WHITE BELIEFS: MYTH OR FACT   What are the main reasons—beliefs, fears, rationalizations—given by white people for rejecting Negroes as neighbors?

(1) *Deteriorating Property Values*   The belief is widespread that entrance of Negroes into an area inevitably causes property values to decline. This belief does not objectively imply any personal prejudice.

(2) *Negro "Bad" Housekeeping and Disorderly Behavior*   These two closely related beliefs held by whites are part of the long-held stereotype of Negroes as inferior people. They serve as logical reasons for not wanting Negroes as neighbors. Whites who hold these beliefs fear deterioration of the physical appearance and moral climate of their neighborhood.

(3) *Interracial Conflict*   Whites express the fear that there will be inter-racial conflict in which their own safety will be endangered.

(4) *Fear of Inundation*   It is commonly believed that once any Negro family moves into their block, others will follow and the neighborhood will become all Negro. As we shall see, it is this belief which stands as the last barrier to developing racially mixed residential areas.

(5) *Fear of Loss of Status*   A revealing illustration of this feeling on the part of whites is seen in this incident:

> A white woman, commenting on a Negro family's purchase of a house a few doors away, observed that it was a "fine" family, the husband was a surgeon, and she had no personal objection to them whatever. But, she added, people driving by see the little boy playing on the sidewalk. "How are they to know he is a doctor's son?" [6]

The widespread belief of whites that the entrance of nonwhites into a neighborhood will automatically cause deterioration of property values has prompted extensive study of this subject. In an investigation by Laurenti,[7] price changes in property values in areas of seven American cities following the entry of nonwhites were compared with price changes in "control areas" of the same cities over the same periods of time. The main finding was that

> ... during the time period and for the cases studied, the entry of non-whites into previously all-white neighborhoods was much more often associated with price improvement or stability than with price weakening. A corollary and possibly more significant finding is that no single or uniform pattern of non-white influence on property prices could be detected. Rather, what happens to prices when non-

[6] *Report of the Commission on Race and Housing*, p. 18.
[7] Luigi Laurenti, *Property Values and Race* (Berkeley and Los Angeles: University of California Press, 1960).

whites enter a neighborhood seems to depend on a variety of circumstances which, on balance, may influence prices upward or downward or leave them unaffected.[8]

The major variables interacting in these local situations appear to be (1) strength of whites' desires to move out; (2) strength of nonwhites' desires to move in; (3) willingness of whites to purchase property in racially mixed neighborhoods; (4) housing choices open to nonwhites; (5) absolute and relative levels of house prices; (6) absolute and relative purchasing power of nonwhites; (7) state of general business conditions; (8) long-run trend values in areas involved; (9) time.[9] The first three of the above variables are not economic factors at all but sociopsychological. Thus what happens to property values when Negroes enter a new area is basically affected by how whites behave in general and the state of race relations in the community at the time.

From the extensive research of the University of California team on race and housing the following three generalizations emerge: (1) Where whites do not move out en masse, there is often little effect on property values, aside from those which might have taken place because of the changing situation of the areas as a whole. (2) It is after the area begins to reach a point of all-Negro occupancy that the less desirable consequences of overcrowding and downgrading of the area begin to set in. The first Negroes to take advantage of a vacancy in the white area tend to be similar in income, education, habits, and manners to their white neighbors. (3) Interracial conflict is generally less in the areas of mixed occupancy after the initial stages. Interracial conflict is more frequent on the borders of Negro-white areas and at the beginning of the entrance of Negroes in new neighborhoods.[10]

In their more detailed findings Glazer and McEntire stress the extent to which the minority develops a middle class which manifests the approved characteristics of the American middle class in general.[11] Such a development undermines the unfavorable stereotype, which is generally more easily applicable to the lower-class members of any minority. This favors the Japanese, for example, who are now largely middle class and have few new lower-class Japanese coming in. While the Negro middle class is growing, it is still disadvantaged by the continued migration of lower-class Negroes from the South, who serve to reinforce the northern white stereotyped image as pertaining to all Negroes. Glazer and McEntire find difficulty in isolating the role of prejudice for evaluation in the racial housing picture. On the one hand, the point that "the decisive factor in this poor housing is Negro economic weakness and white middle class fears of the deteriorating neighborhoods on Negro entry" leads them to state

[8] *Ibid.,* p. 47.

[9] *Ibid.,* pp. 47–48.

[10] See Nathan Glazer and Davis McEntire, *Studies in Housing and Minority Groups,* and Davis McEntire, *Residence and Race* (Berkeley and Los Angeles: University of California Press, 1960).

[11] *Studies in Housing and Minority Groups,* p. 8.

that "Prejudice in its pure form—that is to say as unreasoning and inflexible antipathy—rarely plays a decisive role in the determination of the housing of minority groups." [12] On the other hand, they state that "it is likely that color alone, serving as an almost unmistakable cue to behavior, plays a dynamic role in the situation. And for this reason changes in the character of the Negro group are likely to have less effect on their housing than real changes in the character of the Mexican or Puerto Rican group." [13]

METHODS OF SEGREGATING NEGROES IN HOUSING   The direct process by which Negroes are kept from moving into white areas involves the real estate and financing businesses. Many realtors will not handle transactions involving the entrance of Negroes into white residential areas. Or there is the reverse phenomenon known as "block busting": when one or two Negro families have managed to move into a white neighborhood, realtors have been known to encourage whites to sell and move quickly before the "inevitable decline in property values" begins, and from then on to show the properties for sale only to Negroes.

In general mortgage-lending institutions have been unwilling or most reluctant to finance Negro housing purchases. For the real estate business, the changeover from a white to a Negro area is highly profitable, although the whole community pays heavily for these private gains.[14] Such practices do not necessarily reflect direct prejudice on the part of the buinessman involved but rather judgment based on his understanding of the prejudices of clientele of dominant status. Nevertheless the result—keeping Negroes isolated—is the same.

An increasing number of states and municipalities have been legislating against *de jure* racial discrimination in housing but enforcement has been lax. An attempt to pass a national act for the same purpose was defeated in Congress in 1966. Experience in the varying degrees of reluctance of local authorities in the enforcement of all civil rights legislation suggests considerable caution in expecting any rapid breakthrough in the sensitive area of housing desegregation. Aside from this legislative action, special attention to other action taking place in this connection is pertinent: (1) public housing, (2) privately developed experiments in interracial housing, and (3) community organization to facilitate harmonious adjustment in areas of mixed occupancy.[15]

Experience in all racial integration in housing indicates that the obstacle to success is the fear by whites of inundation. Polls of white attitudes covering twenty years show an increasing willingness of white people to live in an integrated area.[16] But by an integrated area the respondents do not mean one that

---

[12] *Ibid.,* p. 4.

[13] *Ibid.,* p. 10.

[14] See George and Eunice Grier, *Equality and Beyond: Housing Segregation and the Goals of the Great Society* (Chicago: Quadrangle Books, 1966), pp. 34–35.

[15] See Eunice Grier and George Grier, *Privately Developed Interracial Housing: An Analysis of Experience* (Berkeley and Los Angeles: University of California Press, 1960).

[16] Davis McEntire, *Residence and Race,* p. 81.

is largely Negro. The crucial factor in planning mixed areas is to prevent too many Negroes from entering. While "the tipping point" cannot be defined with precision, it appears to be well below 50 percent Negro. In a private interracial development in Concord Park, in the Philadelphia region, the builders hoped for a Negro proportion of about 20 percent. When forty of the first fifty houses built went to Negroes, the management placed a 45 percent limit on sales to Negroes in an effort to preserve the interracial character of the project.[17] We have here an interesting situation. Quotas are illegal; but only by limiting the number of minority people can the goal of truly integrated areas be pushed forward. The term "benign quota" has emerged in this connection, and is more generally applicable than to housing alone,[18] for example, in schools. In an integrated section of Lakeview, Long Island, Negro residents took the initiative themselves in trying to discourage further Negro purchases in the area.

URBAN REDEVELOPMENT AND NEGRO HOUSING   The housing segregation of Negroes (in varying situations, of other minorities) is inextricably interrelated with metropolitan planning. For example, both the erection of low-cost housing developments and higher-class apartments on the fringes of the slums require the displacement of present occupants, who are frequently Negroes. In any building financed by federal funds, suitable relocation of displaced residents is supposed, by law, to be accomplished before new buildings can start, but when the present occupants are Negroes, finding a new residence is a difficult task. Thus either new developments are delayed or the displaced Negro residents face great hardship.

By no means all the Negro residents of Negro areas favor the reconstruction of areas they inhabit for new housing or for nonresidential purposes. It should be pointed out that the flight of whites from inner areas leaves vacant much housing that is not really slum housing. Many Negro families have been able to buy these buildings, become home owners for the first time and resent having to give them up.[19]

Progress in either providing better homes for Negroes or in integrating Negroes in white areas during the 1960's has been meager compared to the size of the problem. Citing a 1965 report for New York City, Piven and Cloward write, "Not only has the supply of low income units diminished, but segregation has increased."[20] The same authors find little immediate prospects for improvement.

---

[17] *Ibid.,* p. 214.

[18] Dan W. Dodson, "Can Intergroup Quotas Be Benign?" *Journal of Intergroup Relations,* Autumn, 1960. Reprinted in Earl Raab, *American Race Relations Today* (Garden City, N.Y.: Doubleday and Co., 1962), pp. 125–134.

[19] In Newark, New Jersey, a proposal to erect a large medical complex in the heart of its major ghetto prompted a protest to the city government by a committee of Negroes against it. Discussion of the proposed plan and the reactions to it took place from the fall of 1966 and into 1967 prior to the Newark riot of July of that year.

[20] Frances Fox Piven and Richard A. Cloward, "Desegregated Housing," *The New Republic,* Dec. 17, 1966, pp. 17–22. See also George and Eunice Grier, *Equality and Beyond,* especially Chapter 2 on the subject.

"Segregation" in Northern Schools

The Supreme Court school decision had less immediate impact on the North, because with some few exceptions segregated schooling for Negroes as an *official* policy had been abandoned wherever it existed. Nevertheless, the decision prompted review of school districting and assignment practices. Since there remains much *de facto* school segregation arising from housing segregation, changes were made in some communities to promote more mixed enrollments. A new concept, "racial imbalance," arose leading to new policies of pupil assignments. Princeton, New Jersey, went the whole way. All the pupils for specified grades were assigned to the same building. Such a procedure is easier to effect in a small, spatially compact community such as Princeton. The efforts of many communities to achieve racial balance often required "bussing" of some students of both races out of their neighborhood school. Strong pressures, sometimes successful, sometimes not, arose against such policies, because of white resistance, reluctance on the part of some Negro parents to send their younger children far away from their neighborhoods, and the extra cost. In 1964, White Plains, New York, adopted a racial balance plan. It closed a predominately Negro elementary school and started to transport its pupils to white schools in other areas. In October, 1967, the White Plains School Board released an evaluation of pupil achievement over three years. The main findings indicated that both Negro and white students were benefiting. Finally, as long as the current racial concentration continues, pupil assignment to achieve desirable ethnic balance is more difficult to achieve. In the inner core of metropolitan areas it becomes almost impossible.[21]

In New York City the percentage of Negro students rose from 18.2 in 1960 to 29.3 in 1966. During the same period the percentage of Puerto Rican pupils rose fro m13.5 to 20.9, so that 1966 marks the first year in which these two ethnic components combined constituted a majority in the city's schools. Considering the problem of ethnic balance, it is instructive to note that the same report shows that in Manhattan, the Bronx, and Brooklyn—the "inner core" boroughs—the ethnic breakdown for elementary schools shows the combined totals of these two components ranging from around 60 to 75 percent. During the same period, white enrollment, excluding Puerto Ricans, dropped by 17 percent.[22] Other metropolitan areas with a larger proportion of Negro population face even a more difficult similar situation.[23]

Economic Inequality

The economic position of Negroes the nation over has improved since 1940

[21] See Nathan Glazer, "Is Integration Possible in the New York City Schools?" *Journal of Intergroup Relations,* Autumn, 1960.
[22] See the *New York Times,* March 17, 1967, pp. 1, 39 for account of *New York City Board of Education Report.*
[23] See Virgil A. Clift, *The American Negro Reference Book,* pp. 390–393.

as measured by income, employment, and occupational distribution. The unequal gap between Negroes and whites has been somewhat narrowed.

Income

As a group Negroes have gained in absolute income along with the national
trend. The median wage and salary incomes of gainfully employed nonwhite
males expressed in actual purchasing power rose threefold from $995 in 1939
to $3,023 in 1962.[24]

Within the Negro group the trend is toward a wide disparity in income between class levels. Brimmer found that "The middle and upper class groups
are getting richer while the lowest income group is getting poorer." [25] But he
also found that "this relatively broad carpet of prosperity rests heavily on the
labor of multiple wage earners." [26]

Employment

The crude rates of unemployment for nonwhites as compared with whites in
recent years run more than 2 to 1. While in part related to the concentration of
Negroes in the least stable occupations, the relatively higher unemployment rate
was found as late as 1962 at each occupational level.[27] In 1962, the unemployment of nonwhite teenagers [28] was nearly 25 percent which when coupled with
the higher school dropout rate among Negro youth has serious implications with
regard to unrest and delinquency.[29]

A special study by the Department of Labor of Negro employment for the
years 1963 through 1966 showed a rise in Negro employment of slightly over
10 percent while white employment was rising slightly over 7.8 percent. Unemployment among Negroes over this period dropped from 10 percent to 7.3
percent while the unemployment rate of whites was dropping from 5 percent
to 3.3 percent.[30]

Occupational Distribution

From 1940 to 1960, the distribution of Negroes by occupational levels
showed a noticeably higher percentage gain for Negroes compared with whites

[24] Leonard Broom and Norval Glenn, *Transformation of the American Negro* (New York:
Harper & Row), p. 105.
[25] Andrew F. Brimmer, "The Negro in the National Economy," in *The American Negro
Reference Book*, p. 267.
[26] *Ibid.*, p. 266.
[27] Dale L. Hiestand, *Economic Growth and Employment Opportunities for Minorities*
(New York: Columbia University Press, 1964), p. 53.
[28] In many government reports, the data for white are compared with nonwhite. While
the data for nonwhite includes other non-Caucasian people, Negroes comprise around
92 percent of any nonwhite data reported in the 1960's.
[29] Joseph H. Douglass, *The American Negro Reference Book*, p. 345.
[30] Arthur M. Ross, Commissioner, Bureau of Labor Statistics, U.S. Dep't of Labor, "The
Changing Patterns of Negro Employment," *Ebony*, July 1, 1967, p. 39.

at all nonfarm occupation levels except the professional and technical level. Negro women wage earners were still highly concentrated in service work, about 59 percent in 1960 as against 68 percent in 1940.[31] The 1966 distribution of Negro workers by occupational levels and the percentage of change in each category which occurred over the period 1963 to 1966 show that the upward occupational mobility is still continuing but that half of all Negro workers remain at the lower rungs of the occupational ladder. More detailed occupational changes revealed in this special Department of Labor report are indicated by Commissioner Arthur M. Ross as follows:

> Greatest gains were made in occupations in the health and medical field; as salaried workers; as clerical workers; craftsmen and foremen; and durable and nondurable goods operatives. But a comparatively low rate of increase was shown for teachers; partly because of the drop in new housing, an even lower rate was evidenced for carpenters; and increases among the ranks of policemen and firemen (protective service workers) were minimal.[32]

In summary, the economic position of American Negroes in the mid-1960's is put by Broom and Glenn thus:

> Negro Americans are on a treadmill. They must keep gaining on whites in education and occupation simply to stay the same distance behind in income. Undoubtedly, this condition adversely affects Negro morale. Many Negroes find it increasingly difficult to get and keep jobs, and many who manage to remain employed most of the time do not share in the general increase in real income in the United States. While their own economic condition becomes worse or improves slowly, their appetite for a more affluent style of life is whetted by direct observation of increased consumption by other Americans (both white and the growing number of middle-class Negroes) and by increased exposure to the mass media of communication. Their feelings of deprivation increase even if their absolute economic condition improves.[33]

Improvement in the economic position of Negroes requires two things: (1) increased education of Negroes in general and specific training for more skilled positions. In addition to the school integration process, various federal and state programs designed to this end were carried on in the mid-sixties, the success of which has yet to be appraised, and which we will discuss in the final chapter. (2) The second requirement is the increased integration of qualified Negroes into all segments of the occupational structure. How rapidly this will take place depends on how rapidly the prejudices of white employers and workers decline. After a detailed analysis of technical factors influencing Negro employment patterns, Ginsberg and Hiestand conclude that discrimination is the basic reason

[31] United States Department of Labor, *The Economic Situation of Negroes in the United States,* October, 1960, Bulletin S-3.
[32] *Ebony,* July 1, 1967, p. 39.
[33] Leonard Broom and Norval Glenn, *Transformation of the American Negro,* pp. 119–120.

for the unfavorable position of nonwhites.[34] While this trend in increased job integration is proceeding, it is inevitable that there will be a lack of adjustment between the availability of qualified Negroes and the openings which decreasing prejudice will afford. Numerous situations of this sort have already occurred.[35]

An alternative possibility—to encourage increased separate professional and business enterprise does not appear to offer much improvement in the Negro occupational pattern.[36] We saw that much of the earlier development in this field was a function of segregation. Given the present emphasis among Negro leaders on more independent self-reliance by Negroes, apparently more attempts to improve the employment pattern by this route will be made.

Integration in Government and The Armed Services

Along with the many other ways in which government has been a major factor in promoting civil rights for minorities, one of the most immediately gainful has been the trend toward increasing employment of Negroes, and especially pertinent, at higher echelon levels. The appointment of Robert Weaver to the cabinet as Secretary of the Department of Housing and Urban Development in 1965 and of Thurgood Marshall as United States Supreme Court Justice in 1967 are the most honorific new "firsts." [37]

An order from President Harry Truman to begin to integrate the armed forces completely was issued in 1948 and, well before the Vietnam fighting, integration was essentially accomplished, more by the Army than by the other branches of the service. While it could not be expected that all race-related incidents between white and Negro troops, reflecting normative reciprocal race attitudes, could be completely eliminated, or that some discrimination in promotion recommendations by the higher echelon could be obviated, the greater problem existed in achieving equal treatment of Negro servicemen and their families in the communities of the nation having military installations, over which the military had no direct control.

Military service in general and now on its integrated basis offers opportunities to Negro men still greatly denied them in civilian life: steady employment on an equal-scale basis; training in skills; post-service education grants and other benefits; and association with whites on an equal, often comradely basis. For those with more ability and education, the service offers opportunity for upward mobility in rank and pay, and the experience of "commanding" whites of lower ranks.

[34] Ginzberg and Hiestand, *The American Negro Reference Book*, p. 243.
[35] The Urban League in 1964 started a "job bank" program to provide a central listing of Negroes already with higher special training and encouraged employers to utilize this service.
[36] See Andrew F. Brimmer, *The American Negro Reference Book*, pp. 291–334, for an extensive account of Negroes as entrepreneurs.
[37] See Eli Ginzberg and Gale Hiestand, *The American Negro Reference Book*, pp. 225–231, for a more detailed account.

As in all other "pressured" integration, while *de jure* integration could be claimed, some *de facto* discrimination has continued through the Korean War and even in Vietnam but with decreasing degree.[38]

The "carryover" effects of the integration of the armed services in the current Negro challenge remain to be studied. How far has this new experience of white servicemen changed their attitudes, and, more pertinently, developed an interest in doing something to further the current trend when they return to civilian life? How will the integrated service and combat experience effect Negroes as they return to a discriminatory civilian life? That some will exploit their new abilities to improve their personal position within the framework of biracialism is obvious. But how many will utilize their improved position in the civil rights movement remains to be seen. Those Negro ex-servicemen who have acquired leadership experience could be most useful to the movement. Those who join the more militant segments can put their training in the methods of military warfare to effective use in "racial warfare," especially those who gained experience in guerrilla tactics, more suitable for the less powerful combatants.

More broadly still, the fact that a substantial military organization has now become a fixed addition to the institutional structure of American life has raised further problems during this period of overt racial conflict. The selective service draft problem is one example. A disproportionate number of Negroes fail to meet the minimum service requirements but this is more than outweighed by the deferment of higher education students which favors the whites.

Discrimination in Law Enforcement and Justice

That Negroes are discriminated against in all aspects of the administration of law in the South has been amply documented.[39] Outside the region no law supports this inequality and discrimination as to jury service or in court trials and it is not easily pinpointed. The chief area of discrimination in justice pertains to police action. Discrimination is found in both the absence of adequate police protection within the Negro community and the excess of roughness in the handling of Negro suspects or arrested persons. The following excerpt summarizes the latter:

> The problem of police brutality seems to arise in four main contexts. The first involves racially motivated police efforts to enforce "segregation." The second, a not entirely separate category, entails brutality in handling Negro prisoners. The third involves coercion to obtain confessions [now illegal]. The fourth concerns unpremeditated, or spontaneous use of unnecessary force in making arrests. Racialism is necessarily involved in the first; it may or may not be present in the others.[40]

[38] See *Time*, May 26, 1967, "Democracy in the Foxhole," pp. 15–19, for an account of race relations in the armed services, particularly in Vietnam.

[39] See any *Annual Report of the United States Commission on Civil Rights.*

[40] Wallace Mendelson, *Discrimination* (Englewood Cliffs, N.J.: Prentice-Hall, 1962), p. 145. The book is based on the report of the United States Commission on Civil Rights of the first five years of its existence, 1957–1961.

While Mendelson cites more Southern than Northern instances of these types of discrimination, indications of police brutality in Detroit and interviews with inmates of prisons in Pennsylvania and New Jersey are cited.

Given the total situation in Negro-white relations it is inevitable that the police will to some extent discriminate against Negroes. This total situation includes these factors: (1) White people discriminate against Negroes generally; (2) While in democratic theory the administration of justice is equal, in practice it is differentially administered with some degree of inequality related to status. This being generally true even in regard to class status, it is even more bound to be the case where dominant-minority status prevails. Dominant-status people are not apt to be deeply concerned about discriminatory police treatment of minority people, and police practice reflects in the long run the attitudes of the dominants. (3) Generally, white police not only share white prejudice but are, because of recruitment from lower-ranking status levels, apt to be drawn from the segments of the white population where the salience of white prejudice is highest.[41] (4) Negro policemen, as Negroes, are less secure and under pressure to conform to white police practices.

The Negro slum dweller's image of the policeman is not that of a protector but of a punisher. Representing white law in which most Negroes have experienced or witnessed discrimination, the policeman is viewed with hostility. The police and Negroes hold reciprocal hostile images of each other: the police look upon the Negro masses as inclined to be lawbreakers; the Negro masses view white police as prejudiced. Thus it is inevitable that mutual distrust will continue to exist as long as the white community generally treats Negroes as a minority.

The foregoing can stand without special reference to the Negro Revolt. But the revolt has given it increasing significance for at least two reasons. The revolt inevitably heightens the salience of the conflict and the increasing polarization of white versus Negro as "enemies." It is not too difficult to understand that many Negroes in such a conflict situation view *any* arrest of a Negro as a discriminatory act even when the arrest is obviously valid. Furthermore, the revolt situation acerbates the occasion for police-Negro conflict. Both from a strictly legal view and from a police administrative view the boundary line between a legally proper "protest" activity and an illegal one is not always easy to draw. To this may be added the tendency of court interpretations to be currently more fluid and unpredictable, which adds to the perplexity of police authorities.

Awareness of this long-standing vicious circle in police-Negro relations has been heightened by the current Negro revolt. "Thus while serious problems of police mistreatment and violence remain new resources are being employed to deal with them. The developing law, more vigorous action by federal, state, and

---

[41] The status ranking of their occupation and the salaries paid make recruitment from this level inevitable.

local officials, and community training programs all afford promise of significant gains in the administration of justice." [42] The results of police training programs do not yet appear promising.[43] Police and military brutality has been widely alleged by Negro groups in all the riots of the 1960's with varying degrees of factual support. (See Chapter 15.)

Topics for Projects and Discussion

1. Design a questionnaire aimed at discovering the attitudes of Northern white people toward having Negroes as neighbors. If you live near a Northern area with a Negro population, try to find some white people who have had the experience of having Negroes as neighbors and probe them in this connection.
2. Discuss the possibilities and problems involved in a national program designed to accomplish the geographic distribution of Negroes throughout the United States in ten percent proportions, plus or minus.
3. Test the validity of this chapter's discussion of "police brutality" by interviewing a number of policemen and a number of Negro people.
4. Study, at first hand if possible, or through any available second-hand source, what has actually happened in any urban area where either public housing or other urban redevelopment programs have been carried out with the view of determining what problems arose in relation to Negro residents and what happened.
5. Interview a number of men who have served in the armed forces since 1950 to probe their attitudes and experience with reference to Negro-white relations in service units. Design a short questionnaire to use for this purpose. If possible, interview Negro servicemen as well as whites.

Suggested Readings

Clark, Kenneth B. *Dark Ghetto.* New York: Harper & Row, 1965.
> *A penetrating analysis of the social dynamics of the ghetto and the psychological effects on the inhabitants, as revealed in Harlem and other New York ghetto areas.*

Dentler, Robert A. "Barriers to Northern School Segregation," in *The Negro American,* eds., Talcott Parsons and Kenneth B. Clark. Boston: Houghton Mifflin Co., 1966.
> *Describes the problems arising in attempts to provide racial balance in Northern cities, including a comparison of smaller and larger cities.*

Glazer, Nathan and Daniel P. Moynihan. *Beyond the Melting Pot.* Cambridge: The M.I.T. Press and Harvard University Press, 1963.
> *Chapter 1 provides a description and analysis of the Negroes of New York as one of the metropolis's five large ethnic components.*

[42] United States Civil Rights Commission, *Freedom to be Free: A Century of Emancipation* (Washington, D.C., 1963), p. 187.

[43] A recent example is a Police-Community Relations Training Program, sponsored by the Human Rights Commission of Newark, New Jersey, where programs providing for police and civilians from the poorer areas (largely Negro) to interact in small groups for the purpose of creating better mutual understanding were undertaken. Access to the unpublished report on this project strongly supports our analysis of this topic. Ironically, the program ended in June, 1967, before the large-scale rioting in Newark in July of that year.

Johnson, Robert B. "Negro Reactions to Minority Group Status" in *Racial and Ethnic Relations: Selected Readings,* Bernard Siegel, ed. New York: Thomas Y. Crowell, 1966.

>*A notable contribution to understanding how Negroes see themselves and their relations to whites, based on intensive research in a middle-sized, middle-Atlantic community.*

Laurenti, Luigi. *Property Values and Race.* Berkeley and Los Angeles: University of California Press, 1960.

>*An excellent research into the crucial problem of minority housing.*

Lowe, Jeanne R. *Cities in a Race for Time.* New York: Random House, 1967.

>*Analyzes the development of large-scale urban renewal programs in five major cities in the post-World War II period and delineates the problems involved, including the interracial aspects.*

McEntire, Davis. *Residence and Race.* Berkeley and Los Angeles: University of California Press, 1960.

>*The final summary of the extensive research into the housing of minority groups conducted by the author and numerous associates.*

15

Negro Challenge to White Dominance: The Negro Revolt

Let us focus on the nationwide challenge to white dominance carried on in the 1960's. This challenge can be divided into two phases: the civil rights movement and the Negro Revolt, even though the two phases overlap in time. The civil rights phase, primarily legislative as we have seen, began in sustained momentum with the school desegregation decision precipitating the Southern crisis and ultimately bringing about change in race relations in the North. As it began to be clear to Negroes that this civil rights legislation alone would not achieve genuine equality, direct action in the protest form emerged. First carried on with the technique of nonviolence, the protest movement may be viewed both as an attempt to bring the civil rights phase to fruition and as a precursor of the Revolt phase. For some segments of the Negro population, the nonviolent protest phase has been superseded by the Black Power movement, briefly stated as the mobilization of all the potential political and economic power that Negroes themselves can bring to bear to force change. In and of itself the Black Power phase is entirely within the normative process of change characteristic of American history, far more so than the technique of nonviolence. That it carries with it the danger of violence and disorder became obvious in the early sixties and was most dramatically illustrated by destructive rioting.

If the mid-sixties phase of the challenge is to be referred to as a *revolt* [1] it should be so only in a delimited sense. Fortunately, for the maintenance of national order, so far and for the most part, these activities have not been a revolt against the formal political structure of the nation (which in fact supports it), or against the economic system, but a revolt against the normative patterns of white dominance. It is called a *Negro* revolt not only because the goals it seeks are for Negroes but because increasingly its leadership and direction is in Negro hands. Our discussion of this massive challenge will be centered around the following topics: (1) the goals of the Negro challenge; (2) the organization of the challenge: the specific organized groups involved and their techniques of

---

[1] See Louis Lomax, *The Negro Revolt* (New York: Harper & Row, 1962).

action; (3) the reaction of the white community to it; and (4) its current trends and prospects. The chapter will conclude with an extended discussion of the long-range bases for the restabilization of Negro-white relations and call attention to certain particular theoretical implications for the sociology of intergroup relations upon which events of the past fifteen years especially bear.

The Goals of the Negro Challenge

Before the current revolt it might have surprised many white Americans to suggest that the ultimate objectives of the Negro challenge were not wholly clear to Negro Americans themselves. Did they want complete assimilation—a situation where Negroid visibility would be irrelevant either as a basis of social relationships or of cultural characteristics, no more significant than that some gentlemen prefer blondes, others brunettes? Did Negroes want "cultural pluralism"? If so, on what bases would "Negro Culture" rest? Or did American Negroes simply want structural pluralism, that is to continue a Negro "community" but have it and them, as persons, reacted to as equals, otherwise being culturally like the WASP prototype? And in this latter alternative what were the chances whites would accord this equality as long as visibility, communal and/or physiognomic, was present?

One index of the state of mind of Negro leadership as to the ultimate goals is provided by Milton Gordon who sounded out the opinions of the leading Negro organizations at the turn of the 1960 decade, along with other "intergroup" agencies with reference to their pluralistic or assimilationist orientation. He found as follows:

> Of the remaining six agencies—that is, those which expressed little interest in or enthusiasm for cultural pluralism—the major Negro agencies bulked large. This does not mean that they are necessarily opposed to the idea for other groups, nor that they have taken an official position on the matter or would oppose Negroes otherwise inclined, but my inference from the interview materials and published statements is that they do not envisage the retention of a Negro subcommunity with its own institutions as a desirable long-range goal for Negroes in the United States—that is, one to be consciously sought. One official of one of the Negro agencies, when asked about the position of his organization on the question of Negro communality, put it this way: "We would like to see complete freedom of choice exist. We stand very firmly on the distinction between public situations and private relationships. As far as friends and associates are concerned, this is a matter of private likes and dislikes. We don't regard this as susceptible to the operations of law. *We believe, however, that eventually, under equal-status contact, these private mixed associations will take place, and we regard this as desirable when taking place naturally.* [And later] *The logic of our position is obviously anti-insularity—anti-communal;* [however] we assume that there will be a definable Negro group in the foreseeable future" (italics mine).[2]

[2] Milton Gordon, *Assimilation in American Life* (New York: Oxford University Press, 1964), p. 14.

Another available measure of what Negro Americans want is found in the Brink-Harris analysis of the 1963 *Newsweek* nationwide survey.[3] A summary of their findings as to what Negro respondents said they wanted is as follows, set forth in the order of highest frequencies: (1) better jobs and at the same pay whites get; (2) strong preference for working in a mixed job force (7 to 1); (3) by a 7 to 1 margin also they want integrated schools, believing that integration itself has a salutary effect on their children's learning; (4) as to integrated housing, the survey found a majority for it but with more mixed feelings (64 percent in favor); and (5) in a more general sense, Negroes want the *right* to integrate.[4] In the repeat survey by *Newsweek* in 1966, substantially the same picture is found on the above matters.[5] We draw further on the analysis of the 1963 findings on points 4 and 5 above where less clear-cut consensus is found.

With reference to housing many of the minority of Negro respondents who prefer all-Negro neighborhoods do so because they would feel uncomfortable living with whites. Concerning the 64 percent of the whole Negro sample who prefer living in mixed neighborhoods, the authors, Brink and Harris, write, "The reason . . . is not the superior facilities of white neighborhoods, rather, it is the more psychological effect of liberation from the ghetto and the deep felt desire to prove to whites that Negroes aren't as bad as they think." [6]

As to the broader question of integration in general, Brink and Harris conclude: "The next question, and a key one, is: just what does the word 'integration' mean for them? Does it mean a massive outpouring of Negroes from their ghettos into white suburbs, schools, restaurants, social organizations and churches? The Negroes' own answer is that this is not his primary or immediate goal." [7] When asked specifically which is more important to them—equal treatment or a "lot of mixing of the races"—Negro respondents chose equal treatment by a better than eight to one margin. This leads the authors to state: "What he wants now is to be treated as a human being; and part and parcel of this is the *right* to integrate." [8]

The Revolt in Action

Direct civil rights activities have grown into a national revolt without any centralized plan, not comparable to the years of conspiratorial planning which characterizes political revolutions. The regionally delimited aspect of it, perhaps best dated from the Montgomery bus revolt, has already been described in Chapter 13. The revolt has been a pluralistic movement involving many different groups with varying immediate objectives and utilizing different methods of ac-

[3] William Brink and Louis Harris, *The Negro Revolution in America* (New York: Simon and Schuster, 1964).
[4] *Ibid.,* Ch. 10 passim.
[5] *Newsweek Magazine,* "Crisis of Color," August 22, 1966, pp. 21–58.
[6] *The Negro Revolution in America,* p. 161.
[7] *Ibid.,* p. 161.
[8] *Ibid.*

tion. And as with any such movement, conflicts have developed between protest groups and their leaders. But despite this pluralistic character, it is appropriate to give these activities the singular term "the revolt" because there is an underlying unanimity. The immediate verbal response of protest of practically all leading Negro national leaders against the refusal of Congress in 1966 to seat Adam Clayton Powell at the beginning of the 99th Congress attests an underlying spiritual unity. This unanimous support was for the position and not the person involved. The plain fact is that Congressman Powell exercized more power over national affairs than any other American Negro.

The March on Washington, August 28, 1963, may be considered as a formal symbol to white America that the revolt was a determined racial effort. Initiated by A. Philip Randolph and organized by Bayard Rustin, some 250,000 Americans held a day long protest before the Lincoln Memorial, perhaps the largest single demonstration in the nation's history. All Negro organizations (aside from the "separatist" groups) were represented, with a number of white supporting organizations and individual sympathizers joining them. Despite the fears of many Washingtonians, the occasion was extremely orderly. While no direct results can be traced to it, the march served notice to the nation that the revolt was on.

The Leading Organizations

Numerous local civil rights organizations have sprung up with .arying degrees of permanence. But the leading organizations in the Negro challenge are the "old-timers"—the National Association for the Advancement of Colored People (NAACP) and the Urban League—and the "newcomers"—the Congress of Racial Equality (CORE), the Southern Christian Leadership Conference (SCLC) and the Student Nonviolent Coordinating Committee (SNCC). As Clark puts it, "All [the above] civil rights organizations are committed to the full inclusion of the Negro in the economic and political life of America without restriction based on race or color." [9] We include the Black Muslims as the major "separatist" organization.

Having earlier discussed the origin and general program of the NAACP and the Urban League, we shall here deal with their role in the current revolt. As will be recalled, it was the former that fought the successful legal battle for school desegregation, as well as subsequent legal battles involved in the Southern crisis. The rise of the new, more radical, organizations has affected the established ones in several ways: (1) While still retaining the methods of litigation, persuasion, and negotiation as their main techniques, the NAACP and the Urban League have adopted more aggressive policies in response to the militant activities of the newer groups. (2) While sometimes critical of the methods employed by the newer organizations, the traditional agencies have on occasion

---

[9] Kenneth Clark, *The Negro American*, p. 619.

supported and lent assistance to them. (3) The greater militancy of the newer groups has changed the viewpoint of the influential segment of the white community toward the older ones. Whereas before the NAACP and, to a lesser degree, the Urban League had been looked upon as troublemakers, they began to be viewed now as moderates and turned to by white officials for aid in working on racial problems. This greater respectability in white eyes has resulted in increasing contributions from white sources enabling them to expand their activities. The Urban League, for example, increased its local chapters from 63 in 1960 to 73 in 1966, and its national staff almost doubled during 1966.[10] Also in the same year news announcements appeared of large grants from established foundations to both of these organizations.

All three of the newer organizations have been concerned with more direct action and, up to recently, dedicated to the principle of nonviolence; they are less well organized than the older ones, but have achieved significant results.

THE CONGRESS OF RACIAL EQUALITY   CORE antedates the Negro Revolt, having been founded in 1942 in Chicago by people who felt that direct action and demonstrations were needed to supplement the previous sorts of challenge to white dominance. It used the "sit-in" technique in a Chicago restaurant in 1943 and in Palisades Amusement Park, New Jersey, in 1947–48, successfully effecting desegregation. But it was not until the Negro Revolt began in earnest that CORE became a major civil rights organization. We have previously cited its "freedom riders" action in the South; the organization has continued direct action demonstrations ever since. CORE has not always been able to control its more militant chapters, as in the case of the somewhat unsuccessful "stall-in" to keep people from the New York World's Fair in April, 1964.[11] It has been the most interracial in membership of all the organizations.

THE SOUTHERN CHRISTIAN LEADERSHIP CONFERENCE   The origin of SCLC was also discussed as part of the Southern Crisis. While it became substantial in size of staff and budget, its organization according to Clark is "amorphous and more symbolic than functional." [12] The charismatic leadership of Dr. Martin Luther King, Jr. in a sense makes the organization. Dr. King's deep commitment to nonviolent resistance is generally well known and resulted in his being awarded a Nobel Peace Prize. While he has been in great demand as a speaker and consultant on Negro civil rights the nation over, the activities of SCLC were largely confined to the South until the summer of 1966 when King organized demonstrations in the Chicago area against segregation in housing.

THE STUDENT NONVIOLENT COORDINATING COMMITTEE   SNCC (or "Snick" as it is often referred to) was organized in 1960 to coordinate the activities of numerous college student groups of both races on behalf of civil rights. Its direct action protests, sit-ins and demonstrations, were successful in desegregating hun-

---

[10] *Urban League News Letter,* Summer, 1966.
[11] Kenneth Clark, *The Negro American,* p. 609.
[12] *Ibid.,* p. 612.

dreds of segregated facilities in Southern cities.[13] Later SNCC has carried on more sustained activities of education and voter registration. It has more successfully identified with the rank and file of Southern Negroes than the other organizations. Many of its members, white and black, have been jailed. As Clark puts it, "SNCC has not overtly repudiated King's philosophy of nonviolence, but it does not root its own acceptance of this strategy in love of the enemy." [14] We shall later note a further trend away even from this.

THE BLACK MUSLIMS   Ever since Marcus Garvey's unsuccessful "Back to Africa" movement, some American Negroes have shared his "separatist" viewpoint and small Black Nationalist organizations have been formed. In essence the philosophy of these movements is that the white man is adamantly opposed to ever giving Negroes genuine equality in white societies and that "Black" Americans should stay apart from white society as much as possible.

The Black Muslims is the largest and most significant of the separatists' movements. It was organized in Detroit in 1930 by Wali Farad, believed to have been born in Mecca about 1877 and an orthodox Moslem. Farad, mysteriously disappeared around 1934 and was succeeded by Elijah Muhammad (born in Sanbornville, Georgia, as Elija Poole) who has remained the organization's leader ever since. Muhammad claimed some 250,000 followers, but outside observers doubt it had more than 100,000 followers in the early 1960's. Since the organization is most secretive, its actual size is difficult to determine. Its seventy to eighty mosques or temples are located in cities with large black ghettos scattered throughout the nation.

The movement is a racial-religious sect. Its membership is recruited from the poorest and most disorganized elements of the black ghettos. The members develop a strong personal discipline, devoting much time and money to the cause. The philosophy is racist. It proclaims the superiority of the black (the term "Negro" is taboo) man over the white. It stereotypes the white race generically as devils by nature. There is no such thing as a "good" white man. Christianity is anathema. To quote the leader, "Love thy neighbor: I have yet to meet one white man that loved his neighbor . . . Thou shalt not kill; I have yet to meet such a Christian," or again, "The white man has 'given you Jesus' while he has robbed you blind." [15] The movement organizes itself as a religion, "The Nation of Islam in the West," and carries on zealously religious meetings and rituals resembling Mohammedanism.

The movement is anti-integrationist; the less Negroes have to do with whites, the better. However, since they have to live in white-controlled society, Black Muslims are enjoined to obey white laws, and to work diligently when employed by whites. The position of the Black Muslims toward violence is ambivalent. While they do not share Dr. King's philosophy of nonviolence, they command

[13] C. Eric Lincoln, *The American Negro Reference Book,* p. 472.
[14] Kenneth Clark, *The Negro American,* p. 616.
[15] *Mr. Muhammad Speaks,* May 2, 1959. (A newspaper published by the movement.)

their followers not to be aggressive toward whites unless attacked. This well may be only a matter of expediency, but Lincoln points out that the movement serves the function of providing "outlets, short of violence, for the aggressive feelings aroused in its members" toward whites.[16] In their policy statement, they have asked that some areas of the United States be given over to Blacks alone, so obviously unrealistic and impossible that it is fair to ponder the motives of Elijah Muhammad in making it.[17] More realistically, the movement has encouraged the development of small businesses all run and patronized by Negroes, which have had modest success.

In its impact on American society, the Black Muslim movement is a paradox.[18] On the one hand, by converting self-respecting, law-abiding (for the time being at least), and more conventionally moral persons out of what was often the opposite in the same qualities, the movement lowers the incidence of "pathologies" in the ghetto populations and reduces the welfare load. On the other hand, in its long-range aim as expressed in its philosophy, it is the most subversive of the organizations here considered. Its long-range effect on the national society depends entirely upon its size, which appears now to be increasing. Despite the low rank order assigned Muhammad by Negro respondents in the *Newsweek* 1963 and 1966 polls [19] (Muhammad received the lowest of all approvals—15 percent in 1963 and 12 in 1966), Lincoln found Muhammad together with Malcolm X approaching the status of folk heroes among militant black youth of Harlem.[20] The defection of Malcolm X to form the Organization of Afro-American Unity, a broadly based movement designed to attract Negroes who do not necessarily subscribe to the religion of Islam but do not believe in integration, was a severe blow to the Black Muslims.[21] Since the assassination of Malcolm X, February 21, 1965, his autobiography has been a sort of "bible" for some non-integrationist Negroes.

In any direct way, the Black Muslim movement was unrelated to the Negro challenge during the Civil Rights phase. It provided continuity to the separatist, Black Nationalist, idea. But its racial as distinct from its religious ideology being more similar to some segments of the current Black Power movement, provides

[16] C. Eric Lincoln, *The Black Muslims in America* (Boston: The Beacon Press, 1961), p. 249.

[17] In a paper read by Charles P. Loomis at the annual convention of the American Sociological Association, in San Francisco, California, August 28, 1967, Dr. Loomis suggested this solution but further suggested finding some place in the less populated areas of South America for this purpose, an "Israel," for those Negroes who want "out" of the United States.

[18] Lincoln, *The Black Muslims in America*. See pp. 248–253 for a fuller discussion of the functions and dysfunctions of this movement for American society.

[19] *Newsweek*, August 22, 1966, p. 34.

[20] *The American Negro Reference Book*, p. 479.

[21] C. Eric Lincoln, *The American Negro Reference Book*, p. 479. Also see the *Autobiography of Malcolm X* (New York: Grove Press, 1965), Ch. 16.

a basis for more cooperation between Black Muslims and other nonintegrationist groups.

Riots

No realistic appraisal of the Negro Revolt can fail to give considerable prominence to rioting. Riots with interracial implications are no new phenomenon. Grimshaw identified thirty-three "major interracial disturbances in the United States between 1900 and 1949." [22] But the 1960's have witnessed an unparalleled number of riots with a substantial number of deaths and injuries, and enormous property losses. *Time* summarized the toll from 1964 to mid-August of 1967 as indicated in Table 15-1.

The significance of this rioting lies in its relation to the Negro Revolt. Writing, as we do, in the midst of riot after riot, it is obviously too soon to give a definitive appraisal of the causes or the consequences. However, it does appear clear that generally rioting arose spontaneously in consequence of fortuitous circumstances, however much small bands of radical agitators may have attempted to exploit the situations.

Advance reports of a two-year study of the Watts riot of 1965 by a team of University of California social scientists both confirm and challenge previous ideas as to the causes of rioting. The restlessness and sense of despair of the residents' underprivileged situation, indicated by such remarks as that of one Watt's inhabitant, "I am still hungry, and a hungry man is a dangerous man," lead the researchers to affirm that jobs *today* are crucial in lessening violence. But the report challenges the belief that it is only the poor, the uneducated, and the recent Southern migrant families who are ready to manifest violence. More than 50 percent of the Watts' sample had completed high school but most were employed at low-level jobs. [23]

Likewise, it is too soon for more definitive appraisals of the consequences of extended rioting. That the immediate effects are costly in economic terms and temporarily increase interracial tension in the communities involved are obvious. Later appraisals will have to include the following considerations. While riots are set off and carried through by impulsive behavior, there are indications that some of the Negro participants consider it as related to the revolt. Bayard Rustin reports a Negro as saying about the Watts, Los Angeles, riot in 1965, "We won." Asked why he considered the damaging of much property in the Negro areas and the injuries and deaths of Negro people (most of the white people injured were innocent passersby, aside from police), as "winning," the reply was "we made the mayor come down and look at the place." [24] A *New Republic* editorial

[22] Allen D. Grimshaw, "A Study in Violence" (Doctoral Dissertation, University of Pennsylvania, 1959, pp. 178–180).

[23] The material of this paragraph was taken from an account of a preliminary report submitted to the Office of Economic Opportunity as appearing in *The Washington Post*, July 28, 1967.

[24] Bayard Rustin, "The Watts Manifesto and the McCone Report," *Commentary*, March 1966, pp. 29–35.

TABLE 15–1. *Riot Toll: 1967 and Before*

	Dead	Injured	Arrested
1964 Eight cities	8	1,056	2,643
1965 Watts, Chicago	35	1,080	4,310
1966 Eighteen areas	12	366	1,647
1967 31 cities to date	86	2,056	11,094

Where & When This Year (1967)

APRIL

	Dead	Injured	Arrested
Nashville, Tenn.		17	80
MAY			
Jackson, Miss	1	2	
Houston	1	3	488
JUNE			
Boston (Roxbury)		45	44
Tampa, Fla.	2	15	68
Dayton, Ohio		6	55
Atlanta	1	6	9
Buffalo		92	205
JUNE–JULY			
Cincinnati	1	70	405
JULY			
Newark	26	1,004	1,397
Jersey City	1	*	34
Minneapolis		9	13
Plainfield, N.J.	1	46	167
Detroit	42	386	5,557
East Harlem, N.Y. [not Negro]	2	14	20
Rochester	2		*
Toledo		85	160
Grand Rapids		44	278
Flint, Mich.			183
Pontiac, Mich.	2	9	300
Saginaw, Mich.		14	73
Poughkeepsie, N.Y.		5	31
Passaic, N.J.		3	69
Peekskill, N.Y.			58
Riviera Beach, Fla.		2	46
South Bend, Ind.		20	99
Hartford, Conn.		11	20
JULY–AUGUST			
Chicago		6	150
Milwaukee	4	101	958
Providence		32	72
Wichita, Kan.		9	55

* Still unknown.

Source: *Time*, August 11, 1967, p. 11. Copyright Time Inc. 1967.

quotes a 24-year-old Bostonian Negro as saying "It's not the agitators who blew up. It's us, all over the place who say it's too late for us to wait when nothing comes anyway." [25] The youth quoted was a school dropout, unemployed, although having tried to find work; he belonged to no civil rights organization. Despite the unorganized character of the rioting, selectivity in the choice of places burned and looted based on local conceptions of which storekeepers were considered more exploitative is noted.

From a larger range viewpoint, it is clearly too soon to assume that rioting will be viewed as entirely dysfunctional to advancing the goal of the Negro Revolt. It is a sociological postulate that basic social change always has costs, and in the history of many nations violence and disorder have frequently been part of the cost. For example, in the United States the establishment of collective bargaining as an institutionalized method of settling management-labor disputes was accompanied by a substantial volume of various forms of violence and disorder. Finally, any future assessment of the functional or dysfunctional role of rioting will have to take into account how the white community reacted to it. This will be subsumed in the following discussion of how white America has reacted to the Negro Revolt in general.

White Reaction to the Negro Revolt

We have seen that an increasing number of white Americans (now a majority, outside the Deep South) claim willingness to accord Negroes equality in the public sectors of American life. One measure of the current white attitude—again from the *Newsweek* 1966 report—shows its extent and the trend. For example: "Three years ago almost one in four whites objected to sitting beside a Negro in a movie. Today one in five says he would object—progress to be sure, but hardly spectacular." [26] We are here, however, more concerned with the reaction of whites to the organized revolt. Here the reaction of whites generally that the "Negroes are trying to move too fast" is attested in the same polls as follows. As against 64 percent of the whites feeling this way in 1963, the percentage had increased to 70 in 1966.[27]

Sociological research generally holds that there is a correlation between white hostility and discrimination and social status: the lower the status (with the possible exception of the lowest), the greater the resistance to integration.[28] To this we would postulate this proposition: in a conflict situation, the stronger the thrust of one opponent, the stronger the counter thrust of the other, provided it possesses the power necessary (as whites usually do). That the white backlash reaction to the Negro Revolt should become more articulate is therefore not at

[25] *The New Republic*, "Blow Up in the Cities," August 5, 1967, p. 5.
[26] *Newsweek*, August 22, 1966, p. 25.
[27] *Ibid.*, pp. 24–26.
[28] See Paul B. Sheatsley, "White Attitudes toward the Negro," in *The Negro American*, p. 315.

all surprising. The first failure in a series of civil rights acts to pass Congress in 1966 (with particular reference to housing); the victory of die-hard segregationists in the South and the upset of racially liberal Congressmen in 1966; the reported increase of the Ku Klux Klan; the development of counter demonstrations of whites against the housing desegregation thrust led by Dr. Martin Luther King in Chicago; and the defeat of the open-occupancy referendum in California all reflect the white backlash. But the studies made since World War II broadly indicate that, outside the South, the hard-core, "racist"-minded segments of the white population constitute a distinct minority; [29] and that the more influential radical right movements are not clearly "racist." [30] Thus with the tendency of government at the federal level and in non-South states to press for the actual adherence to civil rights law, the hard-core white backlash can only impede the Negro Revolt, it cannot stop it.

What is, however, more significant is the substantial negative reaction to Negro protest activities found among whites who are more liberal on the race issue. This is seen in Table 15–2, particularly items B, C, D, E, and F.[31] The data here are arranged on the basis of previous ratings on a Gutman Scale of Pro-Integration Sentiment.[32] It will be noted in item D that of the high-integration white scorers a third replied that they "generally disapprove of action Negroes have taken to obtain civil rights," while an eighth replied that they feel "Negro groups are asking too much"; and that the percentages for the "medium"-scoring white integrationists on the same two questions are 62 percent and 31 percent.

Current Trends and Prospects

Attention now focuses on the current trends in relations between Negro and non-Negro Americans and what these appear to forecast for the years ahead. At the outset it should be emphasized again that any satisfactory stabilization of these relations in the light of the current conflict situation will depend primarily on changes in the attitudes and behavior of white people, and secondarily on what Negroes do. Let us start with this point in mind.

Continued Decline in White Discrimination

Despite some short-term reversals in white attitudes and behavior and differences in the various components of the white population, the overall national trend appears to continue in the same direction indicated in the previous dis-

[29] *Ibid.,* p. 311.
[30] In *The Radical Right* (Garden City, New York: Doubleday and Company, 1963), edited by Daniel Bell, Peter Viereck writes: "Manifestations of ethnic intolerance today tend to decrease in proportion as ideological intolerance increases. In sharp contrast, both bigotries used to increase together." (p. 168)
[31] Paul B. Sheatsley, in *The American Negro,* p. 317, Table 4.
[32] *Ibid.,* p. 310, Table 2.

TABLE 15–2. *White Attitudes Toward Negro Protest Movement in North and*

Percent Who Say:	North	South	Pro-Integration Scale Scores			
			0–2 (High Seg.)	3–4 (Mod. Seg.)	5–6 (Mod. Int.)	7–8 (High Int.)
A. Most Negroes feel strongly about						
The right to vote	80%	77%	79%	76%	84%	79%
Right to hold same jobs as white people	84	81	76	84	85	89
Right to use same parks, hotels, restaurants	84	80	67	82	83	90
Right to send children to same schools as whites	63	35	45	51	59	66
Right to live in white neighborhoods	45	33	42	39	42	44
Right to marry white people ..	10	8	13	9	7	10
Having a separate area of U.S. set aside for Negroes	5	3	7	6	4	2
B. The Negro protest movement has been generally violent rather than peaceful	47%	63%	78%	50%	47%	30%
C. Demonstrations have hurt rather than helped the Negro cause	43%	60%	71%	52%	45%	24%
D. Generally disapprove of actions Negroes have taken to obtain civil rights	59%	78%	89%	73%	62%	33%

cussion of white reaction to the Negro Revolt: continued decline in white discrimination. The broad picture in prospect is put by Sheatsley in these words:

> Certainly there is no evidence that the majority of American whites eagerly look forward to integration. Most are more comfortable in a segregated society, and they would prefer that the demonstrators slow down or go away while things are worked out gradually. But most of them know also that racial discrimination is morally wrong and recognize the legitimacy of the Negro protest. Our survey data persuasively argue that where there is little or no protest against segregation and discrimination, or where these have the sanction of law, racial attitudes conform to the existing situation. But when attention is kept focused on racial injustice and when acts of discrimination become contrary to the law of the land, racial attitudes change. Conversely, there is no persuasive evidence thus far that either demonstration and other forms of direct action, or legal sanctions applied by government, create a backlash effect and foster segregationist sentiment. On the contrary, they may simply demonstrate, ever more conclusively, that it is more costly to oppose integration than to bring it about. The mass of white Americans have shown in many ways that they do not want a racist government and that they will not follow racist leaders. Rather, they are engaged in the painful task of ad-

South, and by Scores on Pro-Integration Scale, December 1963*

Percent Who Say:	North	South	Pro-Integration Scale Scores			
			0–2 (High Seg.)	3–4 (Mod. Seg.)	5–6 (Mod. Int.)	7–8 (High Int.)
E. Negro groups are asking for too much	37%	55%	74%	45%	31%	16%
F. "Others" are really behind the Negro protest movement	39%	52%	56%	46%	43%	24%
Communists are behind it	21	27	30	26	22	12
G. Problem of Negro rights should be left to states rather than federal government	34%	59%	57%	45%	36%	24%
H. Negro-white relations will always be a problem for U.S.	42%	49%	61%	52%	36%	26%
I. Self or family have been affected favorably by integration	4%	1%	—%	2%	4%	7%
Have been affected unfavorably ..	9	11	16	14	4	3
Have not been affected	87	83	82	83	91	87
J. Are around Negroes: Almost every day	29%	39%	33%	28%	31%	35%
Less often than that	45	52	45	47	46	51
Never around Negroes	26	9	22	25	23	14

* Percentages do not always add to 100 percent. Omitted are a small group who answered vaguely or irrelevantly.

Source: *The Negro American*, Table 4, p. 317. Reproduced by permission of *Daedalus* and Houghton Mifflin Co.

justing to an integrated society. It will not be easy for most, but one cannot at this late date doubt the basic commitment. In their hearts they know that the American Negro is right.[33]

Referring to our discussion of Southern trends (Chapter 13) suggests that the above quotation is less applicable to the South, especially the Deep South. It seems safe to predict that if complete integration of Negroes ever comes to the United States, there will be at least a one-generation lag in much of the South.

Continued Migration

Continued migration toward the Northern slum ghettos aggravates slum conditions and keeps racial tension at a high point. The sporadic acceptance of a trickling of middle-class Negro families into white communities is far more than offset by the numerical growth of the Negro ghettos. This migration is ex-

[33] Paul B. Sheatsley, "White Attitudes toward the Negro," in *The Negro American*, Talcott Parsons and Kenneth B. Clark, eds. (Boston: Houghton Mifflin, 1966), pp. 322–323.

pected to continue at least into the mid-1970's, according to several federal bureau studies. Despite the lack of jobs available, the push effect of poor rural conditions in the South encourages continued migration to the more friendly atmosphere within the Northern urban ghettos.[34]

The Negro Class Structure Elaborated

The trend noted for the economic and occupational status of middle-class and educated Negroes to improve is substantial, while that of the Negro masses remains relatively stagnant. Only improved education of lower-class Negro children, and extensive retraining of young adults will develop the sort of continuous steady upward mobility of Negroes that has characterized most other minority groups. Awareness of this has prompted moderately extensive efforts by federal and local governments in this direction. It is too soon to appraise their effectiveness adequately.

Identification for the Negro Upper Classes

The dilemma for the middle-class Negro whether to exploit his more favorable position by disassociating himself from the masses or not is not new, as Frazier so fully elaborated.[35] But it gains poignancy from the Negro Revolt. While numerous instances can be found of middle-class Negroes resolving this dilemma in alternate ways, the trend appears toward identification with, rather than alienation from, the Negro masses.[36] An indication of a growing solidarity of successful Negroes with the Negro cause is the fact that in 1967 a group of Negro millionaires formed an association to raise among them a million dollars a year for the legal defense of Americans (white or Negro) claiming their legal rights. The predicament for the middle and upper-class Negroes is put by Kenneth Clark thus: "The Negro who dares to move outside the ghetto, either physically or psychologically, runs the risk of retaliatory hostility, at worst, or of misunderstanding, at best.... He is in conflict with himself, with whites, and with Negroes, confronted by a sense of guilt, alienation, resentment, and random bitterness directed as much against Negroes, as against whites." [37]

The Increasing Involvement of More Negro Americans

Brink and Harris found in 1963 that the actual participation of the Negro rank and file in various forms of direct action ranged from 12 percent who had marched in demonstrations to 4 percent who had gone to jail. But the results to the question whether these respondents would participate in protest movements

[34] See Will Lissner, reporting in the *New York Times*, August 13, 1967, p. 40.
[35] E. Franklin Frazier, *The Black Bourgeoisie* (New York: The Free Press, 1957).
[36] See Dan Cortz, "The Negro Middle Class Right in the Middle," *Fortune Magazine*, Nov. 1966, pp. 175–180 and passim.
[37] Kenneth B. Clark, *The Dark Ghetto* (New York: Harper & Row, 1965), pp. 194–195. See pp. 193–196.

if asked to do so in the future were as follows: "Among the rank and file, roughly half—and that's almost ten million people—were willing to participate in such action, a figure that puts them much closer to the leadership." [38] The University of California researchers of the Watts riots found a significant number of successful as well as unsuccessful Negroes prepared emotionally for violence as a strategy to resolve the problem of their subordinate status position.

Division in the Revolt Leadership: Militancy

The emergence of the term "Black Power" in 1966 as a widely heralded slogan symbolizes considerable polarization within the Negro leadership as to goals and methods. The timing of this division appears related to the slowing up of the pace of the civil rights movement and the continuing rise of Negro expectation. The main differences among Negro leaders refer to the questions of the degree of militancy in techniques, and in the relative emphasis on integration versus pluralism as the goals.

"Black Power," like all slogans, is an ambiguous term. In a public symposium in 1966 the views of six Negro leaders ranged from disavowing any usefulness for the term to explicit definition by Floyd McKissick of CORE, who put it essentially as follows: Basically Black Power means that black people must decide for themselves what they want and then use all the power they can muster to get it. More specifically, McKissick mentioned political power, and economic power, to be strengthened by developing a black consumer block. To strengthen their power potential, he felt, required improving the Negroes' self-image—pride in race—and development of young militant leadership.[39]

While whites likewise are in doubt as to the meaning and implications of "Black Power," there is among them the common denominator of fear, a feeling which can be advantageously manipulated by the white racist groups.

Since the appearance of more aggressive protest activity of Negroes is one of the more crucial developments in the current scene, it is pertinent to give the subject of militancy a general analysis.

"Militancy" in the civil rights movement ranges along a continuum somewhat as follows: (1) *Legal militancy.* This has in turn divided into attempts to get court rulings on existing laws which would make unconstitutional local discriminatory laws and ban their administration; and to press for the passage of new laws which would prevent practices not explicitly defined as illegal. For example, whether it is or was illegal to refuse to sell a house to a Negro was not explicitly clear until in certain states new legislation was passed specifically defining it as invalid. (2) *Public protests and nonviolence.* Organized protests pursued with nonviolent techniques have characterized the current Negro challenge: demonstrations, picketing, and boycotting of certain businesses are frequent

[38] Brink and Harris, *The Negro Revolution in America,* p. 68.
[39] See "Excerpts from Interviews with Six Civil Rights Leaders on Racial Problems in the U.S.," *New York Times,* Aug. 22, 1966, p. 36.

modes. Nonviolent activity does not preclude deliberate violation of law where the protesters consider the law morally wrong.[40] Another distinction in public protests has been between those directed at specific grievances, and those aimed at calling attention to the general plight of the Negroes. The former was illustrated in Newark, New Jersey, where in 1967 a group of Negroes marched on City Hall to protest the location of a large medical complex in the heart of that city's Negro slum. Protest at the general plight of Negroes is illustrated by the World's Fair blockade of the New York Triborough Bridge with no specific grievance in mind. Waskow has termed these new techniques of protest "creative disorder," creative in the sense that they have sometimes, and may further, contribute to new gains by Negroes.[41] (3) The trend away from total nonviolence. The preceding phrase has been put thus to disabuse any reader of the idea that in public statements the national Negro leaders of main civil rights organizations have positively called on Negroes to initiate attacks on white people. Dr. King still holds to the nonviolent technique both because it is to him morally right and practically feasible. Floyd McKissick, on the other hand, while intimating that nonviolence is a thing of the past, later indicates that he means only that blacks should strike back at white aggressors.[42] In this guarded sense, the latter view expresses a trend away from strict nonviolence as far as the main organizations are concerned.

In unorganized rioting, the use of violence is obvious. Given the "tinder box" climate of all Negro ghettos, rioting in which some white property and some white people will be injured is inevitable, sporadically. News accounts of such riots of the 1960's indicate the four following immediate stimuli to rioting: (1) quarrels between individual persons or small groups, often youthful gangs, involving the two races; (2) a highly provocative reaction by whites—sometimes police—to an organized civil rights activity; (3) an act by whites—sometimes a white policeman legitimately detaining a Negro—which is misperceived by Negroes. Sometimes only a rumor of the above is sufficient. The less militant leaders in public addresses stress their difficulties in influencing Negroes to keep protests within orderly bounds when disorderly means appear to prompt concessions from the white establishment. (4) A fourth dimension in the use of militancy would be a deliberate and planned attack on white people. While there are small splinter groups of Negroes who believe in this approach, up to 1966, such action had not been reported in the national news media. But it

---

[40] A widely publicized example involved Dr. Martin Luther King, Jr., who defied a court order against a demonstration in Birmingham in 1963, was arrested, and sentenced to jail. Legal appeals finally resulted in the U.S. Supreme Court upholding an earlier affirmation of the sentence by a 5 to 4 decision on June 12, 1967. Dr. King, with others, returned voluntarily to Birminghom to serve his sentence in October, 1967.

[41] Arthur I. Waskow, *From Race Riots to Sit-In: 1919 and the 1960's* (Garden City, N.Y.: Doubleday and Co., 1966), especially chapters 15 and 16.

[42] *The New York Times,* Aug. 22, 1966, p. 36.

would not be surprising in the future.[43] In the meantime, some of these real revolutionaries are suspected of feeling obligated to attack moderate Negro leaders. For example, the arrest of 16 Negroes purported to be members of a revolutionary group planning the assassination of the executive secretaries of the N.A.A.C.P. and the Urban League was reported on June 21, 1967.

Trend toward Pluralism

As a final current trend, we note an increasing movement in more militant Negro circles away from a total integrationist goal and toward a pluralistic orientation. While this is not a new phenomenon, as previously seen, it has gained wider acceptance among Negroes since the mid-1960's. If this new trend should gain ascendancy, it would profoundly affect the whole future of the relations between Negro and non-Negro Americans. For this reason, let us explore it at some length in the following section.

The Long-Range Prospect for a Stabilized Race Relations Pattern

The Alternatives

Let us return to consider possible answers to the question pertaining to integration or pluralism raised at the outset of the discussion of the Negro Revolt. Applying to Negro-white relations the same alternatives considered in other minority situations, the possibilities for establishing a stable pattern in this intergroup situation on a coordinate (equal) rather than on a dominant-minority basis are as follows. All these alternatives are based on an assumption that is currently problematical and not certain: that white Americans will ultimately react to Negroes as equals, and thus permit Negroes themselves to decide which alternatives to choose. The choices are

(1) *Total Assimilation* This would involve the disappearance of a separate Negro subcommunity and group identity, ultimately leading to the absorption of Negro genetic strains into the white race.

(2) *Structural Pluralism* The complete integration of Negroes into public sectors of American life with the allocation of occupational and class status strictly on merit and with no reference to race; the opportunity to live anywhere in the community which they can afford; but retaining a separate Negro subcommunity structure where most formal and informal social life would be lived—identifiable as Negro. This would be similar to the structural pluralism of several European nationality groups in large cities, as discussed by Milton

[43] There are always, of course, occasional individuals or gangs who decide to attack, burglarize white people, or vandalize white property. The current climate of race relations encourages more Negro boldness in such action. Certainly there is more fear of such Negro activity on the part of the whites.

Gordon.[44] The culture would be indistinguishable from that of white society and in large measure like the WASP stereotype since most American Negroes are Protestant.

(3) *Cultural-Structural Pluralism* This would involve stabilization of Negro-white relations including the elements of structural pluralism just mentioned but would include some distinctive cultural as well as subcommunal identification. This would bear similarity to the pluralism of Catholic-Protestant-Jew, as developed by Will Herberg.[45]

Having set forth the alternatives we now consider them in reverse order with more extended discussion of the third, not because there is any clear indication that the majority of Negro Americans if given a free choice would choose it, but because, currently, it is more frequently voiced by certain Negro segments as more desirable than integration.

Cultural-Structural Pluralism

If American Negroes are to be ultimately a culturally pluralistic group on a coordinate status basis, what is this Negro culture to be based upon? Three possibilities emerge: one based on African heritage; one based on creative developments from the 350 years of white dominance; or the development of a new subculture, possibly identified or related to twentieth-century Pan-Africanism.

THE AFRICAN HERITAGE As a part of the Negro Protest American Negroes have pressed for a more accurate teaching of the history of the Negro throughout time, including the great African civilizations of the past.[46] But from the sixteenth century on much of the history of Africa is tragic, including slave exportation and colonialism. Essentially what this fact of the great empires demonstrates is the myth of innate genetic superiority of Caucasians, as we pointed out in Chapter 3. The pulverization of tribal heritages was so thorough under slavery that even before the re-establishment of Southern white dominance under caste, the continuity of American Negroes with African culture had been virtually lost. Thus while it may develop some sense of race pride to recall the glorious empires, certainly any subculture of the American Negroes living in twentieth-century urban-industrial society is not to be based on adaptive survivals of either the empires or tribalism.

UNIQUE MINORITY EXPERIENCE OF AMERICAN NEGROES It was inevitable that the enforced separation of the Negro people from the mainstream of social life and the constant humiliating frustration in white-Negro contacts should de-

---

[44] See Milton Gordon, *Assimilation in American Life,* Ch. 7.

[45] *Protestant-Catholic-Jew* (Garden City, N.Y.: Doubleday and Co., 1956), Ch. 3.

[46] See Daniel Chou and Elliot Skinner, *A Glorious Age in Africa* (Garden City, N.Y.: Doubleday and Co., 1960), who state that "at the heights of their power, the great earlier kingdoms of West Africa, Ghana, Mali, and Senegal compared favorably with their contemporary counterparts in Europe and Asia." (p. 116.)

velop some distinctive patterned ways of behavior. But much of these, as we have indicated, are either skillful constructive ways of adapting to the inevitability of minority status or indulging in the "pathologies" found in lesser degree among whites.

Delineating the elements of a possible distinctive American Negro subculture is complicated by class and regional differences. Therefore, any comparison between white and Negro culture must control for these variables. One study meeting these requirements shows Negroes spending their money differently than comparable status whites.[47] Another study concludes that while Southern Negro dialects bear similarity to those of Southern whites, the former do have distinctive features.[48]

Considering the structure of the Negro subcommunity, it will be recalled that Myrdal characterized it as a pathological replica of the white community. The one possible exception is the family. In recent years the lower-class Negro family has been widely studied.[49] We therefore select this for an example of the general question of cultural distinctiveness in the Negro as compared with the white lower class.

The American lower-lower class family [50] in general is characterized as highly unstable; marriage is at a lower age and contracted casually or as a result of an illegitimate pregnancy; marriage involves more role segregation, with far less shared companionship than in other classes; the number of children is relatively large and not planned for; and husbands are at least formally and in their own concept dominant over their wives.

While the lower-lower class Negro family is in many features like the lower-lower white class family, there do appear nuances of difference. Freer expression of sexual behavior from youth on is taken for granted (although not necessarily approved of) and manifests itself in a large volume of illegitimacy. Illegitimate pregnancy far less often leads to marriage. After marriage, especially in young marriages, the spouses frequently continue to live with one or the other spouses' family. This type of family is highly unstable. Moynihan states, "It is probable that not much more than one-third of Negro youth reach eighteen having lived all their lives with both of their parents." [51] Often the children have

[47] L. R. Klein and W. H. Mooney, "Negro-White Differentials and the Consumption Function Problem," *Econometrics*, 21, July 1953, pp. 435–456.

[48] Gordon C. Green, "Negro Dialect, the Last Barrier to Integration," *Journal of Negro Education* (Winter, 1963), pp. 81–83.

[49] See Daniel P. Moynihan, "Employment, Income, and the Negro Family," in *The Negro American*, pp. 134–159; Lee Rainwater, "Crucible of Identity: The Negro Lower Class Family," in *The Negro American*, pp. 160–204; and Jessie Bernard, *Marriage and Family among Negroes* (Englewood Cliffs, N.J.: Prentice-Hall, 1966).

[50] We adapt here a commonly used six-fold class differentiation of upper, middle, and lower class, with upper and lower of each. The upper-lower class family is frequently called the "working" class or "blue-collar" class to distinguish it from the lower-lower class, frequently spoken of as the level most clearly alienated from the mainstream of American society.

[51] Moynihan, in *The Negro American*, p. 150.

as a surrogate father their mother's successive husbands or boy friends. The proportion of fatherless families has increased.[52]

While the lower-class Negro family has been always matrifocal,[53] the present situation in the new ghettos has further denigrated the role of the Negro male and increased the responsibility of the Negro woman. For example, Moynihan found that in March, 1964, 56.7 percent of nonwhite women with children six to seventeen years of age were in the work force—a higher percentage than that of nonwhite women with *no* children under 18 years of age, which was 50.5.[54]

The most creative developments in American Negro culture have been in music, literature, and possibly sports.[55] It is in the field of music that recent summary accounts leave open the possible survival of African heritage, but not too convincingly. For example, Le Roi Jones writes, "it is in American Negro music in most of its forms that the most easily discernible African influence remains to this day." [56] But writing more generally on Negro music in the same volume Zelma George states, "For the Negro, music is the most socially permissive vehicle which he has used as a medium of social comment, criticism, and protest, and to express his aggression. . . . The Negro is a composite character in the American culture. He is American, not African." [57] The major forms of music developed by Negroes have been the spirituals, the special form of "gospel" singing traditional in the Negro churches, and the "blues." All of these may be interpreted as types of music in response to frustration. Apparently, the one most likely to suggest African survival is the antiphonal form that Le Roi Jones finds in the blues and Zelma George in gospel music.

Considering the arts more broadly, Marion E. Brown indicates that in literature, entertainment, and the fine arts Negro artists have been influenced by whites.[58] In the field of letters, Negro poets and writers have concentrated on "racial" themes, largely the plight of the American Negro.[59]

Our conclusion is that there is little possibility for the development of a distinctive American Negro culture based exclusively on their heritage as a minority in the United States.

A "NEW" AMERICAN NEGRO CULTURE   What are the possibilities of the de-

[52] Jessie Bernard, *Marriage and Family Among Negroes*, p. 19.
[53] See E. Franklin Frazer, *The Negro Family*.
[54] *The Negro American*, p. 151.
[55] We are not concerned with the innumerable contributions made by individual Negro persons to the mainstream of American (white) culture. We refer in sports not to the success of Negroes in sports invented by white men—first on a segregated, and later on an integrated basis—but to boxing and "jockeying" which were largely participated in by Negroes in their earlier stages, albeit in a sense as "protegees" of white men. See John P. Davis, *The American Negro Reference Book*, Ch. 23.
[56] Le Roi Jones, "Blues, Jazz and the Negro," *The American Negro Reference Book*, Ch. 21.
[57] Zelma George, *The American Negro Reference Book*, Ch. 20.
[58] *The American Negro Reference Book*, "The Negro in Fine Arts," Ch. 22.
[59] For example, Anna Bontemps cites Braithwhite as being bothered because Claude McKay, the Negro poet, "seemed to waver between the racial and universal notes." *The Negro American Reference Book*, pp. 858–859.

velopment of a new distinctive American Negro culture? One basis might be identification with and pride in the "new" Negroid Africa. This, however, raises difficult problems. Since actually American Negroes know no more—probably less, because of their disadvantaged educational situation—about Africa than most white men, the development of such an interest would require an enormous problem of special education. Second, do the accomplishments of the new independent African states all serve to create pride in identification with them? Third, as the independent African states move into the industrial-urban world society, to what extent are they going to develop distinctive modern cultures or take on Western traits? The answers to the last two questions lie in the future.

Turning to the possibility of the development of a new American Negro cultural pluralism on other bases than identification with the New Africa, one finds equally perplexing questions. Since cultural pluralism in the economic and political fields is ruled out by the requirements of social order, these fields may be dismissed. Some current efforts to develop Negro cooperative economic enterprises are in the nature of temporary aids pending the integration of jobless Negroes into the general economic system. In a day when larger, not smaller, units of economic enterprise are the trend, efforts to develop separate private Negro economic enterprises are at best transitional.

Turning to the expressive areas of culture, religion comes to mind. The major development here has been the Black Muslims' attempt to identify with Mohammedanism. But since the vast majority of American Negroes are nominally Christian and have a large-scale organized network of church organization, is a widespread turn to the Muslims likely? Perhaps in the field of the arts, particularly music, lies the only pluralistic possibility.

Thus this analysis points strongly away from cultural pluralism as a basis for the establishment of coordinate status Negro-white intergroup relations.

Structural Pluralism

An American Negro subcommunity with no distinctive cultural basis clearly would have only the common feature of race as a unifying bond. Such a situation calls for emphasis on the very factor that in general social science has been tending to de-emphasize as having any valid social relevance. It would be retaining by choice the social color line which is now maintained by the actions of white Americans.

Assimilation-Integration

And now, back to the first of the three long-range prospects for the stabilization of Negro-white relations—total assimilation. Put in other words, this calls for solution by elimination of the "color line" completely. Such a development is actually what liberal and academic white America has for some time advocated. We suspect, however, that even this segment of the white population has not realistically envisioned an actual society in which the color "black" [60] is irrelevant. While the full integration of American Negroes into the public sectors of our society on an equal basis is in the process of fulfillment largely through "forced" means, social equality will require a vast alteration of the attitudes of the American white people. This can be accomplished only by a radical change of the socialization process of future cohorts of white children through the family and the school. We see no current prospects for the implementation of the kind of socialization needed on the scale sufficient to the task and thus view with considerable pessimism the prospects for harmonious relations for a considerable period ahead.

The Negro Challenge and Social Science

Further on, particularly in Chapter 19, sociological theory concerning dominant-minority relations at various levels of generalization is systematically considered. In concluding our discussion of the changing trends in Negro-white relations, we call attention to certain long-standing theoretical problems which these events particularly illumine.

Integration

The Negro challenge has led to the emergence of the concept integration in sociological literature in recent years. Its extensive use can substantially be dated from 1954 as the positive way to state the negative connotation of desegregation in the Southern school situation. It arose because of the inadequacies of the previously well-established concepts of acculturation and assimilation to describe the placing of Negroes into a situation alongside whites on equal—at least in formal status—basis. We have seen again and again that the acceptance of a Negro as a fellow schoolmate or a fellow worker has not necessarily meant acceptance as a social equal or the removal of white prejudice. Different from the experience of other minority persons, "integrated" Negroes are acculturated at the outset, but not assimilated. Integration does not have a common definition among social scientists. While the term serves the purpose indicated we see no need to use it as Kenneth Clark does to include the elimination of prejudice which then makes integration synonymous with the term "assimilation." [61]

Relative Deprivation

The proposition that the *feeling* of frustration and deprivation is not measured in absolute terms but rather in relation to the situation of others in a given society is highly useful in interpreting the current interracial scene. In terms of material welfare many Negro families in the United States supported on relief may have a higher standard of living than the majority of people in many

---

[60] Black is here used as a symbol for Negroid visibility in general.
[61] Kenneth B. Clark, "Desegregation: The Role of the Social Sciences," *Teachers College Record*, 1960, 62, pp. 16–17.

of the nonindustrialized, underdeveloped societies. But the feeling of deprivation is greater when one is among the 20 percent of the "poor" in a society where the rest share in the general affluence. The same principle holds at higher levels, the college-educated Negro, for example, who cannot get a position commensurate with his abilities because of discrimination feels highly frustrated despite having a comfortable living in comparison with a Negro school dropout.

Strain toward Cultural Consistency

Social science has postulated that there is a strain toward consistency in each culture. The major values in the United States include freedom, equality, democracy, respect for the individual person, and a somewhat distinctive "moral" orientation.[62] Negro-white relations are grossly inconsistent with these values. Thus ultimately either the basic value system must change to conform to racial discrimination or racial discrimination must be abandoned. In Chapter 1 we noted that this moral dilemma was the basic theme of Myrdal's study, and that he expressed no doubt that racial discrimination would have to give way.

Social Forces vs. Direct Action

Social science finds it useful to distinguish between change that is brought about by pressure of social forces and change brought about by social action— that is, by conscious, planned action. In the last analysis, the adaptive changes encouraged by social factors require social action. The central problem, then, is at what point concerted social action can be introduced to influence trends more directly or immediately. With the balance of social forces in their favor since the mid-century, Negro leadership chose to press for increased, more sustained, and more militant direct action to accelerate the process, up to the mid-sixties with considerable success.

Methods of Social Action

The events of the past twenty years have contributed insight as to the values of various methods of social action.

FORCED STRUCTURAL CHANGE VS. ATTITUDINAL CHANGE: LAW   During the first part of this century, social theory leaned toward the viewpoint, influenced by William G. Sumner, that law is powerless to change mores.[63] Thus during this time, social action against ethnic discrimination was directed generally at changing attitudes and urging people of dominant status to cease discrimination, using education and religio-ethical persuasion. In the past two decades, civil rights movements have relied heavily on law to reduce discrimination. The

---

[62] See Robin Williams, *American Society,* rev. ed. (New York: Alfred A. Knopf, 1965), pp. 415–470.
[63] William G. Sumner, *Folkways* (Boston: Ginn and Co., 1907). The orthodox interpretation of Sumner's views on legislation is challenged in an article by Harry V. Ball, George Eaton Simpson, and Kiyoshi Ikeda, "Law and Social Change: Sumner Reconsidered," *American Journal of Sociology,* March 1962, pp. 532–540.

degree of success achieved by this method has changed sociological thought.[64]

On the basis of our material we would suggest that the events of the postwar challenge indicate that the value of a new law as an instrument of change is relative to the prevalence and intensity of the localized patterns of behavior and supporting institutions for or against it. Law appears to have been more immediately valuable in accelerating change in the North than in the South, and more immediately valuable in the local Southern areas where caste sanctions were less strong.

From another viewpoint, a case can be made that the pressure of outside law against the South by whites was the only means to get some changes started. The resistance to the new legal interpretations in the South and the slow pace of compliance suggest that the white South by itself would have moved quite slowly, if ever, in desegregation.

In addition to law, those social systems which are most autocratic—where the power of decision rests in the top echelon—can bring about desegregation more quickly. Recent examples are seen in the armed services, certain industrial enterprises, and the Roman Catholic Church.

Finally, that law has its limits as an agency of social change in the current crisis has been substantially illustrated in this and the previous chapter.[65]

NONVIOLENT ACTIVITY   Direct protest action with nonviolent techniques has been demonstrated, again with limits, to be an effective technique for a less powerful group in the conflict against the more powerful group. Much has been learned about how to make this technique effective from both its successes and failures. For example, the protesters must be a trained and disciplined group; the technique cannot be used by "mobs."

VIOLENCE   It is significant that it was in the mid-1960's that a distinguished social science journal devoted an issue to the subject of violence. In this volume, Lewis Coser writes:

> American social science has been traditionally remiss in examining social conflict and social violence because of its excessive commitment to models of social harmony; this has resulted in a tame view of social structures. . . . A plea is made that the subject of social violence be given greater emphasis in the future.[66]

The current situation in Negro-white relations in the United States has provided and is continuing to furnish a generous supply of case material for this purpose.

[64] Arnold M. Rose was among the first to indicate this changing view. See his *Race Prejudice and Discrimination: Readings in Intergroup Relations in the United States* (New York: Alfred A. Knopf, 1953), "The Influence of Legislation on Prejudice," pp. 545–555.
[65] See also Alexander M. Bickel, "The Limits of Effective Legal Action," in *Politics and the Warren Report* (New York: Harper & Row, 1964).
[66] "Some Social Functions of Violence," *Patterns of Violence* (Philadelphia: *The Annals of the American Academy of Political and Social Science*, vol. 364, March 1966), p. 8.

Topics for Projects and Discussion

1. Design a questionnaire aimed at discovering whether the attitudes of white people toward Negro Americans have changed in consequence of the large volume of rioting in the sixties. Interview a number of white people and report your results.
2. If there are Negro students in your college or university, study their situation within your academic community. If there are no Negro students, how do you account for this?
3. As a term paper, make a special study of any one of the leading organizations involved in the current Negro challenge to white dominance.
4. Discuss in fuller detail the topics briefly developed in the final section of this chapter, "The Negro Challenge and Social Science."
5. Discuss the prospects for Negro-white relations in the United States for the next decade.

Suggested Readings

The Autobiography of Malcolm X. With an introduction by M. S. Handler. New York: Grove Press, 1965.
> *This autobiography of one of the most charismatic young Negro leaders has become a "bible" of the militant movement.*

Clark, Kenneth B. "The Civil Rights Movement: Momentum and Organization," in *The Negro American.* Boston: Houghton Mifflin Co., 1966, pp. 595–625.
> *Analyzes the Civil Rights movement in the post-World War II period including the role played by the leading participating organizations.*

Drake, St. Clair. "Negro Americans and the Africa Interest." Chapter 16 of *The American Negro Reference Book,* John P. Davis, ed. Englewood Cliffs, N.J.: Prentice-Hall, 1966.
> *Traces the interest and activity of Negro Americans in Africa throughout American history.*

Haydn, Tom. "The Occupation of Newark." A special supplement of *New York Review,* Aug. 14, 1967.
> *An outstanding journalistic day-by-day account of one of the largest ghetto riots of 1967.*

Harris, Louis and William Brink. *Black and White.* New York: Simon and Schuster, 1967.
> *The authors of the 1963 study of Newsweek polls in this book analyze in depth the new poll data gathered up to 1966.*

Keil, Charles. *Urban Blues.* Chicago: University of Chicago Press, 1965.
> *Analyzes the blues singer as a cultural hero and relates the analysis to a broader "pluralistic" viewpoint.*

King, Martin Luther, Jr. *Where Do We Go from Here?* New York: Harper & Row, 1967.
> *This world-known leader in his latest book searches for new programs within the limits of nonviolence.*

16

Indians in the United States

In contrast to the other American minorities we have discussed who migrated or were transported to the Western hemisphere, the subordinate position of Indians is the result of colonial conquest. An account of the relations between the Indians of the Americas and the white Europeans who invaded their domain reveals significant contrasts between the areas dominated by conquerors from the Latin nations and those dominated by the English. The Spaniards employed various devices to force the Indians to work for them. While this exploitation greatly decimated the Indian population, in the Latin-American nations which Gillen has described as Mestizo America, there are to be found today many Indian groups who remain distinctively Indian in their culture. The large mestizo populations of these nations indicate that, to a far greater extent than north of the Rio Grande, the descendants of the Indians of colonial times have been integrated into the general national societies. The general cultures of Mestizo America have pronounced Indian influences.

In contrast, the English settlers in North America pushed the Indians off the land to work it themselves, subsequently with the aid in the South of Negro slaves. As in Latin America, the Indian population in the United States was greatly decimated, but more as a result of unsuccessful warfare with the whites and the expropriation of their land and resources than through harsh conditions of slavery or peonage. Again as in Latin America, many Indian societies survived and retained their tribal cultures. But they survived largely on the fringes of the new North American society, isolated from it rather than a part of it.

The problems arising from these two contrasting patterns of Indian-white relations likewise differ. In Mestizo America, the groups remaining Indian in their way of life constitute substantial portions of the population; and the welfare of such groups effects in high degree the welfare of the nations involved.[1]

---

[1] John Gillen, "Mestizo America," *Most of the World*, ed. Ralph Linton (New York: Columbia University Press, 1949), pp. 156–174. Mestizo America includes all the nations

The problems of the large mestizo group are not peculiarly Indian but are interrelated with the broad problems of class difference and the development of democratic institutions. In the United States and Canada, on the other hand, the Indian problem is in comparison more particularistic and relatively minor. The special character of the Indian problem in the United States is attested by the establishment of the Indian Service as a branch of the federal government with no counterpart in all the other minority situations. Its minor place is seen in the fact that the Service concerns itself with less than 0.5 percent of the total national population.

The Indian Population

Composition of the Population

Estimates of the number of aborigines in the Western Hemisphere at the time of the white man's coming vary widely. Lorimer cites estimates ranging from 8 to 13 million.[2] Means, however, estimates the number of Indians of the Inca Consolidation alone to have been 16 million.[3]

Any estimate of the present Indian population of the Americas is exceedingly unreliable, not only because of inadequate statistical counts but also because persons of varying degrees of Indian ancestry have been so largely incorporated into the common national populations that the lines of racial division have become highly obscured. Lorimer summarizes the situation as follows: "The number of pureblood Indians in the Western Hemisphere may be greater today than at the time of Columbus; with the number of persons usually considered as Indian it is almost certainly greater; and the total Indian stock, including its fractional elements in the whole population, is far greater." [4] The same author further observes: "Mestizos, or Ladinos, who draw their genetic heritage in part from Amerindian and in part from other stocks now outnumber pureblood Indians both in Latin America and in the United States." [5]

Estimates of the number of Indians in 1492 in the area which is now the United States range from 700,000 to 1,000,000. By the time Indians became official wards in 1871 their population had been reduced to less than half a million. It is generally agreed that under the early reservation system the

---

south of the Rio Grande except Argentina and Uruguay, which are practically all Caucasian in composition, and Brazil, where there is a proportionally smaller Indian population, and where Indians have not been as integrated into the total national life as in Spanish America.

[2] Frank Lorimer, "Observations on the Trends of Indian Population in the United States," *The Changing Indian,* ed. Oliver La Farge (Norman: University of Oklahoma Press, 1942), p. 11.

[3] Philip A. Means, *Ancient Civilization of the Andes* (New York: Charles Scribner's Sons, 1931).

[4] Lorimer, "Observations," p. 11. By permission.

[5] *Ibid.,* p. 12.

population declined still further, reaching its lowest around 1900. In the official census count, these trends are reflected in the following figures:

TABLE 16–1. *Indian Population of the United States* [6]

1890	248,253
1920	244,437
1940	333,369
1950	357,499
1960	523,591

Students of Indian affairs have considered the census an underestimate. Thus it may be that the 46.5 percent increase reported in the Indian population between 1950 and 1960 reflects a more accurate count.

The difficulties in determining the actual number of Indians stem from problems of definition, particularly in regard to the classification of mixed bloods. Census enumerators are instructed "to return as Indians, not only those of full Indian blood, but also those of mixed white and Indian blood, except where the percentage of Indian blood is very small or where the individual is regarded as a white person in the community where he lives." [7] However, persons of whatever admixture of Caucasian genetic strains, or in many instances, of Negro-Indian mixture, who have remained in the tribes and therefore on the Indian Service rolls are considered Indian because they live as Indians. The future size of the Indian population depends not only on natural growth but also on the extent to which mixed bloods choose to remain "Indian" or to pass into the white world.

Distribution of the Indian Population

While there are people classified by the census as Indian in nearly every state in the Union, our interest focuses on those who live as Indians in groups. Some Indian landholdings are to be found in 32 of the 50 states. Their distribution has remained generally the same for many years. [8]

1. THE SOUTHWEST   Primarily Arizona and western New Mexico. Major groups are the Navaho, Hopi, Papago, Pueblo, and Apache. In this area live nearly one quarter of the Indians of the United States, numbering about 110,000 in 1960.

2. CALIFORNIA AND THE NORTHWEST   An intermittent scattering of Indian tribes through California, Nevada, and Utah, including many Shoshone and

[6] United States Census data for the specified years.

[7] H. L. Shapiro, "The Mixed-Blood Indian," in *The Changing Indian*, p. 20.

[8] See Sol Tax, "What the Indians Want" in the Chicago *Sunday Sun Times*, June 11, 1961, Section 2, p. 1, for a map showing the numerical distribution of Indians by states. See G. E. E. Lindquist, *The Indians in American Life* (New York: Friendship Press, 1944), for a map showing the distribution of Indian Tribes by area.

Paiute. A further intermittent but less wide scattering of reservations in Washington, Oregon, Idaho, Montana, and Wyoming.

3. THE NORTH CENTRAL   The area of greatest concentration here is in South Dakota with its large Sioux population, followed by substantial reservations in North Dakota and Minnesota and scattered small bands in Nebraska and Iowa on the south and in Wisconsin and Michigan on the east.

4. OKLAHOMA   Next to the Southwest region, this former Indian territory has the largest concentration of Indians, totaling about 52,000 in 1960. Linked with this area are small bands in Northern Kansas.

5. NORTH CAROLINA   While some small Indian groups are located in widely scattered places in Texas, Louisiana, Mississippi, Alabama, Florida, South Carolina, and Virginia, the Cherokee tribes of North Carolina far outnumber all other Indian groups combined in the South.

6. NEW YORK   Of the relatively few Indians to be found in the Northeast, most are located in the rural areas of New York state, including the Seneca, the Onondaga, and the Tonawanda. There are very small bands in Rhode Island and Maine.

Visibility

Anthropologists believe that the Indian peoples migrated to the Western Hemisphere from Asia, but in the 18,000 years that they have inhabited North and South America they have developed a physiognomic type distinguishable from Asiatic peoples. They are brown in skin color, have straight black hair, little facial or body hair. Head shape and nasal index vary widely.[9] Pure-bred Indians are usually distinguishable in their physical appearance even when acculturated to the dominant society.

For many Indians there is also high cultural visibility. This has been reinforced by United States policy which has created the pattern of reservations, and by, in the past and to an extent still, the mistrust Indians feel for dominants in view of their history.[10]

Indigenous Indian cultures, including language, vary widely and are either highly discrete, or loosely related according to the geographic location and historical economic base. Notwithstanding the difficulties of generalizing about such widely varying cultures, certain broad characteristics of Indian societies may be noted, with some reference to their contrast with the cultures of the

[9] A. L. Kroeber, *Anthropolgy* (New York: Harcourt, Brace and Co., 1948), pp. 136–7.
[10] The mistrust may vary according to the particular history of a given Indian community. A student of Dr. Meyer's who had worked summers on both the Papago and the Ute reservations found a more open attitude among Papagos which she ascribed to their long as relatively benign relations to whites since the days of the first Spanish missionaries; the Utes on the other hand had experienced acute conflict with whites. When under the Indian Reorganization Act tribes were allowed to incorporate so that they could borrow money from the government for economic and social programs, the Navaho refused, feeling this was just another trick to give the white man access to their lands and resources.

white invaders. The characteristic features we shall discuss here apply to the Indian people before the period of wardship.

1. The Indian cultures were all preliterate. Thus knowledge and mores were inculcated through the spoken word and the teaching of youth by the elders.

2. While all preliterate societies appear small in contrast with modern societies, Indian societies north of the Rio Grande tended to be small even in the perspective of primitive societies. Tribal relationships were almost entirely personal, and the Indians lacked experience with those secondary, impersonal, formalized relationships characteristic of larger-scale civilization.

3. The Indian economies were primarily hunting and gathering, with fishing in certain areas. In what is now the United States, hoe agriculture was practiced among the Eastern tribes and the Southwest, where maize growing was prevalent. When hoe agriculture was practiced, it was usual for the women to perform the gardening tasks,[11] a point to keep in mind when noting the later efforts to transform Indian men into farmers. The attitudes of nonagricultural Indians toward the land are revealed in the words of Wowoka, a Nevadan Indian who founded a new religion among the Western Indians in the nineteenth century.

> You ask me to plow the ground . . . Shall I take a knife and tear my mother's bosom? Then when I die she will not take me to her bosom to rest. You ask me to cut grass and make hay and sell it, and be rich like white men but how dare I cut my mother's hair? [12]

4. While individuals sometimes owned items of personal adornment and had property rights to certain songs and crests, property with economic value usually belonged to extended kin or tribal groups. It was inconceivable that any individual member of the group should lack necessities as long as they were available to anyone else.

5. Class distinctions were generally less marked than in preliterate societies in other areas, and where they did exist the material standard of living did not vary greatly from commoner to noble.[13] Too, individual power was greatly limited. Thus in comparing the position of chief among four widely contrasting North American tribes, Goldenweiser writes, "in no case is he [the chief] permitted to exercise actual control over the actions of his people—barring such drastic situations as war or other temporary exploits—and . . . in his daily life he is scarcely distinguishable from any of his subjects.[14]

[11] Robert H. Lowie, *Primitive Society* (New York: Liveright Publishing Corporation, 1947), p. 75.
[12] Paul Radin, *The Story of the American Indian,* p. 368. By permission of the Liveright Publishing Corporation, New York City.
[13] See Harold E. Driver, *Indians of North America* (Chicago: the University of Chicago Press, 1961), Ch. 19, "Rank and Social Classes."
[14] Alexander Goldenweiser, *Early Civilization* (New York: Alfred A. Knopf, 1922), p. 120.

The Establishment of Dominance

Period of Community Diplomacy: 1607–1778

During the colonial period each local English or Dutch settlement dealt with the Indians by whatever means seemed best to it.[15] In Virginia the first settlement, which was founded in 1607, lay within the territory of the Powhatan Confederacy, whose chieftain, Waukunsenecaw, left the small white group in peace. When a new wave of settlers appeared, however, his successor, Opechancanough, fought to drive them out. But in 1644 he was decisively beaten.[16] In Massachusetts, peace prevailed between the Indians and the white men for more than ten years, in part because of an illness which heavily depopulated the tribes nearest the shores. Again, however, as the white settlers became more numerous and began to press westward, many tribes grew hostile. While in some cases Indian resistance was temporarily successful, the ultimate outcome was always white victory. The technological superiority of Europeans acted here, as elsewhere throughout the era of colonial expansion, to subjugate indigenous peoples. There was friendly trade and barter when whites needed Indians. When whites "needed" Indian lands there was conflict. For most Europeans this was their first encounter with a preliterate culture and they had no orientation which would enable them to understand the customs and social structure that Indians had developed as their adaptation to environment. During the French and Indian Wars the French made alliance with Indians in their common goal of driving out the English settlers, and this increased fear and antagonism in the colonial era.

In 1754 the British Crown formulated a policy for dealing with the Indians which took jurisdiction away from the individual colonies or border groups. Under this policy, "the tribes were independent nations, under the protection of the Crown; Indian lands were inalienable except through voluntary surrender to the Crown; and any attempt by an individual or group, subject to the Crown, or by a foreign state, to buy or seize lands from Indians, was illegal." [17] The attempt of the British Government to carry out this policy amidst innumerable local violations increased the antagonism of the colonists, especially those in the border area, toward the Crown. Thus the Indians indirectly contributed to the final issue of the American Revolution.

Period of Control by Treaties: 1778–1871

The policy of the British Crown was in essence taken over by the new American Government. For the first hundred years the relation of the Indian

---

[15] The Dutch established the policy of buying the land from the Indians, as in the famous purchase of Manhattan Island for a purported $24. The Quakers in Pennsylvania developed a friendly policy toward the Indians and tended, in the early days at least, to fulfill with scrupulous honesty the bargains they made.

[16] John Collier, *Indians of the Americas* (New York: Mentor Books, The New American Library of World Literature, 1947), p. 114.

[17] *Ibid.*, pp. 116–117.

tribes to the federal government was characterized by treaties, nominally negotiated by the government with so-called sovereign Indian nations. Yet whenever the Indians failed to agree with what the government wanted, they were met with military force. Frequently special local groups moved against the Indians quite independently of the national government, as when the Georgia Legislature passed an act confiscating all Cherokee land and declaring Cherokee tribal laws invalid within the state. Persistently when the white people rode roughshod over their own treaties, the Indians fought back, and a number of Indian wars of considerable dimension took place east of the Mississippi. The Seminole War in Florida and the Black Hawk War in the Illinois Territory, in which Lincoln fought, were among the more famous. The final outcome east of the Mississippi was that most of the Indian tribes were forced into the newly established Indian Territory (now the state of Oklahoma). The exceptions were a few small, relatively harmless bands in Maine, New York, Virginia, and Florida, and a considerable number of Cherokees in North Carolina, who put up so much resistence that they were let alone in the wilds of the Smoky Mountain Region.

West of the Mississippi, much of the story of Indian-white relations centers around, first, the situation in California following the gold rush and, second, the subjugation of the Plains Indians throughout the vast Midwest. In California the white men in search of gold forced the Indians out of any area they wanted. From 1851 on, the federal government negotiated treaties with many local tribes by which the Indians agreed to surrender more than half of California. These treaties, because of frontier political pressure, were never ratified by the Senate, and the government subsequently sold to white people much of the land pledged to the Indians. The subjugation of the Plains Indians beginning about 1870 is described by Collier:

> First there was military assault, on slight pretexts or no pretexts at all, and the government exploited tribal rivalries in order that Indians should kill Indians. The limited and disciplinary war customs of the Plains turned into total warfare, aimed at annihilation, with the United States Army as the driving power. The tribes were finally beaten, however, not through overwhelming numbers or superior armament (though these existed) but through starvation after the whites had destroyed the buffalo. . . . That revelry of slaughter, which had no sportsmanship in it, was recognized as a war measure against the Indians and was deliberately encouraged.[18]

Reservation Period: First Phase; Forced Assimilation

In 1871, Congress decreed that no Indian tribe "shall be acknowledged or recognized as an independent nation, tribe or power, with whom the United States may contract by treaty,"[19] thus marking the beginning of a definitely

[18] *Ibid.*, by permission of the author.
[19] Ray Allen Billington, *Westward Expansion* (New York: The Macmillan Co., 1949), p. 668. Ch. 32, "The Indian Barrier," pp. 651–670, describes the history of Indian-white relations from 1860 to 1887.

new phase in Indian-white relations. The Indians were now wards of the federal government, a unique status for any minority group in the United States. The policy and practices of the Indian Office from this time on were aimed at weakening the tribal organization of the Indians, destroying their culture, and forcing the assimilation of Indians as individuals into the normative American way of life. After several years of public and Congressional debate, a new land policy was adopted with the passage of the famous Dawes Act in 1887. This legislation empowered the President to divide the lands of any tribe by giving allotted individual portions to family heads or other individuals. But the plots so allotted were to be held in trust for twenty-five years, after which they were to become the unrestricted property of each owner. In the meantime they could not be sold. The object of this program was to force each Indian breadwinner to become a self-supporting individual by working his own land. In the meantime the Indians were to be supported directly by the government.

The Dawes Act was the result of crusading efforts on the part of aroused public opinion about the extreme exploitation and decimation of the Indians. It represented a move of the American conscience, but an extremely naïve move, within the ideology of its period. Understanding nothing of Indian social organization, nor recognizing the problems of a nontechnological people, despite the good intentions of crusaders [20] and Congressmen, the land allotment policy was disastrous to the Indians. They lacked the technical knowledge needed to make their holdings pay. They lacked credit to acquire materials (seed and tools) to operate the land. The division of land through inheritance was inimical to most tribes who held land as common property. Under these circumstances they were prey to whites who leased land allotments at below value (ranchers, for example, would lease contiguous allotments for grazing beef cattle for the urban market), and to squatters who impinged on Indian property that was not fenced or cultivated. Over the entire period in which the allotment policy was in effect (1887–1914), the lands held by the Indians were reduced (largely by squatter occupation) from 138 million acres to 47 million acres.[21]

Another phase of the policy of forced assimilation concerned the educational program. Indian children at school age were taken out of their tribal homes and placed in boarding schools, where the use of Indian languages and the practice of Indian ways, such as dress and hair styles, were forbidden. The curricula of the schools were largely that of the white schools, without any adaptation to the particular needs of the Indians. In Macgregor's opinion, what-

---

[20] See Helen Hunt Jackson, *A Century of Dishonor*, which first appeared in 1881 (New York: Harper & Brothers). It has now been reissued by Harper & Row as a Harper Torchbook (1965). Mrs. Jackson is also known for her novel, *Ramona*, which deals with the sad fate of California Indians. She has been sometimes called the Harriet Beecher Stowe of the Indian cause. In her view wardship a..d the Allotment Act were great steps forward for the protection and integration of Indians.

[21] Ward Shepard, "Land Problems of an Expanding Indian Population," in Oliver La Farge, ed., *The Changing Indian* (Norman: University of Oklahoma Press, 1942), p. 11.

ever practical training the Indian children obtained either for making a living or making better homes was gained from the labor they performed to help support the school.[22]

The first period of reservation policy, until the Reorganization Act of 1934 not only failed to understand cultural differences, and the slow rate of cultural change, especially for segregated groups as was *per se* characteristic of reservations, it further fell short of its objective because of inefficient administration. The Indian Service, particularly in its earlier years, was not conspicuous for the high standards of its personnel. Nor was a particular interest in Indians and their welfare a prerequisite for employment in the Service. Furthermore, the appropriations granted it were inadequate. Even when well-intentioned officials attempted to carry out some sort of policy, they were beset with powerful pressures from special interests to twist the policy to the latter's advantage.

During the 1920's constant pressures were brought to bear by certain vested white interests to enact legislation which would have expropriated further the rights of Indians to their resources. These efforts were defeated and as one result of the publicity attending the hearings in this connection, a comprehensive study of the problems of the administration of Indian affairs was undertaken (1927) by a private agency, the Institute for Government Research, at the request of Secretary of the Interior Hubert Work. The findings of this study, usually known as the Merriam Survey, went far to create a more favorable attitude toward the Indians.[23]

Minority Adaptations to Dominance

We have described public policy as it affected Indians into the second decade of the twentieth century. In these 250 years two important strains of American ideology affected the relations of whites to Indians. First, there were important political leaders who saw the development of America as the manifest destiny of the European "bearers of civilization." Two illustrations will serve to show how persistent was this attitude: Benjamin Franklin, in his *Autobiography* says (clearly half-facetiously, but nevertheless):

> And indeed, if it be the design of Providence to extirpate these savages in order to make room for the cultivators of the earth, it seems probable that rum may be the appointed means.[24]

Theodore Roosevelt thought that Helen Hunt Jackson's plea for Indians was "intensely in earnest" and therefore "capable of doing great harm." To the

[22] Gordon Macgregor, "Indian Education in Relation to the Social and Economic Background of the Reservation," *Ibid.*, pp. 116–127.

[23] Institute for Government Research, *The Problem of Indian Administration* (Baltimore: The Johns Hopkins Press, 1928).

[24] Smyth, Albert Henry, ed., *The Writings of Benjamin Franklin* (New York: The Macmillan Co., 1907), Vol. I, p. 376.

young Theodore Roosevelt, a physically delicate upper-echelon New Yorker, the Indian was "cruel beyond belief," a "painted marauder," capable of great treachery.[25]

The other main trend was one of missionary efforts to Christianize and "civilize" Indians. To some extent in the pre-reservation period they had a moderate success.

Accommodation and Acculturation

Accommodation is always the solution of a powerless people. Indians had neither military superiority nor political strength. The only possibility, therefore, was an appeal to the spirit of justice of dominants. The Cherokee Memorial to the United States Congress of December 29, 1835, illustrates the position into which the acculturated Indian was forced:

> In truth, our cause is your own. It is the cause of liberty and of justice. It is based on your own principles, which we have learned from yourselves; for we have gloried to count your Washington and your Jefferson our great teachers.... We have learned your religion also ... we speak to the representatives of a Christian country.... On your kindness, on your benevolence, we rest our hopes...[26]

Acculturation has always occurred for some individual Indians. For groups it has been often resisted or incomplete. With the Chippewas of Minnesota, as a culture that was organized around individual ownership of property, the acculturation process and the move into the larger society has not been as difficult as for some other Indian nations whose culture patterns adapted less well. Often acculturation was retarded by inconsistencies and shifting policy in the Indian Bureau,[27] as well as the persistence through many vicissitudes of traditional structures in Indian societies.

Of course selective acculturation has affected most Indians. Early adoptions of white material culture included the significant items of the horse, the gun, and alcohol. The adoption of the nonmaterial cultural of whites might have been more widespread for more peoples had it not been for the severity in which white Americans sought to impose their ways on Indians.

Separatism

One example of pre-reservation separatism is the Zuni who repeatedly murdered Spanish administrators and priests, resisted Christianity, took refuge

[25] Helen Hunt Jackson, *A Century of Dishonor,* Introduction to the Harper Torchbook edition by Andrew F. Rolle, pp. xv and xx.

[26] William Brandon, *The American Heritage Book of Indians* (New York: Dell Publishing Co., 1961), p. 374.

[27] Morris Edward Opler, "The Creek "Town" and the Problem of Creek Indian Political Reorganization," in Edward H. Spicer, ed., *Human Problems in Technical Change* (New York: The Russell Sage Foundation, 1952), pp. 165–180.

in the mountains to avoid reprisals, and consolidated their villages into one fortified pueblo. Their contacts with the Spanish (1540–1846) left a residue of mistrust so that to the present they will not let neighboring Hispanos witness any of their ceremonials, although some Hispanos come to the government clinic which is at Zuni.[28]

Retreatism

The early period of reservation life produced dependency and demoralization. Perhaps it was hardest on the Plains Indians whose cultures were built around hunting. Their economic base had been destroyed with the killing off of the buffalo and they were moved from their habitats to other land. They did not have the social organization or patterns of childhood training that adapted to the close proximity of village life and as Hagen states, "the first the reservations (for these warlike Indians) were essentially concentration camps." [29] In the case of the Sioux the aggressiveness fostered in children and the strict self-control necessary to survival in a hunting culture was symbolized and compensated for in a central tribal ceremony: the Sun Dance. Since this ceremony involved self-inflicted pain, on the one hand, and orgiastic release, on the other, it was forbidden by the new masters. "The whites, moved by their own values, unwittingly removed the last vestige of meaning from lives whose external base had already been destroyed." [30] The result was demoralization, cultism, and eventually apathy. In 1961 when Hagen visited the reservations of the Dakotas (Dakota is what the Sioux call themselves), the inhabitants seemed to be suffering from a malaise "more pervasive than malnutrition and more penetrating than cold . . . as ghosts walking about, withdrawn, passive, lifeless. . . ." [31]

Reservation Period: Second Phase; the "New Deal"

The phrase, "New Deal," coined to characterize the early years of Franklin D. Roosevelt's administration, was peculiarly apt with reference to Indian affairs. While the time was ripe in 1933 for reorganization of Indian policy, the sweeping character of the changes undertaken at this time was in considerable measure due to a long-standing sympathetic interest in Indians of the new Secretary of the Interior, Harold I. Ickes, and to the appointment of John Collier as Commissioner of the Bureau of Indian Affairs.

Behind the efforts which culminated in the passage of the Indian Reorganization Act, sponsored by Senator Burton Wheeler of Montana, was a new

[28] Evan Z. Vogt and Ethel M. Albert, *People of Rimrock: A Study of Values in Five Cultures* (Cambridge, Mass.: Harvard University Press, 1966), pp. 46–50.
[29] Everett E. Hagen, *On the Theory of Social Change* (Homewood, Ill.: The Dorsey Press, 1962), p. 481. See Chapter 19 for a case study of the Sioux on the reservations.
[30] *Ibid.*
[31] *Ibid.*, p. 484.

philosophy concerning Indians held by the new Commissioner and strongly supported by the new Federal Administration. In essence, this philosophy aimed at integrating Indians into the national life as Indians, to make Indian groups self-sustaining and yet retain as much of their tribal culture and group identification as was consistent with life in a modern civilized nation. Collier not only admired the Indians as persons but felt that much of their culture should be preserved, that there was a place for Indians as Indians in a multigroup democratic society. He expressed his philosophy thus:

> The new Indian policy ... seeks to reinstate the Indians as normally functioning units, individual and group, into the life of the world. It makes them equal in the management of their own affairs and the direction of their own lives.
>
> On the purely cultural side, only sheer fanaticism would decide the further destruction of Indian languages, crafts, poetry, music, ritual, philosophy, and religion. These possessions have a significance and a beauty which grew patiently through endless generations of a people immersed in the life of nature, filled with imaginative and ethical insight into the core of being....[32]

The point of view of the new commissioner was reflected in the Indian Reorganization Act passed by Congress in 1934, the chief provisions of which are as follows:

> 1. With certain qualifications, Indian societies were to be empowered to undertake political, economic, and administrative self-government.
>
> 2. Land allotment was to be stopped, and under certain conditions, additional lands could be added to current holdings.
>
> 3. A system of agricultural and industrial credit was to be established, and the needed funds were authorized.
>
> 4. An Indian Civil Service was to be established and provisions for the training of Indians themselves in administration and the professions were called for.

The Reorganization Act called for the acceptance of its provisions by each tribe individually, determined on the basis of a referendum using secret ballot. Those who voted to accept could organize under it for self-government and could organize themselves as a federal corporation to conduct economic enterprise.[33]

Progress Under the Indian Reorganization Act

The new deal for the Indians meant considerable strides in economic rehabilitation, increasing tribal self-government, and a slow but steady rise in the

[32] From Report of House of Representatives Subcommittee on Appropriations for the Interior Department, 1934.
[33] Collier, *Indians of the Americas*, pp. 157–158.

welfare of Indians as a whole. By 1948 a total of seventy-three tribes had received charters of incorporation, which meant that with the economic assistance of the government and the technical advice and approval of the Indian Service these groups improved their economic welfare and gained experience in helping themselves. Some tribes through loans have been able to purchase additional lands or to put hitherto unused acreage into effective use. One major problem has been to prevent too great a depletion of Indian land resources because of the desire of many Indians to sell their land to non-Indians or to lease it without adequate safeguards against deterioration. Marked increases in the requests by Indians, some with individual holdings, to sell their lands were reported by the Bureau in 1948 and 1949.[34]

By 1948 a total of ninety-three tribes had adopted written constitutions and had begun to assume larger political self-government. Typically there is a Tribal Council which suggests measures of administration and approves or rejects proposals of the Agency staff. It has considerable control of the tribal finances and appoints a Tribal Court of Indian Judges, which tries all cases of criminal law except those involving the ten most serious offenses, over which the Federal court retains jurisdiction. Nevertheless, the great gap between tribal legal and political practices and those of the white democracy could not be closed at once. For example, it was the practice of both the Navaho and the Papago to decide important matters by face-to-face meetings of all concerned in which the issues were discussed until unanimity was reached, in contrast with the system of majority decision under white democracy. It was clear that the goal of self-government for the Indians had to be approached by degrees.

Although Congress enacted a law in 1924 making all Indians citizens, seven states barred Indians from voting until about 1940, either by discriminatory laws or interpretations of laws. Following 1940, five of these states began to allow Indians to vote by not enforcing these statutes. Court decisions in Arizona and New Mexico in 1948 opened the door to full voting privileges for Indians, and since then Indians there have generally had the right to vote.

Education for Indian children has been continually improving. From 1950 to 1960 the number of Indian children enrolled in schools increased from 26,716 to 133,316; over the same period the percentage of Indian children attending public schools, rather than the federally operated schools for Indian pupils alone, increased from 50 percent to 63.5 percent.[35] It is of especial interest to discover that in 1959 some twenty-five tribes themselves provided scholarships in higher education totalling about $500,000.[36]

Despite this improvement the Indians have a long way to go to approximate national norms. The task force assigned by President Kennedy to recommend Indian policy for his administration found that "the bulk of the reservation

[34] *Annual Report of Secretary of the Interior*, 1948, pp. 369–392.
[35] *Annual Report of the Secretary of Interior*, 1960, p. 97.
[36] *Annual Report*, 1959, p. 235.

Indian population is less well educated than other Americans, has a shorter life span, and has a much lower standard of living." [37]

Recent Trends in Official Policy

A considerable reversal in the Indian policy and program occurred in the '50's. Efforts to speed up the process of liquidating the government's responsibility to the Indians took the forms which may be designated as "relocation" and "termination."

RELOCATION In 1952 the Bureau of Indian Affairs started what was called the Voluntary Relocation Program, under which reservation Indians, either individually or in family groups, who desired to move to industrial centers for permanent employment and settlement were offered financial and other assistance to enable them to relocate. A reason for adopting this program was the fact that most Indian tribal lands were inadequate to permit viable economies with a rapidly growing population. By 1960, some 35,000 reservation Indians had thus been relocated in various industrial areas ranging from the West Coast to the Midwest. These relocated Indians are employed at the lowest occupational range and live in the poorer sections of the cities often inhabited largely by other minorities. Estimates of the extent to which the Indians remained in relocation or returned to the reservation vary. The Bureau of Indian Affairs in 1955 put the number of the relocated Indians who had up to this time returned at about 24 percent; The Association on American Indian Affairs on the basis of its survey of the relocation program gives a much higher percentage of returnees.[38]

As with any program of this sort, the results vary with the attitudes and efficiency of the officials operating the program at local levels. Many Indian leaders, as well as such friends of the Indians as The Association on American Indian Affairs, favor this program in principle. This latter organization feels that the program could be improved by (1) making it clear that relocation opportunities are available to those Indians who really want it without any undue pressures being exerted; (2) improving liaison with local community agencies in the cities of relocation in order to facilitate the adjustment of the resettled Indians; and (3) not stressing the point of permanence in relocation.

Even if substantial numbers of relocated Indians do return to the reservations, the experience will have been educational and the returned members may contribute to the improvement of tribal conditions through their increased acculturation. The main concern of the friends of the Indians is, however, that the relocation program shall not be viewed as a "solution" of the Indian problem, that its operation shall not deflect effort from the more basic problem

---

[37] *Report to the Secretary of Interior by the Task Force on Indian Affairs,* July 10, 1961, p. 2.
[38] La Verne Madigan, "The American Indian Relocation Program," The Association on American Indian Affairs, 1956. Based on the findings of a relocation survey team.

of aiding the reservation Indians to develop viable economies, working out their own problems and being free to determine how much of their traditional cultural heritages they wish to retain.[39]

TERMINATION   The termination policy stemmed from a resolution by Congress passed on August 1, 1953, which stated in part:

> ...[I]t is the policy of Congress, as rapidly as possible, to make the Indians within the territorial limits of the United States subject to the same laws and entitled to the same privileges and responsibilities as are applicable to other citizens of the United States, to end their status as wards of the United States, and to grant them all the rights and prerogatives pertaining to American citizenship....[40]

Following passage of this resolution, efforts were made to order or to persuade tribes to request termination of their relation to the federal government. This would have meant in many instances dissolution of tribal organizations and the division of tribal assets among the several members. In view of the lack of acculturation of most Indians to the normative American way of life, especially to the norms of economic self-reliance, termination might well have resulted in the demoralization and pauperization of the Indians of many tribes. Alarmed at this prospect, friends of the Indians protested the policy and it was revised. Indian groups were not to be pressured to terminate unless they themselves wanted it and were developed to a point where they could carry on their own affairs. Thus in fact only a few tribes were actually terminated, the most important being the Klamaths of Oregon and the Menomines of Wisconsin, both owners of large tracts of valuable timber.

The results of termination have not benefited the Menomines or the government. "Termination itself costs the government nearly $3 million. And now a once profitable business operation, which supported this tribe for nearly a century, looks to be on the edge of collapse." [41] The shift from a common property culture to individual ownership has created legal problems, involved Indians with banks and lawyers, forced them into dealing with county and state structures with which they are unfamiliar. Ridgeway predicts that "the tribe is likely to be slowly extinguished, the Indians either moving down to the cities or dying in the woods. The old reservation seems fated to become a state park." [42] Menomines today see termination as just one more hoax of the white government. Brandon sees the effort to force termination as an aspect of "McCarthyism" and quotes the late Felix S. Cohen, the principal government expert on Indian legal affairs: "Like the miner's canary, the Indian marks the shift from fresh air to poison gas in our political atmosphere; and our treatment of Indians,

---

[39] *Ibid.*
[40] House Concurrent Resolution 108, 83rd Congress, 1st Session.
[41] James Ridgeway, "The Lost Indians," *The New Republic,* December 4, 1965, p. 20.
[42] *Ibid.,* p. 20.

even more than our treatment of other minorities, reflects the rise and fall of our democratic faith." [43]

When wholesale termination was anticipated, a special commission for Indian claims was established to clear up unpaid treaty claims, and past fraudulence. Although some of the claims are extreme, out of our 800 claims, twenty-one, totaling some $40 million had been paid by 1960. [44]

In the latter part of the Eisenhower Administration, official policy veered back toward the principles embodied in the 1934 Indian Reorganization Act, particularly removing pressure on tribes to terminate. Governmental policy is now directed toward increased financial aid and technical assistance to Indian tribal corporations to improve their capacity to support themselves; increased education, especially vocational training to enable Indians to increase their income by working off the reservation in nearby white communities; and encouragement of the location of new industries near the reservation for Indian employment. The health functions of the Bureau of Indian Affairs were transferred to the United States Bureau of Public Health in 1955.

The Udall Plan

In April, 1966, Secretary of the Interior, Stewart L. Udall, announced plans to reorganize the Bureau of Indian Affairs. His announcement followed within a week the Senate confirmation of the appointment of the first Indian head of the Bureau in nearly 100 years. The New Commissioner of Indian Affairs is Robert L. Bennett, an Oneida from Wisconsin.

The Udall Plan promised that Indians would be brought increasingly into the decision making processes; that Bureau regulations for supervising tribes would be revised; that Indian education would be sharply upgraded; that internal organization of the Bureau would be streamlined to allow for greater responsiveness to Indian needs and requests. [45]

The Decline of Dominance

Dominant Adjustments

White attitudes toward Indians have been complex and often ambivalent. Like the Negroes, Indians are part of the American conscience. They have also suffered from a similar paternalism, on the one hand, and exploitation on the other. Because most Indians are poor they experience the general status derogation of all the poor. The degree to which racial attitudes enter into Indian-white relationships today is difficult to assess. Historically they have been in a somewhat better position with regard to race prejudice than the Negroes.

[43] Brandon, *The American Heritage Book of the Indians,* p. 369.
[44] *Ibid.*
[45] *The New York Times,* April 16, 1966, pp. 1, 13.

The Indian Service Personnel

The relations of the Agency staff members to their Indian wards have varied with their own personalities and attitudes toward their task, from warm friendships to purely official and impersonal contact. Spicer found that teachers did not usually become intimately integrated with the Indian life in their school community and that the effectiveness of Agency medical workers to get Indian acceptance of modern health methods depended on their attitude toward Indian beliefs. "Nominally, every staff member . . . is accessible to any Indian who desires to talk with him, but relatively few Indians seek such contacts." [46] Kluckhohn and Leighton found that, while some of the employees of the Indian Service were motivated by a genuine desire to help the Indians, many others took the position because it was the best they could get and not because they had real interest in Indians. "Many are highly conventionally prejudiced, and of limited imagination and flexibility." [47] Many of the younger personnel with some background in anthropology are changing the flavor of the Indian service.

The Traders

Because the traders on the reservations are the white people with whom the Indians become best acquainted, they symbolize the white world to the Indians. On the Navaho reservation some traders are very fond of the Indians and perform a wide variety of friendly services; others "have mercilessly and shamefully exploited the Indians' ignorance of markets and of simple arithmetic." [48] While the role of traders is declining as the Indians get to town more often, nevertheless they "are still significant in helping the Navahos market their goods, in encouraging native handicrafts, and in otherwise promoting the economic development of the tribe.[49]

The Missionaries

In their zeal to teach the Indian children English, the mission schools in some instances have forbidden pupils to speak their native tongue anywhere near the school. When Kluckhohn and Leighton found that missionaries had made few practicing converts to Christianity, they attributed the failure in large measure to "their efforts to suppress native custom or to urge strenuously the substitution of white customs, oftentimes in spheres which seem to the Navahos outside the province of the missionaries." [50] The resistance, and some-

[46] Rosamund Spicer, in Joseph, Spicer, and Chesky, *The Desert People* (Chicago: University of Chicago Press, 1949), p. 103.
[47] Clyde Kluckhohn and Dorothea Leighton, *The Navaho* (Cambridge: Harvard University Press, 1947), p. 107.
[48] *Ibid.,* p. 79.
[49] *Ibid.,* p. 80.
[50] *Ibid.,* pp. 81–82.

times ridicule, which the missionaries encounter in trying to make the Navahos give up their traditional ways is illustrated in the following comment of a young mission school graduate:

> That missionary came here today and tried to make my husband buy a marriage license, but my husband said he didn't have a dollar. He has been trying to get my brother to buy a license for a year. The other missionary tried for two years and got tired of it. His wife said, "We're married all right. We don't need any paper. You tell him you don't know, you'll have to ask your wife—then he won't talk so long to you." [51]

White Employers and Neighbors

In the Papago area "the general public looks upon these Indians as a lower-class group with a tendency toward drunkenness, and, though they are not subjected to as marked social discrimination as are Negroes, they must endure a certain amount of racial prejudice." [52] In the vicinity of the Pine Ridge Reservation Macgregor found the neighbors of the Dakotas reacting to Indians in accord with class position. Middle-class whites looked on Indians generally as inferior but were more accepting of the few whose education, employment, and social behavior were more like their own; a certain segment of the lower class tended to accept Indians as equals. [53]

A picture of white-Indian relations in the biracial community of "Fruitland," New Mexico, in 1954 is presented by Sasaki:

> There existed evidences of intergroup tension. On the one hand many whites, mostly persons who employed Navahos or worked with them, expressed considerable resentment over the Indians' irresponsible behavior. On the other hand, the Navahos began to feel that they were being discriminated against by employers and by the police. Many not so directly involved also began to stereotype Navaho behavior because of the activities of a few. The record of arrests appearing three or four times a week in the local newspaper revealed the same Navaho names. Although no open brawls occurred between Navahos and whites, the Indians were frequently arrested for fighting among themselves and for intoxication. The town's general growing pains were affecting the Navahos in particular. [54]

However, certain white officials in Fruitland—"men who had spent several decades as traders to the Navahos and thus were able to speak their language —were all active in their own ways of promoting intercultural understanding. [55]

[51] *Ibid.,* p. 82. Reprinted by permission of the publishers.
[52] Joseph, Spicer, and Chesky, *The Desert People,* p. 110.
[53] See Gordon Macgregor, *Warriors Without Weapons* (Chicago: University of Chicago Press, 1944), p. 84.
[54] Tom T. Sasaki, *Fruitland, New Mexico: A Navaho Community in Transition* (Ithaca, New York: Cornell University Press, 1960), pp. 198–199.
[55] *Ibid.*

They taught the Navahos the value of the vote and helped get their children into public schools.

The Effect of Army Service

In World War II approximately 25,000 Indians served in the armed forces, somewhat more than a third of all able-bodied Indian men of military age. For many this was an opportunity to learn at least GI English, to associate with non-Indians, and to have their first real look at the off-the-reservation world. They came back on the whole as a strong force for innovation and reform in their tribal communities. Some of these were discouraged by the reaction of the 50's, but others succeeded in developing community leadership.

The Cooperation of the Tribes

Although for several decades there has been an ideological Pan-Indian movement, it was largely concerned with utopian oratory and rather small in membership. The emergence, however, of the National Congress of American Indians as a policy and protest organization represents the impact of the younger generation. Some impetus, indeed in a sense a turning point in Indian affairs, came from the conference sponsored by the University of Chicago in the summer of 1961, where this organization, representing 80 tribes was asked to help shape a new inquiry into contemporary Indian problems. As contrasted with the Merriam Report of 1928, this investigation was to be with the participation and judgment of Indians themselves.[56]

Intertribal contacts have of course occurred in the past through trade exchanges with other Indians in the same area, and through off-reservation boarding schools and colleges where able young Indians form friendships, and sometimes marriages, with members of other tribes.[57]

Perhaps one of the most important aspects of the growth of intertribal cooperation is the fact that formerly ancient enemies are able to meet and decide together on common demands and common problems.[58]

[56] Brandon, *The American Heritage Book of Indians,* pp. 369–370.

[57] One such example, which we know of through personal communication, involves the marriage of an able young tribal leader with the daughter of the chief of another tribe. They live in the husband's tribe (on the reservation) where he has become an important community leader, but they claim status from the wife's family. How like the dominant society!

[58] A student in a field placement in Oraibi, the principal Hopi village, described in a personal communication what may have been a historic meeting between Hopi and Navaho leaders (traditional enemy tribes) in the spring of 1965. There was also present a contingent of CORE from Los Angeles. According to our informant the CORE delegation nearly ruined the whole meeting, as their ideology and urban experience did not allow for the slow pace, the nonideological, and the ceremonial aspects of such a meeting between Indians. Despite CORE the Hopi and the Navahos *came to various points of agreement for common action.*

The New Generation

Hopefully the base has been laid in the Bureau of Indian Affairs for a less paternalistic policy and a more highly qualified personnel. Similarly the isolation and splintered situation of American Indians is modifying. The problems for the immediate future involve generational conflicts.

In his case study of the Sioux, Hagan mentions Cato Valandra,[59] who was council secretary for the Rosebud Reservation. He and the council tribal chairman had begun to accomplish various improvements for the reservation. By 1967 Valandra had became president of the United Sioux Council,[60] representing 45,000 Sioux. He expresses a new militancy, as does Vine Deloria, the executive director of the National Congress of American Indians, also a Sioux. When the Bureau of Indian Affairs had a staff meeting in Santa Fe, New Mexico, to hear and consider "the Udall Plan," the National Congress of American Indians called a meeting, housed three blocks away to present their definition of the problems to the Bureau. They mobilized representatives from 62 tribes. They won two concessions from the meeting of the Bureau: the right to let Indian delegations attend the Bureau meetings, and the right to name a committee of elected tribal officials to consult with Secretary Udall on the reorganization of the Bureau of Indian Affairs.[61] But all was not yet clearly a united front. Mr. Chino, an Apache, said his group, although admiring the new Commissioner, doubted whether he could overcome the bureaucratic restrictions of his office. A Menomine said that the older generation would have to face the "reality" that termination was coming, but that it must be more gradual than it had been for the Menomines.[62]

Indians, Poverty, and "The Great Society"

The Indians are presented as the poorest minority in America. There seems to be agreement that the average income is about $1,500, which means that in order to arrive at such an average many are far below this. Forty to forty-five percent of employable Indians are unemployed.[63] The general level of education is poor for most Indians, though the number of Indian young men and women in professional life both in and out of the Indian world has grown remarkably in the past generation.

A number of Indian tribes have had some programs funded by the Office

[59] Hagen, On the Theory of Social Change, p. 499.
[60] The New York Times, Feb. 19, 1967, p. 33.
[61] The New York Times, April 15, 1966, p. 20.
[62] The New York Times, April 17, 1966, p. 81.
[63] The figure of $1,500 is agreed upon by The New York Times (April 17, 1966, p. 81) and the Association on American Indian Affairs, 1967. The Times reported a 40 percent jobless rate (Feb. 19, 1967, p. 33), and the Association on American Indian Affairs reported in 1967 a 45 percent jobless rate. The unemployment rate for the Sioux is reported by The New York Times (Feb. 19, 1967) as 75 percent.

of Economic Opportunity. The success of these programs has varied, depending on whether the project was adequately conceived to begin with, and subsequently whether it was adequately administered.[64] A good deal of effort has been made to involve Indians (including some from Alaska) in job training programs to make them available as members of the general labor force. But thus far the number of those who return to the reservation after taking an outside job may be as high as 50 percent.

It may be that the Indians will benefit, as other poor people, from the present American concern with reducing poverty. How much discrimination will handicap them is hard to estimate until a larger number seek a place in the overall social structure of non-Indian America. There have been charges of police brutality toward Indians,[65] and undoubtedly Indians will encounter discrimination in employment in some areas as they have heretofore. Some money recovered by claims has been set aside by some tribes for economic development. There has been some small movement to begin to develop industry on the reservations but this is beset with problems: the protest of unions, the isolation of reservations, the lack of Indian entrepreneurial skills, and unease with outside enterprise having "control" in the reservation. Nevertheless, the Bulova Watch Company has a small plant at Turtle Mountain Reservation (Chippewa), and the Navaho Tribal Council has started a small electronics enterprise. Navahos also own a large trucking business, and their vans may be seen from coast to coast.

We have cited some conspicuous examples of new leadership and movement toward development. But the speed with which retreatism can be turned into innovation depends on many factors: the history and social structure of the particular Indian nation, the resources available to it, its self-image, and the attitudes of the dominant society surrounding it. Even though more Indians are leaving the reservations than in former times, students of Indian affairs do not anticipate a dissolution of tribal identity in the foreseeable future.

Topics for Projects and Discussion

1. Select one Indian culture and describe its values and social structure. Show how these were functional adaptations to the environment in which the Indians lived before their subjugation by white Americans.
2. Make a study among your friends, classmates, or people in your community of their image of the American Indian. Have they ever known any Indians and if so, under what circumstances?
3. Trace the history of American policy toward the Indians and relate changes in policy to the political climate in which they occurred.
4. To what extent do you believe it is possible for Indians to retain subsocieties of their

[64] Homer Bigart "For the Indian: Squalor in the Great Society," *The New York Times,* March 13, 1966, pp. 1 and 67.
[65] *Ibid.,* p. 67.

own and achieve ultimate economic autonomy? What would the preconditions for this be? Would it be desirable?

5. Compare Helen Hunt Jackson's novel *Ramona* with Harriet Beecher Stowe's *Uncle Tom's Cabin* as examples of polemics that aroused public opinion in behalf of a minority. (Both of them are based on actual people and incidents).

Suggested Readings

Driver, Harold E. *Indians of North America.* Chicago: University of Chicago Press, 1961.
> *A comprehensive comparative description and interpretation of native American cultures.*

Hagan, William T. *American Indians.* Chicago: The University of Chicago Press, 1961.
> *A brief study of Indian-white relations from colonial times to the present.*

Sasaki, Tom. T. *Fruitland, New Mexico: A Navaho Community in Transition.* Ithaca, N.Y.: Cornell University Press, 1960.
> *Studies of acculturation of Navahos under increasing contact with whites.*

Spicer, Edward H., ed. *Human Problems in Technical Change: A Casebook.* New York: The Russell Sage Foundation, 1952.
> *Cases 1, 6, 10, 11, and 12 analyze attempts and results of innovation in several Indian societies.*

Vogt, Evan Z., and Albert, Ethel M. *People of Rimrock: A Study of Values in Five Cultures.*
> *A study of Zuni and Navaho Indians in relation to their Mormon, Hispano, and "Texan" neighbors.*

17

The Peoples of Hawaii

Intergroup relations in Hawaii are unique. Hawaii's extensive ethnic and racial heterogeneity can be seen in Table 17–1, where the ethnic composition at specified dates is shown. Although the dominant status of the white people of Euro-American background over the peoples of Oriental origin was well established when Hawaii became American territory, intergroup relations have continuously been distinguished by the absence of any legal or public discrimination. Nonofficial discrimination, however, by the white residents against both the native Hawaiians and the successive immigrant groups has been equally evident. The absence of formal discrimination has led many writers and students to picture Hawaii as a paradise of interracial relations; the informal discrimination has led others to view it less favorably.

With so many different peoples to consider, the problem of consistent nomenclature arises. With the exception of the Caucasians, the peoples involved can be identified by the names used in Table 17–1. By "Hawaiians" we shall mean the descendants of the native group present in the islands when white contact was first established. All others we shall call by their nationality names. Rather than designating the white dominant group by the racial term "Caucasian," we use the name bestowed on them by the native Hawaiians, "haoles," the meaning of which is "stranger." This label has come to be restricted to the first strangers to appear in Hawaii, the Euro-American whites, and their descendants, and not to others who subsequently immigrated to the islands. It identifies white people of American or northwestern European descent.

Presenting the changing ethnic composition of the population of Hawaii in graphic form offers difficulties. While official figures by ethnic composition have been recorded since 1853, changes in the basis of classification, reflecting changing social realities, have been made over the years, as is illustrated in Table 17–1. The changes are reasonably clear, however. (1) Between the time of first white contact in 1778 to about 1850, there were only small numbers of haoles residing in the Islands, with an essentially homogeneous native Hawaiian population. (2) From about 1850 to 1930, successive waves of immigrant peoples

TABLE 17-1. *Population of Hawaii by Ethnic Components at Specified Intervals and by Percent of Total, 1960*

	1853[1]	1884[1]	1900[1]	1920[1]	1950[1]	1960[2]	1960 % of Total
Hawaiian	70,036	40,414	29,799	23,723	12,245	11,294	1.7
Part Hawaiian	983	4,218	9,857	18,027	73,845	91,169	14.4
Caucasian	1,687	16,579	26,819	49,140	114,793	202,230	31.9
Portuguese	87	9,967	18,272	27,002	—	—	
Other Caucasian	1,600	6,612	8,547	19,708	—	—	
Chinese	304	18,254	25,767	23,507	32,376	38,197	6.3
Japanese		116	61,111	109,274	184,598	203,455	32.1
Korean		—	—	4,950	7,030	—	
Filipino	5	—	—	21,031	61,062	69,070	10.9
Puerto Rican				5,602	9,551		
Negro			233	348	2,651	4,953	0.8
All Other	62	1,397	648	310	1,618	12,305[3]	1.9
Total	73,137	80,578	154,234	255,912	499,769	632,772	100.0

[1] See Andrew Lind, *Hawaii's People* (Honolulu: University of Hawaii Press, 1955), p. 27 for the data through 1950.
[2] U.S. Census, 1960, Non-White Population by Race, *Final Report* (P C 2)—C, p. 254.
[3] The Negro components are subtracted from the above U.S. Census table "All Other" category, leaving the "All Other" largely Korean.

produced wide ethnic heterogeneity. The larger immigrant waves were Chinese, Japanese, and Filipino, in that time order. At various times other ethnics have found their way to Hawaii in response to the demand for plantation labor. Portuguese, Puerto Ricans, and Koreans came in sufficient numbers to be classified as separate groups in earlier population tables. There have been, in addition, Spaniards, Germans, Islanders from scattered areas of the Pacific, and Russians.[1] (3) During this period the native Hawaiian population declined. Outmarriage of Hawaiians with other ethnics was so extensive that by 1930 the "Part-Hawaiian" began to exceed the pure Hawaiian category. (4) During this period also the Japanese came to a position of numerical predominance among all the ethnics. (5) By 1940 the proportions of the ethnic components were showing a tendency to stabilize. (6) Since World War II the proportion of the Caucasian population has been increasing. Whereas in 1950 the Japanese comprised about 37 percent and the Caucasian component 25 percent (including the Puerto Ricans), by 1960 both groups were at about 32 percent. A major factor in the haole increase was the increasing numbers of dependents of military personnel residing in Hawaii and counted as part of the state's population in the 1950 and 1960 census counts. Nearly 40 percent of the Caucasian population growth is attributed to the military dependency category (not counting the military personnel itself). Contributing to the relative loss of first place of the Japanese ethnic component was a net loss of an estimated 17,300 from the interchange through migration and immigration over the decade.[2] Before 1930 migration to the Islands from the mainland was far greater than the opposite. Since then the pattern of migration exchange has been reversed.[3]

The story of ethnic intergroup relations in Hawaii will be divided into three periods: (1) the period of European invasion and the decline of the aboriginal Hawaiian civilization, from 1778 to about 1850, when the immigration of Asiatic people began; (2) the period of haole dominance over both the Hawaiians and the other subsequent immigrant peoples from 1850 to World War II; (3) the period of declining haole dominance, which characterizes the years since World War II.

The Establishment of Haole Dominance

The Decline of the Hawaiians

At the time of the first white contact with Hawaii in 1778, the archipelago was inhabited by a people of Polynesian origin and physiognomic features, who had brown skin, black hair, and were considered handsome by Caucasians.

[1] See Andrew Lind, *An Island Community* (Chicago: University of Chicago Press, 1938), p. 194.

[2] *Components of Change in the Civilian Population by Ethnic Group and Military Dependency, for Hawaii 1950–1960*. Estimated by the Department of Planning and Research from Hawaii 1950 and 1960 Census data and information supplied by the Department of Health and the U.S. Armed Services.

[3] See Robert C. Schmitt, "A Century of Hawaiian Out-Migration," *Social Process in Hawaii*, 1956, 20:38–46.

Their society, though preliterate, was highly elaborated. Early estimates of the native population in 1798 placed the number at about 300,000, but contemporary scholars believe it to have been far less than this. They suggest that the early explorers saw only the settlements near the coast and based their estimates of the total population on the assumption that the interior was just as densely populated. It is now known that the island of Hawaii, for example, where so much of the interior is covered by bare lava, was quite sparsely populated. The Hawaiians had developed a distinctive way of life suitable to themselves and with sufficient resources available to sustain them. Within a century after the coming of the white man, this civilization was virtually destroyed. The population declined almost to the point of extinction and the relatively small group of white newcomers supplanted the natives as the controlling element in the further development of Hawaii as an insular community.

Except for the missionaries, the few Euro-Americans who came to Hawaii before the middle of the nineteenth century were motivated almost entirely by economic interests. First confining themselves to trading, the whites gradually became interested in cattle raising and rice growing—introduced first by the Chinese—and finally in sugar growing, destined to become the economic foundation of the future Hawaii. Thus they came to seek permanent tenure of more and more valuable lands.

The reactions of the Hawaiians to the haoles were compounded chiefly of awe and friendliness, both of which aided the haoles in gaining their immediate ends. The technological superiority of the haole evoked admiration from the natives and helped establish haole prestige. As Burrows writes, "They [the natives] seem to have made the generalization that because the foreigners were superior to them in certain points of technology, they were superior in everything." [4] Although some native groups did oppose the haoles as they encroached on their land, in general, infiltration was accomplished peacefully. In 1845 an act was passed prohibiting aliens from acquiring fee simple title to land.[5] Like the Indians in the United States, however, when this act was repealed in 1850, native Hawaiians sold their land for ready cash.

During the period here under review and beyond it, the native Hawaiian population declined at a staggering rate. From the early explorers' estimate of 300,000 in 1788, the numbers declined so that in 1950 only about 12,000 pure Hawaiians were recorded. The low point for the continued native and part-Hawaiian total was reached in the 1900–1910 decade. Since then the part-Hawaiian group has shown a substantial growth.[6]

[4] Edwin G. Burrows, *Hawaiian Americans* (New Haven: Yale University Press, 1947), p. 17.

[5] *Ibid.*, p. 40. At that time, land was owned by the king. In 1848, a division of the land gave some of it to the people.

[6] This growth should be considered in the light of local procedures for enumerative purposes. All persons with any part-Hawaiian ancestry are counted as part-Hawaiian. For other non-Caucasian groups, the racial background of the father is used for classifying persons of mixed backgrounds. Thus in the case of part-Hawaiians, as well as other ethnic components, the figure is partly an artifact of ethnic definitions used by the census.

Adams has summarized the causes for this phenomenal population decline: (1) the sanguinary wars which continued for seventeen years after Captain Cook's first visit; (2) the introduction by foreigners of diseases new and highly fatal to the natives; (3) the hardship and exposure incident to new relations with foreigners, such as cutting and carrying candlewood, service on whaling ships, and the contributions of foodstuffs required for trade; (4) the serious disorganization of production through trade and contacts with the foreigners; (5) the disruption of the old moral order; and (6) the inability of a primitive people to meet the requirements of the new situation promptly.[7] In short, it is clear that this rapid decimation of the Hawaiian population was influenced by haole infiltration, even though haoles as a group or as individuals did not directly contribute to it nor desire it.

In this early period a pattern of interracial relations began to emerge quite contrary to those established by north Euro-Americans in their imperialist expansion elsewhere. The number of white people in Hawaii was quite small. They came from various nations and no one nation had gained ascendancy. Hawaiian political autonomy, although influenced by white intrigue, was maintained. The power situation called for treating Hawaiians wth due respect and with at least formal equality. Furthermore, the white population was predominantly male, and thus many of those who remained married Hawaiian women. Intermarriage was further facilitated by the freedom regarding marriage within the loosely organized native Hawaiian system.[8] Thus many conditions in the Hawaiian situation conspired against the drawing of a color line by the white people. Haole prestige, obvious even in the early days, was based more on social class position than on race consciousness. For the study of dominant-minority relations, this is the most significant development in the early period.

In the latter half of the nineteenth century, white people established a firm control over Hawaiian society. Nationalistic rivalries among the whites from imperialist nations were resolved in favor of the Americans. Agitation in the islands for annexation to the United States then arose, ultimately producing a revolution and formation of a provisional government favorable to annexation. Official transfer of sovereignty from the Republic of Hawaii to the United States occurred on August 12, 1898.

Economic Dominance

Control over the Hawaiian economy by haoles had been substantially accomplished through the concentration of control over the elaborated plantation system and its auxiliary financial and shipping enterprises. This control was vested substantially in five corporations.

[The Big Five] act in the capacity of factors or agents for all but three of the sugar companies operating in Hawaii, and have substantial stock holdings in these com-

[7] Romanzo Adams, *Interracial Marriage in Hawaii* (New York: The Macmillan Co., 1939), p. 7.
[8] *Ibid.*, pp. 46–48.

panies. Together, the Big Five control about 96 per cent of island sugar production. Largest of these agencies is American Factors, Ltd., which was formed in 1918 to take over the business of the German firm of H. Hackfeld & Company, and which in 1945 represented nine plantations responsible for 30.8 per cent of the total sugar produced. The others are C. Brewer & Company, Ltd., with 23.5 per cent; Alexander & Baldwin, with 20.8 per cent; Castle & Cook, Ltd., with 14.5 per cent; and Theo. H. Davies & Company, Ltd., with 6.9 per cent. The agency system is less used in the pineapple industry, although some of the Big Five have an interest in that industry. The Big Five have holdings in other important enterprises such as public utilities, docks, shipping companies, banks, hotels, department stores, and affiliated concerns. Power is held not only through direct stock ownership but through financing and supply contracts, through holding companies, through complicated land-leasing systems, through control over transportation agencies, through personal interfamily relationships, through trusteeships, and through a web of interlocking directorates.[9]

This great economic development in Hawaii under Euro-American corporate direction would not have been possible without an additional labor supply. But because of the population decline there were not enough Hawaiians. Furthermore, the natives did not make good plantation workers. Burrows writes, "The whole idea of steady work for wages was so foreign to their old culture that it had no value to appeal to them. . . . When an Hawaiian was hired to work on the plantations, he would work, as a rule, only until he had enough money to buy what he wanted at the moment, and to give his friends a good time.[10] The labor problem was solved by the importation, either under contract or by active persuasion, of a succession of immigrants from various parts of Asia and elsewhere. The order of succession of these ethnic groups is seen in the population composition in Table 17–1—the Chinese, the Portuguese, the Japanese, and, considerably later, the Puerto Ricans and Filipinos.

This process of immigration to Hawaii developed into a pattern. The need was for cheap and tractable labor. Each new ethnic group would at first serve as plantation workers. As its members became better adjusted to island life, some, growing discontented with their menial lot, would desert the fields for the city or return home. Thus the planters needed constant replacements. As the numbers of any one ethnic group increased, characteristic antagonism arose, first showing itself among competing workers. The planters' strategy was to try new ethnic sources in order to allay public antagonism against any one group. Another circumstance which suggested this course of action was that the longer any group of workers stayed in Hawaii, the less tractable they became.

While the growth of a strong labor movement in Hawaii is a recent development, there was some organization among workers and some attempted strikes in the early nineteenth century. An ethnically divided working group, however, was not likely to develop strong labor solidarity.

[9] Ralph S. Kuykendall, and A. Grove Day, *Hawaii: A History* (New York: Prentice-Hall, Inc., 1948), pp. 271–272. By permission.
[10] Burrows, *Hawaiian Americans*, pp. 41–43. By permission of the publishers, Yale University Press.

The drawing of racial lines in labor activities has, indeed, been one of the chief causes of lack of labor solidarity. Early in the century, the policy of denying to Orientals membership in the skilled trades unions smashed all hopes for effective organization, for a "one-nationality" union arouses prejudice and may be crippled by competing workers from another national or racial group, who will work for lower wages or even act as strikebreakers. Discrimination has been charged; it was once a common saying in Hawaii that there are three kinds of payment for the same kind of work—what *haoles* pay *haoles,* what *haoles* pay Orientals, and what Orientals pay Orientals. Racial loyalties have conflicted with labor-group loyalties, although racial antagonism in Hawaii has never been acute. Language difficulties and differences in culture and outlook have further divided allegiances to working-class ideals.[11]

Although after annexation contract labor became illegal, the planters still managed to locate and control the inflow of the additional labor supply needed.

Political Dominance

Wherever the economic control of an area is highly concentrated in relatively few hands, the same economic interests in large measure control the politics and government. While it is true that under American rule all the formal democratic institutions of the American governmental system were established, practically all students of Hawaii conclude that the Big Five controlled the political life of the Islands from annexation to World War II. Illustrative are these remarks of Barber:

> Moreover, they [the Big Five] are represented indirectly in the political affairs of the Territory, members of the legislature being linked with the Big Five, either through former association (or as in the case of the Speaker of the lower House, through being legal counsel for the sugar industry), or through the bonds of kinship.[12]

In spite of the fact that the nonhaole groups combined constituted a majority, they did not until about 1930 begin to challenge haole political domination. Although the Japanese were by far the largest of the ethnic groups, "it was not until 1930 that a number of Japanese-American candidates appeared in the primaries." [13] It will be recalled that federal law made foreign-born Orientals ineligible for citizenship.

Intergroup Relations

The pattern of intergroup relations in Hawaii before World War II involved haole social dominance over and discrimination against the nonhaole

[11] Kuykendall and Day, *Hawaii,* p. 275.
[12] From *Hawaii, Restless Rampart,* by Joseph Barber, Jr., copyright 1941, used by special permission of the publishers, The Bobbs-Merrill Company, Inc., p. 46.
[13] Bradford Smith, *Americans From Japan* (Philadelphia: J. B. Lippincott Co., 1948), p. 166.

ethnic groups. The reality of the formal, institutionalized pattern of racial equality in Hawaii is attested by practically all writers on Hawaii. From the start there have been no Jim Crow laws in Hawaii; no segregation in schooling; no laws against intermarriage. However, practically all writers indicate that beneath the surface there was evidence of prejudice and discrimination in which race consciousness was a predominant factor. Burrows writes:

> ... throughout their school years the Hawaiian born of Oriental stock have become more and more American. The process was favored by an atmosphere kindlier toward their race, and more tolerant of racial and cultural differences, than that of the American mainland. But when they got out of school, and set out to win their way toward prosperity, as good Americans are expected to do, they met with a rude shock. They found that the tolerance and friendliness among races, for which Hawaii has been justly celebrated, prevailed only within limits, and at a price. The price demanded by the dominant haoles—never in so many words, but nevertheless insistent—has been cheerful acceptance by other peoples of a subordinate place.[14]

Referring to haole relations with the Japanese, Bradford Smith cites instances of occupational and social discrimination.

> Discrimination appears in social life as well as in business. . . . The principal of a Honolulu school told me that in sixteen years as a teacher . . . he had come to know only three or four haoles well enough to enter their homes, and all of them were from the mainland. Even in the faculty lunch rooms racial lines hold in the table groups.
> Social considerations also affect advancement in jobs. A plantation manager wanted to appoint a Nisei chief electrician. If he did, the Nisei and his family would move into a house in the supervisor's area and his wife would have to be invited to social affairs with the other supervisors' wives. The ladies refused to do this. So the man was not appointed.[15]

The dominance of the haoles over the other ethnic groups was in considerable measure a function of their class position. The upper class was composed almost entirely of haoles. Most of the other haoles were in the middle class. The smaller number of lower-class haoles were, or were descended from, sailors or other occasional travelers who decided to stay there, some of whom belonged in the "beachcomber" category. In occupational upgrading and in wage rates within the same job levels, nonhaoles were discriminated against. How much this discrimination was based on "race consciousness" is a difficult question. Judged by comparison with Euro-Americans on the mainland United States, the haoles certainly showed less negative reaction to "color." Intermarriage between whites and Orientals and Hawaiians occurred frequently throughout the period, in part a consequence of the excess of males in the haole

14 Burrows, *Hawaiian Americans*, p. 85. By permission of the publishers, Yale University Press.
15 Bradford Smith, *Americans from Japan*, p. 166.

group. Before annexation, Hawaii classified its residents on the basis of nationality rather than race. After annexation the territorial government did classify Euro-Americans as Caucasian, and the offspring of a mixed marriage was classified as belonging to the non-Caucasian parent's group. In a plantation community where the differentiation of haoles as the upper class was strongly marked, Norbeck found the distinction between the haoles and the Japanese and the Filipinos to be more often thought of as cultural rather than racial.[16]

Status distinctions developed among the nonhaole groups themselves. The main Hawaiian gradient was haole-Chinese-Japanese-Filipinos. Native Hawaiians were interspersed but generally toward the bottom. Puerto Ricans and Portuguese also had a generally low status. In a study of the race preference of the Japanese in Hawaii, Matsuoka found the first preference to be their own kind, followed by "other Caucasians," Chinese, White-Hawaiians, Korean, Hawaiian, Portuguese, Filipino, Puerto Rican in order. "In general, preference depends not on physiognomy but on socioeconomic status." [17] Within the nonhaole groups, status differences had significance. Among the Hawaiians, the families descended from chiefs were superior to the commoners; among the Chinese, the Punti were superior to the Hakka; and the "regular" Japanese considered themselves above the Okinawans.

Nonhaole Reaction to Haole Dominance

How did nonhaoles as individuals and as groups react to haole dominance? Burrows analyzed three types of reaction by the minorities to the stress and frustration engendered by minority status: aggressiveness, withdrawal, and cooperation.[18]

AGGRESSION   This had not been characteristic of any of the groups except the Hawaiians at the two periods of their maximum stress: around 1830, when the haoles were rapidly assuming dominance, and in the period of the 1880's, when haoles assumed control of the government. The only form of aggression which had been at all common among the minorities was the mildest one of grumbling.

WITHDRAWAL   The extreme forms of withdrawal were more frequent among Hawaiians than among Orientals. Such reactions were manifested in happy-go-lucky apathy, such as drinking extensively and taking life easy—going fishing and strumming the ukulele, for example. Extreme withdrawal was manifested in religious reversion, either in the revival of traditional Hawaiian rites and practices or the embracing of new cults.

According to Burrows, "recreation reversion" gained ground during the

[16] Edward Norbeck, *Pineapple Town* (Berkeley and Los Angeles: University of California Press, 1959), p. 118.
[17] Jitsuichi Matsuoka, "Race Preference in Hawaii," *American Journal of Sociology,* 1935–36, 41:635–641.
[18] Burrows, *Hawaiian Americans,* Part II.

last generation in pronounced forms.[19] This mildest form of withdrawal was illustrated by the revival of interest in the traditional culture of the non-haoles' native lands: among the Hawaiians the revival of ancient pageantry, the hula, and folklore; among the Chinese, the revival of Chinese drama and music; among the Japanese, the revival of Japanese arts, of which dancing was the most popular. While the withdrawal response was more common than aggression, it was still confined to a minority of the persons in the groups involved.

COOPERATION   Cooperation was the main reaction to haole dominance. For the most part, it involved passive conformity to the demands placed on the nonhaoles by the haoles. In fewer instances it took the form of asceticism, where the individual meticulously avoids all that is forbidden and drives himself to do his full duty. During the war this reaction expressed itself often among Japanese-American soldiers who drove themselves to heroic martyrdom in acts "above and beyond the call of duty."

The Acculturation of the Nonhaole Peoples

Despite these reactions, the pattern of acculturation of the minority ethnic groups went on. The children of immigrant Orientals were being acculturated rapidly to the haole way of life. All the native-born were educated in public schools of a modern American type. "By 1940, approximately 65 per cent of the American citizens of Japanese ancestry over the age of twenty-five had completed eight or more years of American schooling as compared with only 30 per cent in the entire population of the Territory." [20] The public-school system encouraged all its pupils to conceive of themselves as full-fledged members of a free and democratic society. As the native-born came of age, which did not occur before 1920 in any considerable number, except for the Chinese and Hawaiians, they began to participate more actively in political life. Illustrative of the American orientation of the native-born Japanese in comparison with their foreign-born parents, is Bradford Smith's comment on Nisei reaction to Issei attitudes toward Japan's informal war against China after 1931. "The Nisei resented the partisanship of their parents. They resented anything which set them apart from other young Americans. They resented the contributions to Japanese militarism. Family arguments grew bitter, family relations more strained." [21]

Like the earlier Chinese, the more enterprising Japanese moved from agricultural work into the cities, and there have shown upward occupational mobility. "By 1930 the Japanese were operating 49 per cent of the retail stores in Hawaii and provided 43 per cent of the salesmen. . . . Fifteen per cent of the Japanese gainfully employed in 1940 were in preferred professional, proprietary,

---

[19] *Ibid.,* pp. 167–198.
[20] Andrew Lind, *Hawaii's Japanese* (Princeton, N.J.: Princeton University Press, 1946), p. 18. By permission of the publishers, Princeton University Press.
[21] Bradford Smith, *Americans from Japan,* p. 147.

and managerial occupations as compared with 13.7 per cent of the total population." [22]

Let us conclude our examination of Hawaii's ethnic relations marked by haole dominance by noting those developments within it which generated social forces leading to the period marked by the decline of haole dominance.

In the relatively short span of less than 200 years, Hawaii changed from an aboriginal, self-sustaining, isolated, stone-age culture to a modern, urbanized, commercial, industrial community linked closely to international trade. In the early part of this process there was a dichotomized, semi-feudalistic type of society, with an upper-class haole component and the natives (with due deference to the native rulers) and the immigrants as lower class. The dominant haoles possessed a value system in which capitalism, political democracy, and Christianity were basic. These values generated social forces that resulted in the rise in status and power of the Asian ethnic groups. Among the noneconomic developments which contributed to this change were (1) the maintenance of political control by native Hawaiians for over a century following discovery; (2) the development of a free and integrated public-school system based on the American model; (3) the introduction of American political concepts with the constitutional guarantees of equality of all before the law; and (4) the missionary influence.

Decline in Dominance

World War II

World War II marked a turning point in Hawaiian intergroup relations. The circumstances of war introduced new tensions, which were of a temporary nature. However, the war further accelerated certain trends that had begun in the period of haole dominance. The exigencies of war brought to the islands an influx of mainland civilian workers and military personnel not accustomed to Hawaii's pattern of race relations. Lind points out that

> As early as 1940 the mounting tide of defense workers, which was to more than double the size of the civilian population of Caucasian ancestry in Hawaii within six years, had begun to make its impact upon the sensitive balance of race relations within the territory. Despite the fairly frequent instances of "shacking up" with local girls, the defense workers generally were highly critical of the free and easy association of the various racial groups in the Islands. Most of them came with fixed ideas, derived from experience with the Negro in the South or with the Oriental and the Filipino on the West Coast. Although living in Hawaii, the psychological barriers they brought with them, along with the limitations imposed by their occupations and

[22] Lind, *Hawaii's Japanese*, pp. 17–18. By permission of the Publishers, Princeton University Press.

their segregated residence, prevented most of them from really becoming "at home" in Hawaii.[23]

The onset of World War II placed the Japanese in Hawaii in a peculiarly difficult situation. As the largest of the archipelago's ethnic groups, the Japanese had always been something of a threat to many of the haole population. It was almost inevitable that in consequence of the attack on Pearl Harbor, suspicion of their possible disloyalty should arise. Andrew Lind, sociologist at the University of Hawaii, in his intensive study of the situation of the Japanese in Hawaii following Pearl Harbor reports that numerous stories of alleged sabotage by Hawaiian Japanese aiding in the success of the Pearl Harbor attack and of other sabotage activities were widely circulated through the islands and on the mainland United States.[24] On the whole, however, he finds that the stories were given more credence on the mainland than in Hawaii itself. As we pointed out in Chapter 9, Hawaiian authorities imposed limited restrictions on those Japanese who were enemy aliens but not on the whole group. As to facts concerning the Japanese, Lind cites from official sources to the effect that there was no evidence of sabotage on the part of Hawaii's Japanese.[25] The generally cooperative behavior of the Japanese, including the service of many Hawaiian Japanese young men and women in the armed forces, demonstrated their loyalty to the United States.

Since World War II, Hawaii's nonhaoles have taken such rapid strides toward assimilation that Lind was able to conclude that "The peoples of Hawaii are becoming Hawaii's people." [26] By 1950 only 15.2 percent were foreign-born, the Koreans with 25 percent and the Filipinos with 55 percent being the only ethnic groups in Hawaii exceeding this.[27] It follows that most of the nonhaoles speak English. The fact that the territorial government stopped collecting data on this after 1930, when 85 percent were literate and 75 percent spoke English, indicates the increasing English literacy. In 1960 approximately 90 percent of the state's population were United States citizens, and about 75 percent were born in Hawaii.[28]

The main changes pertinent to interethnic group relations in the postwar period have been as follows: (1) The extensive rise to middle- and upper-class status of an increasing number of nonhaoles. (2) The nearly complete accultura-

---

[23] Andrew W. Lind, "Recent Trends in Hawaiian Race Relations," *Race Relations,* Vol. V, Numbers 3 & 4 (Dec. 1947, Jan. 1948), p. 60. By permission of the publishers, Fisk University.

[24] Lind, *Hawaii's Japanese* (Princeton: Princeton University Press, 1946).

[25] *Ibid.,* pp. 43–46. Among the authorities quoted are Henry L. Stimson, Secretary of War, the Federal Bureau of Investigation, the Army Intelligence in Hawaii, and the Police Chief of Honolulu.

[26] Lind, *Hawaii's People* (Honolulu: Univ. of Hawaii Press, 1955), p. 107.

[27] *Ibid.,* p. 81.

[28] *U.S. Census,* 1960, vol. 1, Part 13 (Hawaii) Table 13.

tion to haole (Hawaiian American) norms and values. (3) **The decline in haole dominance**, especially in politics, and increasingly in economic control. The above interacting changes all press toward the elimination of "minority" status from Hawaiian life. Concerning other pertinent matters, the evidence is less clear. (4) "Racial tolerance" we have seen has been a tradition in Hawaii. Social changes have "forced" a decline in haole discrimination; but it is less clear how far haole prejudice has declined. (5) Despite the continued amount of interracial marriage, ethnic self-identification and a degree of subethnic communality were certainly observable in 1960.[29] How far this may have declined since then had not been the subject of rigorous research. (6) Finally, we shall raise again the theme of integrated versus pluralistic assimilation as applied to Hawaii in the light of current trends.

Rapid Acculturation and Rise in Haole Status

THE JAPANESE EXAMPLE   Because they are the largest nonhaole group, the example of the Japanese may be taken to illustrate the rapid acculturation of the nonhaoles. Even on a plantation, *Pineapple Town*, traditionally more "feudalistic" than the urban areas, a postwar study gives this picture:

> Western foods are dominant in Nisei diet even though rice is always served. Amusements of the Nisei bear little relation to Japanese pursuits, although social dancing is rare. The higher ranking, supervisory Nisei belong to the golf club and with their wives bridge playing is a mark of social status. While they have all been taught the Japanese language, Nisei are rarely proficient in it because they use it little. While giving their children a Japanese and an English name, Nisei parents usually address them by the latter. Japanese cultural survivals are usually found on ceremonial occasions such as weddings and funerals but this is largely in deference to their parents' wishes.
>
> In basic personality traits, the traditional Japanese cultural influence is noted in the prevalence of the following: punctiliousness in meeting obligations; reciprocity for any favors done; social distance, or reserve in social relations; sensitivity to ridicule; and the undisputed mastery of the husband in the home, however more freely the couple may associate in public.[30]

With reference to the religious acculturation of the Japanese, Kolarz writes:

> Although many of the young second and third generation Japanese are Christians, Buddhism is by no means dead on the islands. . . . But Buddhism has changed in the Hawaiian atmosphere. It is more and more adopting the English language. Certain hymns have similarity to Christian hymns. Some Buddhist temples have introduced pews, candles and pulpits. . . . A Buddhist from Japan would probably be appalled at such a sight.[31]

[29] The U.S. Census in 1960 asked people to identify themselves in ethnic terms with the results for Hawaii indicated in our Table 17–1.
[30] Adapted by permission of the publishers from Edward Norbeck, *Pineapple Town* (Berkeley and Los Angeles: University of California Press, 1959), pp. 96–100.
[31] Walter Kolarz, "The Melting Pot in the Pacific," *Social Process in Hawaii*, 1955, 19: 23–26.

The impact of their experience in World War II and haole reaction to it had consequences for Hawaii's Japanese beyond permanently establishing their loyalty. As Sakumoto writes us:

> The solidarity of the local group *as a group* was reaffirmed and strengthened; that is, now they had a right to act collectively. The war exposed the local Japanese to a world wide community, beyond that of the local and even national community. It hastened their participation in more varied areas of social life, including the arts, travel, and business. (For instance, a prominent local sculptor, Bumpei Akaji, received his discharge from the army in Italy to study.) In short, the war broke the barrier of oceanic isolation.[32]

Beyond this, Sakumoto concludes that the most significant break-through is in politics, which we shall discuss later.

Further indices of the assimilative process going on in Hawaii can be found in occupational differentiation, in income, in residential distribution, and in intermarriage.

OCCUPATIONAL DIFFERENTIATION Each immigrant group started as agricultural laborers (except the Negroes, who are the newest arrivals); successively each group moved urbanward and to other occupations. This occupational shift, which has involved upward mobility as well, had been effected in part by the changing economic structure, especially the decline in the proportion employed in agriculture. Whereas in 1932 there were 51,427 workers employed to produce about a million tons of sugar at a yield of 19.9 tons per acre per employee, in 1952 there were 18,193 workers involved in producing about the same number of tons at a yield of 56.1 tons per employee.[33] By 1961, the number of plantation workers had dropped to about 12,000. With the increasing mechanization of agriculture, both the wage rates and the status of farm workers have risen. A summary of the occupational differentiation is put thus by Lind:

> Within little more than half a century the Chinese have run the full cycle from an immigrant labor group to one in which unskilled labor is almost nonexistent. The Portuguese and Japanese in that order followed the Chinese in pushing out of the laboring class, and by 1930 the Portuguese had only 30.1 per cent of their employed males left in that class, while the Japanese had a somewhat higher proportion. The slower rate of upward movement among the Filipinos is reflected in the fact that twenty-five years after most of them had arrived in Hawaii more than half of their employed men were still in the laboring class. This is obviously no reflection upon the Filipinos, but rather a reflection of the changed economic conditions of the Islands.[34]

[32] Raymond E. Sakumoto of the University of Hawaii has kindly given us permission to quote these observations.
[33] Lind, *Hawaii's People*, p. 66.
[34] *Ibid.*, pp. 73, 75.

Even with the Filipinos the proportion who worked as laborers declined from 80 to 54 percent between 1940 and 1950, whereas the proportion engaged at the operator level increased from 8 to nearly 20 percent. At the highest occupational status level—professional and technical—the continued high ranking position of Caucasians is seen in the 17.0 percent of this group employed. The Chinese come next with 10.7 percent; the Hawaiians and the Japanese are nearly even at 5.7 and 5.5 percent; and the Filipinos are at 1.2 percent.[35]

INCOME   As would follow from the occupational mobility indicated above, the income of the nonhaole peoples has been rising. "Census data available only for 1950 indicate that the sharp distinctions which once existed between the average income of the several ethnic groups are much less clearly drawn than formerly." [36] Acquiring the necessary skills for effective competition has been easier for the immigrant groups than for the Hawaiians; and among the immigrants, the Chinese, the Koreans, and the Japanese have enjoyed an advantage over the Portuguese, Puerto Ricans, and Filipinos, which Lind attributes to the variation in cultural traditions of the various groups.

RESIDENTIAL DIFFERENTIATION   As the successive groups of immigrants moved toward the cities, like immigrants generally, they formed ethnic residential colonies. But in Honolulu at least these colonies tended to fuse more quickly, so that the boundaries between the ethnic colonies have been less sharply marked off than in mainland cities. For example, while Honolulu's "Chinatown" was still visible in 1950, only 10 percent of the city's Chinese population lived there. The Japanese have been able to maintain their separate communities longer than the other ethnic groups because they have a much larger population. The upward economic mobility of the Oriental groups has caused the scattering of a given group in clusters representing economic levels. For example, in the mid-twenties a cluster of better-off Chinese established a neighborhood in a higher-class area. Before long this area was invaded by other Orientals, and some of the most prosperous Chinese moved to still higher-class areas. In summary, Lind states: "All of the five largest ethnic groups are represented in all 61 percent of the census tracts in Honolulu in 1950.[37] With the 1960 census data included, Sakumoto found absent any sharply demarcated ethnically segregated areas in Honolulu which could properly be called "ethnic ghettos." In general, his data indicate that the Caucasian and Filipino groups, with the Chinese close behind, are the most segregated, and the Japanese and Hawaiians significantly less segregated. He further concludes that while ethnic differentiation is reflected in patterns of residential segregation, the extent of it is insufficient *alone* to verify the independence of ethnic variation as a significant factor in Honolulu's social structure.[38]

[35] *Ibid.*, p. 78.
[36] *Ibid.*, p. 95.
[37] *Ibid.*, p. 59.
[38] Raymond E. Sakumoto, "Social Areas of Honolulu: A Study of the Ethnic Dimension in an Urban Social Structure," Ph.D. Dissertation, Northwestern University, 1965.

INTERMARRIAGE   As we turn to consider the ultimate test of the assimilative process, intermarriage, it is pertinent to recall that marriage across ethnic or racial lines has never been prohibited legally in Hawaii. Any disposition toward racial exclusiveness is better reflected in the actual rates of intermarriage. Fortunately, accurate statistics of intermarriage are available since 1912. According to Lind, "They provide a clear and vivid account of the slow but steady process by which the many races of Hawaii are losing their separate identity...." [39] As Table 17-2 shows, for 1912 to 1916, the percentage of all marriages that were interracial was 11.5 percent, whereas from 1957 to 1959, the percentage was 36.4.[40] Over the years the heavy male ratio in each new immigrant group promoted outmarriage, which later tended to decline as the sex ratio of each group became more equitable. But this meant only a temporary reversal of the trend toward intermarriage. By 1950, 18.9 percent of Hawaii's population was considered of mixed racial ancestry.[41] Except for the part-Hawaiians (already mixed) each ethnic category shows an increasing trend toward intermarriage, including the Japanese, who have shown the strongest tendency toward ingroup marriage.[42]

Throughout the years of haole residence in Hawaii, intermarriage first with native Hawaiians and later the Oriental groups has taken place. Over the time in which accurate figures of intermarriage are available, outmarriage of haole males has been increasing. In 1912–1916 the percentage of outmarriage (as a percentage of all marriages involving Caucasians) was for Caucasian males 17.3 percent; during 1962–1965 the comparable percentage had more than doubled, to around 38 percent. The ethnic outmarriage of Caucasian females has been far less frequent, and showed little change until the postwar period. Since 1949, however the percentage of Caucasian brides marrying non-Caucasian grooms has more than doubled. For 1962–1965 the outmarriage rate for Caucasian brides was around 22 percent. The much lower rate of haole female outmarriage as compared with male outmarriage is consistent with the principle that women of a higher status group less often outmarry than do the men. On the other hand, the doubling of the rate of outmarriage of haole women in a decade is substantial testimony to the rising status of nonhaole people. A more precise indication of the possible degree of ethnic prejudices in the matter of marriage requires data on the class distribution of outmarrying Caucasian men, which, unfortunately, is lacking. Of Pineapple Town it is asserted that a "haole should have a spouse who is a haole, speech free of any trace of Pidgin English, and he should avoid intimate social relations with most nonhaoles." [43]

---

[39] Lind, *Hawaii's People,* p. 103.
[40] The figures are not strictly comparable here, since for the earlier period there are twelve ethnic categories and for the later period only eight.
[41] Lind, *Hawaii's People,* p. 25.
[42] See C. K. Chan and Douglas Yamamura, "Interracial Marriage and Divorce in Hawaii," *Social Forces,* October, 1957, 36:77–84, for more detailed discussion of intermarriage.
[43] Norbeck, *Pineapple Town,* p. 118.

TABLE 17–2. *Interracial Marriages as Percentage of All Marriages, 1912–1965*

PERCENT OUTMARRIAGES

		1912–1916*	1920–1930*	1930–1940	1940–1949**	1950–1953†	1957–1959††	1960–1962‡	1963–1965‡
Hawaiian	Grooms	19.4	33.3	55.2	66.3	76.7	87.6	87.4	86.9
	Brides	39.9	52.1	62.7	77.2	78.0	86.6	84.6	85.0
Part-Hawaiian	Grooms	52.1	38.8	41.0	36.9	39.6	42.3	45.9	44.4
	Brides	66.2	57.7	57.9	64.2	58.0	59.0	56.4	56.6
Caucasian	Grooms	17.3	24.3	22.4	33.8	35.6	39.5	35.4	34.2
	Brides	11.7	13.8	10.7	10.2	14.7	19.1	20.1	23.2
Chinese	Grooms	41.7	24.8	28.0	31.2	41.0	49.0	53.5	58.4
	Brides	5.7	15.7	28.5	38.0	42.5	50.0	54.0	60.0
Japanese	Grooms	0.5	2.7	4.3	4.3	7.4	11.2	14.5	18.2
	Brides	0.2	3.1	6.3	16.9	17.6	21.8	24.7	26.5
Korean	Grooms	26.4	17.6	23.5	49.0	68.8	74.0	73.8	78.0
	Brides	0.0	4.9	39.0	66.7	72.3	76.0	78.5	80.0
Filipino	Grooms	21.8	25.6	37.5	42.0	42.0	48.5	51.0	51.4
	Brides	2.8	1.0	4.0	21.0	30.0	42.0	46.6	49.4
Puerto Rican	Grooms	24.4	18.6	29.8	39.5	48.4	47.3	61.1	70.3
	Brides	26.4	39.7	42.8	50.3	59.9	63.0	64.2	70.0
Total		11.5	19.2	22.8	28.6	31.0	36.4	37.1	38.1

* Derived from Romanzo Adams, *Interracial Marriage in Hawaii*, pp. 336–339.
** Bureau of Vital Statistics, July 1, 1940–June 30, 1948, and calendar year 1949.
† Bureau of Health Statistics, calendar years 1950–1953.
†† Bureau of Health Statistics, calendar years 1957–1959. State of Hawaii, Department of Health.
‡ *Annual Reports*, Dep't of Health, State of Hawaii, calendar years 1960–1965.

HAOLE-NONHAOLE RELATIONS Studies following World War II indicated the continuance of subtle discrimination by haoles against nonhaole peoples. One study of a business firm showed that the nonhaole employees felt, and in fact were, discriminated against in getting higher-ranking jobs. The haole top people said there was no discrimination but then went on to defend not appointing "colored" to high position as "good business." A tendency to import mainland Caucasians for top jobs was noted also. The educated nonhaole felt ready for higher position and showed anxiety and tension when it was not forthcoming.[44]

A study of the reactions of nonhaoles to the Wilder murder case further revealed the feeling on the part of Orientals toward discrimination. The case involved the murder of a wealthy white woman by two native Hawaiian prison escapees. Interviews with the nonhaoles brought out their belief that Hawaiian justice was racially unequal. The comparison was made with the lesser penalty imposed on two haole youths who in the same year had murdered two Chinese peddlars. The interviews further revealed a generalized antagonistic attitude toward haoles as "big shots" who took land away from the Hawaiians and exploited immigrants.[45]

A study of ethnicity in relation to housing reported a limited degree of discrimination by owners of private property in the rental market.[46] It was found that 40 percent of the landlords sampled showed no policy of differential treatment on the basis of ethnic preference—that is, they neither preferred any ethnic group as tenants nor rejected outright any group. About 30 percent showed a preference for a single ethnic group, generally their own. Caucasian landlords made more use of the category "restricted" than did the Chinese or Japanese landlords. The highest percentage of rejections as tenants was accorded the Negroes, with Puerto Ricans and Filipinos as the next two most rejected groups; the Hawaiians occupied an intermediate rejected position; and the Japanese, Caucasians, and Chinese received the lowest percentage of rejections (in part related to the fact that these groups are also the landlords). This study was designed to determine the extent of purely economic factors, as well as ethnic discrimination, in affecting the landlord preference in choice of tenants. The findings suggest that neither discrimination nor the lack of it is primarily affected by economic reasons. On the one hand, these researchers feel the study suggests that "the more general practice of non-discrimination was in a large measure the result of a positive orientation toward the moral creed of assimilationism." [47] On the other hand, the same market conditions

---

[44] Evelyn Yama and Margaret Freeman, "Race Relations within a Business Firm in Honolulu," *Social Process in Hawaii*, 1954, 18:19–25.

[45] Bernard L. Hormann, "The Significance of the Wilder or Majors-Palikiko Case," *Social Process in Hawaii*, 1953, 17:1–12.

[46] Harry V. Ball and Douglas S. Yamamura, "Ethnic Discrimination and the Market Place: A Study of Landlords Preferences in a Polyethnic Community," *American Sociological Review*, 1960, 25:687–694.

[47] *Ibid.*, p. 694.

which "permit" individuals to practice discrimination—for example the availability of many Japanese permitting Japanese landlords to prefer Japanese
tenants—also bear on the nondiscriminators.

The major developments in the decline of haole dominance in Hawaii, as
we have seen elsewhere, lie in the technological-economic and political
processes.

Technological and Economic Developments

While agricultural production is still an important part of the Hawaiian
economy, technological changes, greatly accelerated by exigencies of the war,
have resulted in the need for far less manpower and the consequent greater
urbanization of the nonhaole population into nonagricultural occupations.

Of major importance in the alteration of power in the economic sphere
between the haoles and nonhaoles has been the phenomenal rise in labor
unionization. The development of unions started in 1935, reaching a membership of 10,000 by the time of the attack on Pearl Harbor; it was arrested
by the virtual dictation of wages and working conditions by the federal government during World War II, but its postwar growth was rapid. By 1964 the
total union membership was estimated at 55,000, the largest unions being the
International Longshoremen Workers Union (20,200) and the ALF-CIO
(26,500).[48]

The consequences of this rapid unionization on race relations have been
two-fold. It promoted cooperation among the nonhaole laboring groups. "Where
previously the efforts of labor to secure recognition had been confined to the
limited and sporadic demonstrations by workers of a single ethnic group, the
unionized workers were forced into active cooperation without regard to ethnic
background." [49] Furthermore this process at first sharpened the opposition between haoles, especially the large haole employers. But as Lind further observes:

> The more outspoken manifestations of resentments and irritations, particularly
> toward the *Haoles* since World War II, far from reflecting an intensification of
> racial feelings, actually testifies to the removal of restraints and a more normal
> interchange across race lines. Where once the *Haole*, especially on the plantations,
> lived in a world somewhat apart from the non-*Haole* workers and thereby pro-
> tected from their privately held resentments, he is now within easier range of
> normal human intercourse, critical as well as friendly.[50]

The development of large-scale, well-organized unions, having haole leaders,
such as Art Rutledge of the AFL-CIO and Harry Bridges of the ILWU, and

[48] Source: Hawaii Employers' Council.
[49] A. W. Lind, in Jitsuichi Matsuoka and Preston Valien, *Race Relations: Problems and
Theory* (Chapel Hill, N.C.: Univ. of North Carolina Press, 1961), p. 76.
[50] *Ibid.*, p. 77.

the increasing number of haole members at the blue-collar level have tended to blur the previous haole-nonhaole differentiation and, at least at the instrumental level, promote cooperative relations between the two elements.

Political Developments

STATEHOOD Hawaii's admission to statehood in 1959 was a reflection of the general trend in the national civil rights movement; and the polyethnic (predominantly racial) composition of the islands' population had been an important factor in delaying this change. For years Republicans had controlled the territory's politics and haoles were strongly identified with Republicanism. In 1954, for the first time, Democrats gained control of the then territorial legislature and the Japanese became its largest single ethnic component. By 1967, in the 90th United States Congress, Hawaii was represented by one senator of Chinese lineage, a Republican; and another of Japanese lineage, a Democrat; and the state's two House representatives were a woman and a man both of Japanese ancestry—both Democrats.

THE JAPANESE AND THE DEMOCRATIC PARTY That the rise in the political fortunes of the Democratic party in Hawaii is significantly related to the effective participation of the Japanese has been shown by two studies. Digman and Tuttle in a study of the voting in selected districts in the 1954 election conclude "while inferentially this group [the Japanese] does tend to give support to candidates of its own ethnic reference group, such support is considerably below 'en masse' proportion." [51] Sakumoto studied the votes in selected areas of Honolulu in ten key elections in the 1960's, concluding as follows:

> The ethnic factor was most prominent in areas of concentrations particularly of Caucasians and Japanese. Generally speaking, voters in areas of Japanese concentration tended to support Democratic candidates and those in Caucasian areas tended to support Republicans candidates; and this relationship was more pronounced where the opponents were Democrats of Japanese extraction and Republicans of Caucasian background.[52]

More broadly, the same author concludes, "The role of the other ethnic factors in the future, we suspect, will revolve around the Japanese/Democratic-Caucasian/Republican axis." [53]

Two further special features of the Hawaiian scene affecting ethnic relations less basically than the economic and political changes are the large military establishment and tourism.

THE MILITARY ESTABLISHMENT As a military frontier, Hawaii has had a

[51] John M. Digman and Daniel W. Tuttle, "An Interpretation of an Election by Means of Obverse Factor Analysis," *Journal of Social Psychology*, 56:1961, pp. 183–194.
[52] Raymond E. Sakumoto, "Voting Preferences in a Multi-Ethnic Electorate." Paper prepared for the Pacific Sociological Association Conference, March 31, 1967, at Long Beach, California.
[53] *Ibid.*, p. 9.

military establishment ever since annexation in 1898, the size of which was overwhelming during the World War II years, and which has remained at substantial numbers in the years since. Because the large majority of the military personnel and their dependents living there have been mainlanders, Romanze Adams regarded this as a serious threat to the benign race mores of the territory even before Pearl Harbor.[54] Military establishments generally are isolated from the larger community about them and, at the officer level, status conscious. And everywhere the homeless enlisted men seek association with local girls of lower-class status, and generally complain about local economic exploitation in this connection. Finally some intergroup tension emerges. While the former condition—relative isolation—helps to mitigate tensions, the latter always aggravates it (with occasional overt interracial conflict). Lind's appraisal of this phenomenon in Hawaii is that on the one hand, bearing in mind the economic gain which the military brings to the Islands, "Islanders have sometimes compromised with their local code of racial equality," and on the other hand, service personnel have often adjusted to local mores—even to the point of marrying nonhaoles and permanently residing in Hawaii.[55]

Tourism

The influx of thousands of tourists to Hawaii each year inevitably has some influence on the Islands' race relations. The tourist, like the military personnel, often holds mainland racial attitudes; but, contrary to the military, can better afford to express these attitudes freely. As Lind writes, "Theoretically, therefore, the tourists afford a sort of pipe line for the introduction of mainland conceptions of race relations, and the Islanders economically dependent upon their patronage, notably taxi drivers and hotel operators, tend to 'play up' these imported ideas." [56]

Actually, Lind further observes, the tourist in search of new experience and in an uninhibited vacation mood often discards his usual prejudices for the time being at least.[57] The most enthusiastic accounts of the non-Caucasian population frequently come from these outsiders.

Ethnic Assimilation: Integration or Pluralism

It is clear that in no other of the urbanized polyethnic states of the nation is the situation more favorable for complete ethnic assimilation than in Hawaii. Both historical traditions and the formal institutional structure support the trend in this direction. But we find certain questions inadequately researched. (1) To

[54] Romanze Adams, "The Unorthodox Race Doctrine of Hawaii," in *Race and Culture Contacts*, E. B. Reuter, ed. (New York: McGraw-Hill, 1934), p. 159.
[55] A. W. Lind, in Matsuoko and Valien, *Race Relations*, pp. 72–73.
[56] *Ibid.*, p. 73.
[57] *Ibid.*, pp. 73–74.

what extent has the substantially complete acculturation of the nonhaoles (the Filipinos as the latest comers are no doubt catching up with their fellow Asians) been followed by what Gordon has called structural pluralism or "sub-communality"? (See above.) Stated otherwise, within class levels, how much primary (noninstrumental) association occurs between the several Asian lineage components? (2) To what extent have the changes noted above produced, as Yamamura suggested to us in 1961, a nonethnically differentiated middle class? (3) How far have the racial subcommunities that emerged in the larger cities diminished? (4) What in fact has been the effect of the continued interracial marriage upon ethnic identification? In theory, one might expect that before long the division of the Islands' population into such sizable and categorical ethnic components as census counts made up to 1960 provided will become impossible. Interestingly on this point, we understand that for 1970 the Census Bureau plans to omit racial and ethnic data altogether.

Sakumoto offers these impressions as of 1967:

> Persons of part-Hawaiian background tend to identify themselves as Hawaiians, or part-Hawaiian, though they seem to be quite proud of their non-Hawaiian lineage also, especially if it is of European stock. Japanese and Chinese mixtures, that is with others as well as between themselves, tend to be quite marginal, except in the case of marriages with Hawaiians or part-Hawaiians. Overt ethnic identification is most conspicuous among the Hawaiians. Outward ethnic identification is manifested among other groups only in casual or joking relationships. For example, a Japanese politician would never identify himself openly as Japanese to appeal to the ethnic group's vote. The part-Hawaiian politician could sing Hawaiian songs and even do the hula in his campaign, but the Japanese politician would hardly say even a few words in his ethnic language.[58]

(5) Our final question concerns haole-nonhaole relations. It is clear enough that the elaboration of the class structure to include nonhaoles of each lineage at substantially all levels has increased instrumental association between haoles and nonhaoles. But how much association on the primary group basis—"social" relationships—takes place? The data up to 1965 continued to show substantial outmarriage of Caucasian with Asian components. While it has been usual to consider mixed marriages as belonging to the husband's ethnic subgroup, in fact, in what "social circles" do such families interact?

The main hypothesis we venture is that substantially all Hawaii's people consider themselves first of all Americans. If a development paralleling the mainland experience as presented by Gordon of secondary identification (within class) of a subcommunal sort develops, will it be based on specific ethnic lines, e.g., Japanese, Filipino, or will it be based on a dichotomous division of haole and nonhaoles? Suggesting the latter alternative is the political polarization pre-

58 Raymond E. Sakumoto of the University of Hawaii in correspondence with the authors.

viously noted: the haole-Republican and the nonhaole-Democratic axis. Religion as a basis of major subcommunal identification appears ruled out.[59]

As a second generalization, we suggest that it remains true, as in the past, that the Caucasian component of Hawaii's population is less "racial" or "color"-conscious that white Americans elsewhere. Since World War II it has been facing a new test of this trait, the presence of a small but visible Negro component.

A FINAL TEST: NEGROES IN HAWAII   The first enumeration of Negroes in Hawaii was 233 in 1910; by 1940 there were still only 255 recorded; but by 1960 there were 4,943. Lee believes that the failure of the census figures to show a greater increase in the number of Negroes in the Islands between 1910 and 1949 is attributable to the tendency of many of the few Negroes there to "pass" under other ethnic designation—for instance, part-Hawaiian.[60] The substantial Negro growth since 1940 resulted from military and defense assignments. Eventually pressure was brought to bear on federal officials to curb Negro assignments, a pressure coming particularly from the Hawaiians. Lee further found that, while Negroes were definitely at the bottom of the socio-economic hierarchy and tended to be rejected as a group by all the other peoples, nevertheless, when an individual Negro could "transcend his mainland-acquired sensitivity to discrimination" enough to make constructive contributions to the general community life, as an individual he was accepted without discrimination.[61] Kalish studied the comparative attitudes toward Negroes of a mainland and Hawaiian student sample. He found less prejudice among the Hawaiian students toward Negroes than in his mainland sample. The local chapter of the National Association for the Advancement of Colored People disbanded because "there seemed to be no need for it"; yet he noted also the feeling that the Negro is "low man on the totem pole" and that Negro-white intermarriages are strongly frowned on.[62] It will be recalled that a study of ethnic preferences of landlords found more prejudices against Negroes as tenants than for any other ethnic group.[63] Despite this it is significant that only 40 percent of the landlords sampled indicated definite rejection of Negroes as tenants. The tentative conclusion appears to be that the general lesser prejudice in Hawaii against nonwhite people has mitigated the characteristic mainland

[59] While there is a highly heterogeneous differentiation among the Islands' people, most of the nonhaoles are now nominally Christian, ranging a wide gamut of denominations from Roman Catholic, Protestant, and including the smaller "emotionally expressive sects." See A. W. Lind, "Religious Diversity in Hawaii," Social Process in Hawaii, XVL (June, 1952), pp. 11–19.

[60] Lloyd L. Lee, "A Brief Analysis of the Role and Status of the Negro in the Hawaiian Community," American Sociological Review, 1948, 13:419–437.

[61] Ibid.

[62] Richard A. Kalish, "A Comparison of the Hawaiian and Mainland Attitudes toward the Negro." Social Process in Hawaii, 1956, 20:16–22.

[63] Ball and Yamamura, "Ethnic Discrimination and the Market Place: A Study of Landlords' Preferences in a Polyethnic Community," p. 692.

prejudice against Negroes but has not eliminated it. The Hawaii chapter of the N.A.A.C.P. became active again in the late 1960's, and its efforts appear to be focused primarily on the problems of housing of Negroes.

As a concluding comment, we suggest that the ultimate test of Hawaii's highly publicized lack of race-consciousness may be found in the reactions oₗ its citizens with Asian lineage to its citizens of African (in part) lineage.

Some Implications for Theory of Dominant-Minority Relations in Hawaii

The Power of Mores

The power of mores alone in influencing the course of dominant-minority relations is markedly illustrated in the Hawaiian situation. The formal pattern of racial equality developed and maintained from the beginning of haole contact has operated persistently against the many forces pressing in the opposite direction. This stands in contrast to the mainland South, where we have witnessed the power of the established mores of inequality and enforced segregation to resist the nationwide trend toward equality.

The Cumulative Effect of Democratic Political Institutions

The Hawaiian story well illustrates the persistent effect of political democratic institutions in creating still more democracy. It is doubtful that the haole group in Hawaii at the time of annexation foresaw that the introduction of free education and the democratic franchise in Hawaii would, in time, lead to the challenge of haole dominance by the colored peoples of Hawaii. Yet it now seems clear that the rise of nonhaoles to complete equality in status cannot be prevented without explicit reversals in democratic institutions.

Ambivalent Effects of the Private Enterprise Economy

The drive for private profit in the Hawaiian economy led to the search for labor amenable to low wages and easy to control. The fact that this labor was procurable from sources with a degree of minority status based on racial difference further strengthened employer purposes. On the other hand, technological change, shortage of labor in an expanding economy, and the consumption potential of the labor groups in a competitive situation led to increase in the economic welfare of nonhaole groups as a whole and the increasing allocation of higher functional roles to particular nonhaoles. Thus the dynamics of capitalism produced ambivalent effects on interethnic relations.

The Influence of the Size of the Minority

The effect of the numerical size of the minority upon intergroup relations is well illustrated by the numerical predominance of the Japanese descended

Hawaiians among the nonhaole groups. While for a time, and possibly still, the smaller component of Chinese Hawaiians may rank first on the overall ethnic status gradient, the far larger number of Japanese have given them potentially a greater political power which has been used with considerable effect. Their larger numbers also contribute to the lower rate of outgroup marriage by providing a wider field of eligible mate choices within their own group, and may prolong their separate identity.

On the other hand, as class differentiation *within* the large ethnic groups increases the sense of ethnic unity is reduced. This is illustrated by the haole component, now the largest, which is far more class elaborated than in the early years when it was a small, homogeneous upper class and is no longer a single unified bloc; and neither are any of the other groups.

Topics for Projects and Discussion

1. Analyze the relation of the changes in the economy of Hawaii during the twentieth century to the developments in ethnic intergroup relations.
2. Design a list of questions to be used in interviewing mainland Americans who have spent some time in Hawaii aimed at obtaining their reactions to ethnic relations in the islands. If possible, try out your schedule on several persons, selecting those who were there a considerable time.
3. Discuss the question, Why was Hawaii not admitted to statehood earlier? What changes in the situation appear to account for its admission in 1959?
4. Would you expect a substantial increase in migration of Negro Americans to Hawaii in the decade ahead? Explain the reasons for your conclusion.
5. Discuss further the implication for intergroup theory of the topics under this heading at the conclusion of the chapter.

Suggested Reading

Adams, Romanzo. *Interracial Marriage in Hawaii.* New York: The Macmillan Co., 1937.

> *While primarily concerned with intermarriage, the book contains much material on intergroup relations in Hawaii from the beginning of Euro-American contact to the mid-1930's.*

Ball, Harry V., and Yamamura, Douglas S. "Ethnic Discrimination and the Market Place," *American Sociological Review,* 1960, 25:687–694.

> *The findings of research designed to determine the extent of ethnic discrimination in Honolulu as indicated by landlord preferences for or rejection of tenants on the basis of their ethnicity.*

Fuchs, Lawrence H. *Hawaii Pono.* New York: Harcourt, Brace & World, 1961.

> *A social history of Hawaii.*

Lind, Andrew M. *Hawaii's People.* Honolulu: University of Hawaii Press, 1955.

> *The most comprehensive treatment of the trends in ethnic relations in Hawaii, including extensive statistical data up to 1953.*

Lind, Andrew M. "Hawaii's Frontier in Race Relations," ch. 7 in *Race Relations: Problems and Theory,* Matsuoko, Jitsuicki and Valien, Preston (eds.). Chapel Hill, N.C.: University of North Carolina Press, 1961.

    A one-chapter treatment of interethnic relations in Hawaii particularly from the World War II period through the 1950's.

Norbeck, Edward. *Pineapple Town.* Berkeley and Los Angeles: University of California Press, 1959.

    An anthropological study of a pineapple plantation community in Hawaii.

Schmitt, Robert C., and Sousa, Robert A. "Social and Economic Characteristics of Interracial Households in Honolulu," *Social Problems,* Winter, 1963, pp. 264–268.

    Compares racially mixed and non-mixed households in Honolulu based on a sample of 2,500 households.

18

The Jews:
A Historic Minority
in America

We have already presented some facts about Judaism in the United States in Chapter 4, "Religion and Minority Status." The persistence of the Judaic tradition as a minority religion in western Europe from the days of the Roman Empire to the present is one of the greatest demonstrations of the survival of a value system in history. It has also occasioned the development of the most complex pattern of dominant-minority relations in modern times. Territorial conquests have subjected or dispersed the Jewish people throughout their history. With the struggle of non-Jews to establish the power of western Christianity, eastern Christianity, and Islam, the religious issue was kept primary. The Jews experienced recurrent persecution, formal restrictions on residence, occupation, and civic status throughout most of Europe until the seventeenth century and in some areas even longer. Persecution occurred in eastern Europe in the nineteenth and early twentieth centuries and, within living memory, in western Europe in the countries under Nazi domination. Such a remembered past alone, even if there were no other factors, of necessity strengthened Jewish bonds of identity.

The situation of the Jews in various times and places has encompassed every aspect of dominant-minority relations. The history of the Jews in the ancient world included the experience of being a colonially conquered people. Early in the Christian era they were driven out of their homeland. In this period, usually referred to as the Diaspora, or "Dispersion," and in the succeeding eighteen centuries, they were dispersed throughout the whole civilized world. The persistence of segregated colonies of Jews created a pattern of cultural minorities.

The particular historical developments of the twentieth century have added other dimensions to the position of Jews as a minority. When the National Socialist Party undid for Germany all the gains made in western European social thought since the Age of Enlightenment and exterminated six million Jews, the bonds of identity of Jews throughout the world, which had loosened under two centuries of improved civil status, were re-established and intensified.

The founding of the state of Israel has given many Jews a Jewish political identity and affected the feelings of Jews in other countries.

One cannot consider Jewish-Gentile relations without this historical perspective. It accounts for the fact that Jews have been identified, and have identified themselves at various times and in various places, as a religious minority, an ethnic minority, and a "racial" minority.

The rationale for devoting a special chapter to the Jews as a minority, rather than seeing them simply as members of an established religious group, is this very complexity of identity. The Jews have a long history of stabilized minority status in which they have served important functions in the dominant society and incorporated the goals of the dominant society. Jews have attenuated visibility, if any. (Some sectarian religious Jews have high cultural visibility, but this is a small minority). Yet Jews think of themselves as Jews, and they have, however loose, bonds with other Jews. To an extent this is due to "the self will that creates unity"; and to an extent it is the result of "the will of others which imposes unity where hardly any is felt." [1]

The Problem of Jewish Identity

American Jews in the twentieth century have been concerned with the question "Who is a Jew"? Barron cites the frequency with which this has been discussed in general as well as Jewish periodicals and other publications,[2] as well as how difficult the problem of definition has been for the Israeli government.[3]

Are the Jews a Race?

In Chapter 3 we discussed the fact that "race" as used popularly is a social and not a scientific category. We pointed out that present genetic theory accepts only the fact that certain genetic traits are reinforced by isolation and inmarriage. There seems to be little evidence that Jews were ever totally biologically separated from the surrounding peoples. Even initially in Palestine it is probable that the strong prohibitions against outmarriage were a defense against a considerable intermixture. The goal was preserving the religion, not purity of descent, except as this is characteristic of all tribal peoples.

As the Jews dispersed, the people with whom intermixture occurred became progressively more differentiated in physiognomic features. The Ashkenazim, especially, who were dispersed through northern Europe and from

[1] Nathan Glazer and Daniel Patrick Moynihan, *Beyond the Melting Pot: The Negroes, Puerto Ricans, Jews, Italians and Irish of New York City,* (Cambridge, Mass.: The M.I.T. and Harvard University Press, 1963), p. 139.

[2] Milton L. Barron, "Ethnic Anomie," in Milton L. Barron ed., *Minorities in a Changing World* (New York: Alfred A. Knopf, 1967), p. 26, and note 14.

[3] *Ibid.,* p. 27.

whom most American Jews are descended, are a blending of Nordic and Alpine with eastern Mediterranean traits.[4] The other main branch of Jews, the Sephardim, lived long in Spain and the Mediterranean region and through in-marriage tended to develop a degree of physical distinctiveness from other Jews. People of this appearance are often referred to as the "classic" Jewish type, but they are often indistinguishable from other Mediterranean peoples. "The wide range of variation between Jewish populations in their physical characteristics and the diversity of the gene frequencies of their blood groups render any unified racial classification for them a contradiction in terms." [5]

Shapiro, who has examined all the research, anthropological and medical, on the biological traits of Jews, makes the following comment:

> I suppose that one of the reasons, aside from political and cultural ones, that incline many people to accept readily the notion that the Jews are a distinct race, is the fact that some Jews are recognizably different in appearance from the surrounding population. That some are not to be identified in this way is overlooked and the tendency, naturally enough, is to extend to all the stereotype of a part. This process occurs in so many other situations it is scarcely surprising that it does here too.[6]

Are American Jews an Ethnic Group?

It is the fashion today to define any minority as an "ethnic group." As we pointed out in Chapter 2, the term *ethnic* refers to shared culture patterns which are a primary focus of group identification. Many Latin Americans, for example, have a strong sense of cultural foci which are different from those of the United States. There is no overall cultural ethos that distinguishes American Jews from other Americans. To examine this question for American Jews one must consider country of origin, status of Jews in the country from which they migrated, degree of open opportunity in the United States at the time and place of immigration, size and clustering of the migrating group.

In the seventeenth century Sephardic Jews came to the American colonies. This group of Jews originated in the Mediterranian countries, particularly Spain, and dispersed after the Spanish Inquisition to northern Europe and presently to other parts of the world. Those who came to the United States formed a literate, Orthodox elite. Today they still maintain an elegant, modified orthodoxy, if they are the descendants of the early migration. Secularly they are totally assimilated. They have intermarried with descendants of later migrations, but have been a strong force for the maintenance of religious identification for Jews. In the twentieth century there has been a small migration of

---

[4] Carleton S. Coon, "Have the Jews a Racial Identity?" eds. Isacque Graeber and Steuart Henderson Britt, *Jews in a Gentile World* (New York: The Macmillan Co., 1942), p. 33.

[5] Harry L. Shapiro, *The Jewish People: A Biological History* (Paris: UNESCO, 1960), pp. 74–75.

[6] *Ibid.*

Balkan Sephardic Jews who tend to live in clustered pockets of eastern cities. They, however, represent a folk variant of other late migrating village Jews.

The eighteenth and nineteenth centuries saw a considerable migration of Western European Jews, who came at a time of open opportunity, and many of whom had been considerably assimilated into the national cultures of Western Europe from which they migrated. Until the last two decades of the nineteenth century there was real opportunity in rapidly developing America, with little overt discrimination in the large cities, although there were anti-Semitic incidents in the South and the West. The successful German Jewish families maintained close relations with one another, however, intermarried with one another, spoke German at home, and established their pattern of life on the model of the stable, cultured merchant wealth of Europe.[7] These families were, on the whole, strongly behind the movement for Reform Judaism; some were involved in the founding of the Ethical Culture Society, were members of social clubs, felt themselves a true part of American life by the third generation, and were traumatized by the anti-Semitism of the end of the century. They could not in any sense be called an "ethnic" group, although they were forced into a stronger sense of Jewish identity just at the point where they were becoming most American (as contrasted with European).

The largest migration of Jews came between 1880 and 1924. These were primarily from Eastern Europe where they had largely lived in segregated villages or ghettoes of small cities. Most of them were poor and started life in America as skilled and semiskilled workers or small entrepreneurs. Because of the enforced segregation under which most of them had lived in Europe, they maintained a folk orthodoxy in religion which so dominated the daily lives of the villages that it gave this group a cultural uniqueness.[8] Glazer and Moynihan point out that as this was the largest migration of Jews to America it has colored Jewish behavior in many parts of the United States and contributed to the larger culture some of its culturally idiomatic language usages, food, etc.[9] This group of Eastern Jews might have been correctly defined as an ethnic group in the first generation, but today its third-generation descendants have only the most superficial cultural vestiges, if any, and are American "in thought, word, and deed." Partly this is the more true as the group has been economically mobile and the third generation, like other ambitious young Americans, is concerned with status and relatively oblivious to discrimination, actual or potential.[10]

[7] Stephen Birmingham, "Our Crowd": The Great Jewish Families of New York (New York: Harper & Row, 1967).

[8] See Mark Zborowski and Elizabeth Herzog, Life Is With People (New York: International Universities Press, 1952). Two anthropologists have sensitively reconstructed the life in these Jewish villages: a way of life that was destroyed totally by the Nazi conquest of Eastern Europe.

[9] Glazer and Moynihan, Beyond the Melting Pot, pp. 141–142.

[10] Judith R. Kramer and Seymour Levantman, Children of the Gilded Ghetto (New Haven: Yale University Press, 1961).

The Jews Are a Minority

As we have seen the Jews are not a "race," nor can American Jews be subsumed as an ethnic group. Neither are all people who designate themselves as Jewish members of one or another of the denominations of Judaism. Yet the interplay of historic forces has created a centripetal bond which both operates against total assimilation and creates security and varying degrees of mutuality for its members. To be a minority which does not have its sense of identity rooted in strong subcultural values, or in religion, and which competes successfully and seeks admission to full participation in the larger secular society, puts the group in a particularly vulnerable position.[11] Throughout the history of the Jews, economic success and the beginning of social integration have been followed by policies and actions against Jews.[12]

The problems of marginality and ambiguous status for Jews reveal much that is generic to dominant-minority relations, not only in the United States but throughout the world (for example, where developing nations have merchant-minority populations of Indians or Chinese). On the negative side, the burden of tension and alienation for people who are part of both groups can be very great.[13] On the positive side, to the degree that we move toward a more rational-scientific, more equalitarian and more intergroup world, people from such interstitial positions can make great creative contributions toward the resolution of the challenges which confront us.

The American Jews

Size and Distribution of the Population

About 3–5 percent of the American population is Jewish. It is difficult to have an accurate figure as the 1960 Census did not ask about religion, and the yearbooks of religious bodies are able to include only those whom the organization knows or estimates to be of that faith.[14] The Jews then number about five

---

[11] See for example Merton's discussion of in-group virtues that become out-group vices in Robert K. Merton, "The Self Fulfilling Prophecy," *Social Theory and Social Structure*, rev. ed. (Glencoe, Ill.: The Free Press, 1957), p. 426.

[12] Contrast for example the situation of Jews and Gypsies. The Gypsies are as old a minority, originally an Asian religious sect. They were and have remained fundamentally tribal; they have dispersed throughout the whole world of Europe and the Americas. They have had only marginal economic relations with the dominant societies within which they are located and have resisted acculturative or welfare efforts from dominants. Perhaps a major difference lies in the fact that they have no great tradition of literacy and have not contributed to the foundations and development of western European thought and ethic. Usually they have been able to maintain a tolerated (if devalued) status in their environment, although the racialist doctrines of Nazi Germany classified them as "non-Aryan" and sent them to extermination camps.

[13] Barron, "Ethnic Anomie."

[14] See Glazer and Moynihan, *Beyond the Melting Pot*, pp. 137–138, 143, for discussion of the 1957 Census of Religious Bodies and the opposition to release of this data by the American Jewish Committee, presumably for fear it would give ammunition to anti-Semitic groups.

and a half million; they are a little more than a quarter the size of the Negro minority; they will soon be if are not already overtaken in numbers by Spanish-speaking Americans. Their proportion in the population is declining as their rate of reproduction is coherent with other urban groups of equivalent socio-economic status, whereas other minority population groups are increasing.

Approximately 75 percent of the American Jewish population live in large metropolitan areas: Baltimore, Boston, Chicago, Cincinnati, Cleveland, Detroit, Los Angeles, Miami, New York City, Newark, Philadelphia, Pittsburgh, St. Louis and San Francisco.[15] Nearly half of the Jews in the United States live in the New York metropolitan area (the city and its suburbs).[16] About one third of the white, non-Puerto Rican population of New York City proper is Jewish.

One stereotype of the Jews has described them as an urban people, and indeed since the decline of feudalism in Europe this has largely been true for Western European Jews. But such a stereotype has implied that they had no roots in the feudal agricultural world. Contemporary research is beginning to discover that there have been a variety of historical ecological *loci* for Jews: they have been landowners, village craftsmen, administrators for feudal estates, and so on. Jews suffered as scapegoats in the transition and uprooting that characterized the collapse of feudalism and the beginning of the modern era. Many of them sought the cities free of feudal control. In this country, however, relatively few moved into agricultural life until the twentieth century, when intensive farming (poultry and dairy farming) opened a channel of opportunity more coherent with the European agricultural practices they had known than isolated open-country farming of the American expanding West.

There was greater opportunity for Jews in the larger cities as the migration on the whole coincided with urban growth in the United States; there was also the possibility of association with other Jews, which provided a sense of community, made available marriage partners for sons and daughters, and allowed them to fulfill the historic obligation of a good Jew: community responsibility. For second- and third-generation Jews, and indeed for some first-generation migrants, this sense of obligation has extended beyond the "Jewish community" to a responsibility for the welfare of the larger community of which they were a part.

Minority Adaptations to Dominance

We have pointed out that Americans respond to pleas for justice and equality but are uneasy with differences. This is true undoubtedly for any group that associates chiefly with people like themselves. It applies to a minority group's perception of dominants and other minority groups, as well

[15] Ben B. Seligman, et al., "Some Aspects of Jewish Demography," in Marshall Sklare, ed., *The Jews: Social Patterns of an American Group* (Glencoe, Ill.: The Free Press, 1958), p. 46.
[16] Glazer and Moynihan, *Beyond the Melting Pot,* p. 138.

as to dominants' perceptions of minorities. For the majority of Jews in America who are urban and middle class, there has been positive interaction with dominants, and any differences are differences of nuance and of opportunity. It is true that there are some Jews who can and do live out their lives in an ecological cluster which allows them association only with their own "eth-class."[17] But even here, public education, higher education, and work experience are changing the pattern for young people. We would hypothesize that the degree of definable difference in behavior varies with one or more of the following factors: age as related to recency of migration, socioeconomic status, degree of Jewish traditional religious identification, and ecological clustering.

Jewish Institutional and Organizational Patterns

THE JEWISH FAMILY   The cohesiveness of the family is one of the strongest characteristics of the Jewish group. This derives in part from the emphasis in Jewish religion on marriage and family life, as well as adaptations of this tradition in such a practice as early (and, in former times, arranged) marriage, and in part from the mutual aid and protection of the extended kinship. Jewish families on the whole live in the nuclear pattern, keeping in closer touch with their relatives, visiting more frequently, and being more willing to aid a promising relative than is characteristic of the dominant pattern.[18] Among the older generation of eastern European Jews, there is the beloved stereotype of the Jewish mother who will sacrifice everything for her family.

Male and female roles are sharply defined, even though American Jews encourage the education of women and their participation in community affairs. Authority in the family is in the hands of the men. For religious Jews, it is important to have sons, since certain rituals can be carried out only by males. Even where this religious emphasis is no longer stressed, the high valuation of sons seems to persist.

The family not only has had important traditional religious functions to fulfill, it has also been a bulwark for joint economic endeavor. Glazer and Moynihan point out how often Jewish enterprises involve fathers and sons or groups of brothers.[19] There are many such business partnerships, and there are family associations which form investment pools. (This latter is characteristic of the traditional Chinese family system, of many European bourgeois families, but has not been a characteristic of WASP families in America except at the top financial levels since the imposition of income taxes).

[17] The term is one coined by Milton Gordon in *Assimilation in American Life: The Role of Race, Religion and National Origins* (New York: Oxford University Press, 1964).
[18] Stanley R. Brav, *Jewish Family Solidarity: Myth or Fact?* (Vicksburg, Miss.: Nogales Press, 1940).
[19] Glazer and Moynihan, *Beyond the Melting Pot,* p. 154. See also Birmingham, *Our Crowd,* for the involvement of brothers, sons, and sons-in-law in the founding of the great German Jewish fortunes of nineteenth-century America. (Family trees showing descendants and intermarriages are on the end papers of this volume.)

By and large the Jewish family maintains a strong control on outmarriage. Jewish religion takes a firm position on this, and even nonreligious Jews are often afraid that unhappiness because of differences or potential anti-Semitism will destroy the peace of home life. There is probably more outmarriage in communities where there are few Jewish families, and in intellectual circles where there is a primary occupational intergroup bond. As more young Jewish Americans move into professional, technical or other intellectual spheres (the arts, academia, etc.), there may be more intermarriage.

The Jewish Occupational Pattern

Accurate estimates of the occupational distribution of Jews are difficult to make, since they must be compiled from studies of different localities, where the job classifications are often not comparable. Some data, however, can give an indication of the character of the Jewish labor force.

According to Seligman, it appears that a smaller proportion of the total Jewish population is part of the labor force than is true of the general population. It is suggested that this may be related to such factors as the longer period of schooling for Jewish children, or to the emphasis on the domestic role of women.[20]

The Jewish male labor force in most of the communities for which we have data appears to be higher in proportion to the general population in the employer and self-employed class. Classifications by industry indicate a concentration in the wholesale and retail trades. Although it is a popular belief that Jews are found most frequently in the professions, community studies which provide occupational information show the manufacturing (proprietary and managerial) group greater than the professional in most cases.[21] If we consider the nationwide pattern of Jewish occupations, the exclusive occupational emphasis of Jews on the professions seems to be less than has been generally believed. "In more recent years proprietorship has been of first rank in virtually all the Jewish population studies included here, with clerical occupations second and professional work in third position." [22]

Jews as a group have a higher average age than the rest of the population. Since the older age groups in this country have a higher proportion of professional, semiprofessionals, proprietors, managers, and officials, this is a factor which must be taken into account in considering the proportions of the Jewish labor force in these categories. In the female labor force in 1950 the Jewish urban population approaches the proportions found in the general labor force.

Although in the nineteenth and early twentieth century there were prominent Jewish families in finance and industry, there has since been a dispersion. Jewish business fortunes have come from clothing manufacture, merchandizing,

[20] Seligman, "Some Aspects of Jewish Demography," pp. 70–82.
[21] *Ibid.*, p. 73.
[22] *Ibid.*

and the entertainment field. Since the late 1930's an even wider diversification has taken place to include a range of light manufacturing, real estate, and building.[23]

The Jewish businessman, from the small storekeeper to the newer manufacturer in electronics, has had to find those sectors of the economy which were not preempted by white Protestants. As a historic minority Jews have been alert to these opportunities. The strong family system has enabled them to mobilize capital (even if in small sums);[24] even in the culture market of publishing, movies, television, theatre, music, and architecture, both as producers and consumers they have been interested more in the new than in the old and traditional.[25]

The proportion of working-class Jews is declining, although the institutions within the labor world which they created survive. There is, as is to be expected, a higher proportion of Jews in working-class and lower-middle-class occupations in cities like New York where there is such a large Jewish population. In cities where they are perhaps five percent of the population they are more apt to be in middle and upper-middle-class occupations.[26]

The Jews in American Politics

Throughout the nineteenth century Jews could and did participate in any political organization to which their interests inclined them. During the Civil War, Jews were among the partisans of both the North and the South, and within both major parties. The number of Jews before 1880 was so small that they were viewed, and viewed themselves as individual voters rather than as group representatives. Western European Jews who participated in European politics at all after restrictions on political participation were removed, adhered chiefly to the moderate democratic movements of the times.[27] Much of the same spirit permeated Jewish political positions, whatever the party affiliation, in the United States. In this period they tended to recoil from all extreme movements, such as the radical Abolitionist movement or the Know-Nothing Party.[28]

After 1880, however, the immigrants from eastern Europe were strongly influenced by radical intellectuals, and for a period Jewish workers and their leaders formed the backbone of the Anarchist and Socialist movements in this country. Partly this was due to an over-reaction after the suppression of political liberty they had experienced under the Tsarist government. "When the Jewish intellectual came to the United States, he was suddenly given an opportunity to theorize openly and to his heart's content. He took full advantage of it: for

[23] Glazer and Moynihan, *Beyond the Melting Pot*, p. 151.
[24] *Ibid.*, p. 154.
[25] *Ibid.*, p. 174.
[26] *Ibid.*, pp. 144–147.
[27] Werner Cohn, "The Politics of American Jews," in Sklare, ed., *The Jews: Social Patterns of an American Group*, p. 619.
[28] *Ibid.*, p. 620.

many years, the Lower East Eide [in New York City] was one big radical debating society." [29]

Jews have not only been a voting bloc whose liberal voting pattern has been of great persistence,[30] but, where as in New York City there have been large numbers of Jews, there have been the usual urban political careers. Glazer and Moynihan think the Jewish vote is largely ideological and rarely is influenced by whether or not the candidate is Jewish. They give a series of examples where the Jews of New York have preferred a liberal Catholic or Protestant over a conservative or "party machine" Jew.[31]

Jews and Religion

In Chapter 4 we indicated the major denominational divisions of Jewish religion: orthodox, conservative, and reform. These general divisions are based on the degree of emphasis on traditional ritual, both in the temple and in the home, and on the appropriate place of secular learning as contrasted with Jewish scriptural studies. Within each of these divisions there is a great deal of variety bound up with the social-historical experience of the congregation. In addition, there have been revitalization movements which have attempted to bring more emotional commitment to a largely rationalistic religion: the Hassidic movement of eastern Europe, at one extreme, or Reconstructionist Judaism today. It is interesting that the only Jewish theologian in eight centuries to influence Christian thought has been the contemporary, Martin Buber, who in his writings has been concerned with relationship, encounter, and dialogue between God and man, and man and man. One writer, however, feels that Buber has had little impact on American Jewish thought (much less than on contemporary Christian thought).[32] If Himmelfarb is correct the more important influences in the development of Jewish religious life in America stem from nineteenth-century German movements which attempted to find suitable compromises for the dilemma we described in Chapter 4 of "the church and the world," in this instance, the world of "dominants."

Jews like dominants have been affected by the trends toward secularization. Glazer and Moynihan believe that only a minority (of New York City Jews) belong to synagogues.[33] Probably in communities where there are fewer Jews, membership in a synagogue helps validate "respectable status" for many Jews. The rate of conversion is claimed to be small, and probably this is correct with regard to baptism and formal affiliation with Christian churches. But it would

---

[29] *Ibid.*, p. 621.
[30] Glazer and Moynihan, *Beyond the Melting Pot;* see pp. 166–171 for analysis of Jews in New York politics.
[31] *Ibid.*, p. 167.
[32] Milton Himmelfarb, "Introduction" to *The Condition of Jewish Belief: A Symposium Compiled by the Editors of Commentary Magazine* (New York: The Macmillan Company, 1966), p. 3.
[33] Glazer and Moynihan, *Beyond the Melting Pot*, p. 142.

be difficult to assess how many have sought secular anonymity or membership in sectarian religious groups (Quakers, Christian Scientists, etc.) where baptism is not required and is therefore not connotative of betrayal of one's heritage.

The Jewish Community

Wherever any considerable number of Jewish people reside in an American community there has developed a separate Jewish substructure, usually called the "Jewish community," which has a characteristic relation to the larger Gentile community. Sometimes these are actual ecological communities that have developed through residential discrimination or self-clustering; in other cases residence is dispersed, and the network of social and organizational relationships constitutes the Jewish community. There have been many studies of Jewish communities in different parts of the United States. Over 200 communities are affiliated with the Council of Jewish Federations and Welfare Funds, many of which have been studied from one point of view or another.[34]

A large percentage of American Jews have middle-class status and, like the rest of the American urban middle-class, Jews are moving to the suburbs. Let us study briefly the origin and growth of a typical suburban Jewish community.[35]

The Jewish Community of Park Forest

Park Forest is a post-World War II planned community south of Chicago. The men of the community were earning from $4,000 to $10,000 a year in 1949, when the study was made. Among 1,800 families, about 25 percent of them Catholic, the Jewish community numbered just under 150 families. Of these, about 20 (15 of them mixed marriages) rejected all relationships with the formal Jewish community.[36] The Jewish group was made up of young, highly educated, second-generation Jews of eastern European parentage, most of whom had achieved or were likely to achieve with continued prosperity middle-class income status.[37] Park Forest Jews lived like other Park Foresters. They wore the same fashions, ate the same food except on special occasions, and participated with other Park Foresters in the culture of the "young moderns." The Jewish families were scattered, with rarely two Jewish families in adjacent houses.

Soon after these young Jewish families arrived they aligned themselves in a number of cliques, which in a remarkably short time formed a network through which news and gossip could be communicated. Gans points out that "The Jews form a cohesive in-group and tend to behave differently toward a

[34] See Sklare, *The Jews: Social Patterns of an American Group,* for articles based on the reports of many of these studies.
[35] Herbert J. Gans, "The Origin and Growth of a Jewish Community in the Suburbs: A Study of the Jews of Park Forest," in Sklare, pp. 205 ff.
[36] *Ibid.,* p. 206.
[37] *Ibid.,* p. 209.

member of the in-group than toward a non-Jew, in many cases reserving the intimacy of friendship for the former." [38] He then describes the process by which Jews attempted to recognize other Jews. They were aided in this by a Protestant minister who conducted a religious survey and informed interested Jews who the other Jews in their neighborhood were.[39] Although there was no automatic progression from recognition to acquaintance to friendship, in many cases the desire to associate with other Jews was implied from the first. In general it was a matter of only four to eight weeks before people said they had friends whom they saw regularly.

Sociability patterns did not become exclusively Jewish, but in about half the cases it was pointed out that "best friends" were Jewish. This was defended on the ground that sociability as a primary leisure activity should permit relaxation and self-expression, which was more likely when Jews associated with Jews.

The development of the formal community began with the organization of a B'nai B'rith lodge and a chapter of the National Council of Jewish Women. Attendance and active participation in the Council of Jewish Women was soon greater than in B'nai B'rith, reflecting, according to Gans, the women's greater desire for Jewish companionship.[40] Nearly a year after the new suburb of Park Forest had been occupied, some of the leaders in B'nai B'rith met one evening to discuss setting up a Sunday school, which was to be part of a synagogue, either Reform or Conservative. The women in the Council, however, refused to help form a congregation and insisted that all they needed at the time was a Sunday school. Thus began four months of discussion, argument, and conflict.

> In other groups such conflicts can often be explained in terms of power struggles between two socio-economic strata or ideological factions. In the Jewish community, however, they may signify conflicts between groups representing different stages in the ethnic adjustment to American life. . . . In Park Forest, where almost everyone is native born and acculturated to a large and similar extent, the history of the conflict over the Sunday school may be explained as the ascendency of a new type of formal Jewish community, the *child-oriented* one. This contrasts with the traditional Jewish community, which may be described as adult-oriented.[41]

The child-oriented group was successful in creating a school with a historical approach to Judaism rather than a liturgical and theological one. The Sunday school thus became an institution through which to transmit norms of ethnic culture and symbols of identification, whereas the home and family were regulated according to secular, middle-class behavior patterns. Some parents, in expressing their reasons for choosing this kind of Sunday school, pointed out

---

[38] *Ibid.,* p. 210.
[39] *Ibid.,* p. 212.
[40] *Ibid.,* p. 213. However, it should be pointed out that this greater organizational activity of women is a general suburban pattern.
[41] *Ibid.,* p. 215.

that a Jewish child should know how to identify himself in relation to his Catholic and Protestant playmates. A number wanted their children to know the Jewish tradition so that they could later make a choice as to whether or not they wished to remain Jewish. Others saw Sunday school as providing a defense against later psychological hardships arising out of the minority position of Jews. And some parents were concerned about the fact that, although they selected their intimate friends from among the Jewish group, their children chose playmates without regard to ethnic or religious origin. Although a synagogue was not yet established at the time of Gans' study, there was already considerable discussion of one. The reasons for wanting a synagogue were not entirely religious. For many it was to be a symbol of group respectability or of Jewish solidarity.[42]

This suburban community of young Americans reveals facets of Jewish acculturation which contrast with the Jewish subcommunities of a generation earlier. Perhaps this is best shown in the adaptations made in the Park Forest congregation finally established in 1951. The congregation was designated as "Eastern European Reform." It combined a permissive attitude toward practices in the home which involve the sacrifice of secular pleasures (food restrictions and so forth), Conservative ceremonies, Hebrew reading, and responsive singing. The temple kitchen was not kosher but did not serve pork. The rabbi, who was from eastern European background, had been trained as an Orthodox rabbi but later had changed to Reform. A lecture series on secular Jewish topics attracted good attendance. Otherwise, large attendance occurred mainly on the high holy days.

The example of Park Forest shows that there is a reality to the concept of "the Jewish Community" which is bound up with sentiment, preferences, feelings of security, and also with organizational patterns. The Jews are probably the most highly organized of any minority group. There are welfare organizations that are remarkably efficient in helping Jews in many dimensions of need, from the most objective to the most personal; there are organizations from conservative and moderate to militant concerned with improving the opportunity and public image of Jews; there are organizations concerned with helping the State of Israel; there are organizations who are unconcerned with or covertly anti-Israel. All these appeal to the common responsibility of all Jews for other Jews. Many of them have broadened to espouse the situation and needs of other minorities as well as Jews. There are also several major labor unions which in the past have been largely Jewish in membership and still retain Jewish leadership, as well as cultural and benefit societies for the Jewish working class.

The status structure within the Jewish community once was marked by sharp divisions of prestige, paralleling the nineteenth-century criteria of prestige in the dominant society: date of migration, wealth, country of origin. Status differentiation has become more blurred today: this is partially due to the

[42] *Ibid.*, pp. 224–225.

mobility of the descendents of the later migrants, partially due to greater Jewish solidarity evoked by the anti-Semitism of the twentieth century in Europe and America.

Anti-Semitism in the United States

Anti-Semitism as a public issue in the United States is usually dated from 1887. There had been hostile incidents against Jews in various localities from time to time but these were brief local affairs. But in 1877 when the New York banker Joseph Seligman wrote for reservations at the Grand Union Hotel in Saratoga Springs, New York—a fashionable resort hotel where he and his family had often stayed before—he was informed that the hotel had adopted a new policy and "did not accept Israelites." Seligman's had been one of the banking houses that had floated the United States government bond issue of 1870–71 which, in the words of President Grant, "established American credit abroad," [43] after the financial drain of the Civil War. Joseph Seligman was on the platform at President Grant's inauguration, attended the inaugural ball, and was a frequent guest at the White House. He was one of the earliest members of the Union League Club of New York. His refusal at the Grand Union made the national press from coast to coast.[44]

There were many factors in this incident. One was the personal and political animosity between Seligman and the new owner of the Hotel, Judge Hilton. Another was that this hotel was no longer the favorite of the most elite families who had been fellow guests in earlier days with the Seligmans, and the question has been raised as to whether or not Hilton was attempting to recruit a new clientele that was less secure, more *arriviste,* and therefore more anxious to prove their exclusiveness. Whatever the weight of these various factors, the incident and its publicity precipitated a polarization and brought to the surface much latent anti-Semitism. Birmingham thinks the results of the Saratoga Springs incident, in bringing into the open anti-Jewish attitudes, broke Joseph Seligman's spirit. He died within a year.[45]

Anti-Semitism rose in the ensuing decades, probably reaching its peak in the first half of the 1920's, but persisting in organized efforts till World War II. Baltzell, in *The Protestant Establishment,* has traced the role of intellectual and social forces in its development. He delineates the anti-Semitism of the aging Henry Adams who saw the Jews as epitomizing all the evil of industrial America, in which people of his own stratum (the old Protestant leadership of the New England merchant and scholarly occupations) had lost power and took refuge in caste-like exclusiveness.[46] Early American social scientists at the beginning

[43] Birmingham, *Our Crowd,* p. 104.
[44] *Ibid.,* Ch. 18, "The Seligman-Hilton Affair," pp. 141–150.
[45] *Ibid.,* p. 148.
[46] E. Digby Baltzell, *The Protestant Establishment: Aristocracy and Caste in America* (New York: Random House, 1964), pp. 87–93.

of the twentieth century reflected both the influence of European racist thought and the mistrust of growing urbanism and "business ethic," which they linked to industrialization and immigration.[47]

The Populist movement, extolling the virtues of homogeneous rural life, viewed the declining importance of the rural segment of America as due to the manipulations of urban financial power, and the stereotype of the Jewish international financier, involving a conspiracy of power (and usury), emerged.[48] Anti-Semitism was a factor in many pressures to restrict immigration.[49] The fact that anti-Semitism increased concurrently with the large migration of eastern European Jews after 1880 led many people, Gentiles and established Jews, to see the migration as the *cause* of anti-Semitism. Whereas this rationalization may have been important in the minds of some who saw the eastern Jews as more strange and even "unassimilable," [50] as we have seen, anti-Semitism had emerged before this migration began and was rooted in other problems and anxieties associated with social change.

Perhaps the most dramatic example of this is the mob hysteria stirred up by a Southern Populist leader against Leo Frank, a young Jewish factory manager in Georgia, which culminated in his being lynched (August 17, 1915).[51] Mr. Frank came from New York City. He was a graduate of Cornell University. He married into an established circle of Jewish business and banking in Atlanta, and symbolized the alien world of big business and big city.

It is a commonplace that when anti-minority feeling is running high, sexual charges are part of the picture. (This was true of anti-Catholic charges of the immorality of priests and nuns.) Leo Frank was charged with the murder of a very young girl who was employed in his factory. The evidence was of the flimsiest and the trial conducted with a mob milling about outside. Frank was convicted. His case was brought to the Supreme Court where the conviction was upheld, Mr. Justice Holmes writing the dissenting opinion. The Governor of Georgia ruined his political career by commuting the sentence. A day later a mob broke into the jail and transported Frank to another part of the state where he was lynched. Oscar and Mary Handlin feel that the commutation of the sentence appeared to the anti-Semites as proof of the influence on the governor of big business and money.[52] Not the least interesting aspect of the whole case was the cautious attitude of many Jews. On the whole, initially, the Jewish community of Atlanta was frightened. There were five prominent Jews on the grand jury that indicted Frank. Only after the case became a national

[47] *Ibid.*, pp. 104–108.

[48] Richard Hofstadter, *The Age of Reform, From Bryan to F.D.R.* (New York: Alfred A. Knopf, 1955), pp. 70–83.

[49] Baltzell, *The Protestant Establishment*, pp. 204–206.

[50] *Ibid.*, p. 106.

[51] Harry Golden, *A Little Girl Is Dead* (New York: Alfred A. Knopf, 1965). See also "Why Frank was Lynched," *Forum Magazine*, Dec., 1916, p. 678.

[52] Oscar and Mary F. Handlin, *Danger in Discord: Origins of Anti-Semitism in the United States* (New York: Anti-Defamation League of B'nai B'rith, 1959).

issue were more Atlanta Jews willing to come forward in his defense.[53] The fear was there that the national attention would create anti-Semitism where there had been none. The Georgia Chamber of Commerce, in a letter to the *New York Times* denied any anti-Semitism in Atlanta or any prejudice against industrial employers. The *Times,* in an editorial, pointed out that Atlanta was no different from any other American city.[54]

In considering the Leo Frank case it is important to compare the caution of established Jews of Atlanta (and to a degree elsewhere) with the fact that the great Negro leader of the same period, Booker T. Washington, refused to join the newly created NAACP, for he feared for the ultimate result of a militant Negro organization. In thinking of the mob of people involved in violence, displaced or fearing displacement, or subject to frustrated personality needs, it might be useful to compare the action against Mexican Americans in the Los Angeles riots of 1943.

Anti-Semitism similar to that known in Europe, political in its implications, more organized, and more vitriolic in its propaganda, began to arise about 1917. In the few years following the close of World War I, large quantities of anti-Semitic literature identifying Jews with the rising European revolutionary ideology appeared; the new Ku Klux Klan arose in the North, with its generally antiforeign orientation including anti-Semitism; the Fellowship Forum distributed widely copies of the forged Protocols of the Elders of Zion; and Henry Ford commenced his anti-Semitic campaign through the publication of the *Dearborn Independent.*[55]

That these new anti-Semitic activities had an effect is indicated by an increase in various incidents of which the following are illustrative.

> The board of directors of a Milwaukee golf club asked eight Jewish charter members to resign.

> The secretary of the Chamber of Commerce in St. Petersburg, Florida, announced that the time had come to make St. Petersburg "a 100 per cent American gentile City."

> Several large real estate concerns in New Jersey, New York, Georgia, and Florida were found to have restricted new subdivisions against Jewish occupancy.

> Of more than passing interest in this period was President Lowell's graduation address at Harvard in June 1922, in which he advocated quotas against Jews. While the trustees of Harvard later rejected this suggestion, it was painfully apparent that the quota system was spreading.[56]

[53] Golden, *A Little Girl Is Dead,* p. 224; *New York Times,* Aug. 19, 1915, p. 4.
[54] *The New York Times,* March 5, 1914, p. 1; March 6, 1914, p. 10.
[55] Donald S. Strong, *Organized Anti-Semitism in America* (Washington, D.C.: American Council on Public Affairs, 1941), p. 15.
[56] McWilliams, *A Mask for Privilege,* pp. 38–39. By permission of the publisher Little, Brown & Co.

Abating somewhat during the late 1920's, anti-Semitism rose again in the early 1930's as the Depression intensified. Strong has indicated that there were 121 organizations actively spreading anti-Semitic propaganda in the period 1933–1940.[57] In the late 1930's anti-Semitism began to be used for the first time openly in political campaigns. The manager of the nativist third party in the 1936 Presidential election is quoted by McWilliams as stating, "the trouble with this country now is due to the money powers and Jewish politicians." [58]

While the sweeping victory of Franklin D. Roosevelt in 1936 temporarily set back the agitation, it resumed with new intensity in the late 1930's and continued until Pearl Harbor. Involved in this activity were the Christian Front, led by Father Charles Coughlin, and the Silver Shirts, directed by William Pelley. In a period of nineteen months before July 31, 1938, Pelley mailed approximately three and a half tons of anti-Semitic propaganda from his headquarters. All of this organization and propaganda obviously cost a good deal of money, and though the program was conducted by relatively unimportant people, it occasionally received support in high places. For example, McWilliams quotes Congressman John Rankin as stating to Congress that "Wall Street and a little group of our international Jewish brethren are still attempting to harass the President and Congress into plunging us into the European War." [59] It is interesting to note that this new crescendo in anti-Semitic propaganda was correlated with the increasing strength of the Nazi movement in Europe.

During World War II overt manifestations of anti-Semitism disappeared. They were considered inimical to the war effort and were discouraged by the government. Furthermore, the ideological inconsistency of supporting anti-Semitism while fighting the arch Jew-hater, Adolph Hitler, had some deterrent effect. In the few months following the end of World War II, however, the Fair Employment Practices Committee noted an increase in discrimination against Jews in employment. However, a *Fortune* Survey, which had found the incidence of anti-Semitism in the adult population to be about 9.3 percent in 1943, found it to be 8.8 percent in 1946.[60] Organized anti-Semitic activity failed to resume its prewar intensity, although it was far from dormant. The *American Jewish Year Book* for 1950 noted a tendency for individual agitators to combine operations and to favor the distribution of inflammatory literature over holding meetings and demonstrations.[61] These trends indicate that the agitators were having a more difficult time.

This fluctuating course of anti-Semitic behavior suggests that it is more responsive to changes in socioeconomic conditions in the national community than to changes in the behavior of Jews. Such conditions are manifold and we

[57] Strong, *Organized Anti-Semitism in America,* pp. 146–147.
[58] McWilliams, *A Mask for Privilege,* p. 42.
[59] *Ibid.,* p. 46.
[60] *Fortune,* "The Fortune Survey," Feb. 1946, 33:258.
[61] American Jewish Yearbook, 1950, 51:110.

can rarely single out one factor as being the sole determinant. At times it may appear that economic changes have a direct bearing. For example, in the first of the periods of marked discrimination, 1910–1914, the competition of increasingly Americanized Jews for employment in white-collar positions began to be felt by Gentile workers. At other times conflicts in ideologies loomed as the more significant factor. Thus the rise in anti-Semitism following World War I seems related to the spread of radical philosophy in this country, which raised anxiety in the middle class. The sharper political orientation of the anti-Semitism of the 1930's occurred at a time when legislation was enacted which made the position of the working class more secure and, in consequence, increased the anxieties of the other economic levels.

Although there has been a decline in anti-Semitism since World War II, not all has been quiescent. The most dramatic instances have been symbolic acts against institutional property. Acts of vandalism against Jewish property or molestation of Jewish persons are not new. They occurred during World War I and again during the late 20's and early 30's.[62] This particular kind of anti-minority behavior in the post-World War II period seems to reflect other and in some degree more subtle pressures in the society than war, depression, and international tension. A significant example of such outbreaks occurred early in 1960. Beginning with an incident in Cologne, Germany, on December 24, 1959, a wave of vandalism and desecration spread through the United States for nine weeks. There were 643 incidents, nearly two-thirds of which involved only the painting of swastikas. About 60 percent of the incidents occurred in cities with more than 100,000 inhabitants. Not all these acts were directed toward specific Jewish targets. For example, schools and churches were in some instances defaced. The larger the community, the higher the proportion of Jewish targets. The pattern was not consistent throughout the United States; Arizona had an unusually high number of incidents in proportion to its population and its Jewish population, whereas some large cities, such as St. Louis, Newark, New Orleans, Buffalo, and Indianapolis, had hardly any. In the South, states which had made some token effort at desegregation had more incidents than those which had not integrated at all or had made considerable progress in integration.[63]

As for explanations, anxiety in the face of as yet unstructured social change may be inferred as one precipitating factor in the pattern of the Southern outbreaks. The swastika epidemic, however, appealed almost solely to one section of the population—adolescent boys. It was clear from interrogation of the offenders that some of them were expressing direct anti-Semitic feeling. For others, however, this was not the case. It is worth asking what kind of

[62] Charles Wagley and Marvin Harris, *Minorities in the New World* (New York: Columbia University Press, 1958), p. 221.
[63] David Caplovitz and Candace Rogers, *Swastika 1960* (New York: Anti-Defamation League of B'nai B'rith), pp. 28–30, pp. 51–52.

academic, vocational, and personal pressures our society exerts on urban children of this age group that can lead them to engage in this type of destructive activity.

Why Does Anti-Semitism Persist?

There are different degrees of intensity of anti-Semitism, different rationalizations for it, and social science is discovering different levels of motivation. Before we indicate these different levels, it is important to point out that the problem of Jewish-Gentile relations can probably never be divorced entirely from the historical tradition. In our opinion, and contemporary evidence seems to bear this out with regard to the Soviet Union, even a revolutionary reorganization of society will not automatically solve the problem. A literate tradition, unlike the oral tradition of a folk society, can never entirely lose historic attitudes and the awareness of historic problems. This affects Gentile and Jewish thinking alike.

We have already discussed some of the forms in which anti-Semitism expresses itself. We are here interested in the psychological dimension which leads people either spontaneously to express anti-Semitic sentiments, or to be receptive to organized anti-Semitic efforts.

Much of what are popularly considered individual psychological reactions really constitute appropriate behavior within given social-structural situations. All groups with a highly developed sense of identity perceive other groups as different from themselves (ingroup, outgroup relations.) Thus many spontaneous sentiments are construed as anti-Semitic, though they do not necessarily carry with them any inner commitment or virulence. They may, however, lay the base for mobilizable sentiments if a stable situation is in the throes of change.

Another type of anti-Semitism is related to the larger minority problem of competition between those whom the dominant culture favors and the able members of any minority. It is obvious that many less able people are retained in occupational positions by the practice of discrimination. Occupational discrimination furthermore has social concomitants, involving choice of mate, club membership, social admission, and so forth. The local community power structure is reinforced by this web of relationships. The end product is to create an effect on general public policy.

A popular interpretation of anti-Semitism derives from the so-called "scapegoat" theory, which attributes the need to project blame for personal and social difficulties on somebody else. Here the historic position of the Jews makes them particularly vulnerable to being used as scapegoats, although a comparable attitude was not unknown toward the Japanese through World War II among people on the West Coast. There are different levels of insecurity in which this operates, one of which is insecurity of status, such as the threatened loss of middle-class occupation and style of life, where the individuals feel, correctly or incorrectly, that a competitive threat comes from the minority members. Paul Massing has analyzed this factor with regard to the growth of anti-Semitism before the Nazis took over in Germany and in the subsequent support given the Nazi leadership.[64] A recent study of the Nazi leaders has demonstrated that in one way or another these were all marginal men in their societies.[65] What we see from this is that organized anti-Semitism can be aroused in a threatened stratum of the society, and that leaders emerge from those who are less well integrated in the society than the general population of their age group.

The prejudiced personality has been studied from the viewpoint of both sociology and psychiatry. The study of the authoritarian personality which we present in Chapter 19 suggests that certain types of upbringing create this personality need, and that children in authoritative situations where they feel helpless are more apt to be prejudiced than children given freedom to express themselves, to be inventive and exploratory. A person brought up in this manner, it appears, attempts to repress fear, weakness, sex impulses, and aggressive feelings in order to be approved of by the punishing parents. He then compensates by attributing these "bad" repressed impulses to others whom society holds in less esteem, whether or not there is any basis for it in their behavior. Wherever the social situation provides a target for derogation, the repressed wishes will be assigned to the derogated person.

The reduction of anti-Semitism, in the light of what we have said, needs to be approached in different ways, depending on the source of the anti-Semitic attitudes. Thus it may involve varying aspects of social integration or it may be a problem at a deep level of personality structure.

The Decline of Dominance

As we have indicated Jews came to America feeling that here was a new society in which there would be little or none of the heritage of discrimination; this was the more true as Europe had pitched the minority problem primarily on the basis of religion, and America guaranteed, officially at least, freedom of religion. Initially there was little discrimination, though there was some degree of separatism. As anti-Semitism developed, so also did discrimination. The discrimination occurred on economic and social levels, primarily.

The real upsurge in feeling against Jews as economic competitors appears to have started after 1900, reaching a high peak at the outbreak of World War I. In Severson's study of discriminatory want ads, one finds that beginning in 1911 "ads requesting 'Christians only' or 'Gentiles only' appeared at the rate of 0.3 per 1,000, rose to 4 percent in 1921, to 8.8 in 1923, to 13.3 in 1926; averaged 11 percent from 1927 to 1931; dropped to 4.8 percent in 1931, and then rose to 9.4 percent in 1937." Severson's thesis is that it was not immigra-

[64] Paul Massing, *Rehearsal for Destruction* (New York: Harper & Brothers, 1949).
[65] Ithiel da Sola Pool and Daniel K. Lerner, *The Nazi Elite* (Stanford, Calif.: The Stanford University Press, 1956).

tion per se, or cultural conflict, which developed this latent prejudice but rather "that the particular exigency of the occasion was the coming into the clerical labor market, particularly of girls into typing and stenography, of second-generation east European immigrants.[66] The situation could be compared today with discrimination in the employment of Negroes in white-collar occupations. When a minority begins to move up in the competitive areas which affect the broad base of American middle-class security, a more widespread opposition develops.

In the same way there was a period of severe educational discrimination. In public education there has of course been no discrimination, officially. But in elite and professional education there has been until recently, through quota systems, a real discrimination. In 1946, Dodson found in a survey of admissions to 700 liberal arts colleges that the quota system was in effect in nearly all of them (despite official denial).[67] The same situation was, at this period, true of medical schools, though the discrimination against Italians in professional schools was even greater.

This pattern of job discrimination and access to training was the second-last frontier of rising, able minorities. The final frontier has been the admission into the large corporate enterprises characteristic of today's economic power structure.[68] The situation for Jews has been pioneering and the most acute, but it is not in the long run fundamentally different from other religious minorities (Catholics, for example), or ethnic minorities of the later migration (Italians), or "racial" minorities, especially Negroes.

Social discrimination has been a very sensitive point with Jews. Restrictions on residence, hotel and vacation accommodations, country clubs, fraternities in colleges have all been offensive. To the degree that these social-structured groupings affect the acceptance of Jews in other spheres of life this is an important aspect of discrimination. Where such discrimination has existed or does exist it puts a severe burden on people who both wish to be of the society and retain affectionate aspects of their own heritage.

It is clearly true that in the last decade formal discrimination has declined. Part of this is due to the fact that there has always been a segment of the larger society which fought against the crystallization of caste, though when this was of primary significance a generation or two ago it usually did not permeate to "the little man."[69] Part of it has been due to Jewish organizations created to improve Jewish-Gentile relations. There are a number of these and they vary in emphasis and in membership just as organizations of other minorities do. Several of them have furthered both research and action about all

---

[66] Quotation taken from A. L. Severson, "Nationality and Religion in Newspaper Ads," *American Journal of Sociology*, January, 1939, 545.
[67] Dan W. Dodson, "Religious Prejudice in Colleges," *American Mercury*, July, 1946, pp. 5–13.
[68] Glazer and Moynihan, *Beyond the Melting Pot*, pp. 147–148.
[69] Baltzell, *The Protestant Establishment*, Chapters 6, 7, 13.

American minority problems, not merely issues affecting Jews. A third factor has been the success of other minorities in permeating both the corporate business structure and the political power structure on a national level. Whereas this has happened in the national scene, it possibly also has contributed to local-national tension in those localities where change has been slow and where homogeneity of population is still a predominant factor.

Where discrimination persists today, and no one denies that it is still real in some dimensions of life, and particularly in some places, it is usually subtle and hard to document. It is also true that some Jews, because of their history, are hypersensitive to *any* definition of themselves by non-Jews, seeing any recognition of difference as potentially or actually anti-Semitic. In large cities where residents are accustomed to contact with many different kinds of people these definitions may carry no derogation, but are simply part of the present urban drift to acceptance of America as a pluralistic society.[70]

The Outlook

As we have indicated the Jewish group in America is a varied population with important regional and status differences. The choices before individuals and families are rooted in their particular relation to American life of the 1960's, and also in their particular and group history. Now that many of the barriers have been lowered, now that many Jews have been able to benefit from the open opportunity structure of America, they are confronted with discovering an appropriate balance between separation and loss of identity.[71] For many Jews the solution has been to strengthen their religious ties and to see themselves within the total society as members of an American religion. But the secularizing pressures of the larger society have also affected many Jews, who nevertheless do not wish to abandon their sense of being Jewish. For some of these, active alliance with organizations or movements for social reform have provided a structure. Many Jewish middle-class families have followed the larger middle-class trend to the suburbs, but usually, though not always, this operates toward social separatism.

Topics for Projects and Discussion

1. Discuss the effects of the establishment of the State of Israel on the position of Jews in the United States and in the world.
2. Write a biographical sketch of an American Jew who has made a significant contribution to law, humanities, science, business, or the arts. Describe how his interest was aroused and assess his achievement. (Suggested names: Benjamin Cardozo, Albert Einstein, Julius Rosenwald, Leonard Bernstein.)

[70] Herbert J. Gans, *The Urban Villagers: Group and Class in the Life of Italian-Americans* (New York: The Free Press of Glencoe, 1962), p. 36.
[71] See Glazer and Moynihan, *Beyond the Melting Pot*, "Culture and the Future," pp. 171–180.

3. Discuss the role of Jewish Americans in helping other minorities in the United States—for example the activities of the Rosenwald Fund or the Anti-Defamation League of B'nai B'rith.
4. Describe instances of hidden discrimination that you have encountered or read about. How can these be changed?
5. Analyze the types of people attracted to anti-Semitic movements and the social circumstances which give rise to these movements.
6. Discuss generational conflicts of American Jewish young people. Are these similar to the conflict of generations throughout the society, or are they in some way special in the Jewish group?
7. What can you discover about attitudes of Jews and of Gentiles with regard to Jewish-Gentile intermarriage?

Suggested Reading

Birmingham, Stephen. *"Our Crowd": The Great Jewish Families of New York*. New York: Harper & Row, 1967.

> *A lively popular account of the nineteenth-century German Jewish families and their descendants and intermarriages who played an important role in the worlds of finance, enterprise, welfare, and patrons of the arts.*

Commentary. *The Condition of Jewish Belief*. New York: The Macmillan Co., 1966.

> *A symposium of the opinions of thirty-eight rabbis representing a wide range from orthodox to reformed Judaism. Five critical questions were put to each and their answers give a spectrum of the agreements and disagreements of the denominations of Judaism.*

Glanz, Rudolf. *The Jews of California: From the Discovery of Gold until 1880*. New York: Waldon Press, 1960.

> *A scholarly documentation of the early migration and establishment of Jews on the Pacific coast, and their roles and participation in the larger society as well as in "the Jewish Community."*

Glazer, Nathan, and Moynihan, Daniel Patrick. *Beyond the Melting Pot*. Cambridge, Mass.: The M.I.T. and the Harvard Press, 1963.

> *The Jews of New York City in the perspective of other minority groups in the city.*

Gordon, Albert I. *Intermarriage*. Boston: The Beacon Press, 1964.

> *A discussion of trends and problems in Jewish-Gentile marriage.*

Kramer, Judith, and Levantman, Seymour. *Children of the Gilded Ghetto*. New Haven: Yale University Press, 1961.

> *A study of the generations in a Jewish suburban community in the Middle West.*

Rosenthal, Erich. "Jewish Intermarriage in the United States," *Council Women*. New York: National Council of Jewish Women, Nov. 1963.

> *Rosenthal in the early '60's found in his sample that intermarriage between Jews and Gentiles is increasing.*

Shapiro, Harry L. *The Jewish People: A Biological History*. Paris, France: UNESCO, 1960.

*The most complete and up-to-date statement of the physiological traits of
the Jewish people.*

Sklare, Marshall. *The Jews: Social Patterns of an American Group.* Glencoe, Ill.: The
Free Press, 1958.

*A book of readings covering many aspects of Jewish life in the United States—
social, religious, cultural.*

Zborowski, Mark, and Herzog, Elizabeth. *Life Is With People.* New York: International
Universities Press, 1952.

*Two anthropologists reconstruct with great sensitivity and warmth the eastern
European Jewish village as a culture and a way of life.*

19

Sociological Theory and the Analysis of Dominant-Minority Relations

Minority problems occur within the larger frame of social structure and social processes. There is, therefore, no proper separate body of theory of dominant-minority relations. They may, however, be selected as the focus within which a general theory of social relations is developed. This is true of the work of Robert E. Park, to be discussed below. Interethnic relations have also served as illustrative material for the elaboration of key concepts in the analysis of a whole society. It is not surprising that references to the position of minorities occur in most "classical" American sociological theory, as "racial" and ethnic variation are the fabric of the American society which was under the purview of these "founding fathers."

What Is Theory?

Scientific theory is a set of interrelated, testable propositions. Every science is in the process of developing theory. At one level theory is the effort simply to *describe* accurately a set of interrelated phenomena. Thus, for example, the Romans developed a crude theory of physical stress which allowed them, in its application, to build bridges and aqueducts. Essential to this level of developing theory is *common agreement on descriptive terms.* In studying human behavior do we agree on what we mean when we say "role" or "status" or "values" or "institutions"? This is one part of the theoretical task of a science.

At the other extreme there is an attempt to map out the entire social universe. This may be based, methodologically, entirely on *logical deduction* and may develop far beyond any immediate practical application, as, for example, the science of astronomy, before the space age, far outran any practical applications, relevant, say, to navigation.

The sources of insight that lead to theory building occur in several ways. Some may be arrived at from concern about problems demanding action. Sometimes theory evolves out of the accidental observations of a person thinking about the general relationships which the particular incident makes vivid. It is part of the folklore of science, for example, that the observation of an apple falling from a tree crystallized Newton's formulation of the theory of gravity. Much of the advanced development of science is derived from logical, abstract thought, which must then be validated by appropriate testing procedures. Application can be an end product, as well as an initial stimulus to theory building.

Action and theory are not a dichotomy. As action inevitably stimulates speculation, in a scientifically oriented society theory sooner or later must be tested if it is to survive in the accepted system of knowledge. Part of the task of the behavioral sciences in the twentieth century has been to develop increasingly reliable methods of testing propositions. That great gains have been made in reliability and acceptance of scientific investigation in the behavioral fields is attested by the use of an "expert brief," prepared by social psychologists, sociologists, and anthropologists in the United States Supreme Court Decision (Brown vs the Board of Education) on school desegregation.

The Interdisciplinary Nature of Social Science

The "social" or "behavioral" sciences have historically proceeded from different foci to examine the same phenomena. Psychology, psychiatry, anthropology, sociology, and history have all contributed to our understanding of dominant-minority relations. This interdisciplinary linkage is paralleled in the sciences that deal with organic or inorganic matter, as with physical chemistry and biochemistry. Any ultimate solution of all the problems related to dominant-minority relations must take account of the several dimensions that have been the specialties of related behavioral science disciplines. We are beginning to see interdisciplinary efforts, and there has been, of course, much borrowing of ideas, or much use of data from related fields. If, then, in this chapter we concentrate on some theoretical efforts of sociologists that have affected our understanding of dominant-minority relations, it is with the understanding that sociology has not been the only contributor to our current knowledge. Furthermore, since sociology is a very young science, there is not yet any agreed-upon canon of sociological theory, although there is a body of concepts that have become the accepted tools of social analysis.

It is not our intention here to attempt to review all sociological theoretical contributions that have a bearing on dominant-minority relations, nor to develop an integrated theoretical statement of our own. The purpose of this chapter is, rather, to acquaint the student with the nature of the theoretical task and present selected illustrations of how theory building affects our understanding of dominant-minority relations. In approaching this chapter the student may leave the mastery of substantive material presented in the foregoing chapters and be stimulated to speculate with the sociological thinkers about the multi-group world of which he is part.

As we pointed out, theory building occurs at several levels. There is the search for more refined, and therefore more precise, definition of terms (conceptual clarification). There is the attempt to show the interrelatedness of several kinds of propositions (middle-range theory). There are various ways of looking at the same phenomena that are derived from systematic theory of the total society.

"Grand Theory"

We have selected four illustrations of systematic sociological theory to illustrate some of the problems, some of the convergences, and some of the distinctive contributions of the writers cited as they have relevance to dominant-minority relations.

Robert E. Park

Robert E. Park's systematic analysis of society revolved around three postulated basic modes of human *interaction:* cooperation, competition, and conflict. Race and culture contacts were subsumed under this system.[1] He attempted to explore the diversity in race and culture contacts, from those of accommodative peace to those of open conflict. His assumptions were the evolutionary beliefs that were the critical intellectual issues of his period—the early part of this century. With this orientation, Park saw relations between dominants and minorities as moving through a definite cycle, with one outcome, the assimilation of the minority into the dominant society. The sequence of competition, conflict, cooperation was a dynamic process in which Park ignored any volitional elements. This makes him the most deterministic of the theorists we are presenting and the least concerned with psychological and motivational dimensions.

Park's work, together with that of his colleague, Louis Wirth, made the first major impact on theory of dominant-minority relations. The work of these two men and others associated with them as colleagues or students comprise what has been called the Park-Wirth school of thought about "race relations." Several of Park's formulations have been incorporated into all subsequent thinking about minorities and have been validated or expanded by subsequent theory and research. One of the most significant of these is the concept of the marginal man. Park also saw that prejudice is to be separated from discrimination, that it cannot be dispelled by knowledge alone, that it rises in periods of social change as individuals and vested interests resist change in the status of minorities, or, otherwise threatened, vent hostility on a vulnerable minority. Park took cognizance of conflict of interest in the dynamics of social interaction, a dimension neglected by some contemporary theorists. He was also interested in the effect of urbanization on conflict between races and nationality groups. He felt that urbanization increased tension between dominants and minorities. Contempo-

[1] Robert E. Park, *Race and Culture* (Glencoe, Ill.: The Free Press, 1950).

rary research in urban patterns of interaction suggests this may not always be so, depending on other variables.[2]

George C. Homans [3]

A contemporary sociologist whose analysis is on the basis of *interaction* is George C. Homans. The fundamental unit in society, for Homans, is the group as a social system. The elements of group behavior are activities, interaction, and sentiment. These three elements in their various interrelations and priorities constitute the social system.

Homans distinguishes between an "external system" of relationships of those elements which relate primarily to survival in the environment and an "internal system" which is related to liking and preferences. External and internal systems are never wholly independent of one another, but a different order of precedence of the three basic factors governs each system. Essentially what Homans is accounting for is the type of interaction related to survival in the larger society as contrasted with the type of interaction which allows the persistence of widely differentiated subgroups within the society.

Homans derives his three basic elements of behavior from a series of empirical case studies of group behavior, ranging from kinship to occupation. Homans develops some specific propositions, several of which can be applied to dominant-minority relations.

Proposition 1
... persons who interact with one another frequently are more like one another in their activities than they are like other persons with whom they interact less frequently.

Thus, in line with this proposition, which establishes in Homans scheme the basis for group coherence, one would expect that individuals in a minority group or in the dominant group who associate frequently would develop similarities of activities that would identify them both subjectively and objectively with their group. This might serve as a base for the development of stereotypes; but, equally, if group barriers disappear to permit frequent interaction the differences of activity should disappear also.

Proposition 2
... the more frequently persons interact with one another, the stronger their sentiments of friendship for one another are apt to be.

This proposition would be basic to the reduction of intergroup diffidence or antagonism. Antagonism can be dispelled if there is a structured situation within

---

[2] For a re-evaluation of Park by a contemporary sociologist, see Seymour Martin Lipset, "Changing Social Status and Prejudice: The Race Theories of a Pioneering American Sociologist," *Commentary*, May, 1950, pp. 475–479.

[3] George C. Homans, *The Human Group* (New York: Harcourt, Brace, 1950).

which dominants and minorities can interact as equals. Out of interaction sentiments of friendship will develop, as, ideally, with school integration.

Proposition 3

... to the degree that the activities of the other individual in a reciprocal role relationship conform to the norms of one's own group, one will like him.

One might interpret this proposition to suggest that where minority group individuals and dominants carry out their roles in relation to one another with the same standards (for example, two civil servants), they are more likely to conceive of each other as individuals to whom one assigns liking and respect, rather than as representatives of their group.

It is hardly necessary to point out that many efforts at improved intergroup relations operate on one or another of these propositions, whether or not the organizers of programs have ever heard of Homans. Homans' analysis has also stimulated a large development in small group research. His concern is with the dynamics of relationship and he gives greater weight to effective sentiments in his basic schema than do many sociologists. Homans later work moves even closer to psychology.

Robert M. MacIver

Robert M. MacIver must be included in any discussion of general theory particularly relevant to dominant-minority relations for a number of reasons. Perhaps the least significant but most obvious of these is that he has, in addition to general theory, written specifically on dominant-minority relations.[4]

MacIver's contributions to general theory are largely those of precision and emphasis. He is in the tradition of the classical sociologists of continental Europe, England, and America. Like Park, his assumptions are evolutionary; unlike Park, he avoids the value judgment of "progress," nor is he as deterministic as Park in his view of social change. For MacIver, for good or ill, societies evolve from the simple to the complex. Within the broad limits of evolutionary development, however, there is room for voluntaristic action to determine directions of change and solutions to problems created by change.

The complexity of the evolving modern social world intrigues MacIver. His main concerns are with the analysis of social structure as a mechanism for sustaining an appropriate balance of necessary controls and optimum individual creativity. He has coined the term "the multi-group society." MacIver sees the State in a pre-eminent role in modern society (he is also distinguished for his writings in political science). Nevertheless, he is convinced of the limited effectiveness of the State if it intrudes beyond its proper sphere, which is adjudicator of competing interests.

[4] Robert M. MacIver, *The More Perfect Union* (New York: Macmillan, 1948). For MacIver's general analysis of social structure and change, see Robert M. MacIver and Charles H. Page, *Society* (New York: Holt, 1949).

MacIver makes a distinction between like (competing) interests and common interests. The function of the State is to regulate *like* interests. *Common* (cultural) interests, where the pursuit of the interest by some members of the society does not detract from the total available to others, is a sphere in which the State is ill-suited or incapable of functioning.

MacIver, concerned as he is with the institutional regulatory patterns of society, still emphasizes that the social reality is groups and associations of people. For him culture is the vehicle for creative and spontaneous expression. All compulsion in the cultural sphere is deadening. In the society at large there must be room for variation:

> The course of civilization is as irreversible as time itself. We have left behind the one-room habitation of our ancestors. We have built ourselves a house of many mansions. Somehow we must learn to make it ours.[5]

MacIver in his insistence on the independence of the cultural sphere opens the way to a redefintion of the question of cultural pluralism more in harmony with what current research is finding to be the reality.

Talcott Parsons [6]

Talcott Parsons is probably the most abstract, the most influential, and the most controversial of contemporary sociological theorists. Parsons sees a social system as held together by a consensus of central values. The survival of a particular society with its values makes necessary the creation of specific positions which represent the distribution of functions in the society. These might be occupational positions, such as banker, machinist, farmer, private secretary and so forth; or within the kinship patterns, father, aunt, stepmother. These positions are statuses, ranked higher or lower in community evaluation according to how central they are to the preservation of the core values and how limited they are in replaceability. Each status demands the carrying out of a function in a socially defined way. This is role.

Parsons subsumes human behavior in three interrelated systems: the social system, the cultural system, and the personality (or motivational) system. The theoretical sociologists from Park to the present have tended to emphasize social structural problems, anthropologists the cultural dimensions of intergroup relations, and the social psychologists and psychiatrists the motivational aspects. Parsons tries to integrate the analysis of all three. Some of his critics say he is trying to write a theory of the social sciences, not of sociology.

None the less, Parsons' chief focus thus far has been on the *social* system. He sees its institutional structure as regulative, defining the legitimate limits of action, and as relational in its establishment of reciprocal role expectations. In-

---

[5] Robert M. MacIver, *The Web of Government* (New York: Macmillan, 1947), p. 430.
[6] Talcott Parsons, *The Social System* (Glencoe, Ill.: The Free Press, 1950). Parsons has also, incidentally, contributed to specific discussion of minorities. See below, Ch. 20.

stitutions for Parsons translate the private acceptance of values into public commitment, through the carrying out of institutionally defined roles. He sees such problems as negative stereotyping as *deviance by the dominant* from his own institutional norms for the entire society. So long as discrimination is accepted and reinforced within the dominant society, no *single individual has to pay the price for deviance of this kind,* as in other circumstances he would through various kinds of negative sanctions against him.[7]

Critics of Parsons have charged that he is too limited in his emphasis on institutional integration and socially induced personality stress. It is felt that he overlooks real conflict of interest in his concern for the stabilizing regulative mechanisms of society and individual acceptance of or reaction formation against these structures.

In Parsons' own view his most significant theoretical contribution has been in the development of what are generally called "pattern variables." These are five pairs of alternatives which the individual may choose as a way relating to others. Clearly the individual does not choose deliberately, but as a person socialized within a culture and within a given social situation with its expectations of role and status behavior. On a very simple level the pattern variables can delineate dichotomies in expectations as between one culture and another, or a village society and a cosmopolitan society. Some of the variables in their original formulation [8] were

(1) Particularism versus universalism—that is, in a particularistic pattern a person or object is significant, whereas in universalism a precept is significant. For example, Puerto Ricans today, like older ethnic groups in the past, may see employment in terms of getting a relative a job (if they have one and know of another in the same shop). This is particularism. The union, however, is interested in general hiring policies, and seniority privileges regardless of personal or ethnic ties (ideally). This is universalism.

(2) The second pair of variables is affect positive versus affect neutrality. Affect positive means the willingness to risk the expression of feeling in the expectation of a rewarding response. This is characteristic of small groups with frequent interaction of the members, or with very stable small subsocieties. In urban society with its many daily contacts and its multigroup character, it is impossible to risk the psychic burden of affective relationships in all contacts, and a pattern of viable choice develops in which the individual is restrained, cautious, and uninvolved (affect neutral).

Others of the variables need not be elaborated: they are self-interest (individualism) versus collective interest; achievement versus ascription (performance as contrasted with known quality); specificity versus diffuseness (specialization of roles and/or contractually defined limits of obligation versus commitment beyond any defined limit, or roles so loosely defined that they

[7] *Ibid.*, p. 290.
[8] *Ibid.*, p. 67.

encompass many diverse interactions with varying obligation and response patterns depending on the interaction and not on the role definition.)

Parsons has somewhat revised this earliest formulation to make the variables more abstractly stated in the hope of making them more flexible tools for many levels of analysis. In this earliest formulation, however, they already add a considerable dimension for our view of areas of conflict in behavioral expectations as between dominants and cultural minorities, or as between rural and urban patterns of living and evaluating. For example: A small homogeneous village society will not be able to offer wide choices of roles, therefore role specialization is not a realistic choice; or collective interest may be made by the pressure of social norms to take priority over individual self interest. The student might attempt to apply these to the five communities of Rimrock as discussed in Chapters 4, 6, and 16.

The three contemporary theorists we have just presented have taken cognizance, by their respective designations of "like," "external," and "social," of the separation of the secular systems of relationship and the cultural systems of relations. These latter allow, in MacIver's terms, more creative spontaneity; in Homan's terms, more sentiment-engendered interaction; in Parsons' terms, more particularistic values; and in keeping with all three, the possibility of great variety of group life. The cultural sphere is, as it were, terrain for abundant variant flowering, flourishing from a root of common interest, common norms, and established position in the secular order. All three theorists recognize the interdependence of the social and cultural, but all recognize that the spheres are of a different order. Thus the base is laid for the role of culture in our pluralistic society. Even Park, by implication, took this into account in his definition of assimilation as access to and fulfillment only of secular community and citizen roles.

Only the experience of America could produce such a theory. Heretofore cultural pluralism has been discussed as if whole cultures, with their sacred and secular systems intact, were to be incorporated in a quasi-federal fashion. The risks of fragmentation, separation, loss of benefit, and eventual instability of the nation-state have been apparent in this older theory, and aroused grave doubts about the support of that kind of pluralistic society. The solution here presented suggests the appropriateness of separating those functions which are uniquely cultural from the totality, allowing their voluntary development in a variety of patterns and strengthening unity in areas of secular public interest. MacIver feels strongly that such a possibility is inherent in the democratic state. It is in the light of these theories that we can then understand Frazier's vision of cosmopolitan urban societies of the future, in which the interaction of people of varying racial and ethnic identification on the basis of equality will lead to a new flow of human creativity.[9]

[9] E. Franklin Frazier, *Race and Culture Contacts in the Modern World.* (New York: Knopf, 1957).

Theory Building: The Refinement of Concepts

If we are to analyze dominant-minority relations, sociology must come to some agreement about the meaning of terms describing the major modes in which dominants and minorities relate to each other. Park saw these major modes as patterns of *interaction:* competition, conflict, accommodation, assimilation, proceeding through that sequence. If, however, one is interested in the continuing structured relationships between dominants and minorities, the basic terms which need to be agreed upon are those describing *stabilized forms of adaptation,* and *goals,* of minorities in their minority status: accommodation, acculturation, assimilation.

Accommodation

Since Park emphasized the interaction between dominants and minorities, he saw accommodation as a temporary suspension of conflict. A subsequent emphasis is contained in the definition of accommodation by Kimball Young and Raymond W. Mack: "a condition, a state of equilibrium between individuals or groups in which certain working arrangements have been agreed on or accepted." [10] We would stress *accepted* rather than *agreed on,* thus emphasizing that accommodation is a mode of adaptation about which the minority has no choice. It is the adjustment by the minority to conditions over which it has no control. "The Southerner keeps watching all the time for germs of unrest in the Negro community. He preserves the machinery of caste controls in a state of perpetual preparedness, and applies it occasionally as an exercise or demonstration. In this system, Negroes *have* to accommodate individually and as a group." [11] Myrdal's study brings out in various contexts a point often neglected in the discussion of accommodation: that accommodation has two separate but related components, the external or behavioral element, and the internal or attitudinal change. These two levels of adaptation have been much discussed in the literature on acculturation, but it has not been recognized as equally true for minorities who have had to accept an accommodative position. There is ample evidence in the history of slavery and in the subsequent post-Reconstruction history of the Negro that much accommodation was external only.

Another major unexplored area is that of the social effects of accommodation. Whereas social psychiatry has explored a little the effect on minority individuals of living in an accommodative pattern, the study of the effect on the total society, dominants and minorities alike, has not been adequately considered. For example there is some reason to believe that we could find a cor-

---

[10] Raymond W. Mack and Kimball Young, *Sociology and Social Life,* 4th ed. (New York: American Book Company, 1968). See Glossary.
[11] Gunnar Myrdal, *An American Dilemma* (New York: Harper & Brothers, 1944), p. 768. Italics in original.

relation between an accommodative pattern of dominant-minority relations and political apathy of both dominants and minorities within that structure.

Acculturation

All contemporary writing on acculturation takes cognizance of the two levels on which cultural characteristics must be acquired when an individual is divesting himself of one culture and accepting another. These have been described by the terms "manifest" versus "intangible," or "behavioral" versus "attitudinal," or "external" and "internal." Whereas these distinctions are commonplace, little attention has been given to the selectivity involved in taking on new cultural traits, whether external or internal. There is very little known about the resistances that may arise at the introduction of a new culture trait or about specific conditions affecting the traits that are accepted or rejected. For example, there will be a difference of behavioral and/or attitudinal acceptance or resistance according to whether culture traits are forced upon a people or are received voluntarily by them. It will make a difference whether or not there is social or political inequality between groups. The analysis of acculturation must be refined to take cognizance of the situations within which acculturation occurs.[12]

Warner and others have claimed that acculturation is apt to occur more quickly when two cultures are similar. Here the differentiation between behavioral and attitudinal needs also to be made, as is pointed out by Broom and Kitsuse.[13] They call attention to the fact that the manifest behavioral culture traits of a minority may be markedly different from those of the host society, but this does not mean that the attitudinal ones are necessarily disparate. They cite the example of the Japanese, and account in this way for the relatively rapid acculturation of Japanese-Americans despite many different external modes of behavior in Japanese culture.

Broom and Kitsuse also point out that the person who is taking on a new culture must "validate" his acculturation by having *qualified* and been *accepted* in the major institutional patterns of the dominant society.[14] In order to do this he must also give up any privileged protection or immunities which he has enjoyed by virtue of being a member of a minority. This has been recognized by Frazier and others who have described as "vested interests" the resistances to assimilation of certain status groups within the minority, where incorporation into equal competition with dominants might diminish their advantages. Dominants can equally shut out minorities by patterns of overprotection, by making pets of individual minority members to whom they have some

[12] Melville J. Herskovits, *Acculturation: The Study of Culture Contact* (Gloucester, Mass.: Peter Smith, 1958). Appendix, "Outline for the Study of Acculturation," by Robert Redfield, Ralph Linton, and Melville J. Herskovits, p. 133.
[13] Leonard Broom and John Kitsuse, "The Validation of Acculturation," *American Anthropologist,* February, 1955, 57:44 ff.
[14] *Ibid.*

personal tie. In this connection, Margaret Mead, as anthropologist consultant to the Israel Ministry of Health, cautions with regard to the Arab minority:

> ... There seemed to be a tendency to demand for the Arab health services far less local contribution than Jewish communities would make and to treat some Arab nomadic groups with a considerable amount of patronage. I fully realize the delicacy of the problem ... but I think the only safe course of action is to accord the Arab population the same type of expectation, privilege, and responsibility accorded other Israeli citizens, for over-privilege can be as discriminatory as under-privilege, even though there are fewer immediate ill effects.[15]

Validation is the point at which the move to ultimate assimilation will or will not be made. If minority members reject participation in some but not all the major institutional forms of the dominant culture, they have made a choice for stabilized pluralism, with the ensuing development of particular established patterns of interaction with dominants. There is often a generational battle over the choice of stabilized acculturation versus assimilation.

Assimilation

In a definition of assimilation Park states that "an immigrant is ordinarily considered assimilated as soon as he has acquired the language and the social ritual of the native community and can participate, without encountering prejudice in the common life, economic and political. ... Assimilation may in some senses and to a certain degree be described as a function of visibility." [16] A problem arises here as to whether or not a minority person is assimilated if he participates only in the secular community institutions of economic and public life, and is debarred in the sphere of social invitation. Another point of view has been that which stresses the interactional aspect of assimilation. Thus Mack and Young define assimilation as "the fusion of divergent habits, attitudes, and ideas of two or more groups or societies into a common set of habits, attitudes, and ideas." [17] This definition stresses the blending of mutual contributions to the common life. It does not imply that every vestige of the old culture must be abandoned, but it makes no effort to differentiate on what levels old culture sentiments and traits may be retained and a person still be considered assimilated.

Contemporary sociologists stress the fact that, in the end, assimilation depends on dominant acceptance of the minority individual. The question is not only in which spheres of social life a person is accepted; it is also a question of which traits, with what symbolic significance, a host culture will accept, physiognomic or ideological. This last may vary according to the character of the host culture.

[15] Margaret Mead, "Problems of Cultural Accommodations," in *Assignment in Israel*, ed. Bernard Mandelbaum (New York: The Jewish Theological Seminary of America, Harper & Brothers, 1958), p. 113.
[16] Robert E. Park, "Assimilation," *Encyclopedia of the Social Sciences*, Vol. II (New York: The Macmillan Co., 1930), p. 281.
[17] *Sociology and Social Life*, 4th ed., Glossary.

Another closely related problem is whether assimilation is the only goal for minority groups. Park believed that minorities and dominants were caught in the same evolutionary process and had no choice. Louis Wirth, in analyzing the problems of the Jewish minority, also saw assimilation as the inevitable outcome, and any alternatives as temporary delays. However, he put the burden of delay on the minority, who are discouraged by rebuffs, or are overaggressive, thereby intensifying both minority solidarity and dominant discrimination.[18]

In a re-evaluation of Wirth's thesis, Etzioni has challenged the *a priori* assumption of assimilation as the only alternative choice.[19] He holds that America is a pluralistic society, and it is illogical not to include cultural pluralism.

This discussion of assimilation suggests that in the writings about dominant-minority relations there is as yet no clear consensus as to which if any sentiments and traits may be retained when a person of minority origin considers himself assimilated and is accepted in all the range of social relationships accorded to a dominant of the same social status.

Pluralism

When we speak of America as a pluralistic society we mean that there are many groups which retain differences derivative from their tradition and some degree of collective identity. In the case of minority groups, this would include some cultural or physiognomic traits. A pattern of pluralism in dominant-minority relations would require that this pattern be acceptable to the larger society and that members of the groups involved be accorded equality in the overall status scale, regardless of race or ethnicity. Areas in which the validity of pluralism may be tested are religion and education. Unity under conditions of religious pluralism involves treating religion as a matter of private faith and divorcing it from public policy. In the field of education the issue arises as to whether there can be *any* separate but equal education. Certainly not all Americans will agree that exclusively parochial education of whatever kind can give a successful orientation to the larger society.

An example of how concepts change and are used differently to meet the needs of new social situations is illustrated by the term *integration*. The concept of integration assumes a pluralistic society.

Status

The refinement of theory about minorities has increasingly made use of the concepts of *status* and *role*.

It has been a common assumption in theory of stratification that ethnic identification is one of the factors contributing to position in the overall status structure of the society. This applies at various class levels. Thus, for example, an Anglo-Saxon chairman of a union local viewed his potential successor as

[18] Louis Wirth, *The Ghetto* (Chicago, Ill.: University of Chicago Press, 1928).
[19] Amitai Etzioni, "The Ghetto—A Re-evaluation," *Social Forces,* March, 1959, 37: 255 ff.

"Polish, but able." [20] In his study of Philadelphia, Baltzell shows that membership in the exclusive clubs of that city, although open more during the last half-century to men who had achieved their position rather than been placed in it by birth, admitted only "token" Catholics and no Jews.[21]

Another aspect of status is involved when two differently evaluated statuses are represented in one person, where one status has low evaluation and the other high. Everett Hughes cites the example of the Negro physician. In the subsystem he will have high status. In the dominant society as a physician he would also have high status. Does the dominent society treat him as a physician or as a Negro? [22] The answer depends on a number of variables: size of community, region, and so on. In a large Northern metropolitan community Negro physicians are beginning to find a place on hospital staffs where patients are white as well as of other races. It is still rare, however, for a Negro physician in private practice to treat white patients. The more common dominant pattern is, at best, that of treating him as a physician in formal professional associations and as a Negro the rest of the time. Hughes points out that occupational advances of this sort on the part of minority individuals are apt to result in an "elaboration of social segregation." [23]

Warner seems to hold that exclusive membership in the ethnic subsystem is possible only for those who do not rise above the lower middle class in the larger social system. The rise to higher position implies a break from the ethnic identity and eventual assimilation. His prognosis is that nonracial subgroups, under the motivations provided by the American norm of upward mobility, will eventually disappear. Gordon, in criticism of Warner's evidence that one is frozen at the lower-middle-class ceiling if one remains in the ethnic subsystem, states:

> In small towns and cities the number in each ethnic group frequently is so small, in absolute terms, and so few have reached upper-middle class status as a result of general immigration history and the out-migration of many socially mobile members of the second and third generation, that a sub-system composed of upper-middle class ethnics is impossible. Thus those that do reach this status are drawn into Old American social relationships. However, in the larger cities and metropolitan areas, upper middle class and even upper class ethnics are so numerous that they can and do develop their own social systems of primary and associational relationships within the ethnic framework.[24]

[20] Morroe Berger and John Alexander, "The Grass Roots Labor Leader," in *Studies in Leadership,* ed. Alvin Gouldner (New York: Harper & Brothers, 1950), pp. 174 ff.

[21] E. Digby Baltzell, *The Philadelphia Elite: The Making of a National Upper Class* (Glencoe, Ill.: The Free Press, 1958).

[22] Everett Cherrington Hughes, "Dilemmas and Contradictions of Status," *American Journal of Sociology,* March, 1945, 50:353 ff.

[23] *Ibid.*

[24] Milton Gordon, *Social Class in America* (Durham, N.C.: Duke University Press, 1959), pp. 111 ff.

In the literature about social mobility there have been a number of ideas brought out which are relevant to dominant-minority relations and which we can indicate only briefly here. Some recent writing has been concerned with the increase in prejudice and discrimination when the members of either the dominant society or of a particular minority are highly mobile. We might expect that the object of prejudice would vary from one status level to another, depending on which minority was competing with a particular stratum in the dominant society. The suggestion is made by Broom and Kitsuse that status competition is the crucial point of dominant-minority tension.[25] This would be the basis for the stereotype which devalues the minority as being "aggressive" or "clever," when, as Merton says, "ingroup virtues become outgroup vices." [26]

Another dimension of the problem of mobility is that of efforts toward group improvement through collective action. Labor organization is an outstanding example of improved status through this means. One of the subtler problems is the relation of dominants to minorities within such collective bodies, of minorities to each other, and of the carryover, or lack of it, of nondiscriminatory patterns from the work situation to the community.[27]

Marginality

Park was the first sociologist to be concerned with the concept of marginality. He and his students emphasized the role of culture conflict affecting the marginal individual. Thus marginality, in Park's terms, refers to the situation in which an individual finds himself when he still retains values and behavior from the culture group in which he had his early childhood training and subsequently attempts to incorporate other values and ways of behaving derived from experience outside his own group. Stonequist expanded Park's concept of marginality to show alternative individual modes of adaptation to this conflict.[28] The emphasis of these earlier writers was on the conflict engendered in the personality by the attempt to internalize two differing sets of values.

Merton sees marginality as behavior "in which the individual seeks to abandon one membership group for another to which he is socially forbidden access." [29] For Merton the concept of marginality is a special instance of reference group theory.

[25] Broom and Kitsuse, "The Validation of Acculturation," p. 46. See also, in this connection, Higham's analysis of the Saratoga incident described in Chapter 18. Higham argues that at the time Seligman was refused accommodations, Saratoga was no longer the resort of the upper-class elite but rather of the nouveau riche. "Social Discrimination Against Jews in America, 1830–1930," Publication of the American Jewish Historical Society, Vol. XLVII, No. 1 (Sept., 1957).
[26] Robert K. Merton, "The Self-Fulfilling Prophecy," Social Theory and Social Structure, rev. ed. (Glencoe, Ill.: The Free Press, 1957), p. 426.
[27] Daniel Bell and Seymour Martin Lipset, "Trade Unions and Minority Problems," The Journal of Social Issues, Vol. 9, No. 1 (1953), entire issue.
[28] E. V. Stonequist, The Marginal Man (New York: Scribners, 1937).
[29] Robert K. Merton and Alice Rossi, "Contributions to the Theory of Reference Group Behavior," in Robert K. Merton, Social Theory and Social Structure, p. 266.

The term *reference group* was introduced by Herbert Hyman,[30] and has been expanded by Merton and his associates. In his initial article, Hyman pointed out that many individuals tend to identify themselves with a group to which they do not in fact belong but to whom they accord prestige. This group is their point of reference, whose behavior and attitudes they attempt to adopt. Frazier states that in the post-Civil War South there was an invasion of "New England School marms" setting up schools for Negroes, who were able to create a generation of Negroes with the best culture of New England.[31] These teachers were a reference group for their students. But, as Merton comments, such reference group behavior may be dysfunctional to the person's best interests. If his reference group is a closed group to which he can never belong—that is, if he is marginal—his newly adopted behavior may initially lead to confusion.[32] The situation of British and American educated Africans was such until recently.[33] However, if positions in the social structure are open to the person, he will be able to use the new behavior he has learned.

The rigidity or fluidity of the society as a whole will affect how the person is received. If the society has rigid barriers against movement from one group to another, the person adapting to modes of a group other than his own will be rejected and ridiculed by the outside group, as Southerners sometimes speak of educated Negroes as "uppity." If the society is less rigid, a Negro who achieves a good job, good manners, and good speech may, in New York for example, be respected by whites and Negroes alike.

Park and Stonequist's approach to marginality supplied sociological dimensions for the explanation of behavior that had previously been viewed as individual deviance and evaluated in moral terms. They wrote at a time when American society was incorporating large groups of migrants of diverse cultural origins. Under Merton the concept of marginality is enlarged, so that it applies not only to individuals of ethnic or racial subgroups but to any individual who seeks entrance to and is denied admission to a group, a stratum, or a community. Merton stresses the role of the excluding group as a new dimension of Park's original formulation.

Roles

There is an increasing interest in sociological theory in role-behavior. A role, as we have seen, is the appropriate behavior associated with a given position in the society. There are socially expected ways of behaving in each society—a father, a student, a priest, a teacher, a chairman, and so on.

The problem of roles in the older theoretical tradition regarding dominant-minority relations was perceived as part of the problem of culture conflict.

[30] Herbert H. Hyman, "The Psychology of Status," in *Archives of Psychology*, No. 269, 1942.
[31] Frazier, *Race and Culture Contacts in the Modern World*, p. 309.
[32] Robert K. Merton, *Social Theory and Social Structure*, pp. 266 ff.
[33] Frazier, *Race and Culture Contacts*, p. 313.

Handlin has written eloquently on the threatened patriarchal role of the immigrant father, which did not fit the role definition of an "American" father.[34] The first concern with roles, then, was with conflicts in definition of institutional roles between the dominant groups and subcultural groups. Often this may involve the necessity for *role relearning.*

Other writing on minorities has dealt with a second problem of roles: that of *learning new roles,* which are associated with structures and positions that do not exist in the society in which the individual grew up, so that he has had no opportunity to acquire this kind of role behavior in his general social learning. Individuals from folk societies have had to learn the roles appropriate to large-scale technological societies, such as behavior in formal organizations.

Role theory has pointed out that many dilemmas for the individual are contained in the *conflict of roles* he must assume in a complex society. Conflict may occur between the roles of citizen (cooperative in emphasis), entrepreneur (competitive in emphasis), and member of a family (authoritative, or supportive, or subordinate).[35]

Merton has also shown that there may be conflicts within a role-set [36]— that is, the role associated with one position may precipitate conflict because it bears different relations to different reference groups. A school principal has responsibilities to his bureaucratic superiors in the school system, to his teachers, to the children in his school, and to their parents. The interests of these various groups may well contain elements of conflict which affect the principal and can in some circumstances confuse, immobilize, or force difficult decisions upon him.

Role theory is concerned with analyzing roles characteristic of situations found recurrently in comparable situations. Thus Yankee traders invading the Reconstruction South played roles associated with marginal business and were stereotyped with traits similar to the stereotype some Gentiles have of Jews. This passing insight of Lipset's was picked up and expanded by Rinder, who suggested crosscultural similarities in the role of the stranger-trader.[37] Stryker has carried the delineation further in an article that explores the circumstances under which prejudice will develop against these middlemen traders.[38] He compares attitudes toward three groups of these peoples in the nineteenth century: Jews in Germany, Christian Armenians in Turkey, and Parsis in India. Prejudice developed against Jews and Armenians, but the variable within these two societies, which was absent in the case of the Parsis, was emergent militant nationalism.

This discussion of the minority trader and the way his role is perceived by

[34] Oscar Handlin, *The Uprooted* (Boston: Little, Brown & Co., 1951).
[35] Robert K. Merton, *Social Theory and Social Structure,* p. 369.
[36] *Ibid.*
[37] Lipset, "Changing Social Status and Prejudice," p. 477; Irwin D. Rinder, "Strangers in the Land," *Social Problems, Winter,* 1958–1959, 6:253 ff.
[38] Sheldon Stryker, "Social Structure and Prejudice," *Social Problems,* Spring, 1959, **6:** 340 ff.

the dominant society not only shows the value of a wider conceptual frame in making evaluations of particular social behavior, but the sequence of the discussion from Park, to Lipset, to Rinder, to Stryker is an excellent example of how theory is developed.

Theory Building: Middle-Range Theory

Robert K. Merton, who coined the term "middle-range theory," has stated that ". . . theory must advance on . . . interconnected planes: through special theories adequate to limited ranges of social data, and the evolution of a more general conceptual scheme adequate to consolidate groups of special theories." [39] We have just dealt with an array of generalizations based on a limited range of data, and in some instances seen how they have modified or amplified one another. Middle-range theory seeks a consolidation of related insights at a more abstract level than those we have considered thus far in the framework of theory building.

Merton envisages theory growing out of empirical data and an inductive process of reasoning, though he himself has largely worked deductively. Middle-range theory thus far has not stated a relationship to one or another "grand theory," but many of the assumptions underlying it are so derived. In Merton's own work with its emphasis on structure and function one may see his heritage, though modified and made his own, from Parsons.

Middle-range theory had made significant contributions to problems of dominant-minority relations. It now awaits increased testing on comparative material to define accurately which variables are generic to minority situations. To illustrate this level of theory we present two of Merton's theoretical formulations that are now a recognized part of all thinking about minority situations.

"The Self-Fulfilling Prophecy" [40]

In this classic essay Merton explores the phenomenon of the *vicious cycle*. We have already seen in Chapter 2 that Myrdal dealt with this concept and saw it as a spiraling process. Merton is more concerned with analyzing how it gets started and what is inherent in its control. Merton's theory has broader applications than just the vicious cycle, and lends itself equally well to an analysis of, for example, outbreaks of violence.

Starting with the theorem of W. I. Thomas, "If men define situations as real, they are real in their consequences," Merton points out that the trouble begins with an incomplete or false definition of the situation. If this false definition is acted on, it brings about a situation which fits the definition. His first illustration is of how a bank can be caused to fail when a rumor starts that it is shaky. The rumor (false definition) brings about a run on the bank (be-

---

[39] Merton, *Social Theory and Social Structure,* Introduction, pp. 9–10.
[40] *Ibid.,* pp. 421–436.

havior) that precipitates its failure. His second illustration is of unions excluding Negroes because Negroes have been strike breakers; then since they cannot join unions they will obviously have no union loyalty that would keep them from accepting employment in a shop whose workers are on strike. Merton's theory illuminates the nature of stereotypes. The dominant group's beliefs (definitions of situations) result in discriminatory actions that so structure the interacting of dominants and minorities that they force the minority to intensify the derogated behavior and thus give the stereotype validity. Therefore, stereotypes are never wholly false.

Furthermore, Merton points out that when a minority has been enclaved in a stereotype—that is to say, a false definition of character and behavior—the minority individual who behaves in the approved mode of the dominant group is criticized for so doing. The same behavior is defined differently by the dominant group, depending on whether it is displayed by one of their own group or a member of the minority group. What is virtue for the dominant group becomes vice in the eyes of the majority for the stereotyped minority. If, as Merton cites, a Presbyterian rises from rags to riches, he is held up as a model. If a Jew does the same he is condemned as being too acquisitive and too ambitious.

In considering how the circle of self-fulfilling prophecies can be broken, Merton posits that, logically and ideally, one should begin with a redefinition of the situation. This, however, is not a simple act of will or good will, for deep-seated beliefs are themselves the products of social forces. He notes furthermore, the hopelessness of trying to persuade the psychologically disturbed. Similarly, he is less than optimistic about education as the way out. The fact that the educational system is itself part of the normative institutional structure of the dominant society makes it subject to the, at best, "incomplete" definitions that dominants make of minorities.

For this reason, Merton sets his hope for remedy in the deliberate enactment of institutional change. Returning to his initial illustrations of the failure of a bank and action against Negroes, he points out that banking legislation, or the statutory creation of interracial public housing have been effective enacted institutional controls. The original proposition then may be restated in this way: "The self-fulfilling prophecy, whereby fears are translated into reality, operates only in the absence of deliberate institutional controls." [41]

"Social Structure and Anomie" [42]

In this essay Merton shows how the social structure poses problems of adaptation for individuals in the competitive opportunities offered the members of society. He points out that the person who achieves an honored place in

[41] *Ibid.*, p. 436.
[42] *Ibid.*, pp. 131–160. *Anomie* is a term used to describe a condition characterized by lack of norms.

the society is expected to pursue goals which society values, using the means of which the society approves. But other patterns of adjustment occur, depending on opportunity within the society. Some people have incorporated the approved goals into their thinking very early and have been trained appropriately at successive stages in how to pursue them. The boy who goes to a good school, a college of standing, and a recognized school for business or professional training, or becomes associated with a reputable firm may expect, according to his talents, to achieve desirable goals by legitimate means. But the boy who goes to an overcrowded, understaffed school and cannot get into a good college, or any college, will be at a competitive disadvantage in achieving those same goals. He may lower his aspirations but retain the approved means of pursuing such goals as he can attain. He will be good, conscientious, but not so successful. He may on the other hand, retain the goals and abandon the approved means. He may then become a racketeer or robber baron or a canny politician. He may make a fortune, and perhaps his descendants will endow a college or a church. Or if the barriers are too great or too confusing, he may reject both goals and means. He may retreat into reactive movements, cults, daydreams perhaps stimulated by television or other mass escape mechanisms, or opiates.

The final alternative offered in Merton's paradigm is that of rebellion: the attempt to change both the goals and means. This alternative suggests the association with groups supporting "unofficial values" or counter ideologies. (See Chapter 2.)

Merton has prepared a now well-known paradigm [43] which summarizes the choices of adaptation to goals and means.

Modes of Adaptation	Culture Goals	Institutional Means
I. Conformity	+	+
II. Innovation	+	−
III. Ritualism	−	+
IV. Retreatism	−	−
V. Rebellion	±	±

The contribution of this theory is not in labeling the behavior as rebellion or innovation but in providing an explanation of why one might expect to find such behavior more frequently in minority groups than in the dominant group. The explanation, according to Merton, lies in the differential access to the means (education, capital, and so on) for achieving the goals of the dominant culture. According to this theory, as these minorities achieve equality of opportunity, one would expect a decline in such types of deviant behavior.

Theory Building and Empirical Research

No one in sociology today who is trying to work theoretically neglects the growing body of empirical research. Homans derived his entire analysis of the

[43] *Ibid.,* p. 140. By permission.

human group from five empirical case studies in which he found common identifiable basic relationships and identifiable variables in their priorities in differently structured situations. Morris Zelditch, Jr., made a crosscultural comparison of role distribution in the nuclear family in 56 societies to test Parsons' theory of socialization which is incorporated in Parsons, Bales, and others, *Family, Socialization and Interaction Process.*[44]

Another way in which theory is related to research occurs when empirical research has been directed toward a problem that has been identified in society and as a result of the research generalizations are arrived at and theoretical formulations developed without any previous hypotheses to be tested. This was the case with Gunnar Myrdal's study of the American Negro.[45]

To conclude this chapter we cite two examples of theory based on empirical data, the first illustrating the testing of hypotheses, the second demonstrating the formulation of generalizations from field data without previously stated hypotheses.

The Authoritarian Personality [46]

For the last several decades there has been a growing literature bringing together psychological and sociological concepts about personality structure. One of the postulates on which such conceptual integration rests is that the individual's early experiences exert a lasting effect on his personality, what he learns as norms (sociology) and how he reacts emotionally to this learning (psychiatry). There is now a wide range of material to document the different modes of child-rearing in different cultures.[47] Looking toward a crosscultural typology in the field of social structure and personality, one major step has been taken in the formulation of a type: the authoritarian personality. This was first described in the early 1930's by the German philosopher and sociologist Max Horkheimer.[48] The authoritarian personality is one which has been molded by a fear of authority, as for instance in the relationship to a strict patriarchal father whose decisions are binding and often arbitrary, and who punishes for lack of respect. Some cultures, including the Puritan strain in our own, have valued this type of family structure. The child trained in this way responds to all authority as he did to his father, submissively, and as an adult becomes authoritarian in turn. Deeper study of such personalities has shown that obeying arbitrary authority in childhood results in bottled-up fear and resentment. The child who successfully weathers the discipline develops into a man who is

[44] (New York: The Free Press, 1955).
[45] *An American Dilemma.*
[46] T. W. Adorno, Else Frankel-Brunswik, Daniel J. Levinson, R. Nevitt Sanford, *The Authoritarian Personality* (New York: Harper & Brothers, 1950).
[47] For examples see Margaret Mead, *Childhood in Contemporary Culture* (New York: Columbia University Press, 1958).
[48] Max Horkheimer, "Authority and the Family," in Bernard Stern, *The Family, Past and Present* (New York: D. Appleton-Century, 1938), p. 428.

frightened by and morally indignant about (and perhaps covertly envious of) people whose behavior is different from the conduct that he has bitterly achieved. His residue of fear and suppressed wish to retaliate can all too easily be mobilized wherever and whenever an appropriate rationalization is supplied.

This is one example of an analytic concept in the social sciences which has been tested, in at·least one dimension, by a major field study. Under the auspices of the American Jewish Committee, T. W. Adorno, a colleague of Horkheimer, and several associates set out to test the relationship between authoritarian versus nonauthoritarian upbringing and degree of anti-Semitic prejudice. They derive from their empirical work a summary profile of the prejudiced and the nonprejudiced personality. The prejudiced personality tries to repress from his consciousness unacceptable tendencies or impulses in himself; the unprejudiced person shows more awareness of his faults and is more willing to face up to them. The prejudiced person particularly attempts to repress fear, weakness, sex impulses, and aggressive feelings toward those in authority—for example, his parents. He shows also a tendency to compensate for this over-repression by manifesting a drive for power and success along conventional lines. The prejudiced seem to gain less pleasure from emotional experience—companionship, art, or music—than the unprejudiced. Outward conformance to conventions is a marked characteristic of the prejudiced; the unprejudiced are more genuinely concerned with discovering a valid ethical value system for themselves. The prejudiced are more interested in achieving power; the less prejudiced seek love and affection as satisfactory ends in themselves. The high scorers on the prejudice scale are extremely rigid in their standards of behavior, intolerant of any deviation from the conventional codes of morals or manners; in contrast, the low scorers are more flexible in their own adjustments to the mores, more appreciative of the complexities of human behavior, and more sympathetic with those who err.

The basis for these two contrasting personality types was found by these research workers to have been established in the contrasting patterns of family life to which the subjects were exposed in childhood. The prejudiced report rigid discipline, with affection made conditional on the child's approved behavior. In the families of the prejudiced there were clearly defined roles of dominance by parents and submission by children, in contrast with families where equalitarian practices prevailed. As the authors put it: "Forced into a surface submission to parental authority, the child develops hostility and aggression which are poorly channelized. The displacement of a repressed antagonism toward authority may be one of the sources, and perhaps the principal source, of his antagonism

There are social structural implications here which take the analysis of prejudice out of the purely psychological. For even though psychology and psychiatry have given us the insight into the effect of repressed material on toward outgroups." [49]

[49] Adorno, et. al., The Authoritarian Personality, p. 482.

behavior, as sociologists we are interested in the kind of family system which is to be normative for our society. The democratic family is not only logically coherent with the ideal of a democratic society; it is necessary for the functioning of a true democracy.

The theory of the authoritarian personality contributes to an explanation of why some members of the dominant group are prejudiced while others may not be. It also suggests that given this particular type of family structure the individuals who grow up in such a family will have a "need" to be prejudiced, that such prejudice cannot be dispelled by formal education, but that the prejudiced person's behavior toward minority groups may be controlled by the use of authority.

"Yankee City" [50]

A major systematic attempt to delineate the variables in assimilation has been made by Warner and Srole. Their criteria of assimilation are the amount and kind of participation permitted the ethnic group by the dominant group as measured by residential mobility, occupational mobility, social class mobility, and membership in formal associations. On the basis of their research they suggest certain variables as determining the rate of assimilation. In each case the variable mentioned should be read as if preceded with the phrase "other things being equal." They may be summarized as follows:

The Recency Factor   The more recently the ethnic group has come into the community, the slower the degree of assimilation.

The Cultural Similarity Factor   The more divergent the culture of the ethnic group from the normative culture of the dominant status group, the slower the degree of assimilation.

The Concentration Factor   The larger the numerical proportion of the ethnic group in relation to the total population of the area, the slower the degree of assimilation.

The Physiognomic Factor   The "darker" the general physical appearance of the group, the slower the degree of assimilation.

The Permanency Factor   The more temporary the ethnic group conceives its residency in the host society, the slower the degree of assimilation. [51]

These variables lend themselves to the following proposition regarding the assimilation of ethnic groups.

The greater the difference between the host and the immigrant cultures, the greater will be the subordination, the greater the strength of the ethnic social

[50] W. Lloyd Warner and Leo Srole, *The Social Systems of American Ethnic Groups* (Vol. 3 of the Yankee City Series) (New Haven: Yale University Press, 1945).
[51] Compare with the list given by Warner and Srole, p. 102.

systems, and the longer the period necessary for the assimilation of the ethnic group.[52]

Though the work of Warner and Srole was a major step forward in the development of theory in the field of majority-minority relations, it should be noted that the propositions they developed tend to treat the attitudes and behavior of the dominant groups as a dependent variable. The behavior of the dominant group may be in some situations the independent variable determining the rate of assimilation of ethnic groups. For example, the dominant group may be considered as having certain privileges and advantages which it wishes to monopolize. The unwillingness to admit the minority group to equal status thus becomes the crucial factor in assimilation.

Although in this chapter we have limited ourselves to the presentation only of the work of sociologists it seems likely that, in harmony with trends in the behavioral sciences today, the next major breakthrough in theory and research about dominant-minority relations may come from interdisciplinary effort. This will not preclude, however, the continuing sociological effort to validate or modify conceptual schemes through research, or the increasing sophistication of the conceptual frame within which sociological research is undertaken.

Topics for Projects and Discussion

1. Take any two substantive chapters on specific minorities which this book has presented and find what is similar and what is different in their situation. Use some of the concepts elaborated in this brief introduction to theory, to explain the similarities and differences.
2. What interests do you and your friends share that are cultural in MacIver's use of the term? What like interests do you share? What regulates your pursuit of like interests—rules? guilt feelings (internalized norms)? In whom is the regulating authority vested? Why?
3. Take any minority subculture that you know or have read about and see if you can analyze the behavioral patterns according to Parsons' pattern variables. How does the community and the culture help determine which choices within the variables are actually available?
4. Have you had any experience which would test Homans' proposition that frequency of interaction increases sentiments of friendship? Describe how this came about. Do Homans' other two quoted propositions apply also to this experience?
5. What evidence have you found for Park's claim that urbanization increases dominant-minority tension? Is Park's statement adequate or would you like to qualify it? If so, how?

Suggested Readings

Dahlke, H. Otto, "Race and Minority Riots—A Study in the Typology of Violence," *Social Forces*, May, 1952.

[52] *Ibid.*, p. 285.

In this article Dahlke extrapolates the common elements in disparate situations in which riots have occurred. It is a good example of how theoretical hypotheses are developed.

Hughes, Everett C. "Social Change and Status Protest," *Phylon*, Vol. X, First Quarter, 1949.

The author, who has richly contributed to the literature on minorities, anticipates here by nearly two decades some of the phenomena we are now witnessing in the Negro revolt.

(This article is available in a Bobbs-Merrill reprint.)

MacIver, Robert M. *The Web of Government.* New York: The Macmillan Co., 1947.

The entire argument is an elaboration of MacIver's theory of the state, and the last chapter on the "multi-group" society is especially relevant.

Merton, Robert K. *Social Theory and Social Structure*, rev. ed. Glencoe, Ill.: The Free Press, 1957.

Merton's principal contributions to middle-range theory, including elaborations and further thoughts on the self-fulfilling prophecy, social structure and anomie, and reference groups.

Parsons, Talcott. *The Social System.* Glencoe, Ill.: The Free Press, 1950.

Parsons' elaboration of the structure of the social system. Chapter 3 discusses the various combinations of particularistic and universalistic values found in different cultures.

Williams, Robin M., Jr., with the collaboration of John P. Dean and Edward A. Suchman, *Strangers Next Door: Ethnic Relations in American Communities,* Englewood Cliffs, N.J.: Prentice-Hall, Inc., 1964.

A summary volume from the Cornell Studies in Intergroup Relations, including intensive studies of intergroup relations in four cities in different regions of the United States. The last chapter might be profitably read in comparison with this one.

20

Summary Interpretation and Social Policy

In this concluding chapter we shall provide a summary interpretation of the presence of ethnic differentiation on the dominant-minority basis throughout the history of the United States; we will delineate the remaining problem aspects of this phenomenon and consider what social policy may be undertaken to deal with the problem areas. Since minority status is imposed by the dominant segment and change in the status of minorities lies primarily in the dominants' hands, attention will be focused on dominant behavior.

Synthesized Interpretation of Dominant Behavior

Two main generalizations stand out: (1) In every situation where Americans of unquestioned dominant status have come in contact with "other" peoples within the boundaries of the United States, the dominant-minority pattern has been established. (2) This superordinate-subordinate pattern has never remained completely stable, and the long-term trend has been toward the modification and/or elimination of minority status for each of the minorities.[1]

We proceed on the assumption that it is not necessary at this point in the development of social science in the United States to consider points of view now generally discarded. Thus we shall assume that the discussion of race in Chapter 3 is sufficient to rule out any conception that dominant or minority behavior is affected by genetic factors. It is taken for granted, too, that there is no such thing as a "natural" (in the genetic sense) aversion toward people of contrasting somatic appearance. Finally, interpretation proceeds on the assumption that no complex pattern of social relationships can be explained by a single "cause." For this reason we should expect, for example, to find a Marxian interpretation of dominant-minority relations exclusively on the basis

[1] Short-term reversals under conditions of special stress, such as war time, depressions, etc., have, of course, occurred, as in the Japanese evacuation episode.

452

of class struggle as inadequate to explain dominant-minority relations as it has been to explain the course of social history.

Universal Principles of Ethnocentrism

The initial stages of interaction between a dominant and a minority group may be expected to follow the well-established universal sociological principles of ethnocentrism and ingroup—outgroup processes. In order for any society to survive, each member as he grows up must acquire a strong sense of loyalty to and identification with his own people—the ingroup. Through this process also each member acquires the conviction that the culture of his own group, its ways of doing things are the "proper" ones. It is therefore almost inevitable that when two such ingroups find themselves suddenly faced with the problem of living together in the same area, each should consider the other an outgroup and that some antagonism should arise. The immediate harmonious assimilation of two visibly different groups is impossible.[2]

Historical Circumstance

As was pointed out in Chapter 1, other modern nations have had dominant-minority situations as well and many still display ethnic and racial prejudice. But no other nation has had so many different peoples to absorb into its society as our own. Thus the salience of ethnic and racial differentiation in the social life of this country has arisen in part out of historical circumstances.

Superior Power

The unvarying dominance of those Americans of native status resulted from their possession of superior power. In almost all situations, the combination of power factors, superiority in numbers, economic resources, and technological skills is so obvious as to need no elaboration. Thus the opportunity to assign minority status to these other peoples lay with white Nordic Americans, if they so desired. Interpretation of the reasons why dominance was established involves examining the value system and the institutional structure of American society.

The Value Orientation

In broad outline the value orientations of American society focus around four main configurations. (1) The democratic ethos with its stress on equality,

[2] Robin Williams, Jr., has cogently argued that ethnocentrism does not necessarily result in prejudice, but the conditions indicated by Williams in which ethnocentrism does have this effect are all widely present in American society. See his *Strangers Next Door: Ethnic Relations in American Communities* (Englewood Cliffs, N.J.: Prentice-Hall, 1964), pp. 17–27.

freedom, individualism; (2) the belief in private economic enterprise, with the associated traits of activity and work, achievement and success, and material comfort; (3) Judeo-Christian beliefs (with Protestantism dominating) which have developed in the United States, as Williams views them, a somewhat distinctive "moral orientation" not as strongly present in other Western nations; and (4) secularism with its emphasis on rationality, progress, and scientific achievement.[3]

While the above configuration of publicly stated values contains inconsistencies, it would not as a whole point toward racial and ethnic prejudice. As Williams considers it, the presence of "racism and related group-superiority themes" in the value system is based on the development of an organic "genetic"-racist view of mankind. In this connection he cites Mydral as follows: "The race dogma is nearly the only way out for a people so moralistically equalitarian, if it is not prepared to live up to its faith." [4]

The Major Institutional Systems

An examination of the major institutions in the social structure shows them to generate crosscurrents which motivate dominance on the one hand and its reduction on the other.

THE ECONOMIC SYSTEM   Historically, the economic system has moved from mercantile capitalism to finance capitalism. Its essence, however, is still private enterprise, a system in which all individuals strive by competition and bargaining to gain the most for themselves individually. While the belief has been widely held that the indirect result of this pluralistic striving is to provide the greatest economic welfare possible for the society as a whole, our interest concerns the way the economic system influences dominant behavior.

The employer has gained from the presence of minorities cheaper labor. The lack of sophistication of immigrant laborers, as well as their interethnic rivalries, have often held back the process of unionization. But the employer must have labor, and in times of labor shortages he is likely to break the previous customary dominant practices which barred certain minorities from given occupations or prevented their allocation to higher status positions. Sellers may adhere to prevailing prejudices against minority status customers, but if competitive pressures prompt one store owner to break the line, others are motivated to follow suit.

Within the economic system certain special interests gain advantage from the discrimination against minorities, as for example, employers of unskilled labor, particularly agricultural entrepreneurs or real estate operators in housing areas largely restricted to minorities, who can charge higher rents because

[3] Much of our analysis of the value system relies on Robin Williams, Jr. in his *American Society: A Sociological Interpretation* (New York: Knopf, 1951), Ch. 11, "Value Orientation in American Society."

[4] See Williams, *American Society*, p. 439. The quotation is from Myrdal, *et al.*, *An American Dilemma*, Vol. 1, p. 89.

segregation limits minority choice. Ironically, certain minority people themselves stand to gain from segregation patterns, such as undertakers, and Negro beauticians or small storekeepers in ethnic neighborhoods.

Once unionization was established, especially in the skilled trades, the pressure to keep the supply of such workers low resulted in the refusal to admit some minorities to apprenticeships. On the other hand, the bargaining strength of a union is increased when unionization is all-inclusive.

POLITICAL SYSTEM   At the ideal level political democracy expresses what Myrdal has called the "American Creed." The institutional complexes set up to implement it include democratic citizenship, democratic government, and public education.

Democratic citizenship involves both equal opportunity to participate in government and equal protection from it. Participation includes the right to vote, to join a political party, to run for office, and to be appointed to a government job. Protection includes the right to trial by jury, equal treatment by law-enforcing officers, and equal protection from physical harm or property damage. Caucasian immigrants have been able to acquire all these rights through naturalization, and their descendants born here are automatically citizens.

The exercise of civic rights provides minority citizens opportunity to vote in their own interest. In areas of minority group concentration they have elected members of their own group to public office and secured appointment to government positions. Since government is the only institution whose membership embraces the entire population, it is constrained to operate for the benefit of all more than other institutions.

In actual operation the democratic political system falls far short of its idealistic value system. Citizens in the democratic society may be divided into "politicians"—those actively interested in achieving political power or occupational position directly in control of elected officials—and those whose political activity is motivated by other self-interests. The "politician" attempts to make the best judgment of which way the majority of his electorate feels on any issues. In relation to minority problems, this explains the frequent change of position of many politicians, as for example, why politician X appeals to segregationist sentiment to win election, and when faced with the responsibilities of office acts less "racist"-minded.

The emphasis on the "individual" in the American value system has tended to promote unrealistic thinking about the political power of the individual person, as De Gré has analyzed. "A sociological theory of freedom, therefore, must take as its starting point the *socius,* that is, the individual as a member of a group, class, or social type, rather than the abstract individual-as-such that forms the nucleus of Romanticism." [5] He further contends that the greater

[5] Gerard De Gré, "Freedom and the Social Structure," *American Sociological Review,* October, 1946, p. 53.

stability of the pluralist-democratic political structure in comparison with totalitarian and oligarchic regimes lies in the absence of the concentration of sufficient power in any one power bloc to dominate the others. We might note that the current "Black Power" movement is quite in line with the normative political processes. It has been precisely in the South, though less today than earlier, that the overwhelming concentration of power in the hands of whites vis-à-vis Negroes has most nearly nullified the democratic process.

In actual practice the administration of law and government often reflects the prejudice of the officials who administer it; even unprejudiced officials tend to consider how the dominant community wants it administered. Our earlier discussion of the highly sensitive area of policing in Negro areas well illustrates this point.

Finally, our governmental system is itself pluralistic, with separation of powers at the federal, state, and local levels. For example, the governor of a Southern state was quoted as saying in effect, "the federal court has ordered desegregated schools, let them enforce it."

PUBLIC EDUCATION The right of all children to free public education has been profoundly instrumental in undermining minority status. Minority valedictorians deflate the myth of categorical minority inferiority. The contact between dominant and minority children in unsegregated schools is formally on a basis of equality, thus giving dominant status students the experience of associating with minority students on a plane of equality. Despite their handicapped background the abler minority students achieve skills and training enabling upward social mobility.

In actual operation, the public-school system, however, has reflected the pervasive community patterns of dominant-minority intergroup relations. The faculties are disproportionately drawn from the dominant population and in varying degrees hold dominant prejudices which bias, often unconsciously, their relations with minority students. The informal relations among students often manifest prejudice in the formation of cliques and the refusal to elect minority students to certain clubs. Finally, the content of the curriculum often reflects dominant prejudice. A survey of the treatment of minorities in secondary-school textbooks concludes: "A majority of the texts still present a largely white, Protestant, Anglo-Saxon view of history and of the current social scene. The nature and problems of minority groups in America are still very largely neglected." [6]

RELIGIOUS INSTITUTIONS For the purpose of interpreting dominant be-

---

[6] Lloyd Marcus, *The Treatment of Minorities in Secondary School Textbooks* (New York: Anti-Defamation League of B'nai Brith, 1961) p. 59. More specific findings were (1) Treatment of the Jews continues to suffer from an overemphasis on their ancient past and on the theme of persecution. (2) Nazi persecutions of minority groups are inadequately treated. (3) The Negroes' position in contemporary American society is very largely ignored. (4) Immigrants to the continental United States receive considerable attention in American history and social-problems texts.

havior, we may confine our discussion to Protestantism and Catholicism.[7] In both these Christian institutions at least the formal ethical tenets are against racial and ethnic discrimination. In recent years there has been more positive action in both these religious systems to implement their ethical codes in intergroup relations. This positive action has been more unified and manifest by Catholicism than by Protestantism, in part because the authoritative structure of the Roman Catholic church makes it more possible.[8] Currently the ecumenical movement in the major religions may strengthen the efforts of all organized religion in this direction.

In theological aspects, the Christian religious institutions tend to perpetuate prejudice and discrimination indirectly. At least a loose positive association exists between the "fundamentalism" in Protestantism and "bigotry" in ethnic, religious, and racial fields. A recent research finds survivals of doctrine and ritual in Protestantism which still tend to perpetuate the anti-Semitic bias of historic Christianity.[9]

Finally, the "social" aspect of religious institutions cannot realistically be ignored. Church affiliation and activity is in considerable degree a matter of sociability. In the nation at large but more visible at the local community level, there exists a status differentiation between various Protestant denominations, and less strongly, in Catholic church organization. Episcopalians and Presbyterians usually rank higher than Baptists. "Sociability" involves interaction between people of equal status, which partly explains the racial and ethnic segregation seen in local congregations. It has been pointed out that the hour between 11 and 12 on Sunday morning is the most segregated hour of the week.

THE NON-PECUNIARY INTELLECTUAL AND WELFARE COMPLEX We refer here to a congeries of institutions which while considered in some sociological analyses of American society have not generally been thought of as a broad institutional complex. Specifically we refer to research agencies (academic or otherwise), social work agencies (some of which are, of course, in the governmental structure), and Foundations. The major characteristic of this currently vast network which provides a common denominator is the absence of the pecuniary interests, or, positively stated, the presence of either an intellectual interest, the search for truth for its own sake with the hope that

---

[7] Up to World War II we might have omitted Catholicism but on the assumption that Catholicism as well as Judaism has now acquired status equality Catholicism must now be considered.

[8] Lenski found in a Detroit research where the major religious groups were asked to indicate their images of one another that the most favorable image of the Catholic group was held by Negro Protestants. He attributes this to the awareness among Negro Americans of the strong stand taken by the Catholic hierarchy for racial integration. Gerhard Lenski, *The Religious Factor* (New York: Doubleday, 1961), p. 67.

[9] Charles Y. Glock and Rodney Stark, *Christian Beliefs and Anti-Semitism* (New York: Harper & Row, 1966). Chief finding was that one-fourth of those Christians classified as anti-Semitic had a religious basis for their views and only five percent with prejudice against Jews lacked any evidence of a supposed theological self-justification.

the findings will serve some useful purpose, or a humane interest, improving the welfare of society, or both.[10] The research findings in the behavioral field greatly undermine the whole rationale of intergroup prejudice and discrimination; and the work of social agencies alleviates the effects of the underprivilege which discrimination has produced.

What is most crucial is the fact that there are built-in elements in this structure which to a considerable degree, protect the nonpecuniary institutions from the onslaughts of other interests. Neither government itself nor reactionary groups can prevent these truths from publication or humane activities from being pursued. (The McCarthy periods do not last indefinitely.) For example, the devastating criticism of the Boston School System written by an ex-teacher in a ghetto school *was* published, and *was* favorably reviewed by an eminent psychiatrist associated with Harvard University.[11]

THE OPEN-CLASS SYSTEM   Strictly speaking, the class system is not an institution. It is, however, interwoven with the entire institutional structure. Sociological thought generally agrees that status distinctions are inherently part of the nature of the modern industrial-urban society, as they have been in earlier societal forms. But relatively the class system of the modern society is an open system where one's eventual position is in substantial measure *achieved* by one's own efforts as distinct from being *ascribed* at birth.

The open-class system is distinguished from the dominant-minority system in that it is not an imposed phenomenon; and categorical barriers to upward social mobility are absent. If, as many social scientists hold, the open-class system is positively functional for the order of modern societies, its value can be greatly increased by the elimination of the ascribed bases of the dominant-minority system.

The Socialization Process

Once established, the pattern of dominant-minority behavior stabilizes through the process of continuous socialization of the children of the dominant status collectivity. While the socialization process is continuous through life, the primary socialization acquired through the family, the school, and early peer group contacts leave an imprint that is seldom completely changed in later life. Thus discrimination and prejudice toward minorities far from being deviant or abnormal behavior become *normative* psychologically and sociologically. Acquired originally without reflection, dominant prejudices and discriminatory habits simply carry on unless some intervening circumstances challenge them.

---

[10] That persons employed within this broad complex manifest often the pecuniary and status-seeking behavior found in pecuniary institutions is true enough. But there are built-in checks which limit this behavior to a secondary level.

[11] Jonathan Kozol, *Death at an Early Age. The Destruction of the Hearts and Minds of Negro Children in the Boston Public Schools.* (Boston: Houghton Mifflin, 1967.) Reviewed by Robert Coles, a research psychiatrist at Harvard, in *The New York Times Book Review*, October 1, 1967, Section 7, p. 1.

The Problem Areas

Definition of the Situation as a Problem

Whether a situation is a problem or not depends on how people view it. Whenever enough people feel discomfort about a situation—usually brought about by change—they designate the situation a "problem." Once a problem is named, people in Western culture expect action to be taken to solve it. But there is considerable variation in the definition of the nature of the problem and therefore variation in ideas as to ways of solving it. In the American scene four major modes of viewing the "problem" are common: (1) There are those who believe that minorities should remain minorities, that the problem is one of keeping them in that status. (2) There are those who hold that the welfare of the depressed minorities should be improved within the framework of segregation, a philosophy followed by some moderate Southerners concerning the Negro. (3) There are those who see a problem only when tension and hostility between groups disturb the peace of the community through disorderly violence. (4) There are those who define the problem in the light of the American Creed.

It is impossible to discuss social policy without choosing a value frame of reference. We adopt the value frame of reference of the American Creed and define the problem areas of intergroup relations in its terms.

Minority Problems and the American Creed

The value system of the American Creed holds that all members of American society should have equal opportunity without experiencing discrimination based on racial, religious, or nationality identity or on lineage. Thus the total elimination of discrimination on these grounds is the basic problem, and the primary goal of all social policy should be directed to that end.

A secondary problem arises from the integrationist-pluralistic trends in intergroup relations, which we repeatedly analyzed in our discussion of the various minority situations. It may be stated thus: Should the elimination of discrimination against minorities require the elimination of subgroup cultures and social structure? The American Creed answers, "No," with some qualification. The right to retain cultural pluralism or structural pluralism based on religion or ethnicity, and, if racial groups wish it, race, should not be denied. The qualification is that such pluralism should incorporate basic identity with the American value system. All members of the society should be firmly acculturated both externally and internally to the basic core of American values. In short, all should be Americans first and members of subgroups second.[12]

As a corollary to this right to plurality, it should be understood that each person previously identified with minority groups should have the right to de-

[12] Gordon develops this theme cogently in his *Assimilation in American Life* (New York: Oxford University Press, 1964), Ch. 8, "Assessment and Implications for Intergroup Relations," pp. 233–265.

cide for himself whether he wishes to retain subgroup identity or pass over into the main (ideally no longer "dominant") community. Whether, for example, an American of Jewish background wants to retain his Jewish identity or not should be his *own* choice. Social policy should be directed to protecting either choice.

A wide range of problems arise at the tertiary level, such as jobs and better education for Negroes, Mexican Americans and Indians. For convenience we shall refer to these conditions as *Welfare* problems. But such problems while urgently requiring immediate attention should not deflect social policy from the primary and secondary goals stated above.

The Specific Current Problem Areas

Let us review the current situation of the various groups who have had at one time or still possess minority status. For this purpose we present the Chart on p. 461 as a descriptive evaluation of the groups on the basis of (1) the degree of discrimination experienced, (2) the degree of cultural pluralism, (3) the degree of structural pluralism, and (4) the welfare index. At this point we may assume that what is meant by these four indices of the minority situation has been adequately discussed. With reference to discrimination, we mean categorical discrimination involving a derogatory image of an ethnic group and corresponding differentially unequal treatment of the category in general. We have repeatedly dealt with the integrationist-pluralistic axis in the light of theories of assimilation, and, following Gordon, analytically distinguishing cultural from structural pluralism. Welfare indices involve the economic standard of living; the health, physical and mental; and various indices of sociopathology, such as delinquency, disorganizing personal practices, and indices of family disorganization. It should be understood that adequate evidence to support the evaluative judgments indicated are extremely uneven. Concrete data to support the welfare indices are probably the most available, much from government surveys.

The chart on p. 461 suggests the areas of serious problems in the intergroup field: (1) No problems for Caucasian, Protestant Americans of Northern and Western European, non-English, nationality background; and none for non-Caucasian Hawaiian groups. (2) Problems pertaining to the integrationist-pluralist axis of assimilation for Jews, and white Catholics in general; for nationality groups where concentrated in large numbers; and for Puerto Ricans, Mexicans, and Indians. Negro "separatists" may create a new problem in this field. (3) Problems of Discrimination. *Mild.* Possibly Jews but more the ever-present danger of a rise in anti-Semitism in times of crisis; and against descendants of the early Chinese immigrants. *Considerable.* Both the Spanish-speaking groups, Mexicans and Puerto Ricans; and tribal and pure-blood Indians. *Severe.* for Negro Americans. (4) A positive correlation between degrees of discrimination and low welfare.

Group	Discrimination	Degree of Cultural Pluralism	Degree of Structural Pluralism	Welfare Situation
Caucasian, Protestant, North-West European Immigrants	None	None	None	Normative, skewed upward
Caucasian, Catholic, South-East European, Irish Descendant	Little in urban America; declining	Some, varying with socioeconomic status	More in large cities; in interethnic Catholic sub-communities	Highly varied, skewed downward
Jewish American	Subtle, likely to increase in crisis periods; some ascription by descent	Variable, depending on generation	High	Moderately varied, skewed upward
Japanese American	Rapidly declining	Disappearing with the Sansei	Moderate	Varied, skewed upward
Chinese American	Declining	Considerable	Moderate, generational	Normal for descendants of "new" Chinese, low for "old" but improving
Mexican American	Considerable	High	High	Low, small upper classes excepted
Puerto Rican (Mainland)	Considerable	High	High	Low
Negro Americans	Very high, but declining; ascription by descent	Little. "Are culturally Americans"	Very high. Primarily due to imposed segregation	Improving for upper classes; very low for masses
American Indians	Extensive for tribal Indians; no ascription by descent	High for reservation Indians	High for tribal Indians	Very low
Hawaii's non-Caucasion Peoples	Apparently in process of complete assimilation			

Social Policy and Social Action

The term social policy implies awareness that problems exist and that social action needs to be taken to cope with them. Having defined the nature of the problem and delineated the specific problem areas, let us now discuss social policy and social action to implement it.

Social Forces versus Social Action

At many points in preceding chapters reference has been made to broad social forces in the changing society that impinge on minority situations in the absence of any social action directly undertaken. When such a force is working toward the goal desired, direct social action may only be needed to foster it. However, when the social force is operating to impede the goal, social action is needed to cope with it, if possible. For example, the general expanding economy has offered opportunity for the upward mobility of some minority groups, whereas automation has retarded the advance of Negroes. Social action groups should guard against strategic moves which may arrest or temporarily reverse the trend of a force favorable to their goal.

The Agents of Social Action

While, ideally, resolving the problems of minorities is the task of all citizens, in fact social action generally is undertaken by groups and agencies most concerned. The most important agencies are government—legal, legislative, and administrative; and at all levels—federal, state, and local; private welfare agencies; and social action groups, initiated by dominants primarily or exclusively interested in the problems of minorities. In addition, there are certain agencies whose broader field of interest encompasses the minority problem, for example, the American Civil Liberties Union. Again even individuals can effect social policy by their support of action groups or by exemplary nondiscriminatory behavior. Finally, many minorities themselves initiate social action either in groups including dominant status members or in groups exclusively their own, sometimes in behalf of their own groups exclusively, or for other minorities as well as their own. We shall refer to the respective roles in social action of each category of agency in connection with each level of problem.

Indirect Social Action

By indirect social action we mean activities aimed at improving the general conditions in society known to breed prejudice and discrimination. Such conditions are economic changes creating downward mobility in one or more segments of the society; the ever-present efforts of special economic groups to cultivate discrimination for profit; and the failure of certain governmental officials to uphold vigorously and to implement the democratic institutions they are charged with administering. Persons interested primarily in reducing minority discrimination usually support public policy aimed at creating the general conditions favorable to nondiscrimination.

Reducing Discrimination

To start with the primary problem from the value frame of reference of the American Creed, we find it useful to elaborate the distinction between prejudice and discrimination, briefly stated in Chapter 2, by presenting the variable relations between these two concepts as formulated by Merton.[13]

> Type I. *The Unprejudiced Nondiscriminator, or All-Weather Liberal.* Since this type of person believes unequivocally in the Democratic Creed, he practices what he believes consistently. Obviously such people are logical leaders for social action in the same direction. However, Merton considers the all-weather liberal prone to accept three fallacies. The first, the fallacy of group soliloquy, refers to the tendency for such like-minded people to gather in small groups and reinforce each other's attitudes and convictions rather than joining other groups and influencing them in the desired direction. Growing closely out of this is the second fallacy, called the fallacy of unanimity, which is the tendency to exaggerate the extent to which the rest of the community shares their own viewpoint. A third limitation to effective action by all-weather liberals is their addiction to the fallacy of private solutions to social problems. Since he himself has solved the problem, this liberal may not feel compelled to do anything more. Rightly, he feels no guilt for himself.
>
> Type II. *The Unprejudiced Discriminator, or Fair-Weather Liberal.* This is the type of man who has no prejudices against ethnic groups and on the whole believes in the American Creed. But he is primarily a man of expediency, who tends to support discriminatory practices when it is the easier or more profitable course. He does, however, feel guilty about his discrimination. He is therefore capable of cure, because he really wants to be cured.
>
> Type III. *The Prejudiced Nondiscriminator, or Fair-Weather Illiberal.* This type of man does not believe in ethnic equality. Being, however, also a man of expediency, he conforms in situations in which the group sanctions are against discrimination through fear of the penalties which might otherwise ensue. But whenever the pressure against it is removed, he discriminates.
>
> Type IV. *The Prejudiced Discriminator, or the All-Weather Illiberal.* This type is the true bigot. Since he believes firmly that certain minorities ought to be discriminated against, he can be counted on to discriminate as thoroughly as is permitted by the customs and institutions of the community. This type is obviously hardest to change, although the situation varies in relation to the prevailing mores of the area where he lives. When the mores support his position, he is a conformist,

[13] Robert K. Merton, "Discrimination and the American Creed," in MacIver, *Discrimination and National Welfare* (New York: Harper & Brothers, 1949), pp. 99–126. The terms "liberal" and "illiberal" used by Merton are based on the degree to which the types illustrated accept or do not accept and practice the American Creed—that is, "the right of equitable access to justice, freedom, and opportunity, irrespective of race or religion, or ethnic origin."

and change means making himself open to community criticism. When the mores in general are against him, he is a social deviant, and here change on his part would draw him closer into the general community structure.

Two main lines of approach to reducing discrimination are to alter the social structure or to change prejudicial attitudes. Change in either affects the other. Since World War II there has been a marked shift in social action efforts toward the first line of approach. Altering the social structure to require the integration of minorities into specific associations of the main institutional structure affords a shorter route to change than attempting to change prejudicial attitudes. As the Merton paradigm shows, the salience of prejudice varies widely.

Various social action groups have worked for at least a quarter of a century to secure the integration of minority status persons into social structures previously denied them. Research studies of such efforts are numerous and have produced substantive knowledge concerning how such new intergroup contacts may be accomplished most effectively. A summary of the research findings are stated in 27 propositions presented in Dean and Rosen's *A Manual of Intergroup Relations*.[14] Action aimed at new breakthroughs against discrimination may well be guided by the specialized knowledge now available.

These extensive voluntary efforts toward desegregation clearly demonstrated that increasing contact and interaction between dominant and minority persons can be accomplished without serious social disturbance, and that their continuance tends to produce a lessening of prejudice under certain conditions.[15]

Among the conditions favorable to successful integration are that (1) contact takes place in a situation where both are defined as equal; (2) the contact be continuous and intimate enough to challenge the stereotypes of the dominant person; (3) the minority person does not act according to the stereotype; (4) the situation poses no threat to the security of the parties involved; (5) the situation is one in which the two groups involved have a common interest, and (6) the more the community norms, or the norms of the reference groups most influential for the dominant parties, support the new integration, the more effective the process will be.[16]

Efforts to increase integration, especially of Negro Americans prior to 1954, were few and thus progress was slow. Since the basic Supreme Court School Desegregation Decision the employment by social action groups of "forced" integration has greatly increased. By "forced" integration we mean integration

---

[14] John P. Dean and Alex Rosen, with the assistance of Robert B. Johnson, *A Manual of Intergroup Relations* (Chicago: The University of Chicago Press, First Phoenix Edition, 1963).

[15] Among the earlier studies demonstrating this point were Morton Deutsch and Mary C. Collins, *Interracial Housing* (Minneapolis: University of Minnesota Press, 1951), and Gerhart Saenger and E. Gilbert, "Customer Reaction to the Integration of Negro Sales Personnel," *International Journal of Opinion and Attitude Research*, 4 (1950), pp. 57–76.

[16] See Robin Williams, *Strangers Next Door*, Ch. 7, "Social Integration and Intergroup Attitudes" for a fuller discussion.

effected by the order of authoritative agencies or persons with the power to dictate the process without the consent of all the dominants affected by it. Here the social scientist faces the lack of sufficient research to evaluate the results and must rely on broad observations. The causal connection between protest activities and the effective desegregation of many public sectors of the society is clear. On the other hand, even in political jurisdiction with open-occupancy housing laws, successful resistance to residential integration is found; and "forced" integration has increased the articulate expression of prejudice and in some instances prompted counter organized activity on the part of the less liberal-minded dominant public. Nevertheless, the nation is now committed to integration, which will inevitably be accomplished. Social action groups can best attempt to guide this process with strategic expediency toward the ultimate goal.

EDUCATION AND PROPAGANDA In general, social science has found that the educational approach—giving people the facts about dominant-minority rela-tions—has relatively little value in reducing discrimination or prejudice. Further-more, recent researches have tended to question the previous belief that educated people are less prejudiced than the less educated. While generally on attitude tests the more highly educated people respond verbally with less prejudice, and tend to support legal equality, inner feelings of prejudice and discrimination in primary group relations have been revealed in recent studies.[17] Williams puts it this way, "The prejudice of the well educated, when it does exist, may in some ways be harder, colder, more polite and more thoroughly buttressed by rational-izations, but it is less likely to be global, diffuse, and all-or-none in character." [18]

The research on propaganda as a method of reducing prejudice in general points to its limited effect. A major limitation lies in the difficulty of reaching through mass media the "target" public, the most prejudiced.[19]

THE ROLE OF MINORITIES Up to this point we have been discussing social action directed at the dominants and carried on by interethnic agencies. Let us now give special attention to the activity of minorities themselves. For some time social science has held that all minority status persons can facilitate achieving equality. In the form of postulates, Williams' earlier review of the literature found as follows:

> A vulnerable minority can itself help to reduce hostility and conflict insofar as there is group control over individual members, by:
> (a) educating its members to an understanding of the dominant group's reaction to the minority's values and behavior

[17] See, for example, Charles H. Stember, *Education and Attitude Change* (New York: The Institute of Human Relations Press, 1961), and Robin Williams, *Strangers Next Door*, pp. 374–375.

[18] *Strangers Next Door*, p. 375.

[19] For a summary of the literature concerning the effects of propaganda on changing attitudes, see Arthur M. Cohen, *Attitude Change and Social Influence* (New York: Basic Books, 1964).

(b) careful study of the behaviors of its own members which are regarded as objectionable by other groups

(c) minimizing conspicuous display of traits of marked negative-symbol value

(d) participation *as individuals* in wider community activities which are widely regarded as necessary in welfare [20]

Point (a) above is difficult to convey to minority people, especially the less receptive members of the group. We have stressed before that much of dominant discrimination is the result of habit acquired innocently in childhood through the socialization process. Tolerant understanding of this point is a mark of maturity for the minority individual.

New Challenges to Social Action Groups

The vastly altered situation in intergroup relations following from the ongoing Negro Revolt presents new challenges to intergroup social actionists, raising many questions for decision. (1) Is the time now at hand for dominant status leadership—aside from government which represents all—to step aside and encourage the assumption of leadership by minority leaders? The answer may well vary with different minorities. (2) Should the United States adopt a "Marshall Plan" for minorities, especially Negroes, as supported by Whitney M. Young, Jr., and others—an all out and highly costly effort to improve the welfare and status of the Negro population? One controversial aspect of this plan is whether or not policy should involve a form of discrimination in reverse, at least for an interim period. For example, when an equally qualified white and Negro apply for a job, should the employer deliberately select the Negro? (This action should not simply represent "token" evidence of nondiscrimination.) (3) Is the time now at hand when dominant status social actionists should carry on a campaign designed to promote what we shall call *positive invitation* to minorities to integrate. Heretofore effort has been largely directed at persuading or "forcing" dominants to *accept* minorities into a new integrated situation. Positive invitation may be illustrated by encouraging white employers as well as employees to deliberately suggest job openings to minority persons, or calling the attention of a minority person to a suitable house for him to purchase in their neighborhoods. The following by Whitney Young, Jr., is an example of what would be positive encouragement of integration.

> In Baltimore, an important Chamber of Commerce official said to me recently, "Negroes will soon have the political majority in this city and will elect public officials without the aid of other voting factions. How can we be sure that they will elect responsible people to office?"

[20] Robin M. Williams, Jr., *Reducing Intergroup Tensions* (New York: Social Science Research Council, Bulletin 57, 1947), p. 8. This report is a summary of the significant research which up to 1947 had been undertaken in the field of ethnic, racial, and religious group relations. The findings are, of course, not definitive but stand as the best operational hypotheses social science had to offer at that time.

My reply was, "Don't wait! Appoint and elect qualified Negroes to responsible positions now. Give them experience. Because if you wait, you are likely to have a repetition of what happened in Boston when the Irish finally achieved a popular majority. They repeatedly elected James Michael Curley mayor even after he was convicted and sentenced to jail." [21]

(4) Finally, what social policy can cope with the constantly increasing problem of the growth of Negro ghettos in the major metropolitan areas of the nation? Social science has long held that ecological dispersion of a minority population reduces prejudice and discrimination. This has been happening with all the non-Negro minorities except the Indians. We can suggest no easy panacea. However, our concept of "positive invitation" could conceivably be promoted in communities with no sizable present Negro population. The relocation experiments with Japanese, and later Indians, point to a possible way to cope with this problem. An illustration of such positive encouragement by whites for Negroes to relocate occurred in Worthington, Minnesota, where in 1965 a contingent of Negro workers and their families were relocated because of the transfer of a unit of the company for which they worked from Kansas City, Kansas, to Worthington. While the company itself paved the way for the smooth transfer effected, leading white citizens and agencies of this previously all-white small city cooperated in finding housing and helping the newcomers adjust to the community. A year later a report prepared by a social scientist indicated not only an absence of racial problems but also a substantial amount of interpersonal interaction between Negroes and whites.[22]

Finally, the increasingly recognized need for the reconstruction of metropolitan areas, already undertaken although on an inadequate scale in several cities, presents an opportunity to break up the ghetto concentration. But if Negroes are to be uprooted and relocated in mixed racial areas, they will need assurance that their new locations are not only physically better than their old, but that they will be treated as real neighbors.

Welfare Problems

All national states have been class differentiated, and had a lower class with a level of living usually characterized as "poor." But poverty until the nineteenth century was generally viewed as an inevitable part of social life. In the twentieth century, however, as a consequence of the enormous economic and technological development, there has emerged the conviction that poverty, with the associated pathologies of the lower class, constitutes a "problem" that not only should be but can be eliminated. In varying degrees all modern nations have implemented this belief to a degree.

[21] Whitney M. Young, Jr., *To Be Equal* (New York: McGraw-Hill Company, 1964), p. 214.
[22] See David Janson, reporting in *The New York Times*, Nov. 20, 1966, "Negro Families Find Acceptance in White Town in Minnesota," pp. 1, 82.

In the American public there are many beliefs concerning the underprivileged population. For analytical purposes, we shall focus on two contrasting conceptions: (1) The views that the "poor" are poor because they are incapable, either by genetic determination or in consequence of their willful practice of traits considered disorganizing, for example, laziness; and (2) the belief that the causes of this underprivileged condition lie in the malfunctioning of the social order (often quite positively functional to the welfare of other classes). Both the current effect of social forces, especially as seen in the governmental sectors, and the development of the behavioral sciences have tended to establish wider acceptance of the second viewpoint. The full acceptance of the welfare state is retarded, however, by the influence of those who still hold the self-responsible viewpoint of lower-class behavior. Misunderstanding of the facts (perhaps because the truth is unpalatable) causes certain publics to oppose the expansion of welfare benefits to the "irresponsible poor." As Young puts it:

> Often citizens have curious misconceptions about typical relief recipients and resent paying money to "all those able-bodied men." It should be noted that approximately nine out of every ten persons who receive assistance is either too young or too old to work, is disabled or busy caring for youngsters who are receiving ADC —aid to dependent children. Of the remaining 10 percent, most want real jobs rather than work relief or welfare subsistence.[23]

With biting eloquence, Young further deals with the criticism of illegitimacy among Negroes.

> Negro citizens ... resent the suggestion that disproportionate dependency and high rates of illegitimacy stem from inherent moral weakness or flaws. ... For a long time, Negroes had a monopoly on being bell hops, hotel maids, and domestic servants. We were the ones who cleaned out the whiskey bottles with the trash in the mornings. We were the ones asked to procure women at night. If anything, we *learned* immorality from our white masters and employers. Perhaps we did not learn discretion, but then we were not taught to be discreet. Social disorganization even in the ghettos does not reflect attitudes and patterns of behavior in a culture *unique* to the Negro, such situations are no more acceptable to or characteristic of, Negroes than of other citizens.[24]

The most immediate need to cope with the current unrest in the Negro population is to find employment for its unemployed and underemployed, especially of males and youth. Since, however, there is widespread lack of skills, effective job rehabilitation requires extensive training, already initiated in various government programs, such as those developed under the Office of Economic Opportunity.

[23] Whitney M. Young, Jr., *To Be Equal*, p. 165.
[24] *Ibid.*, p. 169. Italics added.

Finally, one notes the unfortunate tendency to associate welfare problems with minorities, currently with Negroes. Gunnar Myrdal has recently pointed out the serious threat to world peace posed by emphasizing race in the relation between poor and rich countries, and similarly the threat to orderly race relations in the United States if the extension of welfare activities is thought of as a Negro problem rather than a problem of Americans of all ethnic, racial, and religious backgrounds.[25]

Some Problems of Strategy

In the past, social action groups have often been faced with the dilemma of whether or not to support a new program which would improve the welfare of minorities on a segregated basis, for example, a new housing project limited to minority occupants. With the current insistence on nondiscriminatory clauses in government-supported programs both as to housing and job placement or training, this problem has taken a slightly different form, which may be illustrated in regard to projects for improved schools. Should social action agencies support a program for improving the quality of ghetto schools as against programs to promote desegregation when this would require "bussing" pupils of dominant and minority status out of their neighborhoods? To refuse support for the improved schools is to deny immediate welfare gains, to accept is to retard the integrative process.

Strong opposition to requiring the use of ethnic, religious, or racial designations on personnel forms in employment, schools, and other records has arisen from minority groups. This opposition has been based on the feeling that such labeling will adversely affect such matters as their opportunity to get a job or the attitude of a teacher toward a student. On the other hand, not to have such data available makes difficult an accurate appraisal of progress being made. The absence of such data greatly handicaps social scientists and government surveys in defining with more precision the extent of the problem areas.

The Problems of Ethnic Pluralism

We have dealt so extensively with the pluralist-integrationist axis of assimilation that in conclusion we relate it briefly to social policy and social action. From the American Creed frame of reference, the problems are twofold: (1) to protect the right of individuals to choose or not to choose to retain ethnic identification without incurring discrimination for either choice, and (2) to keep such ethnic subcommunality from engendering group conflict to the point that it threatens the maintenance of order. It is appropriate to close with Gordon's words:

[25] Address delivered before the American Institute of Planners 50th Anniversary Convention in Washington, D.C., Oct. 3, 1967.

In sum, the basic long-range goal for Americans, with regard to ethnic communality, is fluidity and moderation within the context of equal civic rights for all, regardless of race, religion, or national background, and the option of democratic free choice for both groups and individuals. Ethnic communality will not disappear in the foreseeable future and its legitimacy and rationale should be recognized and respected. By the same token, the bonds that bind human beings together across the lines of ethnicity and the pathways on which people of diverse ethnic origin meet and mingle should be cherished and strengthened. In the last analysis, what is gravely required is a society in which one may say with equal pride and without internal disquietude at the juxtaposition: "I am a Jew, or a Catholic, or a Protestant, or a Negro, or an Indian, or an Oriental, or a Puerto Rican"; "I am an American"; and "I am a man." [26]

The Outlook

The prospects for the future in intergroup relations present a paradox. On the one hand, social forces and social action are rapidly moving the society to a point where all but one of its racial, ethnic, and religious components are being assimilated into the mainstream of American life with a free choice to be accepted as all American, retaining or not, as individual members please, some identification with regard to culture or choice of social affiliation with their lineal backgrounds. The currently subordinate status of the Mexican Americans and mainland Puerto Ricans has to do in part with a time lag. While stabilization of religious and ethnic pluralism will afford bases for conflict in intergroup relations, as has occurred in the past, there do not appear any issues which cannot be accommodated, if not resolved, by the democratic process within orderly bounds. Witness the ecumenical movement in religion; the increasing pride in identifying oneself as an American of non-British lineage; and the growing acceptance of Oriental visibility by white Americans as irrelevant.

On the other hand, the nation faces for some years ahead a *now* unavoidable period of increased racial tension and conflict in Negro-white relations, fraught with the potential of ever larger-scale disorder than already experienced. The intellectual segment of the population has seen this coming for a long time; there are now signs that the white establishment with its considerable power to determine the course of events is becoming aware of it. The extent of conflict in this period will be affected primarily by the interpretation made of its cause. If the responsibility is considered that of Negroes, the prospect is for continued conflict which can conceivably reach the level of "racial warfare." If, however, it is realized that the reason the nation has reached this unfortunate crisis is the as yet inability or unwillingness of white Americans to discard the major social disease of "racism," now polarized on "Black" visibility, the prospects for

[26] Milton M. Gordon, *Assimilation in American Life* (New York: Oxford University Press, 1964), pp. 264–265.

weathering this crisis with less economic cost, personal casualties, and attrition of national prestige are greater.

A particular aspect of white reaction to the Negro Revolt shows current salience. Social science has long noted that as various minorities moved up the rank order of subordination, they tended to act toward those below them like the dominants. Stated otherwise, acculturation has involved adopting the normative prejudice of the dominant WASPS. As an increasing number of former minority status people reach equal status, they find the rules of the game have been changed—that it is now (outside the South) no longer normative to display racial prejudice, openly at least, and that other advantages open to the earlier WASPS, like cheap labor and low taxes, are now not available to them. It is not surprising that such newcomers to dominant status should feel a certain ambivalence between justice and equality on the one hand, and personal competitive advantage on the other. Such people can often be mobilized to do *for* minorities but not *with* minorities, since "with" is a threat to their new and precarious status.

Another unpredictable variable is the outcome of the present struggle for control within the Negro movement. Some degree of militancy is now found in the major Negro organizations: they are saying to white America that the time has now run out. The technique of passive resistance, which may have served a transitional purpose, is now being superceded by more aggressive activity. The NAACP, the Urban League, and CORE press for prompt and large scale action to secure genuine equality of opportunity by legitimate pressures in which they invite white cooperation. However, the more militant Negro groups have given up on white America, and some of these now feel they have only one power left—the power to destroy—and are prepared to use this, even if it means martyrdom.

Likewise unpredictable is the extent to which Negro Americans will adopt the pluralist as distinct from the integrationist orientation. It is now clear that a substantial number will choose pluralism even if, and when white America offers full integration. Our analysis of this issue in Chapter 15 suggested that whether the pluralist course will bring the results all Negroes want is debatable. It may be, however, a necessary intervening stage in the establishment of harmonious relations.

Looking still further ahead, perhaps to the twenty-first century, one final suggestion for social action is this. Since racial prejudice and discrimination are acquired through the socialization process, the present generation of adult Americans could facilitate the adjustment of their children's adult life to a world in which race is considered irrelevant by a drastic revision of the primary socialization process. Since as in many other fields in this complicated modern world, most parents have difficulty in orienting their children to the "facts of life," it is more probable that the school, including its corollary informal associational structure, would have to do the job, with the aid of the churches, and with group social action agencies.

Projects and Topics for Discussion

1. Comment critically on the authors' interpretation of American dominant behavior.
2. Assume the role of a social actionist interested in reducing discrimination and prejudice faced with appointments to speak to a Rotary Club, a labor union, and a Unitarian congregation. Outline the kind of talk you would give to each of these groups, and defend the differences indicated in each case. (Other groups may be added.)
3. Review the discussion of pluralism versus integration in Chapter 15 and relate it to the broader discussion in this chapter.
4. Design a brief questionnaire aimed at determining how white Americans view the problem of high racial tension now current in the United States. Try it out on some available sample and report your results.
5. Compare the positions of various minority groups today with regard to their abilities to solve their own problems.

Suggested Readings

Clark, Kenneth B. "Strategy for Change," Chapter 7 of *Dark Ghetto*. New York: Harper & Row, 1965.
> *Discusses the relative values of the various strategies for change in the current Negro Protest.*

Dean, John P., and Rosen, Alex, with the assistance of Robert B. Johnson, *A Manual of Intergroup Relations*. Chicago: The Univ. of Chicago Press, First Phoenix Ed., 1963.
> *In this new edition is to be found the most complete guide for social action in intergroup work with substantially more support from research findings than in its earlier edition.*

"Liberalism and the Negro," A Round Table Discussion. *Commentary*, 37 (March 1964), pp. 25–42.
> *In this symposium James Baldwin, Nathan Glazer, Sidney Hook, Gunnar Myrdal, and Norman Podhoretz discuss the future of Negro Americans revealing common interest but considerable difference of opinion on goals and strategies.*

Parsons, Talcott. "Full Citizenship for the Negro American?" in Parsons and Kenneth B. Clark, eds. *The Negro American*. Boston: Houghton Mifflin, 1966, pp. 708–754.
> *In the final essay of this distinguished volume, the senior editor ranges widely both historically and theoretically to find the answer to the question.*

Rose, Arnold, and Caroline B. "Proposed Techniques for Eliminating Minority Problems," Part VI of *Minority Problems*. New York: Harper & Row, 1965.
> *Includes selections dealing with several approaches to minority problems.*

Samora, Julian, ed. *La Raza: Forgotten Americans*. Notre Dame, Indiana: Univ. of Notre Dame Press, 1966.

Chapter V and the conclusion of this series of articles are most pertinent to the consideration of social policy with reference to this large Spanish-speaking minority.

Wilson, James Q. "Planning and Politics: Citizen Participation in Urban Renewal," *Journal of the American Institute of Planners*, XXIX, No. 4 (Nov. 1963), pp. 242–249.

Analysis of the problems and possible role of Negro Americans in urban planning.

Young, Whitney M., Jr. *To Be Equal.* New York: McGraw-Hill, 1964.

A highly intelligent and hard-hitting interpretation of the present situation of Negro Americans with specific recommendations for dealing with the entire range of problems involved.

INDEX OF AUTHORS

INDEX OF SUBJECTS

481